THE BOOK ®

Rover 200 Series
Service and Repair Manual

Spencer Drayton and Steve Rendle

Models covered
Rover 211, 214, 216, 218 & 220 Hatchback models with petrol and turbo-diesel engines, including special/limited editions

(3399 - 368 - 5AC1)

Petrol engines: 1.1 litre (1120 cc), 1.4 litre (1396 cc), 1.6 litre (1589 cc) & 1.8 litre (1796 cc)
Turbo-diesel engines: 2.0 litre (1994 cc)

Does not cover 200Vi models with 1.8 litre DOHC 'VVC' engine

WITHDRAWN

© Haynes Publishing 1999

A book in the **Haynes Service and Repair Manual Series**

All rights reserved. No part of this book may be reproduced or transmitted in any form or by any means, electronic or mechanical, including photocopying, recording or by any information storage or retrieval system, without permission in writing from the copyright holder.

ISBN 1 85960 399 8

British Library Cataloguing in Publication Data
A catalogue record for this book is available from the British Library

ABCDE
FGHIJ
KLMNO
PQR

Printed by **J H Haynes & Co Ltd, Sparkford, Nr Yeovil, Somerset BA22 7JJ, England**

Haynes Publishing
Sparkford, Nr Yeovil, Somerset BA22 7JJ, England

Haynes North America, Inc
861 Lawrence Drive, Newbury Park, California 91320, USA

Editions Haynes S.A.
Tour Aurore - La Défense 2, 18 Place des Reflets, 92975 PARIS LA DEFENSE Cedex, France

Haynes Publishing Nordiska AB
Box 1504, 751 45 UPPSALA, Sweden

D0102401

* 000128635 *

Contents

LIVING WITH YOUR ROVER 200

Roadside Repairs

Weekly Checks

Lubricants, Fluids, Capacities and Tyre Pressures

MAINTENANCE

Routine Maintenance and Servicing

Contents

The Rover 200 Hatchback model covered in this Manual is an evolution of the original Rover 214/216 Hatchback model first launched in 1989. At its launch in December 1995, the Rover 200 was available in three and five door Hatchback body styles, powered by 1.4 litre eight-valve, 1.4 litre sixteen-valve and 1.6 litre sixteen-valve variants of the proven 'K-series' petrol engine. A range of diesel-engined models was launched at the same time, powered by two variants of the new 2.0 litre turbocharged 'L-series' diesel engine. The range was extended in 1997 by the inclusion of the 218 model, fitted with a 1.8 litre variant of the sixteen-valve 'K-series' engine, and in 1998 by the addition of the 211 model, powered by a multi-point fuel injected, 1.1 litre variant of the eight-valve 'K-series' engine. The flagship 200Vi model, fitted with a 1.8 litre 'K-series' engine, featuring variable valve control (VVC), is not covered in this Manual.

All petrol engined models are fitted with eight-valve, single overhead camshaft or sixteen-valve double overhead camshaft versions of the 'K' series engine, controlled by the Rover/Motorola Modular Engine Management System (MEMS) with multi-point fuel injection (MPi). All versions of the engine are able to accept a full range of emission control systems, up to and including a three-way regulated catalytic converter.

Two derivatives of the 'L-series' turbocharged diesel engine are available; 220D and 220SD models are fitted with an 86PS version,

employing mechanical fuel injection, whilst 220Di and 220SDi models are fitted with a 105PS version of the same engine, employing an air-to-air intercooler and electronic fuel injection.

Two types of five-speed manual transmission are used; the PG1 unit is fitted to diesel and 1.8 litre petrol models, with the RG65 unit fitted to the remainder of the range. The complete engine/transmission unit is mounted transversely across the front of the car, with the transmission mounted at the left-hand end of the engine. Drive to the front wheels is via unequal-length, solid driveshafts.

The front suspension incorporates coil-over-damper MacPherson struts and an anti-roll bar. The hub carriers are located by tie rods and single transverse lower arms. The rear suspension is of the torsion-beam type, utilising coil-over-damper struts and tubular steel trailing arms linked via a single twist beam axle. The whole assembly is bolted to the underside of the vehicle via composite rubber bushes and angled pivot mountings, which endow the car with 'in-phase, passive rear steering' for improved handling during cornering. Diesel and 1.8 litre petrol models are also fitted with a rear anti-roll bar.

Braking is by discs at the front and drums at the rear, with a dual-circuit hydraulic system. On all models in the range, an Anti-lock Braking System (ABS) was offered as an optional extra. Where ABS is fitted, braking is by discs both at the front and rear.

Rover 216 SLi

Rover 211

Your Rover 200 Manual

The aim of this manual is to help you get the best value from your vehicle. It can do so in several ways. It can help you decide what work must be done (even should you choose to get it done by a garage), provide information on routine maintenance and servicing, and give a logical course of action and diagnosis when random faults occur. However, it is hoped that you will use the manual by tackling the work yourself. On simpler jobs, it may even be quicker than booking the car into a garage and going there twice, to leave and collect it. Perhaps most important, a lot of money can be saved by avoiding the costs a garage must charge to cover its labour and overheads.

The manual has drawings and descriptions to show the function of the various components, so that their layout can be understood. Then the tasks are described and photographed in a clear step-by-step sequence.

References to the 'left' or 'right' of the vehicle are in the sense of a person in the driver's seat facing forward.

Acknowledgements

Thanks are due to Champion Spark Plug who supplied the illustrations showing spark plug conditions, and to Duckhams Oils who provided lubrication data. Thanks are also due to Draper Tools Limited, who supplied some of the workshop tools, and to all those people at Sparkford who helped in the production of this Manual.

We take great pride in the accuracy of information given in this manual, but vehicle manufacturers make alterations and design changes during the production run of a particular vehicle of which they do not inform us. No liability can be accepted by the authors or publishers for loss, damage or injury caused by any errors in, or omissions from the information given.

Working on your car can be dangerous. This page shows just some of the potential risks and hazards, with the aim of creating a safety-conscious attitude.

General hazards

Scalding

• Don't remove the radiator or expansion tank cap while the engine is hot.
• Engine oil, automatic transmission fluid or power steering fluid may also be dangerously hot if the engine has recently been running.

Burning

• Beware of burns from the exhaust system and from any part of the engine. Brake discs and drums can also be extremely hot immediately after use.

Crushing

• When working under or near a raised vehicle, always supplement the jack with axle stands, or use drive-on ramps. *Never venture under a car which is only supported by a jack.*

• Take care if loosening or tightening high-torque nuts when the vehicle is on stands. Initial loosening and final tightening should be done with the wheels on the ground.

Fire

• Fuel is highly flammable; fuel vapour is explosive.
• Don't let fuel spill onto a hot engine.
• Do not smoke or allow naked lights (including pilot lights) anywhere near a vehicle being worked on. Also beware of creating sparks (electrically or by use of tools).
• Fuel vapour is heavier than air, so don't work on the fuel system with the vehicle over an inspection pit.
• Another cause of fire is an electrical overload or short-circuit. Take care when repairing or modifying the vehicle wiring.
• Keep a fire extinguisher handy, of a type suitable for use on fuel and electrical fires.

Electric shock

• Ignition HT voltage can be dangerous, especially to people with heart problems or a pacemaker. Don't work on or near the ignition system with the engine running or the ignition switched on.

• Mains voltage is also dangerous. Make sure that any mains-operated equipment is correctly earthed. Mains power points should be protected by a residual current device (RCD) circuit breaker.

Fume or gas intoxication

• Exhaust fumes are poisonous; they often contain carbon monoxide, which is rapidly fatal if inhaled. Never run the engine in a confined space such as a garage with the doors shut.

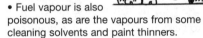

• Fuel vapour is also poisonous, as are the vapours from some cleaning solvents and paint thinners.

Poisonous or irritant substances

• Avoid skin contact with battery acid and with any fuel, fluid or lubricant, especially antifreeze, brake hydraulic fluid and Diesel fuel. Don't syphon them by mouth. If such a substance is swallowed or gets into the eyes, seek medical advice.
• Prolonged contact with used engine oil can cause skin cancer. Wear gloves or use a barrier cream if necessary. Change out of oil-soaked clothes and do not keep oily rags in your pocket.
• Air conditioning refrigerant forms a poisonous gas if exposed to a naked flame (including a cigarette). It can also cause skin burns on contact.

Asbestos

• Asbestos dust can cause cancer if inhaled or swallowed. Asbestos may be found in gaskets and in brake and clutch linings. When dealing with such components it is safest to assume that they contain asbestos.

Special hazards

Hydrofluoric acid

• This extremely corrosive acid is formed when certain types of synthetic rubber, found in some O-rings, oil seals, fuel hoses etc, are exposed to temperatures above 400°C. The rubber changes into a charred or sticky substance containing the acid. *Once formed, the acid remains dangerous for years. If it gets onto the skin, it may be necessary to amputate the limb concerned.*
• When dealing with a vehicle which has suffered a fire, or with components salvaged from such a vehicle, wear protective gloves and discard them after use.

The battery

• Batteries contain sulphuric acid, which attacks clothing, eyes and skin. Take care when topping-up or carrying the battery.
• The hydrogen gas given off by the battery is highly explosive. Never cause a spark or allow a naked light nearby. Be careful when connecting and disconnecting battery chargers or jump leads.

Air bags

• Air bags can cause injury if they go off accidentally. Take care when removing the steering wheel and/or facia. Special storage instructions may apply.

Diesel injection equipment

• Diesel injection pumps supply fuel at very high pressure. Take care when working on the fuel injectors and fuel pipes.

⚠ *Warning: Never expose the hands, face or any other part of the body to injector spray; the fuel can penetrate the skin with potentially fatal results.*

Remember...

DO

• Do use eye protection when using power tools, and when working under the vehicle.

• Do wear gloves or use barrier cream to protect your hands when necessary.

• Do get someone to check periodically that all is well when working alone on the vehicle.

• Do keep loose clothing and long hair well out of the way of moving mechanical parts.

• Do remove rings, wristwatch etc, before working on the vehicle – especially the electrical system.

• Do ensure that any lifting or jacking equipment has a safe working load rating adequate for the job.

DON'T

• Don't attempt to lift a heavy component which may be beyond your capability – get assistance.

• Don't rush to finish a job, or take unverified short cuts.

• Don't use ill-fitting tools which may slip and cause injury.

• Don't leave tools or parts lying around where someone can trip over them. Mop up oil and fuel spills at once.

• Don't allow children or pets to play in or near a vehicle being worked on.

The following pages are intended to help in dealing with common roadside emergencies and breakdowns. You will find more detailed fault finding information at the back of the manual, and repair information in the main chapters.

If your car won't start and the starter motor doesn't turn

☐ If it's a model with automatic transmission, make sure the selector is in 'P' or 'N'.
☐ Open the bonnet and make sure that the battery terminals are clean and tight.
☐ Switch on the headlights and try to start the engine. If the headlights go very dim when you're trying to start, the battery is probably flat. Get out of trouble by jump starting (see next page) using a friend's car.

If your car won't start even though the starter motor turns as normal

☐ Is there fuel in the tank?
☐ Is there moisture on electrical components under the bonnet? Switch off the ignition, then wipe off any obvious dampness with a dry cloth. Spray a water-repellent aerosol product (WD-40 or equivalent) on ignition and fuel system electrical connectors like those shown in the photos. Pay special attention to the ignition coil wiring connector and HT leads. (Note that Diesel engines don't normally suffer from damp.)

A A bad earth can cause intermittent problems in several circuits at the same time and can be difficult to trace. Check that the earth point bolts are secure and free from corrosion

B Check that the spark plug HT lead connections are clean and secure

C Check the security and condition of the battery connections

Check (with the ignition switched off) that all electrical connections are secure and spray them with a water-dispersant spray (such as WD40) if you suspect a problem due to damp

D The ECU wiring connector can cause problems if dirty, or poorly connected

E Check that the ignition distributor cap connections are clean and secure

Jump starting

HAYNES HINT *Jump starting will get you out of trouble, but you must correct whatever made the battery go flat in the first place. There are three possibilities:*

1 *The battery has been drained by repeated attempts to start, or by leaving the lights on.*

2 *The charging system is not working properly (alternator drivebelt slack or broken, alternator wiring fault or alternator itself faulty).*

3 *The battery itself is at fault (electrolyte low, or battery worn out).*

When jump-starting a car using a booster battery, observe the following precautions:

✔ Before connecting the booster battery, make sure that the ignition is switched off.

✔ Ensure that all electrical equipment (lights, heater, wipers, etc) is switched off.

✔ Take note of any special precautions printed on the battery case.

✔ Make sure that the booster battery is the same voltage as the discharged one in the vehicle.

✔ If the battery is being jump-started from the battery in another vehicle, the two vehicles MUST NOT TOUCH each other.

✔ Make sure that the transmission is in neutral (or PARK, in the case of automatic transmission).

1 Connect one end of the red jump lead to the positive (+) terminal of the flat battery

2 Connect the other end of the red lead to the positive (+) terminal of the booster battery.

3 Connect one end of the black jump lead to the negative (-) terminal of the booster battery

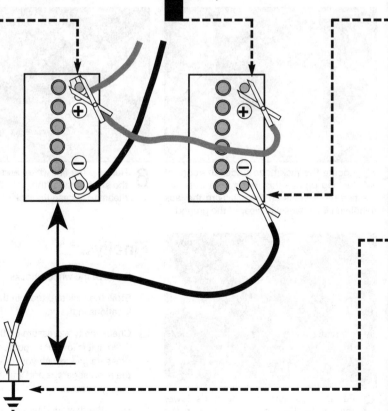

4 Connect the other end of the black jump lead to a bolt or bracket on the engine block, well away from the battery, on the vehicle to be started.

5 Make sure that the jump leads will not come into contact with the fan, drive-belts or other moving parts of the engine.

6 Start the engine using the booster battery and run it at idle speed. Switch on the lights, rear window demister and heater blower motor, then disconnect the jump leads in the reverse order of connection. Turn off the lights etc.

Wheel changing

Some of the details shown here will vary according to model. For instance, the location of the jack is not the same on all cars. However, the basic principles apply to all vehicles.

 Warning: Do not change a wheel in a situation where you risk being hit by another vehicle. On busy roads, try to stop in a lay-by or a gateway. Be wary of passing traffic while changing the wheel - it is easy to become distracted by the job in hand.

Preparation

☐ When a puncture occurs, stop as soon as it is safe to do so.
☐ Park on firm level ground, if possible, and well out of the way of other traffic.
☐ Use hazard warning lights if necessary.

☐ If you have one, use a warning triangle to alert other drivers of your presence.
☐ Apply the handbrake and engage first or reverse gear (or Park on models with automatic transmission.

☐ Chock the wheel diagonally opposite the one being removed – a couple of large stones will do for this.
☐ If the ground is soft, use a flat piece of wood to spread the load under the jack.

Changing the wheel

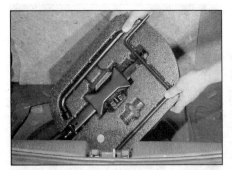

1 Lift up the floor carpet in the boot space and remove the wheel changing toolkit

2 Unscrew the spare wheel retaining cap

3 Use the end of the wheel brace to lever off the wheel trim on the flat tyre

4 Slacken each of the wheel nuts in turn slightly, using the wheel brace

5 Locate the jack head under the correct jacking point - this is the area between the two protrusions on the sill. Turn the jack handle until the wheel is clear of the ground

6 Remove the flat wheel and slide it under the sill in front of the jack; this is a safety measure in case the jack collapses

7 Fit the spare wheel into position

8 Fit the wheel nuts onto the studs, lower the car to the ground and tighten the wheel nuts securely using the wheel brace

Finally...

☐ Remove the wheel chocks.

☐ Stow the jack and tools in the correct locations in the car.

☐ Check the tyre pressure on the wheel just fitted. If it is low, or if you don't have a pressure gauge with you, drive slowly to the nearest garage and inflate the tyre to the right pressure.

☐ Have the damaged tyre or wheel repaired as soon as possible.

Identifying leaks

Puddles on the garage floor or drive, or obvious wetness under the bonnet or underneath the car, suggest a leak that needs investigating. It can sometimes be difficult to decide where the leak is coming from, especially if the engine bay is very dirty already. Leaking oil or fluid can also be blown rearwards by the passage of air under the car, giving a false impression of where the problem lies.

 Warning: Most automotive oils and fluids are poisonous. Wash them off skin, and change out of contaminated clothing, without delay.

HAYNES HiNT *The smell of a fluid leaking from the car may provide a clue to what's leaking. Some fluids are distinctively coloured. It may help to clean the car carefully and to park it over some clean paper overnight as an aid to locating the source of the leak.*
Remember that some leaks may only occur while the engine is running.

Sump oil

Engine oil may leak from the drain plug...

Oil from filter

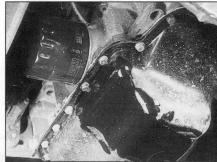

...or from the base of the oil filter.

Gearbox oil

Gearbox oil can leak from the seals at the inboard ends of the driveshafts.

Antifreeze

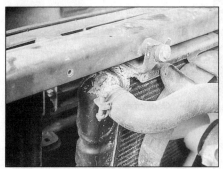

Leaking antifreeze often leaves a crystalline deposit like this.

Brake fluid

A leak occurring at a wheel is almost certainly brake fluid.

Power steering fluid

Power steering fluid may leak from the pipe connectors on the steering rack.

Towing

☐ The Rover 200 is not fitted with towing eyelets. The lashing eyelets fitted to the front and rear of the car are intended for use by emergency services during vehicle recovery and should not be used for any other purpose.

 Warning: Models with automatic transmission must be towed with the front wheels raised from the ground. This is because the transmission is not adequately lubricated without the engine running and could be damaged as a result.

Introduction

There are some very simple checks which need only take a few minutes to carry out, but which could save you a lot of inconvenience and expense.

These "Weekly checks" require no great skill or special tools, and the small amount of time they take to perform could prove to be very well spent, for example;

☐ Keeping an eye on tyre condition and pressures, will not only help to stop them wearing out prematurely, but could also save your life.

☐ Many breakdowns are caused by electrical problems. Battery-related faults are particularly common, and a quick check on a regular basis will often prevent the majority of these.

☐ If your car develops a brake fluid leak, the first time you might know about it is when your brakes don't work properly. Checking the level regularly will give advance warning of this kind of problem.

☐ If the oil or coolant levels run low, the cost of repairing any engine damage will be far greater than fixing the leak, for example.

Underbonnet check points

◄ Rover 214i K8 petrol engine

A *Brake fluid reservoir*

B *Engine oil filler cap*

C *Engine oil level dipstick*

D *Power steering fluid reservoir*

E *Windscreen washer fluid reservoir filler cap*

F *Coolant expansion tank*

G *Battery*

Engine oil level

Before you start
✔ Make sure that your car is on level ground.
✔ Check the oil level before the car is driven, or at least 5 minutes after the engine has been switched off.

 HAYNES HINT *If the oil is checked immediately after driving the vehicle, some of the oil will remain in the upper engine components, resulting in an inaccurate reading on the dipstick.*

The correct oil
Modern engines place great demands on their oil. It is very important that the correct oil for your car is used (see "*Lubricants, fluids and capacities*" on page 0•16).

Car Care
● If you have to add oil frequently, you should check whether you have any oil leaks. Place some clean paper under the car overnight, and check for stains in the morning. If there are no leaks, the engine may be burning oil (see "*Fault Finding*").

● Always maintain the level between the upper and lower dipstick marks. If the level is too low, severe engine damage may occur. Oil seal failure may result if the engine is overfilled by adding too much oil.

1 The dipstick is located at the right-hand end of the engine, next to the power steering fluid reservoir (see "*Underbonnet check points*" on page 0•10 for exact location). Withdraw the dipstick.

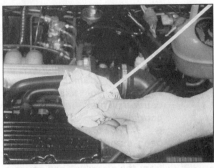

2 Using a clean rag or paper towel, wipe all the oil from the dipstick. Insert the clean dipstick into the tube as far as it will go, then withdraw it again.

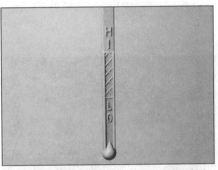

3 Note the oil level on the end of the dipstick, which should be between the upper HI mark and the lower LO mark. Approximately 1.0 litre of oil will raise the level from the lower mark to the upper mark.

4 Oil is added through the filler cap. Rotate the cap through a quarter-turn anti-clockwise and withdraw it. Top-up the level. A funnel may help to reduce spillage. Add the oil slowly, checking the level on the dipstick often. Do not overfill.

Power steering fluid level

Before you start:
✔ Make sure that the car is on level ground.
✔ Set the front roadwheels in the straight-ahead position.
✔ The engine should be stopped.
✔ Do not operate the steering once the engine is stopped.

Safety First!
● If the reservoir requires repeated topping-up, there is a fluid leak somewhere in the system which should be investigated immediately.
● If a leak is suspected, the car should not be driven until the power steering system has been checked.

1 The power steering fluid reservoir is located on the right-hand side of the engine compartment, next to the dipstick. MAX and MIN level marks are indicated on the side of the reservoir and the fluid level should be maintained between these marks at all times.

2 If topping-up is necessary, first wipe the area around the filler cap with a clean rag before removing the cap. When adding fluid, pour it carefully into the reservoir to avoid spillage - be sure to use only the specified fluid. After filling the reservoir to the proper level, make sure that the cap is refitted securely to avoid leaks and the entry of foreign matter into the reservoir.

Brake fluid level

Warning:

● **Brake fluid can harm your eyes and damage painted surfaces, so use extreme caution when handling and pouring it.**

● **Do not use fluid which has been standing open for some time, as it absorbs moisture from the air, which can cause a dangerous loss of braking effectiveness.**

Before you start

✔ Make sure that the car is on level ground.

✔ Cleanliness is of great importance when dealing with the braking system, so take care to clean around the reservoir cap before topping-up. Use only clean brake fluid from a container which has stood for at least 24 hours (to allow air bubbles to separate out).

Safety First!

● If the reservoir requires repeated topping-up, this is an indication of a fluid leak somewhere in the system, which should be investigated immediately.

● If a leak is suspected, the car should not be driven until the braking system has been checked. Never take any risks where brakes are concerned.

1 The brake master cylinder and fluid reservoir is located at the rear right-hand end of the engine compartment. The MAX and MIN level marks are indicated on the side of the reservoir and the fluid level should be maintained between these marks at all times.

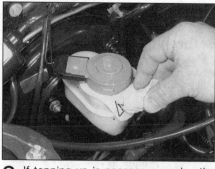

2 If topping-up is necessary, unplug the electrical connector and wipe the area around the filler cap with a clean rag before removing the cap. When adding fluid, pour it carefully into the reservoir to avoid spilling it on surrounding painted surfaces. Be sure to use only the specified brake hydraulic fluid since mixing different types of fluid can cause damage to the system.

3 Before adding fluid it is a good idea to inspect the reservoir. The system should be drained and refilled if deposits, dirt particles or contamination are seen in the fluid.

4 After filling the reservoir to the proper level, make sure that the cap is refitted securely to avoid leaks and the entry of foreign matter. Ensure that the fluid level switch plunger is free to move.

Screen washer fluid level

Car care

● Screenwash additives not only keep the windscreen clean during bad weather, they also prevent the washer system freezing in cold weather - which is when you are likely to need it most. Don't top up using plain water, as the screenwash will become diluted and will freeze in cold weather.

● Check the operation of the windscreen and rear window washers. Adjust the nozzles using a pin if necessary, aiming the spray to a point slightly above the centre of the swept area.

Warning: On no account use engine coolant antifreeze in the screen washer system - this will damage the paintwork.

1 The reservoir for the windscreen and rear window washer systems is located at the front right-hand side of the engine compartment. When topping-up the reservoir, a screenwash additive should be added in the quantities recommended on the bottle.

Coolant level

Warning: Do not attempt to remove the expansion tank pressure cap when the engine is hot, as there is a very great risk of scalding. Do not leave open containers of coolant about, as it is poisonous.

Car Care

● With a sealed-type cooling system, adding coolant should not be necessary on a regular basis. If frequent topping-up is required, it is likely there is a leak. Check the radiator, all hoses and joint faces for signs of staining or wetness, and rectify as necessary.

● It is important that antifreeze is used in the cooling system all year round, not just during the winter months. Don't top up with water alone, as the antifreeze will become diluted.

1 The coolant level varies with the temperature of the engine. When the engine is cold, the coolant level should be between the 'MAX' and 'MIN' markings on the side of the reservoir. When the engine is hot, the level may rise slightly.

2 If topping-up is necessary, wait until the engine is cold, then cover the expansion tank with a thick layer of rag and unscrew the filler cap anti-clockwise. Wait until the hissing ceases, indicating that all pressure is released, then slowly unscrew the filler cap until it can be removed. At all times keep well away from the filler opening.

3 Add a mixture of water and antifreeze through the expansion tank filler neck, until the coolant is up to the 'MAX' level. Refit the cap, turning it clockwise as far as it will go until it is secure.

Wiper blades

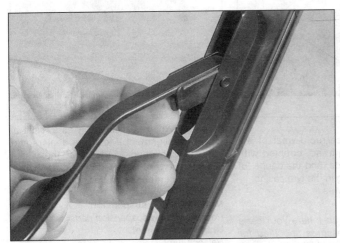

1 Check the condition of the wiper blades. If they are cracked or show any signs of deterioration, or if the glass swept area is smeared, renew them. For maximum clarity of vision, wiper blades should be renewed annually, as a matter of course.

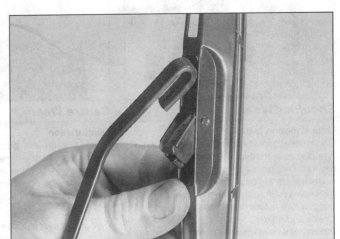

2 To remove a wiper blade, pull the arm fully away from the glass until it locks. Swivel the blade through 90°, press the locking tab with a finger nail and slide the blade out of the arm's hooked end. On refitting, ensure that the blade locks securely into the arm.

Tyre condition and pressure

It is very important that tyres are in good condition, and at the correct pressure - having a tyre failure at any speed is highly dangerous. Tyre wear is influenced by driving style - harsh braking and acceleration, or fast cornering, will all produce more rapid tyre wear. As a general rule, the front tyres wear out faster than the rears. Interchanging the tyres from front to rear ("rotating" the tyres) may result in more even wear. However, if this is completely effective, you may have the expense of replacing all four tyres at once! Remove any nails or stones embedded in the tread before they penetrate the tyre to cause deflation. If removal of a nail does reveal that

the tyre has been punctured, refit the nail so that its point of penetration is marked. Then immediately change the wheel, and have the tyre repaired by a tyre dealer.

Regularly check the tyres for damage in the form of cuts or bulges, especially in the sidewalls. Periodically remove the wheels, and clean any dirt or mud from the inside and outside surfaces. Examine the wheel rims for signs of rusting, corrosion or other damage. Light alloy wheels are easily damaged by "kerbing" whilst parking; steel wheels may also become dented or buckled. A new wheel is very often the only way to overcome severe damage.

New tyres should be balanced when they are fitted, but it may become necessary to re-balance them as they wear, or if the balance weights fitted to the wheel rim should fall off. Unbalanced tyres will wear more quickly, as will the steering and suspension components. Wheel imbalance is normally signified by vibration, particularly at a certain speed (typically around 50 mph). If this vibration is felt only through the steering, then it is likely that just the front wheels need balancing. If, however, the vibration is felt through the whole car, the rear wheels could be out of balance. Wheel balancing should be carried out by a tyre dealer or garage.

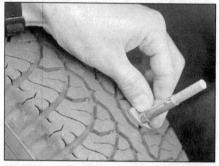

1 **Tread Depth - visual check**
The original tyres have tread wear safety bands (B), which will appear when the tread depth reaches approximately 1.6 mm. The band positions are indicated by a triangular mark on the tyre sidewall (A).

2 **Tread Depth - manual check**
Alternatively, tread wear can be monitored with a simple, inexpensive device known as a tread depth indicator gauge.

3 **Tyre Pressure Check**
Check the tyre pressures regularly with the tyres cold. Do not adjust the tyre pressures immediately after the vehicle has been used, or an inaccurate setting will result.

Tyre tread wear patterns

Shoulder Wear

Underinflation (wear on both sides)
Under-inflation will cause overheating of the tyre, because the tyre will flex too much, and the tread will not sit correctly on the road surface. This will cause a loss of grip and excessive wear, not to mention the danger of sudden tyre failure due to heat build-up.
Check and adjust pressures
Incorrect wheel camber (wear on one side)
Repair or renew suspension parts
Hard cornering
Reduce speed!

Centre Wear

Overinflation
Over-inflation will cause rapid wear of the centre part of the tyre tread, coupled with reduced grip, harsher ride, and the danger of shock damage occurring in the tyre casing.
Check and adjust pressures

If you sometimes have to inflate your car's tyres to the higher pressures specified for maximum load or sustained high speed, don't forget to reduce the pressures to normal afterwards.

Uneven Wear

Front tyres may wear unevenly as a result of wheel misalignment. Most tyre dealers and garages can check and adjust the wheel alignment (or "tracking") for a modest charge.
Incorrect camber or castor
Repair or renew suspension parts
Malfunctioning suspension
Repair or renew suspension parts
Unbalanced wheel
Balance tyres
Incorrect toe setting
Adjust front wheel alignment
Note: *The feathered edge of the tread which typifies toe wear is best checked by feel.*

Battery

Caution: Before carrying out any work on the vehicle battery, read the precautions given in "Safety first!" at the start of this manual.

✔ Make sure that the battery tray is in good condition and that the clamp is tight. Corrosion on the tray, retaining clamp and the battery itself can be removed with a solution of water and baking soda. Thoroughly rinse all cleaned areas with water. Any metal parts damaged by corrosion should be covered with a zinc-based primer, then painted.

✔ Periodically (approximately every three months), check the charge condition of the battery as described in Chapter 5A.

✔ If the battery is flat and you need to jump start your vehicle, see *"Jump starting"*.

HAYNES HiNT

Battery corrosion can be kept to a minimum by applying a layer of petroleum jelly to the clamps and terminals after they are reconnected.

1 The battery is located on the left-hand side of the engine compartment. The exterior of the battery should be inspected periodically for damage such as a cracked case or cover.

3 If corrosion (white fluffy deposits) is evident, remove the cables from the battery terminals, clean them with a small wire brush, then refit them. Automotive stores sell a useful tool for cleaning the battery posts . . .

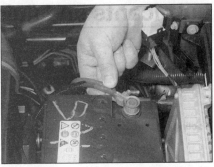

2 Check the tightness of the battery cable clamps to ensure good electrical connections. You should not be able to move them. Also check each cable for cracks and frayed conductors.

4 . . . as well as the cable terminals.

Electrical systems

✔ Check all external lights and the horn. Refer to the appropriate Sections of Chapter 12 for details if any of the circuits are found to be inoperative, and replace the fuse if necessary. Most fuses are located behind a panel at the lower right-hand side of the facia. Other fuses are located in the fusebox on the left-hand side of the engine compartment. To replace a blown fuse, pull it from position, using the plastic tool provided. Fit a new fuse of the same rating. If a second fuse blows, it is important that you find the reason - do not use a fuse with a higher rating.

✔ Visually check all accessible wiring connectors, harnesses and retaining clips for security, and for signs of chafing or damage.

HAYNES HiNT *If you need to check your brake lights and indicators unaided, back up to a wall or garage door and operate the lights. The reflected light should show if they are working properly.*

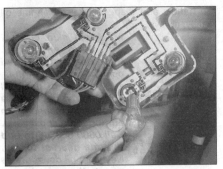

1 If a single indicator light, brake light or headlight has failed, it is likely that a bulb has blown and will need to be replaced. Refer to Chapter 12 for details. If both brake lights have failed, it is possible that the stop lamp switch operated by the brake pedal is faulty. Refer to Chapter 9 for details.

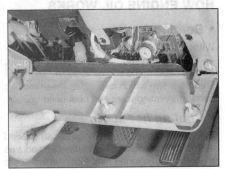

2 If more than one indicator light or headlight has failed, it is likely that either a fuse has blown or that there is a fault in the circuit (see Chapter 12).

Lubricants and fluids

Engine

Petrol .... Multigrade engine oil, viscosity SAE 10W/40 to ACEA A2
(Duckhams QXR Premium Petrol Engine Oil)

Diesel .... Multigrade engine oil, viscosity SAE 10W/40 to ACEA B2
(Duckhams QXR Premium Diesel Engine Oil, or Duckhams Hypergrade
Diesel Engine Oil)

Cooling system .... Antifreeze to spec. BS 6580 and BS 5117. Ethylene-glycol based with
non-phosphate corrosion inhibitors, containing no methanol. Mixture
50% by volume
(Duckhams Antifreeze and Summer Coolant)

Manual transmission

R65 transmission .... Gear oil viscosity SAE 75W-80W to API GL5
(Duckhams Hypoid Gear Oil 75W/80W GL5 - for topping-up only)

PG1 transmission .... Special gearbox oil - refer to your Rover dealer
(Duckhams QXR Premium Petrol or Diesel Engine Oil may be used for
topping-up only)

Automatic transmission .... Special CVT fluid. Refer to your Rover dealer
(Duckhams ATF Autotrans III - for topping-up only)

Braking system .... Hydraulic fluid to spec. SAE J 1703 or DOT 4, but note that Rover
specify brake fluids produced by approved manufacturers only - refer
to your Rover dealer

Power steering system

Topping-up .... Automatic transmission fluid (ATF) to Dexron II D specification
(Duckhams ATF Autotrans III)

Complete refill .... Special power steering fluid - refer to your Rover dealer

General greasing .... Multi-purpose lithium-based grease to NLGI consistency No. 2
(Duckhams LB10)

Choosing your engine oil

Engines need oil, not only to lubricate moving parts and minimise wear, but also to maximise power output and to improve fuel economy. By introducing a simplified and improved range of engine oils, Duckhams has taken away the confusion and made it easier for you to choose the right oil for your engine.

HOW ENGINE OIL WORKS

• Beating friction

Without oil, the moving surfaces inside your engine will rub together, heat up and melt, quickly causing the engine to seize. Engine oil creates a film which separates these moving parts, preventing wear and heat build-up.

• Cooling hot-spots

Temperatures inside the engine can exceed 1000° C. The engine oil circulates and acts as a coolant, transferring heat from the hot-spots to the sump.

• Cleaning the engine internally

Good quality engine oils clean the inside of your engine, collecting and dispersing combustion deposits and controlling them until they are trapped by the oil filter or flushed out at oil change.

OIL CARE - FOLLOW THE CODE

To handle and dispose of used engine oil safely, always:

• **Avoid skin contact with used engine oil. Repeated or prolonged contact can be harmful.**
• **Dispose of used oil and empty packs in a responsible manner in an authorised disposal site. Call 0800 663366 to find the one nearest to you. Never tip oil down drains or onto the ground.**

DUCKHAMS ENGINE OILS

For the driver who demands a premium quality oil for complete reassurance, we recommend synthetic formula **Duckhams QXR Premium Engine Oils.**
For the driver who requires a straightforward quality engine oil, we recommend **Duckhams Hypergrade Engine Oils.**

For further information and advice, call the Duckhams UK Helpline on 0800 212988.

Capacities

Engine oil	4.5 litres - including filter

Cooling system
Petrol engines	5.5 litres (from dry)
Diesel engines	7.0 litres (from dry)

Manual transmission
R65	2.0 litres (from dry)/1.8 litres (drain and refill)
PG1	2.2 litres (from dry)/2.0 litres (drain and refill)

Automatic transmission	5.0 litres (from dry)
Power steering reservoir	0.3 litres
Fuel tank	50 litres
Washer system reservoir	6.5 litres

Tyre pressures (tyres cold)

Note: *This is a selection of typical tyre pressures - refer to your handbook, service station wallchart or Rover dealer for greater detail.*

	Front	Rear
Normal driving conditions		
214, 216 with manual transmission	2.1 bar (30 psi)	2.1 bar (30 psi)
216 Si with automatic transmission	2.2 bar (32 psi)	2.1 bar (30 psi)
220D, SD and SDi diesel models	2.2 bar (32 psi)	2.1 bar (30 psi)
216SLi with automatic transmission	2.3 bar (33 psi)	2.1 bar (30 psi)
Speeds in excess of 100 mph (160 km/h)		
214 models	2.3 bar (33 psi)	2.3 bar (33 psi)
216 models with manual transmission	2.2 bar (32 psi)	2.1 bar (30 psi)
216 Si models with automatic transmission	2.5 bar (36 psi)	2.4 bar (34 psi)
216 SLi models with automatic transmission	2.6 bar (37 psi)	2.4 bar (34 psi)
220D, SD and SDi diesel models	2.4 bar (35 psi)	2.3 bar (33 psi)

Note: *Pressures apply only to original equipment tyres and may vary if any other make or type is fitted. Check with the tyre manufacturer or supplier for correct pressures if necessary. Pressures also vary for increased loads or towing - refer to your car's handbook or Rover dealer .*

Chapter 1 Part A:
Routine maintenance and servicing - petrol models

Contents

Degrees of difficulty

| Easy, suitable for novice with little experience | Fairly easy, suitable for beginner with some experience | Fairly difficult, suitable for competent DIY mechanic | Difficult, suitable for experienced DIY mechanic | Very difficult, suitable for expert DIY or professional 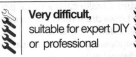 |

Lubricants, fluids and capacities

Refer to the end of "Weekly Checks"

Engine

Oil filter type .... Champion B104

Cooling system

Antifreeze properties - 50% antifreeze (by volume):
    Commences freezing .... - 36°C
    Frozen solid .... - 48°C

Fuel system

Air cleaner filter element .... Champion U631
Idle speed .... 875 ± 50 rpm
Idle mixture (CO content) – engine at normal operating temperature .. Less than 0.5 %
Recommended fuel .... 95 RON premium unleaded

Ignition system

Firing order .... 1-3-4-2 (No 1 cylinder at timing belt end of engine)
Crankshaft rotation .... Clockwise (viewed from timing belt end of engine)
Distributor rotor arm rotation .... Anti-clockwise (viewed from flywheel end of engine)
Ignition timing .... Controlled by engine management system – no adjustment possible
Spark plugs:
    Type .... Champion RC9YCC
    Electrode gap .... 0.8 mm

Braking system

Front and rear brake pad friction material minimum thickness .... 3.0 mm
Rear brake shoe friction material minimum thickness .... 2.0 mm
Handbrake lever travel:
    Models with rear drum brakes .... 8 to 12 clicks
    Models with rear disc brakes .... 10 to 14 clicks

Suspension and steering

Power steering pump drivebelt deflection:
    Used belt .... 7.5 - 8.5 mm
    New belt .... 5.5 - 8.5 mm

Tyre pressures

Refer to the end of "Weekly checks"

Electrical system

Alternator/air conditioning compressor drivebelt deflection:
    With air conditioning .... 9 - 10 mm
    Without air conditioning .... 6 - 8 mm
Wiper blades - front and rear .... Champion X45

Torque wrench settings

	Nm	lbf ft
Engine oil drain plug:		
Steel sump	42	31
Alloy sump	25	18
Fuel pipe-to-fuel filter unions	28	21
Spark plug cover screws (K16 engines)	10	7
Spark plugs	25	18
Alternator mounting bolts	25	18
Alternator/air conditioning compressor drivebelt tensioner pulley bolt	25	18
Manual transmission filler/level plug:		
"R65"-type transmission	25	18
"PG1"-type transmission	40	29
Automatic transmission fluid drain plug	30	22
Brake caliper bleed screws	10	7
Front/rear brake caliper guide pin bolts	27	20
Rear brake drum retaining screws	7	5
Wheel cylinder bleed screws	7	5
Power steering drivebelt tensioner pulley bolt	25	18
Roadwheel nuts	See Chapter 10	

The maintenance intervals in this manual are provided with the assumption that you will be carrying out the work yourself. These are based on the minimum maintenance intervals recommended by the manufacturer for vehicles driven daily. If you wish to keep your vehicle in peak condition at all times, you may wish to perform some of these procedures more often. We encourage frequent maintenance because it enhances the efficiency, performance and resale value of your vehicle.

If the vehicle is driven in dusty areas, used to tow a trailer, or driven frequently at slow speeds (idling in traffic) or on short journeys, more frequent maintenance intervals are recommended.

When the vehicle is new, it should be serviced by a factory-authorised dealer service department, in order to preserve the factory warranty.

Every 250 miles (400 km) or weekly
☐ Refer to *"Weekly Checks"*

Every 6000 miles (10 000 km) or 6 months - whichever comes first
☐ Engine oil and filter renewal (*Section 4*)

Note: *Frequent oil and filter changes are good for the engine. We recommend changing the oil at the mileage specified here, or at least twice a year if the mileage covered is less.*

Every 12 000 miles (20 000 km) or 12 months - whichever comes first
☐ Bodywork corrosion check (*Section 3*)
☐ Engine oil and filter renewal (*Section 4*)
☐ Coolant specific gravity check (*Section 5*)
☐ Manual transmission oil level check (*Section 6*)
☐ Automatic transmission fluid level check (*Section 7*)
☐ Vacuum hose condition check (*Section 8*)
☐ Underbonnet and underbody hose and pipe condition check (*Section 9*)
☐ Air conditioning system check (*Section 10*)
☐ Auxiliary drivebelt tension and condition check (*Section 11*)
☐ Exhaust system check (*Section 12*)
☐ Front brake check (*Section 13*)
☐ Rear brake check (*Section 14*)
☐ Driveshaft and gaiter check (*Section 15*)
☐ Suspension and steering check (*Section 16*)
☐ Handbrake check and adjustment (*Section 17*)
☐ Lock and hinge lubrication (*Section 18*)
☐ Windscreen and numberplate condition check* (*Section 19*)
☐ Seat belt check* (*Section 20*)
☐ Airbag system components check* (*Section 21*)
☐ Oxygen sensor operation check* (*Section 22*)
☐ Exhaust gas CO content check* (*Section 23*)
☐ Road test (*Section 24*)

Rover recommend that these tasks need only be carried out after the first three years/36,000 miles of the vehicle's life and every year/12,000 miles thereafter.

Every 24 000 miles (40 000 km) or 2 years - whichever comes first
Carry out all the items listed for the 12 000 mile/ 12 months service, plus the following:

☐ Automatic transmission fluid renewal (*Section 25*)
☐ Air cleaner filter element renewal (*Section 26*)
☐ Spark plug renewal (*Section 27*)
☐ Coolant renewal* (*Section 28*)
☐ Alarm remote keypad battery renewal (*Section 29*)

If Rover-recommended antifreeze is used exclusively, this task need only be carried out after the first three years/36,000 miles of the vehicle's life and every two years/24,000 miles thereafter.

Every 48 000 miles (80 000 km) or 4 years - whichever comes first
☐ Fuel filter renewal (*Section 30*)

Every 60 000 miles (100 000 km) or 5 years - whichever comes first
☐ Camshaft timing belt renewal (*Section 31*)

Every 2 years, regardless of mileage
☐ Brake fluid renewal (*Section 32*)

Every 10 years, regardless of mileage
☐ Airbag system component renewal (*Section 33*)

Underbonnet view of a Rover 214i with 1.4 litre K8 MPi petrol engine

1 Engine oil dipstick
2 Engine oil filler cap
3 Spark plugs
4 Alternator
5 Washer fluid reservoir cap
6 Power steering fluid reservoir cap
7 Windscreen wiper motor
8 Brake fluid reservoir/master cylinder
9 Fuel filter
10 Coolant expansion tank
11 Throttle body
12 Ignition distributor cap
13 Air filter housing
14 Battery
15 Engine compartment fusebox

Front underbody view of a Rover 214i with 1.4 litre K8 MPi petrol engine

1 Brake caliper
2 Tie bar
3 Suspension lower arm
4 Track rod
5 Power steering gear
6 Anti-roll bar
7 Exhaust system front pipe
8 Suspension front beam
9 Radiator
10 Engine oil filter
11 Sump drain plug
12 Driveshaft

Rear underbody view of a Rover 214i with 1.4 litre K8 MPi petrol engine

1 Handbrake cables
2 Beam axle assembly
3 Beam axle pivot mountings
4 Fuel tank
5 Suspension strut lower mountings
6 Exhaust system tailbox
7 Brake backplates

Maintenance procedures - petrol models

1 Introduction

This Chapter is designed to help the home mechanic maintain his/her vehicle for safety, economy, long life and peak performance.

The Chapter contains a master maintenance schedule, referring to Sections dealing specifically with each task in the schedule, or other Chapters. Visual checks, adjustments, component renewal and other helpful items are included. Refer to the accompanying illustrations of the engine compartment and the underside of the vehicle for the locations of the various components.

Servicing your vehicle in accordance with the mileage/time maintenance schedule and the following Sections will provide a planned maintenance programme, which should result in a long and reliable service life. This is a comprehensive plan, so maintaining some items but not others at the specified service intervals will not produce the same results.

As you service your vehicle, you will discover that many of the procedures can be grouped together, because of the particular procedure being performed, or because of the close proximity of two otherwise-unrelated components to one another. For example, if the vehicle is raised for any reason, the exhaust can be inspected at the same time as the suspension and steering components.

The first step in this maintenance programme is to prepare yourself before the actual work begins. Read through all the Sections relevant to the work to be carried out, then make a list and gather together all the parts and tools required. If a problem is encountered, seek advice from a parts specialist, or a dealer service department.

2 Maintenance

1 If, from the time the vehicle is new, the routine maintenance schedule is followed closely and frequent checks are made of fluid levels and high-wear items, as suggested throughout this Manual, the engine will be kept in relatively good running condition and the need for additional work will be minimised.

2 It is possible that there will be times when the engine is running poorly due to the lack of regular maintenance. This is even more likely if a used vehicle, which has not received regular and frequent maintenance checks, is purchased. In such cases, additional work may need to be carried out, outside of the regular maintenance intervals.

3 If engine wear is suspected, a compression test will provide valuable information regarding the overall performance of the main internal components. Such a test can be used as a basis to decide on the extent of the work to be carried out. If, for example, a compression test indicates serious internal engine wear, conventional maintenance as described in this Chapter will not greatly improve the performance of the engine, and may prove a waste of time and money, unless extensive overhaul work is carried out first.

4 The following series of operations are those most often required to improve the performance of a generally poor-running engine:

Primary operations

a) Clean, inspect and test the battery
b) Check all the engine-related fluids
c) Check the condition and tension of the auxiliary drivebelt(s)
d) Renew the spark plugs
e) Inspect the distributor cap and HT leads - as applicable
f) Check the condition of the air cleaner filter element, and renew if necessary
g) Renew the fuel filter (if fitted)
h) Check the condition of all hoses, and check for fluid leaks
i) Check the idle speed and mixture settings - as applicable

5 If the above operations do not prove fully effective, carry out the following secondary operations:

Secondary operations

a) Check the charging system
b) Check the ignition system
c) Check the fuel system
d) Renew the distributor cap and rotor arm - as applicable
e) Renew the ignition HT leads - as applicable

1A

Every 12 000 miles (20 000 km) or 12 months - whichever comes first

3 Bodywork corrosion check

1 Start at the front of the car and work along each body panel in turn, look for any signs of paintwork damage. It may be possible to repair small scratches with a touch-up pen. These should be purchased from a Rover dealer, to get an accurate colour match.

2 Larger scratches that have penetrated the primer or exposed the bare metal beneath should be repaired professionally. The Rover 200 has an extensive Anti-Corrosion Warranty, the terms of which specify how bodywork repairs must be carried out; failure to adhere to the guidelines may invalidate the Warranty. Have the damage assessed by a Rover Dealer or automotive bodywork specialist at the earliest opportunity.

3 Check each body panel for evidence of corrosion, such as raised blisters behind the paintwork and rust-coloured staining. Pay particular attention to vulnerable areas, including the wheel arches, the front edge of the bonnet , the front valence (under the front bumper) and the lower edges of the doors. Corrosion can quickly destroy bodywork, so have any dubious-looking areas examined by a professional.

4 Jack up the front/rear car and support it securely on axle stands (see "*Jacking and Vehicle Support*").

5 Examine the underside of the car for signs of corrosion. Look for cracking or flaking of the metal floorpan. Pay particular attention to the areas around the suspension and steering components mountings. Look for damage that may have been caused by attempting to jack up the car at incorrect jacking points.

6 Check for corrosion along the length of the side sills, which run between the front and rear wheel arches.

7 The underside of the vehicle is coated with a protective sealant, which helps to prevent corrosion. If this coating has been scraped off at any point, due to an impact or repair work, it must be re-applied as soon as possible, to protect the bodywork beneath.

4 Engine oil and filter renewal

Note: *An oil filter removal tool and a new oil drain plug sealing washer will be required for this operation.*

1 Frequent oil and filter changes are the most important preventative maintenance procedures which can be undertaken by the DIY owner. As engine oil ages, it becomes diluted and contaminated, which leads to premature engine wear.

2 Before starting this procedure, gather together all the necessary tools and materials. Also make sure that you have plenty of clean rags and newspapers handy, to mop up any spills. Ideally, the engine oil should be warm, as it will drain more easily, and more built-up sludge will be removed with it. Take care not to touch the exhaust or any other hot parts of the engine when working under the vehicle. To avoid any possibility of scalding, and to protect yourself from possible skin irritants and other harmful contaminants in used engine oils, it is advisable to wear gloves when carrying out this work.

3 Access to the underside of the vehicle will be greatly improved if it can be raised on a lift, driven onto ramps, or jacked up and supported on axle stands (see "*Jacking and Vehicle Support*"). Whichever method is chosen, make sure that the vehicle remains level, or if it is at an angle, that the drain plug is at the lowest point. The drain plug is located at the front of the sump.

4 Remove the oil filler cap from the cylinder head cover.

5 Using a spanner, or preferably a suitable socket and bar, slacken the drain plug about half a turn **(see illustration)**. Position the draining container under the drain plug, then remove the plug completely. If possible, try to keep the plug pressed into the sump while unscrewing it by hand the last couple of turns.

> **HAYNES HiNT** *As the plug releases from the threads, move it away sharply, so that the stream of oil from the sump runs into the container, not up your sleeve!*

6 Allow some time for the oil to drain, noting that it may be necessary to reposition the container as the oil flow slows to a trickle.

7 After all the oil has drained, wipe the drain plug and the sealing washer with a clean rag. The sealing washer should be renewed as a matter of course. Clean the area around the drain plug opening, and refit the plug complete with the new sealing washer. Tighten the plug securely, preferably to the specified torque, using a torque wrench.

8 The oil filter is located at the right-hand front corner of the engine. Access is most easily obtained by jacking up the front of the vehicle (see "*Jacking and Vehicle Support*") **(see illustration)**.

9 Move the container into position under the oil filter.

10 Use an oil filter removal tool to slacken the filter initially, then unscrew it by hand the rest of the way **(see illustration)**. Empty the oil from the old filter into the container.

11 Use a clean rag to remove all oil, dirt and sludge from the filter sealing area on the engine. Check the old filter to

4.5 Slackening the engine oil drain plug

4.8 Oil filter location (arrowed)

4.10 Slackening the filter using an oil filter removal tool

5.3 Using a hydrometer to measure the specific gravity of the coolant

make sure that the rubber sealing ring has not stuck to the engine. If it has, carefully remove it.

12 Apply a light coating of clean engine oil to the sealing ring on the new filter, then screw the filter into position on the engine. Tighten the filter firmly by hand only - **do not** use any tools.

13 Remove the old oil and all tools from under the vehicle then, if applicable, lower the vehicle to the ground.

14 Fill the engine through the filler hole in the cylinder head cover, using the correct grade and type of oil (see *"Lubricants, fluids and capacities"*). Pour in half the specified quantity of oil first, then wait a few minutes for the oil to drain into the sump. Continue to add oil, a small quantity at a time, until the level is up to the lower mark on the dipstick. Adding approximately 1.0 litre will bring the level up to the upper mark on the dipstick.

15 Start the engine and run it for a few minutes, while checking for leaks around the oil filter seal and the sump drain plug. Note that there may be a delay of a few seconds before the low oil pressure warning light goes out when the engine is first started, as the oil circulates through the new oil filter and the engine oil galleries before the pressure builds up.

16 Stop the engine, and wait a few minutes for the oil to settle in the sump once

Note: It is antisocial and illegal to dump oil down the drain. To find the location of your local oil recycling bank, call this number free.

OIL CARE

OIL BANK LINE 0800 66 33 66

more. With the new oil circulated and the filter now completely full, recheck the level on the dipstick, and add more oil as necessary.

17 Dispose of the used engine oil safely.

5 Coolant specific gravity check

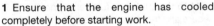

1 Ensure that the engine has cooled completely before starting work.

2 Slowly unscrew the coolant expansion tank cap by about half a turn, allowing any residual pressure in the cooling system to reduce gradually - use a cloth to protect your hands from any escaping steam.

3 Insert a hydrometer into the expansion tank filler neck and measure the specific gravity of the coolant **(see illustration)**. Compare your measurement with the figures given in the Specifications.

4 The hydrometer shown in the photo incorporates an integral syringe, which allows a 'sample' of the coolant to be collected. The coloured indicator balls inside the hydrometer float or sink in the coolant sample, depending on the specific gravity.

5 If the specific gravity is too low, do not try to correct it by adding neat antifreeze, as it may not mix completely with the existing coolant and could lead to 'hot spots' in the cooling system. With reference to Section 28, partially drain the cooling system, then refill it with antifreeze and water mixed in the correct proportions.

6 If the specific gravity is too high, refer to Section 28 and partially drain the cooling system, then top up with clean water.

6 Manual transmission oil level check

1 Ensure that the vehicle is parked on level ground then, where applicable, remove the engine/transmission undershield to gain access to the transmission filler/level plug.

2 Remove all traces of dirt from around the filler/level plug which is located on the left-hand side of the transmission, behind the driveshaft inboard joint. Place a suitable container beneath the plug to catch any escaping oil, then unscrew the plug and recover the sealing washer **(see illustrations)**.

3 Check that the oil is level with the bottom of the filler/level plug hole. Note that oil which has collected behind the filler/level plug will probably trickle out when the plug is removed, which can give a false impression that the level is correct.

4 If necessary, top up using the specified type of oil (see *"Lubricants, fluids and capacities"*). Refilling the transmission is an awkward operation. Allow plenty of time for the oil level to settle properly before checking it. Note that the car must be parked on flat level ground when checking the oil level.

5 Using a tube inserted through the filler/level plug hole, slowly top up the level until the oil reaches the bottom of the filler/level plug hole **(see illustration)**. Allow plenty of time for the level to stabilise.

6 When the level is correct, refit the filler/level plug, using a new sealing washer, and tighten it to the specified torque.

7 Automatic transmission fluid level check

1 The transmission oil level is checked using a dipstick located at the left-hand side of the

1A

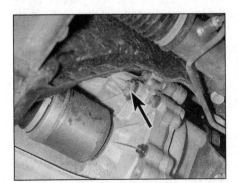

6.2a Transmission filler/level plug (arrowed) – "R65"-type transmission

6.2b Transmission filler/level plug (arrowed) – "PG1"-type transmission

6.5 Topping up the transmission oil level – "PG1"-type transmission

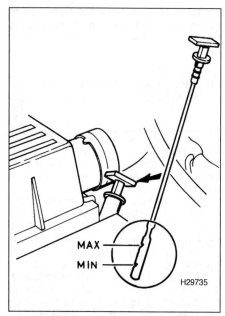

7.1 Automatic transmission fluid level dipstick location (arrowed) and markings

8.1 Check the condition of the brake servo vacuum hose

9.1 Checking the condition of a coolant hose

engine, behind the air cleaner **(see illustration)**.

2 In order to check the fluid level, the transmission must be at operating temperature (take the vehicle on a short run), and the vehicle must be parked on level ground.

3 With the engine running at idle speed, and the handbrake applied, move the gear selector lever through its full range of movement 3 times, starting and finishing in position "N".

4 Withdraw the dipstick, and wipe it with a clean, lint-free cloth, then re-insert the dipstick, and withdraw it once more.

5 Read off the fluid level on the dipstick, which should be between the "maximum" and "minimum" marks.

6 If topping up is necessary, first stop the engine, then top up through the dipstick tube, using the specified type of fluid (see *"Lubricants, fluids and capacities"*). A funnel will help to avoid spillage.

7 Re-check the fluid level as described previously and, if necessary, continue to top up until the fluid level reaches the "maximum" mark on the dipstick.

8 On completion, re-insert the dipstick, and move the selector lever to position "P", then stop the engine.

8 Vacuum hose condition check

1 Open the bonnet and check the condition of the vacuum hose that connects the brake servo to the inlet manifold **(see illustration)**. Look for damage in the form of chaffing,

melting or cracking. Check that the union nuts and T-joints (where applicable) are secure. Also examine the vacuum hoses serving the evaporative loss emission control and fuel pressure regulation systems.

2 Locate the engine control module (ECM) at the left-hand side of the engine compartment. Inspect the vacuum hose that runs from the ECM to the inlet manifold, ensuring that it is secure and free from damage. Remove it from the engine compartment and clean it out using compressed air, to expel any fuel or oil which may have collected inside it. Do not use cleaning fluids, as these may contaminate the ECU pressure sensor.

3 A leak in a vacuum hose means that air is being drawn into the hose (rather than escaping from it) and this makes leakage very difficult to detect. If you suspect that a vacuum hose may be leaking, the following method may help you to pinpoint it. Start the engine and allow it to idle. Hold one end of a length of narrow bore tubing close to your ear, then run the other end along the vacuum hose. If a leak exists, you should be able to hear a hissing noise through the tubing as the air 'escapes' into the hose at the suspected leak.

9 Underbonnet and underbody hose and pipe condition check

Coolant

⚠️ *Warning: Refer to the safety information given in 'Safety First' and Chapter 3, before disturbing any of the cooling system components.*

1 Carefully check the radiator and heater coolant hoses along their entire length. Renew any hose which is cracked, swollen or which shows signs of deterioration. Cracks will show up better if the hose is squeezed **(see illustration)**. Pay close attention to the clips that secure the hoses to the cooling system components. Hose clips that have been over-tightened can pinch and puncture hoses, resulting in leakage.

2 Inspect all the cooling system components (hoses, joint faces etc.) for leaks. Where any problems of this nature are found on system components, renew the component or gasket with reference to Chapter 3.

3 A leak from the cooling system will usually show up as white or rust-coloured deposits, on the area surrounding the leak.

Leaks in the cooling system will usually show up as white or rust coloured deposits around the point of leakage

Fuel

⚠️ *Warning: Refer to the safety information given in 'Safety First' and the relevant part of Chapter 4, before disturbing any of the fuel system components.*

4 Petrol leaks are difficult to pinpoint, unless the leakage is significant and hence easily visible. Fuel tends to evaporate quickly once it comes into contact with air, especially in a hot engine bay. Small drips can disappear before you get a chance to identify the point of leakage. If you suspect that there is a fuel leak from the area of the engine bay, leave the vehicle overnight then start the engine from cold, with the bonnet open. Metal components tend to shrink when they are cold, and rubber seals and hoses tend to harden, so any leaks may be more apparent whilst the engine is warming up from a cold start.

5 Check all fuel lines at their connections to the fuel rail, fuel pressure regulator and fuel

9.5 Check for fuel leaks at the fuel filter unions (arrowed)

9.9 Checking a power steering fluid hose for damage

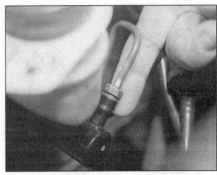

9.15 Checking a master cylinder brake pipe union for leakage

filter **(see illustration)**. Examine each rubber fuel hose along its length for splits or cracks. Check for leakage from the crimped joints between rubber and metal fuel lines. Examine the unions between the metal fuel lines and the fuel filter housing. Also check the area around the fuel injectors for signs of O-ring leakage.

6 To identify fuel leaks between the fuel tank and the engine bay, the vehicle should be raised and securely supported on axle stands (see "*Jacking and Vehicle Support*"). Inspect the petrol tank and filler neck for punctures, cracks and other damage. The connection between the filler neck and tank is especially critical. Sometimes a rubber filler neck or connecting hose will leak due to loose retaining clamps or deteriorated rubber.

7 Carefully check all rubber hoses and metal fuel lines leading away from the petrol tank. Check for loose connections, deteriorated hoses, kinked lines, and other damage. Pay particular attention to the vent pipes and hoses, which often loop up around the filler neck and can become blocked or kinked, making tank filling difficult. Follow the fuel supply and return lines to the front of the vehicle, carefully inspecting them all the way for signs of damage or corrosion. Renew damaged sections as necessary.

Automatic transmission (CVT) fluid

8 Check the hoses leading to the transmission fluid cooler at the front of the engine bay for leakage. Look for deterioration caused by corrosion and damage from grounding, or debris thrown up from the road surface.

Power assisted steering (PAS) fluid

9 Examine the hose running between the fluid reservoir and the power steering pump, and the return hose running from the steering rack to the fluid reservoir. Also examine the high pressure supply hose between the pump and the steering rack **(see illustration)**.

10 Where applicable, check the hoses leading to the PAS fluid cooler at the front of the engine bay. Look for deterioration caused

by corrosion and damage from grounding, or debris thrown up from the road surface.

11 Pay particular attention to crimped unions, and the area surrounding the hoses that are secured with adjustable worm drive clips. Like automatic transmission fluid, PAS fluid is a thin oil, and is usually red in colour.

Air conditioning refrigerant

 Warning: Refer to the safety information given in 'Safety First' and Chapter 3, regarding the dangers of disturbing any of the air conditioning system components.

12 The air conditioning system is filled with a liquid refrigerant, which is retained under high pressure. If the air conditioning system is opened and depressurised without the aid of specialised equipment, the refrigerant will immediately turn into gas and escape into the atmosphere. If the liquid comes into contact with your skin, it can cause severe frostbite. In addition, the refrigerant may contain substances which are environmentally damaging; for this reason, it should not be allowed to escape into the atmosphere.

13 Any suspected air conditioning system leaks should be immediately referred to a Rover dealer or air conditioning specialist. Leakage will be shown up as a steady drop in the level of refrigerant in the system - refer to Section 10 for details.

14 Note that water may drip from the condenser drain pipe, underneath the car, immediately after the air conditioning system has been in use. This is normal, and should not be cause for concern.

Brake fluid

 Warning: Refer to the safety information given in 'Safety First' and Chapter 9, regarding the dangers of handling brake fluid.

15 With reference to Chapter 9, examine the area surrounding the brake pipe unions at the master cylinder for signs of leakage **(see illustration)**. Check the area around the base of fluid reservoir, for signs of leakage caused by seal failure. Also examine the brake pipe unions at the ABS hydraulic unit. Brake fluid is

an effective paint stripper, so if cracked or bubbling paintwork on or around any of the braking system components is found, suspect fluid leakage.

16 If fluid loss is evident, but the leak cannot be pinpointed in the engine bay, the brake calipers and underbody brakelines should be carefully checked with the vehicle raised and supported on axle stands (see "*Jacking and Vehicle Support*"). Leakage of fluid from the braking system is a serious fault that must be rectified immediately.

17 Brake hydraulic fluid is a toxic substance with a watery consistency. New fluid is almost colourless, but it becomes darker with age and use.

Unidentified fluid leaks

18 If there are signs that a fluid of some description is leaking from the vehicle, but you cannot identify the type of fluid or its exact origin, park the vehicle overnight and slide a large piece of card underneath it. Providing that the card is positioned in roughly in the right location, even the smallest leak will show up on the card. Not only will this help you to pinpoint the exact location of the leak, it should be easier to identify the fluid from its colour. Bear in mind, though, that the leak may only be occurring when the engine is running!

Vacuum hoses

19 Refer to Section 8.

10 Air conditioning system check

1 The refrigerant condition and level is checked via the sightglass on the top of the receiver drier. The receiver drier is situated in the engine compartment, just to the left of the radiator.

2 Start the engine then switch on the air conditioning system and allow the engine to idle for a couple of minutes whilst observing the sightglass. If the air conditioning system is operating normally then occasional bubbles should be visible through the sightglass.

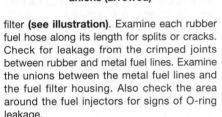

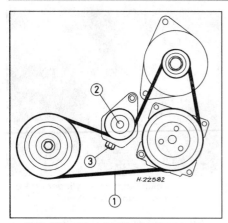

11.8 Alternator drivebelt adjustment - models with air conditioning

1 *Drivebelt tension checking point*
2 *Adjuster pulley spindle bolt*
3 *Adjuster bolt*

3 If a constant stream of bubbles is visible, the refrigerant level is low and must be topped up. If the sightglass has become clouded or streaked, there is a fault in the system. If either condition is present, the vehicle must be taken to a Rover dealer or suitable professional refrigeration specialist for the air conditioning system to be checked further and overhauled.

11 Auxiliary drivebelt tension and condition check

General information

1 Either one or two auxiliary drivebelts may be fitted, depending on model and specification. Both drivebelts are of the flat, multi-ribbed type and take drive from a pulley bolted to the right-hand end of the crankshaft.
2 Where a single belt is fitted, it provides drives to the alternator. The belt is tensioned by means of a manual adjustment mechanism at the base of the alternator, which alters the position of the alternator in relation to engine. On models equipped with air conditioning, the

same belt also drives the refrigerant compressor. In this configuration, the belt is tensioned by means of a manually adjustable roller tensioner assembly.
3 A second (outer) belt is fitted to models with power assisted steering (PAS), to provide drive to the PAS hydraulic pump. The belt is tensioned either by means of a manually adjustable roller tensioner, or an automatic tensioner assembly.

Checking

4 Apply the handbrake then jack up the front of the vehicle and support it on axle stands (see "*Jacking and Vehicle Support*"). Remove the right-hand front roadwheel.
5 From underneath the front of the vehicle, slacken and remove the bolts securing the bumper flange to the body. Remove the bolts securing the front undercover panel to the body and remove the panel.
6 Check the drivebelt(s) for cracks, splitting, fraying or damage, whilst rotating the crankshaft clockwise using a suitable spanner applied to the crankshaft pulley bolt, so that the entire length of each belt is examined. Check also for signs of glazing (shiny patches) and for separation of the belt plies. Renew the belt if worn or damaged, with reference to Chapter 5A or 10 as appropriate.

Adjustment

Alternator drivebelt - models with air conditioning

7 Carry out the operations described in paragraphs 4 and 5.
8 The drivebelt tension is checked by measuring the amount of deflection that takes place when a force of 10 kg is applied (using a spring balance, or similar) midway between the crankshaft and air conditioning pulleys on the belt's lower run. If the deflection measured is more or less than that specified, the drivebelt must be adjusted as follows **(see illustration)**.
9 Slacken the drivebelt adjuster (idler) pulley spindle nut and bolt, then rotate the adjuster bolt (situated on the underside of the pulley assembly) clockwise or anti-clockwise as required to obtain the correct belt tension.
10 When the correct tension is achieved,

tighten the adjuster pulley spindle bolt and nut, and rotate the crankshaft several times to settle the drivebelt. Recheck the belt tension, repeating the adjustment procedure if necessary.
11 Refit the undercover panel and roadwheel, then lower the vehicle to the ground.

Alternator drivebelt - models without air conditioning

12 Carry out the operations described in paragraphs 4 and 5.
13 The drivebelt tension is checked by measuring the amount of deflection that takes place when a force of 10 kg is applied (using a spring balance, or similar) midway between the crankshaft and alternator pulleys on the belt's upper run. If the deflection measured is more or less than that specified, the drivebelt must be adjusted as follows.
14 Slacken both the alternator upper pivot mounting bolts and the lower adjusting arm mounting bolt. Rotate the adjuster bolt clockwise or anti-clockwise as required to obtain the correct belt tension **(see illustrations)**.
15 When the correct tension is achieved, tighten the alternator adjusting arm and pivot bolts to the specified torque and rotate the crankshaft several times to settle the drivebelt. Recheck the belt tension and re-adjust if necessary.
16 Refit the undercover panel and roadwheel, then lower the vehicle to the ground.

Power steering drivebelt - models with manual tensioner

17 The drivebelt tension is checked by measuring the amount of deflection that takes place when a force of 10 kg is applied (using a spring balance, or similar) midway between the crankshaft and PAS pump pulleys on the belt's upper run. If the deflection measured is more or less than that specified, the drivebelt must be adjusted as follows.
18 Slacken the drivebelt adjuster (idler) pulley spindle nut and bolt, then rotate the adjuster bolt (situated on the underside of the pulley assembly) clockwise or anti-clockwise as required to obtain the correct belt tension **(see illustrations)**.

11.14a Slacken the alternator upper pivot mounting bolts (arrowed) . . .

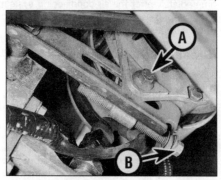

11.14b . . . and lower adjusting arm bolt (A) then rotate adjuster bolt (B) - models without air conditioning

11.18a Slacken the adjuster pulley spindle nut . . .

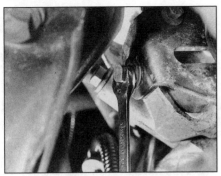

11.18b . . . and rotate the adjuster bolt until the power steering pump drivebelt tension is correct

12.2 Make sure that the exhaust mountings are in good condition

13.2 Front brake pad friction material (arrowed) can be measured through the inspection aperture in caliper body

19 When the correct tension is achieved, tighten the adjuster pulley spindle bolt and nut, and rotate the crankshaft several times to settle the drivebelt. Recheck the belt tension, repeating the adjustment procedure if necessary.

20 Refit the undercover panel and roadwheel, then lower the vehicle to the ground.

Power steering drivebelt - models with automatic tensioner

21 The drivebelt tension is set automatically by the tensioner assembly and requires no adjustment. Refer to Chapter 10 for renewal details.

12 Exhaust system check

1 With the engine cold (at least an hour after the vehicle has been driven), check the complete exhaust system from the engine to the end of the tailpipe. The exhaust system is most easily checked with the vehicle raised on a hoist, or suitably supported on axle stands, so that the exhaust components are readily visible and accessible.

2 Check the exhaust pipes and connections for evidence of leaks, severe corrosion and damage. Make sure that all brackets and mountings are in good condition, and that all relevant nuts and bolts are tight **(see illustration)**. Leakage at any of the joints or in other parts of the system will usually show up as a black sooty stain in the vicinity of the leak.

3 Rattles and other noises can often be traced to the exhaust system, especially the brackets and mountings. Try to move the pipes and silencers. If the components are able to come into contact with the body or suspension parts, secure the system with new mountings. Otherwise separate the joints (if possible) and twist the pipes as necessary to provide additional clearance.

13 Front brake check

1 Firmly apply the handbrake then jack up the front of the vehicle and support it securely on axle stands (see "*Jacking and Vehicle Support*"). Remove the front roadwheels.

2 For a quick check, the thickness of friction material remaining on each brake pad can be measured through the inspection aperture in the front of the caliper body **(see illustration)**. If any pad's friction material is worn to the specified thickness or less, all four pads must be renewed as a set.

3 For a comprehensive check, the brake pads should be removed and cleaned. This will permit the operation of the caliper to be checked and the condition of the brake disc itself to be fully examined on both sides. Refer to Chapter 9 for further information.

14 Rear brake check

Models with rear drum brakes

1 Chock the front wheels then jack up the rear of the vehicle and support it on axle stands (see "*Jacking and Vehicle Support*").

14.2 Remove grommet to check rear brake shoe friction material thickness

2 For a quick check the thickness of friction material remaining on one of the brake shoes can be measured through the slot in the brake backplate that is exposed by prising out its sealing grommet **(see illustration)**. If a rod of the same diameter as the specified minimum thickness is placed against the shoe friction material, the amount of wear can quickly be assessed. If any shoe's friction material is worn to the specified thickness or less, all four shoes must be renewed.

3 For a comprehensive check, the brake drums should be removed and cleaned. This will permit the wheel cylinders to be checked and the condition of the brake drum itself to be fully examined. Refer to Chapter 9 for further information.

Models with rear disc brakes

4 Chock the front wheels then jack up the rear of the vehicle and support it on axle stands (see "*Jacking and Vehicle Support*").

5 For a quick check, the thickness of friction material remaining on each brake pad can be measured through the inspection aperture in the caliper body. If any pad's friction material is worn to the specified thickness or less, all four pads must be renewed as a set.

6 For a comprehensive check, the brake pads should be removed and cleaned. This will permit the operation of the caliper to be checked and the condition of the brake disc itself to be fully examined on both sides. Refer to Chapter 9 for further information.

15 Driveshaft and gaiter check

1 With the vehicle raised and securely supported on axle stands (see "*Jacking and Vehicle Support*"), turn the steering onto full lock then slowly rotate the roadwheel. Inspect the condition of the outer constant velocity (CV) joint rubber gaiters while squeezing the gaiters to open out the folds

1A

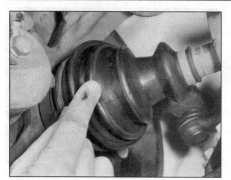

15.1 Inspecting a driveshaft joint rubber gaiter

16.2 Checking the condition of a steering gear rubber gaiter

16.4 Checking the condition of the steering and suspension components by rocking a roadwheel

(see illustration). Check for signs of cracking, splits or deterioration of the rubber which may allow the grease to escape and lead to the entry of water and grit into the joint. Also check the security and condition of the gaiter retaining clips. Repeat these checks on the inner CV joints. If any damage or deterioration is found, then renew the gaiters.

2 Check the general condition of the CV joints by first holding the driveshaft and attempting to rotate the roadwheel. Repeat this check by holding the inner joint and attempting to rotate the driveshaft. Any appreciable movement indicates wear in the joints or driveshaft splines, or a loose driveshaft nut.

16 Suspension and steering check

Front suspension and steering

1 Raise the front of the vehicle and securely support it on axle stands (see *"Jacking and Vehicle Support"*).

2 Inspect the balljoint dust covers and the steering gear rubber gaiters for splits, chafing or deterioration **(see illustration)**. Any wear of these components will cause loss of lubricant, together with dirt and water entry, resulting in rapid deterioration of the balljoints or steering gear.

3 On vehicles equipped with power steering, check the fluid hoses for chafing or deterioration and the pipe and hose unions for fluid leakage. Also check for signs of fluid leakage under pressure from the steering gear rubber gaiters which would indicate failed fluid seals within the steering gear.

4 Grasp the roadwheel at the 12 o'clock and 6 o'clock positions and try to rock it **(see illustration)**. Very slight free play may be felt but if the movement is appreciable then further investigation is necessary to determine the source. Continue rocking the wheel while an assistant depresses the brake pedal. If the movement is now eliminated or significantly reduced, it is likely that the hub bearings are at fault. If the free play is still evident with the

brake pedal depressed, then there is wear in the suspension joints or mountings.

5 Now grasp the roadwheel at the 9 o'clock and 3 o'clock positions and try to rock it as before. Any movement felt now may again be caused by wear in the hub bearings, or in the track rod balljoints. If a balljoint is worn the visual movement will be obvious. If the inner joint is suspect it can be felt by placing a hand over the steering gear rubber gaiter and gripping the track rod. If the wheel is now rocked, movement will be felt at the inner joint if wear has taken place.

6 Using a large screwdriver or flat bar check for wear in the suspension mounting bushes by levering between the relevant suspension component and its attachment point. Some movement is to be expected as the mountings are made of rubber, but excessive wear should be obvious. Also check the condition of any visible rubber bushes, looking for splits, cracks or contamination of the rubber.

7 With the vehicle standing on its wheels, have an assistant turn the steering wheel back and forth about an eighth of a turn each way. There should be very little, if any, lost movement between the steering wheel and the roadwheels. If this is not the case, closely observe the joints and mountings previously described but in addition, check for wear of the steering column universal joint and the steering gear itself.

Rear suspension

8 Chock the front wheels then jack up the rear of the vehicle and support it on axle stands (see *"Jacking and Vehicle Support"*).

9 Working as described for the front suspension, check the rear hub bearings and the trailing arm and lateral link bushes for wear.

17 Handbrake check and adjustment

Checking

1 The handbrake should be capable of holding the parked vehicle stationary, even on steep slopes, when applied with moderate

force. Equally, the handbrake must release properly, or the brakes will bind and overheat when the car is driven.

2 The mechanism should be firm and positive in feel with no trace of stiffness or sponginess from the cables and should release immediately the handbrake lever is released. If the mechanism is faulty in any of these respects then it must be checked immediately.

3 To check the handbrake setting, first apply the footbrake firmly several times to establish correct shoe-to-drum clearance. Applying normal, moderate pressure, pull the handbrake lever to the fully-applied position whilst counting the number of 'clicks' produced by the handbrake ratchet mechanism. Check that the number of clicks produced is as listed in the Specifications. If this is not the case, then adjustment is required.

Adjustment

4 To adjust the handbrake, chock the front wheels then jack up the rear of the vehicle and support it on axle stands (see *"Jacking and Vehicle Support"*).

5 Lift out the ashtray from the rear of the centre console to gain access to the handbrake adjusting nut **(see illustrations)**.

6 Apply the handbrake and check that the equalizer and cables move freely and smoothly, then set the lever on the first notch of the ratchet mechanism. With the lever in this position, rotate the handbrake lever

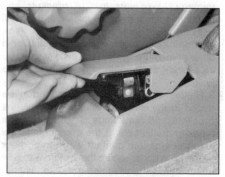

17.5a Remove the ashtray from the rear of the centre console . . .

17.5b ... to gain access to the handbrake cable adjuster nut (arrowed) and equalizer mechanism

adjusting nut until only a slight drag can be felt when the rear wheels are turned by hand. Once this is the case, fully release the handbrake lever and check that the wheels rotate freely. Check adjustment by applying the handbrake fully whilst counting the clicks emitted from the handbrake ratchet. Carry out the adjustment procedure again, if necessary.

7 Once adjustment is correct, refit the ashtray and lower the vehicle to the ground.

18 Lock and hinge lubrication

1 Lubricate the hinges of the bonnet, doors and tailgate with a light duty oil.
2 Lightly grease the bonnet release mechanism and cable.
3 The door and tailgate latches, strikers and locks must be lubricated using only the special Rover Door Lock and Latch Lubricant supplied in small sachets. Inject 1 gram into each lock and wipe off any surplus, then apply a thin film to the latches and strikers.
4 Do not lubricate the steering lock mechanism with oil or any other lubricant which might foul the ignition switch contacts. If the lock is stiff, try the effect of a proprietary electrical contact lubricant, rather than conventional lubricant.
5 If a sunroof is fitted, lubricate very sparingly the seal lip with Rover supplied non-staining seal grease.

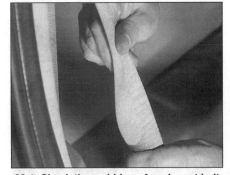

20.1 Check the webbing of each seat belt for signs of fraying, cuts or other damage

19 Windscreen and numberplate condition check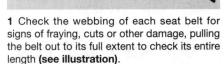

Refer to the MOT pre-test checks described in the *Reference* Chapter, at the end of this manual.

20 Seat belt check

1 Check the webbing of each seat belt for signs of fraying, cuts or other damage, pulling the belt out to its full extent to check its entire length **(see illustration)**.
2 Check the operation of the belt buckles by fitting the belt tongue plate and pulling hard to ensure that it remains locked in position.
3 Check the retractor mechanism (inertia reel only) by pulling out the belt to the halfway point and jerking it downwards **(see illustration)**. The mechanism must lock immediately to prevent any further unreeling but must allow free movement during normal driving.
4 Ensure that all belt mounting bolts are securely tightened. Note that the bolts are shouldered so that the belt anchor points are free to rotate.
5 If there is any sign of damage, or any doubt about a belt's condition, then it must be renewed. If the vehicle has been involved in a collision, then any belt in use at the time must be renewed as a matter of course and all other belts checked carefully.
6 Use only warm water and non-detergent soap to clean the belts.
Caution: Never use any chemical cleaners, strong detergents, dyes or bleaches. Keep the belts fully extended until they have dried naturally and do not apply heat to dry them.

21 Airbag system component check

1 Checking of the airbag system by the home mechanic is limited to a visual inspection of

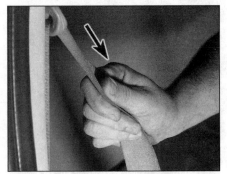

20.3 Checking the operation of the inertia reel locking mechanism

the outer surface of the driver and passenger air bag modules (as applicable). If the surface of the casing has sustained any damage (such as that caused by an impact, or fluid spillage for example) then the air bag system should be checked by a Rover dealer at the earliest opportunity.
2 Sit in the driver's seat and release the steering column lock. On models with power steering, start the engine and allow it to idle. Turn the steering wheel from lock to lock, whilst listening to the rotary coupler at the steering wheel hub. Any noise or roughness in operation could indicate a worn rotary coupler - refer to a Rover dealer for further advice.
3 The SRS warning lamp on the instrument panel should illuminate for about six seconds when the ignition key is turned to the 'II' position and then extinguish. If the lamp fails to extinguish, or does not illuminate at all, there may be a fault with the SRS system; the advice of a Rover dealer should be sought.

22 Oxygen sensor operation check

This check should be carried out by a Rover dealer or suitably-equipped fuel injection specialist.

23 Exhaust gas CO content check

Experienced home mechanics with access to a tachometer and an accurately calibrated exhaust gas analyser may be able to check the exhaust CO level. Follow the instructions supplied with the test equipment. However, if the level is found to be in need of adjustment, the vehicle must be taken to a Rover dealer for further testing.

No manual adjustment of the exhaust CO level is possible.

24 Road test

Instruments and electrical equipment

1 Check the operation of all instruments and electrical equipment.
2 Make sure that all instruments read correctly, and switch on all electrical equipment in turn, to check that it functions properly.

Steering and suspension

3 Check for any abnormalities in the steering, suspension, handling or road 'feel'.
4 Drive the vehicle, and check that there are no unusual vibrations or noises.

1A

5 Check that the steering feels positive, with no excessive 'sloppiness', or roughness, and check for any suspension noises when cornering and driving over bumps.

Drivetrain

6 Check the performance of the engine, clutch, transmission and driveshafts.
7 Listen for any unusual noises from the engine, clutch and transmission.
8 Make sure that the engine runs smoothly when idling, and that there is no hesitation when accelerating.
9 Check that the clutch action is smooth and progressive, that the drive is taken up smoothly, and that the pedal travel is not excessive. Also listen for any noises when the clutch pedal is depressed.
10 Check that all gears can be engaged smoothly without noise, and that the gear lever action is not abnormally vague or 'notchy'.
11 Listen for a metallic clicking sound from the front of the vehicle, as the vehicle is driven slowly in a circle with the steering on full-lock. Carry out this check in both directions. If a clicking noise is heard, this indicates wear in a driveshaft joint (see Chapter 8).

Check the operation and performance of the braking system

12 Make sure that the vehicle does not pull to one side when braking, and that the wheels do not lock prematurely when braking hard.
13 Check that there is no vibration through the steering when braking.
14 Check that the handbrake operates correctly, and that it holds the vehicle stationary on a slope.

Every 24 000 miles (40 000 km) or 2 years - whichever comes first

25 Automatic transmission fluid renewal

Note: *A new fluid drain plug sealing washer will be required on refitting.*
1 In order to drain the transmission fluid, the transmission must be at operating temperature (take the vehicle on a short run). **Caution: Take care when draining the fluid, as it will be very hot!**
2 Release the clips securing the air intake trunking to the throttle body and the air cleaner casing, and remove the trunking.

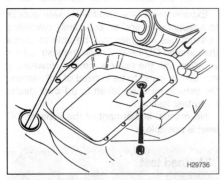

25.5 Automatic transmission fluid pan drain plug location (arrowed)

3 Withdraw the automatic transmission fluid level dipstick.
4 Apply the handbrake, then jack up the front of the vehicle and support securely on axle stands (see *"Jacking and Vehicle Support"*).
5 Using a suitable Allen key or hexagon bit, slacken the fluid drain plug (located at the rear of the fluid pan) about half a turn **(see illustration)**. Position the draining container under the drain plug, then remove the plug completely. If possible, try to keep the plug pressed into the fluid pan while unscrewing it by hand the last couple of turns.

> **HAYNES HiNT** *As the plug releases from the threads, move it away sharply, so that the stream of oil from the sump runs into the container, not up your sleeve!*

6 Allow some time for the oil to drain, noting that it may be necessary to reposition the container as the oil flow slows to a trickle.
7 After all the oil has drained, wipe the drain plug and the sealing washer with a clean rag. The sealing washer should be renewed as a matter of course. Clean the area around the drain plug opening, and refit the plug complete with the new sealing washer.

Tighten the plug securely, preferably to the specified torque, using a torque wrench.
8 Lower the vehicle to the ground, and ensure that it is level.
9 Refill the transmission through the dipstick tube, using the specified type of fluid (see *"Lubricants, fluids and capacities"*). A funnel will help to avoid spillage. Refill the transmission slowly, and check the fluid level on the dipstick at frequent intervals. Add fluid until the level reaches the "minimum" mark on the dipstick.
10 Refit the dipstick, then start the engine, and check the fluid level as described in Section 7. Top up the fluid level if necessary.
11 On completion, refit the air intake trunking.

26 Air cleaner filter element renewal

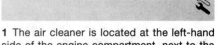

1 The air cleaner is located at the left-hand side of the engine compartment, next to the battery **(see illustration)**.
2 Release the four securing clips, and lift off the air cleaner cover, then lift out the element **(see illustration)**.
3 Wipe out the air cleaner casing and the cover using a clean cloth **(see illustration)**.

26.1 Air cleaner location (arrowed)

26.2 Lifting off the air cleaner cover

26.3 Wiping out the air cleaner casing

26.4 Fitting a new air cleaner element

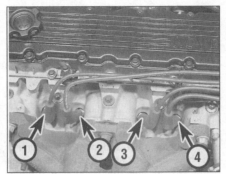

27.3a Spark plug lead identification – K8 engine

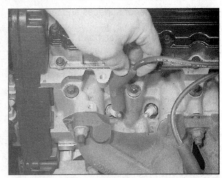

27.3b Pulling the HT lead from No 1 spark plug

4 Fit the new element, then refit the cover and secure with the clips **(see illustration)**.

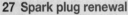

27 Spark plug renewal

1 The correct functioning of the spark plugs is vital for the correct running and efficiency of the engine. It is essential that the plugs fitted are appropriate for the engine (a suitable type is specified at the beginning of this Chapter). If this type is used and the engine is in good condition, the spark plugs should not need attention between scheduled replacement intervals. Spark plug cleaning is rarely necessary, and should not be attempted unless specialised equipment is available, as damage can easily be caused to the firing ends.

2 On K16 engine models, remove the two securing screws, and withdraw the spark plug cover from the centre of the cylinder head cover.

3 If there are no identification marks on the spark plug (HT) leads, label the leads to correspond to the cylinder the lead serves (No 1 cylinder is at the timing belt end of the engine). Pull the leads from the plugs by gripping the end fitting, not the lead, otherwise the lead connection may be fractured **(see illustrations)**.

4 Unscrew the plugs using a spark plug spanner, suitable box spanner or a deep

socket and extension bar. Keep the socket aligned with the spark plug - if it is forcibly moved to one side, the ceramic insulator may be broken off **(see illustration)**. As each plug is removed, examine it as follows.

5 Examination of the spark plugs will give a good indication of the condition of the engine. If the insulator nose of the spark plug is clean and white, with no deposits, this is indicative of a weak mixture or a plug of the wrong temperature grade (a "hot" plug transfers heat away from the electrode slowly, a "cold" plug transfers heat away quickly).

6 If the tip and insulator nose are covered with hard black-looking deposits, then this indicates that the mixture is too rich. Should the plug be black and oily, then it is likely that the engine is fairly worn, as well as the mixture being too rich.

7 If the insulator nose is covered with light tan to greyish-brown deposits, then the mixture is correct and it is likely that the engine is in good condition.

8 The spark plug electrode gap is of considerable importance as, if it is too large or too small, the size of the spark and its efficiency will be seriously impaired. The gap should be measured using a feeler blade and set to the value given in the Specifications at the beginning of this Chapter.

9 To set the gap, bend the outer plug electrode in the required direction, until the correct gap is achieved. The centre electrode should never be bent, as this may crack the insulator and cause plug failure, if nothing

worse. If using feeler blades, the gap is correct when the appropriate-size blade is a firm sliding fit **(see illustration)**.

10 Special spark plug electrode gap adjusting tools are available from most motor accessory shops, or from some spark plug manufacturers **(see illustration)**.

11 Before fitting the spark plugs, check that the threaded connector sleeves are tight, and

HAYNES HINT

It is often difficult to insert spark plugs into their holes without cross-threading them. To avoid this possibility, fit a short length of suitable internal diameter rubber hose over the end of the spark plug. The flexible hose acts as a universal joint to help align the plug with the plug hole. Should the plug begin to cross-thread, the hose will slip on the spark plug, preventing thread damage to the cylinder head.

1A

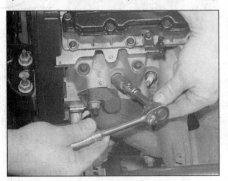

27.4 Unscrewing a spark plug

27.9 Measuring a spark plug gap using a feeler blade

27.10 Adjusting the spark plug gap using a special tool

that the plug exterior surfaces and threads are clean.

12 Remove the rubber hose (if used), and tighten the plug to the specified torque using the spark plug socket and a torque wrench. Refit the remaining spark plugs in the same manner.

13 Connect the HT leads in their correct order. On K16 engines, refit the spark plug cover on completion.

28 Coolant renewal

 Warning: Wait until the engine is completely cold before starting the coolant renewal procedure. Do not allow antifreeze to come into contact with your skin or painted surfaces of the vehicle. Rinse off spills immediately with plenty of water. Never leave antifreeze lying around in an open container or in a puddle in the driveway or on the garage floor. Children and pets are attracted by its sweet smell; and antifreeze can be fatal if ingested.

Antifreeze mixture

1 Antifreeze should always be renewed at the specified intervals. This is necessary not only to maintain the anti-freezing properties of the coolant but also to prevent corrosion which would otherwise occur, as the corrosion inhibitors in the coolant become progressively less effective.

2 Always use an ethylene glycol based antifreeze which is suitable for use in mixed-metal cooling systems.

3 The type of antifreeze and levels of protection afforded are indicated in *"Lubricants, fluids and capacities"* and Specifications. To achieve the recommended 50% concentration, equal quantities of antifreeze and clean, soft water must be mixed together. It is best to make up slightly more than is actually needed to refill the cooling system, so that a supply is available for subsequent topping-up.

Caution: Always pre-mix the antifreeze and water in a suitable container before refilling the cooling system. If the antifreeze and water are poured into the cooling system separately, they may not mix correctly and could cause localised overheating, which may lead to engine damage.

Draining

4 To drain the cooling system, remove the expansion tank filler cap then move the heater air temperature control to the maximum heat position.

5 Place a large drain tray beneath the bottom hose connection, at the bottom left-hand corner of the radiator. Release the hose clip and carefully pull the bottom hose off the radiator stub, allowing the coolant to drain into the container below. Once the system has drained completely, reconnect the bottom hose and secure with the hose clip.

Flushing

6 With time, the cooling system may gradually lose its efficiency due to the radiator core having become choked with rust, scale deposits and other sediment. To minimise this, the system should be flushed as described in the following paragraphs, whenever the coolant is renewed.

7 With the coolant drained, refill the system with fresh water. Refit the expansion tank filler cap, start the engine and warm it up to normal operating temperature, then stop it and (after allowing it to cool down completely) drain the system again. Repeat as necessary until only clean water can be seen to emerge, then refill finally with the specified coolant mixture.

8 If the specified coolant mixture has been used and has been renewed at the specified intervals, the above procedure will be sufficient to keep clean the system for a considerable length of time. If, however, the system has been neglected, a more thorough operation will be required, as follows.

9 First drain the coolant, then disconnect the radiator top and bottom hoses from the radiator. Insert a garden hose into the radiator top hose outlet and allow water (under LOW pressure only) to circulate through the radiator until it runs clean from the bottom outlet.

Caution: Do not flush with water under high pressure, as this may damage the radiator.

10 To flush the engine, insert the garden hose into the top hose and allow water to circulate until it runs clear from the bottom hose. If, after a reasonable period, the water still does not run clear, the cooling system should be flushed with a good proprietary cleaning agent. Bear in mind, however, that any leaks sealed in the past using a cooling system sealant additive may be weakened by this course of action, and could start to leak again.

11 In severe cases of contamination, reverse-flushing of the radiator may be necessary. To do this, remove the radiator, invert it and insert a garden hose into the bottom outlet. Continue flushing (again, using water under LOW pressure only) until clear water runs from the top hose outlet. If necessary, a similar procedure can be used to flush the heater matrix.

12 The use of chemical cleaners should be necessary only as a last resort as regular renewal of the coolant will prevent excessive contamination of the system.

Filling

13 With the cooling system drained and flushed, ensure that all radiator hoses are securely reconnected. Check all hose unions for security and all hoses for condition. Fresh antifreeze has a searching action which will rapidly find any weaknesses in the system.

14 Prepare a sufficient quantity of the specified coolant mixture, allowing for a surplus so as to have a reserve supply for topping-up (see *Antifreeze Mixture* above).

15 Remove the air cleaner assembly (see Chapter 4A) to gain access to the cooling system bleed screw, in the coolant rail underneath the ignition distributor. Slacken the bleed screw fully, to allow trapped air to escape during refilling **(see illustration)**.

16 Remove the expansion tank filler cap, then fill the system slowly through the filler neck **(see illustration)**. When coolant can be seen emerging from the bleed screw in a steady stream, tighten the bleed screw securely. Continue filling until the coolant level reaches the 'MAX' mark on the side of the expansion tank. Refit the filler cap and tighten it securely.

17 Start the engine and run it at no more than idle speed until it has warmed up to normal operating temperature and the radiator electric cooling fan has cut in once. Watch the temperature gauge to check for signs of overheating.

18 Stop the engine and allow it to cool down completely, then remove the expansion tank filler cap carefully and top up the tank to the

28.15 Slackening the cooling system bleed screw, to allow trapped air to escape during refilling

28.16 Remove the expansion tank filler cap, then fill the system slowly through the filler neck

28.18 Top up the expansion tank to the 'MAX' level

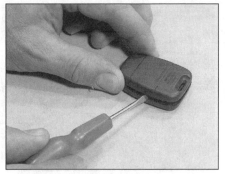

29.1a Using a flat-bladed screwdriver, carefully prise the two halves of the keypad apart . . .

29.1b . . . to expose the battery

'MAX' level **(see illustration)**. Refit the filler cap and wash off any spilt coolant from the engine compartment and bodywork with plenty of clean water.

19 After refilling, check carefully all system components for signs of coolant leaks. A label should now be attached to the radiator or expansion tank stating the type and concentration of antifreeze used and the date installed. Any subsequent topping-up should be made with the same type and concentration of antifreeze.

20 If, after draining and refilling the system, symptoms of overheating are found which did not occur previously, then the fault is almost certainly due to trapped air at some point in the system causing an air-lock and restricting the flow of coolant. Usually air is trapped because the system was refilled too quickly. In some cases, air-locks can be released by tapping or squeezing the appropriate coolant hose. If the problem persists, stop the engine and allow it to cool down completely before unscrewing the bleed screw and expansion

tank filler cap, to allow the trapped air to escape.

29 Alarm remote keypad battery renewal

1 Place the keypad on work surface and using a flat-bladed screwdriver, carefully prise the two halves of the keypad apart **(see illustrations)**. Take care to avoid damaging the rubber seal and internal components with the screwdriver blade.

2 Remove the battery from the terminal clips, noting which way up it is. Press each keypad button in turn and hold it down for a few seconds, to fully discharge the electronic components inside.

3 Obtain a new battery of the correct type and insert it between the terminal clips, ensuring that it is fitted the correct way around (the positive '+' side faces upwards). Avoid touching the contact surfaces of the battery as

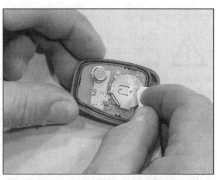

29.3 Fit the new battery, handling it with a piece of tissue paper to avoid touching the battery contact surfaces

you do this, by handling it with a piece of tissue paper; moisture from fingertips can cause the battery surfaces to corrode **(see illustration)**.

4 Press the two halves of the keypad back together, ensuring that the rubber seal is correctly located, then check the operation of the keypad.

1A

Every 48 000 miles (80 000 km) or 4 years - whichever comes first

30 Fuel filter renewal

> ⚠ **Warning: Petrol is extremely flammable – great care must be taken during this procedure. Before carrying out any operation on the fuel system, refer to the precautions given in "Safety first!", and follow them implicitly. Petrol is a highly-dangerous and volatile liquid, and the precautions necessary when handling it cannot be overstressed.**

1 The fuel filter is located on the bulkhead at the rear of the engine compartment **(see illustration)**.

2 Disconnect the battery negative lead.

3 Release the charcoal canister from its mounting bracket, and move it to one side, to improve access to the fuel filter **(see illustration)**.

4 Position a wad of absorbent cloth beneath the inlet pipe union on the bottom of the fuel filter.

5 Counterhold the union on the fuel filter,

30.1 Fuel filter location (arrowed)

30.3 Move the charcoal canister to one side

30.5 Slackening the fuel inlet pipe union

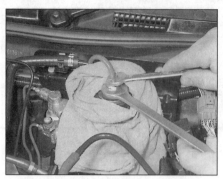

30.7 Disconnect the fuel outlet pipe . . .

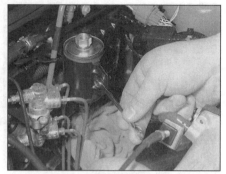

30.8a . . . then slacken the filter clamp bolt . . .

and **slowly** slacken the fuel pipe union nut using a second spanner (**see illustration**).

 Warning: Be prepared for the escape of some fuel. Take adequate fire precautions.

6 Allow the fuel pressure to dissipate, then fully unscrew the union nut, and disconnect the fuel inlet pipe. If the new filter is not going to be fitted immediately, cover the open end of the fuel pipe union to prevent dirt entry.

7 Repeat the procedure to disconnect the fuel outlet pipe from the top of the fuel filter (**see illustration**).

8 Slacken the filter clamp bolt, then withdraw the filter from the mounting bracket (**see illustrations**).

9 Collect the fuel from the filter, then dispose of the filter safely.

30.8b . . . and withdraw the filter from the mounting bracket

10 Fit the new filter using a reversal of the removal procedure, but ensure that the flow direction arrow on the side of the filter is

30.10 Ensure that the flow direction arrow on the side of the filter is pointing upwards

pointing upwards, and tighten the fuel unions securely (**see illustration**).

Every 60 000 miles (100 000 km) or 5 years - whichever comes first

31 Camshaft timing belt renewal

The procedure is described in Chapter 2A.

Every 2 years, regardless of mileage

32 Brake fluid renewal

1 This procedure is similar to that described for the bleeding of the hydraulic system, as described in Chapter 9, except that the brake fluid reservoir should be emptied by syphoning and allowance should be made for all old fluid to be expelled when bleeding a section of the circuit.

2 Working as described in Chapter 9, open

the first bleed nipple in the sequence and pump the brake pedal gently until nearly all the old fluid has been emptied from the master cylinder reservoir. Top up to the MAX level on the reservoir with new fluid and continue pumping until only new fluid remains in the reservoir and new fluid can be seen emerging from the bleed nipple. Old hydraulic fluid is much darker in colour than new fluid, making it easy to distinguish between them.

3 Tighten the nipple and top the reservoir level up to the MAX level line.

4 Work through all the remaining nipples in

the sequence until new fluid can be seen emerging from all of them. Be careful to keep the master cylinder reservoir topped up to above the MIN level at all times, or air may enter the system and greatly increase the length of the task.

5 When the operation is complete, check that all nipples are securely tightened and that their dust caps are refitted. Wash off all traces of spilt fluid and recheck the master cylinder reservoir fluid level.

6 Check the operation of the brakes before taking the vehicle on the road.

Every 10 years, regardless of mileage

33 Airbag system component renewal

1 The Supplementary Restraint System (SRS), which incorporates the airbag and seat belt pre-tensioning systems, has components which contain pyrotechnic materials. Because these materials degrade with age, Rover specify that the following components must be renewed every ten years:

   a) *The passenger airbag module*

   b) *The driver airbag module*

2 Chapter 12 contains information relating to the removal and refitting of these components. However, given the safety-critical nature of the SRS components, and the fact that the correct operation of the SRS can only be verified using dedicated electronic test equipment, we strongly recommend that these operations are entrusted to a Rover dealer.

1A

Notes

Chapter 1 Part B:
Routine maintenance and servicing - diesel models

Contents

Degrees of difficulty

Easy, suitable for novice with little experience	**Fairly easy,** suitable for beginner with some experience	**Fairly difficult,** suitable for competent DIY mechanic	**Difficult,** suitable for experienced DIY mechanic	**Very difficult,** suitable for expert DIY or professional

Lubricants, fluids and capacities

Refer to the end of "Weekly Checks"

Cooling system

Antifreeze properties - 50% antifreeze (by volume):
    Commences freezing .... - 36°C
    Frozen solid .... - 48°C

Fuel system

Idle speed (for reference only):
    Models without intercooler .... 850 ± 50 rpm
    Models with intercooler .... 805 ± 50 rpm

Braking system

Front and rear brake pad friction material minimum thickness .... 3.0 mm
Rear brake shoe friction material minimum thickness .... 2.0 mm
Handbrake lever travel:
    Models with rear drum brakes .... 8 to 12 clicks
    Models with rear disc brakes .... 10 to 14 clicks

Tyre pressures

Refer to the end of "Weekly checks"

Electrical system

Wiper blades - front and rear .... Champion X45

Torque wrench settings

	Nm	lbf ft
Engine		
Engine oil drain plug	25	18
Manual transmission		
Filler/level plug	40	29
Drain plug	45	33
Brake system		
Caliper bleed screws	10	7
Front/rear brake caliper guide pin bolts	27	20
Rear brake drum retaining screws	7	5
Wheel cylinder bleed screws	7	5
Suspension and steering		
Roadwheel nuts	See Chapter 10	

The maintenance intervals in this manual are provided with the assumption that you will be carrying out the work yourself. These are based on the minimum maintenance intervals recommended by the manufacturer for vehicles driven daily. If you wish to keep your vehicle in peak condition at all times, you may wish to perform some of these procedures more often. We encourage frequent maintenance because it enhances the efficiency, performance and resale value of your vehicle.

If the vehicle is driven in dusty areas, used to tow a trailer, or driven frequently at slow speeds (idling in traffic) or on short journeys, more frequent maintenance intervals are recommended.

When the vehicle is new, it should be serviced by a factory-authorised dealer service department, in order to preserve the factory warranty.

Every 250 miles (400 km) or weekly
- [ ] Refer to *"Weekly Checks"*

Every 6000 miles (10 000 km) or 6 months - whichever comes first
- [ ] Engine oil and filter renewal (*Section 4*)

Note: *Frequent oil and filter changes are good for the engine. We recommend changing the oil at the mileage specified here, or at least twice a year if the mileage covered is less.*

Every 12 000 miles (20 000 km) or 12 months - whichever comes first
- [ ] Bodywork corrosion check (*Section 3*)
- [ ] Engine oil and filter renewal (*Section 4*)
- [ ] Coolant specific gravity check (*Section 5*)
- [ ] Manual transmission oil level check (*Section 6*)
- [ ] Vacuum hose condition check (*Section 7*)
- [ ] Underbonnet and underbody hose and pipe condition check (*Section 8*)
- [ ] Air conditioning system check (*Section 9*)
- [ ] Auxiliary drivebelt tension and condition check (*Section 10*)
- [ ] Exhaust system check (*Section 11*)
- [ ] Front brake check (*Section 12*)
- [ ] Rear brake check (*Section 13*)
- [ ] Driveshaft check (*Section 14*)
- [ ] Suspension and steering check (*Section 15*)
- [ ] Handbrake check and adjustment (*Section 16*)
- [ ] Lock and hinge lubrication (*Section 17*)
- [ ] Windscreen and numberplate condition check* (*Section 18*)
- [ ] Seat belt check* (*Section 19*)
- [ ] Drain water from fuel filter (*Section 20*)
- [ ] Airbag system components check*(*Section 21*)
- [ ] Exhaust smoke emission check* (*Section 22*)
- [ ] Road test (*Section 23*)

* These tasks need only be carried out after the first three years/36,000 miles of the vehicle's life and every two years/12,000 miles thereafter.

Every 24 000 miles (40 000 km) or 2 years - whichever comes first
Carry out all the items listed for the 12 000 mile/ 12 months service, plus the following:

- [ ] Manual transmission oil renewal (*Section 24*)
- [ ] Air cleaner filter element renewal (*Section 25*)
- [ ] Coolant renewal* (*Section 26*)
- [ ] Alarm remote keypad battery renewal (*Section 27*)
- [ ] Fuel filter renewal (*Section 28*)

*If Rover-recommended antifreeze is used exclusively, this task need only be carried out after the first three years/36,000 miles of the vehicle's life and every two years/24,000 miles thereafter.

1B

Every 36 000 miles (60 000 km) or 3 years - whichever comes first
- [ ] Camshaft timing belt renewal (*Section 29*)

Note: *The manufacturer recommends that the timing belt is changed every 72 000 miles (120 000 km). However, we strongly advise that this belt is replaced sooner, as extensive damage may occur, if the belt fails under certain driving conditions.*

Every 2 years, regardless of mileage
- [ ] Brake fluid renewal (*Section 30*)

Every 10 years, regardless of mileage
- [ ] Airbag system component renewal (*Section 31*)

Underbonnet view of a Rover 220 SDi with 2.0 l turbocharged, intercooled L-series diesel engine

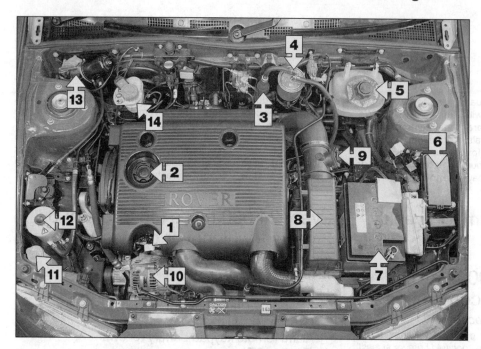

1 Engine oil level dipstick
2 Engine oil filler cap
3 Fuel system priming bulb
4 Fuel filter
5 Coolant expansion tank
6 Engine compartment fusebox
7 Battery
8 Air cleaner
9 Air mass meter
10 Alternator/vacuum pump
11 Washer fluid reservoir cap
12 Power steering fluid reservoir
13 Windscreen wiper motor
14 Brake fluid reservoir/master cylinder

Front underbody view of a Rover 220 SDi with 2.0 l turbocharged, intercooled L-series diesel engine

1 Engine oil sump drain plug
2 Engine oil filter
3 Tie bar
4 Brake caliper
5 Suspension lower arm
6 Track rod
7 Driveshaft
8 Exhaust system front pipe
9 Anti-roll bar
10 Power steering gear

Rear underbody view of a Rover 220 SDi with 2.0 l turbocharged, intercooled L-series diesel engine

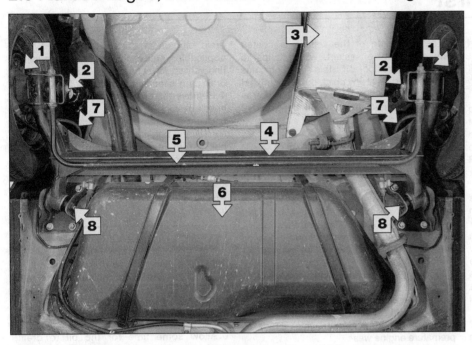

1 Brake backplate
2 Suspension strut lower mounting
3 Exhaust system tailbox
4 Anti-roll bar
5 Beam axle assembly
6 Fuel tank
7 Handbrake cables
8 Beam axle pivot mountings

Maintenance procedures - diesel models

1 Introduction

This Chapter is designed to help the home mechanic maintain his/her vehicle for safety, economy, long life and peak performance.

The Chapter contains a master maintenance schedule, referring to Sections dealing specifically with each task in the schedule, or other Chapters. Visual checks, adjustments, component renewal and other helpful items are included. Refer to the accompanying illustrations of the engine compartment and the underside of the vehicle for the locations of the various components.

Servicing your vehicle in accordance with the mileage/time maintenance schedule and the following Sections will provide a planned maintenance programme, which should result in a long and reliable service life. This is a comprehensive plan, so maintaining some items but not others at the specified service intervals will not produce the same results.

As you service your vehicle, you will discover that many of the procedures can be grouped together, because of the particular procedure being performed, or because of the close proximity of two otherwise-unrelated components to one another. For example, if the vehicle is raised for any reason, the exhaust can be inspected at the same time as the suspension and steering components.

The first step in this maintenance programme is to prepare yourself before the actual work begins. Read through all the Sections relevant to the work to be carried out, then make a list and gather together all the parts and tools required. If a problem is encountered, seek advice from a parts specialist, or a dealer service department.

2 Maintenance

1 If, from the time the vehicle is new, the routine maintenance schedule is followed closely and frequent checks are made of fluid levels and high-wear items, as suggested throughout this Manual, the engine will be kept in relatively good running condition and the need for additional work will be minimised.
2 It is possible that there will be times when the engine is running poorly due to the lack of regular maintenance. This is even more likely if a used vehicle, which has not received regular and frequent maintenance checks, is purchased. In such cases, additional work may need to be carried out, outside of the regular maintenance intervals.
3 If engine wear is suspected, a compression test will provide valuable information regarding the overall performance of the main internal components. Such a test can be used as a basis to decide on the extent of the work to be carried out. If, for example, a compression test indicates serious internal engine wear, conventional maintenance as described in this Chapter will not greatly improve the performance of the engine, and may prove a waste of time and money, unless extensive overhaul work is carried out first.
4 The following series of operations are those most often required to improve the performance of a generally poor-running engine:

Primary operations

a) Clean, inspect and test the battery.
b) Check all the engine-related fluids.
c) Check the condition and tension of the auxiliary drivebelt(s).
d) Check the condition of the air filter, and renew if necessary.
e) Check the fuel filter and drain off all water.
f) Check the condition of all hoses, and check for fluid leaks.

5 If the above operations do not prove fully effective, carry out the following secondary operations:

Secondary operations

a) Check the charging system (see relevant Part of Chapter 5).
b) Check the fuel system (see relevant Part of Chapter 4).
c) Check the preheating system (see relevant Part of Chapter 5).

Every 12 000 miles (20 000 km) or 12 months - whichever comes first

3 Bodywork corrosion check

1 Start at the front of the car and work along each body panel in turn, look for any signs of paintwork damage. It may be possible to repair small scratches with a touch-up pen. These should be purchased from a Rover dealer, to get an accurate colour match.

2 Larger scratches that have penetrated the primer or exposed the bare metal beneath should be repaired professionally. The Rover 200 has an extensive Anti-Corrosion Warranty, the terms of which specify how bodywork repairs must be carried out; failure to adhere to the guidelines may invalidate the Warranty. Have the damage assessed by a Rover Dealer or automotive bodywork specialist at the earliest opportunity.

3 Check each body panel for evidence of corrosion, such as raised blisters behind the paintwork and rust-coloured staining. Pay particular attention to vulnerable areas, including the wheel arches, the front edge of the bonnet , the front valence (under the front bumper) and the lower edges of the doors. Corrosion can quickly destroy bodywork, so have any dubious-looking areas examined by a professional.

4 Jack up the front/rear car and support it securely on axle stands (see *"Jacking and Vehicle Support"*).

5 Examine the underside of the car for signs of corrosion. Look for cracking or flaking of the metal floorpan. Pay particular attention to the areas around the suspension and steering components mountings. Look for damage that may have been caused by attempting to jack up the car at incorrect jacking points.

6 Check for corrosion along the length of the side sills, which run between the front and rear wheel arches.

7 The underside of the vehicle is coated with a protective sealant, which helps to prevent corrosion. If this coating has been scraped off at any point, due to an impact or repair work, it must be re-applied as soon as possible, to protect the bodywork beneath.

4 Engine oil and filter renewal

Note: *On diesel engines we strongly recommend the oil and filter are changed every 6000 miles (10 000 km) or 6 months.*
Note: *An oil filter removal tool and a new oil drain plug sealing washer will be required for this operation.*

1 Frequent oil and filter changes are the most important preventative maintenance procedures which can be undertaken by the DIY owner. As engine oil ages, it becomes diluted and contaminated, which leads to premature engine wear.

2 Before starting this procedure, gather together all the necessary tools and materials. Also make sure that you have plenty of clean rags and newspapers handy, to mop up any spills. Ideally, the engine oil should be warm, as it will drain more easily, and more built-up sludge will be removed with it. Take care not to touch the exhaust or any other hot parts of the engine when working under the vehicle. To avoid any possibility of scalding, and to protect yourself from possible skin irritants and other harmful contaminants in used engine oils, it is advisable to wear gloves when carrying out this work.

3 Access to the underside of the vehicle will be greatly improved if it can be raised on a lift, driven onto ramps, or jacked up and supported on axle stands (see *"Jacking and Vehicle Support"*). Whichever method is chosen, make sure that the vehicle remains level, or if it is at an angle, that the

drain plug is at the lowest point. Where applicable, remove the engine/transmission undershield for access to the drain plug. The drain plug is located at the rear of the sump.

4 Remove the oil filler cap from the cylinder head cover.

5 Using a spanner, or preferably a suitable socket and bar, slacken the drain plug about half a turn **(see illustration)**. Position the draining container under the drain plug, then remove the plug completely. If possible, try to keep the plug pressed into the sump while unscrewing it by hand the last couple of turns.

 HAYNES HINT *As the plug releases from the threads, move it away sharply, so that the stream of oil from the sump runs into the container, not up your sleeve!*

6 Allow some time for the oil to drain, noting that it may be necessary to reposition the container as the oil flow slows to a trickle.

7 After all the oil has drained, wipe the drain plug and the sealing washer with a clean rag. The sealing washer should be renewed as a matter of course. Clean the area around the drain plug opening, and refit the plug complete with the new sealing washer **(see illustration)**. Tighten the plug securely, preferably to the specified torque, using a torque wrench.

8 The oil filter is located at the right-hand rear corner of the engine. Access is most easily obtained by jacking up the front of the vehicle (see *"Jacking and Vehicle Support"*) **(see illustration)**.

9 Move the container into position under the oil filter.

10 Use an oil filter removal tool to slacken the filter initially, then unscrew it by hand the rest

4.5 Slackening the engine oil drain plug

4.7 Refit the drain plug using a new sealing washer

4.8 Oil filter location (arrowed)

4.10 Loosening the oil filter using an oil filter removal tool

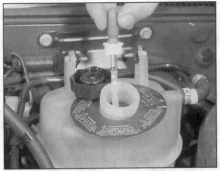

5.3 Using a hydrometer to measure the specific gravity of the coolant

4 The hydrometer shown in the photo incorporates an integral syringe, which allows a 'sample' of the coolant to be collected. The coloured indicator balls inside the hydrometer float or sink in the coolant sample, depending on the specific gravity.

5 If the specific gravity is too low, do not try to correct it by adding neat antifreeze, as it may not mix completely with the existing coolant and could lead to 'hot spots' in the cooling system. With reference to Section 26, partially drain the cooling system, then refill it with antifreeze and water mixed in the correct proportions.

6 If the specific gravity is too high, refer to Section 26 and partially drain the cooling system, then top up with clean water.

of the way **(see illustration)**. Empty the oil from the old filter into the container.

11 Use a clean rag to remove all oil, dirt and sludge from the filter sealing area on the engine. Check the old filter to make sure that the rubber sealing ring has not stuck to the engine. If it has, carefully remove it.

12 Apply a light coating of clean engine oil to the sealing ring on the new filter, then screw the filter into position on the engine. Tighten the filter firmly by hand only - **do not** use any tools.

13 Remove the old oil and all tools from under the vehicle then, if applicable, lower the vehicle to the ground.

14 Fill the engine through the filler hole in the cylinder head cover, using the correct grade and type of oil (see *"Lubricants, fluids and capacities"*). Pour in half the specified quantity of oil first, then wait a few minutes for the oil to drain into the sump. Continue to add oil, a small quantity at a time, until the level is up to the lower mark on the dipstick. Adding approximately 1.0 litre will bring the level up to the upper mark on the dipstick.

15 Start the engine and run it for a few minutes, while checking for leaks around the oil filter seal and the sump drain plug. Note that there may be a delay of a few seconds before the low oil pressure warning light goes out when the engine is first started, as the oil circulates through the new oil filter and the engine oil galleries before the pressure builds up.

16 Stop the engine, and wait a few minutes

for the oil to settle in the sump once more. With the new oil circulated and the filter now completely full, recheck the level on the dipstick, and add more oil as necessary.

17 Dispose of the used engine oil safely.

OIL CARE
FOLLOW THE CODE
OIL BANK LINE
0800 66 33 66

Note: It is antisocial and illegal to dump oil down the drain. To find the location of your local oil recycling bank, call this number free.

5 Coolant specific gravity check

1 Ensure that the engine has cooled completely before starting work.

2 Slowly unscrew the coolant expansion tank cap by about half a turn, allowing any residual pressure in the cooling system to reduce gradually - use a cloth to protect your hands from any escaping steam.

3 Insert a hydrometer into the expansion tank filler neck and measure the specific gravity of the coolant **(see illustration)**. Compare your measurement with the figures given in the Specifications.

6 Manual transmission oil level check

1 Ensure that the vehicle is parked on level ground then, where applicable, remove the engine/transmission undershield to gain access to the transmission filler/level plug.

2 Remove all traces of dirt from around the filler/level plug which is located on the left-hand side of the transmission, behind the driveshaft inboard joint **(see illustration)**. Place a suitable container beneath the plug to catch any escaping oil, then unscrew the plug and recover the sealing washer.

3 Check that the oil is level with the bottom of the filler/level plug hole. Note that oil which has collected behind the filler/level plug will probably trickle out when the plug is removed, which can give a false impression that the level is correct.

4 If necessary, top up using the specified type of oil (see *"Lubricants, fluids and capacities"*). Refilling the transmission is an awkward operation. Allow plenty of time for the oil level to settle properly before checking it. Note that the car must be parked on flat level ground when checking the oil level.

5 Using a tube inserted through the filler/level plug hole, slowly top up the level until the oil reaches the bottom of the filler/level plug hole **(see illustration)**. Allow plenty of time for the level to stabilise.

6 When the level is correct, refit the filler/level plug, using a new sealing washer, and tighten it to the specified torque.

7 Vacuum hose condition check

1 Open the bonnet and check the condition of the vacuum hose that connects the brake servo to the vacuum pump **(see**

6.2 Transmission filler/level plug (arrowed) – "PG1"-type transmission

6.5 Topping up the transmission oil level – "PG1"-type transmission

1B

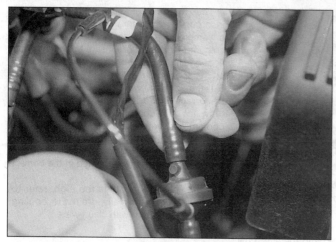

7.1 Check the condition of the brake servo vacuum hose

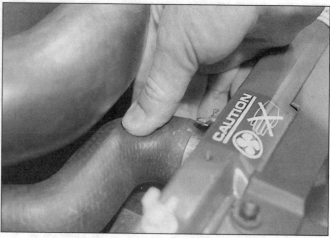

8.1 Checking the condition of a coolant hose

illustration). Look for damage in the form of chaffing, melting or cracking. Check that the union nuts and T-joints (where applicable) are secure. Also examine the vacuum hoses serving the evaporative loss emission control and fuel pressure regulation systems.

2 Locate the engine management system ECU at the left-hand side of the engine compartment. Inspect the vacuum hose that runs from the ECU to the inlet manifold, ensuring that it is secure and free from damage. Remove it from the engine compartment and clean it out using compressed air, to expel any fuel or oil which may have collected inside it. Do not use cleaning fluids, as these may contaminate the ECU pressure sensor.

3 A leak in a vacuum hose means that air is being drawn into the hose (rather than escaping from it) and this makes leakage very difficult to detect. If you suspect that a vacuum hose may be leaking, the following method may help you to pinpoint it. Start the engine and allow it to idle. Hold one end of a length of narrow bore tubing close to your ear, then run the other end along the vacuum hose. If a leak exists, you should be able to hear a hissing noise through the tubing as the air 'escapes' into the hose at the suspected leak.

8 Underbonnet and underbody hose and pipe condition check

Coolant

 Warning: *Refer to the safety information given in 'Safety First' and Chapter 3, before disturbing any of the cooling system components.*

1 Carefully check the radiator and heater coolant hoses along their entire length. Renew any hose which is cracked, swollen or which shows signs of deterioration. Cracks will show

up better if the hose is squeezed **(see illustration)**. Pay close attention to the clips that secure the hoses to the cooling system components. Hose clips that have been over-tightened can pinch and puncture hoses, resulting in leakage.

2 Inspect all the cooling system components (hoses, joint faces etc.) for leaks. Where any problems of this nature are found on system components, renew the component or gasket with reference to Chapter 3.

3 A leak from the cooling system will usually show up as white or rust-coloured deposits, on the area surrounding the leak.

Leaks in the cooling system will usually show up as white or rust coloured deposits around the point of leakage

Fuel

 Warning: *Refer to the safety information given in 'Safety First' and the relevant part of Chapter 4, before disturbing any of the fuel system components.*

4 Unlike petrol leaks, diesel leaks are fairly easy to pinpoint; diesel fuel tends to settle on the surface around the point of leakage collecting dirt, rather than evaporate. If you suspect that there is a fuel leak from the area of the engine bay, leave the vehicle overnight then start the engine from cold, and allow it to idle with the bonnet open. Metal components

tend to shrink when they are cold, and rubber seals and hoses tend to harden, so any leaks may be more apparent whilst the engine is warming up from a cold start.

5 Check all fuel lines at their connections to the fuel injection pump and fuel filter **(see illustration)**. Examine each rubber fuel hose along its length for splits or cracks. Check for leakage from the crimped joints between rubber and metal fuel lines. Examine the unions between the metal fuel lines and the fuel filter housing. Also check the area around the fuel injectors for signs of leakage.

6 To identify fuel leaks between the fuel tank and the engine bay, the vehicle should be raised and securely supported on axle stands (see "*Jacking and Vehicle Support*"). Inspect the fuel tank and filler neck for punctures, cracks and other damage. The connection between the filler neck and tank is especially critical. Sometimes a rubber filler neck or connecting hose will leak due to loose retaining clamps or deteriorated rubber.

7 Carefully check all rubber hoses and metal fuel lines leading away from the fuel tank. Check for loose connections, deteriorated hoses, kinked lines, and other damage. Pay particular attention to the vent pipes and hoses, which often loop up around the filler neck and can become blocked or kinked, making tank filling difficult. Follow the fuel supply and return lines to the front of the

8.5 Check for fuel leaks at the fuel filter unions

vehicle, carefully inspecting them all the way for signs of damage or corrosion. Renew damaged sections as necessary.

Engine oil

8 Check the hoses leading to the engine oil cooler at the front of the engine bay for leakage. Look for deterioration caused by corrosion and damage from grounding, or debris thrown up from the road surface.

Power assisted steering (PAS) fluid

9 Examine the hose running between the fluid reservoir and the power steering pump, and the return hose running from the steering rack to the fluid reservoir. Also examine the high pressure supply hose between the pump and the steering rack **(see illustration)**.

10 Where applicable, check the hoses leading to the PAS fluid cooler at the front of the engine bay. Look for deterioration caused by corrosion and damage from grounding, or debris thrown up from the road surface.

11 Pay particular attention to crimped unions, and the area surrounding the hoses that are secured with adjustable worm drive clips. Like automatic transmission fluid, PAS fluid is a thin oil, and is usually red in colour.

Air conditioning refrigerant

 Warning: Refer to the safety information given in 'Safety First' and Chapter 3, regarding the dangers of disturbing any of the air conditioning system components.

12 The air conditioning system is filled with a liquid refrigerant, which is retained under high pressure. If the air conditioning system is opened and depressurised without the aid of specialised equipment, the refrigerant will immediately turn into gas and escape into the atmosphere. If the liquid comes into contact with your skin, it can cause severe frostbite. In addition, the refrigerant may contain substances which are environmentally damaging; for this reason, it should not be allowed to escape into the atmosphere.

13 Any suspected air conditioning system leaks should be immediately referred to a Rover dealer or air conditioning specialist. Leakage will be shown up as a steady drop in the level of refrigerant in the system - refer to Section 9 for details.

14 Note that water may drip from the condenser drain pipe, underneath the car, immediately after the air conditioning system has been in use. This is normal, and should not be cause for concern.

Brake fluid

 Warning: Refer to the safety information given in 'Safety First' and Chapter 9, regarding the dangers of handling brake fluid.

15 With reference to Chapter 9, examine the area surrounding the brake pipe unions at the master cylinder for signs of leakage **(see illustration)**. Check the area around the base

8.9 Checking a power steering fluid hose for damage

of fluid reservoir, for signs of leakage caused by seal failure. Also examine the brake pipe unions at the ABS hydraulic unit. Brake fluid is an effective paint stripper, so if cracked or bubbling paintwork on or around any of the braking system components is found, suspect fluid leakage.

16 If fluid loss is evident, but the leak cannot be pinpointed in the engine bay, the brake calipers and underbody brakelines and should be carefully checked with the vehicle raised and supported on axle stands (see "Jacking and Vehicle Support"). Leakage of fluid from the braking system is serious fault that must be rectified immediately.

17 Brake hydraulic fluid is a toxic substance with a watery consistency. New fluid is almost colourless, but it becomes darker with age and use.

Unidentified fluid leaks

18 If there are signs that a fluid of some description is leaking from the vehicle, but you cannot identify the type of fluid or its exact origin, park the vehicle overnight and slide a large piece of card underneath it. Providing that the card is positioned in roughly in the right location, even the smallest leak will show up on the card. Not only will this help you to pinpoint the exact location of the leak, it should be easier to identify the fluid from its colour. Bear in mind, though, that the leak may only be occurring when the engine is running!

Vacuum hoses

19 Refer to Section 7.

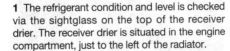
9 Air conditioning system check

1 The refrigerant condition and level is checked via the sightglass on the top of the receiver drier. The receiver drier is situated in the engine compartment, just to the left of the radiator.

2 Start the engine then switch on the air conditioning system and allow the engine to idle for a couple of minutes whilst observing the sightglass. If the air conditioning system is operating normally then occasional bubbles should be visible through the sightglass.

3 If a constant stream of bubbles is visible, the refrigerant level is low and must be topped

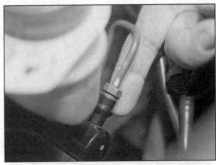

8.15 Checking a master cylinder brake pipe union for leakage

up. If the sightglass has become clouded or streaked, there is a fault in the system. If either condition is present, the vehicle must be taken to a Rover dealer or suitable professional refrigeration specialist for the air conditioning system to be checked further and overhauled.

10 Auxiliary drivebelt tension and condition check

General information

1 On all diesel models, a single flat, multi-ribbed-type auxiliary drivebelt is fitted. Drive is taken from a pulley bolted to the right-hand end of the crankshaft.

2 The belt provides drives to the power steering pump, alternator (which incorporates the vacuum pump), and the air conditioning compressor (where applicable). The belt is tensioned by means of a spring-loaded automatic tensioner assembly.

Checking

3 Apply the handbrake then jack up the front of the vehicle and support it on axle stands (see "Jacking and Vehicle Support"). Remove the right-hand front roadwheel.

4 From underneath the front of the vehicle, slacken and remove the bolts securing the bumper flange to the body. Remove the bolts securing the front undercover panel to the body and remove the panel.

5 Check the drivebelt(s) for cracks, splitting, fraying or damage **(see illustration)**, whilst

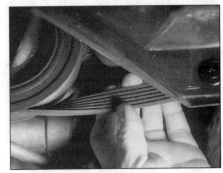

10.5 Checking the condition of the auxiliary drivebelt

1B

10.6 Auxiliary drivebelt wear indicator markings

11.2 Check that the exhaust mountings are secure

rotating the crankshaft clockwise using a suitable spanner applied to the crankshaft pulley bolt, so that the entire length of each belt is examined. Check also for signs of glazing (shiny patches) and for separation of the belt plies. Renew the belt if worn or damaged, with reference to Chapter 9 or 10 as appropriate.

6 The drivebelt tension is set automatically by the tensioner assembly and requires no manual adjustment. Belt wear can be assessed by observing the markings on the tensioner assembly **(see illustration)**. If the belt is too slack through excessive wear, the line marking on the section of the tensioner nearest the engine will fall outside of the marking on the other section of the tensioner.

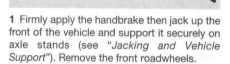

11 Exhaust system check

1 With the engine cold (at least an hour after the vehicle has been driven), check the complete exhaust system from the engine to the end of the tailpipe. The exhaust system is most easily checked with the vehicle raised on a hoist, or suitably supported on axle stands, so that the exhaust components are readily visible and accessible.

12.2 Front brake pad friction material (arrowed) can be measured through the inspection aperture in caliper body

2 Check the exhaust pipes and connections for evidence of leaks, severe corrosion and damage. Make sure that all brackets and mountings are in good condition, and that all relevant nuts and bolts are tight **(see illustration)**. Leakage at any of the joints or in other parts of the system will usually show up as a black sooty stain in the vicinity of the leak.

3 Rattles and other noises can often be traced to the exhaust system, especially the brackets and mountings. Try to move the pipes and silencers. If the components are able to come into contact with the body or suspension parts, secure the system with new mountings. Otherwise separate the joints (if possible) and twist the pipes as necessary to provide additional clearance.

12 Front brake check

1 Firmly apply the handbrake then jack up the front of the vehicle and support it securely on axle stands (see "*Jacking and Vehicle Support*"). Remove the front roadwheels.

2 For a quick check, the thickness of friction material remaining on each brake pad can be measured through the inspection aperture in the front of the caliper body **(see illustration)**.

13.2 Remove grommet to check rear brake shoe friction material thickness

If any pad's friction material is worn to the specified thickness or less, all four pads must be renewed as a set.

3 For a comprehensive check, the brake pads should be removed and cleaned. This will permit the operation of the caliper to be checked and the condition of the brake disc itself to be fully examined on both sides. Refer to Chapter 9 for further information.

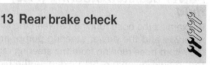

13 Rear brake check

Models with rear drum brakes

1 Chock the front wheels then jack up the rear of the vehicle and support it on axle stands (see "*Jacking and Vehicle Support*").

2 For a quick check, the thickness of friction material remaining on one of the brake shoes can be measured through the slot in the brake backplate that is exposed by prising out its sealing grommet **(see illustration)**. If a rod of the same diameter as the specified minimum thickness is placed against the shoe friction material, the amount of wear can quickly be assessed. If any shoe's friction material is worn to the specified thickness or less, all four shoes must be renewed.

3 For a comprehensive check, the brake drums should be removed and cleaned. This will permit the wheel cylinders to be checked and the condition of the brake drum itself to be fully examined. Refer to Chapter 9 for further information.

Models with rear disc brakes

4 Chock the front wheels then jack up the rear of the vehicle and support it on axle stands (see "*Jacking and Vehicle Support*").

5 For a quick check, the thickness of friction material remaining on each brake pad can be measured through the inspection aperture in the caliper body. If any pad's friction material is worn to the specified thickness or less, all four pads must be renewed as a set.

6 For a comprehensive check, the brake pads should be removed and cleaned. This will permit the operation of the caliper to be checked and the condition of the brake disc itself to be fully examined on both sides. Refer to Chapter 9 for further information.

14 Driveshaft check

1 With the vehicle raised and securely supported on axle stands (see "*Jacking and Vehicle Support*"), turn the steering onto full lock then slowly rotate the roadwheel. Inspect the condition of the outer constant velocity (CV) joint rubber gaiters while squeezing the

14.1 Inspecting a driveshaft joint rubber gaiter

15.2 Checking the condition of a steering gear rubber gaiter

9 Working as described for the front suspension, check the rear hub bearings and the trailing arm and lateral link bushes for wear.

16 Handbrake check and adjustment

Checking

1 The handbrake should be capable of holding the parked vehicle stationary, even on steep slopes, when applied with moderate force. Equally, the handbrake must release properly, or the brakes will bind and overheat when the car is driven.
2 The mechanism should be firm and positive in feel with no trace of stiffness or sponginess from the cables and should release immediately the handbrake lever is released. If the mechanism is faulty in any of these respects then it must be checked immediately.
3 To check the handbrake setting, first apply the footbrake firmly several times to establish correct shoe-to-drum clearance. Applying normal, moderate pressure, pull the handbrake lever to the fully-applied position whilst counting the number of 'clicks' produced by the handbrake ratchet mechanism. Check that the number of clicks produced is as listed in the Specifications. If this is not the case, then adjustment is required.

Adjustment

4 To adjust the handbrake, chock the front wheels then jack up the rear of the vehicle and support it on axle stands (see "Jacking and Vehicle Support").
5 Lift out the ashtray from the rear of the centre console to gain access to the handbrake adjusting nut **(see illustrations)**.
6 Apply the handbrake and check that the equalizer and cables move freely and smoothly, then set the lever on the first notch of the ratchet mechanism. With the lever in this position, rotate the handbrake lever adjusting nut until only a slight drag can be

gaiters to open out the folds **(see illustration)**. Check for signs of cracking, splits or deterioration of the rubber which may allow the grease to escape and lead to the entry of water and grit into the joint. Also check the security and condition of the gaiter retaining clips. Repeat these checks on the inner CV joints. If any damage or deterioration is found, then renew the gaiters.
2 Check the general condition of the CV joints by first holding the driveshaft and attempting to rotate the roadwheel. Repeat this check by holding the inner joint and attempting to rotate the driveshaft. Any appreciable movement indicates wear in the joints or driveshaft splines, or a loose driveshaft nut.

15 Suspension and steering check

Front suspension and steering

1 Raise the front of the vehicle and securely support it on axle stands (see "Jacking and Vehicle Support").
2 Inspect the balljoint dust covers and the steering gear rubber gaiters for splits, chafing or deterioration **(see illustration)**. Any wear of these components will cause loss of lubricant, together with dirt and water entry, resulting in rapid deterioration of the balljoints or steering gear.
3 On vehicles equipped with power steering, check the fluid hoses for chafing or deterioration and the pipe and hose unions for fluid leakage. Also check for signs of fluid leakage under pressure from the steering gear rubber gaiters which would indicate failed fluid seals within the steering gear.
4 Grasp the roadwheel at the 12 o'clock and 6 o'clock positions and try to rock it **(see illustration)**. Very slight free play may be felt but if the movement is appreciable then further investigation is necessary to determine the source. Continue rocking the wheel while an assistant depresses the brake pedal. If the movement is now eliminated or significantly reduced, it is likely that the hub bearings are at fault. If the free play is still evident with the brake pedal depressed, then there is wear in the suspension joints or mountings.

5 Now grasp the roadwheel at the 9 o'clock and 3 o'clock positions and try to rock it as before. Any movement felt now may again be caused by wear in the hub bearings, or in the track rod balljoints. If a balljoint is worn the visual movement will be obvious. If the inner joint is suspect it can be felt by placing a hand over the steering gear rubber gaiter and gripping the track rod. If the wheel is now rocked, movement will be felt at the inner joint if wear has taken place.
6 Using a large screwdriver or flat bar check for wear in the suspension mounting bushes by levering between the relevant suspension component and its attachment point. Some movement is to be expected as the mountings are made of rubber, but excessive wear should be obvious. Also check the condition of any visible rubber bushes, looking for splits, cracks or contamination of the rubber.
7 With the vehicle standing on its wheels, have an assistant turn the steering wheel back and forth about an eighth of a turn each way. There should be very little, if any, lost movement between the steering wheel and the roadwheels. If this is not the case, closely observe the joints and mountings previously described but in addition, check for wear of the steering column universal joint and the steering gear itself.

Rear suspension

8 Chock the front wheels then jack up the rear of the vehicle and support it on axle stands (see "Jacking and Vehicle Support").

15.4 Checking the condition of the steering and suspension components by rocking a roadwheel

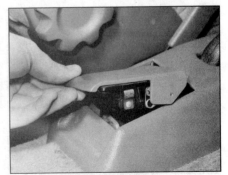

16.5a Remove the ashtray from the rear of the centre console . .

16.5b . . . to gain access to the handbrake cable adjuster nut (arrowed) and equalizer mechanism

felt when the rear wheels are turned by hand. Once this is the case, fully release the handbrake lever and check that the wheels rotate freely. Check adjustment by applying the handbrake fully whilst counting the clicks emitted from the handbrake ratchet. Carry out the adjustment procedure again, if necessary.

7 Once adjustment is correct, refit the ashtray and lower the vehicle to the ground.

17 Lock and hinge lubrication

1 Lubricate the hinges of the bonnet, doors and tailgate with a light duty oil.
2 Lightly grease the bonnet release mechanism and cable.
3 The door and tailgate latches, strikers and locks must be lubricated using only the special Rover Door Lock and Latch Lubricant supplied in small sachets. Inject 1 gram into each lock and wipe off any surplus, then apply a thin film to the latches and strikers.
4 Do not lubricate the steering lock mechanism with oil or any other lubricant which might foul the ignition switch contacts. If the lock is stiff, try the effect of a proprietary electrical contact lubricant, rather than conventional lubricant.

5 If a sunroof is fitted, lubricate very sparingly the seal lip with Rover supplied non-staining seal grease.

18 Windscreen and numberplate condition check

Refer to the MOT pre-test checks described in the *Reference* Chapter, at the end of this manual.

19 Seat belt check

1 Check the webbing of each seat belt for signs of fraying, cuts or other damage, pulling the belt out to its full extent to check its entire length **(see illustration)**.
2 Check the operation of the belt buckles by fitting the belt tongue plate and pulling hard to ensure that it remains locked in position.
3 Check the retractor mechanism (inertia reel only) by pulling out the belt to the halfway point and jerking it downwards **(see illustration)**. The mechanism must lock immediately to prevent any further unreeling but must allow free movement during normal driving.
4 Ensure that all belt mounting bolts are securely tightened. Note that the bolts are shouldered so that the belt anchor points are free to rotate.
5 If there is any sign of damage, or any doubt about a belt's condition, then it must be renewed. If the vehicle has been involved in a collision, then any belt in use at the time must be renewed as a matter of course and all other belts checked carefully.
6 Use only warm water and non-detergent soap to clean the belts.
Caution: Never use any chemical cleaners, strong detergents, dyes or bleaches. Keep the belts fully extended until they have dried naturally and do not apply heat to dry them.

20 Drain water from fuel filter

1 A water drain screw is provided at the base of the fuel filter. To make draining easier, a suitable tube can be attached to the drain screw, then the water/fuel can be more easily directed into a container.
2 Place a suitable container beneath the filter.
3 Open the drain screw by turning it anti-clockwise, and allow fuel and water to drain into the container until fuel, free from water, emerges from the end of the tube **(see illustration)**. Close the drain screw and tighten it securely.
4 Dispose of the drained fuel safely.
5 Start the engine. If difficulty is experienced, bleed the fuel system as described in Chapter 4B.

21 Airbag system component check

1 Checking of the airbag system by the home mechanic is limited to a visual inspection of the outer surface of the driver and passenger air bag modules (as applicable). If the surface of the casing has sustained any damage (such as that caused by an impact, or fluid spillage for example) then the air bag system should be checked by a Rover dealer at the earliest opportunity.
2 Sit in the driver's seat and release the steering column lock. On models with power steering, start the engine and allow it to idle. Turn the steering wheel from lock to lock, whilst listening to the rotary coupler at the steering wheel hub. Any noise or roughness in operation could indicate a worn rotary coupler - refer to a Rover dealer for further advice.
3 The SRS warning lamp on the instrument panel should illuminate for about six seconds when the ignition key is turned to the 'II' position and then extinguish. If the lamp fails to extinguish, or does not illuminate at all, there may be a fault with the SRS system; the advice of a Rover dealer should be sought.

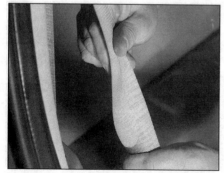

19.1 Check the webbing of each seat belt for signs of fraying, cuts or other damage

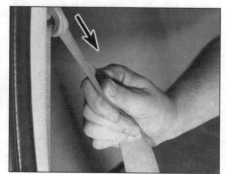

19.3 Checking the operation of the inertia reel locking mechanism

20.3 Drain fuel and water from the fuel filter into a container such as a plastic cup (arrowed)

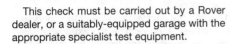

22 Exhaust smoke emission check

This check must be carried out by a Rover dealer, or a suitably-equipped garage with the appropriate specialist test equipment.

23 Road test

Instruments and electrical equipment

1 Check the operation of all instruments and electrical equipment.
2 Make sure that all instruments read correctly, and switch on all electrical equipment in turn, to check that it functions properly.

Steering and suspension

3 Check for any abnormalities in the steering, suspension, handling or road 'feel'.
4 Drive the vehicle, and check that there are no unusual vibrations or noises.
5 Check that the steering feels positive, with no excessive 'sloppiness', or roughness, and check for any suspension noises when cornering and driving over bumps.

Drivetrain

6 Check the performance of the engine, clutch, transmission and driveshafts.
7 Listen for any unusual noises from the engine, clutch and transmission.
8 Make sure that the engine runs smoothly when idling, and that there is no hesitation when accelerating.
9 Check that the clutch action is smooth and progressive, that the drive is taken up smoothly, and that the pedal travel is not excessive. Also listen for any noises when the clutch pedal is depressed.

10 Check that all gears can be engaged smoothly without noise, and that the gear lever action is not abnormally vague or 'notchy'.
11 Listen for a metallic clicking sound from the front of the vehicle, as the vehicle is driven slowly in a circle with the steering on full-lock. Carry out this check in both directions. If a clicking noise is heard, this indicates wear in a driveshaft joint (see Chapter 8).

Check the operation and performance of the braking system

12 Make sure that the vehicle does not pull to one side when braking, and that the wheels do not lock prematurely when braking hard.
13 Check that there is no vibration through the steering when braking.
14 Check that the handbrake operates correctly, and that it holds the vehicle stationary on a slope.

Every 24 000 miles (40 000 km) or 2 years - whichever comes first

24 Manual transmission oil renewal

Refer to *"Manual transmission oil – draining and refilling"* in Chapter 7A.

25 Air cleaner filter element renewal

1 The air cleaner is located at the left-hand side of the engine compartment, next to the battery.
2 Release the coolant pipe from the clips on the air cleaner (**see illustration**).
3 Release the four securing clips, then lift up the air cleaner cover sufficiently to enable the element to be lifted out (**see illustrations**).

4 Wipe out the air cleaner casing and the cover using a clean cloth.
5 Fit the new element, then refit the cover and secure with the clips, and clip the coolant pipe into position on the air cleaner.

26 Coolant renewal

⚠️ **Warning: Wait until the engine is completely cold before starting the coolant renewal procedure. Do not allow antifreeze to come into contact with your skin or painted surfaces of the vehicle. Rinse off spills immediately with plenty of water. Never leave antifreeze lying around in an open container or in a puddle in the driveway or on the garage floor. Children and pets are attracted by its sweet smell; and antifreeze can be fatal if ingested.**

Antifreeze mixture

1 Antifreeze should always be renewed at the specified intervals. This is necessary not only to maintain the anti-freezing properties of the coolant but also to prevent corrosion which would otherwise occur, as the corrosion inhibitors in the coolant become progressively less effective.
2 Always use an ethylene glycol based antifreeze which is suitable for use in mixed-metal cooling systems.
3 The type of antifreeze and levels of protection afforded are indicated in *"Lubricants, fluids and capacities"* and Specifications. To achieve the recommended 50% concentration, equal quantities of antifreeze and clean, soft water must be

1B

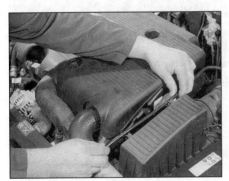

25.2 Release the coolant pipe from the clips on the air cleaner

25.3a Release the air cleaner cover securing clips . . .

25.3b . . . then lift the cover and lift out the element

mixed together. It is best to make up slightly more than is actually needed to refill the cooling system, so that a supply is available for subsequent topping-up.

Caution: Always pre-mix the antifreeze and water in a suitable container before refilling the cooling system. If the antifreeze and water are poured into the cooling system separately, they may not mix correctly and could cause localised overheating, which may lead to engine damage.

Draining

4 To drain the cooling system, remove the expansion tank filler cap then move the heater air temperature control to the maximum heat position.

5 Place a large drain tray beneath the bottom hose connection, at the bottom left-hand corner of the radiator. Release the hose clip and carefully pull the bottom hose off the radiator stub, allowing the coolant to drain into the container below. Once the system has drained completely, reconnect the bottom hose and secure with the hose clip.

Flushing

6 With time, the cooling system may gradually lose its efficiency due to the radiator core having become choked with rust, scale deposits and other sediment. To minimise this, the system should be flushed as described in the following paragraphs, whenever the coolant is renewed.

7 With the coolant drained, refill the system with fresh water. Refit the expansion tank filler cap, start the engine and warm it up to normal operating temperature, then stop it and (after allowing it to cool down completely) drain the system again. Repeat as necessary until only clean water can be seen to emerge, then refill finally with the specified coolant mixture.

8 If the specified coolant mixture has been used and has been renewed at the specified intervals, the above procedure will be sufficient to keep clean the system for a considerable length of time. If, however, the system has been neglected, a more thorough operation will be required, as follows.

9 First drain the coolant, then disconnect the radiator top and bottom hoses from the radiator. Insert a garden hose into the radiator top hose outlet and allow water (under LOW pressure only) to circulate through the radiator until it runs clean from the bottom outlet.

Caution: Do not flush with water under high pressure, as this may damage the radiator.

10 To flush the engine, insert the garden hose into the top hose and allow water to circulate until it runs clear from the bottom hose. If, after a reasonable period, the water still does not run clear, the cooling system should be flushed with a good proprietary cleaning agent. Bear in mind, however, that any leaks sealed in the past using a cooling system sealant additive may be weakened by this course of action, and could start to leak again.

11 In severe cases of contamination, reverse-flushing of the radiator may be necessary. To do this, remove the radiator, invert it and insert a garden hose into the bottom outlet. Continue flushing (again, using water under LOW pressure only) until clear water runs from the top hose outlet. If necessary, a similar procedure can be used to flush the heater matrix.

12 The use of chemical cleaners should be necessary only as a last resort as regular renewal of the coolant will prevent excessive contamination of the system.

Filling

13 With the cooling system drained and flushed, ensure that all radiator hoses are securely reconnected. Check all hose unions for security and all hoses for condition. Fresh antifreeze has a searching action which will rapidly find any weaknesses in the system.

14 Prepare a sufficient quantity of the specified coolant mixture, allowing for a surplus so as to have a reserve supply for topping-up (see *Antifreeze Mixture* above).

15 Remove the expansion tank filler cap, then fill the system slowly through the filler neck. Continue filling until the coolant level reaches the 'MAX' mark on the side of the expansion tank. Refit the filler cap and tighten it securely.

16 Start the engine and run it at no more than idle speed until it has warmed up to normal operating temperature and the radiator electric cooling fan has cut in once. Watch the temperature gauge to check for signs of overheating.

17 Stop the engine and allow it to cool down completely, then remove the expansion tank filler cap carefully and top up the tank to the 'MAX' level **(see illustrations)**. Refit the filler cap and wash off any spilt coolant from the engine compartment and bodywork with plenty of clean water.

18 After refilling, check carefully all system components for signs of coolant leaks. A label should now be attached to the radiator or expansion tank stating the type and concentration of antifreeze used and the date installed. Any subsequent topping-up should be made with the same type and concentration of antifreeze.

19 If, after draining and refilling the system, symptoms of overheating are found which did not occur previously, then the fault is almost certainly due to trapped air at some point in the system causing an air-lock and restricting the flow of coolant. Usually air is trapped because the system was refilled too quickly. In some cases, air-locks can be released by tapping or squeezing the appropriate coolant hose. If the problem persists, stop the engine and allow it to cool down completely before unscrewing the expansion tank filler cap, to allow the trapped air to escape.

27 Alarm remote keypad battery renewal

1 Place the keypad on work surface and using a flat-bladed screwdriver, carefully prise the two halves of the keypad apart. Take care to avoid damaging the rubber seal with the screwdriver blade **(see illustrations)**.

2 Remove the battery from the terminal clips, noting which way up it is. Press each keypad button in turn and hold them down for a few seconds, to fully discharge the electronic components inside.

26.17a **Remove the expansion tank filler cap and carefully top up the tank . . .**

26.17b **. . . to the 'MAX' level**

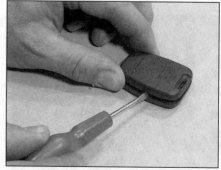

27.1a **Using a flat bladed screwdriver, carefully prise the two halves of the keypad apart . . .**

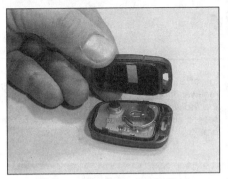

27.1b . . . to expose the battery

27.3 Fit the new battery, handling it with a piece of tissue paper to avoid touching the battery contact surfaces

28.3 Disconnect the fuel inlet hose . . .

3 Obtain a new battery of the correct type and insert it between the terminal clips, ensuring that it is fitted the correct way around (the positive '+' side faces the keypad backplate). Avoid touching the contact surfaces of the battery as you do this, by handling it with a piece of tissue paper; moisture from fingertips can cause the battery surfaces to corrode **(see illustration)**.

4 Press the two halves of the keypad back together, ensuring that the rubber seal is correctly located, then check the operation of the keypad.

28 Fuel filter renewal

⚠️ **Warning: Petrol is extremely flammable – great care must be taken during this procedure. Before carrying out any operation on the fuel system, refer to the precautions given in "Safety first!", and follow them implicitly. Petrol is a highly-dangerous and volatile liquid, and the precautions necessary when handling it cannot be overstressed.**

28.4 . . . and the fuel outlet hose . . .

28.5a . . . then slacken the clamp bolt . . .

1 The fuel filter is located on the bulkhead at the rear of the engine compartment.

2 Position a wad of absorbent cloth beneath the fuel filter.

3 Release the hose clip, and disconnect the fuel inlet hose from the top of the fuel filter **(see illustration)**. If the new filter is not going to be fitted immediately, clamp or cover the open end of the fuel hose to prevent dirt entry and fuel loss.

4 Repeat the procedure to disconnect the fuel outlet hose from the top of the filter **(see illustration)**.

5 Slacken the fuel filter clamp bolt, and withdraw the filter from the clamp bracket **(see illustrations)**.

6 Collect the fuel from the filter, then dispose of the filter safely.

7 Fit the new filter using a reversal of the removal procedure, but ensure that the hoses are correctly reconnected – fuel flow direction arrows are stamped into the filter adjacent to the fuel pipes **(see illustration)**. Ensure that the hose clips are tight and, on completion, prime the fuel system as described in Chapter 4B.

1B

28.5b . . . and withdraw the fuel filter

28.7 Note the fuel flow arrows stamped into the top of the filter

Every 36 000 miles (60 000 km) or 3 years - whichever comes first

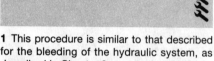

29 Camshaft timing belt renewal

The procedure is described in Chapter 2B.

Note: *Although the normal interval for timing belt renewal is 72 000 miles (120 000 km), it is strongly recommended that the interval is halved to 36 000 miles (60 000 km) on vehicles which are subjected to intensive use, ie. mainly short journeys or a lot of stop-start driving. The actual belt renewal interval is therefore very much up to the individual owner, but bear in mind that severe engine damage will result if the belt breaks.*

Every 2 years, regardless of mileage

30 Brake fluid renewal

1 This procedure is similar to that described for the bleeding of the hydraulic system, as described in Chapter 9, except that the brake fluid reservoir should be emptied by syphoning and allowance should be made for all old fluid to be expelled when bleeding a section of the circuit.
2 Working as described in Chapter 9, open the first bleed nipple in the sequence and pump the brake pedal gently until nearly all the old fluid has been emptied from the master cylinder reservoir. Top up to the MAX level on the reservoir with new fluid and continue pumping until only new fluid remains in the reservoir and new fluid can be seen emerging from the bleed nipple. Old hydraulic fluid is much darker in colour than new fluid, making it easy to distinguish between them.
3 Tighten the nipple and top the reservoir level up to the MAX level line.
4 Work through all the remaining nipples in the sequence until new fluid can be seen emerging from all of them. Be careful to keep the master cylinder reservoir topped up to above the MIN level at all times, or air may enter the system and greatly increase the length of the task.
5 When the operation is complete, check that all nipples are securely tightened and that their dust caps are refitted. Wash off all traces of spilt fluid and recheck the master cylinder reservoir fluid level.
6 Check the operation of the brakes before taking the vehicle on the road.

Every 10 years, regardless of mileage

31 Airbag system component renewal

1 The Supplementary Restraint System (SRS), which incorporates the airbag and seat belt pre-tensioning systems, has components which contain pyrotechnic materials. Because these materials degrade with age, Rover specify that the following components must be renewed every ten years:
a) The passenger airbag module
b) The driver airbag module
2 Chapter 12 contains information relating to the removal and refitting of these components. However, given the safety-critical nature of the SRS components, and the fact that the correct operation of the SRS can only be verified using dedicated electronic test equipment, we strongly recommend that these operations are entrusted to a Rover dealer.

Chapter 2 Part A:
K-series petrol engine in-car repair procedures

Contents

Degrees of difficulty

Easy, suitable for novice with little experience	**Fairly easy,** suitable for beginner with some experience	**Fairly difficult,** suitable for competent DIY mechanic 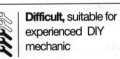

Difficult, suitable for experienced DIY mechanic	**Very difficult,** suitable for expert DIY or professional

2A

Specifications

General

Engine type	Four-cylinder in-line, four-stroke, liquid-cooled
Designation:	
8-valve engines	K8
16-valve engines	K16
Bore:	
1.1 and 1.4 litre engines	75.00 mm
1.6 and 1.8 litre engines	80.00 mm
Stroke:	
1.1 litre engine	63.25 mm
1.4 and 1.6 litre engines	79.00 mm
1.8 litre engine	89.30 mm
Capacity:	
1.1 litre engine	1120 cc
1.4 litre engine	1396 cc
1.6 litre engine	1589 cc
1.8 litre engine	1796 cc
Firing order	1-3-4-2 (No 1 cylinder at timing belt end)
Direction of crankshaft rotation	Clockwise (seen from right-hand side of vehicle)
Compression ratio:	
1.1 litre engine	9.75 : 1
1.4 litre K8 engine	9.90 : 1
1.4 litre K16 engine	10.4:1
1.6 and 1.8 litre engines	10.5:1
Minimum compression pressure (typical value)	10.0 bar
Maximum compression pressure difference between cylinders (typical value)1.5 bar	

Camshaft

Drive	Toothed belt
Number of bearings	6
Bearing journal running clearance:	
Standard	0.060 to 0.094 mm
Service limit	0.150 mm
Camshaft endfloat:	
Standard	0.060 to 0.190 mm
Service limit	0.300 mm
Hydraulic tappet outside diameter	32.959 to 32.975 mm

Lubrication system

System pressure	1.7 to 3.5 bar @ idle speed
Pressure relief valve opening pressure	4.1 bar
Low oil pressure warning light comes on	0.3 to 0.5 bar
Oil pump clearances:	
Rotor endfloat	0.02 to 0.06 mm
Outer rotor-to-body clearance	0.28 to 0.36 mm
Rotor lobe clearance	0.05 to 0.13 mm

Torque wrench settings

	Nm	lbf ft
Timing belt cover bolts	10	7
Timing belt tensioner backplate clamp bolt	10	7
Timing belt tensioner pulley screw	45	33
Camshaft sprocket bolt:		
M8 bolt	35	26
M10 bolt	65	48
Rear camshaft cover plate bolts (K16 engines)	25	18
Crankshaft pulley bolt	163	120
Right-hand engine mounting:		
1.1 and 1.4 litre engines:		
Engine mounting-to-engine bracket nuts	100	74
Engine mounting-to-body through-bolt	80	59
1.6 and 1.8 litre engines:		
Mounting bracket-to-engine bolts	160	118
Restraint bar securing nuts	45	33
Mounting-to-body nut	45	33
Mounting-to-mounting bracket nut	85	63
Steady bar-to-mounting bracket bolt	80	59
Left-hand engine/transmission mounting:		
1.1 and 1.4 litre engines:		
Engine/transmission mounting-to-body bolts	55	41
Engine/transmission mounting bracket-to-body bolts	55	41
Engine/transmission mounting-to-mounting bracket bolts	60	44
1.6 and 1.8 litre engines with manual transmission:		
Engine/transmission mounting-to-transmission bracket bolts	100	74
Engine/transmission mounting-to-body bracket through-bolt	85	63
Automatic transmission models:		
Mounting bracket-to-body bolts	55	41
Transmission mounting bracket-to-engine/transmission		
mounting nut1	60	118
Mounting-to-mounting bracket nuts	45	33
Engine/transmission steady bar-to-transmission/sump bolt	45	33
Engine/transmission steady bar-to-subframe bolt	80	59
Oil pressure warning light switch	15	11
Cylinder head bolts:		
Stage 1	20	15
Stage 2	Angle-tighten through a further 180°	
Stage 3	Angle-tighten through a further 180°	
Alternator top mounting bracket nut/bolt	25	18
Cylinder head cover bolts	9	6
Engine lifting bracket bolts	9	6
Flywheel bolts*	85	63
Torsion damper-to-flywheel bolts (automatic transmission models) . . .	22	16
Flywheel lower cover bolts	9	6
Oil pump-to-cylinder block bolts	9	6

Torque wrench settings (continued)

	Nm	lbf ft
Sump bolts:		
Steel sump:		
M6 bolts	10	7
M8 bolts	25	18
Alloy sump	25	18
Engine oil drain plug:		
Steel sump	42	31
Alloy sump	25	18
Spark plug cover screws (K16 engines)	10	7
Spark plugs	25	18
Camshaft bearing carrier bolts	10	7
Big-end bolts:		
Stage 1	25	18
Stage 2	Angle-tighten through a further 45°	
Main bearing ladder-to-cylinder block bolts:		
Stage 1	5	4
Stage 2	15	11
Oil rail-to-main bearing ladder bolts	5	4

*Use new bolts

1 General information and precautions

How to use this Chapter

This Part of the Chapter describes those repair procedures that can reasonably be carried out on the engine whilst it remains in the vehicle. If the engine has been removed from the vehicle and is being dismantled as described in Part C of this Chapter, any preliminary dismantling procedures can be ignored.

Note that whilst it may be possible physically to overhaul items such as the piston/connecting rod assemblies with the engine in the vehicle, such tasks are not usually carried out as separate operations and usually require the execution of several additional procedures (not to mention the cleaning of components and of oilways). For this reason, all such tasks are classed as major overhaul procedures and are described in Part C of this Chapter.

Engine description

The engine is of four-cylinder, in-line type, mounted transversely at the front of the vehicle with the clutch and transmission at its left-hand end. The K8 engine is of eight-valve single overhead camshaft type, and the K16 engine is of sixteen-valve double overhead camshaft type.

The main structure of the engine consists of three major castings - the cylinder head, the cylinder block/crankcase, and the crankshaft main bearing ladder.

The three major castings are made from aluminium alloy, and are clamped together by ten long through-bolts which perform the dual role of cylinder head bolts and crankshaft main bearing bolts. An oil rail is fitted under the main bearing ladder, and to avoid disturbing the bottom end of the engine when removing the through-bolts, the oil rail is

secured independently to the main bearing ladder (by two nuts), and the main bearing ladder is secured to the cylinder block/crankcase (by ten bolts).

The crankshaft runs in five main bearings. Thrustwashers are fitted to the centre main bearing (upper half) to control crankshaft endfloat.

The connecting rods rotate on horizontally-split bearing shells at their big-ends. The pistons are attached to the connecting rods by gudgeon pins which are an interference fit in the connecting rod small-end eyes. The aluminium alloy pistons are fitted with three piston rings, comprising two compression rings and an oil control ring.

The cylinder bores are formed by replaceable wet liners which locate in the cylinder block/crankcase at their top ends. A bead of sealant around each liner prevents the escape of coolant into the sump.

The inlet and exhaust valves are each closed by coil springs and operate in guides pressed into the cylinder head. The valve seat inserts are pressed into the cylinder head and can be renewed separately if worn.

The camshaft(s) is/are driven by a toothed timing belt, and operate(s) the valves via self-adjusting hydraulic tappets, thus eliminating the need for routine checking and adjustment of the valve clearances. The camshaft rotates in bearings which are line-bored directly into the cylinder head and the (bolted-on) bearing carrier. This means that the bearing carrier and cylinder head are matched, and cannot be renewed independently. The distributor is driven from the rear (flywheel end) of the camshaft. The fuel pump is electrically-operated.

The coolant pump is driven by the timing belt.

Lubrication is by means of an eccentric-rotor type pump driven directly from the front (timing belt end) of the crankshaft. The pump draws oil through a strainer located in the sump, and then forces it through an externally-mounted full-flow cartridge-type oil

filter into galleries in the oil rail and the cylinder block/crankcase, from where it is distributed to the crankshaft (main bearings) and camshaft. The big-end bearings are supplied with oil via internal drillings in the crankshaft, while the camshaft bearings and the hydraulic tappets receive a pressurised supply via drillings in the cylinder head. The camshaft lobes and valves are lubricated by oil splash, as are all other engine components.

Repair operations possible with the engine in the car

The following work can be carried out with the engine in the vehicle:

a) Compression pressure - testing.
b) Cylinder head cover - removal and refitting.
c) Crankshaft pulley - removal and refitting.
d) Timing belt covers - removal and refitting.
e) Timing belt - removal, refitting and adjustment.
f) Timing belt tensioner and sprockets - removal and refitting.
g) Camshaft oil seal(s) - renewal.
h) Camshaft(s) and hydraulic tappets - removal, inspection and refitting.
i) Cylinder head - removal and refitting.
j) Cylinder head and pistons - decarbonising.
k) Sump - removal and refitting.
l) Oil pump - removal, overhaul and refitting.
m) Crankshaft oil seals - renewal.
n) Engine/transmission mountings - inspection and renewal.
o) Flywheel - removal, inspection and refitting.

Precautions

Note that a side-effect of the through-bolt engine design is that the crankshaft cannot be rotated once the through-bolts have been slackened. During any servicing or overhaul work the crankshaft must always be rotated to the desired position before the bolts are disturbed.

2A

2 Compression test – description and interpretation

Note: *A suitable compression tester will be required for this test.*

1 When engine performance is down, or if misfiring occurs which cannot be attributed to the ignition or fuel systems, a compression test can provide diagnostic clues as to the engine's condition. If the test is performed regularly it can give warning of trouble before any other symptoms become apparent.

2 The engine must be fully warmed up to normal operating temperature, the battery must be fully charged and the spark plugs must be removed. The aid of an assistant will be required.

3 Disable the ignition system by disconnecting the ignition HT coil lead from the distributor cap and earthing it on the cylinder block. Use a jumper lead or similar wire to make a good connection.

4 Fit a compression tester to the No 1 cylinder spark plug hole. The type of tester which screws into the plug thread is preferred.

5 Have the assistant hold the throttle wide open and crank the engine on the starter motor. After one or two revolutions, the compression pressure should build up to a maximum figure and then stabilise. Record the highest reading obtained.

6 Repeat the test on the remaining cylinders, recording the pressure in each.

7 All cylinders should produce very similar pressures. Any difference greater than that specified indicates the existence of a fault. Note that the compression should build up quickly in a healthy engine. Low compression on the first stroke, followed by gradually increasing pressure on successive strokes, indicates worn piston rings. A low compression reading on the first stroke, which does not build up during successive strokes, indicates leaking valves or a blown head gasket (a cracked head could also be the cause). Deposits on the undersides of the valve heads can also cause low compression.

8 If the pressure in any cylinder is reduced to the specified minimum or less (Rover do not specify figures, the figures given in the Specifications are typical figures for a petrol engine), carry out the following test to isolate the cause. Introduce a teaspoonful of clean oil into that cylinder through its spark plug hole and repeat the test.

9 If the addition of oil temporarily improves the compression pressure, this indicates that bore or piston wear is responsible for the pressure loss. No improvement suggests that leaking or burnt valves, or a blown head gasket, may be to blame.

10 A low reading from two adjacent cylinders is almost certainly due to the head gasket having blown between them and the presence of coolant in the engine oil will confirm this.

11 If one cylinder is about 20 percent lower than the others and the engine has a slightly rough idle, a worn camshaft lobe could be the cause.

12 If the compression reading is unusually high, the combustion chambers are probably coated with carbon deposits. If this is the case, the cylinder head should be removed and decarbonised.

13 On completion of the test, refit the spark plugs and reconnect the HT lead to the distributor cap.

3 Engine timing marks – general information

1 The crankshaft pulley, crankshaft and camshaft sprockets are provided by the factory with clear marks which align only at 90° BTDC. This positions the pistons half-way up the bores so that there is no risk of damage as the engine is reassembled after dismantling. These marks **do not** indicate TDC.

2 For all engine overhaul procedures, the engine should be positioned with No 1 piston at the 90° BTDC position, as follows.

3 Apply the handbrake and ensure that the transmission is in neutral, then jack up the front of the vehicle and support it securely on axle stands (see *"Jacking and Vehicle Support"*). Remove the right-hand roadwheel. Where applicable, remove the splash shield for access to the crankshaft pulley.

4 Remove the upper outer timing belt cover, as described in Section 6.

5 On K8 engines, using a spanner or socket and extension bar applied to the crankshaft pulley bolt, rotate the crankshaft clockwise until the timing mark (usually marked "EX") on the camshaft sprocket is aligned horizontally with the top face of the cylinder head. The timing mark should be positioned on the right-hand side of the sprocket when viewed from the timing belt end of the engine **(see illustration)**.

6 On K16 engines, using a spanner or socket and extension bar applied to the crankshaft pulley bolt, rotate the crankshaft clockwise until the timing marks on the camshaft sprockets are aligned horizontally with the top face of the cylinder head (there is usually a line marked on the rear timing belt cover which represents the top face of the cylinder head). The timing marks should be positioned on the right-hand side of the sprockets when viewed from the timing belt end of the engine, and the "EXHAUST" arrow markings should point towards the rear of the vehicle **(see illustration)**.

7 On all engines, when the camshaft timing marks are aligned, the notch in the crankshaft pulley inboard rim should be aligned with the 90° BTDC mark on the outer timing belt cover. This mark is positioned vertically above the pulley. If the crankshaft pulley has been removed, the timing marks on the crankshaft sprocket can be used, and in this case, the two punched dots on the crankshaft sprocket should be positioned either side of the raised flange on the oil pump, vertically above the sprocket **(see illustrations)**.

3.5 Camshaft sprocket timing mark (A) aligned with cylinder head top surface (B) – K8 engine

3.6 Camshaft sprocket timing marks (A) aligned with mark (B) on timing belt cover – K16 engine

3.7a Crankshaft pulley timing mark aligned with 90° BTDC mark on outer timing belt cover

3.7b Crankshaft sprocket dots (A) positioned on each side of raised rib (B) on oil pump body

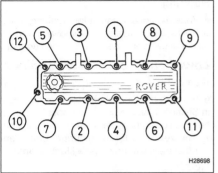

4.9 Cylinder head cover bolt tightening sequence – K8 engines

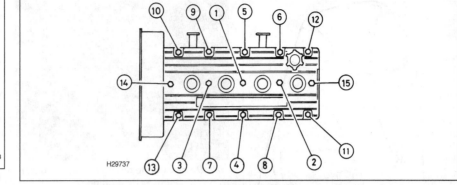

4.19 Cylinder head cover bolt tightening sequence – K16 engines

4 Cylinder head cover – removal and refitting

K8 engines

Removal

1 Disconnect the battery negative lead.
2 Using a suitable pair of pliers, release the retaining clips and disconnect the breather hoses from the cylinder head cover.
3 Working progressively and in the **reverse** of the tightening sequence **(see illustration 4.9)**, slacken and remove the cylinder head cover retaining bolts.
4 Remove the cover, complete with the rubber seal. The seal should remain attached to the camshaft cover as it is removed – do not separate the cylinder head cover and seal unless the seal is in obvious need of renewal.

Refitting

5 Before commencing refitting, check the condition of the cylinder head cover rubber seal, without removing it from the cylinder head cover. Do not remove the seal unless it is damaged and in need of renewal.
6 Thoroughly clean the mating faces of the cylinder head cover and the cylinder head.
7 If a new rubber seal is being fitted, fit the seal to the cylinder head cover.
8 Refit the cover to the cylinder head, ensuring that the seal remains seated in its groove. Fit all the retaining bolts, and tighten them finger-tight.
9 Tighten the bolts to the specified torque in the sequence shown **(see illustration)**.
10 Reconnect the breather hoses to the cylinder head cover and secure in position with the retaining clips, then reconnect the battery negative lead.

K16 engines

Removal

11 Proceed as described in paragraphs 1 and 2.
12 Undo the two spark plug cover retaining screws and lift off the cover. Disconnect the HT leads from the spark plugs and withdraw

them from the cylinder head, along with the clip plate and the grommet which is fitted to the left-hand end of the cylinder head cover.
13 Working progressively and in the **reverse** of the tightening sequence **(see illustration 4.19)**, slacken and remove the cylinder head cover retaining bolts.
14 Remove the cover, complete with the gasket. The gasket should remain attached to the camshaft cover as it is removed – do not separate the cylinder head cover and gasket unless the gasket is in obvious need of renewal.

Refitting

15 Before commencing refitting, check the condition of the cylinder head cover gasket, without removing it from the cylinder head cover. Do not remove the gasket unless it is damaged and in need of renewal.
16 Thoroughly clean the mating faces of the cylinder head cover and the cylinder head.
17 If a new gasket is to be fitted, press it onto the cover locating dowels so that if it were laid on the camshaft bearing carrier its stamped markings would be legible. The "TOP" mark should be nearest the inlet manifold and the "EXHAUST MAN SIDE" mark should have its arrows pointing to the exhaust manifold.
18 Refit the cover to the cylinder head, ensuring that the gasket remains correctly seated. Fit all the retaining bolts, and tighten them finger-tight.
19 Tighten the bolts to the specified torque in the sequence shown **(see illustration)**.

5.6 Align the notch (arrowed) in the crankshaft pulley with the lug on the sprocket

20 Reconnect the HT leads to the spark plugs, then locate the clip plate and grommet in the left-hand end of the cylinder head cover. Ensure the HT leads are correctly routed then refit the spark plug cover and tighten its retaining screws to the specified torque.
21 Reconnect the breather hoses to the cylinder head cover and secure in position with the retaining clips, then reconnect the battery negative lead.

5 Crankshaft pulley – removal and refitting

Removal

1 Apply the handbrake then jack up the front of the vehicle and support it securely on axle stands (see "Jacking and Vehicle Support"). Remove the right-hand roadwheel. Where applicable, remove the splash shield for access to the crankshaft pulley.
2 If necessary, rotate the crankshaft until the relevant timing marks align (see Section 3).
3 Remove the auxiliary drivebelt as described in Chapter 1A.
4 To prevent crankshaft rotation while the pulley bolt is unscrewed, on manual transmission models, select top gear and have an assistant apply the brakes firmly. Alternatively, lock the flywheel by removing the starter motor (see Chapter 5A), and using a suitable tool or a large screwdriver engaged with the starter ring gear teeth.
5 Unscrew the pulley bolt, and recover the washer, then remove the pulley from the crankshaft.

Refitting

6 Fit the pulley to the crankshaft, aligning the notch in the pulley with the locating lug on the sprocket, then refit the bolt and the washer **(see illustration)**. Make sure that the larger diameter side of the washer is against the pulley.
7 Lock the crankshaft using the method used on removal, and tighten the pulley retaining bolt to the specified torque setting.

2A

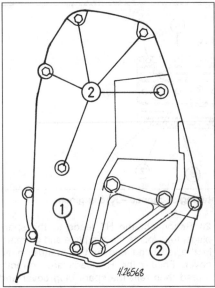

6.2 Timing belt upper outer cover securing bolts – K8 engines

1 Slacken bolt (cover is slotted)
2 Remove bolts

8 Refit and tension the auxiliary drivebelt as described in Chapter 1A.
9 Refit the roadwheel, then lower the vehicle to the ground.

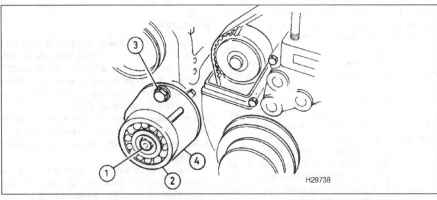

6.10 Power steering pump drivebelt tensioner mounting details – K16 engines

1 Pulley securing nut   2 Pulley   3 Tensioner securing bolt   4 Tensioner

6.16a Rear timing belt cover securing bolts (arrowed) – K8 engine

6.16b Removing the rear timing belt cover – K16 engine

6.7 Removing the timing belt lower outer cover – K8 engines

6 Timing belt covers – removal and refitting

Upper outer cover

Removal

1 Unscrew the lower bolt securing the upper cover to the engine.
2 Unscrew the upper bolts securing the upper cover to the rear cover **(see illustration)**.
3 Lift off the upper cover, and recover the rubber seal if it is loose.

Refitting

4 Wipe the cover clean before refitting.
5 Refitting is a reversal of removal, but make sure that the rubber seal is positioned correctly.

Lower outer cover – K8 engines
Removal

6 Remove the crankshaft pulley as described in Section 5, and remove the upper timing belt cover as described previously in this Section.
7 Unscrew the three securing bolts, and remove the lower cover **(see illustration)**.

Refitting

8 Refitting is a reversal of removal, but refit the crankshaft pulley as described in Section 5.

Lower outer cover – K16 engines
Removal

9 Remove the crankshaft pulley as described in Section 5.
10 Unscrew the nut (and recover the washer) securing the power steering pump drivebelt tensioner pulley to the tensioner. Remove the tensioner pulley **(see illustration)**.
11 Unscrew the three bolts securing the drivebelt tensioner to the power steering pump mounting bracket, then remove the drivebelt tensioner.
12 Unscrew the three bolts securing the lower timing belt cover to the engine. Withdraw the lower cover, and recover the seal.

Refitting

13 Refitting is a reversal of removal, but refit the crankshaft pulley as described in Section 5.

Rear cover
Removal

14 Remove the outer timing belt covers as described previously in this Section.
15 Remove the camshaft sprocket(s) and the timing belt tensioner as described in Section 8.
16 Unscrew the securing bolts, and withdraw the timing belt rear cover **(see illustrations)**.

Refitting

17 Refitting is a reversal of removal, but refit the timing belt tensioner and the camshaft sprocket(s) as described in Section 8, and tighten all fixings to the specified torque wrench settings.

7 Timing belt – removal, inspection, refitting and adjustment

Removal

1 Disconnect the battery negative lead.
2 Apply the handbrake, then jack up the front of the vehicle and support securely on axle stands (see *"Jacking and Vehicle Support"*). Remove the right-hand roadwheel.
3 Remove the upper outer timing belt cover, with reference to Section 6 **(see illustrations)**.

1 Timing belt upper outer cover
2 Seal
3 Bolt
4 Bolt
5 Bolt
6 Shouldered bolt
7 Timing belt lower
   outer cover
8 Seal
9 Seal
10 Bolt
11 Bolt
12 Crankshaft pulley
13 Washer
14 Crankshaft pulley bolt
15 Timing belt tensioner
   pulley assembly
16 Tensioner pulley
   Allen screw
17 Tensioner backplate
   clamp bolt
18 Tensioner pulley
   spring
19 Sleeve
20 Anchor bolt
21 Timing belt
22 Crankshaft sprocket
23 Camshaft sprocket
24 Camshaft sprocket bolt
25 Washer
26 Timing belt rear cover
27 Bolt - cover to water pump
28 Bolt

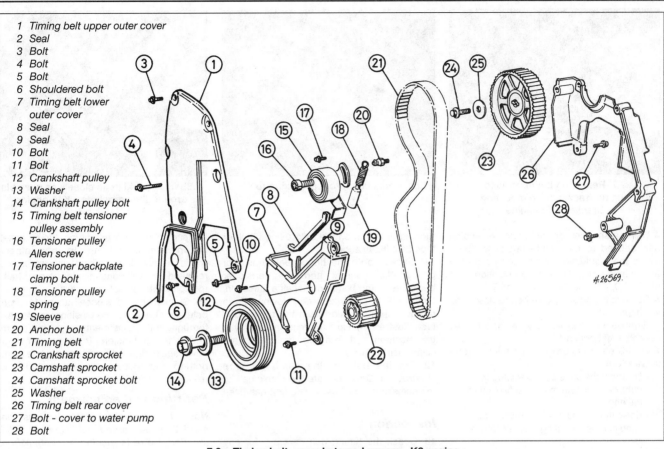

7.3a Timing belt, sprockets and covers - K8 engine

1 Timing belt upper outer
   cover
2 Bolt
3 Seal
4 Bolt
5 Timing belt lower outer
   cover
6 Seal
7 Bolt
8 Bolt
9 Crankshaft pulley
10 Washer
11 Crankshaft pulley bolt
12 Timing belt
13 Camshaft sprockets
14 Bolt
15 Washer
16 Timing belt tensioner pulley
   assembly
17 Tensioner pulley Allen
   screw
18 Tensioner pulley spring
19 Sleeve
20 Anchor bolt
21 Tensioner backplate clamp
   bolt
22 Crankshaft sprocket
23 Timing belt rear cover
24 Bolt

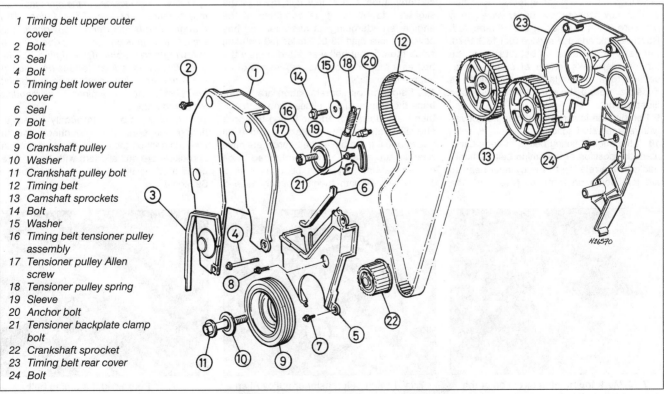

7.3b Timing belt, sprockets and covers - K16 engine

2A

7.7 Removing the right-hand engine/transmission mounting bracket – K8 engine

7.8a Camshaft sprocket locking tool . . .

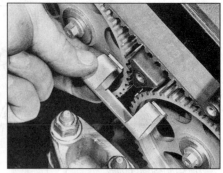

7.8b . . . should fit as closely as possible around the sprockets – K16 engine

4 Using a spanner, or socket and extension bar, applied to the crankshaft pulley bolt, rotate the crankshaft clockwise to align the timing marks with No 1 piston positioned at 90° BTDC, as described in Section 3.

5 Remove the auxiliary drivebelt as described in Chapter 1A.

6 Remove the right-hand engine mounting as described in Section 17.

7 On K8 engines, proceed as follows **(see illustration)**.

 a) *Unscrew the three bolts securing the right-hand engine mounting bracket to the engine.*

 b) *Raise the engine slightly until the right-hand engine mounting bracket can be removed.*

8 On K16 engines, a suitable tool should be used to lock the camshaft sprockets together, so that they cannot move under valve spring pressure when the timing belt is removed. Rover technicians use service tool 18G 1570, but an acceptable substitute can be fabricated from a length of steel square-section tube, or similar to fit as closely as possible around the sprocket spokes **(see illustrations)**.

9 Remove the lower outer timing belt cover, with reference to Section 6.

10 If the original timing belt is to be re-used, mark the position of the timing belt tensioner backplate in relation to the cylinder head to aid tensioning on refitting. Also mark the

running direction on the belt, using chalk or tape **(see illustration)**.

11 Slacken both the timing belt tensioner pulley Allen screw and the tensioner backplate clamp bolt through half a turn each, then push the pulley assembly downwards to remove all the tension from the timing belt **(see illustration)**. Hold the tensioner pulley in this position and re-tighten the backplate clamp bolt securely.

12 Slip the belt off the sprockets **(see illustration)**. **Do not** rotate the crankshaft or the camshaft(s) until the timing belt has been refitted.

Inspection

13 Check the timing belt carefully for any signs of uneven wear, splitting or oil contamination and renew it if there is the slightest doubt about its condition. If the engine is undergoing an overhaul and has covered more than 48 000 miles (80 000 km) since the original belt was fitted, renew the belt as a matter of course, regardless of its apparent condition.

14 If signs of oil contamination are found, trace the source of the oil leak and rectify it, then wash down the engine timing belt area and all related components to remove all traces of oil. If the timing belt sprockets have been subjected to prolonged oil contamination, they must be soaked in a suitable solvent bath, then thoroughly washed

in clean solvent before refitting (the sprockets are manufactured from a porous material which will absorb oil – the oil will eventually be released and will contaminate the new belt if the sprockets are not cleaned).

15 Slacken the tensioner backplate clamp bolt, and check that the tensioner move freely throughout its adjustment range, and returns under spring tension. Push the tensioner down again, and tighten the backplate clamp bolt to secure the tensioner in the fully-released position.

Refitting and adjustment

Note: *The manufacturer states that tensioning need only be carried out when a belt is (re)fitted. No re-tensioning is recommended once a belt has been fitted and therefore this operation is not included in the manufacturer's maintenance schedule. If the timing belt is thought to be incorrectly tensioned, then adjust the tension as described in the following paragraphs. If the timing belt has been disturbed, adjust its tension following the same procedure, omitting as appropriate the irrelevant preliminary dismantling/ reassembly steps.*

16 On reassembly, thoroughly clean the timing belt sprockets and check that the timing marks on the camshaft and crankshaft sprockets are still aligned, with No 1 piston positioned at 90° BTDC, as described in Section 3.

7.10 Mark the running direction of the timing belt if it is to be re-used

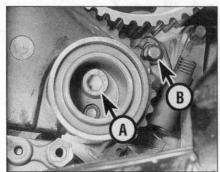

7.11 Timing belt tensioner pulley Allen screw (A) and backplate clamp bolt (B)

7.12 Removing the timing belt – K16 engine

17 If a used belt is being refitted, ensure that the direction mark made on removal points in the normal direction of rotation. Fit the timing belt over the crankshaft and camshaft sprockets, ensuring that the belt front run is taut, ie: all slack is on the tensioner pulley side of the belt, then fit the belt over the coolant pump sprocket and tensioner pulley. Do not twist the belt sharply during refitting and ensure that the belt teeth are correctly seated centrally in the sprockets and that the timing marks remain in alignment.

18 On K16 engines, remove the tool used to lock the camshaft sprockets together.

19 Refit the lower timing belt cover, then refit and tighten the securing bolts.

20 Refit the crankshaft pulley, with reference to Section 5, but do not refit the auxiliary drivebelt at this stage.

21 On K8 engine models, refit the right-hand engine mounting bracket, and tighten the securing bolts. If necessary, raise the engine slightly to allow the bracket to be fitted.

22 Refit the right-hand engine mounting bracket, and tighten the securing bolts to the specified torque, then refit the engine mounting, as described in Section 17.

23 Proceed as follows according to whether the original timing belt or a new timing belt is being fitted.

Existing timing belt

24 Unhook the tensioner spring from the spring anchor bolt.

25 Move the tensioner to align the mark made on the tensioner backplate before removal with the corresponding mark on the cylinder head.

26 Tighten the tensioner backplate clamp bolt and then the tensioner pulley screw to the specified torque.

27 Reconnect the tensioner spring to the anchor bolt.

28 Proceed to paragraph 34.

New timing belt

29 Slacken the tensioner backplate clamp bolt and tension the belt by applying finger pressure to the tensioner backplate, pushing the tensioner pulley against the timing belt.

30 Hold the tensioner in position and tighten the backplate bolt to the specified torque.

31 Using a suitable spanner or socket on the crankshaft pulley bolt, rotate the crankshaft two full turns clockwise to settle and tension the belt. Realign the crankshaft pulley (90° BTDC) mark with the mark on the timing belt cover, and check that the sprocket timing mark is still correctly aligned (see Section 3).

32 Slacken the tensioner backplate clamp bolt, and check that tension is still being applied by the tensioner spring.

33 Tighten the tensioner backplate clamp bolt and then the tensioner pulley screw to the specified torque.

All timing belts

34 Refit the timing belt upper cover, with reference to Section 6, then refit and tension

the auxiliary drivebelt as described in Chapter 1A.

35 Refit the roadwheel, and lower the vehicle to the ground, then reconnect the battery negative lead.

8 Timing belt tensioner and sprockets – removal, inspection and refitting

Camshaft sprocket – K8 engines

Removal

1 Disconnect the battery negative lead.

2 Remove the timing belt as described in Section 7. Note that there is no need to remove the timing belt completely, provided that it is slipped from the camshaft sprocket. **Do not** rotate the crankshaft or the camshaft until the timing belt has been refitted.

3 Slacken the camshaft sprocket retaining bolt and remove it, along with its washer. To prevent the camshaft from rotating, Rover technicians use service tool 18G 1521, but an acceptable substitute can be fabricated from two lengths of steel strip (one long, the other short) and three nuts and bolts. One nut and bolt should form the pivot of a forked tool with the remaining two nuts and bolts at the tips of the forks to engage with the sprocket spokes, as shown in illustration 8.7.

4 Withdraw the sprocket from the camshaft, noting the locating roll-pin **(see illustration)**. If the roll-pin is a loose fit in the end of the camshaft, remove it and store it with the sprocket for safe-keeping.

Inspection

5 Clean the sprocket thoroughly, and renew it if it shows signs of wear, damage or cracks.

Refitting

6 Where applicable, refit the roll-pin to the end of the camshaft, ensuring that its split is facing the centre of the camshaft, then refit the sprocket (ensure that it engages with the roll-pin) so that the "EX" line and the mark stamped on the sprocket rim are pointing towards the front of the vehicle and aligned exactly with the cylinder head top surface.

7 Prevent the sprocket from rotating by using the method employed on removal, then tighten the sprocket retaining bolt to the specified torque setting **(see illustration)**. Check that the sprocket timing marks are still aligned.

8 Refit and tension the timing belt as described in Section 7, then reconnect the battery negative lead.

Camshaft sprockets – K16 engines

Removal

9 Proceed as described in paragraphs 1 and 2.

10 Slacken the relevant camshaft sprocket retaining bolt and remove it, along with its washer. The tool used to lock the sprockets together during the timing belt removal procedure (Section 7) should prevent the sprockets rotating as the sprocket retaining bolt is unscrewed.

11 Remove the sprocket from the end of the camshaft, noting the locating roll-pin If the roll-pin is a loose fit in the end of the camshaft, remove it and store it with the sprocket for safe-keeping. If both camshaft sprockets are being removed, although the sprockets are identical, it is good practise to mark them (inlet and exhaust) so that they can be refitted in their original positions.

Inspection

12 Clean the sprocket thoroughly, and renew it if it shows signs of wear, damage or cracks.

Refitting

13 Where applicable, refit the roll pin to the end of the camshaft, ensuring that its split is facing the centre of the camshaft, then refit the sprocket (ensure that it engages with the roll-pin). The timing marks should be positioned on the right-hand side of the sprockets when viewed from the timing belt end of the engine, and the "EXHAUST" arrow markings should point towards the rear of the vehicle. Ensure that the appropriate sprocket keyway engages the camshaft roll-pin, ie, if refitting the inlet camshaft sprocket, engage the "IN" keyway with the roll-pin, and if refitting the exhaust camshaft sprocket,

2A

8.4 Removing the camshaft sprocket (roll-pin arrowed) – K8 engine

8.7 Using a fabricated tool to hold the camshaft sprocket stationary as the bolt is tightened – K8 engine

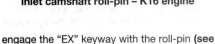

8.13 Engage "EX" keyway with exhaust camshaft roll-pin, and "IN" keyway with inlet camshaft roll-pin – K16 engine

8.14 Using a fabricated tool to hold the camshaft sprockets stationary as the inlet camshaft sprocket bolt is tightened – K16 engine

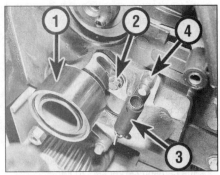

8.21 Timing belt tensioner components

1 *Tensioner pulley*
2 *Tensioner backplate clamp bolt*
3 *Tensioner spring*
4 *Anchor bolt*

engage the "EX" keyway with the roll-pin **(see illustration)**.
14 Proceed as described in paragraphs 7 and 8 **(see illustration)**.

Crankshaft sprocket

Removal

15 Proceed as described in paragraphs 1 and 2.
16 Remove the sprocket from the crankshaft.

Inspection

17 Clean the sprocket thoroughly, and renew it if it shows signs of wear, damage or cracks.

Refitting

18 Refit the sprocket to the crankshaft, ensuring that it locates correctly on the crankshaft flattened section. Note that the sprocket flange must be innermost. Check that the sprocket timing marks align - the two dots on the sprocket must be positioned on each side of the raised rib on the oil pump body (see Section 3).
19 Refit and tension the timing belt as described in Section 7, then reconnect the battery negative lead.

Tensioner assembly

Removal

20 Proceed as described in paragraphs 1 and 2.
21 Using a suitable pair of pliers, unhook the tensioner spring from the anchor bolt **(see illustration)**.
22 Unscrew the tensioner pulley Allen screw and the tensioner backplate clamp bolt, then withdraw the tensioner assembly from the engine.

Inspection

23 Clean the tensioner assembly but do not use any strong solvent which may enter the pulley bearing. Check that the pulley rotates freely on the backplate, with no sign of stiffness or of free play. Renew the assembly if there is any doubt about its condition or if there are any obvious signs of wear or damage. The same applies to the tensioner

spring, which should be checked with great care as its condition is critical for the correct tensioning of the timing belt.

Refitting

24 Refit the tensioner pulley assembly and tighten the pulley Allen screw and the backplate clamp bolt lightly. Hook the tensioner spring over the anchor bolt and check that the tensioner is free to move under spring tension and that the pulley bears correctly against the timing belt (lay the timing belt in position over the sprockets).
25 Refit and tension the timing belt as described in Section 7, then reconnect the battery negative lead.

9	Camshaft oil seals – renewal	⚙️

Note: *If a front oil seal is to be renewed with the timing belt still in place, then check that the belt is free from oil contamination. Renew the belt if signs of oil contamination are found. Cover the belt to protect it from contamination while work is in progress and ensure that all traces of oil are removed from the area before the belt is refitted.*

Front (timing belt end) seal

1 Remove the camshaft sprocket as described in Section 8.

9.4 Fitting a new inlet camshaft front oil seal – K16 engine

2 Punch or drill two small holes opposite each other in the oil seal. Screw a self-tapping screw into each hole, and pull on the screws with pliers to extract the seal.
3 Clean the seal housing and polish off any burrs or raised edges which may have caused the seal to fail.
4 Lubricate the lips of the new seal with clean engine oil and drive it into position until it seats on its locating shoulder. Use a suitable tubular drift, such as a socket, which bears only on the hard outer edge of the seal **(see illustration)**. Take care not to damage the seal lips during fitting and note that the seal lips should face inwards.
5 Refit the camshaft sprocket as described in Section 8.

Rear (distributor end) seal – K8 engines

6 At the rear of the camshaft, sealing is provided by the distributor O-ring. Refer to Chapter 5B for details.

Exhaust camshaft rear (distributor end) seal – K16 engines

7 Disconnect the battery negative lead.
8 Remove the air cleaner assembly as described in Chapter 4A.
9 Unscrew the two bolts securing the rear camshaft cover plate to the bearing carrier, and remove the cover plate **(see illustration)**.

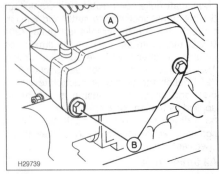

9.9 Exhaust camshaft rear cover plate (A) and securing bolts (B) – K16 engines

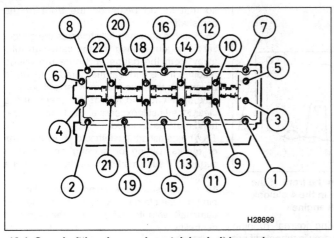

10.4 Camshaft bearing carrier retaining bolt loosening sequence – K8 engines

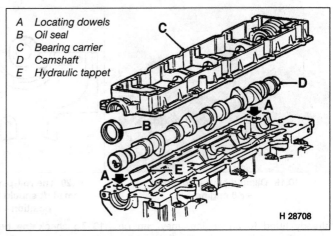

A Locating dowels
B Oil seal
C Bearing carrier
D Camshaft
E Hydraulic tappet

10.5 Camshaft and bearing carrier components – K8 engines

10 Proceed as described in paragraphs 2 to 4.

11 Thoroughly clean the mating faces of the bearing carrier and the camshaft cover plate, then refit the cover plate and tighten the securing bolts to the specified torque setting.

12 Refit the air cleaner, then reconnect the battery negative lead.

Inlet camshaft rear (distributor end) seal – K16 engines

13 Disconnect the battery negative lead.

14 Remove the air cleaner assembly as described in Chapter 4A.

15 Remove the distributor cap, rotor arm and shield, with reference to Chapter 5B.

16 Proceed as described in paragraphs 2 to 4.

17 Refit the shield, rotor arm and distributor cap.

18 Refit the air cleaner, then reconnect the battery negative lead.

---

10 Camshaft(s) and hydraulic tappets – removal, inspection and refitting

---

> **HAYNES HINT**
> *If faulty tappets are diagnosed and the engine's service history is unknown, it is always worth trying the effect of renewing the engine oil and filter (using only good quality engine oil of the recommended viscosity and specification) before going to the expense of renewing any of the tappets.*

K8 engines

Note: *Prior to removing the camshaft(s), obtain Rover sealant kit LVV 10002 which also contains a plastic scraper and a foam action sealant remover to clean the mating surfaces. Read the instructions supplied with the kit and*

take care not to allow the sealant to contact the fingers, as it will bond the skin. A new camshaft front oil seal should be used on refitting.

Removal

1 Remove the cylinder head cover, with reference to Section 4.

2 Remove the distributor cap, rotor arm and shield, as described in Chapter 5B.

3 Remove the camshaft sprocket as described in Section 8.

4 Working in the sequence shown (see illustration), slacken the camshaft bearing carrier retaining bolts progressively, by one turn at a time, to release the pressure of the valve springs on the bearing caps gradually and evenly.

5 Lift the camshaft bearing carrier from its locating dowels (see illustration). Store the bearing carrier carefully to avoid any possibility of damage to the bearings.

6 Carefully lift the camshaft from the cylinder head, and withdraw the oil seal from the front of the camshaft.

7 Obtain eight small, clean plastic containers and number them from 1 to 8.

8 Using a hydraulic sucker, withdraw each hydraulic tappet in turn, invert it to prevent oil loss and place it in its respective container, which should then be filled with clean engine

oil (see illustration). **Do not** interchange the hydraulic tappets, and do not allow the hydraulic tappets to lose oil, as they will take a long time to refill with oil on restarting the engine, which could result in incorrect valve clearances.

Inspection

Note: *To measure the camshaft bearing running clearance, an American product known as Plastigage can be used. This consists of a fine thread of perfectly round plastic which is compressed between the bearing surface and the camshaft journal. When the bearing carrier is removed, the plastic is deformed and can be measured with a special card gauge supplied with the kit. The running clearance is determined from this gauge. Plastigage is sometimes difficult to obtain, but enquiries at one of the larger specialist motor factors should produce the name of a stockist in your area.*

9 Check each hydraulic tappet for signs of obvious wear (scoring, pitting, etc) and for ovality. Renew if necessary. Using a micrometer, measure the outside diameter of the tappets – if the diameter of any tappet is outside the specified limits, it must be renewed. Note that modified tappets have been introduced in production (see illustration). When the modified tappets are

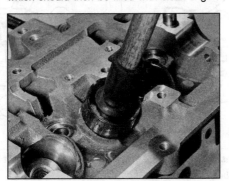

10.8 Using a hydraulic sucker to withdraw a hydraulic tappet – K8 engine

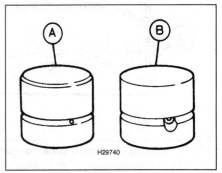

10.9 Earlier (A) and modified (B) hydraulic tappets

2A

10.19 Oiling a hydraulic tappet – K8 engine

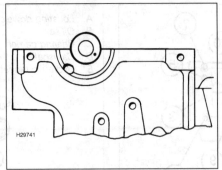

10.20 The roll-pin in the front of the camshaft should be in the 4 o'clock position – K8 engines

already fitted to an engine, they can be renewed on an individual basis. If the earlier type tappets are fitted to the engine, and an individual tappet is to be renewed, both tappets for the relevant cylinder must be renewed and replaced with the modified tappets (ie, if the exhaust tappet for No 1 cylinder is to be renewed, both inlet and exhaust tappets must be renewed and replaced with the modified tappets).

10 If the engine's valve clearances have sounded noisy, particularly if the noise persists after initial start-up from cold, then there is reason to suspect a faulty hydraulic tappet. Only a good mechanic experienced in these engines can tell whether the noise level is typical, or if renewal is warranted of one or more of the tappets.

11 If the operation of any tappet is faulty, then it must be renewed.

12 Carefully remove all traces of old sealant from the mating surfaces of the camshaft bearing carrier and cylinder head by using a plastic scraper - use the solvent supplied in the Rover sealant kit to remove any stubborn traces of sealant. Examine the camshaft bearing journals and the cylinder head and bearing carrier bearing surfaces for signs of obvious wear or pitting. If any such signs are evident, renew the component(s) concerned.

13 To check the bearing journal running clearance, remove the hydraulic tappets (if not already done), carefully clean the bearing surfaces and refit the camshaft and bearing carrier with a strand of Plastigage across each journal, parallel with the camshaft running axis (see Note at the beginning of this sub-Section). Tighten the bearing carrier bolts, in the specified order **(see illustration 10.23)**, to the specified torque wrench setting, whilst taking great care not to rotate the camshaft, then remove the bearing carrier and use the scale provided with the Plastigage kit to measure the width of each compressed strand.

14 If the running clearance of any bearing is found to be beyond the specified service limit or beyond the specified service limit, fit a new camshaft and repeat the check. If the clearance is still excessive, then the cylinder head (and matched bearing carrier) must be renewed.

15 To check camshaft endfloat, remove the hydraulic tappets (if not already done), carefully clean the bearing surfaces and refit the camshaft and bearing carrier. Tighten the bearing carrier bolts, in the specified order **(see illustration 10.23)**, to the specified torque wrench setting, then measure the endfloat using a Dial Test Indicator (DTI) or dial gauge mounted on the cylinder head,

so that its tip bears on the front of the camshaft.

16 Tap the camshaft fully towards the gauge, zero the gauge, then tap the camshaft fully away from the gauge and note the gauge reading. If the endfloat measured is found to be greater than the maximum specified, fit a new camshaft and repeat the check. If the clearance is still excessive, then the cylinder head must be renewed.

17 The camshaft itself should show no signs of marks, pitting or scoring on the lobe surfaces. If such marks are evident, renew the camshaft.

18 If a camshaft is renewed, extract the roll-pin from the old one and fit the pin to the new camshaft, with its split towards the camshaft centreline.

Refitting

19 Liberally oil the cylinder head hydraulic tappet bores and the tappets **(see illustration)**. Note that if new tappets are being fitted, they must be charged with clean engine oil before installation. Carefully refit the tappets to the cylinder head, ensuring that each tappet is refitted to its original bore and is the correct way up. Some care will be required to enter the tappets squarely into their bores.

20 Liberally oil the camshaft bearings and lobes then refit the camshaft. Position the shaft so that its No 1 cylinder lobes are pointing away from their valves and the roll-pin in the front of the camshaft is in the 4 o'clock position when viewed from the timing belt end of the engine **(see illustration)**.

21 Ensure that the two locating dowels are pressed firmly into the bearing carrier. Check that the mating surfaces of the cylinder head and bearing carrier are completely clean, unmarked and free from oil, then apply a continuous bead of the recommended sealant to the mating surfaces of the bearing carrier as shown **(see illustration)**. Spread the sealant to an even film using a brush or roller, taking care not to allow any sealant to enter

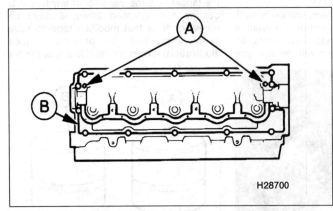

10.21 Application of sealant to camshaft carrier

A Locating dowels   B Continuous bead of sealant

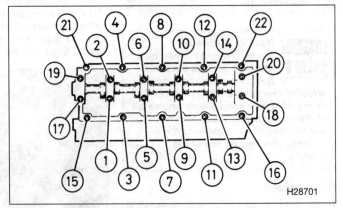

10.23 Camshaft bearing carrier bolt tightening sequence – K8 engines

Lightly tighten bolts 1, 2, 13 and 14 before tightening all bolts to the specified torque setting

the lubrication grooves. Note that once the sealant has been applied, assembly must be completed within 20 minutes.

22 Refit the carrier to the cylinder head, pushing it firmly into position. Fit the bearing carrier securing bolts, and tighten them finger-tight.

23 Lightly tighten the four bolts indicated then, working in the sequence shown, progressively tighten the securing bolts to the specified torque wrench setting to evenly apply pressure to the valve springs and the bearings **(see illustration)**.

24 Carefully wipe off all surplus sealant to that none is left to find its way into the oilways. Follow the sealant manufacturer's recommendations as to the time needed for curing – usually at least an hour must be allowed between application of the sealant and the starting of the engine.

25 Fit a new camshaft oil seal, using a suitable tube or socket, with reference to Section 9.

26 Refit the camshaft sprocket as described in Section 8.

27 Refit the shield, rotor arm and distributor cap, with reference to Chapter 5B if necessary.

28 Refit the cylinder head cover, with reference to Section 4.

K16 engines

Note: *Prior to removing the camshaft(s), obtain Rover sealant kit LVV 10002 which also contains a plastic scraper and a foam action sealant remover to clean the mating surfaces. Read the instructions supplied with the kit and take care not to allow the sealant to contact the fingers, as it will bond the skin. A new camshaft front oil seal should be used on refitting.*

Removal

29 Remove the cylinder head cover, with reference to Section 4.

30 Remove the distributor cap, rotor arm and shield, as described in Chapter 5B.

31 Remove the camshaft sprockets as described in Section 8.

32 Unscrew the two rear timing belt cover upper securing bolts so that the top of the cover can be pulled slightly away from the cylinder head.

33 Where applicable, unbolt the air intake duct support bracket from the cylinder head.

34 Working in the **reverse** of the tightening sequence **(see illustration 10.42)**, evenly and progressively slacken the camshaft bearing carrier bolts by one turn at a time. Once all valve spring pressure has been relieved, remove the bolts.

35 Withdraw the camshaft bearing carrier, noting the positions of the locating dowels, then lift out the camshafts and slide off the oil seals. The inlet camshaft can be identified by the distributor rotor arm drive spindle (or its location), therefore there is no need to mark the camshafts.

36 Obtain sixteen small, clean plastic containers, number them 1 to 16, and then fill them with clean engine oil. Using a rubber sucker, withdraw each hydraulic tappet in turn, and place it in its respective container, to prevent oil loss. Do not interchange the hydraulic tappets, or the rate of wear will be much increased. Do not allow the oil to drain from the tappets, or they will take a long time to refill with oil on restarting the engine, resulting in incorrect valve clearances.

Inspection

37 Proceed as described in paragraphs 9 to 18.

Refitting

38 Liberally oil the cylinder head hydraulic tappet bores and the tappets. Note that if new tappets are being fitted, they must be charged with clean engine oil before installation. Carefully refit the tappets to the cylinder head, ensuring that each tappet is refitted to its original bore and is the correct way up. Some care will be required to enter the tappets squarely into their bores.

39 Liberally oil the camshaft bearings and lobes and refit the camshafts to the cylinder head. Position each camshaft so that its No 1 cylinder lobes are pointing away from their valves. With the shafts in this position, the

10.39 The camshaft roll-pins should be positioned as shown when refitting the bearing carrier – K16 engines

roll-pin in the front end of the inlet camshaft will be in the 4 o'clock position when viewed from the right-hand end of the engine, while that of the exhaust camshaft will be in the 8 o'clock position **(see illustration)**.

40 Ensure that the locating dowels are pressed firmly into their recesses, check that the mating surfaces are completely clean, unmarked and free from oil, then apply a thin bead of the recommended sealant to the mating surfaces of the camshaft carrier as shown **(see illustration)**. Carefully follow the instructions supplied with the sealant kit. Spread the sealant to an even film using a brush or roller, taking care not to allow any sealant to enter the lubrication grooves. Note that once the sealant has been applied, assembly must be completed within 20 minutes.

41 Refit the carrier to the cylinder head, pushing it firmly into position. Fit the bearing carrier securing bolts, and tighten them finger-tight.

42 Working in the sequence shown **(see illustration)**, progressively tighten the camshaft carrier bolts by one turn at a time until the carrier touches the cylinder head evenly. Now go round again, working in the same sequence, tightening all bolts to the specified torque setting. Work only as described, to apply the pressure of the valve springs gradually and evenly on the carrier.

2A

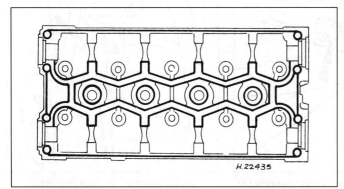

10.40 Apply a thin bead of sealant to the camshaft carrier mating surface along the paths shown by the heavy black lines – K16 engines

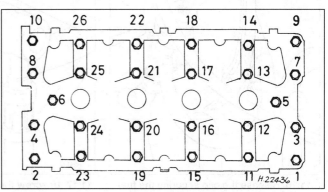

10.42 Camshaft bearing carrier bolt tightening sequence – K16 engines

Wipe off all surplus sealant so that none is left to find its way into any oilways. Follow the sealant manufacturer's recommendations as to the time needed for curing – usually at least an hour must be allowed between application of the sealant and the starting of the engine.

43 Fit new camshaft oil seals, using a suitable tube or socket, with reference to Section 9, then refit the rear timing cover retaining bolts.

44 Refit the camshaft sprockets as described in Section 8.

45 Refit the shield, rotor arm and distributor cap, with reference to Chapter 5B if necessary.

46 Refit the cylinder head cover, with reference to Section 4.

47 Refit the air intake duct support bracket, tightening its screws to their specified torque wrench setting then, where applicable, refit the rubber strap to secure the air intake duct.

---

11 Cylinder head –
removal and refitting

Caution: Before commencing any servicing or overhaul work on the engine, the crankshaft must always be rotated to the desired position before the cylinder head bolts are disturbed.

Note: *Due to the design of the engine, it will become very difficult, almost impossible, to turn the crankshaft once the cylinder head bolts have been slackened. The manufacturer accordingly states that the crankshaft will be "tight" and should not be rotated more than absolutely necessary once the head has been removed. If the crankshaft cannot be rotated, then it must be removed for overhaul work to proceed. With this in mind, during any servicing or overhaul work, the crankshaft must always be rotated to the desired position before the bolts are disturbed. Suitable tools will be required to clamp the cylinder liners in position during this procedure (see text), and a*

new cylinder head gasket and a new timing belt must be used on refitting. A new fuel feed pipe-to-fuel rail O-ring and suitable silicone grease will be required on refitting.

K8 engines
Removal

1 Disconnect the battery negative lead.

2 Drain the cooling system, as described in Chapter 1A.

3 Remove the air cleaner as described in Chapter 4A.

4 Remove the exhaust manifold as described in Chapter 4A.

5 Remove the camshaft sprocket, and the timing belt tensioner, as described in Section 8, noting that the timing belt should be discarded.

6 Unscrew the securing bolts, and withdraw the timing belt rear cover.

7 Working at the front left-hand corner of the cylinder head, slacken the hose clips, and disconnect the coolant hoses from the coolant elbow.

8 Disconnect the wiring plugs from the coolant sensors mounted in the coolant elbow.

9 Disconnect the end of the throttle cable from the throttle linkage, with reference to Chapter 4A.

10 Release the clip securing the charcoal canister vacuum pipe to the inlet manifold, then disconnect the pipe from the manifold.

11 Disconnect the engine control module (ECM) vacuum hose from the inlet manifold.

12 Depress the collar on the quick-release connector, and disconnect the brake servo vacuum hose from the inlet manifold.

13 Slacken the hose clip, and disconnect the coolant hose from the inlet manifold.

14 Position a large wad of absorbent cloth around the fuel outlet union on the fuel filter.

15 Slowly slacken the fuel filter outlet union to relieve the pressure in the fuel system (counterhold the union on the filter using a second spanner) **(see illustration)**. Be prepared for fuel leakage, and take adequate

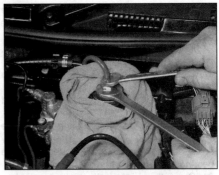

11.15 Slacken the fuel filter outlet union to relieve the fuel pressure

fire precautions. Once the pressure has been relieved, re-tighten the fuel union securely.

16 Release the clip securing the fuel return hose to the fuel rail, then disconnect the hose and, where applicable, release it from the two clips underneath the inlet manifold **(see illustration)**. Plug or clamp the open ends of the hose and fuel rail to prevent dirt entry and further fuel loss.

17 Unscrew the two bolts securing the fuel feed pipe to the fuel rail, then disconnect the pipe, and recover the O-ring **(see illustration)**. Again, take suitable fire precautions and plug the open ends of the pipe and fuel rail. Discard the O-ring, a new one must be used on refitting.

18 Release the fuel injector wiring harness wiring connector from the bracket under the throttle body, then separate the two halves of the connector.

19 Disconnect the following wiring plugs.
a) *Inlet air temperature sensor wiring plug.*
b) *Throttle position sensor wiring plug.*
c) *Idle air control valve wiring plug.*
d) *Distributor coil HT lead.*

20 Unscrew the bolt securing the inlet manifold to the support bracket **(see illustration)**.

21 Unscrew the three bolts securing the HT lead brackets to the cylinder head, and remove the brackets, noting their locations.

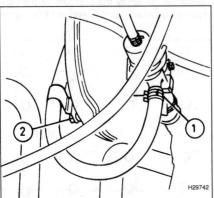

11.16 Release the clip securing the fuel return hose (1) to the fuel rail and release the hose from the clips (2) underneath the manifold

11.17 Unscrew the two bolts securing the fuel feed pipe to the fuel rail

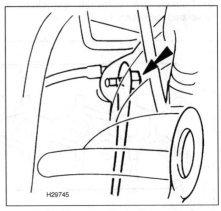

11.20 Unscrew the bolt (arrowed) securing the inlet manifold to the support bracket

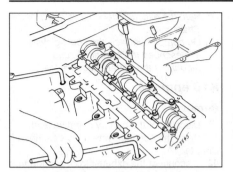

11.25 Using two cranked bars to break the cylinder head-to-cylinder block joint by rocking

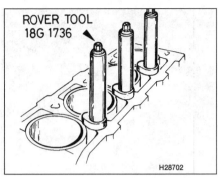

11.27 Cylinder liner clamps secured by cylinder head bolts

11.29 Checking the length of a cylinder head bolt

22 Remove the cylinder head cover as described in Section 4.

23 Working in the **reverse** of the tightening sequence **(see illustration 11.38a)**, progressively unscrew (ie, slacken each bolt by one turn at a time) the cylinder head bolts. Withdraw the bolts, and store them in order, so that they can be refitted in their original locations. The bolts can be stored by pushing them through a clearly-marked cardboard template.

24 The joint between the cylinder head and gasket and the cylinder block/crankcase must now be broken without disturbing the cylinder liners. Although these liners are better located and sealed than some wet liner engines, there is still a risk of coolant and foreign matter leaking into the sump if the cylinder head is lifted carelessly. If care is not taken and the liners are moved, there is also a possibility of their seals being disturbed, causing leakage after refitting the head.

25 To break the joint, obtain two L-shaped metal bars which fit into the cylinder head bolt holes and gently rock the cylinder head free towards the front of the vehicle **(see illustration)**. Do not try to swivel the head on the cylinder block/crankcase as it is located by dowels as well as by the tops of the liners.

26 When the joint is broken, lift the cylinder head away, using assistance if possible as it is a heavy assembly, especially if complete with the manifolds. Remove the gasket, noting the two locating dowels, and discard it. Support the cylinder head on wooden blocks or stands – do not rest the lower face of the cylinder head on the work surface.

27 Note that further to the warnings given in the note at the beginning of this Section, **do not** attempt to rotate the crankshaft with the cylinder head removed, otherwise the liners may be displaced. Operations that require the rotation of the crankshaft (eg: cleaning the piston crowns) can be carried out after fitting cylinder liner clamps. The manufacturer's liner clamps are secured by the cylinder head bolts as shown **(see illustration)**. Equivalents can be improvised using large washers and tubular spacers.

28 If the cylinder head is to be dismantled, remove the camshaft, as described in Section 10, then refer to the relevant Sections of Part C of this Chapter.

Cylinder head bolt examination

29 Check the condition of the cylinder head bolts, particularly their threads. Keeping all bolts in their correct fitted order, wash them and wipe dry. Check each bolt for any sign of visible wear or damage, renewing as necessary. Note that if cylinder head bolts have been used to secure the cylinder liner clamps, each bolt and clamp should be removed one at a time for checking, and refitted immediately the bolt has been tested. Lightly oil the threads of each bolt, carefully enter it into its original hole (**do not** drop the bolt into the hole) and screw it in, by hand only until finger-tight. Measure the distance from the cylinder block/crankcase gasket surface to the lower surface of the bolt head **(see illustration)**.

30 If the distance measured is under 97 mm, the bolt may be re-used. If the distance measured is more than 97 mm, the bolt must be renewed. Considering the task these bolts perform and the pressures they must withstand, owners should consider renewing all the bolts as a matched set if more than one of the original bolts fail inspection or are close to the limit.

Refitting

31 The mating faces of the cylinder head and cylinder block/crankcase must be perfectly clean before refitting the head. Use a hard plastic or wood scraper to remove all traces of gasket and carbon. Also clean the piston crowns. Take particular care, as the soft aluminium alloy is damaged easily. Also, make

sure that the carbon is not allowed to enter the oil and water passages – this is particularly important for the lubrication system, as carbon could block the oil supply to any of the engine components. Using adhesive tape and paper, seal the water, oil and bolt holes in the cylinder block/crankcase. To prevent carbon entering the gap between the pistons and bores, smear a little grease in the gap. After cleaning each piston, use a small brush to remove all traces of grease and carbon from the gap, then wipe away the remainder with a clean cloth. Clean all the pistons in the same way. Take great care not to move the pistons during this procedure.

32 Check the mating surfaces of the cylinder block/crankcase and the cylinder head for nicks, deep scratches and other damage. If slight, they may be removed carefully with a file, but if excessive, machining may be the only alternative to renewal.

33 If warpage of the cylinder head gasket surface is suspected, use a straight-edge to check it for distortion. Refer to Part C of this Chapter if necessary.

34 Wipe clean the mating surfaces of the cylinder head and cylinder block/crankcase. Check that the two locating dowels are in position at each end of the cylinder block/crankcase surface.

35 Position a new gasket on the cylinder block/crankcase surface so that its "TOP" mark is uppermost and the "FRONT" arrow points to the timing belt end **(see illustrations)**.

11.35a Fit a new cylinder head gasket over the locating dowels (arrowed) . . .

11.35b . . . so that the "TOP" marking is uppermost and the "FRONT" marking points towards the timing belt end of the engine

2A

11.38a Cylinder head bolt tightening sequence – K8 engines

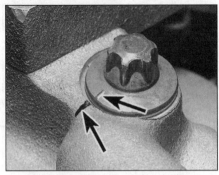

11.38b Mark the position of each bolt head radial mark on the cylinder head to aid angle-tightening of the bolts

36 Refit the cylinder head, locating it on the dowels.

37 Keeping all the cylinder head bolts in their correct fitted order, wash them and wipe dry. Lightly oil under the head and on the threads of each bolt, carefully enter it into its original hole and screw it in, by hand only, until finger-tight. **Do not** drop the bolts into their holes.

38 Working progressively and in the sequence shown **(see illustrations)**, use first a torque wrench, then an ordinary socket extension bar to tighten the cylinder head bolts through the specified stages – ie, tighten all bolts progressively to Stage 1, then tighten all bolts to Stage 2, and so on. To tighten the bolts through the specified angles, simply use a felt-tip pen or similar to mark the position on the cylinder head of each bolt head radial mark. The second stage torque can then be achieved by tightening each bolt through half-a-turn so that the mark on the bolt head faces away from the corresponding mark on the cylinder head.

To tighten to the third stage, tighten each bolt through a further half-a-turn so that the bolt head mark is aligned with the corresponding mark on the cylinder head again. If any bolt is overtightened beyond the mark on the cylinder head, slacken the bolt by a quarter-turn, then re-tighten until the marks align.

39 Further refitting is a reversal of removal, bearing in mind the following points.

a) Refit the cylinder head cover with reference to Section 4.
b) Ensure that all wiring plugs and hoses are correctly reconnected.
c) Use a new O-ring when reconnecting the fuel feed pipe to the fuel rail, and lubricate the O-ring with a little silicone grease.
d) Reconnect and, if necessary adjust the throttle cable as described in Chapter 4A.
e) Refit the timing belt tensioner and the camshaft sprocket as described in Section 8, then fit a **new** timing belt as described in Section 7.

f) Refit the exhaust manifold as described in Chapter 4A.
g) On completion, refill the cooling system as described in Chapter 1A, and reconnect the battery negative lead.

K16 engines

Removal

40 Disconnect the battery negative lead.
41 Drain the cooling system, as described in Chapter 1A.
42 Disconnect the exhaust front section from the manifold, with reference to Chapter 4A.
43 Proceed as described in paragraphs 5 to 8, noting that both camshaft sprockets must be removed.
44 On models with air conditioning, proceed as follows.

a) Remove the alternator, as described in Chapter 5A.
b) Unbolt the alternator heat shield from the alternator mounting bracket and the stud on the cylinder head.
c) Remove the alternator top mounting bracket.

45 Disconnect the following wiring plugs.

a) Inlet air temperature sensor wiring plug.
b) Throttle position sensor wiring plug.
c) Idle air control valve wiring plug.
d) Distributor coil HT lead.
e) Fuel injector harness wiring plug.
f) Oxygen sensor wiring plug.

46 Release the oxygen sensor wiring plug, and the coil HT lead from their locating clips.
47 Release the hose clip, and disconnect the air intake trunking from the throttle body.
48 Proceed as described in paragraphs 14 to 17.
49 Release the hose clip, and disconnect the charcoal canister hose from the throttle body.
50 Disconnect the end of the throttle cable from the throttle linkage, with reference to Chapter 4A. Release the throttle cable from the clip on the inlet manifold **(see illustration)**.
51 Depress the collar on the quick-release connector, and disconnect the brake servo vacuum hose from the inlet manifold.
52 Disconnect the vacuum hose from the right-hand end of the inlet manifold.
53 Slacken the hose clip, and disconnect the coolant expansion tank hose from the inlet manifold.
54 Disconnect the HT leads from the spark plugs (label them 1 to 4, if not already done, to ensure correct refitting), then remove the distributor cap and HT leads as an assembly, with reference to Chapter 5B if necessary.
55 Remove the cylinder head cover as described in Section 4.
56 Working in the **reverse** of the tightening sequence **(see illustration 11.60)**, progressively unscrew (ie, slacken each bolt by one turn at a time) the cylinder head bolts. Withdraw the bolts, and store them in order, so that they can be refitted in their original locations. The bolts can be stored by pushing

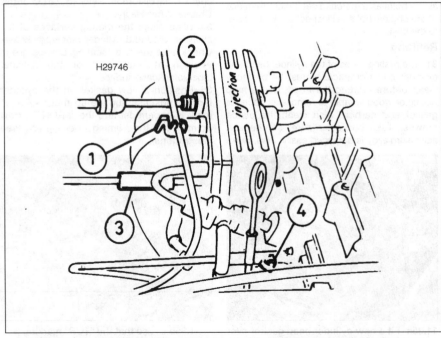

11.50 Release the throttle cable from the clip (1), then disconnect the brake servo vacuum hose (2), the vacuum hose (3) and the expansion tank hose (4)

them through a clearly-marked cardboard template.

57 Proceed as described in paragraphs 24 to 28.

Cylinder head bolt examination

58 Proceed as described in paragraphs 29 and 30.

Refitting

59 Proceed as described in paragraphs 31 to 37.

60 Working progressively and in the sequence shown **(see illustration)**, use first a torque wrench, then an ordinary socket extension bar to tighten the cylinder head bolts through the specified stages – ie, tighten all bolts progressively to Stage 1, then tighten all bolts to Stage 2, and so on. To tighten the bolts through the specified angles, simply use a felt-tip pen or similar to mark the position on the cylinder head of each bolt head radial mark. The second stage torque can then be achieved by tightening each bolt through half-a-turn to that the mark on the bolt head faces away from the corresponding mark on the cylinder head. To tighten to the third stage, tighten each bolt through a further half-a-turn so that the bolt head mark is aligned with the corresponding mark on the cylinder head again. If any bolt is overtightened beyond the mark on the cylinder head, slacken the bolt by a quarter-turn, then re-tighten until the marks align.

61 Further refitting is a reversal of removal, bearing in mind the following points.

a) *Refit the cylinder head cover with reference to Section 4.*

b) *Ensure that all wiring plugs and hoses are correctly reconnected.*

c) *Where applicable, refit the alternator with reference to Chapter 5A.*

d) *Reconnect and, if necessary adjust the throttle cable as described in Chapter 4A.*

e) *Refit the timing belt tensioner and the camshaft sprocket as described in Section 8, then fit a* **new** *timing belt as described in Section 7.*

f) *Reconnect the exhaust front section to the exhaust manifold as described in Chapter 4A.*

g) *On completion, refill the cooling system as described in Chapter 1A, and reconnect the battery negative lead.*

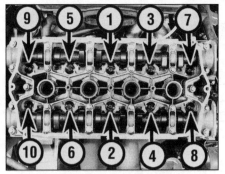

11.60 Cylinder head bolt tightening sequence – K16 engines

12 Sump –
removal and refitting

1.1 and 1.4 litre engines

Removal

Note: *A new sump gasket may be required on refitting.*

1 Disconnect the battery negative lead.

2 Drain the engine oil (with reference to Chapter 1A if necessary), then clean and refit the engine oil drain plug, tightening it to the specified torque wrench setting. If the engine is nearing its service interval when the oil and filter are due for renewal, it is recommended that the filter is also removed and a new one fitted. After reassembly, the engine can then be refilled with fresh engine oil.

3 Apply the handbrake, then jack up the front of the vehicle and support it securely on axle stands (see *"Jacking and Vehicle Support"*). Remove the right-hand roadwheel.

4 Remove the exhaust front section as described in Chapter 4A.

5 Unscrew the three retaining bolts and remove the flywheel lower cover plate **(see illustration)**.

6 Progressively slacken the sump retaining bolts then remove them.

7 Break the joint by striking the sump with the palm of the hand, then lower the sump and withdraw it **(see illustration)**.

12.5 Removing the flywheel lower cover plate – 1.1 and 1.4 litre engines

8 With the sump is removed, take the opportunity to unbolt the oil pump pick-up/strainer pipe and clean it using a suitable solvent (see Part C of this Chapter). Inspect the strainer mesh for signs of clogging or splitting and renew if necessary.

Refitting

9 Clean all traces of gasket from the mating surfaces of the cylinder block/crankcase and sump, then use a clean rag to wipe out the sump and the engine interior. If the oil pump pick-up/strainer pipe was removed, fit a new sealing O-ring to its end and refit the pipe, tightening its retaining bolts to the specified torque setting.

10 If the sump gasket is damaged or shows signs of deterioration, then it must be renewed. Fit the gasket to the sump mating surface so that its 7 locating pegs fit into the holes in the sump **(see illustration)**.

11 Offer up the sump to the cylinder block/crankcase then refit the sump retaining bolts, and tighten the bolts finger-tight only.

12 Working in the sequence shown **(see illustration)**, tighten the sump bolts to the specified torque setting.

13 Refit the flywheel lower cover plate and tighten the securing bolts to the specified torque wrench setting.

14 Refit the exhaust front section with reference to Chapter 4A.

15 Lower the vehicle to the ground and reconnect the battery negative lead.

16 Refill the engine with oil as described in Chapter 1A.

2A

12.7 Removing the sump – 1.1 and 1.4 litre engines

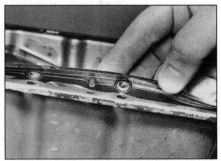

12.10 The sump gasket pegs must engage with the holes in the sump – 1.1 and 1.4 litre engines

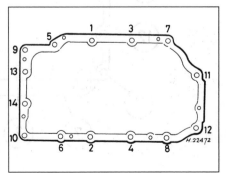

12.12 Sump bolt tightening sequence – 1.1 and 1.4 litre engines

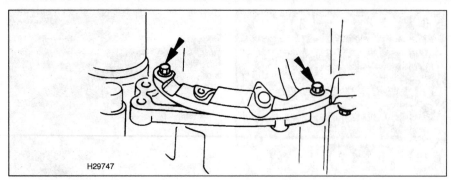

12.19 Unscrew the two bolts (arrowed) securing the sump to the transmission

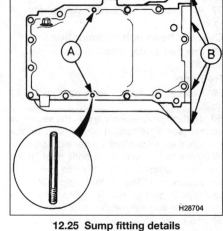

**12.25 Sump fitting details
– 1.6 and 1.8 litre engines**

A   *Alignment pin locations*
B   *Sump flange-to-cylinder block rear face
    alignment*

1.6 and 1.8 litre engines

Note: *Two improvised alignment pins (see text) and suitable RTV sealant will be required on refitting.*

Removal

17 Proceed as described in paragraphs 1 to 4.

18 Slacken the bolt securing the engine steady bar to the subframe, then unscrew and remove the bolt securing the steady bar to the bracket on the sump.

19 Unscrew the two bolts securing the sump to the transmission **(see illustration)**.

20 Progressively slacken the sump retaining bolts then remove them.

21 Break the joint by striking the sump with the palm of the hand, then lower the sump and withdraw it.

22 With the sump is removed, take the opportunity to unbolt the oil pump pick-up/strainer pipe and clean it using a suitable solvent (see Part C of this Chapter). Inspect the strainer mesh for signs of clogging or

splitting and renew if necessary. If desired, the engine steady bar bracket can be unbolted from the sump.

Refitting

23 Clean all traces of sealant from the mating surfaces of the cylinder block/crankcase and sump, then use a clean rag to wipe out the sump and the engine interior. If the oil pump pick-up/strainer pipe was removed, fit a new sealing O-ring to its end and refit the pipe, tightening its retaining bolts to the specified torque setting.

24 Apply a continuous 2.0 mm wide bead of RTV sealant to the sump mating face, running the bead inside the bolt holes, then spread the sealant to an even film using a brush or roller.

25 Make up two alignment pins using lengths of M8 studding or by cutting the heads off two M8 bolts. Fit the pins in the positions shown, before carefully placing the sump over them, and pressing it firmly into position **(see illustration)**.

26 Insert the sump-to-main bearing ladder

securing bolts (with the exception of the two which fit in the alignment pin locations), and tighten them finger-tight only.

27 Remove the alignment pins, and fit the two remaining sump-to-bearing ladder securing bolts.

28 Using a straight-edge, check that the machined face of the sump flange is level with the rear face of the cylinder block. Tap the sump gently to reposition it if necessary.

29 Working in the sequence shown, progressively tighten the sump securing bolts to the specified torque setting **(see illustration)**.

30 Refit the sump-to-transmission securing bolts, and tighten to the specified torque.

31 Reconnect the engine steady bar to the bracket on the sump, then refit the securing bolt, and tighten to the specified torque setting.

32 Tighten the engine steady bar-to-subframe bolt to the specified torque.

33 Proceed as described in paragraphs 14 to 16.

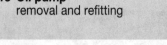

13 Oil pump –
removal and refitting

Removal

Note: *The oil pressure relief valve can be dismantled without removing the oil pump from the vehicle - see Section 14 for details. A new oil pump gasket and a new crankshaft front oil seal will be required on refitting, and suitable thread-locking compound will be required to coat the pump securing bolts.*

1 Remove the crankshaft sprocket as described in Section 8, and secure the timing belt clear of the working area so that it cannot be contaminated with oil.

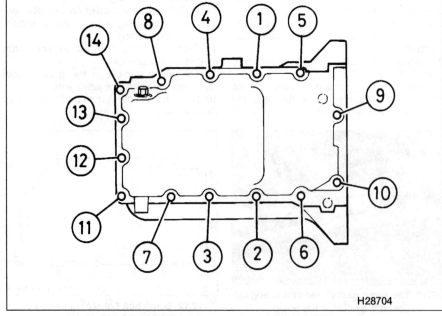

12.29 Sump bolt tightening sequence – 1.6 and 1.8 litre engines

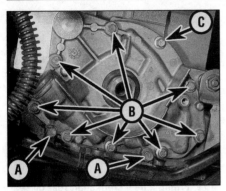

13.4 Oil pump securing mounting details

A   *Wiring harness guide bolts*
B   *Oil pump bolts*
C   *M6 x 20 mm oil pump bolt*

2 Drain the engine oil, then clean and refit the engine oil drain plug, tightening it to the specified torque wrench setting. If the engine is nearing its service interval when the oil and filter are due for renewal, it is recommended that the filter is also removed and a new one fitted. After reassembly, the engine can then be refilled with fresh engine oil.

3 Unscrew the two bolts securing the engine wiring harness guide to the oil pump, then move the guide clear of the oil pump.

4 Unscrew the oil pump retaining bolts, and withdraw the oil pump **(see illustration)**, noting that it is located on dowels. Note the location of the M6 x 20 mm bolt. Recover the pump gasket and discard it, then carefully lever the crankshaft front oil seal out of the oil pump. The oil seal should be renewed whenever it is disturbed.

Refitting

5 Thoroughly clean the mating faces of the oil pump and cylinder block/crankcase. Use a thin smear of grease to stick a new gasket in place on the cylinder block. Clean the oil seal running surface on the crankshaft.

6 Carefully clean out the oil pump retaining bolt holes in the cylinder block, using a suitable tap. Take care not to allow any debris to enter the crankcase.

7 Prime the pump before installation by

injecting clean engine oil into it and turning it by hand.

8 Offer up the pump, ensuring that its inner gear engages fully with the crankshaft flats, then push the pump fully into position on the locating dowels.

9 Thoroughly clean and then dry the threads of the pump securing bolts, then coat the threads with thread-locking compound. Fit the bolts, and tighten them progressively to the specified torque wrench setting. Ensure that the M6 x 20 mm bolt is refitted to the correct location as noted before removal.

10 Fit a new crankshaft front oil seal, using a suitable tube or socket, with reference to Section 15 if necessary.

11 Secure the engine wiring harness guide to the oil pump using the two securing bolts.

12 Refit the crankshaft sprocket as described in Section 8, then refit and tension the timing belt as described in Section 7.

13 On completion, refill the engine with oil as described in Chapter 1A.

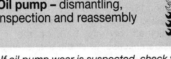

14 Oil pump – dismantling, inspection and reassembly

Note: *If oil pump wear is suspected, check the cost and availability of new parts (only available in the form of a repair kit) against the cost of a new pump. Examine the pump as described in this Section and then decide whether renewal or repair is the best course of action. A new pump cover sealing ring, and a new pressure relief valve plug sealing ring will be required on refitting.*

Dismantling

1 Remove the oil pump as described in Section 13.

2 Unscrew the Torx screws and remove the pump cover plate. Discard the sealing ring.

3 Note the identification marks on the outer rotor then remove both the rotors from the body.

4 The oil pressure relief valve can be dismantled, if required, without disturbing the pump. If this is to be done with the pump in

position and the engine still installed in the vehicle, it will first be necessary to jack up the front of the vehicle and remove the right-hand roadwheel to gain access to the valve **(see illustration)**.

5 To dismantle the valve, unscrew the threaded plug and recover the valve spring and plunger **(see illustration)**. Discard the plug sealing washer.

Inspection

6 Inspect the rotors for obvious signs of wear or damage and renew if necessary. If the pump body or cover plate is scored or damaged, then the complete oil pump assembly must be renewed.

7 Using feeler blades of the appropriate thickness, measure the clearance between the outer rotor and the pump body, then between the tips of the inner and outer rotor lobes (a and b respectively) **(see illustration)**.

8 Using feeler blades and a straight-edge placed across the top of the pump body and the rotors, measure the rotor endfloat (c).

9 If any measurement is outside the specified limits, the complete pump assembly must be renewed.

10 If the pressure relief valve plunger is scored, or if it does not slide freely in the pump body bore, then it must be renewed, using all the components from the repair kit.

11 Thoroughly clean the threads of the pump cover plate securing screws.

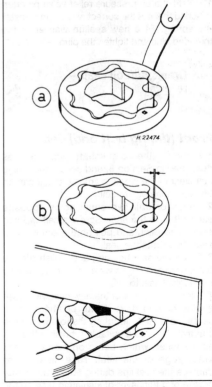

14.7 Checking oil pump rotors for wear – see text for details

14.4 Unscrewing the oil pressure relief valve threaded plug using a spanner and drain plug key

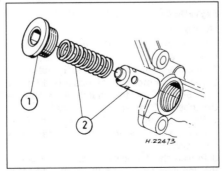

14.5 Oil pressure relief valve components

1   *Threaded plug*
2   *Valve spring and plunger*

2A

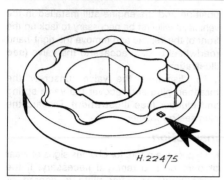

14.12 Oil pump outer rotor identification mark (arrowed)

15.4 Fitting a new crankshaft front oil seal – shown with engine removed

15.9 Fitting a new crankshaft rear oil seal – shown with engine removed and inverted

Reassembly

12 Lubricate the pump rotors with clean engine oil and refit them to the pump body, ensuring that the identification mark on the outer rotor faces outwards (ie, towards the pump cover) **(see illustration)**.

13 Lubricate a new sealing ring with clean engine oil, then fit the sealing ring to the pump body and refit the cover plate. Apply thread-locking compound to the threads of the cover plate screws and tighten them securely to the specified torque wrench setting.

14 Check that the pump rotates freely, then prime it by injecting oil into its passages and rotating it. If a long time elapses before the pump is refitted to the engine, prime it again before installation.

15 Refit the oil pressure relief valve plunger, ensuring that it is the correct way up, then install the spring. Fit a new sealing washer to the threaded plug and tighten the plug securely.

15 Crankshaft oil seals – renewal

Front (timing belt end) seal

1 Remove the crankshaft sprocket as described in Section 8, and secure the timing belt clear of the working area so that it cannot be contaminated with oil.

2 Punch or drill two small holes opposite each other in the seal. Screw a self-tapping screw into each and pull on the screws with pliers to extract the seal.

3 Clean the seal housing and polish off any burrs or raised edges which may have caused the original seal to fail.

4 Lubricate the lips of the new seal with clean engine oil and drive it into position until it seats on its locating shoulder **(see illustration)**. Use a suitable tubular drift, such as a socket, which bears only on the hard outer edge of the seal. Take care not to damage the seal lips during fitting. Use either grease or a thin layer of insulating tape on the crankshaft to protect the seal lips from the edges of the crankshaft flats, but be careful to remove all traces of tape and to lubricate the

seal lips if the second method is used. Note that the seal lips should face inwards.

5 Wash off any excess oil, then refit the crankshaft sprocket as described in Section 8, and refit and tension the timing belt as described in Section 7.

Rear (flywheel end) seal

6 Remove the flywheel as described in Section 16.

7 Taking care not to mark either the crankshaft or any part of the cylinder block/crankcase, lever the seal evenly out of its housing, using a large flat-bladed screwdriver or similar tool.

8 Clean the seal housing and polish off any burrs or raised edges which may have caused the original seal to fail.

9 Grease the lips of the new seal and the crankshaft shoulder, then offer up the seal to the cylinder block/crankcase **(see illustration)**.

10 Ease the sealing lip of the seal over the crankshaft shoulder, by hand only, then press the seal evenly into its housing until its outer flange seats evenly on the housing lip. If necessary, a soft-faced mallet can be used to tap the seal gently into place.

11 Wash off any excess oil, then refit the flywheel as described in Section 16.

16 Flywheel/driveplate/torsion damper – removal, inspection and refitting

Flywheel

Removal

Note: *New flywheel retaining bolts must be used on refitting.*

1 Remove the torsion damper (automatic transmission models), as described later in this Section, or the clutch assembly as described in Chapter 6, as applicable.

2 Remove the crankshaft position (CKP) sensor, with reference to Chapter 4A if necessary.

3 Prevent the flywheel from turning by locking the ring gear teeth **(see illustration 16.11)** or by bolting a strap between the flywheel and the cylinder block/crankcase, if not already done.

4 Slacken and remove the flywheel retaining bolts and discard them The bolts must be renewed whenever they are disturbed.

5 Remove the flywheel. Do not drop it, as it is very heavy.

Inspection

6 If the flywheel clutch mating surface (where applicable) is deeply scored, cracked or otherwise damaged, then the flywheel must be renewed, unless it is possible to have it surface ground. Seek the advice of a Rover dealer or engine reconditioning specialist.

7 If the ring gear is badly worn or has missing teeth, then it must be renewed. This job is best left to a Rover dealer or engine reconditioning specialist. The temperature to which the new ring gear must be heated for installation (350°C - shown by an even light blue colour) is critical and, if not done accurately, the hardness of the teeth will be destroyed.

8 Examine the reluctor ring (fitted to the rear of the flywheel) for signs of damage. If the reluctor ring is damaged, then the flywheel must be renewed.

Refitting

9 Clean the mating surfaces of the flywheel and crankshaft. Clean any remaining adhesive from the threads of the crankshaft threaded holes by carefully using a suitable tap.

10 Position the flywheel over the locating dowel in the end of the crankshaft, press it into place and fit six **new** bolts **(see illustration)**.

16.10 Use new bolts when refitting the flywheel

16.11 Using a fabricated tool to lock the flywheel when tightening bolts

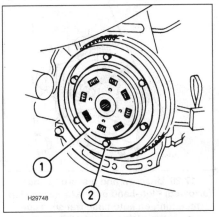

16.16 Torsion damper (1) and securing bolt (2) – automatic transmission models

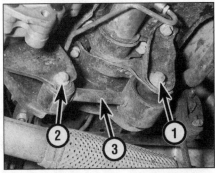

17.6 Engine/transmission steady bar mounting details – 1.1 and 1.4 litre engines

1 Steady bar-to-subframe through-bolt
2 Steady bar-to-transmission through-bolt
3 Steady bar

11 Lock the flywheel using the method employed on dismantling then, working in a diagonal sequence, progressively tighten the retaining bolts to the specified torque wrench setting **(see illustration)**.
12 Where applicable, refit the crankshaft position (CKP) sensor as described in Chapter 4A.
13 Refit the clutch assembly as described in Chapter 6, or the torsion damper (automatic transmission models), as described later in this Section, as applicable.

Torsion damper (automatic transmission models)

Removal

14 Remove the automatic transmission as described in Chapter 7B.
15 Lock the flywheel in position, by applying a suitable tool to the flywheel ring gear teeth. One of the transmission-to-engine bolts can be used to bolt the tool in place.
16 Progressively slacken and remove the bolts securing the torsion damper to the flywheel, then withdraw the torsion damper **(see illustration)**.

Inspection

17 Check that the torsion damper centre splines are unworn, and that the torsion springs are in good condition. Renew the torsion damper if there is evidence of damage or deterioration to the torsion springs.

Refitting

18 Refitting is a reversal of removal, but tighten the securing bolts to the specified torque, and refit the automatic transmission as described in Chapter 7B.

17 Engine/transmission mountings – inspection and renewal

Inspection

1 If improved access is required, raise the front of the vehicle and support it securely on axle stands (see "Jacking and Vehicle Support").
2 Check the mounting rubber to see if it is cracked, hardened or separated from the metal at any point. Renew the mounting if any such damage or deterioration is evident.
3 Check that all mounting fasteners are securely tightened. Use a torque wrench to check, if possible.
4 Using a large screwdriver or a pry bar, check for wear in the mounting by carefully levering against it to check for free play. Where this is not possible, enlist the aid of an assistant to move the engine/gearbox unit back and forth or from side to side while you watch the mounting. While some free play is to be expected even from new components, excessive wear should be obvious. If excessive free play is found, check first that the fasteners are correctly secured, then renew any worn components as described below.

Renewal

Engine/transmission steady bar

5 Apply the handbrake, then jack up the front of the vehicle and support securely on axle stands (see "Jacking and Vehicle Support").
6 Working under the vehicle, unscrew the through-bolt securing the engine steady bar to the subframe **(see illustration)**.
7 Unscrew the through-bolt securing the steady bar to the transmission or the bracket on the sump (as applicable), then withdraw the steady bar.
8 Refitting is a reversal of removal, but tighten the through-bolts to the specified torque.

Left-hand engine/transmission mounting - 1.1 and 1.4 litre engines

9 Apply the handbrake, then jack up the front of the vehicle and support securely on axle stands (see "Jacking and Vehicle Support").
10 Place a trolley jack under the transmission, with a block of wood positioned between the jack and transmission, then raise the jack to just take the weight of the engine/transmission unit.
11 Remove the air cleaner assembly as described in Chapter 4A.
12 Disconnect the clutch cable from the clutch release lever, as described in Chapter

6, then release the cable from the bracket on the transmission, and position the cable to one side.
13 Unscrew the two bolts securing the engine/transmission mounting to the transmission mounting bracket **(see illustration)**.
14 Unscrew the two bolts securing the mounting to the body.
15 Unscrew the two bolts securing the mounting to the mounting bracket.
16 Slacken the two bolts securing the mounting bracket to the body.
17 Carefully lower the engine, using the jack, and remove the mounting.

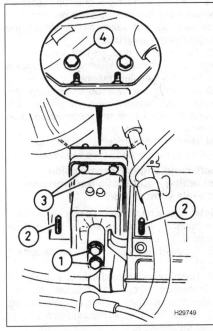

17.13 Left-hand engine/transmission mounting details – 1.1 and 1.4 litre engines

1 Mounting-to-transmission mounting bracket bolts
2 Mounting-to-body bolts
3 Mounting-to-mounting bracket bolts
4 Mounting bracket-to-body bolts

2A

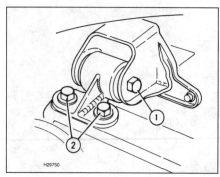

17.22 Left-hand engine/transmission mounting details – 1.6 and 1.8 litre engines with manual transmission

1 Through-bolt
2 Mounting-to-mounting bracket bolts

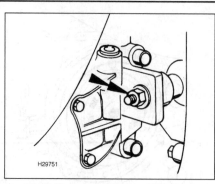

17.26 Unscrew and discard the nut (arrowed) - left-hand engine/transmission mounting on automatic transmission models without ABS

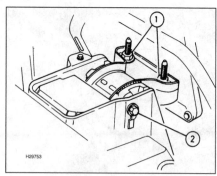

17.52 Right-hand engine mounting details – 1.1 and 1.4 litre engines

1 Mounting-to-engine nuts
2 Through-bolt

18 Refitting is a reversal of removal, bearing in mind the following points.
a) Tighten all fixings to the specified torque.
b) Reconnect and if necessary adjust the clutch cable with reference to Chapter 6.

Left-hand engine/transmission mounting - 1.6 and 1.8 litre engines with manual transmission

19 Apply the handbrake, then jack up the front of the vehicle and support securely on axle stands (see "Jacking and Vehicle Support").
20 Remove the air cleaner assembly as described in Chapter 4A.
21 Place a trolley jack under the transmission, with a block of wood positioned between the jack and transmission, then raise the jack to just take the weight of the engine/transmission unit.
22 Unscrew the through-bolt securing the engine/transmission mounting to the bracket on the body **(see illustration)**.
23 Unscrew the two bolts securing the engine/transmission mounting to the mounting bracket on the transmission, then withdraw the mounting.
24 Refitting is a reversal of removal, but tighten all fixings to the specified torque.

Left-hand engine/transmission mounting - automatic transmission models without ABS

Note: A new transmission mounting bracket-to-mounting Nyloc nut will be required on refitting.

25 Proceed as described in paragraphs 9 to 11.
26 Unscrew and discard the nut securing the transmission mounting bracket to the engine/transmission mounting **(see illustration)**.
27 Lower the engine/transmission unit to clear the mounting.
28 Unscrew the four bolts securing the engine/transmission mounting bracket to the body, then withdraw the engine mounting and bracket assembly.
29 Unscrew the two nuts securing the bracket to the mounting, and remove the mounting.

30 Commence reassembly by fitting the mounting to the mounting bracket, but **do not** tighten the securing nuts.
31 Offer the mounting/bracket assembly into position in the engine compartment, then refit the lower two bolts securing the bracket to the body, and tighten to the specified torque setting.
32 Refit the upper two bolts securing the bracket to the body, and tighten to the specified torque.
33 Raise the engine/transmission unit to engage the transmission mounting bracket with the mounting, then fit a **new** Nyloc nut, and tighten to the specified torque setting.
34 Tighten the two nuts securing the mounting to the mounting bracket, to the specified torque setting.
35 Refit the air cleaner, then withdraw the jack, and lower the vehicle to the ground.

Left-hand engine/transmission mounting - automatic transmission models with ABS

36 Apply the handbrake, then jack up the front of the vehicle and support securely on axle stands (see "Jacking and Vehicle Support").
37 Remove the air cleaner assembly as described in Chapter 4A.
38 Remove the ABS hydraulic modulator, as described in Chapter 9.
39 Unscrew the two bolts and the nut securing the ABS hydraulic modulator mounting bracket to the body.
40 Unscrew the bolt securing the modulator mounting bracket and the engine/ transmission mounting bracket to the body, then release the brake fluid pipes from the clips on the modulator mounting bracket, and withdraw the modulator mounting bracket.
41 Place a trolley jack under the engine sump, with a block of wood positioned between the jack and sump, then raise the jack to just take the weight of the engine/transmission unit.
42 Unscrew and discard the nut securing the transmission mounting bracket to the engine/transmission mounting.

43 Lower the engine/transmission unit to clear the mounting.
44 Unscrew the three bolts securing the engine mounting bracket to the body, then withdraw the mounting/bracket assembly.
45 Unscrew the two nuts securing the mounting to the bracket, and withdraw the mounting.
46 Proceed as described in paragraphs 30 to 34.
47 Refit the ABS hydraulic modulator mounting bracket, then refit and tighten the securing bolts and nut. Tighten the bolt which secures the modulator mounting bracket and the engine/transmission mounting bracket to the specified torque setting.
48 Refit the ABS hydraulic modulator as described in Chapter 9.
49 Refit the air cleaner, and lower the vehicle to the ground.

Right-hand engine mounting - 1.1 and 1.4 litre engines

50 Disconnect the battery negative lead.
51 Place a trolley jack under the engine sump, with a block of wood positioned between the engine and sump, then raise the jack to just take the weight of the engine/transmission unit.
52 Unscrew the nuts securing the engine mounting to the engine, and discard them. New nuts must be used on refitting **(see illustration)**.
53 Unscrew the through-bolt securing the engine mounting to the body, then withdraw the mounting and remove the two rubber washers from the mounting.
54 Refitting is a reversal of removal, bearing in mind the following points.
a) Fit the rubber washers to the mounting before fitting the mounting.
b) Do not tighten the mounting through-bolt until the nuts securing the mounting to the engine have been fitted.
c) Use new nuts to secure the mounting to the engine.
d) Tighten all fixings to the specified torque.

Right-hand engine mounting – 1.6 and 1.8 litre engines

55 Proceed as described in paragraphs 50 and 51.

56 Unscrew the bolt securing the right-hand engine steady bar to the engine mounting bracket **(see illustration)**.

57 Unscrew the two bolts securing the mounting bracket to the engine.

58 Unscrew the nut securing the mounting bracket to the mounting.

59 Unscrew the nut securing the engine mounting and the restraint bar to the body.

60 Slacken the nut securing the restraint bar to the body, and move the restraint bar to one side. Remove the engine mounting bracket.

61 Unscrew the nut securing the engine mounting to the body, then remove the mounting.

62 Commence refitting by fitting the mounting to the body, and tightening the securing nut finger-tight.

63 Refit the engine mounting bracket, then align the bracket with the engine, and refit and tighten the bracket-to-engine bolts to the specified torque setting.

64 Move the restraint bar into position, then refit the securing nuts and tighten to the specified torque setting.

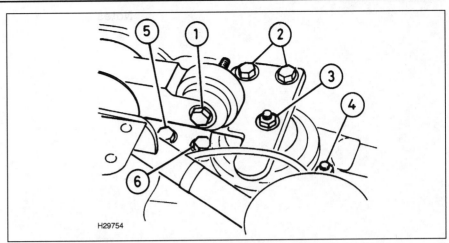

17.56 Right-hand engine mounting details – 1.6 and 1.8 litre engines

1 *Steady bar-to-mounting bracket bolt*
2 *Mounting bracket-to-engine bolts*
3 *Mounting bracket-to-mounting nut*
4 *Mounting and restraint bar-to-body nut*
5 *Restraint bar-to-body nut*
6 *Mounting-to-body nut*

65 Tighten the nut securing the mounting to the body to the specified torque setting.

66 Refit the nut securing the mounting to the mounting bracket, and tighten to the specified torque setting.

67 Refit the bolt securing the steady bar to the engine mounting bracket, and tighten to the specified torque setting.

68 Withdraw the jack, and lower the vehicle to the ground.

2A

Notes

Chapter 2 Part B:
Diesel engine in-car repair procedures

Contents

Degrees of difficulty

| Easy, suitable for novice with little experience | 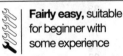 | Fairly easy, suitable for beginner with some experience | | Fairly difficult, suitable for competent DIY mechanic | | Difficult, suitable for experienced DIY mechanic | | Very difficult, suitable for expert DIY or professional | 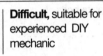 |

Specifications

General

Engine type	Four-cylinder in-line, four-stroke, liquid-cooled
Designation:	
Models without intercooler	20T2R
Models with intercooler	20T2N
Bore	84.00 mm
Stroke	89.00 mm
Capacity	1994 cc
Firing order	1-3-4-2 (No 1 cylinder at timing belt end)
Direction of crankshaft rotation	Clockwise (seen from right-hand side of vehicle)
Compression ratio	19.5 : 1
Minimum compression pressure (typical figure)	18 to 20 bars
Maximum compression pressure difference between	
cylinders (typical figure)	3 bars
Maximum power (EEC):	
Models without intercooler	86 Ps (63 kW) @ 4500 rpm
Models with intercooler	105 Ps (77 kW) @ 4200 rpm
Maximum torque (EEC):	
Models without intercooler	170 Nm (124 lbf ft) @ 2000 rpm
Models with intercooler	210 Nm 153 lbf ft) @ 2000 rpm

Camshaft

Drive	Toothed belt
Number of bearings	6
Bearing journal running clearance	0.043 to 0.094 mm
Camshaft endfloat (maximum)	0.510 mm
Hydraulic tappet outside diameter	34.959 to 34.975 mm

Timing belt tensioner

Spring free length	65.0 mm

2B

Lubrication system

System pressure	0.7 bar @ idle speed
Pressure relief valve opening pressure	4.5 bar
Low oil pressure warning light comes on	0.4 to 0.7 bar
Oil pump clearances:	
Rotor endfloat	0.03 to 0.08 mm
Outer rotor-to-body clearance	0.05 to 0.10 mm
Rotor lobe clearance	0.025 to 0.120 mm
Pressure relief valve spring free length	38.9 mm

Torque wrench settings

	Nm	lbf ft
Cylinder head cover bolts	12	9
Outer timing belt cover bolts	5	4
Rear timing belt cover bolts	8	6
Timing belt tensioner pulley bolt	55	41
Timing belt idler pulley nut	45	33
Timing belt idler pulley stud	12	9
Camshaft sprocket bolt*:		
Stage 1	20	15
Stage 2	Angle-tighten through a further 90°	
Crankshaft pulley bolt:		
Stage 1	63	46
Stage 2	Angle-tighten through a further 90°	
Fuel injection pump drivebelt tensioner pulley bolt	44	32
Fuel injection pump drivebelt backplate bolts	8	6
Fuel injection pump drive (camshaft) sprocket*:		
Stage 1	20	15
Stage 2	Angle-tighten through a further 90°	
Fuel injection pump drive (camshaft) sprocket (adjuster) bolts	25	18
Camshaft bearing carrier bolts	11	8
Right-hand engine mounting cover plate nuts	35	26
Right-hand engine mounting cover plate bolts	45	33
Right-hand engine mounting:		
Mounting bracket-to-engine bolts	100	74
Restraint bar securing nuts	45	33
Mounting-to-body nut	45	33
Mounting-to-mounting bracket nut	85	63
Steady bar-to-mounting bracket bolt	80	59
Left-hand engine/transmission mounting:		
Engine/transmission mounting-to-transmission bracket bolts	100	74
Engine/transmission mounting-to-body bracket through-bolt	85	63
Engine/transmission steady bar-to-engine bolt	85	63
Engine/transmission steady bar-to-subframe bolt	60	44
Oil pressure warning light switch	16	12
Cylinder head bolts:		
Stage 1	30	22
Stage 2	65	48
Stage 3	Angle-tighten through a further 90°	
Stage 4	Angle-tighten through a further 90°	
Flywheel bolts*:		
Stage 1	15	11
Stage 2	Angle-tighten through a further 90°	
Oil pump-to-cylinder block bolts:		
M6 bolts	8	6
M10 bolt	45	33
Oil pump thermostatic valve plug	35	26
Sump bolts	25	18
Oil pump pick-up/strainer pipe bolts	8	6
Engine oil drain plug	25	18
Main bearing cap bolts	112	83
Big-end nuts (see text)	48	35
Big-end bolts (see text):		
Stage 1	20	15
Stage 2	Angle-tighten through a further 85°	
Crankshaft rear oil seal housing bolts	8	6
Piston oil spray jet bolts	12	9
Transmission adapter plate-to-cylinder block bolts	45	33
Oil cooler:		
M8 bolts	25	18
M10 bolts	45	33

*Use new bolts

1 General information and precautions

How to use this Chapter

This Part of the Chapter describes those repair procedures that can reasonably be carried out on the engine whilst it remains in the vehicle. If the engine has been removed from the vehicle and is being dismantled as described in Part D of this Chapter, any preliminary dismantling procedures can be ignored.

Note that whilst it may be possible physically to overhaul items such as the piston/connecting rod assemblies with the engine in the vehicle, such tasks are not usually carried out as separate operations and usually require the execution of several additional procedures (not to mention the cleaning of components and of oilways). For this reason, all such tasks are classed as major overhaul procedures and are described in Part D of this Chapter.

Engine description

The engine is of four-cylinder, in-line type, mounted transversely at the front of the vehicle with the clutch and transmission at its left-hand end. The engine is of eight-valve single overhead camshaft type.

The crankshaft runs in five main bearings. Thrustwashers are fitted to the centre main bearing (upper half) to control crankshaft endfloat. Individual main bearing caps are used, which are bolted directly to the cylinder block.

The connecting rods rotate on horizontally-split bearing shells at their big-ends. The pistons are attached to the connecting rods by fully floating gudgeon pins. The gudgeon pins are retained by circlips at each end. The aluminium alloy pistons are fitted with three piston rings, comprising two compression rings and an oil control ring.

The cylinders are bored directly into the cast iron cylinder block.

The inlet and exhaust valves are each closed by coil springs and operate in guides pressed into the cylinder head. The valve seat inserts are pressed into the cylinder head and can be renewed separately if worn.

The camshaft is driven by a toothed timing belt, and operates the valves via self-adjusting hydraulic tappets, thus eliminating the need for routine checking and adjustment of the valve clearances. The camshaft rotates in bearings which are line-bored directly into the cylinder head and the (bolted-on) bearing carrier. This means that the bearing carrier and cylinder head are matched, and cannot be renewed independently.

Unusually, the coolant pump is driven, via a drive dog from the rear of the power steering pump, which is itself driven by the auxiliary drivebelt.

Lubrication is by means of an eccentric-rotor type pump driven directly from the front (timing belt end) of the crankshaft. The pump draws oil through a strainer located in the sump, and then forces it through an externally-mounted full-flow cartridge-type oil filter into galleries in the oil rail and the cylinder block/crankcase, from where it is distributed to the crankshaft (main bearings) and camshaft. The big-end bearings are supplied with oil via internal drillings in crankshaft, while the camshaft bearings and the hydraulic tappets receive a pressurised supply via drillings in the cylinder head. The camshaft lobes and valves are lubricated by oil splash, as are all other engine components.

Repair operations possible with the engine in the car

The following work can be carried out with the engine in the vehicle:

a) Compression pressure - testing.
b) Cylinder head cover - removal and refitting.
c) Crankshaft pulley - removal and refitting.
d) Timing belt covers - removal and refitting.
e) Timing belt - removal, refitting and adjustment.
f) Timing belt tensioner and sprockets - removal and refitting.
g) Camshaft oil seals - renewal.
h) Camshaft and hydraulic tappets - removal, inspection and refitting.
i) Cylinder head - removal and refitting.
j) Cylinder head and pistons - decarbonising.
k) Sump - removal and refitting.
l) Oil pump - removal, overhaul and refitting.
m) Crankshaft oil seals - renewal.
n) Engine/transmission mountings - inspection and renewal.
o) Flywheel - removal, inspection and refitting.

2 Compression and leakdown tests – description and interpretation

Compression test

Note: *A compression tester designed for diesel engines must be used for this test.*

1 When engine performance is down, or if misfiring occurs which cannot be attributed to the ignition or fuel systems, a compression test can provide diagnostic clues as to the engine's condition. If the test is performed regularly, it can give warning of trouble before any other symptoms become apparent.

2 A compression tester specifically intended for diesel engines must be used, because of the higher pressures involved. The tester is connected to an adapter which screws into the glow plug or injector hole. On these engines, an adapter suitable for use in the injector holes is preferable. It is unlikely to be worthwhile buying such a tester for occasional use, but it may be possible to borrow or hire one - if not, have the test performed by a garage.

3 Unless specific instructions to the contrary are supplied with the tester, observe the following points.

a) *The battery must be in a good state of charge, the air filter must be clean, and the engine should be at normal operating temperature.*
b) *All the injectors or glow plugs should be removed before starting the test.*
c) *The stop solenoid must be disconnected, to prevent the engine from running or fuel from being discharged.*

4 There is no need to hold the throttle pedal down during the test, because the diesel engine air inlet is not throttled.

5 Crank the engine on the starter motor. After one or two revolutions, the compression pressure should build up to a maximum figure, and then stabilise. Record the highest reading obtained.

6 Repeat the test on the remaining cylinders, recording the pressure in each.

7 The cause of poor compression is less easy to establish on a diesel engine than on a petrol one. The effect of introducing oil into the cylinders ("wet" testing) is not conclusive, because there is a risk that the oil will sit in the swirl chamber or in the recess in the piston crown instead of passing to the rings. However, the following can be used as a rough guide to diagnosis.

8 All cylinders should produce very similar pressures; a difference of more than 3.0 bars between any two cylinders usually indicates a fault. Rover do not specify compression pressure figures, so the figures given in the Specifications are typical figures for a diesel engine. Note that the compression should build up quickly in a healthy engine; low compression on the first stroke, followed by gradually-increasing pressure on successive strokes, indicates worn piston rings. A low compression reading on the first stroke, which does not build up during successive strokes, indicates leaking valves or a blown head gasket (a cracked head could also be the cause). Deposits on the undersides of the valve heads can also cause low compression.

9 A low reading from two adjacent cylinders is almost certainly due to the head gasket having blown between them; the presence of coolant in the engine oil will confirm this.

10 If the compression reading is unusually high, the combustion chambers are probably coated with carbon deposits. If this is the case, the cylinder head should be removed and decarbonised.

11 On completion of the test, refit the injectors or the glow plugs, and reconnect the stop solenoid.

Leakdown test

12 A leakdown test measures the rate at which compressed air fed into the cylinder is lost. It is an alternative to a compression test,

2B

and in many ways is better, since the escaping air provides easy identification of where a pressure loss is occurring (piston rings, valves or head gasket).

13 The equipment needed for leakdown testing is unlikely to be available to the home mechanic. If poor compression is suspected, have the test performed by a suitably-equipped garage.

3 Engine timing marks – general information

Note: *A suitable timing pin (which can be improvised using a 6.5 mm diameter twist drill) will be required for this operation.*

1 Locate the timing pin hole in the transmission mounting plate, at the rear left-hand corner of the engine. Access is difficult, and it may be necessary to move surrounding hoses and wiring to one side for access.

2 Remove the upper outer timing belt cover as described in Section 6.

3 Using a suitable socket or spanner on the crankshaft pulley bolt, turn the crankshaft until the timing mark on the camshaft sprocket is aligned with the raised rib on the rear timing belt cover **(see illustration)**.

4 It should now be possible to insert a 6.5 mm twist drill through the timing pin hole in the transmission mounting plate to engage with the timing hole in the flywheel **(see**

3.3 The timing mark (1) on the camshaft sprocket should be aligned with the raised rib on the rear timing belt cover (2)

illustration). The crankshaft is now locked in position with No 1 piston at TDC.

4 Cylinder head cover – removal and refitting

Engines without intercooler

Note: *A new cylinder head cover gasket will be required on refitting.*

Removal

1 Unscrew the bolts securing the engine acoustic cover to the top of the cylinder head cover, then remove the acoustic cover from the engine.

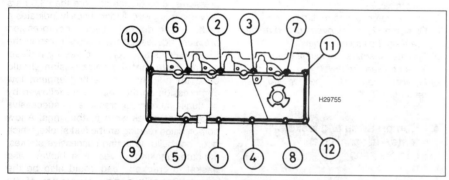

4.7 Cylinder head cover bolt tightening sequence

3.4 6.5 mm twist drill inserted through timing pin hole into flywheel

2 Slacken the hose clip, and disconnect the engine breather hose from the cylinder head cover.

3 Unscrew the bolt securing the brake servo vacuum pipe to the cylinder head cover, and move the pipe to one side.

4 Working in the reverse of the tightening sequence **(see illustration 4.7)** unscrew the cylinder head cover securing bolts.

5 Lift off the cylinder head cover, and recover the gasket. Discard the gasket - a new one must be used on refitting.

Refitting

6 Thoroughly clean the mating faces of the camshaft bearing carrier and the cylinder head cover.

7 Fit a new gasket to the cylinder head cover, then refit the securing bolts, and tighten to the specified torque setting in the sequence shown **(see illustration)**.

8 Further refitting is a reversal of removal.

Engines with intercooler

Note: *A new cylinder head cover gasket, and a new intake pipe-to-inlet manifold gasket will be required on refitting.*

Removal

9 Proceed as described in paragraph 1 **(see illustrations)**.

10 Loosen the hose clip, and disconnect the intercooler top hose from the intercooler **(see illustration)**.

11 Unscrew the two bolts securing the

4.9a Remove the securing bolts . . .

4.9b . . . and remove the acoustic cover from the engine

4.10 Disconnecting the top hose from the intercooler

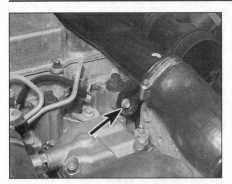

4.11a Unscrew the bolts (arrowed) securing the turbocharger pipe to the cylinder head . . .

4.11b . . . and the engine lifting bracket . . .

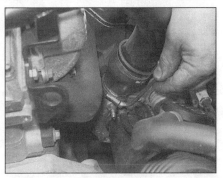

4.12 . . . then loosen the clip securing the hose to the turbocharger

4.13 Disconnect the intercooler bottom hose from the inlet manifold intake pipe

4.14 Unscrew the two bolts securing the EGR recirculation pipe

4.15a Unscrew the bolt securing the inlet manifold intake pipe to the cylinder head cover . . .

turbocharger pipe to the cylinder head and the engine lifting bracket **(see illustrations)**.

12 Loosen the hose clip securing the hose to the turbocharger, then remove the turbocharger pipe **(see illustration)**.

13 Loosen the hose clip, and disconnect the intercooler bottom hose from the inlet manifold intake pipe **(see illustration)**.

14 Unscrew the two bolts securing the EGR recirculation pipe to the inlet manifold intake pipe **(see illustration)**.

15 Unscrew the bolt securing the inlet manifold intake pipe to the cylinder head cover, then unscrew the two bolts securing the intake pipe to the inlet manifold. Remove the intake pipe, and recover the gasket **(see illustrations)**. Discard the gasket – a new one must be used on refitting.

16 Proceed as described in paragraphs 2 to 5.

Refitting

17 Proceed as described in paragraphs 6 to 8, noting that a new gasket should be used when reconnecting the intake pipe to the inlet manifold.

5 Crankshaft pulley –
removal and refitting

Removal

1 Disconnect the battery negative lead.

2 Apply the handbrake, then jack up the front of the vehicle and support securely on axle stands (see *"Jacking and Vehicle Support"*). Remove the right-hand front roadwheel.

3 Remove the auxiliary drivebelt as described in Chapter 1B.

4 Using a suitable socket or spanner applied to the crankshaft pulley bolt, rotate the crankshaft clockwise to bring No 1 piston to TDC, and lock the crankshaft in position using the timing pin as described in Section 3.

5 Alternatively, have an assistant select first gear, and apply the footbrake to prevent the crankshaft from rotating.

6 With the crankshaft held securely in place, unscrew the pulley bolt, then remove the pulley from the crankshaft **(see illustrations)**.

2B

4.15b . . . then unscrew the two bolts securing the intake pipe . . .

4.15c . . . and remove the intake pipe

5.6a Unscrew the securing bolt . . .

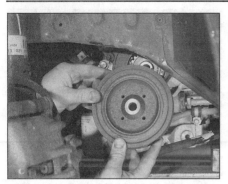

5.6b ... and remove the crankshaft pulley

6.1a Unscrew the securing bolts ...

6.1b ... and remove the upper outer timing belt cover

Refitting

7 Fit the pulley to the crankshaft.

8 Ensure that the timing pin is still in position, then tighten the pulley retaining bolt to the specified torque setting. Remove the timing pin once the pulley bolt has been tightened.

9 Refit and tension the auxiliary drivebelt as described in Chapter 1B.

10 Refit the roadwheel, then lower the vehicle to the ground.

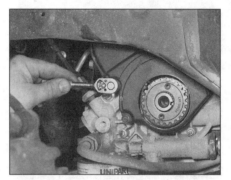

6.7a Unscrew the securing bolts ...

6.7b ... and remove the lower outer timing belt cover

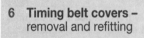
6 Timing belt covers –
  removal and refitting

Upper outer cover

Removal

1 Unscrew the four bolts securing the upper outer timing cover to the rear cover, and withdraw the cover **(see illustrations)**.

Refitting

2 Refitting is a reversal of removal, but make sure that the sealing strips are correctly located in the cover.

Lower outer cover

Removal

3 Disconnect the battery negative lead.

4 Apply the handbrake, then jack up the front of the vehicle and support securely on axle stands (see *"Jacking and Vehicle Support"*). Remove the right-hand front roadwheel.

5 Remove the upper outer timing belt cover, as described previously in this Section.

6 Remove the crankshaft pulley as described in Section 5.

7 Unscrew the securing bolts, and withdraw the lower outer cover **(see illustrations)**.

Refitting

8 Refitting is a reversal of removal, bearing in mind the following points.

 a) *Make sure that the sealing strips are correctly located in the timing belt covers.*

 b) *Note that the three longer bolts fit at the bottom of the lower timing belt cover.*

 c) *Refit the crankshaft pulley with reference to Section 5.*

Upper rear cover

Removal

9 Remove the outer timing belt covers as described previously in this Section.

10 Remove the timing belt as described in Section 7.

11 Remove the camshaft sprocket as described in Section 8.

12 Where applicable, release the three clips securing the engine wiring harness to the rear timing belt cover **(see illustration)**.

13 Unscrew the five securing bolts, and remove the upper rear cover. Recover the sealing strip **(see illustrations)**.

6.12 Release the clips securing the wiring harness to the timing belt cover

6.13a Unscrew the upper rear timing belt cover securing bolts (arrowed) – viewed with engine removed ...

6.13b ... then remove the upper rear timing belt cover

Refitting

14 Examine the sealing strip, and renew if necessary.

15 Refit the upper rear cover, noting that the shorter securing bolts are used to secure the top of the cover to the camshaft bearing carrier. Make sure that the sealing strip is correctly located.

16 Where applicable, clip the engine wiring harness into position on the rear timing belt cover.

17 Refit the timing belt tensioner and the camshaft sprocket as described in Section 8.

18 Refit the timing belt as described in Section 7.

19 Refit the outer timing belt covers, as described previously in this Section.

Lower rear cover

Removal

20 Remove the outer timing belt covers, as described previously in this Section.

21 Remove the timing belt as described in Section 7, and the timing belt tensioner assembly as described in Section 8.

22 Unscrew the nut securing the timing belt idler pulley, and remove the pulley. Note that the mounting stud may be unscrewed with the nut.

23 Unscrew the two securing bolts, and remove the lower rear timing belt cover **(see illustrations)**. Recover the sealing strips.

Refitting

24 If the idler pulley stud was unscrewed with the nut, unscrew the nut from the stud (clamp the stud in a vice if necessary to allow the nut to be unscrewed).

25 Where applicable, clean the threads of the idler pulley stud, and the corresponding threads in the cylinder block, then apply thread-locking compound to the stud threads which screw into the cylinder block. Screw the stud into position, and tighten to the specified torque.

26 Examine the timing belt cover sealing strips, and renew if necessary.

27 Refit the lower rear timing belt cover, and tighten the securing bolts. Make sure that the sealing strips are correctly located.

6.23a Unscrew the two securing bolts (arrowed) . . .

28 Thoroughly clean the threads of the idler pulley nut, then coat the threads with thread-locking compound.

29 Refit the idler pulley to the stud, then refit the nut and tighten to the specified torque.

30 Refit the timing belt as described in Section 7.

31 Refit the outer timing belt covers as described previously in this Section.

---

7 Timing belt – removal, inspection, refitting and adjustment

Removal

Note: *Rover tool No 18G 1719 or a suitable equivalent (see text) will be required to release the timing belt tensioner during this procedure.*

1 Disconnect the battery negative lead.

2 Lock the crankshaft at TDC (No1 cylinder) as described in Section 3. Remove the crankshaft pulley as described in Section 5.

3 Working on the right-hand side of the engine compartment, unscrew the bolt securing the power steering fluid pipe bracket to the body, then move the pipes to one side, to improve access to the timing belt end of the engine **(see illustration)**.

4 Remove the right-hand engine mounting as described in Section 20.

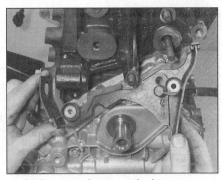

6.23b . . . and remove the lower rear timing belt cover

5 Remove the outer timing belt covers, with reference to Section 6.

6 Unscrew the four securing nuts and two bolts, and remove the engine mounting cover plate **(see illustration)**.

7 If the original timing belt is to be re-used, mark the running direction on the belt, using chalk or tape.

8 Slacken the bolt securing the timing belt tensioner pulley **(see illustration)**.

9 Prise the timing belt tensioner access plug from the lower rear timing belt cover **(see illustration)**.

10 A suitable tool will now be required to release the timing belt tensioner. Rover technicians use service tool 18G 1719, but a suitable alternative can be improvised using a

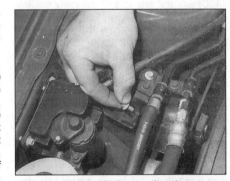

7.3 Unscrew the bolt securing the power steering fluid pipe bracket to the body

7.6 Removing the engine mounting cover plate

7.8 Slackening the bolt securing the timing belt tensioner pulley - engine removed for clarity

7.9 Prise the access plug from the rear timing belt cover – engine removed for clarity

2B

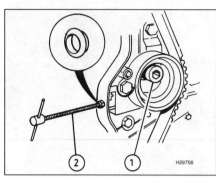
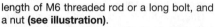

7.10 Slacken the timing belt tensioner pulley bolt (1), then use Rover tool 18G 1719 (2) or a suitable alternative to release the tensioner – engine removed for clarity

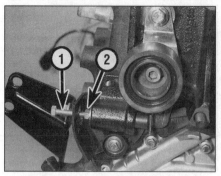

7.11 Screw the bolt (1) into the tensioner plunger, then tighten the nut (2) to draw the plunger back – engine removed for clarity

7.13 Removing the timing belt

length of M6 threaded rod or a long bolt, and a nut **(see illustration)**.

11 Insert the tool through the hole in the lower rear timing belt cover, then screw the threaded rod or bolt into the tensioner plunger, and turn the nut on the tool to draw the plunger back, relieving the tension on the timing belt tensioner pulley **(see illustration)**.

12 Once the tensioner plunger has been released, tighten the tensioner pulley bolt.

13 Slide the timing belt from the sprockets and remove the belt **(see illustration)**. **Do not** rotate the crankshaft or the camshaft until the timing belt has been refitted.

Inspection

14 Check the timing belt carefully for any signs of uneven wear, splitting or oil contamination and renew it if there is the slightest doubt about its condition. If the engine is undergoing an overhaul and has covered more than 42 000 miles (65 000 km) since the original belt was fitted, it is advisable to renew the belt as a matter of course, regardless of its apparent condition. Note that the manufacturers recommend that the timing belt is renewed every 72 000 miles (116 000 km).

15 If signs of oil contamination are found, trace the source of the oil leak and rectify it, then wash down the engine timing belt area and all related components to remove all traces of oil. If the timing belt sprockets have been subjected to prolonged oil

contamination, they must be soaked in a suitable solvent bath, then thoroughly washed in clean solvent before refitting (the sprockets are manufactured from a porous material which will absorb oil – the oil will eventually be released and will contaminate the new belt if the sprockets are not cleaned).

Refitting and adjustment

Note: *The manufacturer states that tensioning need only be carried out when a belt is (re)fitted. No re-tensioning is recommended once a belt has been fitted and therefore this operation is not included in the manufacturer's maintenance schedule. If the timing belt is thought to be incorrectly tensioned, then adjust the tension as described in the following paragraphs. If the timing belt has been disturbed, adjust its tension following the same procedure, omitting as appropriate the irrelevant preliminary dismantling/ reassembly steps.*

16 Ensure that the timing marks on the camshaft sprocket and the rear timing belt cover are still aligned, and that the crankshaft is still locked in position using the timing pin inserted into the flywheel (see Section 3).

17 If a used belt is being refitted, ensure that the direction mark made on removal points in the normal direction of rotation. Fit the timing belt over the crankshaft and camshaft sprockets and around the idler pulley, ensuring that the belt front run is taut, ie: all slack is on the tensioner pulley side of the

belt, then fit the belt around the tensioner pulley. Do not twist the belt sharply during refitting and ensure that the belt teeth are correctly seated centrally in the sprockets and that the timing marks remain in alignment (see Section 3).

18 Refit the engine mounting cover plate, and tighten the securing nuts and bolts to the specified torque **(see illustration)**.

19 Refit the lower outer timing belt cover and tighten the securing bolts to the specified torque **(see illustration)**.

20 Refit the right-hand engine mounting as described in Section 20.

21 Refit the crankshaft pulley, with reference to Section 5 (do not refit the roadwheel or lower the vehicle to the ground at this stage).

22 Refit and tension the auxiliary drivebelt as described in Chapter 1B.

23 Slacken the timing belt tensioner pulley bolt.

24 Using the special tool, release the timing belt tensioner plunger, then remove the tool.

25 Lightly tighten the tensioner pulley bolt.

26 Remove the timing pin from the flywheel.

27 Using a spanner or a socket and extension bar on the crankshaft pulley bolt, rotate the crankshaft through two complete revolutions clockwise until the timing marks on the camshaft sprocket and the rear timing belt cover are aligned again.

28 Refit the timing pin, and engage it with the flywheel.

29 Slacken the timing belt tensioner pulley bolt, and allow the tensioner to push against the belt under the force of the plunger.

30 Tighten the timing belt tensioner pulley bolt to the specified torque.

Caution: Do not exceed the specified torque setting for the tensioner pulley bolt.

31 Remove the timing pin from the flywheel.

32 Refit the upper outer timing belt cover.

33 Refit the timing belt tensioner access plug to the lower rear timing belt cover.

34 Refit the power steering fluid pipe bracket securing bolt.

35 Refit the roadwheel and lower the vehicle to the ground, then reconnect the battery negative lead.

7.18 Refit the engine mounting cover plate – engine removed for clarity

7.19 Refitting the lower outer timing belt cover – engine removed for clarity

Using an improvised tool to prevent the camshaft from rotating whilst unscrewing the sprocket bolt

8.4a Withdraw the camshaft sprocket . . .

8.4b . . . and recover the roll-pin (arrowed) if it is loose

8 Timing belt tensioner and sprockets – removal, inspection and refitting

Camshaft sprocket

Note: *A new camshaft sprocket securing bolt will be required on refitting.*

Removal

1 Disconnect the battery negative lead.
2 Remove the timing belt as described in Section 7. Note that there is no need to remove the timing belt completely, provided that it is slipped from the camshaft sprocket. **Do not** rotate the crankshaft or the camshaft until the timing belt has been refitted.
3 Slacken the camshaft sprocket retaining bolt and remove it, along with its washer. To prevent the camshaft from rotating, Rover technicians use service tool 18G 1521, but an acceptable substitute can be fabricated from two lengths of steel strip (one long, the other short) and three nuts and bolts. One nut and bolt should form the pivot of a forked tool with the remaining two nuts and bolts at the tips of the forks to engage with the sprocket spokes **(see Tool Tip). Do not** allow the camshaft to rotate as the sprocket bolt is being loosened. Discard the sprocket bolt – a new one must be used on refitting.

4 Withdraw the sprocket from the camshaft, noting the locating roll-pin **(see illustrations)**. If the roll-pin is a loose fit in the end of the camshaft, remove it and store it with the sprocket for safe-keeping.

Inspection

5 Clean the sprocket thoroughly, and renew it if it shows signs of wear, damage or cracks.

Refitting

6 Where applicable, refit the roll-pin to the end of the camshaft, ensuring that its split is facing the centre of the camshaft, then refit the sprocket (ensure that it engages with the roll-pin), ensuring that the timing marks on the sprocket and rear timing belt cover are still aligned.
7 Prevent the sprocket from rotating by using the method employed on removal, then fit a **new** sprocket securing bolt, and tighten the bolt to the specified torque setting. **Do not** allow the camshaft to turn as the bolt is tightened.
8 Refit and tension the timing belt as described in Section 7, then reconnect the battery negative lead.

Crankshaft sprocket

Removal

9 Remove the timing belt as described in section 7.
10 Remove the sprocket from the crankshaft **(see illustration)**.

Inspection

11 Clean the sprocket thoroughly, and renew it if it shows signs of wear, damage or cracks.

Refitting

12 Refit the sprocket to the crankshaft, ensuring that it locates correctly on the crankshaft flattened section. Note that the sprocket flange must be innermost. Note that the notch in the sprocket flange should be pointing vertically upwards.
13 Refit and tension the timing belt as described in Section 7, then reconnect the battery negative lead.

Tensioner assembly

Removal

14 Remove the timing belt as described in Section 7.
15 Unscrew the tensioner pulley backplate securing bolt, and the tensioner pulley bolt, and remove the tensioner – take care, as the tensioner spring and plunger will be released from their housing as the tensioner is removed **(see illustration)**.
16 Lift out the tensioner spring and plunger **(see illustration)**.

Inspection

17 Clean the tensioner assembly but do not use any strong solvent which may enter the pulley bearing. Check that the pulley rotates freely on the backplate, with no sign of stiffness or of free play. Renew the assembly

2B

8.10 Removing the crankshaft sprocket – engine removed for clarity

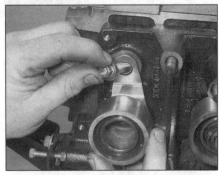

8.15 Removing the timing belt tensioner pulley assembly . . .

8.16 . . . and the spring and plunger – engine removed for clarity

9.3a Unscrew the securing bolts . . .

9.3b . . . and remove the fuel injection pump drivebelt cover

10.6 A 9.5 mm diameter twist drill (arrowed) can be used to lock the fuel injection pump sprocket in position

if there is any doubt about its condition or if there are any obvious signs of wear or damage. The same applies to the tensioner spring, which should be checked with great care as its condition is critical for the correct tensioning of the timing belt.

18 Check the tensioner spring for signs of distortion, and check the spring free-length. If the free-length is not as specified, the spring must be renewed, as its condition is critical for the correct tensioning of the timing belt.

19 Check the tensioner plunger and the housing for signs of wear and corrosion. If there is any evidence of corrosion, the housing and the plunger must be renewed – **do not** attempt to remove corrosion using emery paper or by scraping.

Refitting

20 Thoroughly clean the tensioner components, paying particular attention to the plunger and the housing.

21 Smear the plunger with a little molybdenum disulphide-based grease, then locate the spring and plunger in the housing.

22 Position the tensioner on the engine, then refit the backplate securing bolt, and the tensioner pulley bolt. Tighten the backplate securing bolt to the specified torque, but do not tighten the pulley bolt at this stage.

23 Refit and tension the timing belt as described in Section 7.

9 Fuel injection pump drivebelt cover – removal and refitting

Removal

1 Unscrew the bolts securing the engine acoustic cover to the top of the cylinder head cover, then remove the acoustic cover from the engine.

2 Remove the air cleaner assembly as described in Chapter 4B.

3 Unscrew the six bolts securing the fuel injection pump drivebelt cover to the backplate, and remove the cover **(see illustrations)**.

Refitting

4 Refitting is a reversal of removal.

10 Fuel injection pump drivebelt – removal, inspection, refitting and adjustment

Removal

Note: A reversible torque wrench will be required for this operation.

1 Disconnect the battery negative lead.

2 Apply the handbrake, then jack up the front of the vehicle and support securely on axle stands (see *"Jacking and Vehicle Support"*). Remove the right-hand front roadwheel.

3 Remove the fuel injection pump drivebelt cover, as described in Section 9.

4 Rotate the crankshaft to bring No 1 piston to TDC, and insert the timing pin to lock the crankshaft in position, as described in Section 3.

5 A suitable locking pin must now be used to lock the fuel injection pump sprocket in position. Rover technicians use service tool 18G 1717, but an acceptable substitute can be improvised, using a 9.5 mm twist drill.

6 Push the locking tool through the hole in the fuel injection pump sprocket until it engages with the hole in the transmission mounting plate **(see illustration)**.

7 If the original fuel injection pump drivebelt is to be re-used, mark the running direction on the belt, using chalk or tape.

8 A suitable tool will now be required to hold the camshaft stationary. Rover technicians use service tool 18G 1521, but alternatively, a 3/8 inch drive breaker bar can be used – engage the square drive end of the bar with the square cut-out in the sprocket. Hold the camshaft stationary, and slacken the four (adjuster) bolts securing the fuel injection pump drive sprocket to the camshaft **(see illustrations)**. Do not allow the camshaft to rotate as the bolts are slackened.

9 Slacken the bolt securing the fuel injection pump drivebelt tensioner pulley, then move the tensioner away from the belt, and tighten the pulley bolt **(see illustration)**.

10.8a Engage a breaker bar with the square cut-out (arrowed) in the fuel injection pump drive sprocket . . .

10.8b . . . to hold the sprocket stationary whilst slackening the sprocket adjuster bolts

10.9 Slacken the bolt securing the fuel injection pump drivebelt tensioner pulley

10 Slide the drivebelt from the sprockets **(see illustration)**. Do not rotate the camshaft or the fuel injection pump until the drivebelt has been refitted and tensioned.

Inspection

11 Check the fuel injection pump drivebelt carefully for any signs of uneven wear, splitting or oil contamination and renew it if there is the slightest doubt about its condition. Although the manufacturers suggest that the belt has a service life of 84 000 miles (135 000 km), if the engine is undergoing an overhaul and has covered more than 42 000 miles (65 000 km) since the original belt was fitted, renew the belt as a matter of course, regardless of its apparent condition.

12 If signs of oil contamination are found, trace the source of the oil leak and rectify it, then wash down the engine timing belt area and all related components to remove all traces of oil. If the timing belt sprockets have been subjected to prolonged oil contamination, they must be soaked in a suitable solvent bath, then thoroughly washed in clean solvent before refitting (the sprockets are manufactured from a porous material which will absorb oil – the oil will eventually be released and will contaminate the new belt if the sprockets are not cleaned).

Refitting and adjustment

Note: *The manufacturer states that tensioning need only be carried out when a belt is (re)fitted. No re-tensioning is recommended once a belt has been fitted and therefore this operation is not included in the manufacturer's maintenance schedule. If the belt is thought to be incorrectly tensioned, then adjust the tension as described in the following paragraphs. If the belt has been disturbed, adjust its tension following the same procedure, omitting as appropriate the irrelevant preliminary dismantling/reassembly steps.*

13 Make sure that the four (adjuster) bolts securing the fuel injection pump drive sprocket to the camshaft are just slack enough to allow the sprocket to rotate within its elongated slots – the sprocket should not be able to tip on the end of the camshaft.

14 If a used belt is being refitted, ensure that

10.10 Slide the fuel injection pump drivebelt from the sprockets

the direction mark made on removal points in the normal direction of rotation. Fit the belt over the fuel injection pump sprocket, then rotate the sprocket on the camshaft fully clockwise within the elongated slots, then anti-clockwise, until the belt locates in the sprocket teeth – this procedure must be carried out to ensure correct belt tensioning **(see illustration)**. Ensure that the lower belt run is taut, ie, all slack is on the tensioner pulley side of the belt, then fit the belt around the tensioner pulley. Do not twist the belt sharply during refitting and ensure that the belt teeth are correctly seated centrally in the sprockets.

15 Slacken the tensioner pulley bolt.

16 Engage a torque wrench, with a suitable square-drive extension, with the square hole in the tensioner backplate, and apply a torque of 6 Nm (4 lbf ft), whilst tightening the tensioner pulley bolt **(see illustration)**.

17 Hold the camshaft stationary, using the tool engaged with the camshaft (timing belt) sprocket, as during removal, then tighten the four fuel injection pump drive sprocket (adjuster) bolts to the specified torque.

18 Remove the locking pins from the flywheel and the fuel injection pump sprocket.

19 Rotate the crankshaft through two complete turns clockwise, then refit the locking pin to the flywheel.

20 Check that the camshaft timing mark is aligned with the mark on the rear timing belt cover (see Section 3).

10.14 Rotate the sprocket fully clockwise, then anti-clockwise until the belt locates in the sprocket teeth

21 Slacken the four (adjuster) bolts securing the fuel injection pump drive sprocket to the camshaft, then refit the locking pin to the fuel injection pump sprocket.

22 Slacken the tensioner pulley bolt, then re-engage the torque wrench with the square hole in the tensioner backplate, and again apply a torque of 6 Nm (4 lbf ft).

23 Tighten the tensioner pulley bolt to the specified torque.

24 It is now necessary to apply an **anti-clockwise** torque to the fuel injection pump drive sprocket to ensure that the lower run of the belt is taught as the sprocket adjuster bolts are tightened. If a second torque wrench is available, apply an **anti-clockwise** torque of 25 Nm (18 lbf ft) to the sprocket centre bolt, whilst tightening the four sprocket adjuster bolts to the specified torque using a second torque wrench. If a second torque wrench is not available, apply a moderate anti-clockwise load to the sprocket centre bolt using a suitable spanner or socket, whilst tightening the sprocket adjuster bolts to the specified torque **(see illustration)**.

25 Remove the locking pins from the flywheel and the fuel injection pump sprocket.

26 Refit the fuel injection pump drivebelt cover as described in Section 9.

27 Refit the roadwheel, then lower the vehicle to the ground and reconnect the battery negative lead.

2B

11 Fuel injection pump drivebelt sprockets and tensioner – removal, inspection and refitting

Fuel injection pump drive (camshaft) sprocket

Removal

Note: *A new sprocket securing bolt must be used on refitting.*

1 Remove the fuel injection pump drivebelt as described in Section 10.

2 A suitable tool will now be required to hold the camshaft stationary. Rover technicians use service tool 18G 1521, but an acceptable substitute can be fabricated from two lengths of steel strip (one long, the other short) and

10.16 Engage a torque wrench with the square hole in the tensioner backplate and apply the specified torque whilst tightening the tensioner pulley bolt

10.24 Applying an anti-clockwise load to the pump drive sprocket centre bolt whilst tightening the adjuster bolts to the specified torque

11.3 Removing the fuel injection pump drive (camshaft) sprocket

11.12 Make sure that the peg (arrowed) on the engine engages with the hole in the tensioner backplate

three nuts and bolts. One nut and bolt should form the pivot of a forked tool with the remaining two nuts and bolts at the tips of the forks to engage with the camshaft front (timing belt) sprocket spokes **(see Tool Tip in Section 8)**. **Do not** allow the camshaft to rotate as the sprocket bolt is being loosened.

3 Hold the camshaft stationary, and slacken the centre bolt securing the fuel injection pump drive sprocket. Remove the bolt, and withdraw the sprocket from the end of the camshaft **(see illustration)**. Discard the sprocket bolt, a new bolt must be used on refitting.

Inspection

4 Clean the sprocket thoroughly, and renew it if it shows signs of wear, damage or cracks.

Refitting

5 Coat the threads of the new sprocket securing bolt with clean engine oil.
6 Locate the sprocket on the end of the camshaft, then prevent the camshaft from turning, as during removal, fit the sprocket securing bolt, and tighten the bolt to the specified torque in the two stages given (see *Specifications*).
7 Refit the fuel injection pump drivebelt as described in Section 10.

Fuel injection pump sprocket

8 The procedure is described as part of the fuel injection pump removal procedure in Chapter 4B.

Tensioner

Removal

9 Remove the fuel injection pump drivebelt as described in Section 10.
10 Unscrew the tensioner pulley bolt and remove the tensioner.

Inspection

11 Clean the tensioner assembly but do not use any strong solvent which may enter the pulley bearing. Check that the pulley rotates freely on the backplate, with no sign of stiffness or of free play. Renew the assembly if there is

any doubt about its condition or if there are any obvious signs of wear or damage.

Refitting

12 Refitting is a reversal of removal, but make sure that the peg on the engine engages with the hole in the tensioner backplate **(see illustration)**. Refit the fuel injection pump drivebelt as described in Section 10.

12 Camshaft oil seals – renewal

Front (timing belt end) seal

1 Remove the camshaft sprocket as described in Section 8.
2 Punch or drill two small holes opposite each other in the oil seal. Screw a self-tapping screw into each hole, and pull on the screws with pliers to extract the seal.
3 Clean the seal housing and polish off any burrs or raised edges which may have caused the seal to fail.
4 Lubricate the lips of the new seal with clean engine oil and draw the seal into position using a suitable socket, and a long M12 bolt, or threaded rod and nut. Screw the bolt or

12.8 Using a socket, a length of M12 threaded rod and a nut to draw the camshaft rear oil seal into position – cylinder head removed

threaded rod into the end of the camshaft, and turn the end of the bolt, or the nut to draw the seal into position **(see illustration 12.8)**. Alternatively, drive the seal into position using a suitable tubular drift, such as a socket, which bears only on the hard outer edge of the seal. Take care not to damage the seal lips during fitting and note that the seal lips should face inwards.
5 Refit the camshaft sprocket as described in Section 8.

Rear (flywheel end) seal

6 Remove the fuel injection pump drive sprocket from the end of the camshaft, and remove the fuel injection pump drivebelt tensioner, as described in Section 11.
7 Unscrew the three securing bolts, and remove the fuel injection pump drivebelt backplate.
8 Proceed as described in paragraphs 2 to 4. Ensure that the seal is fully seated in its recess **(see illustration)**.
9 Thoroughly clean the fuel injection pump drivebelt backplate and camshaft bearing carrier and cylinder head mating faces, then refit the backplate, and tighten the securing bolts to the specified torque.
10 Refit the fuel injection pump drivebelt tensioner, then refit the pump drive sprocket, as described in Section 11.

13 Camshaft and hydraulic tappets – removal, inspection and refitting

If faulty tappets are diagnosed and the engine's service history is unknown, it is always worth trying the effect of renewing the engine oil and filter (using only good quality engine oil of the recommended viscosity and specification) before going to the expense of renewing any of the tappets.

13.4a Unscrew the securing bolts . . .

13.4b . . . and remove the fuel injection pump drivebelt backplate

13.8 Lifting off the camshaft bearing carrier

Removal

Note: *Prior to removing the camshaft, obtain Rover sealant kit GUG 705548 GM. Read the instructions supplied with the kit and take care not to allow the sealant to contact the fingers, as it may bond the skin. New camshaft oil seals should be used on refitting.*

1 Remove the cylinder head cover, with reference to Section 4.

2 Remove the upper rear timing belt cover as described in Section 6.

3 Remove the fuel injection pump drive sprocket from the camshaft, and remove the fuel injection pump drivebelt tensioner, as described in Section 11.

4 Unscrew the three securing bolts, and remove the fuel injection pump drivebelt backplate **(see illustrations)**. Note the location of the bracket secured by one of the bolts.

5 Working in the **reverse** order of the tightening sequence **(see illustration 13.26)**, progressively slacken the camshaft bearing carrier securing bolts by 2 to 3 turns – **do not** fully slacken the bolts at this stage.

6 Using a soft-faced mallet, gently tap the bearing carrier upwards to break the sealant bond between the bearing carrier and the cylinder head. Note that the bearing carrier is located on dowels.

7 Using the same reverse sequence **(see illustration 13.26)**, continue to progressively slacken the bearing carrier securing bolts until all the load on the bearing carrier is relieved

13.12 Measuring the outside diameter of a hydraulic tappet using a micrometer

(the load is due to the pressure of the valve springs pushing the camshaft upwards against the bearing carrier).

Caution: If the bolts are removed completely before the load on the bearing carrier is relieved, the carrier may be suddenly released, which may cause damage to the bearing surfaces and/or the camshaft.

8 Finally remove the bolts, and lift the bearing carrier from the camshaft and cylinder head **(see illustration)**.

9 Carefully lift out the camshaft, then remove and discard the front and rear camshaft oil seals.

10 Obtain eight small, clean plastic containers and number them from 1 to 8.

11 Using a hydraulic sucker, or a small magnet, withdraw each hydraulic tappet in turn, invert it to prevent oil loss and place it in its respective container, which should then be filled with clean engine oil. **Do not** interchange the hydraulic tappets, and do not allow the hydraulic tappets to lose oil, as they will take a long time to refill with oil on restarting the engine, which could result in incorrect valve clearances.

Inspection

Note: *To measure the camshaft bearing running clearance, an American product known as Plastigage can be used. This consists of a fine thread of perfectly round plastic which is compressed between the*

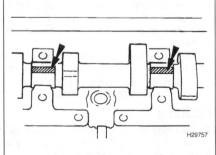

13.16 Position a strand of Plastigage (arrowed) across each camshaft bearing journal

bearing surface and the camshaft journal. When the bearing carrier is removed, the plastic is deformed and can be measured with a special card gauge supplied with the kit. The running clearance is determined from this gauge. Plastigage is sometimes difficult to obtain, but enquiries at one of the larger specialist motor factors should produce the name of a stockist in your area.

12 Check each hydraulic tappet for signs of obvious wear (scoring, pitting, etc) and for ovality. Renew if necessary. Using a micrometer, measure the outside diameter of the tappets – if the diameter of any tappet is outside the specified limits, it must be renewed **(see illustration)**.

13 If the engine's valve clearances have sounded noisy, particularly if the noise persists after initial start-up from cold, then there is reason to suspect a faulty hydraulic tappet. Only a good mechanic experienced in these engines can tell whether the noise level is typical, or if renewal is warranted of one or more of the tappets.

14 If the operation of any tappet is faulty, then it must be renewed.

15 Carefully remove all traces of old sealant from the mating surfaces of the camshaft bearing carrier and cylinder head, using a plastic scraper and suitable solvent if necessary. Examine the camshaft bearing journals and the cylinder head and bearing carrier bearing surfaces for signs of obvious wear or pitting. If any such signs are evident, renew the component(s) concerned.

16 To check the bearing journal running clearance, remove the hydraulic tappets (if not already done), carefully clean the bearing surfaces and refit the camshaft and bearing carrier with a strand of Plastigage across each journal (see Note at the beginning of this sub-Section) **(see illustration)**. Tighten the bearing carrier bolts, in the specified order **(see illustration 13.26)**, to the specified torque wrench setting, whilst taking great care not to rotate the camshaft, then remove the bearing carrier and use the scale provided with the Plastigage kit to measure the width of each compressed strand.

17 If the running clearance of any bearing is

2B

13.18 Checking camshaft endfloat using a dial gauge

13.22 Liberally oil the tappets

13.23 Position the camshaft so that the roll-pin (arrowed) at the timing belt end is in the 2 o'clock position

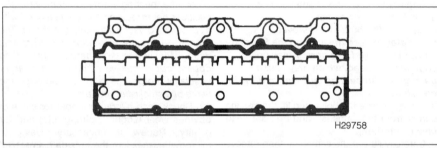

13.24a Apply a bead of sealant to the area indicated by the heavy black line

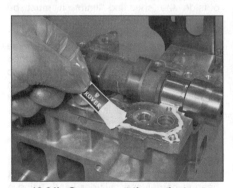

13.24b Squeeze out the sealant . . .

13.24c . . . then spread to an even film using a brush

found to be beyond the specified service limit or beyond, fit a new camshaft and repeat the check. If the clearance is still excessive, then the cylinder head (and matched bearing carrier) must be renewed.

18 To check camshaft endfloat, remove the hydraulic tappets (if not already done), carefully clean the bearing surfaces and refit the camshaft and bearing carrier. Tighten the bearing carrier bolts, in the specified order **(see illustration 13.26)**, to the specified torque wrench setting, then measure the endfloat using a Dial Test Indicator (DTI) or dial gauge mounted on the cylinder head, so that its tip bears on the front of the camshaft **(see illustration)**.

19 Tap the camshaft fully towards the gauge, zero the gauge, then tap the camshaft fully away from the gauge and note the gauge reading. If the endfloat measured is found to

be greater than the maximum specified, fit a new camshaft and repeat the check. If the clearance is still excessive, then the cylinder head must be renewed.

20 The camshaft itself should show no signs of marks, pitting or scoring on the lobe surfaces. If such marks are evident, renew the camshaft.

21 If a camshaft is renewed, extract the roll-pins from the old one and fit the pins to the new camshaft, with the split in each roll-pin towards the camshaft centreline.

Refitting

22 Liberally oil the cylinder head hydraulic tappet bores and the tappets **(see illustration)**. Note that if new tappets are being fitted, they must be charged with clean engine oil before installation. Carefully refit the tappets to the cylinder head, ensuring that

each tappet is refitted to its original bore and is the correct way up. Some care will be required to enter the tappets squarely into their bores.

23 Liberally oil the camshaft bearings and lobes, then refit the camshaft. Position the camshaft so that the roll-pin in the front (timing belt sprocket end) of the camshaft is in the 2 o'clock position when viewed from the right-hand end of the engine **(see illustration)**.

24 Ensure that the locating dowels are pressed firmly into their recesses, check that the mating surfaces are completely clean, unmarked and free from oil, then apply a thin bead of the recommended sealant to the cylinder head mating surfaces of the camshaft bearing carrier as shown. Carefully follow the instructions supplied with the sealant kit. Spread the sealant to an even film using a brush or roller, taking care not to allow any sealant to enter the lubrication grooves **(see illustrations)**. Note that once the sealant has been applied, assembly must be completed within 20 minutes.

25 Refit the bearing carrier to the cylinder head, pushing it firmly into position. Fit the bearing carrier securing bolts, and tighten them finger-tight.

26 Working in the sequence shown **(see illustration)**, progressively tighten the

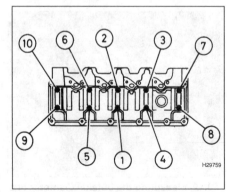

13.26 Camshaft bearing carrier securing bolt tightening sequence

camshaft bearing carrier bolts by one turn at a time until the carrier touches the cylinder head evenly. Now go round again, working in the same sequence, tightening all bolts to the specified torque setting. Work only as described, to apply the pressure of the valve springs gradually and evenly on the carrier. Wipe off all surplus sealant so that none is left to find its way into any oilways. Follow the sealant manufacturer's recommendations as to the time needed for curing – usually at least an hour must be allowed between application of the sealant and the starting of the engine.

27 Fit new camshaft oil seals, using a suitable tube or socket, with reference to Section 12.

28 Refit the fuel injection pump drivebelt backplate, then refit and tighten the securing bolts, making sure that the bracket is in place on the relevant bolt, as noted before removal.

29 Refit the fuel injection pump drivebelt tensioner and refit the pump drive sprocket to the camshaft, as described in Section 11.

30 Refit the upper rear timing belt cover as described in Section 6.

31 Refit the cylinder head cover, with reference to Section 4.

14 Cylinder head – removal and refitting

Models without intercooler

Note: *A new cylinder head gasket, a new turbocharger oil return pipe gasket, and new turbocharger oil feed pipe sealing washers will be required. New cylinder head bolts may be required – see text. A dial test indicator will be required to determine the thickness of the new cylinder head gasket required.*

Removal

1 Disconnect the battery negative lead.

2 Drain the cooling system as described in Chapter 1B.

3 Apply the handbrake, then jack up the front of the vehicle and support securely on axle stands (see *"Jacking and Vehicle Support"*).

14.10 Disconnect the MAP sensor vacuum pipe from the turbocharger

4 Remove the fuel injection pump drivebelt as described in Section 10.

5 Remove the fuel injection pump drive sprocket from the camshaft, and remove the fuel injection pump drivebelt tensioner, as described in Section 11.

6 Unscrew the three securing bolts, and remove the fuel injection pump drivebelt backplate. Note the location of the bracket secured by one of the bolts.

7 Remove the upper rear timing belt cover, as described in Section 6.

8 Slacken the hose clip, and disconnect the breather hose from the cylinder head cover.

9 Disconnect the exhaust front section from the exhaust manifold as described in Chapter 4B.

10 Disconnect the MAP sensor vacuum pipe from the turbocharger **(see illustration)**.

11 Disconnect the vacuum pipe from the exhaust gas recirculation valve **(see illustration)**.

12 Place a suitable container beneath the turbocharger to catch escaping oil, then unscrew the union bolt securing the oil feed pipe to the turbocharger. Disconnect the pipe from the turbocharger, and recover the two sealing washers from the union bolt **(see illustration)**.

13 Similarly, working under the vehicle, unscrew the two securing bolts, and disconnect the oil return pipe from the

14.11 Disconnect the vacuum pipe from the exhaust gas recirculation valve

14.12 Unscrew the union bolt (arrowed) and disconnect the oil feed pipe from the turbocharger. Note cloth in turbocharger outlet to prevent objects from falling in

turbocharger **(see illustration)**. Recover the gasket, and discard it.

14 Disconnect the airflow meter wiring plug, then slacken the hose clip, and disconnect the air intake hose from turbocharger. Remove the air intake hose/airflow meter assembly **(see illustration)**.

15 Remove the inlet and exhaust manifolds, as described in Chapter 4B.

16 Slacken the hose clip, and disconnect the hose from the brake servo vacuum pipe **(see illustration)**.

17 Unscrew the bolts securing the brake servo vacuum pipe to the coolant outlet elbow and the cylinder head cover, then move the

2B

14.13 Unscrew the two bolts (arrowed) securing the oil return pipe to the turbocharger

14.14 Remove the air intake hose/airflow meter assembly

14.16 Disconnect the hose from the brake servo vacuum pipe . . .

14.17 . . . then unscrew the bolts securing the pipe to the coolant outlet elbow and the cylinder head cover

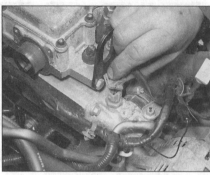

14.19 Disconnect the wiring plug from the engine coolant temperature (ECT) sensor

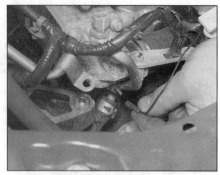

14.20 Disconnect the wiring from the coolant temperature gauge sender

vacuum pipe to one side, clear of the cylinder head **(see illustration)**.

18 On models with air conditioning, unscrew the bolt securing the alternator to its top mounting bracket, then unscrew the two securing bolts, and remove the alternator top mounting bracket.

19 Disconnect the wiring plug from the engine coolant temperature (ECT) sensor, mounted in the coolant outlet elbow **(see illustration)**.

20 Disconnect the wiring from the coolant temperature gauge sender **(see illustration)**.

21 Slacken the hose clips, and disconnect the radiator top hose from the coolant outlet

elbow, and the radiator, then remove the hose.

22 Unscrew the bolt securing the engine oil level dipstick tube bracket to the coolant outlet elbow **(see illustration)**.

23 Release the fuel injector needle lift sensor wiring connector from the bracket on the fuel injection pump, then separate the two halves of the connector **(see illustration)**.

24 Place plenty of absorbent cloth around the fuel injectors, then slacken the union bolts securing the fuel leak-off hoses to the fuel injectors. Be prepared for fuel spillage. Recover the union washers if they are loose **(see illustration)**.

25 Pull the fuel leak-off hose from the fuel injection pump pipe, then remove the fuel leak-off hose assembly.

26 Unscrew the union nuts, and disconnect the fuel feed pipes from the fuel injectors. Counterhold the union on each injector using a second spanner **(see illustration)**. Be prepared for fuel spillage, and cover the open ends of the pipes and fuel injectors to prevent dirt entry.

27 Unscrew the bolt securing the fuel injection pump wiring connector to the pump, then move the connector to one side to allow access to the fuel pipe unions on the pump.

28 Repeat the procedure in paragraph 26, to disconnect the fuel pipes from the fuel injection pump, then remove the pipes. Again, cover or plug the open ends of the fuel pipes and the fuel injection pump.

29 Unscrew the securing nut, and disconnect the feed wiring from the No 2 cylinder glow plug **(see illustration)**.

30 Remove the cylinder head cover, with reference to Section 4.

31 Working in the reverse order of the tightening sequence **(see illustration 14.55)**, progressively unscrew (ie, slacken each bolt by one turn at a time) the cylinder head bolts. Withdraw the bolts, and store them in order, so that they can be refitted in their original locations **(see**

14.22 Unscrew the bolt securing the engine oil level dipstick tube bracket

14.23 Separate the two halves of the fuel injector needle lift sensor wiring connector

14.24 Disconnect the fuel leak-off hoses from the fuel injectors

14.26 Counterhold the union on each injector when unscrewing the injector pipe union nuts

14.29 Unscrew the nut securing the feed wiring to No 2 cylinder glow plug

14.31 Withdraw the cylinder head bolts . . .

14.33 . . . then lift off the cylinder head

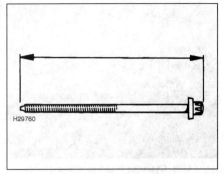

14.36 Measure the overall length of each cylinder head bolt

illustration). **Do not** remove the washers from the bolts. The bolts can be stored by pushing them through a clearly-marked cardboard template.

32 Release the cylinder head from the cylinder block and locating dowels by rocking it. Do not prise between the mating faces of the cylinder head and block, as this may damage the gasket faces.

33 Ideally, an assistant will now be required to help lift the cylinder head from the block – take care as the cylinder head is heavy **(see illustration)**. Recover the cylinder head gasket, and discard it.

Caution: Support the cylinder head on wooden blocks or stands – do not rest the lower face of the cylinder head on the work surface. The tips of the fuel injectors and the glow plugs protrude below the lower face of the cylinder head, and will be damaged if the cylinder head is rested face-down on a work surface.

34 If the cylinder head is to be dismantled, remove the camshaft, then refer to the relevant Sections of Part D of this Chapter.

Cylinder head bolt examination

35 Check the condition of the cylinder head bolts, particularly their threads. Keeping all bolts in their correct fitted order, wash them and wipe dry. **Do not** remove the washers from the bolts. Check each bolt for any sign of visible wear or damage, renewing as necessary.

36 Measure the overall length of each

cylinder head bolt **(see illustration)**. If the length of any of the bolts exceeds 243.41 mm, then **all** the bolts must be renewed. Considering the task these bolts perform and the pressures they must withstand, owners should consider renewing all the bolts as a matter of course.

Cylinder head gasket selection

Note: *A dial test indicator will be required during this procedure.*

37 Three thicknesses of cylinder head gasket are available. In order to ensure that the correct thickness of gasket is fitted, it is necessary to measure the protrusion of each piston above the top face of the cylinder block.

38 Temporarily refit the crankshaft pulley bolt and, where applicable, remove the timing pin from the flywheel.

39 Rotate the crankshaft (use a spanner or socket on the pulley bolt) to bring No 1 piston to TDC.

40 Position a dial test indicator (dial gauge) on the top face of the cylinder block, near No 1 piston location, and zero the gauge on the block top face.

41 Re-position the dial gauge probe on the front edge (the edge nearest the timing belt end of the engine) of No 1 piston crown, then slowly turn the crankshaft back-and-forth past TDC, noting the highest reading on the gauge **(see illustration)**. Record this reading. Re-position the dial gauge probe on the rear edge (the edge nearest the flywheel end of the

engine) of No 1 piston crown, and repeat the measurement. Take the highest of the two readings as the piston protrusion for No 1 piston.

42 Repeat the measurement procedure described in paragraph 39 and 40 on No 4 piston, then turn the crankshaft half-a-turn (180°), and repeat the procedure on Nos 2 and 3 pistons.

43 If a dial test indicator is not available, piston protrusion may be measured using a straight-edge and feeler blades or vernier calipers. However, these methods are inevitably less accurate, and cannot therefore be recommended.

44 Ascertain the greatest piston protrusion measurement, and use this to determine the correct cylinder head gasket thickness from the following table. Note that the gasket thickness identification holes are located adjacent to the No 2 cylinder location at the engine oil level dipstick side of the gasket **(see illustration)**.

Piston protrusion	Gasket identification
0.10 to 0.25 mm	*1 hole*
0.25 to 0.40 mm	*2 holes*
0.40 to 0.55 mm	*3 holes*

Refitting

45 The mating faces of the cylinder head and cylinder block/crankcase must be perfectly clean before refitting the head. Use a hard plastic or wood scraper to remove all traces of gasket and carbon. Also clean the piston crowns. Take particular care, as the soft aluminium alloy is damaged easily. Also, make sure that the carbon is not allowed to enter the oil and water passages – this is particularly important for the lubrication system, as carbon could block the oil supply to any of the engine components. Using adhesive tape and paper, seal the water, oil and bolt holes in the cylinder block/crankcase. To prevent carbon entering the gap between the pistons and bores, smear a little grease in the gap. After cleaning each piston, use a small brush to remove all traces of grease and carbon from the gap, then wipe away the remainder with a clean cloth. Clean all the pistons in the same way.

46 Check the mating surfaces of the cylinder

2B

14.41 Measuring the protrusion of No 1 piston, using a dial gauge

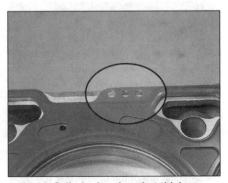

14.44 Cylinder head gasket thickness identification marking

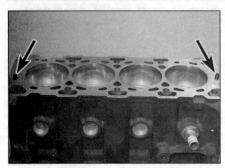

14.48 Cylinder head locating dowel locations (arrowed) in cylinder head

14.51 Cylinder head gasket "TOP" marking

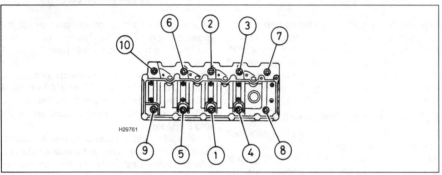

14.55 Cylinder head bolt tightening sequence

c) Ensure that the fuel pipes are correctly reconnected and that the unions are securely tightened.

d) Refit the fuel injection pump drive sprocket and the fuel injection pump drivebelt tensioner, as described in Section 11.

e) Refit the inlet and exhaust manifolds as described in Chapter 4B.

f) Use a new gasket when reconnecting the turbocharger oil return pipe, and use new sealing washers when reconnecting the turbocharger oil feed pipe.

g) Reconnect the exhaust front section to the manifold with reference to Chapter 4B.

h) Refit the upper rear timing belt cover as described in Section 6, but before refitting the timing belt, rotate the crankshaft **clockwise** until the timing pin can be engaged with the flywheel (see Section 3). **Do not** rotate the crankshaft too far, as the pistons may contact the valves.

i) Refit the fuel injection pump drivebelt as described in Section 10.

j) On completion, refill the cooling system as described in Chapter 1B and, if necessary, bleed the fuel system as described in Chapter 4B.

Models with intercooler

Note: A new cylinder head gasket, a new turbocharger oil return pipe gasket, and new turbocharger oil feed pipe sealing washers will be required. New cylinder head bolts may be required – see text. A dial test indicator will be required to determine the thickness of the new cylinder head gasket required.

Removal

57 Proceed as described in paragraphs 1 to 11.

58 Slacken the hose clip, and disconnect the intercooler top hose from the intercooler **(see illustration)**.

59 Unscrew the two bolts securing the turbocharger pipe to the cylinder head and the engine lifting bracket, then slacken the clip securing the pipe to the turbocharger, and remove the pipe **(see illustrations)**.

block/crankcase and the cylinder head for nicks, deep scratches and other damage. If slight, they may be removed carefully with a file, but if excessive, machining may be the only alternative to renewal.

47 If warpage of the cylinder head gasket surface is suspected, use a straight-edge to check it for distortion. Refer to Part D of this Chapter if necessary.

48 Wipe clean the mating surfaces of the cylinder head and cylinder block/crankcase. Check that the two locating dowels are in position at each end of the cylinder block/crankcase surface **(see illustration)**.

49 Temporarily refit the crankshaft pulley bolt, and rotate the crankshaft anti-clockwise until Nos 1 and 4 pistons are approximately 25 mm below the top face of the cylinder block/crankcase.

50 Temporarily refit the camshaft sprocket to the camshaft, and rotate the camshaft until the camshaft sprocket locating roll-pin is at the 2 o'clock position, then remove the sprocket. **Do not** rotate the camshaft and crankshaft until just before the timing belt is to be refitted (see paragraph 56).

51 Fit the new cylinder head gasket to the cylinder block (make sure that the correct gasket has been selected – see paragraphs 37 to 44), ensuring that it locates correctly over the dowels, with the "TOP" marking visible at the flywheel end of the engine **(see illustration)**.

52 Lower the cylinder head into position, locating it on the dowels.

53 Apply a light film of clean engine oil to the cylinder head bolt threads, and to the

underside of the bolt heads – **do not** oil the underside of the washers.

54 Keeping all the cylinder head bolts in their correct fitted order, carefully enter each bolt into its original hole and screw it in, by hand only, until finger-tight. **Do not** drop the bolts into their holes.

55 Working progressively and in the sequence shown **(see illustration)**, use first a torque wrench, then an ordinary socket extension bar with an angle gauge, to tighten the cylinder head bolts through the specified stages – ie, tighten all bolts progressively to Stage 1, then tighten all bolts to Stage 2, and so on.

56 Further refitting is a reversal of removal, bearing in mind the following points.

a) Refit the cylinder head cover with reference to Section 4.

b) Ensure that all wiring plugs and hoses are correctly reconnected.

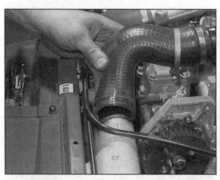

14.58 Disconnect the intercooler top hose

14.59a Unscrew the bolt (arrowed) securing the turbocharger pipe to the cylinder head . . .

14.59b . . . and the bolt securing the pipe
to the engine lifting bracket

14.60 Disconnect the intercooler bottom
hose from the air intake pipe

14.61 Unscrew the bolts securing the
exhaust gas recirculation (EGR) pipe to the
inlet manifold air intake pipe

60 Slacken the hose clip and disconnect the
intercooler bottom hose from the inlet
manifold air intake pipe **(see illustration)**.
61 Unscrew the two bolts securing the
exhaust gas recirculation (EGR) pipe to the
inlet manifold air intake pipe **(see illustration)**.
62 Unscrew the bolt securing the inlet
manifold air intake pipe to the camshaft cover,
then unscrew the two bolts securing the
intake pipe to the inlet manifold, and remove
the intake pipe **(see illustrations)**. Recover
the gasket and discard it.
63 Disconnect the wiring plug from the intake
air temperature (IAT) sensor **(see illustration)**.
64 Proceed as described in paragraphs 12
to 34.

**Cylinder head bolt examination and
cylinder head gasket selection**

65 Proceed as described in paragraphs 35
to 44.

Refitting

66 Proceed as described in paragraphs 45
to 56.

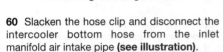

15 Sump –
removal and refitting

Removal

Note: *Prior to removing the sump, obtain
Rover sealant kit GUG 705548 GM. A new
engine oil filter will be required on refitting.*

14.62a Unscrew the bolt securing the air
intake pipe to the camshaft cover . . .

1 Apply the handbrake, then jack up the front
of the vehicle and support securely on axle
stands (see *"Jacking and Vehicle Support"*).
2 Drain the engine oil (with reference to
Chapter 1B if necessary), then clean and refit
the engine oil drain plug, tightening it to the
specified torque wrench setting. If the engine
is nearing its service interval when the oil and
filter are due for renewal, it is recommended
that the filter is also removed and a new one
fitted. After reassembly, the engine can then
be refilled with fresh engine oil.
3 Remove the oil filter, with reference to
Chapter 1B.
4 Remove the engine/transmission steady
bar, as described in Section 20.
5 Unscrew the bolt securing the sump to the

14.62b . . . and the two bolts securing the
intake pipe to the inlet manifold

transmission support bracket **(see
illustration)**.
6 Slacken the hose clip, and disconnect the
brake vacuum pump oil drain pipe from the
sump **(see illustration)**.
7 Unscrew the bolt securing the oil pipe
bracket to the sump.
8 Working in the reverse order to the
tightening sequence **(see illustration 15.16)**,
progressively slacken the sump retaining bolts
then remove them.
9 Break the joint by striking the sump with the
palm of the hand, then lower the sump and
withdraw it. Recover the gasket and discard it.
10 With the sump removed, take the
opportunity to unbolt the oil pump pick-
up/strainer pipe and clean it using a suitable

2B

14.63 Disconnect the wiring plug from the
intake air temperature (IAT) sensor

15.5 Unscrew the bolt (arrowed) securing
the sump to the transmission support
bracket

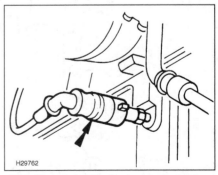

15.6 Disconnect the brake vacuum pump
oil drain pipe (arrowed) from the sump

15.10a Unscrew the securing bolts (arrowed) . . .

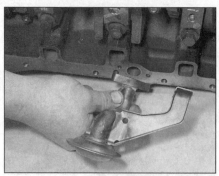

15.10b . . . and remove the oil pump pick-up/strainer pipe

15.12 Refit the oil pump pick-up/strainer pipe using a new O-ring

15.13 Apply sealant to the grooves on each side of the front main bearing cap and the joints between the bearing cap and the cylinder block

15.14 Apply sealant to the joints between the crankshaft rear oil seal housing, the rear main bearing cap and the cylinder block

solvent **(see illustrations)**. Recover the O-ring, and inspect the strainer mesh for signs of clogging or splitting - renew if necessary.

Refitting

11 Clean all traces of gasket from the mating surfaces of the cylinder block/crankcase and sump, then use a clean rag to wipe out the sump and the engine interior. Clean all traces of sealant from the crankshaft rear oil seal housing, front and rear main bearing caps, and cylinder block.

12 Refit the oil pump pick-up/strainer pipe, using a new O-ring, and tighten the securing bolts to the specified torque **(see illustration)**.
13 Using the specified sealant (see Note at the beginning of this Section), fill the grooves on each side of the front main bearing cap, and the joints between the bearing cap and the cylinder block **(see illustration)**.
14 Apply a 1 mm thick bead of sealant to the joints between the crankshaft rear oil seal housing, the rear main bearing cap and the cylinder block **(see illustration)**.

Note: *Do not apply the sealant until immediately prior to refitting the sump, and do not spread the bead of sealant.*
15 Fit a new gasket to the sump, ensuring that the lugs on the gasket engage with the corresponding holes in the sump, then offer up the sump to the cylinder block/crankcase then refit the sump retaining bolts, and tighten the bolts finger-tight only.
16 Working in the sequence shown **(see illustration)**, tighten the sump bolts to the specified torque setting.
17 Further refitting is a reversal of removal, bearing in mind the following points.
a) *Tighten the bolt securing the sump to the transmission support bracket to the specified torque.*
b) *Refit the engine/transmission steady bar, as described in Section 20.*
c) *Fit a new oil filter and, on completion, refill the engine with oil as described in Chapter 1B.*

16 Oil pump – removal and refitting

Removal

Note: *Rover sealant kit GUG 705548 GM will be required when refitting the oil pump. A new oil pump gasket will be required, and new oil cooler pipe and turbocharger oil feed pipe O-rings will be required. If the original pump is to be refitted, a new crankshaft front oil seal will be required. The oil pressure relief valve can be dismantled without removing the oil pump from the vehicle - see Section 17 for details.*
1 Drain the engine oil as described in Chapter 1B.
2 Remove the upper and lower rear timing belt covers as described in Section 6.
3 Remove the crankshaft sprocket from the front of the crankshaft.
4 Place a suitable container beneath the oil cooler pipe connections on the oil pump housing, then unscrew the unions and disconnect the oil cooler pipes **(see**

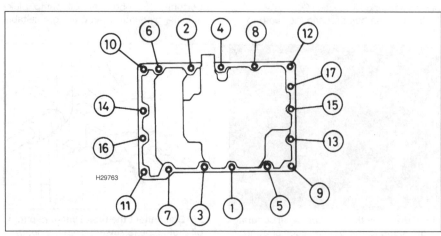

H29763

15.16 Sump bolt tightening sequence

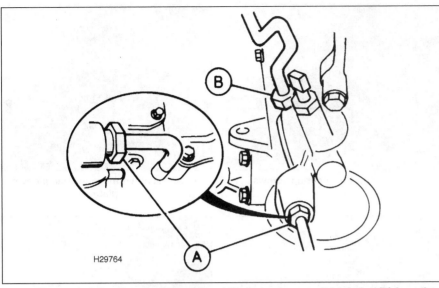

16.4 **Disconnect the oil cooler pipes (A) and the turbocharger oil feed pipe (B) from the oil pump housing**

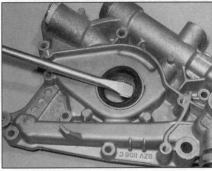

16.11 **Prise the crankshaft oil seal from the oil pump**

illustration). Recover the O-rings from the pipes and discard them.

5 Similarly, slacken the union, and disconnect the turbocharger oil feed pipe from the oil pump housing. Recover the O-ring and discard it.

6 Disconnect the wiring plug from the oil pressure switch.

7 Working in the reverse order to the tightening sequence **(see illustration 16.20)**, unscrew the oil pump securing bolts, noting the location of the single longer securing bolt at the bottom of the pump.

8 Withdraw the pump from the cylinder block, and recover the Woodruff key from the crankshaft if it is loose. Recover the gasket and discard it.

Refitting

9 Make sure that the oil pump bolt holes in the cylinder block are clean and dry.

10 Clean all traces of gasket from the cylinder block and oil pump mating faces, and remove all traces of sealant from the front main bearing cap.

11 If the original oil pump is to be refitted, prise the crankshaft front oil seal from the pump, and discard it **(see illustration)**.

12 Lubricate the oil seal running surface on the crankshaft with clean engine oil.

13 Refit the Woodruff key to the crankshaft.

14 Using the specified sealant (see Note at the beginning of this Section), apply a 1 mm thick bead of sealant to the joints between the front main bearing cap and the cylinder block **(see illustrations)**.

15 Fit a new oil pump gasket to the cylinder block **(see illustration)**.

16 If a new oil pump is being fitted, it will be supplied with a new crankshaft oil seal already fitted. In this case, lubricate the lips of the oil seal.

17 Turn the oil pump inner rotor as necessary to align the slot in the rotor with the Woodruff key in the crankshaft.

18 Slide the oil pump over the crankshaft, ensuring that the Woodruff key engages with the slot in the oil pump inner rotor.

19 Apply thread-locking compound to the oil pump securing bolts, then refit the securing bolts, ensuring that the single longer bolt is

located at the bottom of pump in the position noted before removal.

20 Tighten the bolts to the specified torque, in the sequence shown, noting the different torque setting for the longer bolt **(see illustration)**.

21 If the original oil pump has been refitted, fit a new crankshaft front oil seal with reference to Section 18.

22 Further refitting is a reversal of removal, bearing in mind the following points.

a) *Use new O-rings when reconnecting the turbocharger oil feed pipe and the oil cooler pipes to the pump housing.*

b) *Refit the upper and lower rear timing belt covers as described in Section 6.*

c) *Refill the engine with oil as described in Chapter 1B.*

2B

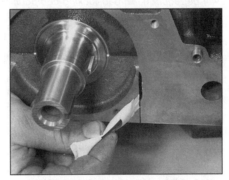

16.14a **Apply a bead of sealant . . .**

16.14b **. . . to the joints between the front main bearing cap and the cylinder block – viewed with engine removed**

16.15 **Fit a new gasket to the cylinder block – viewed with engine removed**

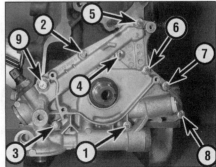

16.20 **Oil pump bolt tightening sequence**

17.3a Some oil pumps have a "TOP" marking at the top of the cover plate

17.3b Unscrew the securing screws . . .

17.3c . . . and remove the pump cover plate

17.4 Lift out the oil pump rotors

17.6a Unscrew the oil pressure relief valve threaded plug (using an oil plug drain key and a spanner) . . .

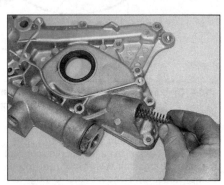

17.6b . . . then recover the valve spring . . .

17 Oil pump – dismantling, inspection and reassembly

1 The oil pump can be dismantled and checked as described in the following paragraphs, but no spare parts are available, and if wear or damage is found, the pump must be renewed as a complete unit.

Dismantling

Note: *Loctite 573 sealant, or a suitable equivalent will be required to seal the pump cover plate to the pump body on reassembly. A new pressure relief valve threaded plug, and a new thermostatic valve plug sealing washer* will be required. Thread-locking compound will be required to coat the threads of the pump cover plate securing screws, and the thermostatic valve plug.

2 Remove the oil pump as described in Section 16.
3 Make alignment marks between the pump cover plate and the pump body (note that some pumps have a "TOP" mark stamped at the top of the cover plate), then unscrew the Torx screws and remove the pump cover plate **(see illustrations)**.
4 Lift out the oil pump rotors, noting the punched identification marks on the front faces of the rotors, which face away from the cover plate **(see illustration)**.
5 The oil pressure relief valve can be

dismantled, if required, without disturbing the pump. If this is to be done with the pump in position and the engine still installed in the vehicle, it will first be necessary to jack up the front of the vehicle and remove the right-hand roadwheel to gain access to the valve (see "*Jacking and Vehicle Support*").
6 To dismantle the valve, unscrew the threaded plug and recover the valve spring and plunger **(see illustrations)**. Discard the threaded plug – a new one must be used on refitting.
7 Similarly, the thermostatic valve (which diverts the oil to the oil cooler) can be dismantled as follows **(see illustrations)**.
  a) Unscrew the thermostatic valve plug.
    Recover the sealing washer and discard it.

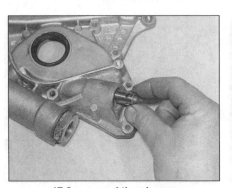

17.6c . . . and the plunger

17.7a Unscrew the thermostatic valve plug . . .

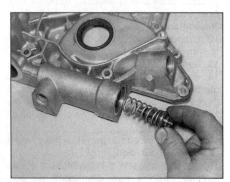

17.7b . . . then withdraw the spring and valve assembly

17.9a Measure the clearance between the outer rotor and the pump body . . .

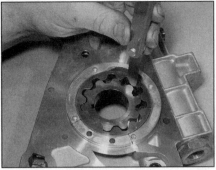

17.9b . . . and between the tips of the inner and outer rotors

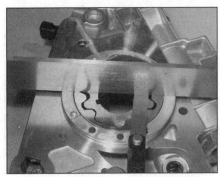

17.10 Measuring the rotor endfloat

b) *Withdraw the spring and valve assembly from the oil pump body. Do not attempt to separate the spring from the valve.*

Inspection

8 Inspect the rotors for obvious signs of wear or damage and renew if necessary. If the pump body or cover plate is scored or damaged, then the complete oil pump assembly must be renewed.

9 Using feeler blades of the appropriate thickness, measure the clearance between the outer rotor and the pump body, then between the tips of the inner and outer rotor **(see illustrations)**.

10 Using feeler blades and a straight-edge placed across the top of the pump body and the rotors, measure the rotor endfloat **(see illustration)**.

11 If any measurement is outside the specified limits, the complete pump assembly must be renewed.

12 If the pressure relief valve plunger is scored, or if it does not slide freely in the pump body bore, then it must be renewed. Check the free length of the relief valve spring, which should be as specified **(see illustration)**.

13 Check the thermostatic valve spring for distortion and corrosion, and check that the valve slides freely in the pump body bore. If there are any signs of damage or wear to the spring or valve, the spring and valve assembly must be renewed. Thoroughly clean the

threads of the valve plug, and the plug threads in the oil pump body.

Reassembly

14 Clean all traces of sealant from the mating faces of the oil pump body and the cover plate. Thoroughly clean the threads of the cover plate securing bolts, and ensure that the cover plate bolt threads in the pump body are clean and dry – **do not** use a tap to clean the threads.

15 Lubricate the pump rotors with clean engine oil and refit them to the pump body, ensuring that the punched marks on the faces of the rotors face away from the pump cover plate **(see illustration)**.

16 Apply a 1 mm bead of the specified sealant (see Note at the beginning of this Section) to the edge of the pump cover plate, then refit the cover plate, ensuring that the marks made on the cover plate and pump body before removal are aligned (where applicable, the "TOP" marking should on the cover plate should be at the top of the pump).

17 Coat the threads of the cover plate securing screws with thread-locking compound, then refit and tighten the screws.

18 Check that the pump rotates freely, then prime it by injecting oil into its passages and rotating it. If a long time elapses before the pump is refitted to the engine, prime it again before installation.

19 Lubricate the oil pressure relief valve bore, and the spring and plunger with clean engine

oil. Refit the oil pressure relief valve plunger, ensuring that it is the correct way up, then install the spring. Fit a new threaded plug, and tighten the plug securely.

20 Lubricate the thermostatic valve, spring and the valve bore in the oil pump body with clean engine oil.

21 Clamp the oil pump body in a vice, with the thermostatic valve bore facing vertically upwards. The valve bore must be as near vertical as possible.

22 Insert the valve and spring assembly into the valve bore in the oil pump body, ensuring that the assembly is positioned centrally in the bore. The valve will not seat correctly in the valve plug if it is not positioned centrally.

23 Fit a new sealing washer to the valve plug, then coat the threads of the plug with thread-locking compound, and screw the plug into position by hand, making sure that the valve is not displaced as the plug is tightened.

24 When the plug has been fully screwed down, tighten it to the specified torque.

25 Refit the oil pump as described in Section 16.

18 Crankshaft oil seals – renewal

Front (timing belt end) seal

1 Remove the timing belt as described in Section 7.

2 Remove the crankshaft sprocket.

3 Punch or drill two small holes opposite each other in the seal. Screw a self-tapping screw into each and pull on the screws with pliers to extract the seal.

4 Clean the seal housing and polish off any burrs or raised edges which may have caused the original seal to fail.

5 Lubricate the lips of the new seal with clean engine oil and drive it into position until it seats on its locating shoulder. Use a suitable tubular drift, such as a socket, which bears only on the hard outer edge of the seal. Take care not to damage the seal lips during fitting. Use either grease or a thin layer of insulating tape on the crankshaft to protect the seal lips

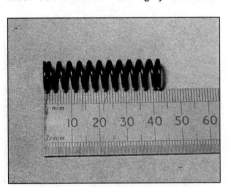

17.12 Measure the free length of the oil pressure relief valve spring

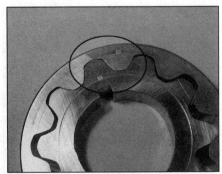

17.15 The punched marks on the faces of the rotors must face away from the pump cover plate

2B

18.11 Slide the protector sleeve, oil seal and housing assembly over the end of the crankshaft – viewed with engine removed

18.13 Crankshaft rear oil seal housing bolt tightening sequence

from the edges of the crankshaft flats, but be careful to remove all traces of tape and to lubricate the seal lips if the second method is used. Note that the seal lips should face inwards.

6 Wash off any excess oil, then refit the crankshaft sprocket, and refit and tension the timing belt as described in Section 7.

Rear (flywheel end) seal

Note: *The oil seal is integral with the oil seal housing. When renewing the oil seal, a complete new housing/seal assembly must be fitted. Prior to removing the seal, obtain Rover sealant kit GUG 705548 GM.*

7 Remove the flywheel as described in Section 19.

8 Remove the sump as described in Section 15.

9 Unscrew the securing bolts, and remove the crankshaft rear oil seal housing.

10 Thoroughly clean the oil seal running surface on the crankshaft, the oil seal housing mating faces on the cylinder block, and the bolt and dowel holes in the cylinder block.

⚠ *Warning: Do not lubricate the oil seal or the seal running surfaces on the crankshaft. The new oil seal/housing assembly will be supplied fitted with a seal protector. Do not separate the protector sleeve from the oil seal, and do not touch the oil seal lip. If*

the seal is inadvertently touched, it must not be fitted, as the coating applied to the seal during manufacture will be destroyed, and this may result in oil leakage.

11 Carefully slide the seal protector sleeve, oil seal and housing assembly over the end of the crankshaft, taking care not to touch the seal lip **(see illustration)**.

12 Locate the housing against the cylinder block, noting that the oil seal protector will be pushed out as the housing/seal assembly is pushed into position.

13 Refit the housing securing bolts, and tighten them to the specified torque in the order shown **(see illustration)**.

14 Apply a 1 mm thick bead of the specified sealant to the joint between the oil seal housing, the rear main bearing cap, and the cylinder block. **Do not** apply the sealant until immediately before the sump is to be fitted.

15 Refit the sump as described in Section 15.

16 Refit the flywheel as described in Section 19.

19 Flywheel – removal, inventory inspection and refitting

Removal

Note: *New flywheel retaining bolts must be used on refitting.*

1 Remove the clutch assembly as described in Chapter 6.

2 If not already done, turn the crankshaft until the locking pin can be inserted into the flywheel, as described in Section 3. Additionally, lock the flywheel by bolting a suitable tool to the transmission mounting plate, to engage with the flywheel ring gear teeth.

3 Slacken and remove the flywheel retaining bolts and discard them **(see illustration)**. The bolts must be renewed whenever they are disturbed.

4 Remove the flywheel **(see illustration)**. Do not drop it, as it is very heavy.

Inspection

5 If the flywheel clutch mating surface is deeply scored, cracked or otherwise damaged, then the flywheel must be renewed, unless it is possible to have it surface ground. Seek the advice of a Rover dealer or engine reconditioning specialist.

6 If the ring gear is badly worn or has missing teeth, then it must be renewed. This job is best left to a Rover dealer or engine reconditioning specialist. The temperature to which the new ring gear must be heated for installation (350°C - shown by an even light blue colour) is critical and, if not done accurately, the hardness of the teeth will be destroyed.

Refitting

7 Clean the mating surfaces of the flywheel and crankshaft. Clean any remaining adhesive from the threads of the crankshaft threaded holes by carefully using a suitable tap.

8 Position the flywheel over the locating dowel in the end of the crankshaft, press it into place and fit six **new** bolts **(see illustration)**.

9 Lock the flywheel using the method employed on dismantling then, working in a diagonal sequence, progressively tighten the retaining bolts to the specified torque wrench setting in the two stages given **(see illustrations)**.

10 Refit the clutch assembly as described in Chapter 6.

19.3 Unscrewing a flywheel bolt – note tool (arrowed) to prevent flywheel from turning

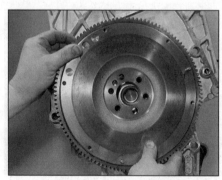

19.4 Lifting off the flywheel

19.8 Fit new flywheel securing bolts

19.9a Tighten the flywheel bolts to the specified torque . . .

19.9b . . . then through the specified angle

20.7 Unscrew the through-bolt (arrowed) securing the engine steady bar to the subframe

20 Engine/transmission mountings – inspection and renewal

Inspection

1 If improved access is required, raise the front of the vehicle and support it securely on axle stands (see *"Jacking and Vehicle Support"*).

2 Check the mounting rubber to see if it is cracked, hardened or separated from the metal at any point. Renew the mounting if any such damage or deterioration is evident.

3 Check that all mounting fasteners are securely tightened. Use a torque wrench to check, if possible.

4 Using a large screwdriver or a pry bar, check for wear in the mounting by carefully levering against it to check for free play. Where this is not possible, enlist the aid of an assistant to move the engine/gearbox unit back and forth or from side to side while you watch the mounting. While some free play is to be expected even from new components, excessive wear should be obvious. If excessive free play is found, check first that the fasteners are correctly secured, then renew any worn components as described below.

Renewal

Engine/transmission steady bar

5 Apply the handbrake, then jack up the front

of the vehicle and support securely on axle stands (see *"Jacking and Vehicle Support"*).

6 Remove the engine undershield, with reference to Chapter 11 if necessary.

7 Working under the vehicle, unscrew the through-bolt securing the engine steady bar to the subframe **(see illustration)**.

8 Unscrew the through-bolt securing the steady bar to the bracket on the sump, then withdraw the steady bar **(see illustration)**.

9 Refitting is a reversal of removal, but tighten the through-bolts to the specified torque.

Left-hand engine/transmission mounting

10 Apply the handbrake, then jack up the front of the vehicle and support securely on axle stands (see *"Jacking and Vehicle Support"*).

11 Remove the air cleaner as described in Chapter 4B.

12 Remove the engine control module (ECM) and the engine management relay module, as described in Chapter 4B.

13 Remove the battery as described in Chapter 5A.

14 Unscrew the bolt securing the fusebox to the battery tray, then unscrew the bolt securing the fusebox to the body, and move the fusebox to one side.

15 Unscrew the four upper bolts securing the battery tray to the body, and slacken the three lower bolts securing the battery tray to the body.

16 Where applicable, release the ABS fuse holder from the battery tray, then remove the battery tray.

17 Place a trolley jack under the transmission, with a block of wood positioned between the jack and transmission, then raise the jack to just take the weight of the engine/transmission unit.

18 Unscrew the through-bolt securing the engine/transmission mounting to the bracket on the body **(see illustration)**.

19 Unscrew the two bolts securing the engine/transmission mounting to the mounting bracket on the transmission, then withdraw the mounting.

20 Refitting is a reversal of removal, but tighten all fixings to the specified torque.

Right-hand engine mounting

21 Apply the handbrake, then jack up the front of the vehicle and support securely on axle stands (see *"Jacking and Vehicle Support"*).

22 Remove the engine undershield.

23 Place a trolley jack under the engine sump, with a block of wood positioned between the engine and sump, then raise the jack to just take the weight of the engine/transmission unit.

24 Unscrew the bolt securing the right-hand engine steady bar to the engine mounting bracket **(see illustration)**.

25 Unscrew the bolt securing the steady bar

2B

20.8 Unscrew the through-bolt (arrowed) securing the engine steady bar to the sump

20.18 Unscrew the through-bolt securing the left-hand engine/transmission mounting to the bracket on the body

20.24 Unscrew the bolt securing the engine steady bar to the engine mounting bracket

20.25a Unscrew the bolt securing the steady bar to the body . . .

20.25b . . . and remove the steady bar

20.26a Unscrew the two nuts . . .

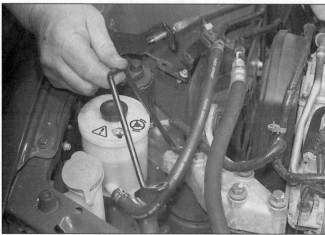

20.26b . . . and remove the engine mounting bracket restraint bar

20.27 Unscrew the nut securing the mounting bracket to the mounting

to the body and remove the steady bar **(see illustrations)**.

26 Unscrew the two nuts and remove the engine mounting bracket restraint bar **(see illustrations)**.

27 Unscrew the nut securing the mounting bracket to the mounting **(see illustration)**.

28 Unscrew the three bolts securing the

mounting bracket to the engine, and remove the bracket **(see illustrations)**.

29 Unscrew the remaining bolt securing the engine mounting to the body, and remove the engine mounting.

30 Commence refitting by fitting the mounting to the body, and tightening the securing bolt finger-tight.

31 Refit the engine mounting bracket, then align the bracket with the engine, and refit and tighten the bracket-to-engine bolts to the specified torque setting.

32 Move the mounting bracket restraint bar into position, then refit the securing nuts and tighten to the specified torque setting.

33 Refit the nut securing the mounting to the

20.28a Unscrew the three bolts securing the mounting bracket to the engine . . .

20.28b . . . and remove the mounting bracket

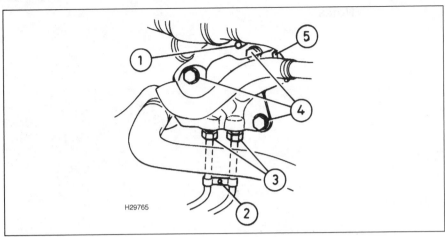

21.2 Oil cooler mounting details

1 Thermostat coolant hose
2 Oil cooler pipe clamp bolt
3 Oil cooler pipe unions
4 Oil cooler securing bolts
5 Radiator bottom hose connection

mounting bracket, and tighten to the specified torque setting.

34 Refit the bolts securing the steady bar to the engine mounting bracket and the body, and tighten to the specified torque setting.

35 Withdraw the jack, then refit the engine undershield, and lower the vehicle to the ground.

21 Engine oil cooler – removal and refitting

Removal

Note: *New oil cooler pipe O-rings will be required on refitting. Thread-locking compound will be required to coat the threads of the oil cooler securing bolts.*

1 Remove the radiator as described in Chapter 3.

2 Slacken the hose clip, and disconnect the left-hand coolant hose from the thermostat **(see illustration)**.

3 Position a suitable container beneath the oil cooler to catch escaping oil.

4 Slacken the clamp bolt securing the two oil cooler pipes together.

5 Slacken the unions, and disconnect the oil cooler pipes from the oil cooler. Recover the O-rings from the pipes and discard them. Allow the oil to drain into the container.

6 Unscrew the three bolts securing the oil cooler to the cylinder block, then withdraw the oil cooler/hose assembly **(see illustration)**. If

21.6 Removing the oil cooler, complete with pipes

the oil cooler has been removed for access to the engine or surrounding components, there is no need to carry out further dismantling.

7 If desired, slacken the hose clips and disconnect the radiator bottom hose and the thermostat hose from the oil cooler, then remove the oil cooler.

Refitting

8 Refitting is a reversal of removal, bearing in mind the following points.

a) *Thoroughly clean the threads of the oil cooler securing bolts, and coat the threads with thread-locking compound before refitting. Tighten the bolts to the specified torque.*

b) *Use new O-rings when reconnecting the oil cooler pipes.*

c) *Refit the radiator as described in Chapter 3.*

d) *On completion, check the engine oil level, and top up if necessary, as described in "Weekly Checks".*

2B

Notes

Chapter 2 Part C:
Petrol engine removal and general overhaul procedures

Contents

Degrees of difficulty

Easy, suitable for novice with little experience	Fairly easy, suitable for beginner with some experience	Fairly difficult, suitable for competent DIY mechanic	Difficult, suitable for experienced DIY mechanic	Very difficult, suitable for expert DIY or professional

Specifications

Cylinder block/crankcase

Material . . . . Aluminium alloy
Cylinder liner bore diameter - 65 mm from top of bore:
   1.1 and 1.4 litre engines:
      Standard - grade A (Red) . . . . 74.970 to 74.985 mm
      Standard - grade B (Blue) . . . . 74.986 to 75.000 mm
   1.6 and 1.8 litre engines:
      Standard – grade A (Red) . . . . 80.000 to 80.015 mm
      Standard – grade B (Blue) . . . . 80.016 to 80.030 mm

Crankshaft

Number of main bearings 5
Main bearing journal diameter . . . . 47.979 to 48.000 mm
Main bearing journal sizes:
    Grade 1 . . . . 47.993 to 48.000 mm
    Grade 2 . . . . 47.986 to 47.993 mm
    Grade 3 . . . . 47.979 to 47.986 mm
Big-end journal diameter:
    1.1, 1.4 and 1.6 litre engines . . . . 42.986 to 43.007 mm
    1.8 litre engine . . . . 47.986 to 48.007 mm
Big-end journal size grades:
    1.1, 1.4 and 1.6 litre engines:
        Grade A . . . . 43.000 to 43.007 mm
        Grade B . . . . 42.993 to 43.000 mm
        Grade C . . . . 42.986 to 42.993 mm
    1.8 litre engine:
        Grade A . . . . 48.000 to 48.007 mm
        Grade B . . . . 47.993 to 48.000 mm
        Grade C . . . . 47.986 to 47.993 mm
Main bearing and big-end bearing journal maximum ovality . . . . 0.010 mm
Main bearing and big-end bearing running clearance . . . . 0.021 to 0.049 mm
Crankshaft endfloat:
    Standard . . . . 0.10 to 0.30 mm
    Service limit . . . . 0.40 mm
Thrustwasher thickness . . . . 2.61 to 2.65 mm

Pistons and piston rings

Piston diameter:
    1.1 and 1.4 litre engines:
        Grade A . . . . 74.940 to 74.955 mm
        Grade B . . . . 74.956 to 74.970 mm
    1.6 and 1.8 litre engines:
        Grade A . . . . 79.975 to 79.990 mm
        Grade B . . . . 79.991 to 80.005 mm
Piston-to-bore clearance:
    1.1 and 1.4 litre engines . . . . 0.015 to 0.045 mm
    1.6 and 1.8 litre engines . . . . 0.010 to 0.040 mm
Piston ring end gaps (fitted 20 mm from top of bore):
    1.1 and 1.4 litre engines:
        Top compression ring . . . . 0.17 to 0.37 mm
        Second compression ring . . . . 0.37 to 0.57 mm
        Oil control ring . . . . 0.15 to 0.40 mm
    1.6 and 1.8 litre engines:
        Top compression ring . . . . 0.20 to 0.35 mm
        Second compression ring . . . . 0.28 to 0.48 mm
        Oil control ring . . . . 0.15 to 0.40 mm
Piston ring-to-groove clearance:
    1.1 and 1.4 litre engines:
        Top compression ring . . . . 0.040 to 0.080 mm
        Second compression ring . . . . 0.030 to 0.062 mm
        Oil control ring - all models . . . . 0.044 to 0.055 mm
    1.6 and 1.8 litre engines:
        Top compression ring . . . . 0.040 to 0.072 mm
        Second compression ring . . . . 0.030 to 0.062 mm
        Oil control ring . . . . 0.010 to 0.180 mm

Cylinder head

Material . . . . Aluminium alloy
Height . . . . 118.95 to 119.05 mm
Reface limit . . . . 0.20 mm
Maximum acceptable gasket face distortion . . . . 0.05 mm
Valve seat angle . . . . 45°
Valve seat width . . . . 1.5 mm
Valve stem installed height:
    K8 engines:
        New . . . . 38.95 to 40.81 mm
        Service limit . . . . 41.06 mm
    K16 engines:
        New . . . . 38.93 to 39.84 mm
        Service limit . . . . 40.10 mm

Valves

Stem diameter:
  K8 engines:
    Inlet . . . . 6.960 to 6.975 mm
    Exhaust . . . . 6.952 to 6.967 mm
  K16 engines:
    Inlet . . . . 5.952 to 5.967 mm
    Exhaust . . . . 5.947 to 5.962 mm
Guide inside diameter:
  K8 engines . . . . 7.000 to 7.025 mm
  K16 engines . . . . 6.000 to 6.025 mm
Stem-to-guide clearance:
  K8 engines:
    Inlet:
      Standard . . . . 0.025 to 0.065 mm
      Service limit . . . . 0.070 mm
    Exhaust:
      Standard . . . . 0.033 to 0.073 mm
      Service limit . . . . 0.110 mm
  K16 engines:
    Inlet;
      Standard . . . . 0.033 to 0.063 mm
      Service limit . . . . 0.070 mm
    Exhaust:
      Standard . . . . 0.038 to 0.078 mm
      Service limit . . . . 0.110 mm
Valve spring free length:
  K8 engines . . . . 46.2 mm
  K16 engines . . . . 50.0 mm
Valve guide fitted height:
  K8 engines . . . . 10.3 mm
  K16 engines . . . . 6.0 mm

Torque wrench settings

Refer to Part A of this Chapter

2C

1 General information

Included in this part of the Chapter are details of removing the engine/transmission unit from the vehicle and general overhaul procedures for the cylinder head, cylinder block/crankcase and all other engine internal components.

The information given ranges from advice concerning preparation for an overhaul and the purchase of replacement parts to detailed step-by-step procedures covering removal, inspection, renovation and refitting of engine internal components.

After Section 6, all instructions are based on the assumption that the engine has been removed from the vehicle. For information concerning in-car engine repair, as well as the removal and refitting of those external components necessary for full overhaul, refer to Part A of this Chapter and to Section 6. Ignore any preliminary dismantling operations described in Part A that are no longer relevant once the engine has been removed from the vehicle.

2 Engine overhaul – general information

It is not always easy to determine when, or if, an engine should be completely overhauled, as a number of factors must be considered.

High mileage is not necessarily an indication that an overhaul is needed, while low mileage does not preclude the need for an overhaul. Frequency of servicing is probably the most important consideration. An engine which has had regular and frequent oil and filter changes, as well as other required maintenance, should give many thousands of miles of reliable service. Conversely, a neglected engine may require an overhaul very early in its life. If a complete service does not remedy any problems, major mechanical work is the only solution.

Excessive oil consumption is an indication that piston rings, valve seals and/or valve guides are in need of attention. Make sure that oil leaks are not responsible before deciding that the rings and/or guides are worn. Perform a compression test to determine the likely cause of the problem (see Part A of this Chapter).

Check the oil pressure with a gauge fitted in place of the oil pressure switch and compare it with that specified (see Part A Specifications). If it is extremely low, the main and big-end bearings and/or the oil pump are probably worn out.

Loss of power, rough running, knocking or metallic engine noises, excessive valve gear noise and high fuel consumption may also point to the need for an overhaul, especially if they are all present at the same time.

An engine overhaul involves restoring all internal parts to the specification of a new engine. During an overhaul, the cylinder liners, the pistons and the piston rings are renewed. New main and big-end bearings are generally fitted and, if necessary, the crankshaft may be renewed to restore the journals. The valves are serviced as well, since they are usually in less than perfect condition at this point. While the engine is being overhauled, other components, such as the distributor, starter and alternator, can be overhauled as well. The end result should be an as-new engine that will give many trouble-free miles.

Critical cooling system components such as the hoses, thermostat and coolant pump should be renewed when an engine is overhauled. The radiator should be checked carefully to ensure that it is not clogged or leaking. Also it is a good idea to renew the oil pump whenever the engine is overhauled.

Before beginning the engine overhaul, read through the entire procedure to familiarise yourself with the scope and requirements of the job. Overhauling an engine is not difficult if you follow carefully all of the instructions, have the necessary tools and equipment and pay close attention to all specifications. However, it can be time-consuming. Plan on the vehicle being off the road for a minimum of two weeks, especially if parts must be taken to an engineering works for repair or reconditioning. Check on the availability of parts and make sure that any necessary special tools and equipment are obtained in advance. Most work can be done with typical hand tools, although a number of precision measuring tools are required for inspecting parts to determine if they must be renewed. Often the engineering works will handle the inspection of parts and offer advice concerning reconditioning and renewal.

Always wait until the engine has been completely dismantled and all components, especially the cylinder block/crankcase, the cylinder liners and the crankshaft have been inspected before deciding what service and repair operations must be performed by an engineering works. Since the condition of these components will be the major factor to consider when determining whether to overhaul the original engine or buy a reconditioned unit, do not purchase parts or have overhaul work done on other components until they have been thoroughly inspected. As a general rule, time is the primary cost of an overhaul, so it does not pay to fit worn or substandard parts.

As a final note, to ensure maximum life and minimum trouble from a reconditioned engine, everything must be assembled with care in a spotlessly clean environment.

3 Engine/transmission removal – methods and precautions

If you have decided that the engine must be removed for overhaul or major repair work, several preliminary steps should be taken.

Locating a suitable place to work is extremely important. Adequate work space, along with storage space for the vehicle, will be needed. If a shop or garage is not available, at the very least a flat, level, clean work surface is required.

Cleaning the engine compartment and engine/transmission before beginning the removal procedure will help keep things clean and organised.

An engine hoist or A-frame will also be necessary. Make sure the equipment is rated in excess of the combined weight of the engine and transmission. Safety is of primary importance, considering the potential hazards involved in lifting the engine/transmission unit out of the vehicle. The engine/transmission unit is removed by lifting it out from above the engine compartment.

If the engine/transmission unit is being removed by a novice, a helper should be available. Advice and aid from someone more experienced would also be helpful. There are many instances when one person cannot simultaneously perform all of the operations required when lifting the unit out of the vehicle.

Plan the operation ahead of time. Before starting work, arrange for the hire of or obtain all of the tools and equipment you will need. Some of the equipment necessary to perform engine/transmission removal and installation safely and with relative ease are (in addition to an engine hoist) a heavy duty trolley jack, complete sets of spanners and sockets as described at the front of this Manual, wooden blocks and plenty of rags and cleaning solvent for mopping up spilled oil, coolant and fuel. If the hoist must be hired, make sure that you arrange for it in advance and perform all of the operations possible without it beforehand. This will save you money and time.

Plan for the vehicle to be out of use for quite a while. An engineering works will be required to perform some of the work which the do-it-yourselfer cannot accomplish without special equipment. These places often have a busy schedule, so it would be a good idea to consult them before removing the engine in order to accurately estimate the amount of time required to rebuild or repair components that may need work.

Always be extremely careful when removing and refitting the engine/transmission unit. Serious injury can result from careless actions. Plan ahead, take your time and a job of this nature, although major, can be accomplished successfully.

4 Engine/manual transmission – removal and refitting

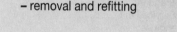

K8 engine

Note: *A suitable engine hoist and adjustable lifting tackle will be required for this operation. A new fuel rail feed pipe O-ring, and suitable silicone grease will be required on refitting.*

Removal

1 Apply the handbrake, then jack up the front of the vehicle and support securely on axle stands (see *"Jacking and Vehicle Support"*). Remove the front roadwheels.

2 Drain the engine oil and coolant, as described in Chapter 1A.

3 Drain the transmission oil as described in Chapter 7A.

4 Remove the air cleaner assembly as described in Chapter 4A.

5 Remove the engine control module (ECM) and the engine management relay module, as described in Chapter 4A.

6 Unscrew the two bolts securing the air intake resonator to the battery tray, and remove the resonator **(see illustration)**.

7 Remove the battery, with reference to Chapter 5A if necessary.

8 Remove the engine compartment fusebox as follows **(see illustrations)**.

a) *Unscrew the two bolts securing the fusebox to the body.*

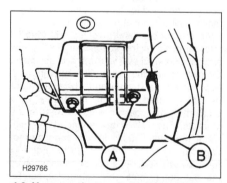

4.6 Unscrew the two bolts (A) and remove the air intake resonator (B) – K8 engine

4.8a Remove the two screws (arrowed) securing the positive leads to the fusebox – K8 engine

4.8b Disconnect the five wiring plugs (arrowed) from the fusebox – K8 engine

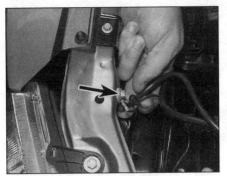

4.14 Unscrew the bolt (arrowed) securing the earth lead to the body front panel

b) *Release the clip and remove the fusebox cover.*
c) *Release the two securing clips and remove the fusebox inner cover.*
d) *Remove the two screws securing the positive leads to the fusebox.*
e) *Disconnect the five wiring plugs from the connectors on the fusebox, then remove the fusebox.*

9 Unscrew the four upper bolts and the three lower bolts securing the battery tray, then remove the battery tray.
10 Slacken the hose clip and disconnect the radiator top hose from the coolant outlet elbow on the engine.
11 Similarly, disconnect the heater coolant hose from the coolant outlet elbow, then move the hose to one side.
12 Slacken the hose clip and disconnect the radiator bottom hose from the coolant rail at the left-hand end of the engine.
13 Disconnect the clutch cable from the clutch release lever, with reference to Chapter 6 if necessary, then release the cable from the transmission bracket, and move the cable to one side.
14 Unscrew the bolt securing the earth lead to the body front panel **(see illustration)**.
15 Disconnect the wiring plug from the radiator cooling fan.
16 Working under the fusebox location on the left-hand side of the engine compartment, push the locking clip, and separate the two halves of the cylindrical engine wiring harness connector **(see illustration)**.

4.17 Oxygen sensor wiring connector location (arrowed) – K8 engine

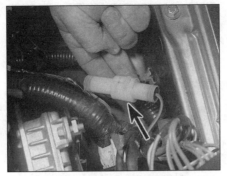

4.16 Main engine wiring harness connector (arrowed) – K8 engine

17 Trace the wiring back from the oxygen sensor, and separate the two halves of the wiring connector, then disconnect the exhaust front section from the manifold, as described in Chapter 4A **(see illustration)**.
18 Disconnect the throttle cable, and release the cable from the bracket on the throttle body/inlet manifold, as described in Chapter 4A.
19 Remove the charcoal canister as described in Chapter 4C.
20 Release the locking collar, and disconnect the brake servo vacuum hose from the inlet manifold.
21 Disconnect the engine control module (ECM) vacuum pipe from the inlet manifold.
22 Slacken the hose clip and disconnect the coolant hose from the inlet manifold.
23 Similarly, disconnect the coolant hose from the thermostat housing.
24 Disconnect the three engine wiring harness connectors from the main wiring harness at the bracket on the engine compartment bulkhead **(see illustration)**.
25 Disconnect the wiring plug from the fuel cut-off inertia switch on the engine compartment bulkhead, next to the brake vacuum servo, and release the wiring from the locating clip.
26 Slacken the hose clip and disconnect the

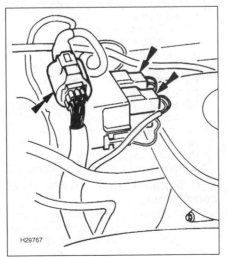

4.24 Engine wiring harness connector locations (arrowed) – K8 engine

coolant hose from the thermostat housing at the right-hand end of the engine, behind the rear timing belt cover.
27 Place a wad of absorbent cloth around the fuel filter outlet union, at the top of the filter, then slowly slacken the fuel pipe union (counterhold the union on the filter using a second spanner) to relieve the pressure in the fuel system. Be prepared for fuel spillage. Re-tighten the union once the fuel pressure has been relieved.
28 Similarly, place a wad of rag around the fuel rail feed pipe union. Unscrew the two securing bolts, then disconnect the fuel feed pipe from the fuel rail. Be prepared for fuel spillage, and take adequate fire precautions. Plug the open ends of the pipe and the fuel rail to prevent dirt entry and further fuel loss. Recover and discard the O-ring.
29 Slacken the hose clip, and disconnect the fuel return hose from the fuel rail. Again, be prepared for fuel spillage, and plug the open ends of the hose and fuel rail. Release the return hose from the clips under the inlet manifold, and move the hose to one side, clear of the engine.
30 Disconnect both driveshafts from the transmission, as described in Chapter 8. Note that there is no need to disconnect the driveshafts from the hubs. Support the driveshafts using wire or string, to avoid placing any strain on the driveshaft joints or gaiters.
31 Using a large flat-bladed screwdriver, carefully prise the gear linkage rod balljoints from the gear selector levers on the transmission, taking care not to damage the balljoints or their gaiters.
32 It is now necessary to make up two suitable engine lifting brackets. The brackets should be made from steel plate, and must be sufficiently strong to carry the combined load of the engine and transmission.
33 The lifting brackets can be attached to the cylinder head using the tapped holes provided at the right-hand rear (above the dipstick tube), and at the left-hand front (behind the HT lead clips) **(see illustrations)**. Make sure that the lifting brackets are securely bolted into position, but take care not to overtighten the securing bolts.

2C

4.33a Left-hand engine lifting bracket bolt location (arrowed) – K8 engine

4.33b Right-hand engine lifting bracket bolt location (arrowed) – K8 engine

4.38 Unscrew the through-bolt (arrowed) securing the right-hand engine mounting to the body – K8 engine

34 Connect an engine hoist and lifting tackle to the engine lifting brackets. The lifting tackle should be adjustable to enable the engine/transmission assembly to be tilted during the removal procedure. Raise the host to just take the weight of the engine.

35 Make a final check to ensure that all relevant pipes, hoses and wires have been disconnected and moved clear to allow removal of the engine/transmission assembly.

36 Working under the vehicle, slacken the through-bolt securing the engine/transmission steady bar to the subframe, then unscrew the bolt securing the steady bar to the transmission, and move the steady bar clear of the transmission.

37 Remove the left-hand engine/transmission mounting as described in Part A of this Chapter.

38 Unscrew the through-bolt securing the right-hand engine mounting to the body **(see illustration)**.

39 Adjust the lifting tackle to tilt the engine/transmission assembly, with the transmission as low as possible.

40 With the aid of an assistant, raise the hoist to manoeuvre the engine/transmission assembly out from the engine compartment. **Caution: Take care not to damage surrounding components as the assembly is removed.**

41 Lower the assembly to the ground, or onto a suitable work bench, and support the assembly on wooden blocks.

42 To separate the engine and transmission, first remove the starter motor.

43 Unbolt the flywheel front, lower and rear cover plates.

44 Ensure that the engine and transmission are adequately supported, then unscrew the four engine-to-transmission bolts.

45 Carefully withdraw the transmission from the engine (the transmission locates on dowels in the engine main bearing ladder), ensuring that the weight of the transmission is not allowed to hang on the input shaft while it is engaged with the clutch friction disc.

Refitting

46 Commence refitting by checking that the

clutch friction disc is centralised as described in Chapter 6.

47 Apply a little high melting-point grease to the splines of the transmission input shaft. Do not apply too much, as this may contaminate the clutch.

48 Ensure that the locating dowels are in place in the engine main bearing ladder, then carefully offer the transmission to the engine, until the locating dowels are engaged, ensuring that the weight of the transmission is not allowed to hang on the input shaft as it is engaged with the clutch friction disc.

49 Refit the engine-to-transmission bolts, and tighten them securely.

50 Further refitting is a reversal of removal, bearing in mind the following points.

a) Tighten all fixings to the specified torque setting, where applicable.

b) Make sure that all pipes, hoses and wires are correctly reconnected and routed as noted before removal.

c) Unbolt the engine lifting brackets once the engine/transmission assembly is in place and supported by the engine/transmission mountings.

d) Reconnect the driveshafts to the transmission as described in Chapter 8.

e) Use a new O-ring when reconnecting the fuel rail feed pipe, and lubricate the O-ring with a little silicone grease.

f) Reconnect and adjust the throttle cable as described in Chapter 4A.

g) Reconnect the exhaust front section to the manifold with reference to Chapter 4A.

h) Reconnect the clutch cable as described in Chapter 6.

i) Refill the transmission with oil as described in Chapter 7A.

j) Refill the cooling system, and refill the engine with oil as described in Chapter 1A.

K16 engine – models without air conditioning

Note: *A suitable engine hoist and adjustable lifting tackle will be required for this operation. A new power steering pump outlet pipe O-ring and, on 1.8 litre models, a new gear selector rod-to-selector shaft roll-pin will be required on refitting.*

Removal

51 Proceed as described in paragraphs 1 to 7.

52 Remove the engine compartment fusebox as follows.

a) Unscrew the bolt securing the fusebox to the body, and the bolt securing the fusebox to the battery tray.

b) Release the clip and remove the fusebox cover.

c) Release the two securing clips and remove the fusebox inner cover.

d) Remove the two screws securing the positive leads to the fusebox.

e) Disconnect the five wiring plugs from the connectors on the fusebox, then remove the fusebox.

53 Where applicable, release the ABS fuseholder from the battery tray, then unscrew the four upper bolts and the three lower bolts securing the battery tray, and remove the battery tray.

54 Proceed as described in paragraphs 10 to 16.

55 Remove the exhaust front section as described in Chapter 4A.

56 Proceed as described in paragraphs 18 to 26, noting that there are four engine wiring harness connectors which must be disconnected from the main wiring harness at the bulkhead bracket.

57 Place a wad of absorbent cloth around the fuel filter outlet union, at the top of the filter, then slowly slacken the fuel pipe union (counterhold the union on the filter using a second spanner) to relieve the pressure in the fuel system. Be prepared for fuel spillage. Disconnect the outlet pipe from the filter, and move it to one side. Plug the open ends of the pipe and filter to prevent dirt entry and further fuel loss.

58 Slacken the hose clip, and disconnect the fuel return hose from the fuel rail. Again, be prepared for fuel spillage, and plug the open ends of the hose and fuel rail. Move the hose to one side, clear of the engine.

59 Slacken the hose clip and disconnect the coolant feed hose from the expansion tank.

60 Place a suitable container beneath the power steering pump to catch escaping fluid, then slacken the hose clip, and disconnect the fluid inlet hose from the power steering pump. Plug the open ends of the hose and pump to prevent dirt entry and further fluid loss.

61 Unscrew the bolt securing the power steering pump fluid outlet hose to the locating bracket, then unscrew the outlet pipe union (counterhold the union on the pump using a second spanner), and disconnect the outlet pipe from the pump. Recover the O-ring and discard it. Plug the open ends of the pipe and pump.

62 Disconnect both driveshafts from the transmission, as described in Chapter 8. Note that there is no need to disconnect the driveshafts from the hubs.

4.64a Unscrewing the bolt securing the gearchange steady bar to the transmission

4.64b Driving out the roll-pin securing the gear selector rod to the selector shaft

63 On 1.4 and 1.6 litre models, using a large flat-bladed screwdriver, carefully prise the gear linkage rod balljoints from the gear selector levers on the transmission, taking care not to damage the balljoints or their gaiters.

64 On 1.8 litre models, proceed as follows **(see illustrations)**.

a) *Unscrew the bolt securing the gearchange steady bar to the transmission. Recover the two washers.*

b) *Remove the metal clip from the gear selector rod-to-selector shaft joint to expose the roll-pin.*

c) *Drive out the roll-pin using a suitable pin punch, then release the selector rod from the selector shaft, and suspend the rod and the gearchange steady bar clear of the working area.*

65 It is now necessary to make up two suitable engine lifting brackets. The brackets should be made from steel plate, and must be sufficiently strong to carry the combined load of the engine and transmission.

66 The right-hand lifting bracket can be attached to the cylinder head using the tapped hole provided at the right-hand rear (above the dipstick tube). To secure the left-hand end lifting bracket, remove one of the bolts from the exhaust camshaft cover plate, and use the cover plate bolts to secure the lifting bracket **(see illustrations)**. Make sure that the lifting brackets are securely bolted into position, but take care not to overtighten the securing bolts.

67 Connect an engine hoist and lifting tackle to the engine lifting brackets. The lifting tackle should be adjustable to enable the engine/transmission assembly to be tilted during the removal procedure. Raise the host to just take the weight of the engine.

68 Make a final check to ensure that all relevant pipes, hoses and wires have been disconnected and moved clear to allow removal of the engine/transmission assembly.

69 Working under the vehicle, slacken the through-bolt securing the engine/transmission steady bar to the subframe, then unscrew the bolt securing the steady bar to transmission, or the bracket on the sump (as applicable).

70 Remove the right-hand and left-hand engine mountings, as described in Part A of this Chapter.

71 Adjust the lifting tackle to tilt the engine/transmission assembly, with the transmission as low as possible.

72 With the aid of an assistant, raise the hoist to manoeuvre the engine/transmission assembly out from the engine compartment. Take care not to damage surrounding components (particularly the brake pipes/ABS modulator pipes, as applicable), as the assembly is removed.

73 Lower the assembly to the ground, or onto a suitable work bench, and support the assembly on wooden blocks.

74 To separate the engine and transmission, first remove the starter motor.

75 On 1.4 and 1.6 litre models, proceed as follows.

a) *Unbolt the flywheel front, lower and rear cover plates.*

b) *Ensure that the engine and transmission are adequately supported, then unscrew the four engine-to-transmission bolts.*

76 On 1.8 litre models, proceed as follows.

a) *Unscrew the two upper engine-to-transmission bolts, and remove the mounting bracket.*

b) *Unscrew the two lower engine-to-transmission bolts.*

c) *Unscrew the bolt at the rear of the engine, securing the engine to the transmission.*

d) *Unscrew the two nuts and bolts securing the flywheel cover plate, then remove the cover plate, then unscrew the remaining transmission-to-engine nut and bolt.*

77 Carefully withdraw the transmission from the engine (the transmission locates on dowels in the engine main bearing ladder), ensuring that the weight of the transmission is not allowed to hang on the input shaft while it is engaged with the clutch friction disc.

Refitting

78 Proceed as described in paragraphs 46 to 49.

79 Further refitting is a reversal of removal, bearing in mind the following points.

a) *Tighten all fixings to the specified torque setting, where applicable.*

b) *Make sure that all pipes, hoses and wires are correctly reconnected and routed as noted before removal.*

c) *Refit the right-hand and left-hand engine mountings as described in Part A of this Chapter.*

d) *Unbolt the engine lifting brackets once the engine/transmission assembly is in place and supported by the engine/transmission mountings. Thoroughly clean the exhaust camshaft rear cover plate before refitting.*

e) *On 1.8 litre models, use a new roll-pin when reconnecting the gear selector rod to the selector shaft.*

f) *Reconnect the driveshafts to the transmission as described in Chapter 8.*

g) *Use a new O-ring when reconnecting the power steering pump outlet pipe.*

h) *Reconnect and adjust the throttle cable as described in Chapter 4A.*

i) *Refit the exhaust front section as described in Chapter 4A.*

j) *Reconnect the clutch cable as described in Chapter 6.*

k) *Refill the transmission with oil as described in Chapter 7A.*

l) *Refill the cooling system, and refill the engine with oil as described in Chapter 1A.*

K16 engine – models with air conditioning
Removal

Note: *The air conditioning system must be discharged bay a Rover dealer or a qualified air conditioning specialist. Do not attempt to*

4.66a Left-hand engine lifting bracket bolt location (arrowed) – K16 engine

4.66b Right-hand engine lifting bracket bolt location (arrowed) – K16 engine

2C

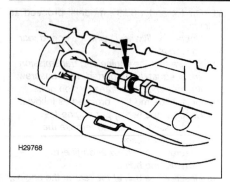

4.83 Slacken the union nut (arrowed) and disconnect the air conditioning compressor pipe from the evaporator pipe

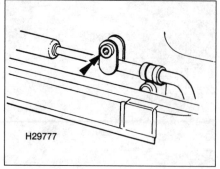

4.84 Unscrew the bolt (arrowed) securing the compressor pipe to the condenser pipe

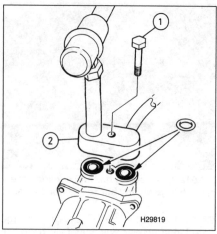

4.85 Unscrew the bolt (1) securing the air conditioning refrigerant pipe union (2) to the compressor

discharge the system yourself – refer to Chapter 3 for precautions to be observed when working on the air conditioning system components. During this procedure, all air conditioning refrigerant pipes and connections should be plugged immediately after disconnection to prevent dirt and moisture from entering the system. A suitable engine hoist and adjustable lifting tackle will be required for this operation. A new power steering pump outlet pipe O-ring, and new air conditioning refrigerant pipe O-rings will be required on refitting. On 1.8 litre models, a new gear selector rod-to-selector shaft roll-pin will be required.

80 Have the air conditioning system refrigerant discharged by a Rover dealer or an air conditioning system specialist.

81 Proceed as described in paragraphs 51 to 61.

82 Unscrew the bolt securing the air conditioning refrigerant pipe to the bracket on the flywheel housing.

83 Slacken the union nut (counterhold the union using a second spanner), and disconnect the air conditioning compressor pipe from the evaporator pipe **(see illustration)**. Recover the O-ring from the compressor pipe and discard it. Position the compressor pipe to one side, clear of the engine. Plug the open ends of the pipes.

84 Unscrew the bolt securing the compressor pipe to the condenser pipe, then release the compressor pipe from the condenser pipe **(see illustration)**. Recover the O-ring from the condenser pipe and discard it. Plug the open ends of the pipes.

85 Unscrew the bolt securing the air conditioning refrigerant pipe union to the compressor, then release the pipe union from the compressor **(see illustration)**. Withdraw the air conditioning refrigerant pipes, then remove the two O-rings from the compressor and discard them. Plug the open ends of the pipes and the compressor.

86 Proceed as described in paragraphs 62 to 77.

Refitting

87 Proceed as described in paragraphs 78 and 79, noting the following additional points.

a) Renew all O-rings when reconnecting the air conditioning refrigerant pipes. The new O-rings should be lubricated with fresh air conditioning refrigerant before fitting.

b) On completion, have the air conditioning system recharged with refrigerant by a Rover dealer or a qualified air conditioning specialist.

5 Engine/automatic transmission – removal and refitting

Models without air conditioning

Removal

Note: The following procedure is similar to that described in Section 4 for models with manual transmission – refer to the illustrations in Section 4 for guidance during the following procedure. A suitable engine hoist and adjustable lifting tackle will be required for this operation. A new power steering pump outlet pipe O-ring, and new transmission fluid oil cooler pipe O-rings will be required on refitting.

1 Apply the handbrake, then jack up the front of the vehicle and support securely on axle stands (see "Jacking and Vehicle Support"). Remove the front roadwheels.

2 Drain the engine oil and coolant, as described in Chapter 1A.

3 Drain the transmission oil as described in Chapter 1A.

4 Remove the air cleaner assembly as described in Chapter 4A.

5 Remove the engine control module (ECM) and the engine management relay module, as described in Chapter 4A.

6 Unscrew the two bolts securing the air intake resonator to the battery tray, and remove the resonator.

7 Remove the battery, with reference to Chapter 5A if necessary.

8 Remove the engine compartment fusebox as follows.

a) Unscrew the bolt securing the fusebox to the body, and the bolt securing the fusebox to the battery tray.

b) Release the clip and remove the fusebox cover.

c) Release the two securing clips and remove the fusebox inner cover.

d) Remove the two screws securing the positive leads to the fusebox.

e) Disconnect the five wiring plugs from the connectors on the fusebox, then remove the fusebox.

9 Where applicable, release the ABS fuseholder from the battery tray, then unscrew the four upper bolts and the three lower bolts securing the battery tray, and remove the battery tray.

10 Slacken the hose clip and disconnect the radiator top hose from the coolant outlet elbow on the engine.

11 Similarly, disconnect the heater coolant hose from the coolant outlet elbow, then move the hose to one side.

12 Slacken the hose clip and disconnect the radiator bottom hose from the coolant rail at the left-hand end of the engine.

13 Unscrew the bolt securing the earth lead to the body front panel.

14 Disconnect the wiring plug from the radiator cooling fan.

15 Working under the fusebox location on the left-hand side of the engine compartment, push the locking clip, and separate the two halves of the cylindrical engine wiring harness connector.

16 Remove the exhaust front section as described in Chapter 4A.

17 Disconnect the throttle cable, and release the cable from the bracket on the inlet manifold/throttle body, as described in Chapter 4A.

18 Remove the charcoal canister as described in Chapter 4C.

19 Release the locking collar, and disconnect the brake servo vacuum hose from the inlet manifold.

20 Disconnect the engine control module (ECM) vacuum pipe from the inlet manifold.

21 Slacken the hose clip and disconnect the coolant hose from the inlet manifold.

22 Similarly, disconnect the coolant hose from the thermostat housing.

23 Disconnect the four engine wiring harness connectors from the main wiring harness at the bracket on the engine compartment bulkhead.

24 Disconnect the wiring plug from the fuel cut-off inertia switch on the engine compartment bulkhead, next to the brake vacuum servo, and release the wiring from the locating clip.

25 Slacken the hose clip and disconnect the coolant hose from the thermostat housing at the left-hand end of the engine, behind the rear timing belt cover.

26 Place a wad of absorbent cloth around the fuel filter outlet union, at the top of the filter, then slowly slacken the fuel pipe union (counterhold the union on the filter using a second spanner) to relieve the pressure in the fuel system. Be prepared for fuel spillage. Disconnect the outlet pipe from the filter, and move it to one side. Plug the open ends of the pipe and filter to prevent dirt entry and further fuel loss.

27 Slacken the hose clip, and disconnect the fuel return hose from the fuel rail. Again, be prepared for fuel spillage, and plug the open ends of the hose and fuel rail. Move the hose to one side, clear of the engine.

28 Slacken the hose clip and disconnect the coolant feed hose from the expansion tank.

29 Place a suitable container beneath the power steering pump to catch escaping fluid, then slacken the hose clip, and disconnect the fluid inlet hose from the power steering pump. Plug the open ends of the hose and pump to prevent dirt entry and further fluid loss.

30 Unscrew the bolt securing the power steering pump fluid outlet hose to the locating bracket, then unscrew the outlet pipe union (counterhold the union on the pump using a second spanner), and disconnect the outlet pipe from the pump. Recover the O-ring and discard it. Plug the open ends of the pipe and pump.

31 Disconnect the selector cable from the transmission, as described in Chapter 7B.

32 Slacken the two unions, and disconnect the transmission fluid cooler pipes from the transmission. Recover and discard the union O-rings.

33 Disconnect both driveshafts from the transmission, as described in Chapter 8. Note that there is no need to disconnect the driveshafts from the hubs.

34 It is now necessary to make up two suitable engine lifting brackets. The brackets should be made from steel plate, and must be sufficiently strong to carry the combined load of the engine and transmission.

35 The lifting brackets can be attached to the cylinder head using the tapped hole provided at the right-hand rear (above the dipstick tube). To secure the left-hand end lifting bracket, unbolt the cover plate from the rear of the exhaust camshaft, and use the two cover plate bolts to secure the lifting bracket. Make sure that the lifting brackets are securely bolted into position, but take care not to overtighten the securing bolts.

36 Connect an engine hoist and lifting tackle to the engine lifting brackets. The lifting tackle should be adjustable to enable the engine/transmission assembly to be tilted during the removal procedure. Raise the host to just take the weight of the engine.

37 Make a final check to ensure that all relevant pipes, hoses and wires have been disconnected and moved clear to allow removal of the engine/transmission assembly.

38 Working under the vehicle, slacken the through-bolt securing the engine/transmission steady bar to the subframe, then unscrew the bolt securing the steady bar to the transmission, or the bracket on the sump (as applicable).

39 Remove the right-hand and left-hand engine mountings, as described in Part A of this Chapter.

40 Adjust the lifting tackle to tilt the engine/transmission assembly, with the transmission as low as possible.

41 With the aid of an assistant, raise the hoist to manoeuvre the engine/transmission assembly out from the engine compartment.

Caution: Take care not to damage surrounding components (particularly the brake pipes/ABS modulator pipes, as applicable), as the assembly is removed.

42 To separate the engine and transmission, first remove the starter motor.

43 Unbolt the flywheel rear cover plate.

44 Ensure that the engine and transmission are adequately supported, then unscrew the four engine-to-transmission bolts.

45 Carefully withdraw the transmission from the engine (the transmission locates on dowels in the engine main bearing ladder), ensuring that the weight of the transmission is not allowed to hang on the input shaft while it is engaged with the flywheel torsion damper.

Refitting

46 Ensure that the locating dowels are in place in the engine main bearing ladder, then carefully offer the transmission to the engine, until the locating dowels are engaged, ensuring that the weight of the transmission is not allowed to hang on the input shaft as it is engaged with the flywheel torsion damper. **Do not** grease the splines of the input shaft.

47 Refit the engine-to-transmission bolts, and tighten them securely.

48 Further refitting is a reversal of removal, bearing in mind the following points.

a) *Tighten all fixings to the specified torque setting, where applicable.*

b) *Make sure that all pipes, hoses and wires are correctly reconnected and routed as noted before removal.*

c) *Refit the right-hand and left-hand engine mountings as described in Part A of this Chapter.*

d) *Unbolt the engine lifting brackets once the engine/transmission assembly is in place and supported by the engine/transmission mountings. Thoroughly clean the exhaust camshaft rear cover plate before refitting.*

e) *Reconnect the driveshafts to the transmission as described in Chapter 8.*

f) *Use new O-rings when reconnecting the transmission fluid cooler pipes.*

g) *Reconnect the selector cable to the transmission, and adjust if necessary, as described in Chapter 7B.*

h) *Use a new O-ring when reconnecting the power steering pump outlet pipe.*

i) *Reconnect and adjust the throttle cable as described in Chapter 4A.*

j) *Refit the exhaust front section as described in Chapter 4A.*

k) *Refill the transmission with oil as described in Chapter 1A.*

l) *Refill the cooling system, and refill the engine with oil as described in Chapter 1A.*

Models with air conditioning

Removal

Note: *The air conditioning system must be discharged by a Rover dealer or a qualified air conditioning specialist. Do not attempt to discharge the system yourself – refer to Chapter 3 for precautions to be observed when working on the air conditioning system components. During this procedure, all air conditioning refrigerant pipes and connections should be plugged immediately after disconnection to prevent dirt and moisture from entering the system. A new power steering pump outlet pipe O-ring, new air conditioning refrigerant pipe O-rings, and new automatic transmission fluid cooler pipe O-rings will be required on refitting.*

49 Have the air conditioning system refrigerant discharged by a Rover dealer or an air conditioning system specialist.

50 Proceed as described in paragraphs 1 to 30.

51 Unscrew the bolt securing the air conditioning refrigerant pipe to the bracket on the flywheel housing.

52 Slacken the union nut (counterhold the union using a second spanner), and disconnect the air conditioning compressor pipe from the evaporator pipe. Recover the O-ring from the compressor pipe and discard it. Position the compressor pipe to one side, clear of the engine. Plug the open ends of the pipes.

53 Unscrew the bolt securing the compressor pipe to the condenser pipe, then release the compressor pipe from the condenser pipe. Recover the O-ring from the condenser pipe and discard it. Plug the open ends of the pipes.

54 Unscrew the bolt securing the air conditioning refrigerant pipe union to the compressor, then release the pipe union from the compressor. Withdraw the air conditioning

2C

refrigerant pipes, then remove the two O-rings from the compressor and discard them. Plug the open ends of the pipes and the compressor.

55 Proceed as described in paragraphs 31 to 45, but additionally, note the location of the air conditioning refrigerant pipe bracket on one of the engine-to-transmission bolts.

Refitting

56 Proceed as described in paragraphs 46 to 48, noting the following additional points.

a) Make sure that the refrigerant pipe bracket is in position on the engine-to-transmission bolt as noted before removal.

b) Renew all O-rings when reconnecting the air conditioning refrigerant pipes. The new O-rings should be lubricated with fresh air conditioning refrigerant before fitting.

c) On completion, have the air conditioning system recharged with refrigerant by a Rover dealer or a qualified air conditioning specialist.

6 Engine overhaul – dismantling sequence

Note: When removing external components from the engine, pay close attention to details that may be helpful or important during refitting. Note the fitted position of gaskets, seals, spacers, pins, washers, bolts and other small items.

1 It is much easier to work on the engine if it is mounted on a portable engine stand. These stands can often be hired from a tool hire shop. Before the engine is mounted on a stand, the flywheel should be removed so that the stand bolts can be tightened into the end of the cylinder block/crankcase (**not** the main bearing ladder).

2 If a stand is not available, it is possible to dismantle the engine with it blocked up on a sturdy workbench or on the floor. Be extra careful not to tip or drop the engine when working without a stand.

3 If you are going to obtain a reconditioned engine, all external components must be removed for transfer to the replacement engine (just as if you are doing a complete engine overhaul yourself). These components include the following:

a) Alternator mounting brackets.
b) Power steering pump and air conditioning compressor brackets (where fitted).
c) Distributor components, HT leads and spark plugs.
d) Thermostat and housing, coolant rail, coolant outlet elbow.
e) Dipstick tube.
f) Fuel injection system components.
g) All electrical switches and sensors.
h) Inlet and exhaust manifolds.
i) Oil filter.
j) Engine mountings.
k) Flywheel.

4 If you are obtaining a short motor (which consists of the engine cylinder block/crankcase and main bearing ladder, crankshaft, pistons and connecting rods all assembled), then the cylinder head, sump, oil pump, and timing belt will have to be removed also.

5 If you are planning a complete overhaul, the engine can be dismantled and the internal components removed in the following order:

a) Inlet and exhaust manifolds.
b) Timing belt, sprockets, tensioner and timing belt inner cover.
c) Cylinder head.
d) Flywheel.
e) Sump.
f) Oil pump.
g) Piston/connecting rod assemblies.
h) Crankshaft.

6 Before beginning the dismantling and overhaul procedures, make sure that you have all of the correct tools necessary. Refer to the introductory pages at the beginning of this Manual for further information.

7 Cylinder head – dismantling

Note: New and reconditioned cylinder heads are available from the manufacturer and from engine overhaul specialists. Due to the fact that some specialist tools are required for dismantling and inspection, and new components may not be readily available, it may be more practical and economical for the home mechanic to purchase a reconditioned head rather than dismantle, inspect and recondition the original. A valve spring compressor tool will be required for this operation.

1 With the cylinder head removed, if not already done, remove the inlet manifold as described in Chapter 4A.

2 Remove the camshaft(s) and hydraulic tappets, as described in Part A of this Chapter.

3 Using a valve spring compressor tool, compress each valve spring in turn until the split collets can be removed. Release the compressor and lift off the spring retainer and spring, then use a pair of pliers to extract the spring lower seat/stem seal (**see illustrations**).

> **HAYNES HiNT**
> If, when the valve spring compressor is screwed down, the spring retainer refuses to free and expose the split collets, gently tap the top of the tool directly over the retainer with a light hammer. This will free the retainer.

4 Withdraw the valve through the combustion chamber.

5 It is essential that each valve is stored together with its collets, retainer and spring, and that all valves are kept in their correct sequence, unless they are so badly worn that they are to be renewed. If they are going to be kept and used again, place each valve assembly in a labelled polythene bag or similar small container (**see illustration**). Note that No 1 valve is nearest to the timing belt end of the engine. On K16 engines, label the valves No 1 inlet, No 1 exhaust, etc, to avoid confusion.

8 Cylinder head and valves – cleaning and inspection

Note: If the engine has been severely overheated, it is best to assume that the cylinder head is warped and to check carefully for signs of this.

7.3a Using a valve spring compressor to release the split collets

7.3b Extracting the spring lower seat/stem seal

7.5 Use a labelled plastic bag to keep together and identify the valve components

8.6a Checking a cylinder head gasket surface for distortion

Note: Be sure to perform all the following inspection procedures before concluding that the services of a machine shop or engine overhaul specialist are required. Make a list of all items that require attention.

1 Thorough cleaning of the cylinder head and valve components, followed by a detailed inspection, will enable you to decide how much valve service work must be carried out during the engine overhaul.

Cleaning

2 Scrape away all traces of old gasket material and sealing compound from the cylinder head.

3 Scrape away all carbon from the combustion chambers and ports, then wash the cylinder head thoroughly with paraffin or a suitable solvent.

4 Scrape off any heavy carbon deposits that may have formed on the valves, then use a power-operated wire brush to remove deposits from the valve heads and stems.

Inspection

Cylinder head

5 Inspect the head very carefully for cracks, evidence of coolant leakage and other damage. If cracks are found, a new cylinder head should be obtained.

6 Use a straight-edge and feeler blade to check that the cylinder head surface is not distorted **(see illustrations)**. If it is, it may be possible to resurface it, provided that the specified reface limit is not exceeded in so doing, or that the cylinder head is not reduced to less than the specified height.

7 Examine the valve seats in each of the combustion chambers. If they are severely pitted, cracked or burned, then they will need to be renewed or re-cut by an engine overhaul specialist. If they are only slightly pitted, this can be removed by grinding-in the valve heads and seats with fine valve-grinding compound as described below. To check for excessive wear, refit each valve and measure the installed height of the stem tip above the cylinder head upper surface **(see illustration)**. If the measurement is above the specified limit, repeat the test using a new valve. If the measurement is still excessive, renew the seat insert.

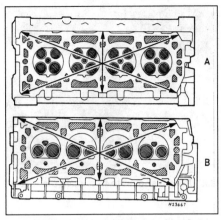

8.6b Check the cylinder head gasket surface for distortion along the paths shown

A K16 engine   B K8 engine

8 If the valve guides are worn, indicated by a side to side motion of the valve, new guides must be fitted. Measure the diameter of the existing valve stems (see below) and the bore of the guides, then calculate the clearance and compare the result with the specified value. If the clearance is excessive, renew the valves or guides as necessary.

9 Valve guide renewal is best carried out by an engine overhaul specialist. If the work is to be carried out at home, then use a stepped, double-diameter drift to drive out the worn guide towards the combustion chamber. On fitting the new guide, place it first in a deep-freeze for one hour, then drive it into the cylinder head bore from the camshaft side until it projects the specified amount above the spring lower seat/stem seal surface.

10 If the valve seats are to be re-cut, this must be done only after the guides have been renewed.

Valves

11 Examine the head of each valve for pitting, burning, cracks and general wear, then check the valve stem for scoring and wear ridges. Rotate the valve and check for any obvious indication that it is bent. Look for pits and excessive wear on the tip of each valve stem. Renew any valve that shows any such signs of wear or damage.

8.12 Measuring valve stem diameter

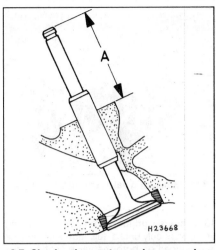

8.7 Check valve seat wear by measuring valve stem installed height (A)

12 If the valve appears satisfactory at this stage, measure the valve stem diameter at several points by using a micrometer **(see illustration)**. Any significant difference in the readings obtained indicates wear of the valve stem. Should any of these conditions be apparent, the valve(s) must be renewed.

13 If the valves are in satisfactory condition they should be ground (lapped) into their respective seats to ensure a smooth gas-tight seal. If the seat is only lightly pitted, or if it has been re-cut, fine grinding compound only should be used to produce the required finish. Coarse valve-grinding compound should not be used unless a seat is badly burned or deeply pitted. If this is the case, the cylinder head and valves should be inspected by an expert to decide whether seat re-cutting or even the renewal of the valve or seat insert is required.

14 Valve grinding is carried out as follows. Place the cylinder head upside down on a bench.

15 Smear a trace of (the appropriate grade of) valve-grinding compound on the seat face and press a suction grinding tool onto the valve head. With a semi-rotary action, grind the valve head to its seat, lifting the valve occasionally to redistribute the grinding compound **(see illustration)**. A light spring placed under the valve head will greatly ease this operation.

2C

8.15 Grinding-in a valve seat

8.19 Measuring valve spring free-length

9.2 Using a socket to fit a valve stem seal

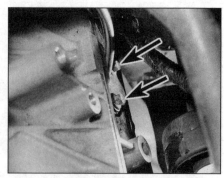

10.5a Dipstick tube retaining bolts (arrowed)

16 If coarse grinding compound is being used, work only until a dull, matt even surface is produced on both the valve seat and the valve, then wipe off the used compound and repeat the process with fine compound. When a smooth unbroken ring of light grey matt finish is produced on both the valve and seat, the grinding operation is complete. Do not grind in the valves any further than absolutely necessary, or the seat will be prematurely sunk into the cylinder head.

17 To check that the seat has not been over-ground, measure the valve stem installed height, as described in paragraph 7.

18 When all the valves have been ground-in, carefully wash off all traces of grinding compound using paraffin or a suitable solvent.

Valve components

19 Examine the valve springs for signs of damage and discoloration and also measure their free length using vernier calipers or by comparing each existing spring with a new component **(see illustration)**.

20 Stand each spring on a flat surface and check it for squareness. If any of the springs are damaged, distorted or have lost their tension, then obtain a complete new set of springs.

21 Check the hydraulic tappets as described in Part A of this Chapter.

9 Cylinder head – reassembly

Note: *A valve spring compressor tool will be required for this operation. New valve spring lower seat/stem oil seals will be required.*

1 Lubricate the valve stems with clean engine oil and insert each valve into its original location. If new valves are being fitted, insert them into the locations to which they have been ground.

2 Working on the first valve, dip the **new** spring lower seat/stem seal in clean engine oil then carefully locate it over the valve and onto the guide. Take care not to damage the seal as it is passed over the valve stem. Use a suitable socket or metal tube to press the seal firmly onto the guide **(see illustration)**.

3 Locate the spring on the seat, followed by the spring retainer.

4 Compress the valve spring and locate the split collets in the recess in the valve stem. Use a little grease to hold the collets in place. Release the compressor, then repeat the procedure on the remaining valves.

5 With all the valves installed, rest the cylinder head on wooden blocks or stands (**do not** rest the head flat on a bench) and, using a hammer and interposed block of wood, tap the end of each valve stem to settle the components.

6 Refit the hydraulic tappets and camshaft(s) as described in Part A of this Chapter.

10 Piston/connecting rod assembly – removal

Note: *Due to the design of the engine, it will become very difficult, almost impossible, to turn the crankshaft once the cylinder head bolts have been slackened. The manufacturer accordingly states that the crankshaft will be 'tight' and should not be rotated more than absolutely necessary once the head has been removed. If the crankshaft cannot be rotated, then it must be removed for overhaul work to proceed. With this in mind, during any servicing or overhaul work the crankshaft must always be rotated to the desired position before the bolts are disturbed. Whenever the piston/connecting rod assemblies are removed, the cylinder liners should be removed and re-sealed as a precaution against leakage after reassembly (see Section 13).*

Removal - without removing crankshaft

1 Remove the timing belt, the camshaft sprocket(s) and timing belt tensioner, and the timing belt rear cover, as described in Part A of this Chapter.

2 Remove the camshaft(s) and hydraulic tappets, as described in Part A of this Chapter.

3 If not already done, rotate the crankshaft (if

necessary temporarily refit the crankshaft pulley bolt and use a spanner or socket to turn the crankshaft) through a quarter-turn clockwise, until Nos 1 and 4 cylinder pistons are at TDC (No 1 piston should have been positioned 90° BTDC to remove the timing belt).

4 Remove the cylinder head, as described in Part A of this Chapter. The crankshaft cannot now be rotated. Note that there is no need to fit cylinder liner clamps, as the cylinder liners should be removed and re-sealed whenever the piston/connecting rod assemblies are removed.

5 Slacken and remove the two dipstick tube retaining bolts and remove the tube from the cylinder block/crankcase **(see illustrations)**.

6 Remove the sump and unbolt the oil pump pick-up/strainer pipe from the oil rail, as described in Part A of this Chapter.

7 Unscrew the two retaining nuts and remove the oil rail **(see illustration)**.

8 Using a hammer and centre punch, paint or similar, mark each connecting rod big-end bearing cap with its respective cylinder number on the flat, machined surface provided. If the engine has been dismantled before, note carefully any identifying marks made previously **(see illustration)**. Note that No 1 cylinder is at the timing belt end of the engine.

9 Unscrew and remove the No 2 cylinder big-end bearing cap bolts and withdraw the cap, complete with bearing shell, from the connecting rod. If only the bearing shells are being attended to, push the connecting rod up and off the crankpin, ensuring that the connecting rod big-ends do not mark the cylinder bore walls, then remove the upper bearing shell. Keep the cap, bolts and (if they are to be refitted) the bearing shells together in their correct sequence. Repeat the procedure to disconnect No 3 cylinder big-end.

10 With Nos 2 and 3 cylinder big-ends disconnected, repeat the procedure (exercising great care to prevent damage to any of the components) to disconnect Nos 1 and 4 cylinder big-ends.

11 Remove the ridge of carbon from the top of each cylinder bore. Push each

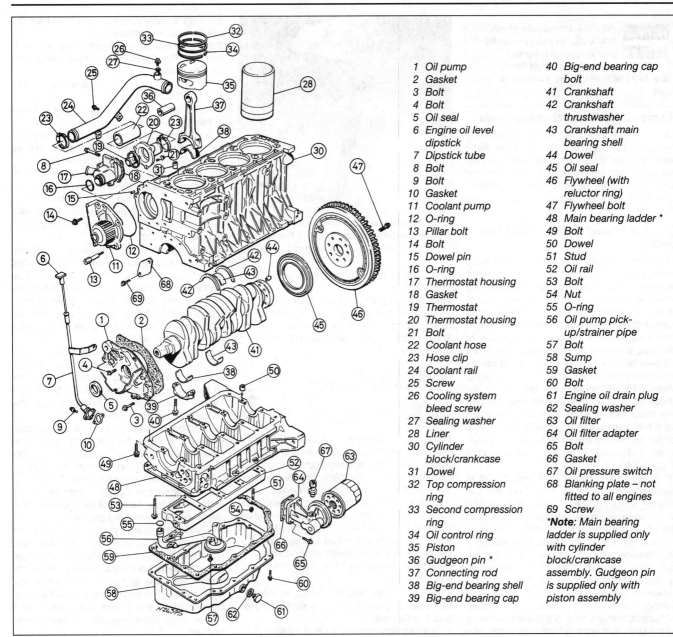

1 Oil pump	40 Big-end bearing cap bolt
2 Gasket	41 Crankshaft
3 Bolt	42 Crankshaft thrustwasher
4 Bolt	43 Crankshaft main bearing shell
5 Oil seal	44 Dowel
6 Engine oil level dipstick	45 Oil seal
7 Dipstick tube	46 Flywheel (with reluctor ring)
8 Bolt	47 Flywheel bolt
9 Bolt	48 Main bearing ladder *
10 Gasket	49 Bolt
11 Coolant pump	50 Dowel
12 O-ring	51 Stud
13 Pillar bolt	52 Oil rail
14 Bolt	53 Bolt
15 Dowel pin	54 Nut
16 O-ring	55 O-ring
17 Thermostat housing	56 Oil pump pick-up/strainer pipe
18 Gasket	57 Bolt
19 Thermostat	58 Sump
20 Thermostat housing	59 Gasket
21 Bolt	60 Bolt
22 Coolant hose	61 Engine oil drain plug
23 Hose clip	62 Sealing washer
24 Coolant rail	63 Oil filter
25 Screw	64 Oil filter adapter
26 Cooling system bleed screw	65 Bolt
27 Sealing washer	66 Gasket
28 Liner	67 Oil pressure switch
30 Cylinder block/crankcase	68 Blanking plate – not fitted to all engines
31 Dowel	69 Screw
32 Top compression ring	*Note: Main bearing ladder is supplied only with cylinder block/crankcase assembly. Gudgeon pin is supplied only with piston assembly
33 Second compression ring	
34 Oil control ring	
35 Piston	
36 Gudgeon pin *	
37 Connecting rod	
38 Big-end bearing shell	
39 Big-end bearing cap	

2C

10.5b Engine bottom end components

piston/connecting rod assembly up and remove it from the top of the bore, ensuring that the connecting rod big-ends do not mark the cylinder bore walls.

12 Note that the number previously stamped on each bearing cap should match the cylinder number stamped (by the manufacturers) on each connecting rod, which can be read once the connecting rod has been removed. If the mark stamped on any connecting rod does not match its correct cylinder, mark or label the connecting rod immediately to avoid confusion, so that each piston/connecting rod assembly can be refitted to its original bore.

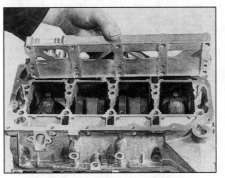

10.7 Removing the oil rail

10.8 Mark the big-end bearing caps before removal – No 4 cylinder cap shown

HAYNES HiNT *Fit the bearing cap, shells and bolts to each removed piston/connecting rod assembly, so that they are all kept together as a matched set.*

Removal - alternative methods

13 If the engine is being completely dismantled and the cylinder head has been removed, either unbolt the main bearing ladder so that the crankshaft can be rotated with care, or remove the crankshaft completely and then remove the connecting rods and pistons.

Cylinder head bolts - condition check

14 Check the condition of the cylinder head bolts, particularly their threads. (Note that if only the cylinder head has been removed, the bolts can be checked as described in Part A of this Chapter). Keeping all bolts in their correct fitted order, wash them and wipe dry. Check each bolt for any sign of visible wear or damage, renewing as necessary. Note that if cylinder head bolts have been used to secure the cylinder liner clamps, each bolt and clamp should be removed one at a time for checking, and refitted immediately the bolt has been tested. Lightly oil the threads of each bolt, carefully enter it into its original hole in the oil rail (**do not** drop the bolt into the hole), and screw it in, by hand only until finger-tight.

15 If the full length of the bolt thread is engaged with the hole in the oil rail, the bolt may be re-used. If the full length of the thread is not engaged, measure the distance from the upper surface of the oil rail to the lower surface of the bolt head (**see illustration**). If the distance measured is under 378 mm, the bolt may be re-used. If the distance measured is more than 378 mm, the bolt must be renewed. Considering the task these bolts perform and the pressures they must withstand, owners should consider renewing all the bolts as a matched set if more than one

10.15 Measure the distance from the upper surface of the oil rail to the lower surface of the bolt head

of the original bolts fail inspection or are close to the limit.

16 Note that if any of the cylinder head bolt threads in the oil rail are found to be damaged, then the oil rail must be renewed. Thread inserts are not an acceptable repair in this instance.

11 Crankshaft – removal

Note: The following procedure assumes that the crankshaft alone is being removed and therefore uses a slightly different sequence of operations to that given for the piston/connecting rod removal procedure in Section 10. Depending on the reason for dismantling, either sequence may be adapted as necessary. If the crankshaft endfloat is to be checked, this must be done when the crankshaft is free to move. If a dial gauge is to be used, check after paragraph 1, but if feeler blades are to be used, check after paragraph 10.

1 Remove the timing belt, sprockets, tensioner, and rear cover, as described in Part A of this Chapter.

2 Slacken and remove the two dipstick tube

retaining bolts and remove the tube from the cylinder block/crankcase.

3 Remove the cylinder head, as described in Part A of this Chapter. The crankshaft cannot now be rotated.

4 Remove the oil pump, as described in Part A of this Chapter.

5 Remove the flywheel as described in Part A of this Chapter.

6 Remove the sump and unbolt the oil pump pick-up/strainer pipe from the oil rail, as described in Part A of this Chapter.

7 If cylinder liner clamps have been fitted, temporarily remove them (this is necessary because the cylinder head bolts used to secure the liner clamps screw into the oil rail), then unscrew the two retaining nuts and remove the oil rail.

8 Working in the sequence shown, progressively unscrew the main bearing ladder retaining bolts by a turn at a time, then withdraw the ladder. Note the locations of the two locating dowels, and the main bearing shells, which should be removed from the ladder and stored in their correct fitted order (**see illustrations**).

9 If the cylinder liners are to be left in place in the cylinder block, refit the liner clamps, noting that suitable nuts and spacers will have to be screwed onto the lower ends of the cylinder head bolts to retain the clamps (the oil rail has now been removed).

10 Using a hammer and centre punch, paint or similar, mark each connecting rod big-end bearing cap with its respective cylinder number on the flat, machined surface provided. If the engine has been dismantled before, note carefully any identifying marks made previously. Note that No 1 cylinder is at the timing belt end of the engine.

11 Working on each cylinder in turn, unscrew and remove the big-end bearing cap bolts and withdraw the cap, complete with the lower bearing shell (**see illustration**). Push the connecting rods up and off their crankpins, then remove the upper bearing shells. Keep the cap, bolts and (if they are to be refitted) the bearing shells together in their correct sequence.

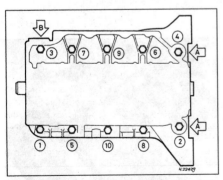

11.8a Crankshaft main bearing ladder bolt slackening sequence

A Bolts hidden in ladder flanges
B Location of single longer bolt

11.8b Removing the main bearing ladder – locating dowels arrowed

11.11 Removing No 1 cylinder big-end bearing cap and lower bearing shell

11.12 Lifting out the crankshaft

12 Carefully lift out the crankshaft **(see illustration)**.

13 Withdraw the two thrustwashers from the No 3 main bearing location in the cylinder block.

14 Remove the upper main bearing shells from the cylinder block, noting their locations. The bearing shells must be kept in order, along with the lower bearing shells, so that they can be refitted (if applicable) in their original locations.

15 Check the condition of the cylinder head bolts as described in Section 10.

12 Cylinder block/crankcase – cleaning and inspection

Note: *During any cleaning operations, take care not to score the mating surfaces of the cylinder block/crankcase, bearing ladder and oil rail. It may be necessary to use a foam action gasket remover.*

Cleaning

1 For complete cleaning, remove the cylinder liners, all external components and all electrical switches/sensors.

2 Scrape all traces of gasket from the cylinder block/crankcase, bearing ladder and oil rail, taking care not to damage the gasket/sealing surfaces.

3 Remove all oil gallery plugs (where fitted). The plugs are usually very tight and may have to be drilled out and the holes re-tapped. Use new plugs when the engine is reassembled.

4 If any of the castings are extremely dirty, all should be steam-cleaned.

5 After the castings have been steam-cleaned, clean all oil holes and oil galleries one more time. Flush all internal passages with warm water until the water runs clear, then dry thoroughly and apply a light film of oil to all mating faces and to the liner surfaces to prevent rusting. If you have access to compressed air, use it to speed up the drying process and to blow out all the oil holes and galleries.

 Warning: Wear eye protection when using compressed air!

6 If the castings are not very dirty, you can do an adequate cleaning job with hot soapy water and a stiff brush. Take plenty of time and do a thorough job. Regardless of the cleaning method used, be sure to clean all oil holes and galleries very thoroughly and to dry all components well. Protect the liners as described previously to prevent rusting.

7 All threaded holes must be clean to ensure accurate torque readings during reassembly. To clean all threads, run the proper size tap into each of the holes to remove rust, corrosion, thread sealant or sludge, and to restore damaged threads. If possible, use compressed air to clear the holes of debris produced by this operation. A good alternative is to inject aerosol-applied water-dispersant lubricant into each hole, using the long spout usually supplied. Always wear eye protection when cleaning out holes in this way. After cleaning, ensure that all threaded holes in the cylinder block are dry. If not already done, now is a good time to check the condition of the cylinder head bolts, as described in Section 10.

8 Apply suitable sealant to the new oil gallery plugs, and insert them into the holes in the block. Tighten them securely.

9 If the engine is not going to be reassembled right away, cover it with a large plastic bag to keep it clean. Protect the cylinder liners as described previously to prevent rusting.

Inspection

10 Inspect all castings for cracks and corrosion. Look for stripped threads. If there has been any history of internal coolant leakage, it may be worthwhile having an engine overhaul specialist check the cylinder block/crankcase with special equipment. If defects are found, have them repaired, if possible, or renew the assembly.

11 Check the bore of each cylinder liner for scuffing and scoring. If the cylinder liner walls are badly scuffed or scored, obtain new cylinder liners.

12 Measure the diameter of each cylinder liner bore 65 mm from the top of the bore, both parallel to the crankshaft axis and at right angles to it. Compare the diameter with that specified. If any measurement exceeds the service limit, then the liner must be renewed.

13 To measure the piston-to-bore clearance, either measure the relevant cylinder liner bore (as described above) and piston skirt (as described in Section 14) and subtract the skirt diameter from the bore measurement, or insert each piston into the original cylinder liner bore, select a feeler blade and slip it into the bore along with the piston. The piston must be aligned exactly in its normal attitude and the feeler blade must be between the piston and bore on one of the thrust faces, 20 mm from the bottom of the bore.

14 If the piston-to-bore clearance is excessive, new cylinder liners and corresponding pistons will be required. If the

piston binds at the lower end of the bore and is loose towards the top, then the bore is tapered. If tight spots are encountered as the piston/feeler blade is rotated in the bore, then the bore is out-of-round. In either case, new liners and pistons will be required.

15 Repeat the checking procedure for the remaining pistons and cylinder liners.

16 If the bores are in reasonably good condition and not worn to the specified limits, and if the piston-to-bore clearances can be maintained properly, then it may only be necessary to renew the piston rings. In this case, **do not** attempt to hone the cylinder liner bores to allow the new rings to bed-in.

13 Cylinder liners – removal and refitting

Removal

Note: *If desired, the cylinder liners can be removed with the main bearing ladder and the crankshaft fitted. "Hylomar" or a suitable equivalent sealant will be required on refitting.*

1 With the pistons removed, if not already done, remove the cylinder liner clamps.

2 If the original liners are to be refitted, make alignment marks between each liner and the cylinder block to ensure that each liner can be refitted in its exact original position. Use a felt-tipped pen or paint to make the marks – **do not** etch or stamp the liners.

3 Lay the cylinder block on its side, then use hand pressure to push the cylinder liners out from the top of the cylinder block. If the liners are to be re-used, mark each one using a piece of masking tape and writing the cylinder number on the tape.

Refitting

Note: *To enable cylinder liner retaining clamps to be fitted when the liners are fitted to the cylinder block, the crankshaft and main bearing ladder must be fitted to the cylinder block.*

4 If not already done, fit the crankshaft and main bearing ladder, as described in Section 19.

5 Support the cylinder block upright on blocks of wood.

6 If not already done, thoroughly clean the cylinder liner mating faces of the cylinder block, and clean away all traces of the cylinder liner sealant. If the original liners are to be refitted, also clean all sealant from the liners, and clean the liner mating faces, taking care not to remove the alignment and identification marks made during removal.

7 Ensure that the cylinder block and liners are dry.

8 Working on the first liner to be refitted, apply a continuous 2 mm bead of "Hylomar" (or a suitable equivalent) sealant around the

2C

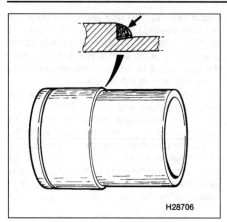

13.8 Apply a 2 mm bead of Hylomar (or a suitable equivalent) to the shoulder (arrowed) of the cylinder liner

13.12a Rover cylinder liner clamps fitted to top face of cylinder block

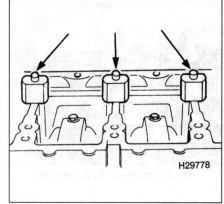

13.12b Rover cylinder liner clamps are retained by screwing the cylinder head bolts into nylon blocks underneath the cylinder block

shoulder of the cylinder liner **(see illustration)**.

9 If the original liners are being refitted, use the marks made on removal to ensure that each liner is refitted in its original bore, in its original location.

10 Insert each liner into its bore in the cylinder block/crankcase, ensuring that the liner is "square" to the bore. If the original liner is being refitted, make sure that the marks made on the liner and the cylinder block are aligned. Push the liner fully down until the shoulder on the liner seats against the cylinder block. **Do not** drop the liner into position.

11 Repeat the procedure to refit the three remaining cylinder liners.

12 Cylinder liner clamps should now be fitted to prevent the liners from being disturbed before the cylinder head is refitted. The manufacturer's liner clamps are secured by the cylinder head bolts as shown **(see illustrations)**. Equivalents can be improvised using large washers, tubular spacers and nuts.

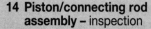

14 Piston/connecting rod assembly – inspection

Cleaning

1 Before the inspection process can begin, the piston/connecting rod assemblies must be cleaned, and the original piston rings removed from the pistons.

2 Carefully expand the old rings over the top of the pistons. The use of two or three old feeler blades will be helpful in preventing the rings dropping into empty grooves **(see illustration)**. Be careful not to scratch the piston with the ends of the ring. The rings are brittle, and will snap if they are spread too far. They are also very sharp - protect your hands

and fingers. Note that the third ring incorporates an expander. Always remove the rings from the top of the piston. Keep each set of rings with its piston if the old rings are to be re-used. Note which way up each ring is fitted to ensure correct refitting.

3 Scrape away all traces of carbon from the top of the piston. A hand-held wire brush (or a piece of fine emery cloth) can be used, once the majority of the deposits have been scraped away.

4 Remove the carbon from the ring grooves in the piston, using an old ring. Break the ring in half to do this (be careful not to cut your fingers - piston rings are sharp). Be careful to remove only the carbon deposits - do not remove any metal, and do not nick or scratch the sides of the ring grooves.

5 Once the deposits have been removed, clean the piston/connecting rod assembly with paraffin or a suitable solvent, and dry thoroughly.

Inspection

6 If the pistons and cylinder liner bores are not damaged or worn excessively, the original pistons can be refitted. Measure the piston diameters, and check that they are within limits for the corresponding bore diameters. Measure the diameter of each piston at right-

14.2 Using a feeler blade to aid removal of the piston rings

angles to the gudgeon pin axis, 8 mm up from the bottom of the skirt.

7 If the piston-to-bore clearance is excessive (see Section 12), new cylinder liners and pistons will have to be fitted. Normal piston wear shows up as even vertical wear on the piston thrust surfaces, and slight looseness of the top ring in its groove. New piston rings should always be used when the engine is reassembled. Note that the piston and bore size grades are stamped on the piston crowns, and on the outer diameters of the cylinder liners.

8 Carefully inspect each piston for cracks around the skirt, around the gudgeon pin holes, and at the piston ring "lands" (between the ring grooves).

9 Look for scoring and scuffing on the piston skirt, holes in the piston crown, and burned areas at the edge of the crown. If the skirt is scored or scuffed, the engine may have been suffering from overheating, and/or abnormal combustion which caused excessively high operating temperatures. The cooling and lubrication systems should be checked thoroughly. Scorch marks on the sides of the pistons show that blow-by has occurred. A hole in the piston crown, or burned areas at the edge of the piston crown, indicates that abnormal combustion (pre-ignition, knocking, or detonation) has been occurring. If any of the above problems exist, the causes must be investigated and corrected, or the damage will occur again. The causes may include incorrect ignition timing, inlet air leaks or incorrect air/fuel mixture.

10 Corrosion of the piston, in the form of pitting, indicates that coolant has been leaking into the combustion chamber and/or the cylinder liner. Again, the cause must be corrected, or the problem may persist in the rebuilt engine.

11 Check the piston-to-bore clearance by measuring the cylinder bore (see Section 12) and the piston diameter. Measure the piston 8 mm from the bottom of the skirt, at a 90°

14.11 Measuring piston diameter

angle to the gudgeon pin **(see illustration)**. If the piston-to-bore clearance is excessive, new cylinder liners and corresponding pistons will be required.

12 Examine each connecting rod carefully for signs of damage, such as cracks around the big-end and small-end bearings. Check that the rod is not bent or distorted. Damage is highly unlikely, unless the engine has been seized or badly overheated. Detailed checking of the connecting rod assembly can only be carried out by a Rover dealer or engine repair specialist with the necessary equipment.

13 Note that the pistons and connecting rods are only available as an assembly. If a piston or connecting rod is to be renewed, it is therefore necessary to renew all four complete piston/connecting rod assemblies – it is not possible to fit a new piston to an existing connecting rod.

15 Crankshaft – inspection

Checking endfloat

1 If crankshaft endfloat is to be checked, this must be done when the crankshaft is still installed in the cylinder block/crankcase but is free to move.

2 Check endfloat by using a dial gauge in contact with the end of the crankshaft. Push the crankshaft fully one way and then zero the gauge. Push the crankshaft fully the other way and check the endfloat. The result can be compared with the specified amount and will give an indication as to whether new thrustwashers are required.

3 If a dial gauge is not available, feeler blades can be used. First push the crankshaft fully towards the flywheel end of the engine, then use feeler blades to measure the gap between the web of No 3 crankpin and the thrustwasher.

Inspection

4 Clean the crankshaft using paraffin or a suitable solvent, and dry it, preferably with compressed air if available. Be sure to clean

the oil holes with a pipe cleaner or similar probe, to ensure that they are not obstructed.

 Warning: Wear eye protection when using compressed air!

5 Check the main and big-end bearing journals for uneven wear, scoring, pitting and cracking.

6 Big-end bearing wear is accompanied by distinct metallic knocking when the engine is running (particularly noticeable when the engine is pulling from low speed) and some loss of oil pressure.

7 Main bearing wear is accompanied by severe engine vibration and rumble - getting progressively worse as engine speed increases - and again by loss of oil pressure.

8 Check the bearing journal for roughness by running a finger lightly over the bearing surface. Any roughness (which will be accompanied by obvious bearing wear) indicates that the crankshaft requires regrinding (where possible) or renewal.

9 If the crankshaft has been reground, check for burrs around the crankshaft oil holes (the holes are usually chamfered, so burrs should not be a problem unless regrinding has been carried out carelessly). Remove any burrs with a fine file or scraper, and thoroughly clean the oil holes as described previously.

10 Using a micrometer, measure the diameter of the main and big-end (crankpin) bearing journals, and compare the results with the *Specifications* **(see illustration)**. By measuring the diameter at a number of points around each journal's circumference, you will be able to determine whether or not the journal is out-of-round. Take the measurement at each end of the journal, near the webs, to determine if the journal is tapered. The main bearing size grades are marked on the crankshaft front web, and the big-end bearing size grades are marked on the crankshaft rear web. In each case, the first letter or number relates to the No 1 bearing, the second to No 2, and so on.

11 Check the oil seal contact surfaces at each end of the crankshaft for wear and damage. If the seal has worn a deep groove in the surface of the crankshaft, consult an engine overhaul

15.10 Measuring a crankshaft main bearing journal diameter

specialist; repair may be possible, but otherwise a new crankshaft will be required.

12 If the crankshaft journals are damaged, tapered, out-of-round or worn beyond the limits specified, the crankshaft must be renewed unless an engine overhaul specialist can be found who will regrind it and supply the necessary undersize bearing shells.

16 Main and big-end bearings – inspection

1 Even though the main and big-end bearings should be renewed during the engine overhaul, the old bearings should be retained for close examination, as they may reveal valuable information about the condition of the engine. The bearing shells are graded by thickness, the grade of each shell being indicated by the colour code marked on it.

2 Bearing failure can occur due to lack of lubrication, the presence of dirt or other foreign particles, overloading the engine, or corrosion **(see illustration)**. Regardless of the cause of bearing failure, the cause must be corrected (where applicable) before the engine is reassembled, to prevent it from happening again.

3 When examining the bearing shells, remove them from the cylinder block/crankcase, the main bearing ladder, the connecting rods and the connecting rod big-end bearing caps. Lay them out on a clean surface in the same general position as their location in the engine. This will enable you to match any bearing problems with the corresponding crankshaft journal.

Caution: Do not touch any shell's bearing surface with your fingers while checking it, or the delicate surface may be scratched.

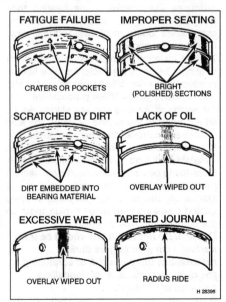

16.2 Typical bearing shell failures

2C

4 Dirt and other foreign matter gets into the engine in a variety of ways. It may be left in the engine during assembly, or it may pass through filters or the crankcase ventilation system. It may get into the oil, and from there into the bearings. Metal chips from machining operations and normal engine wear are often present. Abrasives are sometimes left in engine components after reconditioning, especially when parts are not thoroughly cleaned using the proper cleaning methods. Whatever the source, these foreign objects often end up embedded in the soft bearing material, and are easily recognised. Large particles will not embed in the bearing, and will score or gouge the bearing and journal. The best prevention for this cause of bearing failure is to clean all parts thoroughly, and keep everything spotlessly-clean during engine assembly. Frequent and regular engine oil and filter changes are also recommended.

5 Lack of lubrication (or lubrication breakdown) has a number of interrelated causes. Excessive heat (which thins the oil), overloading (which squeezes the oil from the bearing face) and oil leakage (from excessive bearing clearances, worn oil pump or high engine speeds) all contribute to lubrication breakdown. Blocked oil passages, which usually are the result of misaligned oil holes in a bearing shell, will also oil-starve a bearing, and destroy it. When lack of lubrication is the cause of bearing failure, the bearing material is wiped or extruded from the steel backing of the bearing. Temperatures may increase to the point where the steel backing turns blue from overheating.

6 Driving habits can have a definite effect on bearing life. Full-throttle, low-speed operation (labouring the engine) puts very high loads on bearings, tending to squeeze out the oil film. These loads cause the bearings to flex, which produces fine cracks in the bearing face (fatigue failure). Eventually, the bearing material will loosen in pieces, and tear away from the steel backing.

7 Short-distance driving leads to corrosion of bearings, because insufficient engine heat is produced to drive off the condensed water and corrosive gases. These products collect in the engine oil, forming acid and sludge. As the oil is carried to the engine bearings, the acid attacks and corrodes the bearing material.

8 Incorrect bearing installation during engine assembly will lead to bearing failure as well. Tight-fitting bearings leave insufficient bearing running clearance, and will result in oil starvation. Dirt or foreign particles trapped behind a bearing shell result in high spots on the bearing, which lead to failure. *Caution: Do not touch any shell's bearing surface with your fingers during reassembly; there is a risk of scratching the delicate surface, or of depositing particles of dirt on it.*

9 As mentioned at the beginning of this Section, the bearing shells should be renewed as a matter of course during engine overhaul;

to do otherwise is false economy. Refer to Sections 19 and 20 for details of bearing shell selection.

17 Engine overhaul – reassembly sequence

1 Before reassembly begins, ensure that all new parts have been obtained and that all necessary tools are available. Read through the entire procedure to familiarise yourself with the work involved and to ensure that all items necessary for reassembly of the engine are at hand. In addition to all normal tools and materials, it will be necessary to obtain suitable thread-locking compound, and various Rover sealants – refer to the relevant Sections in this Part of the Chapter and Part A for details. Carefully read the instructions supplied with the appropriate sealant kit.

2 In order to save time and avoid problems, engine reassembly can be carried out in the following order, referring to Part A of this Chapter when necessary. Where applicable, use new gaskets and seals when refitting the various components.

  a) *Crankshaft.*
  b) *Piston/connecting rod assemblies.*
  c) *Oil pump.*
  d) *Sump.*
  e) *Flywheel.*
  f) *Cylinder head.*
  g) *Timing belt rear cover, tensioner and sprockets, and timing belt.*
  h) *Engine external components.*

3 At this stage, all engine components should be absolutely clean and dry, with all faults repaired, and should be laid out (or in individual containers) on a completely clean work surface.

18 Piston rings – refitting

1 Before fitting new piston rings, the ring end gaps must be checked as follows.

2 Lay out the piston/connecting rod assemblies and the new piston ring sets, so

18.4 Measuring a piston ring end gap

that the ring sets will be matched with the same piston and cylinder during the end gap measurement and subsequent engine reassembly.

3 Insert the top ring into the first cylinder liner bore, and push it down the bore using the top of the piston. This will ensure that the ring remains square with the cylinder walls. Position the ring 20 mm from the top of the bore. Note that the top and second compression rings are different. The second ring is easily identified by the step on its lower surface.

4 Measure the end gap using feeler blades. Compare the measurements with the figures given in the *Specifications* **(see illustration)**.

5 If the gap is too small (unlikely if genuine Rover parts are used), it must be enlarged, or the ring ends may contact each other during engine operation, causing serious damage. Ideally, new piston rings providing the correct end gap should be fitted. As a last resort, the end gap can be increased by filing the ring ends very carefully with a fine file. Mount the file in a vice equipped with soft jaws, slip the ring over the file with the ends contacting the file face, and slowly move the ring to remove material from the ends. Take care, as piston rings are sharp, and are easily broken.

6 With new piston rings, it is unlikely that the end gap will be too large. If the gaps are too large, check that you have the correct rings for your engine and for the particular cylinder bore size.

7 Repeat the checking procedure for each ring in the first cylinder, and then for the rings in the remaining cylinders. Remember to keep rings, pistons and cylinders matched up.

8 Once the ring end gaps have been checked and if necessary corrected, the rings can be fitted to the pistons.

9 Check the ring-to-groove clearance by inserting the outside of each ring into the relevant groove, together with a feeler blade between the top surface of the ring and the piston land **(see illustration)**. If the grooves in the piston are excessively worn, new pistons may be required.

10 Fit the piston rings using the same technique as for removal. Fit the bottom (oil control) ring first, and work up. When fitting the oil control ring, first insert the wire expander, then fit the ring with its gap

18.9 Measuring piston ring-to-groove clearance

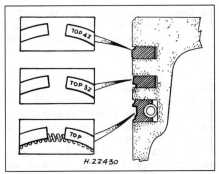

18.10a Piston ring fitting details and top surface markings

positioned 180° from the protruding wire ends of the expander. The oil control expander and ring gaps should be offset 30° either side of the gudgeon pin axis. Ensure that the rings are fitted the correct way up - the top surface of the rings is normally marked "TOP" **(see illustrations)**. Arrange the gaps of the top and second compression rings 120° from each other, away from the thrust side of the piston. **Note:** *Always follow any instructions supplied with the new piston ring sets - different manufacturers may specify different procedures. Do not mix up the top and second compression rings, as they have different cross-sections.*

19 Crankshaft – refitting and main bearing running clearance check

Selection of bearing shells

1 The main bearing running clearance is controlled in production by selecting one of three grades of bearing shell. The grades are

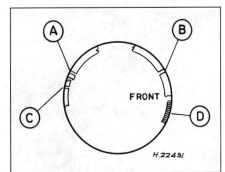

18.10b Piston ring end gap locations

A Top compression ring
B Second compression ring
C Oil control ring
D Oil control ring expander

indicated by a colour-coding marked on the edge of each shell which governs the shell's thickness, as follows:
  a) Green - Thin.
  b) Blue - Intermediate.
  c) Red - Thick.
2 If shells of differing grades are to be fitted to the same journal, the thicker shell must always be fitted to the main bearing ladder location. Bear this carefully in mind when ordering replacement shells for Nos 2, 3 and 4 bearings.
3 If the bearing shells are to be renewed, first check and record the main bearing code letters stamped on the right-hand front face of the main bearing ladder **(see illustration)**. The letters are read with the ladder inverted, No 1 bearing code letter at the top, then No 2 and so on (No 1 bearing is at the timing belt end of the engine).
4 Check and record the crankshaft journal grade code numbers stamped on the

crankshaft front web, No 1 journal code first, then No 2, and so on. If the original crankshaft is to be re-used, the size grade can be checked by direct measurement, as described in Section 15.
5 Note that if the crankshaft is found to be excessively worn, then it must be renewed, and the code numbers of the new crankshaft must be used instead to select a new set of bearing shells.
6 Matching the codes noted to the following table, select a new set of bearing shells.

Ladder code letter	Crankshaft code number	Shells
A	1	Blue, Blue
A	2	Red, Blue
A	3	Red, Red
B	1	Blue, Green
B	2	Blue, Blue
B	3	Red, Blue
C	1	Green, Green
C	2	Blue, Green
C	3	Blue, Blue

Main bearing running clearance check

7 Clean the backs of the bearing shells and the bearing locations in both the cylinder block/crankcase and the main bearing ladder.
8 Press the bearing shells into their locations, ensuring that the tab on each shell engages in the notch in the cylinder block/crankcase or main bearing ladder location. Take care not to touch any shell bearing surface with your fingers.
9 Press the bearing shells with the oil grooves into the upper locations (in the cylinder block/crankcase). Note the following points:
  a) On all engines, grooved bearing shells are fitted to Nos 2, 3 and 4 upper bearing locations. Note the central locating tabs of the grooved shells.
  b) If bearing shells of differing grades are to be fitted to the same journal, the thicker shell must always be fitted to the main bearing ladder location (see paragraph 1).
  c) On all engines, if the original main bearing shells are being re-used, these must be refitted to their original locations in the cylinder block/crankcase and main bearing ladder.
10 The main bearing running clearance should be checked if there is any doubt about the amount of crankshaft wear that has taken place, if the crankshaft has been reground and is to be refitted with non-Rover undersized bearing shells, or if non-genuine bearing shells are to be fitted. If the original crankshaft or a Rover replacement part is to be installed, the shell selection procedure given above will produce the correct clearances, and a further check will not be necessary. If the clearance is to be checked, it can be done in either of two ways. Bear in mind that in order to check the bearing running clearance, the cylinder head must be refitted, and the cylinder head bolts must be tightened to the specified torque and stages.

2C

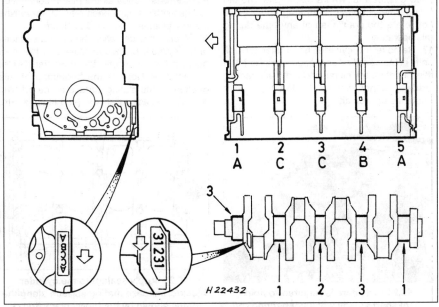

19.3 Crankshaft main bearing size code locations

19.14 Lay a length of Plastigauge on the journal to be measured, parallel to the crankshaft centre-line

19.18 Using the scale on the Plastigauge envelope to check (at widest point) the width of crushed Plastigauge

Use the old cylinder head gasket when refitting the cylinder head (if a new one is used, it will effectively be destroyed when the cylinder head bolts are tightened, and cannot be used for final engine reassembly). If new cylinder head bolts are to be fitted during final reassembly, use the old bolts to secure the cylinder head for this check.

11 The first method (which will be difficult to achieve without a range of internal micrometers or internal/external expanding calipers) is to refit the main bearing ladder to the cylinder block/crankcase (where applicable remove the cylinder liner clamps), with bearing shells in place. With the ladder retaining bolts tightened to the specified torque setting in the two stages given and in the specified sequence **(see illustration 19.26)**, refit the oil rail and the cylinder head (see Part A of this Chapter), then measure the internal diameter of each assembled pair of bearing shells. If the diameter of each corresponding crankshaft journal is measured and then subtracted from the bearing internal diameter, the result will be the main bearing running clearance.

12 The second (and more accurate) method is to use product known as Plastigauge. This consists of a fine thread of perfectly round plastic which is compressed between the bearing shell and the journal. When the shell is removed, the plastic is deformed and can be measured with a special card gauge supplied with the kit. The running clearance is

determined from this gauge. Plastigauge is sometimes difficult to obtain, but enquiries at one of the larger specialist quality motor factors should produce the name of a stockist in your area. The procedure for using Plastigauge is as follows.

13 With the main bearing upper shells in place, carefully lay the crankshaft in position. **Do not** use any lubricant. The crankshaft journals and bearing shells must be perfectly clean and dry.

14 Cut several lengths of the appropriate size Plastigauge (they should be slightly shorter than the width of the main bearings) and place one length on each crankshaft journal axis **(see illustration)**.

15 With the main bearing lower shells in position, refit the main bearing ladder (where applicable, remove the cylinder liner clamps) and tighten the retaining bolts to the specified torque setting in the two stages given and in the specified sequence **(see illustration 19.26)**. Take care not to disturb the Plastigauge.

16 Refit the oil rail and the cylinder head (see Part A of this Chapter). Use the old cylinder head gasket and, where applicable, the old cylinder head bolts – see paragraph 10). Do not rotate the crankshaft at any time during this operation.

17 Remove the cylinder head (slacken the bolts in the specified sequence – see Part A of this Chapter), the oil rail and the main bearing ladder. Do not disturb the Plastigauge or rotate the crankshaft.

18 Compare the width of the crushed Plastigauge on each journal to the scale printed on the Plastigauge envelope to obtain the main bearing running clearance **(see illustration)**.

19 If the clearance is not as specified, the bearing shells may be the wrong grade (or excessively worn if the original shells are being re-used). Before deciding that different grade shells are needed, make sure that no dirt or oil was trapped between the bearing shells and the ladder or cylinder block/crankcase when the clearance was measured. If the Plastigauge was wider at one end than at the other, the journal may be tapered.

20 Carefully scrape away all traces of the Plastigauge material from the crankshaft and bearing shells using a fingernail or other object which is unlikely to score the shells.

Final crankshaft refitting

Note: *Rover sealant kit No LVV 10002 will be required for this operation.*

21 Carefully lift the crankshaft out of the cylinder block once more.

22 Using a little grease, stick the thrustwashers to each side of the No 3 main bearing upper location in the cylinder block/crankcase. Ensure that the oilway grooves on each thrustwasher face outwards.

23 Place the bearing shells in their correct locations, as described in paragraphs 7 to 9. If new shells are being fitted, ensure that all traces of the protective grease are cleaned off using paraffin. Wipe the shells dry with a lint-free cloth. Liberally lubricate each bearing shell in the cylinder block/crankcase, then lower the crankshaft into position so that Nos 2 and 3 cylinder crankpins are at TDC.

24 Refit the piston/connecting rod assemblies, with reference to Section 20 **(see illustrations)**. Once all the piston/connecting rod assemblies have been refitted, leave Nos 1 and 4 pistons at the TDC position.

25 Thoroughly degrease the mating surfaces of the cylinder block/crankcase and the main bearing ladder. Apply the specified Rover sealant (see Note at the beginning of this Section) to the mating surface of the cylinder block/crankcase as shown **(see illustration)**,

19.24a If piston/connecting rod assemblies are refitted before main bearing ladder . . .

19.24b . . . care is required to hold crankshaft steady while connecting rod big-end cap bolts are tightened

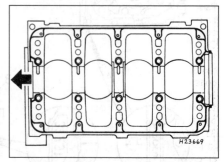

H23669

19.25 Apply sealant to the cylinder block/crankcase mating surface along the paths shown by the heavy black lines – arrow indicates timing belt end of engine

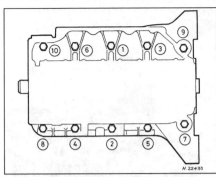

19.26 Crankshaft main bearing ladder bolt tightening sequence

then spread the sealant to an even film using a brush or roller. Carefully follow the instructions supplied with the sealant kit. Assembly must be completed as soon as possible after the sealant has been applied (maximum of 20 minutes).

26 Lubricate the bearing shells in the main bearing ladder, then refit the bearing ladder, ensuring that the shells are not displaced and that the locating dowels engage correctly. Working progressively, by a turn at a time and in the sequence shown **(see illustration)**, tighten the ladder bolts to the specified torque wrench setting in the two stages given – ie, tighten all bolts in sequence to the Stage 1 setting, then tighten all bolts in sequence to the Stage 2 setting. The crankshaft cannot now be rotated.

27 Thoroughly degrease the mating surfaces of the oil rail and the main bearing ladder. Apply the Rover sealant to the oil rail mating surface as shown **(see illustration)**. Carefully follow the instructions supplied with the sealant kit.

28 Refit the oil rail, tightening the nuts to the specified torque wrench setting.

29 Refit the oil pump pick-up/strainer pipe and the sump, as described in Part A of this Chapter.

30 Fit a new crankshaft rear oil seal, then refit the flywheel, as described in Part A of this Chapter.

31 Refit the oil pump and fit a new crankshaft front oil seal, as described in Part A of this Chapter.

32 Refit the cylinder head, as described in Part A of this Chapter. Rotate the crankshaft to position No 1 piston to the 90° BTDC position (see Section 3 in Part A of this Chapter).

33 Refit the dipstick tube to the cylinder block/crankcase, and tighten the securing bolts.

34 Refit the timing belt rear cover, the sprockets and timing belt tensioner, and the belt itself.

35 Using a torque wrench and socket applied to the crankshaft pulley bolt, check that the amount of force required to rotate the crankshaft does not exceed 31 Nm (23 lbf ft). If the effort required is greater than this, the engine must be dismantled again to trace and

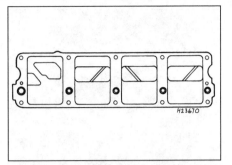

19.27 Apply sealant to the oil rail mating surfaces along the paths shown by the heavy black lines

rectify the cause. This value takes into account the increased friction of a new engine and is much higher than the actual pressure required to rotate a run-in engine, so do not make allowances for tight components.

20 Piston/connecting rod assembly – refitting and big-end bearing running clearance check

Selection of bearing shells

1 The big-end bearing running clearance is controlled in production by selecting one of three grades of bearing shell. The grades are indicated by a colour-coding marked on the edge of each shell which governs the shell's thickness, as follows:
a) Yellow - Thin.
b) Blue - Intermediate.
c) Red - Thick.

2 If shells of differing grades are to be fitted to the same journal, the thicker shell must always be fitted to the big-end bearing cap location.

3 If the bearing shells are to be renewed, first check and record the codes stamped on the front face of each big-end bearing cap and connecting rod. The number stamped on the big-end bearing cap is the bearing size code, the number stamped on the connecting rod is the piston/rod assembly's cylinder number and the letter stamped on the connecting rod is the weight code **(see illustration)**.

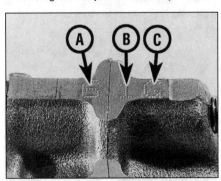

20.3 Big-end bearing size code number (A – on cap) , cylinder number (B) and connecting rod weight code letter (C)

4 Secondly, check and record the crankpin/big-end journal code letters stamped on the crankshaft rear web **(see illustration)**, No 1 journal code first, then No 2, and so on. If the original crankshaft is to be re-used, the code letter can be checked by direct measurement.

5 If the crankshaft is found to be excessively worn, then it must be renewed and the code letters of the new component must be used instead to select a new set of bearing shells.

6 Matching the codes noted to the following table, select a new set of bearing shells.

Cap code number	Crankshaft code letter	Shells
5	A	Blue, Blue
5	B	Red, Blue
5	C	Red, Red
6	A	Blue, Yellow
6	B	Blue, Blue
6	C	Red, Blue
7	A	Yellow, Yellow
7	B	Blue, Yellow
7	C	Blue, Blue

Big-end bearing running clearance check

7 The big-end bearing running clearance should be checked if there is any doubt about the amount of crankshaft wear that has taken place, if the crankshaft has been reground and is to be refitted with non-Rover undersized bearing shells, or if non-genuine bearing shells are to be fitted. If the original crankshaft or a Rover replacement part is to be installed, the shell selection procedure given previously will produce the correct clearances, and a further check will not be necessary. If the clearance is to be checked, it can be done in either of two ways.

8 The first method is to refit the big-end bearing cap to the connecting rod, with bearing shells in place. With the cap retaining bolts tightened to the specified torque, use an internal micrometer or vernier caliper to measure the internal diameter of each assembled pair of bearing shells. If the diameter of each corresponding crankshaft journal is measured and then subtracted from

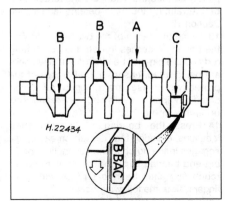

20.4 Crankpin/big-end journal size code location

2C

the bearing internal diameter, the result will be the big-end bearing running clearance.

9 The second method is to use Plastigauge (see Section 19). Place a strand of Plastigauge on each (cleaned) crankpin journal and refit the (clean) piston/connecting rod assemblies, shells and big-end bearing caps, tightening the bolts to the specified torque wrench setting. Take care not to damage the internal surfaces of the cylinder liner bores, and take care not to disturb the Plastigauge. **Do not** rotate the crankshaft during this procedure. Dismantle the assemblies without rotating the crankshaft, and compare the width of the crushed Plastigauge on each journal to the scale printed on the Plastigauge envelope to obtain the main bearing running clearance.

10 If the clearance is not as specified, the bearing shells may be the wrong grade (or excessively worn if the original shells are being re-used). Before deciding that different grade shells are needed, make sure that no dirt or oil was trapped between the bearing shells and the ladder or cylinder block/crankcase when the clearance was measured. If the Plastigauge was wider at one end than at the other, the journal may be tapered.

11 On completion of the measurement, carefully scrape off all traces of Plastigauge from the journals and shells using a fingernail or other object which will not score the components.

Final piston/connecting rod assembly refitting

Note: *Rover sealant kit No LVV 10002 will be required for this operation, and a piston ring compressor tool will be required.*

12 Note that the following procedure assumes that the cylinder liners have been refitted to the cylinder block/crankcase (see Section 13), and that the crankshaft and main bearing ladder are in place. It is of course possible to refit the piston/connecting rod assemblies to the cylinder liner bores, to refit the crankshaft and to reassemble the piston/connecting rods on the crankshaft before refitting the main bearing ladder (see Section 19).

13 Clean the backs of the bearing shells and the bearing recesses in both the connecting rod and the big-end bearing cap. If new shells are being fitted, ensure that all traces of the protective grease are cleaned off using paraffin. Wipe the shells and connecting rods dry with a lint-free cloth.

14 Press the bearing shells into their locations, ensuring that the tab on each shell engages in the notch in the connecting rod or big-end bearing cap, and taking care not to touch any shell bearing surface with your fingers. Note the following points.

a) *If bearing shells of differing grades are to be fitted to the same journal, the thicker shell must always be fitted to the big-end bearing cap location (see paragraph 1).*

20.17a Arrow of "FRONT" marking on piston crown must point to timing belt end of engine

b) *On all engines, if the original big-end bearing shells are being re-used, these must be refitted to their original locations in the relevant connecting rod and big-end bearing cap.*

15 Lubricate the cylinder bores, the pistons and piston rings, then lay out each piston/connecting rod assembly in its respective position.

16 Starting with assembly No 1, make sure that the piston rings are still correctly spaced (see Section 18), then clamp them in position with a piston ring compressor.

17 Insert the piston/connecting rod assembly into the top of liner No 1, ensuring that the arrow or "FRONT" marking on the piston crown faces the timing belt end of the engine. Note that the stamped marks on the connecting rod and big-end bearing cap should face the front (alternator bracket side) of the engine. Using a block of wood or a hammer handle against the piston crown, tap the assembly into the liner until the piston crown is flush with the top of the liner **(see illustrations)**.

18 Ensure that the bearing shell is still correctly installed in the connecting rod. Taking care not to mark the liner bores, liberally lubricate the crankpin and both bearing shells, then pull the piston/connecting rod assembly down the bore and onto the crankpin. Noting that the faces with the stamped marks must match (which means that the bearing shell locating tabs abut each other), refit the big-end bearing cap, tightening the bolts finger-tight at first.

20.17b Using a piston ring compressor tool to clamp the piston rings

19 Use a torque wrench to tighten the bolts evenly to the (stage 1) torque wrench setting specified, then use an angular torque gauge to tighten the bolts evenly through the (stage 2) angle specified **(see illustrations)**.

20 Repeat the procedure for the remaining three piston/connecting rod assemblies, but do not attempt to rotate the crankshaft.

21 Thoroughly degrease the mating surfaces of the oil rail and the main bearing ladder. Apply the specified Rover sealant to the oil rail mating surface **(see illustration 19.27)**. Carefully follow the instructions supplied with the sealant kit.

22 Refit the oil rail, tightening the nuts to the specified torque wrench setting.

23 Refit the oil pump pick-up/strainer pipe and the sump, as described in Part A of this Chapter.

24 Refit the cylinder head, as described in Part A of this Chapter.

25 Rotate the crankshaft to bring No 1 piston to the 90° BTDC position so that the crankshaft sprocket timing marks align (see Section 3 in Part A of this Chapter).

26 Refit the dipstick tube to the cylinder block/crankcase, and tighten the bolts securely.

27 Refit the hydraulic tappets and the camshaft(s), as described in Part A of this Chapter.

28 Refit the timing belt rear cover, sprocket(s), tensioner and the belt itself, as described in Part A of this Chapter.

20.19a Tighten the connecting rod big-end cap bolts to the specified torque setting . . .

20.19b . . . then through the specified angle

29 Finally, using a torque wrench, check that the amount of force required to rotate the crankshaft does not exceed 31 Nm (23 lbf ft). If the effort required is greater than this, the engine must be dismantled again to trace and rectify the cause. This value takes into account the increased friction of a new engine and is much higher than the actual pressure required to rotate a run-in engine, so do not make allowances for tight components.

21 Engine –
initial start-up after overhaul

1 With the engine refitted to the vehicle, double-check the engine oil and coolant levels. Make a final check to ensure that everything has been reconnected and that there are no tools or rags left in the engine compartment.

2 With the spark plugs removed and the ignition system disabled by earthing the ignition coil HT lead with a jumper lead, turn the engine over on the starter until the oil pressure warning lamp goes out.

3 Refit the spark plugs and connect all the spark plug HT leads.

4 Start the engine, noting that this may take a little longer than usual due to the fuel system components being empty.

5 While the engine is idling, check for fuel, coolant and oil leaks. Do not be alarmed if there are some odd smells and smoke from parts getting hot and burning off oil deposits.

If the hydraulic tappets have been disturbed, some valve gear noise may be heard at first; this should disappear as the oil circulates fully around the engine and normal pressure is restored in the tappets.

6 Keep the engine idling until hot coolant is felt circulating through the radiator top hose, check the ignition timing and idle speed and mixture (as appropriate), then stop the engine.

7 After a few minutes, recheck the oil and coolant levels and top up as necessary.

8 If new pistons, rings or crankshaft bearings have been fitted, the engine must be run-in for the first 500 miles (800 km). Do not operate the engine at full throttle or allow it to labour in any gear during this period. It is recommended that the oil and filter be changed at the end of this period.

2C

Notes

Chapter 2 Part D:
Diesel engine removal and general overhaul procedures

Contents

Degrees of difficulty

Easy, suitable for novice with little experience	Fairly easy, suitable for beginner with some experience	Fairly difficult, suitable for competent DIY mechanic	Difficult, suitable for experienced DIY mechanic	Very difficult, suitable for expert DIY or professional

2D

Specifications

Cylinder block/crankcase
Material	Cast iron
Cylinder bore diameter	84.442 to 84.460 mm

Crankshaft
Number of main bearings	5
Main bearing journal diameter	60.703 to 60.719 mm
Big-end journal diameter	57.683 to 57.696 mm
Main bearing and big-end bearing running clearance	0.005 mm
Crankshaft endfloat	0.03 to 0.26 mm
Thrustwasher thickness	2.31 to 2.36 mm

Pistons and piston rings
Piston diameter	84.262 mm
Piston-to-bore clearance	0.18 to 0.20 mm
Piston ring end gaps (rings fitted 30 mm from top of bore):	
Top compression ring	0.25 to 0.27 mm
Second compression ring	0.40 to 0.42 mm
Oil control ring	0.30 to 0.32 mm
Piston ring end gaps (rings fitted to pistons):	
Top compression ring	0.30 to 0.50 mm
Second compression ring	0.40 to 0.60 mm
Oil control ring	0.25 to 0.50 mm
Piston ring-to-groove clearance:	
Top compression ring	0.115 to 0.135 mm
Second compression ring	0.050 to 0.082 mm
Oil control ring - all models	0.050 to 0.082 mm

Gudgeon pins
Diameter	29.995 to 30.000 mm

Cylinder head

Maximum acceptable gasket face distortion	0.010 mm
Valve seat angle:	
Inlet	60°
Exhaust	58° to 62°
Valve seat width	1.5 mm
Inlet	35.697 mm
Exhaust	31.05 to 31.55 mm
Cylinder head bolt length	243.41 mm

Valves

Stem diameter:	
Inlet	6.907 to 6.923 mm
Exhaust	6.897 to 6.913 mm
Guide inside diameter	6.950 to 6.963 mm
Stem-to-guide clearance (measured at valve head, with valve head extended 10 mm from seat):	
Inlet	0.056 mm
Exhaust	0.066 mm
Valve spring free length	37.0 mm
Valve guide fitted height	61.1 to 61.7 mm
Valve head recess below cylinder head face:	
Inlet	1.45 mm
Exhaust	1.35 mm

Torque wrench settings

Refer to Part B of this Chapter

---

1 General information

Included in this part of the Chapter are details of removing the engine/transmission unit from the vehicle and general overhaul procedures for the cylinder head, cylinder block/crankcase and all other engine internal components.

The information given ranges from advice concerning preparation for an overhaul and the purchase of replacement parts to detailed step-by-step procedures covering removal, inspection, renovation and refitting of engine internal components.

After Section 5, all instructions are based on the assumption that the engine has been removed from the vehicle. For information concerning in-car engine repair, as well as the removal and refitting of those external components necessary for full overhaul, refer to Part B of this Chapter and to Section 5. Ignore any preliminary dismantling operations described in Part B that are no longer relevant once the engine has been removed from the vehicle.

2 Engine overhaul – general information

It is not always easy to determine when, or if, an engine should be completely overhauled, as a number of factors must be considered.

High mileage is not necessarily an indication that an overhaul is needed, while low mileage does not preclude the need for an overhaul. Frequency of servicing is probably the most important consideration. An engine which has had regular and frequent oil and filter changes, as well as other required maintenance, should give many thousands of miles of reliable service. Conversely, a neglected engine may require an overhaul very early in its life. If a complete service does not remedy any problems, major mechanical work is the only solution.

Excessive oil consumption is an indication that piston rings, valve seals and/or valve guides are in need of attention. Make sure that oil leaks are not responsible before deciding that the rings and/or guides are worn. Perform a compression or leakdown test to determine the likely cause of the problem (see Part B of this Chapter).

Check the oil pressure with a gauge fitted in place of the oil pressure switch and compare it with that specified. If it is extremely low, the main and big-end bearings and/or the oil pump are probably worn out.

Loss of power, rough running, knocking or metallic engine noises, excessive valve gear noise and high fuel consumption may also point to the need for an overhaul, especially if they are all present at the same time.

An engine overhaul involves restoring all internal parts to the specification of a new engine. During an overhaul, the cylinder liners, the pistons and the piston rings are renewed. New main and big-end bearings are generally fitted and, if necessary, the crankshaft may be renewed to restore the journals. The valves

are serviced as well, since they are usually in less than perfect condition at this point. While the engine is being overhauled, other components, such as the distributor, starter and alternator, can be overhauled as well. The end result should be an as-new engine that will give many trouble-free miles.

Critical cooling system components such as the hoses, thermostat and coolant pump should be renewed when an engine is overhauled. The radiator should be checked carefully to ensure that it is not clogged or leaking. Also it is a good idea to renew the oil pump whenever the engine is overhauled.

Before beginning the engine overhaul, read through the entire procedure to familiarise yourself with the scope and requirements of the job. Overhauling an engine is not difficult if you follow carefully all of the instructions, have the necessary tools and equipment and pay close attention to all specifications. However, it can be time-consuming. Plan on the vehicle being off the road for a minimum of two weeks, especially if parts must be taken to an engineering works for repair or reconditioning. Check on the availability of parts and make sure that any necessary special tools and equipment are obtained in advance. Most work can be done with typical hand tools, although a number of precision measuring tools are required for inspecting parts to determine if they must be renewed. Often the engineering works will handle the inspection of parts and offer advice concerning reconditioning and renewal.

Always wait until the engine has been completely dismantled and all components, especially the cylinder block/crankcase, the cylinder liners and the crankshaft have been inspected before deciding what service and repair operations must be performed by an engineering works. Since the condition of these components will be the major factor to consider when determining whether to overhaul the original engine or buy a reconditioned unit, do not purchase parts or have overhaul work done on other components until they have been thoroughly inspected. As a general rule, time is the primary cost of an overhaul, so it does not pay to fit worn or substandard parts.

As a final note, to ensure maximum life and minimum trouble from a reconditioned engine, everything must be assembled with care in a spotlessly clean environment.

3 Engine/transmission removal – methods and precautions

If you have decided that the engine must be removed for overhaul or major repair work, several preliminary steps should be taken.

Locating a suitable place to work is extremely important. Adequate work space, along with storage space for the vehicle, will be needed. If a workshop or garage is not available, at the very least a flat, level, clean work surface is required.

Cleaning the engine compartment and engine/transmission before beginning the removal procedure will help keep things clean and organised.

An engine hoist or A-frame will also be necessary. Make sure the equipment is rated in excess of the combined weight of the engine and transmission. Safety is of primary importance, considering the potential hazards involved in lifting the engine/transmission unit out of the vehicle. The engine/transmission unit is removed by lowering it out from under the front of the vehicle.

If the engine/transmission unit is being removed by a novice, a helper should be available. Advice and aid from someone more experienced would also be helpful. There are many instances when one person cannot simultaneously perform all of the operations

required when lowering the unit out of the vehicle.

Plan the operation ahead of time. Before starting work, arrange for the hire of or obtain all of the tools and equipment you will need. Some of the equipment necessary to perform engine/transmission removal and installation safely and with relative ease are (in addition to an engine hoist) a heavy duty trolley jack, complete sets of spanners and sockets as described at the front of this Manual, wooden blocks and plenty of rags and cleaning solvent for mopping up spilled oil, coolant and fuel. If the hoist must be hired, make sure that you arrange for it in advance and perform all of the operations possible without it beforehand. This will save you money and time.

Plan for the vehicle to be out of use for quite a while. An engineering works will be required to perform some of the work which the do-it-yourselfer cannot accomplish without special equipment. These places often have a busy schedule, so it would be a good idea to consult them before removing the engine in order to accurately estimate the amount of time required to rebuild or repair components that may need work.

Always be extremely careful when removing and refitting the engine/transmission unit. Serious injury can result from careless actions. Plan ahead, take your time and a job of this nature, although major, can be accomplished successfully.

4 Engine/manual transmission – removal and refitting

Models without air conditioning

Note: *A suitable engine hoist and adjustable lifting tackle will be required for this operation. In order to allow the engine/transmission assembly to pass out from under the vehicle, the front of the vehicle must be raised to a height of 770 mm (measured from the ground to the lower edge of the front bumper) – ensure that suitable axle stands are available to enable the vehicle to be raised to this height. A new gear selector rod-to-selector*

4.1 Raise the vehicle sufficiently high to withdraw the engine/transmission unit from under the front of the vehicle

shaft roll-pin, and a new power steering pump pressure hose-to-intermediate pipe O-ring will be required on refitting.

Removal

1 Apply the handbrake, then jack up the front of the vehicle and support securely on axle stands (see *"Jacking and Vehicle Support"*). Remove the front roadwheels. Note that the vehicle must be jacked up sufficiently high to enable the engine/transmission unit to be withdrawn from under the front of the vehicle – see Note at the beginning of this Section **(see illustration)**.

2 Drain the engine oil and coolant, as described in Chapter 1B.

3 Drain the transmission oil as described in Chapter 7A.

4 Unscrew the bolts securing the engine acoustic cover to the top of the cylinder head cover. Remove the engine oil filler cap, then remove the seal from the acoustic cover, and remove the acoustic cover from the engine.

5 Remove the air cleaner assembly as described in Chapter 4B.

6 Remove the engine control module (ECM) and the engine management relay module, as described in Chapter 4B.

7 Remove the battery, with reference to Chapter 5A if necessary.

8 Remove the engine compartment fusebox as follows **(see illustrations)**.

a) *Release the clip and remove the fusebox cover.*

2D

4.8a Remove the fusebox inner cover . . .

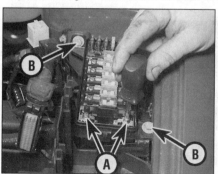

4.8b . . . unscrew the two screws (A) securing the positive leads to the fusebox and the fusebox securing bolts (B)

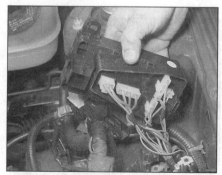

4.8c Disconnect the wiring plugs from the connectors on the bottom of the fusebox

4.9a Unscrew the upper battery tray securing bolts (arrowed)

4.9b Removing the battery tray

4.13 Releasing the preheating (glow plug) relay from its mounting bracket

b) *Release the two securing clips and remove the fusebox inner cover.*
c) *Remove the two screws securing the positive leads to the fusebox.*
d) *Unscrew the bolt securing the fusebox to the body, and the bolt securing the fusebox to the battery tray.*
e) *Disconnect the wiring plugs from the connectors on the bottom of the fusebox, then remove the fusebox.*

9 Unscrew the four upper bolts and slacken the three lower bolts securing the battery tray, then remove the battery tray **(see illustrations)**.

10 Disconnect the clutch cable from the clutch release lever, as described in Chapter 6, then release the cable from the transmission bracket, and move the cable to one side.

11 Unscrew the bolt securing the earth lead to the transmission.

12 Remove the mass airflow (MAF) sensor, with reference to Chapter 4B.

13 Release the preheating (glow plug) relay from its mounting bracket **(see illustration)**.

14 Working under the fusebox location on the left-hand side of the engine compartment, push the locking clip, and separate the two halves of the cylindrical engine wiring harness connector **(see illustration)**.

15 Unscrew the bolt securing the earth lead to the body front panel **(see illustration)**.

16 Remove the radiator cooling fan as described in Chapter 3.

17 Slacken the hose clip and disconnect the top hose from the radiator.

18 Slacken the hose clip and disconnect the

expansion tank hose from the radiator, then position the hose to one side **(see illustration)**.

19 On models without an intercooler, disconnect the throttle cable from the throttle linkage and mounting bracket, and position it to one side, as described in Chapter 4B.

20 On models with an intercooler, unclip the throttle position sensor wiring connector from the support bracket, then separate the two halves of the connector **(see illustration)**.

21 Slacken the hose clip and disconnect the brake servo vacuum hose from the vacuum pipe at the timing belt end of the engine.

22 Disconnect the vacuum pipe from the exhaust gas recirculation (EGR) valve.

23 Disconnect the wiring plugs from the exhaust gas recirculation (EGR) solenoid valve and the manifold absolute pressure (MAP) sensor on the engine compartment bulkhead.

24 Slacken the hose clip, and disconnect the coolant hose from the heater valve at the rear of the engine compartment **(see illustration)**.

25 Disconnect the coolant hose from the coolant pipe at the left-hand side of the engine.

26 Have a container ready to catch escaping fluid, then slacken the union securing the power steering pump pressure hose to the intermediate pipe, at the right-hand side of the engine compartment. Counterhold the union on the pipe using a second spanner **(see**

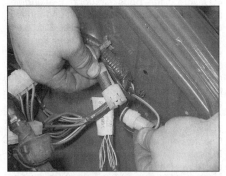

4.14 Separate the two halves of the engine wiring harness connector

4.15 Unscrew the bolt securing the earth lead to the front body panel

4.18 Disconnect the expansion tank hose from the radiator

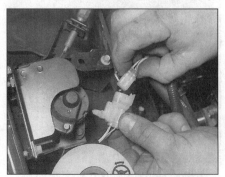

4.20 Separating the two halves of the throttle position sensor wiring connector

4.24 Disconnect the coolant hose from the heater valve

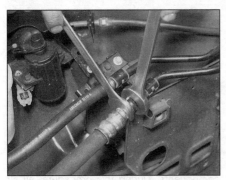

4.26 Disconnect the power steering pump pressure hose from the intermediate pipe

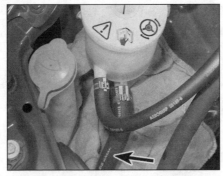

4.27 Disconnect the power steering pump fluid feed hose (arrowed) from the reservoir

4.28 Unbolt the engine wiring harness bracket and separate the two halves of each connector

illustration). Disconnect the hose from the pipe, then recover and discard the O-ring seal. Plug the open ends of the pipe and hose to prevent dirt entry and further fluid loss.

27 Again, have a container ready to catch the escaping fluid, then slacken the hose clip and disconnect the power steering fluid feed hose from the fluid reservoir **(see illustration)**.

28 Unbolt the engine wiring harness plug bracket from the left-hand side of the engine compartment bulkhead, then separate the two halves of each wiring connector (the engine harness connectors and bracket are removed complete with the wiring harness when the engine is removed) **(see illustration)**.

29 Slacken the hose clip, and disconnect the fuel filter hose from the fuel feed pipe at the left-hand side of the engine **(see illustration)**. *Caution: Be prepared for fuel spillage!*

30 Similarly, disconnect the hose from the fuel return pipe.

31 Remove the exhaust front section as described in Chapter 4B.

32 Working under the vehicle, unscrew the bolt securing the gearchange steady bar to the transmission **(see illustration)**. Recover the two washers.

33 Remove the metal clip from the gear selector rod-to-selector shaft joint to expose the roll-pin. Using a suitable pin-punch, drive out the roll-pin, then disconnect the selector rod from the selector shaft, and suspend the

selector rod and the gearchange steady bar to one side, clear of the transmission **(see illustration)**.

34 Unscrew the bolt securing the engine/transmission steady bar to the bracket on the engine **(see illustration)**.

35 Remove the front suspension beam, and the tie-bars as described in Chapter 10.

36 Disconnect both driveshafts from the transmission, as described in Chapter 8. Note that there is no need to disconnect the driveshafts from the hubs.

37 Make a final check to ensure that all relevant pipes, hoses and wires have been disconnected and moved clear to allow removal of the engine/transmission assembly.

4.29 Disconnect the fuel hoses from the pipes

38 Connect an engine hoist and lifting tackle to the engine lifting brackets on the cylinder head. The lifting tackle should be adjustable to enable the engine/transmission assembly to be tilted during the removal procedure. Raise the host to just take the weight of the engine.

39 Remove the right-hand engine mounting bracket, and the left-hand engine/transmission mounting as described in Chapter 2B.

40 With the aid of an assistant, lower the hoist to manoeuvre the engine/transmission assembly out from under the engine compartment **(see illustration)**. Take care not to damage surrounding components as the

4.32 Unscrewing the bolt securing the gearchange steady bar to the transmission

4.33 Driving out the roll-pin securing the gear selector rod to the selector shaft

4.34 Unscrew the bolt securing the engine/transmission steady bar to the engine bracket

4.40 Lower the engine/transmission assembly from the engine compartment

2D

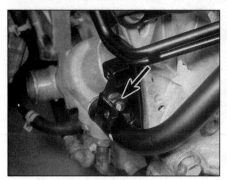

4.43a Unscrew the nut (arrowed) . . .

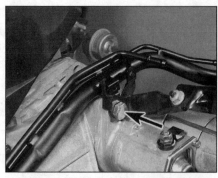

4.43b . . . and the bolt (arrowed) securing the coolant pipe/fuel pipe assembly to the transmission and mounting plate

assembly is removed. Again, with the aid of the assistant, lower the assembly onto a stout trolley or a wooden board supported by a trolley jack – take great care not to allow the assembly to fall onto the floor.

41 Withdraw the assembly from under the front of the vehicle, then lower the assembly to the ground, or move it onto a suitable work bench, and support the assembly on wooden blocks.

42 Disconnect the reversing light switch wiring connectors and, where applicable the vehicle speed sensor wiring plug, then release the wiring harnesses from the clips and brackets on the engine and transmission, and remove the wiring harnesses. Take note of the harness routing to aid refitting.

43 Unscrew the nut and the bolt securing the coolant pipe/fuel pipe assembly to the transmission and the transmission mounting plate. Where applicable, disconnect the fuel and coolant hoses from the pipes and remove the pipe assembly from the engine/transmission assembly **(see illustrations)**.

44 Unscrew the three lower bolts securing the transmission to the transmission mounting plate and the engine/transmission reinforcing bracket.

45 Unscrew the bolt at the rear of the engine, securing the transmission to the mounting plate.

46 Unscrew the two nuts and bolts securing the transmission to the mounting plate, then unscrew the remaining bolt securing the transmission to the mounting plate.

47 Carefully withdraw the transmission from the engine (the transmission locates on dowels in the mounting plate), ensuring that the weight of the transmission is not allowed to hang on the input shaft while it is engaged with the clutch friction disc.

Refitting

48 Commence refitting by checking that the clutch friction disc is centralised as described in Chapter 6.

49 Apply a little high melting-point grease to the splines of the transmission input shaft. Do not apply too much, as this may contaminate the clutch.

50 Ensure that the locating dowels are in place, then carefully offer the transmission to the engine, until the locating dowels are engaged, ensuring that the weight of the transmission is not allowed to hang on the input shaft as it is engaged with the clutch friction disc.

51 Refit the engine-to-transmission nuts and bolts, and tighten them securely.

52 Further refitting is a reversal of removal, bearing in mind the following points.

a) Tighten all fixings to the specified torque setting, where applicable.

b) Make sure that all pipes, hoses and wires are correctly reconnected and routed as noted before removal.

c) Refit the right-hand and left-hand engine mountings as described in Part B of this Chapter.

d) Reconnect the driveshafts to the transmission as described in Chapter 8.

e) Refit the front suspension beam and the tie-rods, with reference to Chapter 10.

f) Use a new roll-pin when reconnecting the gear selector rod to the selector shaft.

g) Refit the exhaust front section as described in Chapter 4B.

h) Use a new O-ring when reconnecting the power steering pump pressure hose to the intermediate pipe.

i) Reconnect and adjust the throttle cable as described in Chapter 4B.

j) Reconnect the clutch cable as described in Chapter 6.

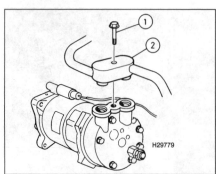

4.55 Unscrew the bolt (1) securing the air conditioning refrigerant pipe union (2) to the compressor

k) Refill the transmission with oil as described in Chapter 7A.

l) Refill the cooling system, and refill the engine with oil as described in Chapter 1B.

Models with air conditioning

Removal

Note: The air conditioning system must be discharged by a Rover dealer or a qualified air conditioning specialist. **Do not** attempt to discharge the system yourself – refer to Chapter 3 for precautions to be observed when working on the air conditioning system components. During this procedure, all air conditioning refrigerant pipes and connections should be plugged immediately after disconnection to prevent dirt and moisture from entering the system. A suitable engine hoist and adjustable lifting tackle will be required for this operation. In order to allow the engine/transmission assembly to pass out from under the vehicle, the front of the vehicle must be raised to a height of 770 mm (measured from the ground to the lower edge of the front bumper) – ensure that suitable axle stands are available to enable the vehicle to be raised to this height. A new gear selector rod-to-selector shaft roll-pin, and a new power steering pump pressure hose-to-intermediate pipe O-ring and new air conditioning refrigerant pipe O-rings will be required on refitting.

53 Have the air conditioning system refrigerant discharged by a Rover dealer or an air conditioning system specialist.

54 Proceed as described in paragraphs 1 to 18.

55 Unscrew the bolt securing the air conditioning refrigerant pipe union to the compressor, then release the pipe union from the compressor **(see illustration)**. Withdraw the air conditioning refrigerant pipes, then remove the two O-rings from the compressor and discard them. Plug the open ends of the pipes and the compressor.

56 Unscrew the bolt securing the compressor pipe to the evaporator pipe, then release the compressor pipe from the evaporator pipe **(see illustration)**. Recover the O-ring from the evaporator pipe and discard it. Plug the open ends of the pipes.

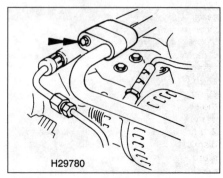

4.56 Unscrew the bolt (arrowed) securing the compressor pipe to the evaporator pipe

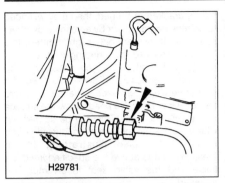

4.57 Slacken the nut (arrowed) securing the air conditioning compressor pipe to the condenser pipe

5.3a Unscrew the securing bolts (arrowed) . . .

5.3b . . . and remove the transmission mounting plate

57 Slacken the union nut (counterhold the union using a second spanner), and disconnect the air conditioning compressor pipe from the condenser pipe **(see illustration)**. Recover the O-ring from the compressor pipe and discard it. Plug the open ends of the pipes.

58 Remove the air conditioning refrigerant pipes, noting their locations to aid refitting.

59 Proceed as described in paragraphs 19 to 47.

Refitting

60 Proceed as described in paragraphs 48 to 52, noting the following additional points.

a) Renew all O-rings when reconnecting the air conditioning refrigerant pipes. The new O-rings should be lubricated with fresh air conditioning refrigerant before fitting.

b) On completion, have the air conditioning system recharged with refrigerant by a Rover dealer or a qualified air conditioning specialist.

5 Engine overhaul – dismantling sequence

Note: *When removing external components from the engine, pay close attention to details that may be helpful or important during refitting. Note the fitted position of gaskets, seals, spacers, pins, washers, bolts and other small items.*

1 It is much easier to work on the engine if it is mounted on a portable engine stand. These stands can often be hired from a tool hire shop. Before the engine is mounted on a stand, the flywheel should be removed so that the stand bolts can be tightened into the end of the cylinder block/crankcase.

2 If a stand is not available, it is possible to dismantle the engine with it blocked up on a sturdy workbench or on the floor. Be extra careful not to tip or drop the engine when working without a stand.

3 If you are going to obtain a reconditioned engine, all external components must be removed for transfer to the replacement engine (just as if you are doing a complete engine overhaul yourself). These components include the following **(see illustrations):**

a) Alternator/brake vacuum pump assembly.
b) Air conditioning compressor (where applicable).
c) Power steering pump/coolant pump assembly.
d) Coolant outlet elbow.
e) Dipstick tube.
f) Fuel injection pump, drivebelt, fuel injectors, glow plugs, and associated fuel system components.
g) All electrical switches and sensors.
h) Inlet and exhaust manifolds.
i) Oil pipes, coolant pipes and brackets.
j) Oil cooler.
k) Oil filter.
l) Engine mounting brackets.
m) Flywheel.
n) Transmission mounting plate.
o) Ancillary mounting brackets.

4 If you are obtaining a short motor (which consists of the engine cylinder block/crankcase, crankshaft, pistons and connecting rods all assembled), then the fuel injection pump drivebelt, timing belt, cylinder head, sump, oil pump, and oil cooler will have to be removed also.

5 If you are planning a complete overhaul, the engine can be dismantled and the internal components removed in the following order:

a) Inlet and exhaust manifolds.
b) Timing belt, sprockets, tensioner, and timing belt rear covers.
c) Cylinder head.
d) Flywheel.
e) Sump.
f) Oil pump.
g) Piston/connecting rod assemblies.
h) Crankshaft.

6 Before beginning the dismantling and overhaul procedures, make sure that you have all of the correct tools necessary. Refer to the introductory pages at the beginning of this Manual for further information.

6 Cylinder head – dismantling

Note: *New and reconditioned cylinder heads are available from the manufacturer and from engine overhaul specialists. Due to the fact that some specialist tools are required for dismantling and inspection, and new components may not be readily available, it may be more practical and economical for the home mechanic to purchase a reconditioned head rather than dismantle, inspect and recondition the original. A valve spring compressor tool will be required for this operation.*

1 With the cylinder head removed, if not already done, remove the fuel injectors (see Chapter 4B) and the glow plugs (see Chapter 5C), then proceed as follows.

2 Remove the camshaft and hydraulic tappets, as described in Part B of this Chapter.

3 Using a valve spring compressor tool, compress each valve spring in turn until the split collets can be removed. Release the compressor and lift off the spring retainer and spring, then use a pair of pliers to extract the spring lower seat/stem seal **(see illustrations)**.

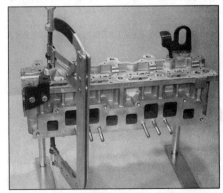

6.3a Using a valve spring compressor tool . . .

2D

6.3b . . . compress the valve spring until the split collets can be removed

HAYNES HiNT *If, when the valve spring compressor is screwed down, the spring retainer refuses to free and expose the split collets, gently tap the top of the tool directly over the retainer with a light hammer. This will free the retainer.*

4 Withdraw the valve through the combustion chamber.
5 It is essential that each valve is stored together with its collets, retainer and spring, and that all valves are kept in their correct sequence, unless they are so badly worn that they are to be renewed. If they are going to be kept and used again, place each valve assembly in a labelled polythene bag or similar small container **(see illustration)**. Note that No 1 valve is nearest to the timing belt end of the engine.

7   Cylinder head and valves –
cleaning and inspection

Note: *If the engine has been severely overheated, it is best to assume that the cylinder head is warped and to check carefully for signs of this.*
Note: *Be sure to perform all the following inspection procedures before concluding that the services of a machine shop or engine*

6.5 Place each valve assembly in a labelled polythene bag

overhaul specialist are required. Make a list of all items that require attention.
1 Thorough cleaning of the cylinder head and valve components, followed by a detailed inspection, will enable you to decide how much valve service work must be carried out during the engine overhaul.

Cleaning
2 Scrape away all traces of old gasket material and sealing compound from the cylinder head.
3 Scrape away all carbon from the combustion chambers and ports, then wash the cylinder head thoroughly with paraffin or a suitable solvent.
4 Scrape off any heavy carbon deposits that may have formed on the valves, then use a power-operated wire brush to remove deposits from the valve heads and stems.

Inspection
Cylinder head
5 Inspect the head very carefully for cracks, evidence of coolant leakage and other damage. If cracks are found, a new cylinder head should be obtained.
6 Use a straight-edge and feeler blade to check that the cylinder head surface is not distorted **(see illustration)**. Note that the cylinder head cannot be refaced, and must be renewed if the surface is distorted beyond the specified limit.
7 Examine the valve seats in each of the combustion chambers. If they are severely

pitted, cracked or burned, then they will need to be renewed or re-cut by an engine overhaul specialist. If they are only slightly pitted, this can be removed by grinding-in the valve heads and seats with fine valve-grinding compound as described below. To check for excessive wear, refit each valve and measure the recess of the valve head below the surface of the cylinder head. This can be carried out with a dial gauge, or with a straight-edge and feeler blades **(see illustration)**. If the measurement is above the specified limit, the valve and the valve seat insert must be renewed.
8 If the valve guides are worn, indicated by a side to side motion of the valve, new guides and valves must be fitted. Measure the diameter of the existing valve stems (see below) and the bore of the guides, then calculate the clearance and compare the result with the specified value. If the clearance is excessive, renew the valves and guides as necessary. Note that the valve guides can only be renewed twice – if the guides need to be renewed for the third time, the cylinder head must be renewed. A mark on the camshaft side of the cylinder head, adjacent to the valve guide will be present if the valve guide has been renewed before – "+" indicates that the guide has been renewed once before, and "-" indicates that the guide has been renewed twice before.
9 Valve guide renewal is best carried out by an engine overhaul specialist, as the cylinder head must be evenly heated to remove and fit the guides, and the guides must be accurately reamed once fitted.

Valves
10 Examine the head of each valve for pitting, burning, cracks and general wear, then check the valve stem for scoring and wear ridges. Rotate the valve and check for any obvious indication that it is bent. Look for pits and excessive wear on the tip of each valve stem. Renew any valve that shows any such signs of wear or damage.
11 If the valve appears satisfactory at this stage, measure the valve stem diameter at several points by using a micrometer **(see illustration)**. Any significant difference in the

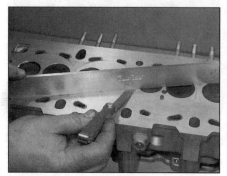

7.6 Use a straight-edge and feeler blade to check the cylinder head for distortion

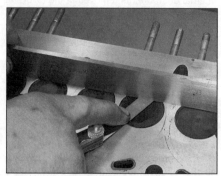

7.7 Checking the recess of a valve head below the surface of the cylinder head

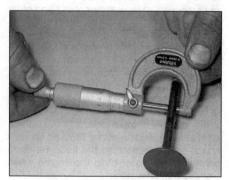

7.11 Measuring a valve stem diameter

Diesel engine removal and general overhaul procedures 2D•9

readings obtained indicates wear of the valve stem. Should any of these conditions be apparent, the valve(s) must be renewed.

12 If the valves are in satisfactory condition they should be ground (lapped) into their respective seats to ensure a smooth gas-tight seal. If the seat is only lightly pitted, or if it has been re-cut, fine grinding compound only should be used to produce the required finish. Coarse valve-grinding compound should not be used unless a seat is badly burned or deeply pitted. If this is the case, the cylinder head and valves should be inspected by an expert to decide whether seat re-cutting or even the renewal of the valve or seat insert is required.

13 Valve grinding is carried out as follows. Place the cylinder head upside down on a bench.

14 Smear a trace of (the appropriate grade of) valve-grinding compound on the seat face and press a suction grinding tool onto the valve head. With a semi-rotary action, grind the valve head to its seat, lifting the valve occasionally to redistribute the grinding compound **(see illustration)**. A light spring placed under the valve head will greatly ease this operation.

15 If coarse grinding compound is being used, work only until a dull, matt even surface is produced on both the valve seat and the valve, then wipe off the used compound and repeat the process with fine compound. When a smooth unbroken ring of light grey matt finish is produced on both the valve and seat, the grinding operation is complete. Do not grind in the valves any further than absolutely necessary, or the seat will be prematurely sunk into the cylinder head.

16 To check that the seat has not been over-ground, measure the valve head recess, as described in paragraph 7.

17 When all the valves have been ground-in, carefully wash off all traces of grinding compound using paraffin or a suitable solvent.

Valve components

18 Examine the valve springs for signs of damage and discoloration and also measure their free length using vernier calipers or a rule, or by comparing each existing spring with a new component **(see illustration)**.

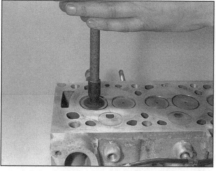

7.14 Grinding-in a valve using a suction grinding tool

19 Stand each spring on a flat surface and check it for squareness. If any of the springs are damaged, distorted or have lost their tension, then obtain a complete new set of springs.

20 Check the hydraulic tappets as described in Part B of this Chapter.

8 Cylinder head – reassembly

Note: A valve spring compressor tool will be required for this operation. New valve spring lower seat/stem oil seals will be required.

1 Lubricate the valve stems with clean engine oil and insert each valve into its original location **(see illustration)**. If new valves are

8.1 Lubricate the valve stems with clean engine oil

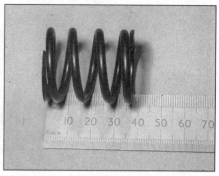

7.18 Measuring a valve spring free length

being fitted, insert them into the locations to which they have been ground.

2 Working on the first valve, dip the **new** spring lower seat/stem seal in clean engine oil then carefully locate it over the valve and onto the guide. Take care not to damage the seal as it is passed over the valve stem. Press the seal firmly onto the guide **(see illustration)**.

3 Locate the spring on the seat, followed by the spring retainer **(see illustrations)**.

4 Compress the valve spring and locate the split collets in the recess in the valve stem. Use a little grease to hold the collets in place **(see illustration)**. Release the compressor, then repeat the procedure on the remaining valves.

5 With all the valves installed, rest the cylinder head on wooden blocks or stands (**do not** rest the head flat on a bench) and, using a

8.2 Fitting a valve spring lower seat/stem seal

8.3a Refit the spring . . .

8.3b . . . followed by the spring retainer

8.4 Use a little grease to hold the split collets in place

2D

9.3 Connecting rod and big-end cap identification markings

9.4 Removing a big-end bearing cap

10 Crankshaft – removal

Note: *A dial gauge will be required to check crankshaft endfloat.*

1 Remove the flywheel, and the crankshaft rear oil seal, as described in Chapter 2B.

2 Remove the pistons and connecting rods, as described in Section 9.

3 Remove the oil pump as described in Chapter 2B.

4 Invert the cylinder block so that the crankshaft is uppermost.

5 Before removing the crankshaft, check the endfloat using a dial gauge in contact with the end of the crankshaft. Push the crankshaft fully one way, and then zero the gauge. Push the crankshaft fully the other way, and check the endfloat **(see illustration)**. The result should be compared with the specified limit, and will give an indication as to whether new thrust bearing shells are required.

6 The main bearing caps are normally numbered 1 to 5 from the timing belt end of the engine **(see illustration)**. If the bearing caps are not marked, centre-punch them to indicate their locations, and note to which side of the engine the marks face.

7 Starting with the centre bearing cap, and working progressively outwards, unscrew and remove the main bearing cap bolts. Keep all the bolts in their fitted order.

8 Using the fingers only, rock each main bearing cap until it is released from its locating dowels **(see illustration)**. **Do not** tap the bearing caps sideways to release them. Recover the bearing shells if they are loose, and tape them to their respective caps.

9 Lift the crankshaft from the crankcase. Take care, the crankshaft if heavy! Take care not to damage the piston oil spay jets fitted to the cylinder block.

10 Extract the upper bearing shells, and identify them for position. Similarly, extract the two thrust washers from the centre bearing location **(see illustration)**.

hammer and interposed block of wood, tap the end of each valve stem to settle the components.

6 Refit the hydraulic tappets and camshaft as described in Part B of this Chapter.

9 Piston/connecting rod assembly – removal

Note: *The big-end bearing caps may be secured to the connecting rods by nuts, or bolts, depending on engine type. On engines where the big-end bearing caps are secured by bolts, "fracture-split" connecting rod/bearing cap assemblies are fitted (big-end bearing caps secured by bolts) – each connecting rod/bearing cap is manufactured as a one-piece component, and then "fractured" to give the connecting rod and bearing cap. On engines with "fracture-split" assemblies, each bearing cap is therefore perfectly matched to its respective connecting rod, and the big-end bolts are offset to prevent incorrect fitting of the bearing cap.*

1 Remove the cylinder head as described in Chapter 2B.

2 Remove the sump and oil pick-up pipe, as described in Chapter 2B.

3 If the connecting rods and big-end caps are not marked to indicate their positions in the cylinder block (ie marked with cylinder numbers), centre-punch them at adjacent points either side of the cap/rod joint. Note to which side of the engine the marks face **(see illustration)**.

4 Unscrew the big-end cap nuts or bolts (as applicable) from the first connecting rod, and remove the cap **(see illustration)**. Tape the cap and the shell together to enable subsequent examination. Similarly, the big-end cap nuts or bolts (as applicable) must be kept in their original locations, with their original connecting rod/bearing cap assemblies (refit the nuts/bolts once the relevant piston/connecting rod assembly has been removed).

5 Check the top of the cylinder bore for a wear ridge. If evident, carefully scrape it away with a ridge reamer tool, otherwise the piston rings may jam against the ridge as the piston is pushed out of the block.

6 Place the wooden handle of a hammer against the bottom of the connecting rod, and push the piston/rod assembly up and out of the cylinder bore. Take care to keep the connecting rods clear of the cylinder bore walls, and be careful not to damage the piston oil spray jets fitted to the cylinder block. Recover the bearing shell, and tape it to the connecting rod if it is to be re-used.

7 Remove the remaining three assemblies in a similar way. Rotate the crankshaft as necessary to bring the big-end nuts or bolts (as applicable) to the most accessible position.

10.5 Checking crankshaft endfloat using a dial gauge

10.6 Main bearing cap identification markings

10.8 Removing a main bearing cap

10.10 Extract the thrust washers from the centre main bearing location

11.1 Removing a piston oil spray jet

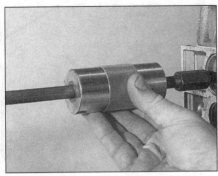

11.2 Removing a core plug using a slide hammer

11 Cylinder block/crankcase – cleaning and inspection

Cleaning

1 Before proceeding, unscrew the securing bolts, and remove the piston oil spray jets from the cylinder block **(see illustration)**. Note that each spray jet is located by a roll-pin.

2 For complete cleaning, ideally the core plugs should be removed, where fitted. Drill a small hole in the plugs, then insert a self-tapping screw, and pull out the plugs using a pair of grips or a slide hammer **(see illustration)**. Also remove all external components (senders, sensors, brackets, etc).

3 Scrape all traces of gasket from the cylinder block, taking particular care not to damage the cylinder head and sump mating faces.

4 Remove all oil gallery plugs, where fitted. The plugs are usually very tight - they may have to be drilled out and the holes re-tapped. Use new plugs when the engine is reassembled.

5 If the block is extremely dirty, it should be steam-cleaned.

6 If the block has been steam-cleaned, clean all oil holes and oil galleries one more time on completion. Flush all internal passages with warm water until the water runs clear. Dry the block thoroughly, and wipe all machined surfaces with a light oil. If you have access to compressed air, use it to speed the drying process, and to blow out all the oil holes and galleries.

 Warning: Wear eye protection when using compressed air!

7 If the block is relatively clean, an adequate cleaning job can be achieved with hot soapy water and a stiff brush. Take plenty of time, and do a thorough job. Regardless of the cleaning method used, be sure to clean all oil holes and galleries very thoroughly, dry the block completely, and coat all machined surfaces with light oil.

8 The threaded holes in the cylinder block must be clean, to ensure accurate torque readings when tightening fixings during reassembly. Run the correct-size tap (which can be determined from the size of the relevant bolt) into each of the holes to remove rust, corrosion, thread sealant or other contamination, and to restore damaged threads **(see illustration)**. If possible, use compressed air to clear the holes of debris produced by this operation. Do not forget to clean the threads of all bolts and nuts as well.

9 After coating the mating surfaces of the new core plugs with suitable sealant, fit them to the cylinder block. Make sure that they are driven in straight and seated correctly, or leakage could result. Special tools are available to fit the core plugs, but a large socket, with an outside diameter which will just fit into the core plug, will work just as well.

10 Where applicable, apply suitable sealant to the new oil gallery plugs, and insert them into the relevant holes in the cylinder block. Tighten the plugs securely.

11 Thoroughly clean the piston oil spray jets and their securing bolts. Examine the spray jets for damage or distortion, and renew if necessary. Ensure that the oil spray jets are clear, and that the locating roll-pins are in position in the cylinder block, then refit the spray jets, ensuring that they locate with the

roll-pins. Apply a little thread-locking fluid to the threads of each oil spray jet securing bolt, then refit the bolt and tighten to the specified torque **(see illustration)**.

Caution: Ensure that the thread-locking fluid does not enter the oil hole in the oil spray jet securing bolt.

12 If the engine is to be left dismantled for some time, refit the main bearing caps, tighten the bolts finger-tight, and cover the cylinder block with a large plastic bag to keep it clean and prevent corrosion.

Inspection

13 Visually check the block for cracks, rust and corrosion. Look for stripped threads in the threaded holes (it may be possible to re-cut stripped threads using a suitable tap). If there has been any history of internal coolant leakage, it may be worthwhile asking an engine overhaul specialist to check the block using special equipment. If defects are found, have the block repaired if possible, otherwise a new block may be the only option.

14 Examine the cylinder bores for taper, ovality, scoring and scratches. Start by carefully examining the top of the cylinder bores. If they are at all worn, a very slight ridge will be found on the thrust side. This marks the top of the piston ring travel.

2D

11.8 Clean out the threaded holes in the cylinder block using the correct-size tap

11.11 Apply thread-locking fluid to the oil spray jet securing bolts

11.15 Measuring a cylinder bore diameter using an internal micrometer

12.2 Removing a piston ring with the aid of a feeler blade

15 Measure the bore diameter of each cylinder approximately 70 mm from the top of the bore, parallel to the crankshaft axis **(see illustration)**.

16 Next, measure the bore diameter at right-angles to the crankshaft axis. Compare the results with the figures given in the Specifications.

17 Repeat the procedure for the remaining cylinders.

18 If the cylinder wear exceeds the permitted tolerances, or if the cylinder walls are badly scored or scuffed, then the cylinder block and pistons **must** be renewed. Note that it is not possible to rebore the cylinder block, as only one size of piston is available for this engine. Similarly, **do not** attempt to hone or "glaze-bust" the cylinder bores.

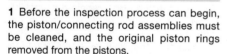

12 Piston/connecting rod assembly – inspection

1 Before the inspection process can begin, the piston/connecting rod assemblies must be cleaned, and the original piston rings removed from the pistons.

2 Carefully expand the old rings over the top of the pistons. The use of two or three old feeler blades will be helpful in preventing the rings dropping into empty grooves **(see illustration)**. Take care, however, as piston rings are sharp.

3 Scrape away all traces of carbon from the top of the piston. A hand-held wire brush, or a piece of fine emery cloth, can be used once the majority of the deposits have been scraped away.

4 Remove the carbon from the ring grooves in the piston, using an old ring. Break the ring in half to do this (be careful not to cut your fingers - piston rings are sharp). Be very careful to remove only the carbon deposits - do not remove any metal, and do not nick or scratch the sides of the ring grooves.

5 Once the deposits have been removed, clean the piston/connecting rod assembly with paraffin or a suitable solvent, and dry

thoroughly. Make sure that the oil return holes in the ring grooves are clear.

6 If the pistons and cylinder bores are not damaged or worn excessively, the original pistons can be refitted. Normal piston wear shows up as even vertical wear on the piston thrust surfaces, and slight looseness of the top ring in its groove. New piston rings should always be used when the engine is reassembled.

7 Carefully inspect each piston for cracks around the skirt, at the gudgeon pin bosses, and at the piston ring lands (between the ring grooves).

8 Look for scoring and scuffing on the thrust faces of the piston skirt, holes in the piston crown, and burned areas at the edge of the crown. If the skirt is scored or scuffed, the engine may have been suffering from overheating, and/or abnormal combustion ('pinking') which caused excessively-high operating temperatures. The cooling and lubrication systems should be checked thoroughly. A hole in the piston crown, or burned areas at the edge of the piston crown indicates that abnormal combustion (pre-ignition, 'pinking', knocking, or detonation) has been occurring. If any of the above problems exist, the causes must be investigated and corrected, or the damage will occur again. The causes may include incorrect fuel injection pump timing, inlet air leaks, or a faulty fuel injector.

9 Corrosion of the piston, in the form of

pitting, indicates that coolant has been leaking into the combustion chamber and/or the crankcase. Again, the cause must be corrected, or the problem may persist in the rebuilt engine.

10 Check the piston-to-bore clearance by measuring the cylinder bore (see Section 11) and the piston diameter. Measure the piston 44 mm from the bottom of the skirt, at a 90° angle to the gudgeon pin. Note that the measurement should be made on the bar metal surfaces of the piston skirt, **not** on the graphite-coated areas **(see illustrations)**. Subtract the piston diameter from the bore diameter to obtain the clearance. If this is greater than the figures given in the Specifications, and the cylinder bore diameter is within limits, new pistons must be fitted. If the cylinder bore is worn beyond the specified limits, the block and pistons **must** be renewed. Note that it is not possible to rebore the cylinder block, as only one size of piston is available for this engine. Similarly, **do not** attempt to hone or "glaze-bust" the cylinder bores.

11 Alternatively, the piston-to-bore clearance can be measured as follows. Invert the piston, and slide it into the relevant cylinder bore, with the arrow on the piston crown pointing towards the flywheel end of the cylinder block. Position the piston with the bottom of the skirt 25 mm below the top of the cylinder bore. Using a feeler blade, measure the clearance between the piston skirt and the left-hand side of the cylinder bore (when viewed with the cylinder block inverted, from the timing belt end of the cylinder block).

12 Examine each connecting rod carefully for signs of damage, such as cracks around the big-end and small-end bearings. Check that the rod is not bent or distorted. Damage is highly unlikely, unless the engine has been seized or badly overheated. Detailed checking of the connecting rod assembly can only be carried out by a Rover dealer or engine repair specialist with the necessary equipment.

13 The gudgeon pins are of the floating type, secured in position by two circlips. The pistons and connecting rods can be separated as follows.

12.10a Measure the diameter of the pistons . . .

12.10b . . . across the bare metal surfaces (arrowed) of the piston skirt

12.14a Prise out the circlips . . .

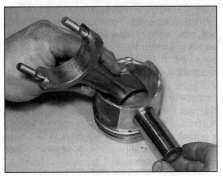

12.14b . . . and push the gudgeon pin from the piston

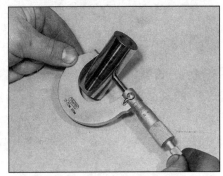

12.17 Measuring the diameter of a gudgeon pin

14 Using a small flat-bladed screwdriver, prise out the circlips, and push out the gudgeon pin **(see illustrations)**. Hand pressure should be sufficient to remove the pin. Identify the piston and rod to ensure correct reassembly. Discard the circlips - new ones **must** be used on refitting.

15 Examine the gudgeon pin and connecting rod small-end bearing for signs of wear or damage. It should be possible to push the gudgeon pin through the connecting rod bush by hand, without noticeable play. If the connecting rod bush is worn, the connecting rod must be renewed – it is not possible to renew the bushes.

16 Similarly, check the fit of the gudgeon pin in its relevant piston. The pin must be a tight sliding fit, with no perceptible side play.

17 Measure the diameter of the gudgeon pin **(see illustration)**. If the diameter is less than the specified limit, or if excessive side play in the piston is evident, the gudgeon pin and piston must be renewed as an assembly.

18 Repeat the checking procedure for the

remaining pistons, connecting rods and gudgeon pins.

19 The connecting rods themselves should not be in need of renewal, unless seizure or some other major mechanical failure has occurred. Check the alignment of the connecting rods visually, and if the rods are not straight, take them to an engine overhaul specialist for a more detailed check.

20 Examine all components, and obtain any new parts from your Rover dealer. If new pistons are purchased, they will be supplied complete with gudgeon pins and circlips. Circlips can also be purchased individually. Note that on models with "fracture split" connecting rod/bearing cap assemblies (big-end bearing caps secured by bolts), if a connecting rod requires renewal, it can only be renewed as an assembly with the relevant bearing cap.

21 Position the piston in relation to the connecting rod, as follows **(see illustrations)**.

a) **On models where the big-end bearing caps are secured by nuts**, the bearing shell tag recess in the connecting rod should be positioned to the left of the arrow on the piston crown, when the piston is viewed from the rear (flywheel end).

b) **On models where the big-end bearing caps are secured by bolts**, the cast boss on the connecting rod should be positioned on the same side of the assembly as the arrow on the piston crown.

22 Apply a smear of clean engine oil to the gudgeon pin. Slide it into the piston and through the connecting rod small-end. Check that the piston pivots freely on the rod, then secure the gudgeon pin in position with two new circlips. Ensure that each circlip is correctly located in its groove in the piston.

23 On engines where the big-end bearing caps are secured by nuts, using the fingers only, check that each big-end bearing cap nut rotates freely on the threads of its respective bolt. If any nut is tight, then both bolts and nuts from the relevant connecting rod must be renewed.

24 On engines where the big-end bearing caps are secured by bolts, using the fingers only, check that each bolt turns freely in its connecting rod. If there is any sign of binding in the threads, the bolts must be renewed.

2D

13 Crankshaft – inspection

1 Clean the crankshaft using paraffin or a suitable solvent, and dry it, preferably with compressed air if available.

> ⚠️ *Warning: Wear eye protection when using compressed air! Be sure to clean the oil holes with a pipe cleaner or similar probe, to ensure that they are not obstructed.*

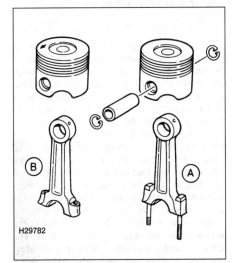

H29782

12.21a Piston and connecting rod identification

A Assembly with big-end bearing cap secured by nuts
B Assembly with big-end bearing cap secured by bolts

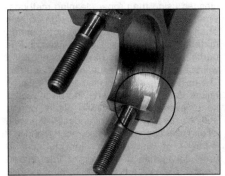

12.21b Where the bearing caps are secured by nuts, the bearing shell tag recess in the connecting rod . . .

12.21c . . . should be positioned to the left of the arrow on the piston crown when the piston is viewed from the rear (flywheel end)

13.6 Measuring the diameter of a crankshaft big-end bearing journal

2 Check the main and big-end bearing journals for uneven wear, scoring, pitting and cracking.

3 Big-end bearing wear is accompanied by distinct metallic knocking when the engine is running (particularly noticeable when the engine is pulling from low revs), and some loss of oil pressure.

4 Main bearing wear is accompanied by severe engine vibration and rumble - getting progressively worse as engine revs increase - and again by loss of oil pressure.

5 Check the bearing journal for roughness by running a finger lightly over the bearing surface. Any roughness (which will be accompanied by obvious bearing wear) indicates the that the crankshaft requires replacing.

6 Using a micrometer, measure the diameter of the main and big-end bearing journals, and compare the results with the Specifications at the beginning of this Chapter **(see illustration)**. By measuring the diameter at a number of points around each journal's circumference, you will be able to determine whether or not the journal is out-of-round. Take the measurement at each end of the

journal, near the webs, to determine if the journal is tapered. If the crankshaft journals are damaged, tapered, out-of-round or excessively-worn, the crankshaft must be renewed. It is not possible to regrind the crankshaft.

7 Check the oil seal contact surfaces at each end of the crankshaft for wear and damage. If the seal has worn an excessive groove in the surface of the crankshaft, consult an engine overhaul specialist, who will be able to advise whether a repair is possible, or whether a new crankshaft is necessary.

14 Main and big-end bearings – inspection

1 Even though the main and big-end bearings **must** be renewed during the engine overhaul, the old bearings should be retained for close examination, as they may reveal valuable information about the condition of the engine.

2 Bearing failure can occur due to lack of lubrication, the presence of dirt or other foreign particles, overloading the engine, or corrosion **(see illustration)**. Regardless of the cause of bearing failure, the cause must be corrected (where applicable) before the engine is reassembled, to prevent it from happening again.

3 When examining the bearing shells, remove them from the cylinder block/crankcase, the main bearing caps, the connecting rods and the connecting rod big-end bearing caps. Lay them out on a clean surface in the same general position as their location in the engine. This will enable you to match any bearing problems with the corresponding crankshaft journal.

4 Dirt and other foreign matter gets into the engine in a variety of ways. It may be left in the engine during assembly, or it may pass through filters or the crankcase ventilation system. It may get into the oil, and from there into the bearings. Metal chips from machining operations and normal engine wear are often present. Abrasives are sometimes left in engine components after reconditioning, especially when parts are not thoroughly cleaned using the proper cleaning methods. Whatever the source, these foreign objects often end up embedded in the soft bearing material, and are easily recognised. Large particles will not embed in the bearing, and will score or gouge the bearing and journal. The best prevention for this cause of bearing failure is to clean all parts thoroughly, and keep everything spotlessly-clean during engine assembly. Frequent and regular engine oil and filter changes are also recommended.

5 Lack of lubrication (or lubrication breakdown) has a number of interrelated causes. Excessive heat (which thins the oil), overloading (which squeezes the oil from the bearing face) and oil leakage (from excessive bearing clearances, worn oil pump or high

engine speeds) all contribute to lubrication breakdown. Blocked oil passages, which usually are the result of misaligned oil holes in a bearing shell, will also oil-starve a bearing, and destroy it. When lack of lubrication is the cause of bearing failure, the bearing material is wiped or extruded from the steel backing of the bearing. Temperatures may increase to the point where the steel backing turns blue from overheating.

6 Driving habits can have a definite effect on bearing life. Full-throttle, low-speed operation (labouring the engine) puts very high loads on bearings, tending to squeeze out the oil film. These loads cause the bearings to flex, which produces fine cracks in the bearing face (fatigue failure). Eventually, the bearing material will loosen in pieces, and tear away from the steel backing.

7 Short-distance driving leads to corrosion of bearings, because insufficient engine heat is produced to evaporate off the condensed water and corrosive gases. These products collect in the engine oil, forming acid and sludge. As the oil is carried to the engine bearings, the acid attacks and corrodes the bearing material.

8 Incorrect bearing installation during engine assembly will lead to bearing failure as well. Tight-fitting bearings leave insufficient bearing running clearance, and will result in oil starvation. Dirt or foreign particles trapped behind a bearing shell result in high spots on the bearing, which lead to failure.

9 As mentioned at the beginning of this Section, the bearing shells must be renewed during engine overhaul, regardless of their condition.

15 Engine overhaul – reassembly sequence

1 Before reassembly begins, ensure that all new parts have been obtained and that all necessary tools are available. Read through the entire procedure to familiarise yourself with the work involved and to ensure that all items necessary for reassembly of the engine are at hand. In addition to all normal tools and materials, it will be necessary to obtain suitable thread-locking compound, and various Rover sealants – refer to the relevant Sections in this Part of the Chapter and Part B for details. Carefully read the instructions supplied with the appropriate sealant kit.

2 In order to save time and avoid problems, engine reassembly can be carried out in the following order, referring to Part B of this Chapter when necessary. Where applicable, use new gaskets and seals when refitting the various components.

 a) *Crankshaft.*
 b) *Piston/connecting rod assemblies.*
 c) *Oil pump.*
 d) *Sump.*
 e) *Crankshaft rear oil seal and flywheel.*

FATIGUE FAILURE

CRATERS OR POCKETS

IMPROPER SEATING

BRIGHT (POLISHED) SECTIONS

SCRATCHED BY DIRT

DIRT EMBEDDED INTO BEARING MATERIAL

LACK OF OIL

OVERLAY WIPED OUT

EXCESSIVE WEAR

OVERLAY WIPED OUT

TAPERED JOURNAL

RADIUS RIDE

H 28395

14.2 Typical bearing failures

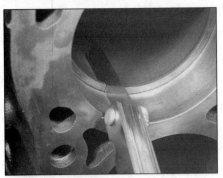

16.4 Measuring a piston ring end gap

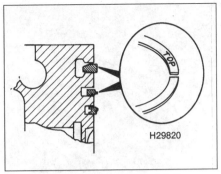

16.9 Piston ring fitting details

surface of the rings is normally marked "TOP" **(see illustration)**. Arrange the gaps of the top and second compression rings 120° from each other, away from the thrust side of the piston. **Note:** *Always follow any instructions supplied with the new piston ring sets - different manufacturers may specify different procedures. Do not mix up the top and second compression rings, as they have different cross-sections.*

17 Crankshaft – refitting

f) *Cylinder head.*
g) *Timing belt rear cover, tensioner and sprockets, and timing belt.*
h) *Engine external components.*

3 At this stage, all engine components should be absolutely clean and dry, with all faults repaired, and should be laid out (or in individual containers) on a completely clean work surface.

16 Piston rings – refitting

1 Before fitting new piston rings, the ring end gaps must be checked as follows.
2 Lay out the piston/connecting rod assemblies and the new piston ring sets, so that the ring sets will be matched with the same piston and cylinder during the end gap measurement and subsequent engine reassembly.
3 Insert the top ring into the first cylinder liner bore, and push it down the bore using the top of the piston. This will ensure that the ring remains square with the cylinder walls. Position the ring 30 mm from the top of the bore. Note that the top and second compression rings are different. The second ring is easily identified by the step on its lower surface.
4 Measure the end gap using feeler blades **(see illustration)**. Compare the

measurements with the figures given in the *Specifications*.
5 If the gap is too small (unlikely if genuine Rover parts are used), it must be enlarged, or the ring ends may contact each other during engine operation, causing serious damage. Ideally, new piston rings providing the correct end gap should be fitted. As a last resort, the end gap can be increased by filing the ring ends very carefully with a fine file. Mount the file in a vice equipped with soft jaws, slip the ring over the file with the ends contacting the file face, and slowly move the ring to remove material from the ends.

Caution: Take care, as the piston rings are sharp, and are easily broken.

6 With new piston rings, it is unlikely that the end gap will be too large. If the gaps are too large, check that you have the correct rings for your engine and for the particular cylinder bore size.
7 Repeat the checking procedure for each ring in the first cylinder, and then for the rings in the remaining cylinders. Remember to keep rings, pistons and cylinders matched up.
8 Once the ring end gaps have been checked and if necessary corrected, the rings can be fitted to the pistons.
9 Fit the piston rings using the same technique as for removal. Fit the bottom (oil control) ring first, and work up. Ensure that the rings are fitted the correct way up - the top

Note: *New main bearing shells must be fitted on reassembly.*

1 After inspecting the crankshaft, and renewing it if necessary, as described in Section 13, proceed as follows.
2 Check that the main bearing cap locating dowels are in position in the cylinder block, and that the main bearing cap bolt holes are clean and dry.
3 Clean the backs of the new bearing shells, and the bearing locations in both the cylinder block/crankcase and the main bearing caps. Ensure that all traces of the protective grease are cleaned off the new bearing shells using paraffin. Wipe the shells dry with a lint-free cloth.
4 Press the bearing shells into their locations in the cylinder block and bearing caps, noting that the bearing shells with the oil grooves fit into the upper locations (in the cylinder block/crankcase). Take care not to touch any shell bearing surface with your fingers. Ensure that the tab on each lower shell engages in the notch in the main bearing cap. The shells in the cylinder block/crankcase have no locating tabs, so make sure that they are located centrally and squarely in their respective positions **(see illustrations)**.
5 Using a little grease, stick the thrustwashers to each side of the centre main bearing upper location in the cylinder block/crankcase. Ensure that the oilway

2D

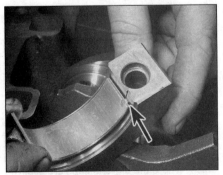

17.4a Ensure that the tab (arrowed) engages with the notch in the main bearing cap

17.4b Press the bearing shells into their locations in the cylinder block . . .

17.4c . . . making sure that they are located centrally

17.5 Ensure that the grooves (arrowed) on the thrustwashers face outwards

17.6 Lubricate the bearing shells in the cylinder block/crankcase

17.8 Oil the threads of the main bearing cap bolts

grooves on each thrustwasher face outwards **(see illustration)**.

6 Liberally lubricate each bearing shell in the cylinder block/crankcase, then lower the crankshaft into position **(see illustration)**.

7 Lubricate the bearing shells in the bearing caps, and the crankshaft journals, then fit the bearing caps, ensuring that they engage with the locating dowels.

8 Ensure that the threads of the main bearing cap bolts are clean, then oil the threads of the bolts, and screw them into their original locations, finger-tight only at this stage **(see illustration)**.

9 Working from the centre main bearing cap outwards, progressively tighten the bearing cap bolts to the specified torque **(see illustration)**.

10 Now rotate the crankshaft, and check that it turns freely, with no signs of binding or tight spots.

11 Check the crankshaft endfloat with reference to Section 10. If the endfloat exceeds the specified limit, remove the crankshaft and fit new thrust washers. If, with the new thrust washers fitted, the endfloat is still excessive, the crankshaft must be renewed.

12 Refit the oil pump as described in Chapter 2B.

13 Refit the pistons and connecting rods as described in Section 18.

14 Refit the crankshaft rear oil seal and the flywheel as described in Chapter 2B.

18 Piston/connecting rod assembly – refitting

Note: *New big-end bearing shells must be fitted on reassembly.*

Caution: Two different types of big-end bearing shells are available, one type for models with "fracture-split" connecting rod/big-end cap assemblies (big-end bearing caps secured by bolts), and one for models with conventional connecting rod/big-end cap assemblies (big-end bearing caps secured by nuts). The two bearing shell types are not interchangeable, and it is vital that the correct bearing shells are fitted, depending on engine type – if in doubt, refer to a Rover dealer for advice.

1 After inspecting the crankshaft, and renewing it if necessary, as described in Section 13, proceed as follows.

2 Clean the backs of the new bearing shells, and the bearing locations in both the connecting rods and the big-end bearing caps. Ensure that all traces of the protective

grease are cleaned off the new bearing shells using paraffin. Wipe the shells dry with a lint-free cloth.

3 Press the bearing shells into their locations. On models where the big-end caps are secured by nuts, ensure that the locating tab on each shell engages with the notch in the connecting rod or big-end cap. On models where the big-end caps are secured by bolts, the shells have no locating tabs, so make sure that they are located centrally and squarely in their respective positions in the connecting rods and bearing caps **(see illustrations)**. Take care not to touch any shell bearing surface with your fingers.

4 Liberally lubricate the big-end bearing journals on the crankshaft.

5 Lubricate No 1 piston and piston rings, and check that the ring gaps are correctly positioned. The gaps of the top and second compression rings should be arranged 120° from each other, away from the thrust side of the piston.

6 Liberally lubricate the cylinder bore with clean engine oil.

7 Fit a ring compressor to No 1 piston, then insert the piston and connecting rod into the cylinder bore so that the base of the compressor stands on the block. With the crankshaft big-end bearing journal positioned at its lowest point, tap the piston carefully into the cylinder bore with the wooden handle of a

17.9 Tighten the main bearing cap bolts to the specified torque

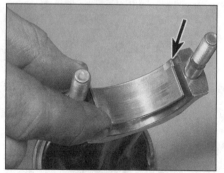

18.3a Where the big-end caps are secured by nuts, the locating tab (arrowed) on each shell must engage with the notch in the connecting rod

18.3b Where the big-end caps are secured by bolts, the bearing shells must be located centrally in the bearing caps

18.7 Refitting a piston/connecting rod assembly using a piston ring compressor and a hammer handle

18.9 Tightening a big-end bearing cap nut to the specified torque

hammer **(see illustration)**. Note that the arrow on the piston crown must point towards the timing belt end of the engine. Check that the cut-out in the piston skirt is positioned above the oil spray jet location. Take care not to allow the connecting rod (and the big-end bolts) to contact the cylinder bore.

8 Guide the connecting rod onto the big-end bearing journal, taking care not to displace the bearing shell, then refit the big-end bearing cap. On engines where the big-end bearing caps are secured by nuts, make sure that the tapered portion of the machined flat on the cap is facing towards the timing belt end of the engine. On engines where the big-end bearing caps are secured by bolts, make sure that the identification marks on the connecting rod and big-end cap are on the same side of the engine.

9 Lubricate the threads of the big-end studs or bolts (as applicable) with clean engine oil,

then fit the nuts or bolts (as applicable), and tighten to the specified torque wrench setting **(see illustration)**.

Note: *The torque wrench setting for engines where the big-end bearing caps are secured by nuts is different to that for engines where the bearing caps are secured by bolts.*

10 Repeat the procedure to refit the remaining three piston/connecting rod assemblies.

11 Refit the oil pick-up pipe and the sump, as described in Chapter 2B.

12 Refit the cylinder head as described in Chapter 2B.

19 Engine – initial start-up after overhaul

1 With the engine refitted to the vehicle,

double-check the engine oil and coolant levels. Make a final check to ensure that everything has been reconnected and that there are no tools or rags left in the engine compartment.

2 Disconnect the wiring from the stop solenoid on the fuel injection pump (see Chapter 4B), then turn the engine over on the starter until the oil pressure warning lamp goes out. Reconnect the wiring to the stop solenoid.

3 Prime the fuel system as described in Chapter 4B.

4 Start the engine (after the pre-heating warning light has gone out), noting that this may take a little longer than usual due to the fuel system components being empty.

5 While the engine is idling, check for fuel, coolant and oil leaks. Do not be alarmed if there are some odd smells and smoke from parts getting hot and burning off oil deposits. If the hydraulic tappets have been disturbed, some valve gear noise may be heard at first; this should disappear as the oil circulates fully around the engine and normal pressure is restored in the tappets.

6 Keep the engine idling until hot coolant is felt circulating through the radiator top hose, then stop the engine.

7 After a few minutes, recheck the oil and coolant levels and top up as necessary.

8 If new pistons, rings or crankshaft bearings have been fitted, the engine must be run-in for the first 500 miles (800 km). Do not operate the engine at full throttle or allow it to labour in any gear during this period. It is recommended that the oil and filter be changed at the end of this period.

2D

Notes

Chapter 3
Cooling, heating and ventilation systems

Contents

Degrees of difficulty

| Easy, suitable for novice with little experience | | Fairly easy, suitable for beginner with some experience | | Fairly difficult, suitable for competent DIY mechanic | | Difficult, suitable for experienced DIY mechanic | | Very difficult, suitable for expert DIY or professional | 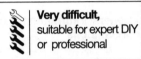 |

Specifications

System
Type . . . . Pressurised, pump-assisted thermo-syphon with front mounted radiator and thermostatically-controlled electric cooling fan

Thermostat
Type . . . . Wax
Start of opening temperature:
  Petrol models . . . . 88 ± 2°C
  Diesel models . . . . n/a
Fully open temperature:
  Petrol models . . . . 100 ± 2°C
  Diesel models . . . . 82 ± 5°C

Expansion tank
Cap opening pressure . . . . 0.9 to 1.2 bar

Cooling fan

	On	Off
Operating temperature (petrol models):		
Models without air conditioning	104°C	98°C
Models with air conditioning:		
Low speed	104°C	98°C
High speed	112°C	106°C
Operating temperature (86 PS diesel models):		
Models without air conditioning	104°C	94 °C
Models with air conditioning:		
Low speed	98°C	94°C
High speed	112°C	104°C
Operating temperature (105 PS diesel models):		
Models without air conditioning	105°C	94°C
Models with air conditioning:		
Low speed	105°C	94°C
High speed	112°C	103°C

3

Torque wrench settings

	Nm	lbf ft
Cooling system		
Coolant pump bolts	10	7
Coolant rail-to-cylinder block/crankcase bolts	9	6
Cooling fan housing bolts	9	6
Expansion tank bolts	5	4
Intercooler-to-radiator bolts	25	18
Radiator upper mounting bracket bolts (petrol models)	9	6
Radiator upper mounting bracket mounting bolts (diesel models)	25	18
Temperature gauge sender unit	15	11
Thermostat housing cover bolts	9	6
Heating system		
Heater blower motor mounting screw	10	7
Heater lower mounting nut	22	16
Air conditioning system		
Bonnet lock upright mounting bolts	9	6
Compressor mounting bolts	45	33
Compressor refrigerant pipe union bolt	35	26
Condenser mounting bolts	9	6
Condenser refrigerant pipe union screws	6	4
Receiver/drier clamp bracket screws	10	7
Receiver/drier refrigerant pipe union	5	4
Trinary switch	12	9

1 General information and precautions

General information

The cooling system is of the pressurised, pump-assisted thermo-syphon type. It consists of the front-mounted radiator, a translucent expansion tank mounted on the right-hand inner wing, a thermostatically-controlled electric cooling fan mounted on the rear of the radiator, a thermostat and a centrifugal coolant pump, as well as the connecting hoses. The coolant pump is driven by the engine timing belt on petrol models. On diesel models, the coolant pump arrangement is unusual: the pump itself is mounted in a housing that is shared with the power steering pump. Drive is taken indirectly from the auxiliary drive belt via a shaft that extends into the coolant pump housing from the rear of the power steering pump.

The cooling system is of the by-pass type, allowing coolant to circulate around the engine while the thermostat is closed. With the engine cold, the thermostat closes off the coolant feed from the bottom radiator hose. Coolant is then drawn into the engine via the heater matrix, inlet manifold and from the top of the cylinder block. This allows some heat transfer, by convection, to the radiator through the top hose whilst retaining the majority of heat within the cylinder block.

The siting of the thermostat in the intake rather than the outlet side of the system ensures that the engine warms up quickly by circulating a small amount of coolant around a shorter tract. This also prevents temperature build-up in the cylinder head prior to the thermostat opening.

When the coolant reaches a predetermined temperature, the thermostat opens and the coolant is allowed to flow freely through the top hose to the radiator. As the coolant circulates through the radiator, it is cooled by the in-rush of air when the vehicle is in forward motion. Airflow is supplemented by the action of the electric cooling fan when necessary. Upon reaching the bottom of the radiator, the coolant is now cooled and the cycle is repeated.

With the engine at normal operating temperature, the coolant expands and some of it is displaced into the expansion tank. This coolant collects in the tank and is returned to the radiator when the system cools.

The electric cooling fan mounted behind the radiator is controlled by a thermostatic switch located in the radiator side tank. At a predetermined coolant temperature the switch contacts close, thus actuating the fan.

Precautions

Cooling system

When the engine is hot, the coolant in the cooling system is under high pressure. The increased pressure raises the boiling point of the coolant and this allows the coolant to circulate at temperatures close to 100°C without actually boiling. If the pressure is reduced suddenly, e.g. by removing the expansion tank filler cap, the coolant will boil very rapidly, resulting in boiling water and steam being ejected through the expansion tank filler neck. This can happen very quickly and the risk of scalding is high.

For this reason, **do not** attempt to remove the expansion tank filler cap or to disturb any part of the cooling system whilst the engine is hot. Allow the engine to cool for several hours after switching off. When removing the expansion tank filler cap, as a precaution cover the cap with a thick layer of cloth, to avoid scalding, and slowly unscrew the filler cap until a hissing sound can be heard. When the hissing has stopped, showing that pressure is released, slowly unscrew the filler cap until it can be removed. If more hissing sounds are heard, wait until they have stopped before unscrewing the cap completely. At all times keep well away from the filler opening.

Do not allow antifreeze to come in contact with your skin or painted surfaces of the vehicle. Rinse off spills immediately with plenty of water. Never leave antifreeze lying around, it is fatal if ingested.

If the engine is hot, the electric cooling fan may start rotating even if the engine is not running, so be careful to keep hands, hair and loose clothing well clear when working in the engine compartment.

Air conditioning system

On models equipped with an air conditioning system, it is necessary to observe special precautions whenever dealing with any part of the system, its associated components and any items which necessitate disconnection of the system. If for any reason the system must be disconnected, entrust this task to your Rover dealer or a refrigeration engineer.

The air conditioning system pipes contains pressurised liquid refrigerant. The refrigerant is potentially dangerous, and should only be handled by qualified persons. If it is splashed onto the skin, it can cause severe frostbite. It is not itself poisonous, but in the presence of a naked flame (including a cigarette), it forms a poisonous gas. Uncontrolled discharging of the refrigerant is dangerous and is also extremely damaging to the environment. For these reasons, disconnection of any part of the system without specialised knowledge and equipment is not recommended.

Electric cooling fan

If the engine is hot, the electric cooling fan may start rotating without warning even if the engine and ignition are switched off. Be careful to keep your hands, hair, and any loose clothing well clear when working in the engine compartment.

2 Cooling system hoses - renewal

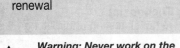

⚠️ **Warning: Never work on the cooling system when it is hot. Release any pressure from the system by loosening the expansion tank cap, having first covered it with a cloth to avoid any possibility of scalding.**

1 If inspection of the cooling system reveals a faulty hose, then it must be renewed as follows.
2 First drain the cooling system. If the coolant is not due for renewal, it may be re-used if collected in a clean container.
3 To disconnect any hose, use a screwdriver to slacken the clips then move them along the hose clear of the outlet. Carefully work the hose off its outlets. Do not attempt to disconnect any part of the system when still hot.
4 Note that the radiator hose outlets are fragile. Do not use excessive force when attempting to remove the hoses. If a hose proves stubborn, try to release it by rotating it on its outlets before attempting to work it off. If all else fails, cut the hose with a sharp knife then slit it so that it can be peeled off in two pieces. Although expensive, this is preferable to buying a new radiator.
5 When refitting a hose, first slide the clips

3.4 Disconnect the expansion tank hose from the radiator stub (8-valve petrol and intercooled diesel models)

onto the hose then work the hose onto its outlets.

> **HAYNES HiNT** *If the hose is stiff, use soap as a lubricant or soften it by first soaking it in boiling water whilst taking care to prevent scalding.*

6 Work each hose end fully onto its outlet, check that the hose is settled correctly and is properly routed, then slide each clip along the hose until it is behind the outlet flared end before tightening it securely.
7 Refill the system with coolant.
8 Check carefully for leaks as soon as possible after disturbing any part of the cooling system.

3 Radiator and expansion tank - removal, inspection and refitting

Removal
Radiator

1 On intercooled diesel models, carry out the following preliminary operations:
  a) *Remove the fixings and lower the undertray away from the underside of the engine bay.*

3.5 Disconnect the top hose from the radiator stub

  b) *Refer to Chapter 4B and remove the intercooler from the radiator.*
2 Refer to Chapter 1A or 1B and drain the cooling system.
3 On all diesel models, remove the air cleaner assembly, with reference to Chapter 4B.
4 On 8-valve petrol models and intercooled diesel models, slacken the hose clip and disconnect the expansion tank hose from the radiator stub **(see illustration)**.
5 Slacken the hose clip and disconnect the top hose from the radiator stub **(see illustration)**.
6 Remove the electric cooling fan with reference to Section 6.
7 On intercooled diesel models, disconnect the wiring from the thermostatic switch(es) which are fitted to the upper rear surface of the radiator (refer to Section 7).
8 Slacken the hose clip and disconnect the bottom hose from the radiator stub **(see illustration)**. Position the top and bottom hoses clear of the radiator so that they do not hinder removal.
9 Undo the two bolts securing the radiator upper mounting brackets to the bonnet platform and remove the brackets from the radiator **(see illustrations)**. On models with air conditioning, remove the bolt and detach the refrigerant pipe from the radiator upper mounting bracket.
10 Disengage the radiator from its lower mounting points and carefully manoeuvre it

3

3.8 Disconnect the bottom hose from the radiator stub

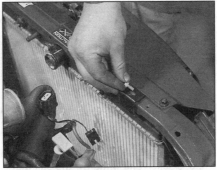

3.9a Undo the radiator upper mounting bracket bolts . . .

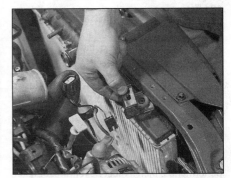

3.9b . . . and remove the brackets from the radiator

out of the engine compartment **(see illustration)**. Note that on intercooled diesel models without air conditioning, the radiator and intercooler are removed as a single assembly and can be separated by removing the two securing screws.

Expansion tank

11 Siphon as much coolant as possible from the expansion tank using an old syringe or poultry baster.

12 Position a container under the expansion tank to catch any spilt fluid, then slacken the retaining clips then disconnect both coolant hoses from the expansion tank.

13 Slacken and remove the two bolts securing the expansion tank to the body, then remove the tank from the vehicle.

Inspection

Radiator

14 If the radiator was removed because of clogging (causing overheating) then try reverse flushing or, in severe cases, use a radiator cleanser strictly in accordance with the manufacturer's instructions. Ensure that the cleanser is suitable for use in a copper/brass radiator. Refer to Chapter 1 for further information

15 Use a soft brush and an air line or low pressure garden hose to clear the radiator matrix of leaves, insects etc.

> **HAYNES HiNT** *Minor leaks from the radiator can be cured using a suitable sealant with the radiator in situ.*

16 Major leaks or extensive damage should be repaired by a specialist, or the radiator should be renewed or exchanged for a reconditioned unit.

17 Examine the mounting rubbers for signs of damage or deterioration and renew if necessary.

Expansion tank

18 Empty any remaining coolant from the tank and flush it with fresh water to clean it. If the tank is leaking it must be renewed but it is worth first attempting a repair using a proprietary sealant or suitable adhesive.

19 The expansion tank cap should be cleaned and checked whenever it is removed. Check that its sealing surfaces and threads are clean and undamaged and that they mate correctly with those of the expansion tank.

20 The cap's performance can only be checked by using a cap pressure-tester (cooling system tester) with a suitable adaptor. On applying pressure, the cap's pressure relief valve should hold until the specified pressure is reached, at which point the valve should open.

21 If there is any doubt about the cap's performance, then it must be renewed. Ensure that the replacement is of the correct type and rating for your engine.

3.10 Carefully manoeuvre the radiator out of the engine compartment

Refitting

Radiator

22 Refitting is the reverse of the removal procedure whilst noting the following:
  a) *Ensure that the radiator is seated correctly and without strain on its mountings.*
  b) *Ensure that the radiator hoses are securely held by the retaining clips.*
  c) *Tighten the radiator upper mounting brackets to the specified torque setting.*
  d) *Ensure that all wiring connectors are correctly routed so that they are clear of the cooling fan and are retained by any necessary clips or ties.*
  e) *On diesel models, refit the air cleaner (and intercooler, where applicable) with reference to Chapter 4B.*
  f) *Refill the cooling system as described in Chapter 1.*

Expansion tank

23 Refitting is the reverse of the removal procedure whilst noting the following:
  a) *Ensure that all hoses are correctly routed with no kinks or sharp bends and are securely held by the retaining clips.*
  b) *Tighten the tank bolts to the specified torque setting.*
  c) *Top up the expansion tank as described in Chapter 1.*

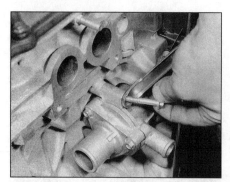

4.3 Slacken and withdraw the bolt that secures the thermostat housing to the engine block

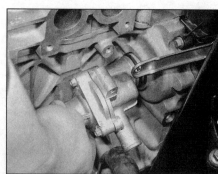

4.2 Disconnect the coolant rail and heater return hoses (arrowed) from the rear of the thermostat housing

4 Thermostat - removal, testing and refitting

Removal

Petrol models

1 Note that access to the thermostat is very limited. Depending on the tools available, it may be easier to raise the front of the vehicle and to work from underneath, ensuring that the vehicle is securely supported on axle stands. In all cases, access is better if the air cleaner is removed.

2 Unbolt the coolant rail from the rear of the cylinder block/crankcase, then slacken the clips and disconnect the heater return hose and coolant rail hose from the thermostat housing **(see illustration)**.

3 Slacken and withdraw the bolt that secures the thermostat housing to the engine block. Note that on some models, the bolt also secure the dipstick tube support bracket in place **(see illustration)**.

4 Release the thermostat housing from the coolant pump and remove it from the vehicle **(see illustration)**.

5 Remove the O-ring seals from the housing stubs and discard them - new seals must be used on refitting.

6 Slacken and remove the three thermostat

4.4 Release the thermostat housing from the pump and remove it from the vehicle (inlet manifold removed)

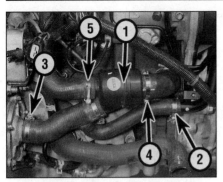

4.8 Thermostat and associated hose connections - diesel models (engine removed)

1 *Thermostat housing*
2 *Coolant rail hose*
3 *Coolant pump hose*
4 *Oil cooler return hose*
5 *Radiator top hose*

housing cover bolts, then lift off the housing cover. Remove the thermostat together with its rubber seal.

Diesel models

7 Refer to Section 3 and remove the radiator.
8 Loosen the hose clip and disconnect the outlet hose from the rear of the coolant pump. Similarly, loosen the hose clip and disconnect the outlet hose from the rigid coolant rail **(see illustration)**.
9 Slacken the hose clips and disconnect the radiator top hose and the oil cooler coolant return hose from the thermostat housing.
10 Remove the thermostat housing and hose assembly from the engine bay. On all diesel models, the thermostat and housing assembly is a sealed unit and cannot be dismantled or serviced. If the operation of the thermostat is thought to be suspect, a complete new assembly must be obtained.

Testing

Note: *This procedure applies primarily to petrol models. On diesel models, the thermostat and its housing are a sealed unit, making the operation of the thermostat difficult to observe.*

11 If the thermostat remains in the open position at room temperature, then it is faulty and must be renewed.

4.15 Correctly refitted thermostat and housing (petrol models)

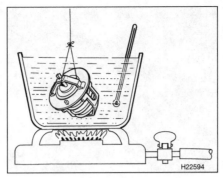

4.12 Testing the thermostat

12 To test it fully, suspend the (closed) thermostat on a length of string in a container of cold water, with a thermometer beside it. Ensure that neither touches the side of the container **(see illustration)**.
13 Heat the water and check the temperature at which the thermostat begins to open. Compare this value with that specified. Continue to heat the water until the thermostat is fully open. The temperature at which this should happen is stamped in the unit's end **(see illustration)**. Remove the thermostat and measure the height of the fully opened valve, then allow the thermostat to cool down and check that it closes fully.
14 If the thermostat does not open and close as described, if it sticks in either position, or if it does not open at the specified temperature, then it must be renewed.

Refitting

Petrol models

15 Refitting is the reverse of the removal procedure, noting the following **(see illustration)**:
a) *Clean the thermostat housing, housing cover and cylinder block/crankcase mating surfaces thoroughly.*
b) *Ensure that the thermostat is correctly seated on the shoulder machined into the housing mating surface.*
c) *Fit a new rubber seal to the thermostat, and new O-ring seals to the thermostat housing stubs.*

5.6 Removing the coolant pump (petrol models)

4.13 The stamped marking (arrowed) indicates the temperature at which the thermostat starts to open

d) *Tighten all bolts to their specified torque wrench settings (where given).*
e) *Ensure the coolant hose clips are positioned so that they do not foul any other component, then tighten them securely.*
f) *Refit any components removed for improved access.*
g) *Refill the cooling system as described in Chapter 1A.*

Diesel models

16 Refitting is the reverse of the removal procedure, noting the following:
a) *Ensure the coolant hose clips are positioned so that they do not foul any other component, then tighten them securely.*
b) *Refer to Section 3 and refit the radiator.*
c) *On completion, refill the cooling system as described in Chapter 1B.*

**5 Coolant pump -
removal and refitting**

3

Removal

Petrol models

1 Coolant pump failure is usually indicated by coolant leaking from the gland behind the pump bearing, or by rough and noisy operation, usually accompanied by excessive pump spindle play. If the pump shows any of these symptoms then it must be renewed as follows.
2 Drain the cooling system, with reference to Chapter 1A.
3 Remove the timing belt, with reference to Chapter 2A.
4 Unscrew the five bolts securing the coolant pump to the cylinder block/crankcase. There are three flange bolts and two pillar bolts; note their relative positions to ensure correct refitting.
5 Unscrew the single bolt securing the pump to the upper left-hand timing belt inner cover.
6 Withdraw the coolant pump and discard its sealing ring (which should be renewed whenever it is disturbed) **(see illustration)**.

5.11 Loosen the clip and disconnect the hose (arrowed) from the rear of the coolant pump (diesel models)

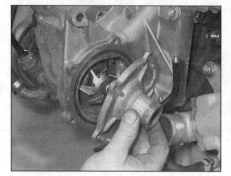

5.12 Removing coolant pump housing cover (diesel models)

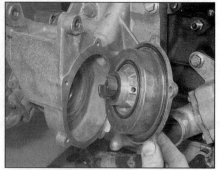

5.13 Withdrawing the coolant pump from its housing (diesel models)

7 Carefully clean the cylinder block/crankcase and coolant pump mating surfaces.

Diesel models without air conditioning

8 Drain the cooling system, with reference to Chapter 1B.

9 Raise the front of the vehicle and support it securely on axle stands (see "*Jacking and Vehicle Support*").

10 Refer to Chapter 10 and remove the front suspension front beam.

11 Loosen the clip and disconnect the hose from the rear of the coolant pump **(see illustration)**.

12 Progressively slacken and withdraw the five securing bolts then remove the coolant pump housing cover. Collect the O-ring seal from the housing and discard it - a new seal must be used on refitting **(see illustration)**.

13 Withdraw the coolant pump from its housing. Collect the two O-ring seals and discard them - new seals must be used on refitting **(see illustration)**.

Diesel models with air conditioning

⚠️ **Warning: This procedure involves discharging the refrigerant from the air conditioning system. This is a hazardous operation which MUST be carried out by a Rover dealer or air conditioning specialist. Note that the**

receiver/drier unit must be renewed whenever the air conditioning system is discharged.

14 Refer to Chapter 5A and remove the alternator.

15 Drain the cooling system, with reference to Chapter 1B.

16 Slacken the hose clip, disconnect the intercooler air intake hose from the inlet manifold, and move it to one side.

17 Slacken the three hose clips, then disconnect and remove the coolant hose assembly from the radiator, coolant outlet elbow and the thermostat housing.

18 Loosen the clip, disconnect the hose from the front of the coolant pump and move the hose to one side.

19 Have the refrigerant discharged from the air conditioning system by a suitably equipped expert - refer to the Warning given in Section 1 and the information given at the beginning of this sub-Section.

20 Slacken and withdraw the bolt that secures the refrigerant pipe union to the ports at the top of the air conditioning compressor. Remove the O-ring seals from the compressor ports and discard them - new seals must be used on refitting.

21 With reference to Chapter 9, unscrew the union and disconnect the vacuum pump oil supply from the cylinder block tapping.

22 Progressively slacken and withdraw the

five securing bolts then remove the coolant pump housing cover. Collect the O-ring seal from the housing and discard it - a new seal must be used on refitting.

23 Withdraw the coolant pump from the housing. Collect the two O-ring seals and discard them - new seals must be used on refitting.

Refitting

Petrol models

24 On refitting, install the pump using a new sealing ring and tighten all bolts to the specified torque wrench settings.

25 The remainder of the refitting procedure is the reverse of removal.

Diesel models without air conditioning

26 Refitting is a reversal of removal, noting the following points **(see illustrations)**:

a) Use new O-ring seals and coat them with Loctite 405 sealing compound.

b) Ensure that the power steering pump drive lugs engage with those on the front of the coolant pump.

c) Tighten all bolts to the specified torque setting.

d) Refit the suspension front beam with reference to Chapter 10.

e) Refill the cooling system with reference to Chapter 1B.

5.26a Fit new O-ring seals (arrowed) to the coolant pump . . .

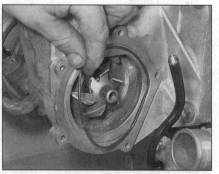

5.26b . . . and the pump housing cover

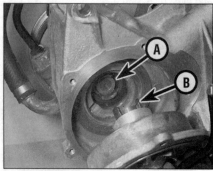

5.26c Power steering pump drive lugs (A) must engage with those on the front of the coolant pump (B)

6.4a Undo the four nuts (upper nuts arrowed) securing the cooling fan cowling to the rear of the radiator . . .

6.4b . . . and manoeuvre the fan assembly out of the engine compartment

6.9 Unplug the wiring from the cooling fan at the multiway connector

Diesel models with air conditioning

27 Refitting is a reversal of removal, noting the following points:

a) *Use new O-ring seals and coat them with Loctite 405 sealing compound.*

b) *Ensure that the power steering pump drive lugs engage with those on the front of the coolant pump.*

c) *Fit new O-ring seals to the air conditioning compressor and tighten the union securing bolt to the specified torque.*

d) *Tighten all bolts to the specified torque setting.*

e) *Refit the alternator with reference to Chapter 5A.*

f) *Fit a new receiver/drier unit with reference to Section 12.*

g) *Refill the cooling system with reference to Chapter 1B.*

h) *Have the air conditioning system recharged by a Rover dealer or air conditioning specialist.*

---

6 Electric cooling fan - removal and refitting

Petrol models

Removal

1 On models with air conditioning, carry out the following:

a) *Drain the cooling system, with reference to Chapter 1A.*

b) *Jack up the front of the vehicle and support it securely on axle stands (see "Jacking and Vehicle Support").*

c) *Refer to Chapter 10 and remove the front suspension front beam.*

2 Release the radiator top hose from the clip at the top of the cooling fan cowling.

3 Disconnect the battery negative cable and position it away from the terminal, then disconnect the radiator cooling fan wiring connector.

4 Undo the four nuts securing the cooling fan cowling to the rear of the radiator and manoeuvre the fan assembly out of the engine

compartment **(see illustrations)**. On models with air conditioning, the fan is removed from below the front of the engine compartment. On all other models, the fan is lifted out over the top of the radiator.

5 If a new fan assembly is to be fitted, undo the three nuts which secure the heat shielding to the cooling fan housing and transfer it to the new assembly.

Refitting

6 Refitting is a reverse of the removal procedure, noting the following:

a) *Ensure that the fan motor wiring is securely reconnected.*

b) *Ensure that the radiator hose is securely held by its retaining clips.*

c) *On models with air conditioning, refer to Chapter 10 and refit the suspension front beam.*

d) *Where applicable, refill the cooling system as described in Chapter 1A.*

Diesel models without air conditioning

Removal

7 Disconnect the battery negative cable and position it away from the terminal.

8 On intercooled models, carry out the following:

a) *Slacken the clips and remove the intercooler supply and return hoses from the engine compartment.*

6.10a Remove the two bolts (arrowed) securing the cooling fan assembly to the radiator . . .

b) *Disconnect the wiring from the thermostatic switch mounted at the top of the radiator.*

9 Unplug the wiring from the cooling fan at the multiway connector **(see illustration)**.

10 Remove the two bolts securing the cooling fan assembly to the radiator, release the cooling fan housing from the spigot on the radiator then manoeuvre the assembly around the radiator top hose and lift it from the engine compartment **(see illustrations)**.

Refitting

11 Refitting is a reversal of removal. On intercooled models, ensure that the thermostatic switch wiring is securely reconnected, then refit the intercooler hoses with reference to Chapter 4B.

Diesel models with air conditioning

Removal

12 Disconnect the battery negative cable and position it away from the terminal.

13 Refer to Chapter 1B and drain the cooling system.

14 Working underneath the front of the vehicle, remove the bolts securing the cover panel to the underside of the engine compartment and remove the panel.

15 On intercooled models, slacken the clips and remove the intercooler supply and return hoses from the engine compartment.

6.10b . . . then manoeuvre the assembly around the radiator top hose and lift it from the engine compartment

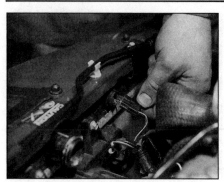

7.3a Unplug the wiring connector from the switch (diesel model without air conditioning shown) . . .

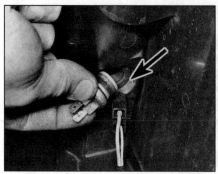

7.3b . . . then release the locking ring and withdraw the switch and sealing ring (arrowed) from the radiator (petrol models)

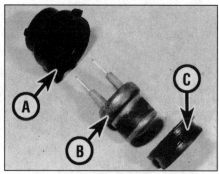

7.17 Cooling fan switch components

A *Locking ring*   C *Sealing ring*
B *Switch body*

16 Loosen the hose clips and disconnect the top hose and expansion tank hose from the radiator stubs.

17 Disconnect the wiring from the thermostatic switch(es) mounted at the top and right hand side of the radiator.

18 Unplug the wiring from the cooling fan at the multiway connector.

19 Slacken and remove the two bolts securing the cooling fan assembly to the radiator, release the cooling fan housing from the spigot on the radiator then manoeuvre the assembly around the radiator top hose and lift it from the engine compartment.

Refitting

20 Refitting is a reversal of removal, noting the following points:

a) *Ensure that the wiring harness plugs are securely reconnected to the thermostatic switches and cooling fan.*

b) *On intercooled models, refit the intercooler hoses with reference to Chapter 4B.*

c) *On completion, refill the cooling system with reference to Chapter 1B.*

7 Cooling system electrical switches - removal, testing and refitting

Note: *On models equipped with air conditioning, there are two switches fitted to the right-hand side of the radiator, the lower of these is the cooling fan switch.*

Removal

Cooling fan thermostatic switch

1 With the engine and radiator cold, either drain the cooling system down to the level of the sender unit, or unscrew the expansion tank filler cap to release any remaining pressure and have a suitable plug ready that can be used to stop the escape of coolant while the switch is removed.

2 Disconnect the battery negative lead.

3 Unplug the wiring connector from the switch then rotate the locking ring to release it. Withdraw the switch and sealing ring from the radiator **(see illustrations)**.

Coolant temperature gauge sender unit

4 With the engine and radiator cold, either drain the cooling system down to the level of the sender unit, or unscrew the expansion tank filler cap to release any remaining pressure and have a suitable plug ready that can be used to stop the escape of coolant while the unit is removed.

5 Disconnect the battery negative lead.

6 Where applicable, release the locking clip then pull the wiring connector from the sender. Unscrew the sender from the coolant outlet elbow (or cylinder head on diesel models).

Coolant temperature sensor (fuel injection system)

7 Refer to Chapter 4A or 4B as applicable.

Testing

Cooling fan thermostatic switch

8 To carry out a thorough test of the switch, use two spare lengths of wire to connect to it either a multimeter (set to the resistance function) or a battery and bulb test circuit.

9 Suspend the switch in a pan of water which is being heated. Measure the temperature of the water with a thermometer. Do not let either the switch or the thermometer touch the pan itself.

10 The switch contacts should close to the ON position (ie: continuity should exist) when the water reaches the temperature specified. Stop heating the water and allow it to cool down. The switch contacts should open.

11 If the switch's performance is significantly different from that specified, or if it does not work at all, then it must be renewed.

Coolant temperature gauge sender unit

12 The coolant temperature gauge mounted in the instrument panel is fed with a stabilised voltage supply from the instrument panel feed, its earth path being controlled by the sender unit.

13 The sender unit is screwed into the coolant outlet elbow mounted on the left-hand end of the cylinder head, underneath the distributor. It contains a thermistor with a negative temperature coefficient, which is an element whose electrical resistance

decreases at a predetermined rate as its temperature rises. Thus, when the coolant is cold, the sender's resistance is high, current flow through the gauge is reduced and the gauge needle points to the C (cold) end of the scale. If the unit is faulty it must be renewed.

14 If the gauge develops a fault, check first the other instruments. If they do not work at all, check the instrument panel feed. If the readings are erratic, there may be a fault in the voltage stabiliser which will necessitate the renewal of the gauge unit or printed circuit. If the fault is in the temperature gauge alone, check it as follows.

15 If the gauge needle remains at the C end of the scale, disconnect the sender unit wire and earth it to the cylinder head. If the needle then deflects when the ignition is switched on, then the sender unit is proven faulty and must be renewed. If the needle still does not move, remove the instrument panel and check the continuity of the green/blue wire between the gauge and the sender unit and the feed to the gauge unit. If continuity is shown and the fault still exists, then the gauge is faulty and must be renewed.

16 If the gauge needle remains at the H end of the scale, disconnect the sender unit wire. If the needle then returns to the C end of the scale when the ignition is switched on, then the sender unit is proven faulty and must be renewed. If the needle still does not move, check the remainder of the circuit as described above.

Refitting

Cooling fan thermostatic switch

17 On refitting, renew the sealing ring if it is worn or compressed and carefully clean the radiator seat before pressing in the sealing ring and switch **(see illustration)**. Refit the locking ring and rotate it to tighten it securely. Reconnect the switch and battery, then replenish the cooling system.

Coolant temperature gauge sender unit

18 On refitting, apply a suitable sealant to the unit threads and tighten it to its specified torque wrench setting. Reconnect the unit and battery, then replenish the cooling system.

8.2a Heater coolant supply and return hoses (arrowed) on engine compartment bulkhead

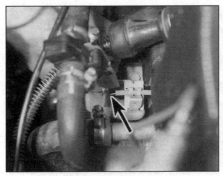

8.2b Heater valve control cable (arrowed)

8.2c Heater unit lower mounting nut (arrowed) on engine compartment bulkhead

8 Heater components - removal and refitting

Removal

Heater unit

1 Drain the cooling system.
2 Working in the engine compartment, slacken the hose clips and disconnect the heater supply and return hoses from the matrix outlets on the bulkhead. Disconnect the cable inner from the heater valve and free the cable outer from its retaining clip. Slacken and remove the heater lower mounting nut which is situated just to the left of the matrix outlets **(see illustrations)**.
3 Working inside the vehicle, remove the facia (see Chapter 11).
4 Release the vehicle wiring harness from the clip at the front of the heater unit **(see illustration)**.
5 Remove the securing screws and detach the heater duct from the heater outlet and blower motor **(see illustrations)**.
6 Unscrew the nuts that secure the heater

unit to the mounting studs on the bulkhead **(see illustration)**.
7 Extract the stud fastener and separate the heater unit from centre console ducting **(see illustration)**.
8 Carefully lift the heater unit off its mounting studs and remove it from the vehicle **(see illustration)**. Keep the unit upright to prevent any coolant still inside the heater matrix from leaking out.

Heater matrix

9 Remove the heater unit (see the previous sub-Section).
10 Undo the screw securing the matrix outlet

8.4 Release the vehicle wiring harness from the clip (arrowed) at the front of the heater unit

8.5a Remove the securing screws (arrowed) . . .

8.5b . . . and detach the heater duct from the heater outlet and blower motor

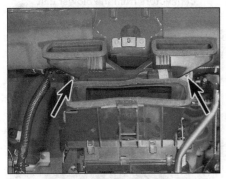

8.6 Unscrew the nuts (arrowed) that secure the heater unit to the mounting studs on the bulkhead

8.7 Extract the stud fastener (arrowed) and separate the heater unit from centre console ducting

8.8 Carefully lift the heater unit off its mounting studs and remove it from the vehicle

3

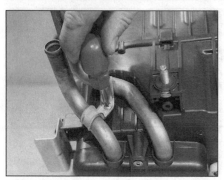

8.10a Undo the screw securing the matrix outlet pipe bracket to the heater unit . . .

8.10b . . . and remove the bracket

8.11a Slacken and remove the two matrix cover retaining screws . . .

pipe bracket to the heater unit and remove the bracket **(see illustrations)**.

11 Slacken and remove the two matrix cover

8.11b . . . then remove the cover . . .

retaining screws, then remove the cover and withdraw the matrix from the heater unit **(see illustrations)**.

12 If the matrix is leaking, it is best to obtain a new or reconditioned unit as home repairs are seldom successful. If it is blocked, it can sometimes be cleared by reverse flushing using a garden hose. Use a proprietary radiator cleaning product if absolutely necessary.

Heater blower motor

13 Disconnect the negative cable battery and position it away from the terminal.

14 Refer to Chapter 11 and remove the facia.

15 Release the radio antenna cable from the clip at the front of the heater unit.

16 Unplug the motor and resistor wiring

harness connectors from the blower unit **(see illustrations)**.

17 Extra clearance may be gained by loosening the facia end support bracket bolts.

18 Slacken and withdraw the bolt that secures the blower unit to the end support bracket.

19 Undo and remove the two nuts securing the blower unit to its mounting studs **(see illustration)**.

20 Remove the securing screw, separate the blower unit from the heater unit duct then remove the blower unit from the vehicle **(see illustration)**.

21 To remove the blower motor, slacken the three securing screws and withdraw the motor from the blower unit. Disconnect the cooling hose from the motor body as it become accessible **(see illustrations)**.

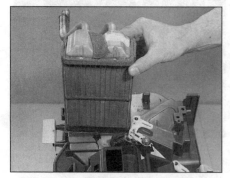

8.11c . . . and withdraw the matrix from the heater unit

8.16a Unplug the motor . . .

8.16b . . . and resistor wiring harness connectors from the blower unit

8.19 Blower unit mounting nuts and bolts (arrowed)

8.20 Removing the blower unit from the vehicle

8.21a Slacken and remove the three blower motor securing screws (arrowed) . . .

8.21b ... and withdraw the blower motor assembly

8.21c Disconnect the cooling hose (arrowed) from the motor body as it become accessible

8.23a Undo the two retaining screws (arrowed) ...

Heater blower motor resistor

22 Refer to Chapter 11 and remove the glovebox from the facia.

23 Unplug the wiring connector, then undo the two retaining screws and remove the resistor from the front of the heater assembly **(see illustrations)**.

Heater valve

24 Working in the engine compartment, disconnect the cable inner from the heater valve and free the cable outer from the retaining clip.

25 Slacken and remove the screws securing the heater valve to its mounting bracket, at the engine compartment bulkhead.

26 Either drain the cooling system or clamp the coolant hoses on each side of the coolant valve to minimise the loss of coolant.

27 Slacken the hose retaining clips, then disconnect both hoses from the heater valve and remove the valve from the engine compartment **(see illustration)**. Mop up any spilt coolant immediately.

Refitting

Heater unit

28 Refitting is a reverse of the removal procedure, noting the following:

a) *Ensure that the heater ducts are securely connected to the unit so that there are no air leaks or gaps.*

b) *Check the operation of all heater cables before refitting the facia, ensuring that the relevant component moves smoothly from the fully open to the fully closed position. If necessary, adjustments can be made by releasing the relevant retaining clip and repositioning the cable outer.*

c) *Ensure that the heater hoses are correctly reconnected and are securely held by the retaining clips.*

d) *Tighten the heater lower mounting nut to the specified torque setting.*

e) *Refill the cooling system as described in Chapter 1A or B as applicable.*

Heater matrix

29 Refitting is a reverse of the removal procedure.

8.23b ... and remove the resistor from the front of the heater assembly

Heater blower motor

30 Refitting is a reversal of the removal sequence, noting the following:

a) *Ensure that the cooling hose is reconnected to the motor casing.*

b) *Tighten the blower motor mounting screws to the specified torque setting.*

c) *Ensure that the air recirculation cable and flap functions correctly before refitting the glovebox. If necessary, adjust by releasing the cable retaining clip and repositioning the cable outer.*

Heater blower motor resistor

31 Refitting is a reverse of the removal procedure.

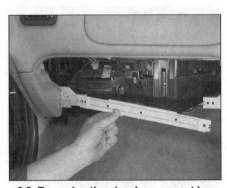

9.2 Removing the glovebox support bar

8.27 Slacken the heater valve hose retaining clips (arrowed) then disconnect both hoses from the valve

Heater valve

32 Refitting is a reversal of the removal procedure. On completion, check the heater cable operates smoothly and replenish the cooling system (see Chapter 1A or 1B).

3

9 Heater/ventilation intake filter - renewal

1 Refer to Chapter 11 and remove the glovebox from the facia.

2 Slacken and remove the screws then lift off the glovebox support bar **(see illustration)**.

3 Release the clip and remove the cover from the side of the heater unit **(see illustration)**.

9.3 Release the clip and remove the cover from the side of the heater unit

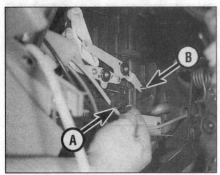

10.3 Disconnect the air distribution control cable (A) from the heater unit lever and release the heater control cable (B) from the guide

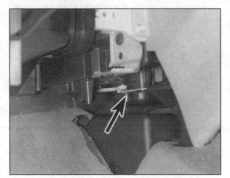

10.4a Disconnect the purple fresh air ventilation flap control cable from the lever at the underside of the heater unit

10.4b Disconnect the (short) yellow fresh air ventilation flap control cable from the lever at the underside of the heater unit

4 Grasp the end of the filter element and withdraw it from the heater unit.
5 Refitting is a reversal of removal.

10 Heater controls - removal, refitting and adjustment

Removal

1 Refer to Chapter 11 and remove the centre console assembly and glovebox from the facia.
2 Release the stud fasteners by turning them

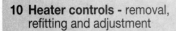

10.5 Release the (long) yellow air recirculation control cable from the blower assembly

through a quarter of a turn, then remove the fuse box cover from the underside of the facia.
3 Disconnect the brown air distribution control cable from the lever at the right hand side of the heater unit. Release the green heater control cable from the guide on the side of the unit. Make a note of each cable fitted position to aid refitting **(see illustration)**.
4 Disconnect the purple and the (short) yellow fresh air ventilation flap control cables from the levers at the underside of the heater unit **(see illustrations)**.
5 Release the (long) yellow air recirculation control cable from the blower assembly **(see illustration)**.
6 Working in the engine compartment, disconnect the green heater control cable from the heater valve and release it from the bulkhead mounting clip (see Section 8 for details).
7 Slacken and remove the four securing screws and withdraw the heater control panel from the facia slightly **(see illustration)**.
8 Unplug the multiway connectors from the rear of the heater control panel as they become accessible (2 connectors on models with a conventional heating system, 3 on models with air conditioning) **(see illustration)**.
9 Fully withdraw the control panel from the facia, feeding the control cables through the facia aperture **(see illustration)**.

10 If the control panel is to renewed, proceed as described from paragraphs 11 onwards.
11 Release the control cables from the heater control panel by slackening the clamp bracket screws and unhooking the cable end fittings from their respective control levers.
12 Carefully prise the rotary and slider knobs from the front of the control panel. Unclip the trim panel , the remove the two screws and remove the two-piece dial bezel.
13 Remove the two securing screws and withdraw the heater fan switch from the rear of the control panel.
14 Transfer the fan switch, bezel, trim panel, knobs and control cables to the replacement heater control panel.

Refitting and adjustment

15 Refitting is a reversal of removal, noting the following points:
a) Set the heater valve to the closed position before reconnecting the control cable.
b) Set the heater control knob and the heater control lever on the heater unit to the cool positions before refitting the control cable.
c) Set the air distribution control slider and the distribution control lever on the heater unit to the ventilation positions before refitting the control cable.
d) Check the operation of all heater controls before refitting the centre console and glovebox.

10.7 Remove the four securing screws (arrowed) and withdraw the heater control panel from the facia slightly

10.8 Unplug the multiway connectors from the rear of the heater control panel as they become accessible

10.9 Fully withdraw the control panel, feeding the control cables through the facia aperture

11 Air conditioning compressor drivebelt - inspection, adjustment and renewal

Inspection and adjustment

1 Refer to Chapter 1A or B as applicable.

Renewal

2 On petrol models, the air conditioning compressor is driven by the same drivebelt as the alternator; refer to the information given in Chapter 5A. On diesel models, all ancillaries are driven by a single auxiliary drivebelt; its renewal is described in Chapter 10 under 'Power steering pump drivebelt - renewal'.

12 Air conditioning system components - removal and refitting

Note: *All O-ring seals must be renewed on refitting and lubricated with a suitable refrigerant oil (such as Unipart SP-10)*

Compressor

⚠️ **Warning: The air conditioning system must be professionally discharged before carrying out this procedure. Cap or plug the pipe lines as soon as they are disconnected to prevent the entry of moisture. Note that the receiver/drier unit must be renewed whenever the air conditioning system is discharged.**

Removal - petrol models

1 Disconnect the battery negative cable and position it away from the terminal.
2 Raise the front of the vehicle and position it securely on axle stands (see *"Jacking and Vehicle Support"*).
3 Refer to Chapter 10 and remove the front suspension front beam
4 Refer to Chapter 5A and remove the alternator.
5 Unplug the compressor clutch wiring at the connector, located on the top of the compressor casing.
6 Slacken and withdraw the refrigerant pipe union bolt. Release the union from the compressor and recover the O-ring seals. Note that new seals must be used on refitting. Cover the exposed unions immediately to prevent the ingress of dirt and moisture.
7 Slacken and withdraw the four compressor mounting bolts (two upper, two lower), then remove the compressor via the underside of the engine compartment.

Refitting - petrol models

8 Refitting is a reverse of the removal sequence, noting the following points:
a) *Tighten the compressor mounting bolts to the specified torque setting.*
b) *Fit new O-ring seals to the compressor refrigerant pipes.*

c) *Tighten the refrigerant pipe union bolt to the specified torque.*
d) *Refit the suspension front beam with reference to Chapter 10.*
e) *Refit the clutch compressor wiring connector securely.*
f) *Refit and adjust the compressor drivebelt as described in Chapters 5A and 1A respectively.*
g) *Fit a new receiver/drier unit, as described later in this Section.*
h) *On completion, have the air conditioning system recharged by a refrigeration specialist or suitably-equipped Rover dealer.*

Removal - diesel models

9 Disconnect the battery negative cable and position it away from the terminal.
10 Refer to Section 3 and remove the radiator.
11 Refer to Chapter 10 and remove the auxiliary drivebelt.
12 Slacken and remove the three securing bolts and remove the bonnet lock upright. Move the upright to one side, leaving the wiring and lock release cable attached.
13 Remove the condenser cooling fan, followed by the condenser itself, as described later in this Section.
14 Unplug the compressor clutch wiring at the connector, located on the top of the compressor casing.
15 Slacken and withdraw the refrigerant pipe union bolt. Release the union from the compressor and recover the O-ring seals. Note that new seals must be used on refitting. Cover the exposed unions immediately to prevent the ingress of dirt and moisture
16 Refer to Chapter 10 and remove the front suspension front beam.
17 Slacken and withdraw the compressor lower mounting nuts and bolts.
18 Position a trolley jack underneath the engine. Position a block of wood in the jack head, then raise the jack until it is just supporting the weight of the engine.
19 With reference to Chapter 2B, remove the right hand engine mounting and the rear engine steady bar. Raise the engine slightly using the jack, then slacken and withdraw the air conditioning compressor upper mounting nut and through bolt. On completion, lower the engine using the jack to its normal height.
20 Manoeuvre the compressor from the vehicle via the underside of the engine compartment.

Refitting - diesel models

21 Refitting is a reverse of the removal sequence, noting the following points:
a) *Tighten the compressor mounting bolts to the specified torque setting.*
b) *Fit new O-ring seals to the compressor and condenser refrigerant pipes.*
c) *Tighten the refrigerant pipe union bolt(s) to the specified torque.*
d) *Refit the suspension front beam with reference to Chapter 10.*

e) *Refit the clutch compressor wiring connector securely.*
f) *Refit the compressor drivebelt as described in Chapter 10.*
g) *Fit a new receiver/drier unit, as described later in this Section.*
h) *Refill the cooling system as described in Chapter 1B.*
i) *On completion, have the air conditioning system recharged by a refrigeration specialist or suitably-equipped Rover dealer.*

Condenser

⚠️ **Warning: The air conditioning system must be professionally discharged before carrying out this procedure. Cap or plug the pipe lines as soon as they are disconnected to prevent the entry of moisture. Note that the receiver/drier unit must be renewed whenever the air conditioning system is discharged.**

Removal

22 Refer to the following sub-Section and remove the condenser cooling fan.
23 Undo the securing bolts and disconnect the refrigerant pipes from the rear of the condenser. Remove the O-ring seals (2 per pipe) and discard them - new seals must be used on refitting.
24 Release the condenser from its mounting points and manoeuvre it away from the vehicle.

Refitting

25 Prior to refitting, check the condenser mounting rubbers for signs of damage or deterioration and renew as necessary.
26 Refitting is a direct reversal of the removal procedure, noting the following points:
a) *Renew the pipe union O-ring seals.*
b) *Tighten the pipe union bolts to the specified torque setting.*
c) *Refit the condenser cooling fan and tighten the securing screws to the specified torque.*
d) *On completion, have the air conditioning system recharged by a refrigeration specialist or a suitably equipped Rover dealer.*

Condenser cooling fan

Removal

27 Disconnect the battery negative cable and position it away from the terminal.
28 Refer to Chapter 11 and remove the front bumper assembly.
29 Slacken and remove the three securing bolts, then lift off the bonnet lock upright and move it to one side, leaving the lock release cable and wiring in place.
30 Undo the bolts and remove the cooling fan housing mounting brackets.
31 Unplug the wiring harness from the cooling fan at the connector.
32 Remove the securing bolts and separate the cooling fan housing from the condenser.

3

33 Release the cooling fan from its lower mountings and remove it from the engine compartment.

Refitting

34 Refitting is a reverse of the removal procedure, noting the following points:
  a) *Ensure that the motor wiring is securely retained by the cowling clips and is clear of the condenser fan.*
  b) *Refit the bumper with reference to Chapter 11.*
  c) *Tighten the bonnet lock upright mounting bolts to the specified torque.*

Receiver/drier unit

 Warning: The air conditioning system must be professionally discharged before carrying out this procedure. Cap or plug the pipe lines as soon as they are disconnected to prevent the entry of moisture. Note that the receiver/drier unit must be renewed whenever the air conditioning system is discharged.

Removal

35 Refer to Chapter 11 and remove the front bumper assembly.
36 Disconnect the wiring harness from the trinary switch at the connector.
37 Slacken the screws and disconnect the refrigerant pipes from the receiver/drier noting the O-rings which are fitted to the pipe unions. Discard the O-rings as they must be renewed whenever they are disturbed. The refrigerant pipe unions must be capped immediately after they are disconnected and must remain capped until they are to be reconnected.
38 Unscrew the trinary switch, renew the O-ring and transfer it to the new receiver/drier unit.
39 Slacken the receiver/drier clamp screws then slide the unit out of the retaining clamp and remove it from the engine compartment.

Refitting

40 Refitting is a direct reversal of the removal sequence, tightening the refrigerant pipe union screws to the specified torque setting. On completion, have the system recharged by a refrigeration specialist or suitably-equipped Rover dealer.

Trinary switch

41 Refer to the information given in the previous sub-Section.

4A•1

Chapter 4 Part A:
Fuel and exhaust systems – petrol engines

Contents

Air cleaner assembly – removal and refitting 2
Air cleaner filter element renewal .... See Chapter 1A
Exhaust gas CO content check .... See Chapter 1A
Exhaust system check .... See Chapter 1A
Exhaust system – general information and
  component renewal 13
Fuel filter renewal .... See Chapter 1A
Fuel injection system – depressurising and priming 7
Fuel injection system – general information 6
Fuel injection system – testing and adjustment 9

Fuel injection system components – removal and refitting 11
Fuel pump/fuel gauge sender unit – removal and refitting 8
Fuel tank and filler neck – removal, inspection and refitting 3
General information and precautions 1
Manifolds – removal and refitting 12
Oxygen sensor operation check .... See Chapter 1A
Throttle body – removal and refitting 10
Throttle cable – removal, refitting and adjustment 4
Throttle pedal – removal and refitting 5
Vacuum hose condition check .... See Chapter 1A

Degrees of difficulty

Easy, suitable for novice with little experience	**Fairly easy,** suitable for beginner with some experience	**Fairly difficult,** suitable for competent DIY mechanic	**Difficult,** suitable for experienced DIY mechanic	**Very difficult,** suitable for expert DIY or professional

Specifications

General
System type .... Rover modular engine management system (MEMS) indirect multi-point fuel injection system integrated with ignition system

4A

Fuel pump
Maximum delivery pressure .... 4.1 bar
Regulated injection pressure .... 3.0 ± 0.2 bar

Idle settings (not adjustable - for reference only)
Idle speed .... 875 ± 50 rpm
Idle mixture (CO content) .... Less than 0.5 %

Torque wrench settings	Nm	lbf ft
Crankshaft position sensor-to-flywheel housing bolt	6	4
Engine control module (ECM)-to-bracket nuts	4	3
Engine coolant temperature (ECT) sensor-to-housing	15	11
Exhaust joint nuts and bolts	50	37
Exhaust manifold securing nuts	45	33
Fuel feed pipe-to-fuel rail bolts	10	7
Fuel pump/gauge sender-to-fuel tank nuts	9	7
Fuel rail-to-manifold bolts	5	4
Heated oxygen sensor (HO2S)-to-manifold/exhaust system	55	41
Idle air control valve (IACV)-to-manifold screws	8	6
Inlet manifold plenum chamber-to-manifold bolts (K8 engines)	25	18
Inlet manifold securing nuts and bolts	25	18
Intake air temperature (IAT) sensor-to-manifold	7	5
Throttle body-to-inlet manifold bolts	7	5
Throttle position sensor securing screws	1.5	1.0

1 General information and precautions

General information

The operation of the fuel injection system is described in more detail in Section 6.

Fuel is supplied from a tank mounted under the rear of the vehicle, by an electric fuel pump mounted in the tank. The fuel pump also incorporates the fuel level gauge sender unit. The fuel passes through a filter, to the fuel injection system, which incorporates various sensors, actuators, and an engine control module (ECM).

The inducted air passes through an air cleaner, which incorporates a paper filter element to filter out potentially-harmful particles (serious internal engine damage can be caused if foreign particles enter through the air intake system).

The engine control module (ECM) controls both the fuel injection system and the ignition system, integrating the two into a complete engine management system. Refer to Chapter 5B for details of the ignition side of the system.

The exhaust system incorporates a catalytic converter to reduce exhaust gas emissions. Further details can be found in Chapter 4C, along with details of the other emission control systems and components.

Precautions

Before disconnecting any fuel lines, or working on any part of the fuel system, the system must be depressurised as described in Section 7.

Care must be taken when disconnecting the fuel lines. When disconnecting a fuel union or hose, loosen the union or clamp screw slowly, to avoid sudden uncontrolled fuel spillage. Take adequate fire precautions.

When working on fuel system components, scrupulous cleanliness must be observed, and care must be taken not to introduce any foreign matter into fuel lines or components.

After carrying out any work involving disconnection of fuel lines, it is advisable to check the connections for leaks; pressurise the system by switching the ignition on and off several times.

Electronic control units are very sensitive components, and certain precautions must be taken to avoid damage to these units as follows.

When carrying out welding operations on the vehicle using electric welding equipment, the battery and alternator should be disconnected.

Although the underbonnet-mounted modules will tolerate normal underbonnet conditions, they can be adversely affected by excess heat or moisture. If using welding equipment or pressure-washing equipment in the vicinity of an electronic module, take care not to direct heat, or jets of water or steam, at the module. If this cannot be avoided, remove the module from the vehicle, and protect its wiring plug with a plastic bag.

Before disconnecting any wiring, or removing components, always ensure that the ignition is switched off.

Do not attempt to improvise fault diagnosis procedures using a test lamp or multi-meter, as irreparable damage could be caused to the module.

After working on fuel injection/engine management system components, ensure that all wiring is correctly reconnected before reconnecting the battery or switching on the ignition.

Leaded fuel will damage the catalytic converter, so unleaded fuel must be used at all times. In addition, if unburnt fuel enters the catalytic converter, this may result in overheating and irreparable damage to the catalytic converter.

Damage to the catalytic converter may result if the following precautions are not observed:

a) *Consult an approved dealer as soon as possible in the event of misfiring, irregular engine running after a cold start, a significant loss of engine power, or any other malfunction which may indicate a fault in the ignition system. If it is necessary to continue driving, do so for a short time at low engine speed, without labouring the engine.*

b) *Avoid frequent cold starts one after another.*

c) *Avoid actuation of the starter for an unnecessarily long time during starting.*

d) *Do not allow the fuel tank to become empty.*

e) *Do not attempt to start the engine by push- or tow-starting - use jump leads (see "Jump starting").*

⚠ **Warning: Many of the procedures in this Chapter require the disconnection of fuel line connections, and the removal of components, which may result in some fuel spillage. Before carrying out any operation on the fuel system, refer to the precautions given in 'Safety first!' at the beginning of this manual, and follow them implicitly. Petrol is a highly-dangerous and volatile liquid, and the precautions necessary when handling it cannot be overstressed.**

3.4 Unscrew the bolt (arrowed) securing the handbrake cable to the H-frame mounting

2 Air cleaner assembly – removal and refitting

Removal

1 Remove the battery as described in Chapter 5A.
2 Release the hose clip, and disconnect the air intake trunking from the throttle body.
3 Unscrew the two bolts securing the air cleaner to the battery tray.
4 Release the air intake tube from the bottom of the air cleaner, then remove the air cleaner assembly from the engine compartment.

Refitting

5 Refitting is a reversal of removal.

3 Fuel tank and filler neck – removal, inspection and refitting

Fuel tank

Removal

Note: *During removal, note the locations and routing of all hoses to aid refitting.*

1 Disconnect the battery negative lead.
2 Chock the front wheels, then jack up the rear of the vehicle and support securely on axle stands (see *"Jacking and Vehicle Support"*).
3 Siphon the fuel from the tank into a clean metal container which can be sealed. Alternatively, working under the car, disconnect an accessible fuel line connection at the tank, and drain the fuel into a suitable container.
4 Unscrew the bolt securing the handbrake cable to the left-hand rear suspension H-frame mounting, and release the cable from the mounting **(see illustration)**.
5 Remove the screw securing the fuel tank filler neck to the body. Note that the screw also secures the rear wheel arch liner.
6 Slacken the hose clip and disconnect the breather hose from the fuel filler neck **(see illustration)**.

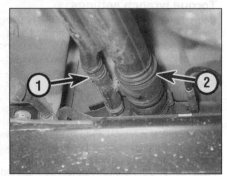

3.6 Disconnect the breather (1) and filler (2) hoses from the fuel filler neck

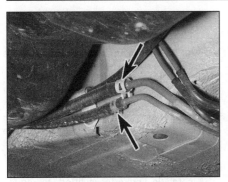

3.8 Disconnect the fuel feed and return hoses (arrowed) from the pipes

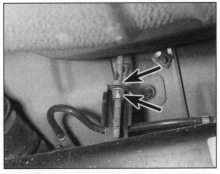

3.11 Fuel tank strap locknut and securing nut (arrowed)

3.19 Pulling out the fuel filler neck surround

7 Slacken the hose clip and disconnect the filler hose from the fuel filler neck **(see illustration 3.6)**.

8 Slacken the hose clips and disconnect the fuel feed and return hoses from the pipes under the rear of the vehicle **(see illustration)**. Plug or cover the open ends of the hoses and pipes to prevent dirt entry.

9 Release the connector and disconnect the breather hose from the pipe.

10 Place a trolley jack under the fuel tank, with a block of wood between the jack and the tank.

11 Working at the rear of the fuel tank, unscrew the locknuts, then unscrew the two fuel tank strap securing nuts **(see illustration)**.

12 Ensure that the jack is supporting the fuel tank, then release the fuel tank straps from the brackets on the body.

13 Lower the fuel tank until the fuel pump/gauge sender unit wiring connector can be reached, then separate the two halves of the connector, and withdraw the fuel tank from under the vehicle.

Inspection

14 If the tank contains sediment or water, it may be cleaned out using two or three rinses with paraffin. Shake vigorously using several changes of paraffin, but before doing so remove the fuel pump/gauge sender unit (see Section 8).

> ⚠ *Warning: This procedure should be carried out in a well-ventilated area, and it is vital to*

take adequate fire precautions – refer to "Safety first!" for further details.

15 Any repairs to the fuel tank should be carried out by a professional. Do not under any circumstances attempt to weld or solder a fuel tank. Removal of residual fuel vapour requires several hours of specialist cleaning.

Refitting

16 Refitting is a reversal of removal, but ensure that all hoses are reconnected to their correct locations as noted before removal, and use new hose clips if necessary.

Fuel filler neck

Removal

17 Chock the front wheels, then jack up the rear of the vehicle and support securely on axle stands (see *"Jacking and Vehicle Support"*). Remove the left-hand rear roadwheel.

18 Remove the securing screws, and withdraw the rear left-hand wheel arch liner.

19 Remove the fuel filler cap, then reach up behind the filler neck and depress the three lugs securing the filler neck surround to the body and filler neck. Pull out the filler neck surround **(see illustration)**.

20 Working under the vehicle, slacken the hose clips, and disconnect the breather hose and the filler hose from the fuel filler neck.

> ⚠ *Warning: Be prepared for fuel spillage, and have a suitable container ready to catch any fuel which may be released as the filler hose is disconnected.*

21 Withdraw the filler neck assembly from under the wheel arch.

Refitting

22 Refitting is a reversal of removal.

---

4 Throttle cable – removal, refitting and adjustment 🔧

Removal

1 Slide the cable adjuster from the bracket on the throttle body/inlet manifold **(see illustration)**.

2 Slide the cable end fitting from the groove in the throttle lever, and disconnect the cable from the lever **(see illustration)**.

3 Release the cable from the clip on the inlet manifold.

4 Working at the engine compartment bulkhead, turn the collar on the throttle cable through 90°, and release the cable from the bulkhead.

5 Working in the driver's footwell, release the two securing clips, and remove the lower facia trim panel.

6 Reach up under the facia, and pull the end of the cable forwards from the pedal, then squeeze the securing lugs and remove the plastic cable securing clip from the end of the pedal. Release the end of the cable from the pedal **(see illustration)**.

4A

4.1 Slide the cable adjuster from the bracket . . .

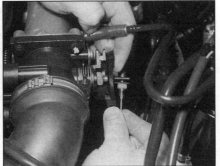

4.2 . . . then slide the cable end fitting from the throttle lever – K8 engines

4.6 Depress the plastic clips (arrowed) and release the end of the throttle cable from the pedal

7 Pull the cable through the bulkhead into the engine compartment, and withdraw the cable from the vehicle.

Refitting

8 Refitting is a reversal of removal, but smear the bulkhead grommet with rubber grease and, on completion, check the cable adjustment as described in the following paragraphs.

Adjustment

Note: *Do not attempt to adjust the throttle stop screw during this procedure.*

9 Slide the cable adjuster from the bracket on the inlet manifold/throttle body, then position the cable adjuster against the rear of the bracket.

10 Hold the throttle lever on the throttle body in the fully closed position, ensuring that the cam on the throttle lever rests against the throttle stop screw.

11 Turn the cable adjuster as necessary until all freeplay is removed from the cable, without moving the throttle lever.

12 Slide the adjuster back into position in the bracket.

13 Have an assistant fully depress the throttle pedal, and check that the throttle lever moves to the fully open position, and returns to the fully closed position when the pedal is released.

5 Throttle pedal – removal and refitting

Removal

1 Disconnect the end of the throttle cable from the pedal as described in Section 4.

2 Using a suitable pair of pliers, unhook the return spring from the pedal **(see illustration)**.

3 Working at the left-hand side of the pedal pivot shaft, prise off the securing clip, then slide the pedal assembly from the mounting bracket towards the right-hand side of the vehicle, until it can be removed **(see illustration)**.

Refitting

4 Refitting is a reversal of removal, but make sure that the securing clip is securely refitted.

6 Fuel injection system – general information

The system is under the overall control of the modular engine management system (MEMS), which also controls the ignition system (see Chapter 5B).

Fuel is supplied from the rear-mounted fuel tank by an electric pump mounted in the tank, via a fuel filter, to the fuel rail. A fuel pressure regulator mounted on the fuel rail maintains a constant fuel pressure to the fuel injectors. Excess fuel is returned from the regulator to the tank.

The fuel rail acts as a reservoir for the four fuel injectors, which inject fuel into the cylinder inlet tracts, upstream of the inlet valves. The injectors operate in pairs - the injectors for Nos 1 and 4 cylinders operate simultaneously, as do the injectors for Nos 2 and 3 cylinders.

The duration of the electrical pulses supplied to the fuel injectors determine the time for which the injectors are open, and hence the quantity of fuel injected. Pulse duration is computed by the engine control module (ECM) on the basis of information received from the following sensors:

a) *Throttle position sensor (TPS) - informs the ECM of throttle position, and the rate of throttle opening/closing.*

b) *Manifold absolute pressure (MAP) sensor - informs the ECM of the load on the engine (expressed in terms of inlet manifold vacuum).*

c) *Crankshaft position (CKP) sensor - informs the ECM of the crankshaft speed and position.*

d) *Engine coolant temperature (ECT) sensor - informs the ECM of engine temperature.*

e) *Intake air temperature (IAT) sensor - informs the ECM of the temperature of air entering the inlet manifold.*

f) *Heated oxygen sensor (HO2S) - informs the ECM of the oxygen content in the exhaust gases (and hence the air/fuel mixture ratio).*

The signals from the various sensors are processed by the ECM, and the optimum fuelling and ignition settings are selected for the prevailing engine operating conditions.

Idle speed is controlled by the idle air control valve (IACV), which regulates the quantity of air bypassing the throttle valve. The valve is controlled directly by the ECM; there is no provision for direct adjustment of idle speed.

Similarly, the fuel/air mixture is controlled within fine limits (to avoid damage to the catalytic converter) by the ECM, via the fuel injectors. No manual adjustment of fuel/air mixture is possible.

A catalytic converter is fitted, to reduce harmful exhaust gas emissions. Details of this and other emissions control system equipment are given in Chapter 4C.

If certain sensors fail, and send abnormal signals to the ECM, the ECM has a back-up programme. In this event, the abnormal signals are ignored, and a pre-programmed value is substituted for the sensor signal, allowing the engine to continue running, albeit at reduced efficiency. If the ECM enters its back-up mode, the engine system warning light on the instrument panel will illuminate, and a fault code will be stored in the ECM memory. This fault code can be read using specialist Rover dedicated test equipment.

All vehicle are fitted with a fuel inertia cut-off switch (see Section 11), which cuts off the fuel supply in the event of the vehicle being involved in an impact. The engine cannot be started if the switch is activated - the switch must be reset manually.

7 Fuel injection system – depressurising and priming

Depressurising

1 Disconnect the battery negative lead.

2 Position a wad of absorbent cloth around the outlet pipe union on the top of the fuel filter.

3 Counterhold the union on the fuel filter, and **slowly** slacken the fuel pipe union nut using a second spanner **(see illustration)**.

5.2 Unhook the return spring (arrowed) from the pedal

5.3 Prise off the throttle pedal securing clip (arrowed)

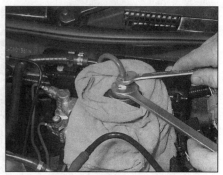

7.3 Slackening the fuel outlet pipe union to relieve the fuel pressure

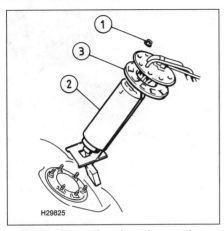

8.5 Fuel pump/sender unit mounting details

1 Securing nut   2 Fuel pump   3 Seal

⚠️ **Warning: Be prepared for the escape of some fuel. Take adequate fire precautions.**

4 Allow the fuel pressure to dissipate, then re-tighten the union nut.

Priming

5 The system is self-priming. Switch on the ignition, and wait for a few seconds before attempting to start the engine. There may be a short delay before the engine starts, as the fuel system components refill with fuel.

8 Fuel pump/fuel gauge sender unit – removal and refitting

Removal

1 The fuel pump/fuel gauge sender unit is mounted in the top of the fuel tank, and cannot be accessed with the tank in place.
2 Remove the fuel tank as described in Section 3.
3 Release the hose clamps, and disconnect the fuel feed and return hoses from the pipes at the top of the pump/sender unit. Plug or cover the open ends of the hoses and pipes to prevent dirt entry.

10.8 Two of the throttle body securing bolts (arrowed) – K8 engines

4 Unscrew the six nuts securing the pump/sender unit to the fuel tank.
5 Carefully slide the pump/sender unit from the fuel tank, taking care not to damage the sender unit float **(see illustration)**. Recover the seal.

Refitting

6 Examine the condition of the sealing ring, and renew if necessary, then thoroughly clean the mating faces of the tank and the pump/sender unit.
7 Refitting is a reversal of removal, tightening the pump/sender unit nuts to the specified torque setting. If necessary, renew the fuel hose clips and on completion, refit the fuel tank with reference to Section 3.

9 Fuel injection system – testing and adjustment

Testing

1 If a fault appears in the fuel injection system, first ensure that all the system wiring connectors are securely connected and free from corrosion. Ensure that the fault is not due to poor maintenance; ie, check that the air cleaner filter element is clean, that the spark plugs are in good condition and correctly gapped (see Chapter 1A), that the cylinder compression pressures are correct (see Chapter 2A), and that the engine breather hoses are clear and undamaged (see Chapter 4C).
2 If the engine will not start, check that the fuel inertia cut-off switch has not operated (see Section 11). Push the switch button to reset if necessary.
3 If these checks fail to reveal the cause of the problem, the vehicle should be taken to a Rover dealer for testing. A wiring connector is provided on a bracket behind the centre console, into which a special electronic diagnostic tester can be plugged. The tester should locate the fault quickly and simply, avoiding the need to test all the system components individually, which is time-consuming, and also carries a risk of damaging the ECM.

Adjustment

4 Experienced home mechanics with access

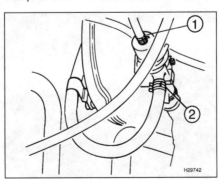

11.3 Disconnect the pressure regulator vacuum hose (1) and the fuel return hose (2) – K8 engines

to a tachometer and an accurately calibrated exhaust gas analyser may be able to check the exhaust CO level and the idle speed. However, if either of these settings is found to be in need of adjustment, the vehicle must be taken to a Rover dealer for further testing.
5 No manual adjustment of the exhaust CO level or idle speed is possible.

10 Throttle body – removal and refitting

Removal

Note: *A new throttle body-to-inlet manifold O-ring will be required on refitting. Silicone grease will be required to lubricate the O-ring.*
1 Disconnect the battery negative lead.
2 Slacken the hose clip securing the air intake trunking to the throttle body, and disconnect the trunking from the throttle body.
3 Disconnect the hose from the idle air control valve (IACV).
4 Disconnect the wiring plug from the throttle position sensor (TPS).
5 Release the hose clip(s), and disconnect the breather hose(s) from the throttle body.
6 Slide the cable adjuster from the bracket on the inlet manifold/throttle body.
7 Slide the cable end fitting from the groove in the throttle lever, and disconnect the cable from the lever.
8 Unscrew the four securing bolts, and withdraw the throttle body from the inlet manifold **(see illustration)**. Recover the O-ring and discard it.

Refitting

9 Thoroughly clean the mating faces of the throttle body and the inlet manifold.
10 Lubricate a new O-ring with a little silicone grease, then fit the O-ring to the throttle body.
11 Further refitting is a reversal of removal, but check the adjustment of the throttle cable as described in Section 4.

11 Fuel injection system components – removal and refitting

Fuel rail and fuel injectors – K8 engines

Note: *New fuel injector seals and a new fuel feed pipe-to-fuel rail O-ring will be required on refitting. Silicone grease will be required to lubricate the fuel feed pipe-to-fuel rail O-ring.*

Removal

1 Depressurise the fuel system as described in Section 7.
2 Remove the inlet manifold plenum chamber, as described in Section 12.
3 Release the hose clip and disconnect the vacuum hose from the fuel pressure regulator **(see illustration)**.

4A

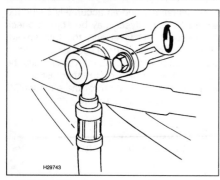

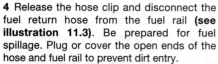

11.5 Fuel feed pipe connection securing bolt (arrowed) – K8 engines

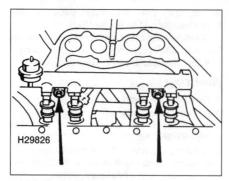

11.7 Fuel rail securing bolts (arrowed) – K8 engines

11.9 Fuel injector with seals removed

4 Release the hose clip and disconnect the fuel return hose from the fuel rail **(see illustration 11.3)**. Be prepared for fuel spillage. Plug or cover the open ends of the hose and fuel rail to prevent dirt entry.

5 Position a wad of absorbent cloth around the fuel feed connection to the fuel rail. Unscrew the two bolts securing the fuel feed pipe to the fuel rail, and disconnect the fuel feed pipe. Recover the O-ring and discard it **(see illustration)**. Be prepared for fuel spillage. Plug the open ends of the pipe and fuel rail to prevent dirt entry and further fuel spillage.

6 Disconnect the wiring plugs from the fuel injectors.

7 Unscrew the two bolts securing the fuel rail to the inlet manifold **(see illustration)**.

8 Carefully pull the fuel rail, complete with the fuel injectors, from the inlet manifold.

9 To remove the fuel injectors, carefully prise off the metal securing clips using a screwdriver, then pull the injectors from the fuel rail. Remove the seals from the fuel injectors and discard them **(see illustration)**.

10 Note that overhaul of the fuel injectors is not possible. If faulty, an injector must be renewed.

Refitting

11 Commence refitting by fitting new seals to both ends of each fuel injector.

12 Refitting is a reversal of removal,

tightening the fuel rail securing bolts to the specified torque setting. Use a new O-ring when reconnecting the fuel feed pipe to the fuel rail (lubricate the O-ring with a little silicone grease) and refit the inlet manifold plenum chamber with reference to Section 12.

Fuel rail and fuel injectors – K16 engines

Note: *New fuel injector seals and a new fuel feed pipe-to-fuel rail O-ring will be required on refitting. Silicone grease will be required to lubricate the fuel feed pipe-to-fuel rail O-ring.*

Removal

13 Depressurise the fuel system as described in Section 7.

14 Release the hose clips, and disconnect the two breather hoses from the cylinder head cover, then disconnect the hoses from the inlet manifold, and remove them **(see illustration 11.17)**.

15 Disconnect the wiring plug from the idle air control valve (IACV) **(see illustration 11.17)**.

16 Release the hose clip and disconnect the vacuum hose from the fuel pressure regulator.

17 Release the hose clip and disconnect the fuel return hose from the fuel rail **(see illustration)**. Be prepared for fuel spillage, and plug or cover the open ends of the hose and fuel rail to prevent dirt entry and further fuel loss.

18 Unscrew the bolt securing the fuel injector harness wiring plug bracket to the inlet

manifold, then disconnect the wiring plug, and remove the bracket.

19 Remove the engine oil level dipstick.

20 Proceed as described in paragraphs 5 to 10.

Refitting

21 Commence refitting by fitting new seals to both ends of each fuel injector.

22 Refitting is a reversal of removal, tightening the fuel rail securing bolts to the specified torque setting. Use a new O-ring when reconnecting the fuel feed pipe to the fuel rail (lubricate the O-ring with a little silicone grease).

Fuel pressure regulator

23 The fuel pressure regulator is integral with the fuel rail, and cannot be removed separately. If the fuel regulator is faulty, the complete fuel rail/regulator assembly must be renewed.

Idle air control valve (IACV)

Note: *A new O-ring and suitable silicone grease will be required on refitting.*

Removal

24 The idle air control valve is located at the rear of the engine.

25 Disconnect the battery negative lead, then disconnect the wiring plug from the valve **(see illustration)**.

26 Remove the two screws securing the valve to the inlet manifold, then withdraw the

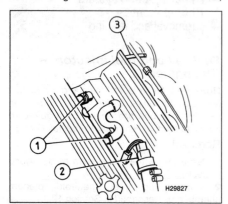

11.17 Disconnect the breather hoses (1), the idle air control valve (IACV) wiring plug (2) and the fuel return hose (3) – K16 engines

11.25 Disconnecting the wiring plug from the idle air control valve (IACV) – K8 engines

11.26 Idle air control valve (IACV) securing screws (arrowed) – K8 engines

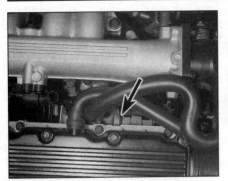

11.28 Intake air temperature (IAT) sensor location (arrowed) – K8 engines

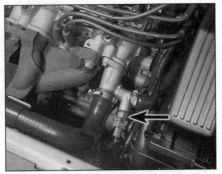

11.32 Engine coolant temperature (ECT) sensor location (arrowed)

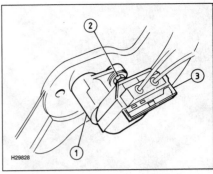

11.38 Crankshaft position (CKP) sensor (1), securing bolt (2) and wiring plug (3)

valve from the manifold **(see illustration)**. Recover the O-ring and discard it.

Refitting

27 Refitting is a reversal of removal, tightening the valve securing screws to the specified torque setting. Use a new O-ring and lubricate the O-ring with a little silicone grease.

Intake air temperature (IAT) sensor

Removal

28 The sensor is mounted at the left-hand rear of the inlet manifold **(see illustration)**.
29 Disconnect the battery negative lead, then disconnect the wiring plug from the sensor.
30 Unscrew the sensor from the inlet manifold.

Refitting

31 Thoroughly clean the threads and mating faces on the sensor and manifold, then refit the sensor using a reversal of the removal procedure and tightening it to the specified torque setting.

Engine coolant temperature (ECT) sensor

Note: *Suitable sealant will be required on refitting.*

Removal

32 The sensor is located in the coolant elbow

at the front left-hand corner of the engine **(see illustration)**.
33 Disconnect the battery negative lead, then disconnect the wiring plug from the sensor.
34 Position a container beneath the sensor to catch escaping coolant, then unscrew the sensor from its housing.

Refitting

35 Thoroughly clean the threads and mating faces on the sensor and manifold, then coat the sensor threads with sealant (Loctite 577, or a suitable equivalent).
36 Refit the sensor to its housing tightening it to the specified torque setting. Reconnect the sensor wiring plug and the battery negative lead, then check the coolant level as described in *"Weekly checks"* and top up if necessary.

Crankshaft position (CKP) sensor

Removal

37 Disconnect the battery negative lead.
38 The sensor is mounted at the rear of the flywheel housing (at the left-hand end of the engine) **(see illustration)**. To improve access to the sensor, apply the handbrake, then jack up the front of the vehicle and support securely on axle stands (see *"Jacking and Vehicle Support"*).
39 Disconnect the wiring plug from the sensor.

40 Unscrew the bolt securing the sensor to the flywheel housing, then remove the sensor.

Refitting

41 Thoroughly clean the mating faces on the sensor and housing, then refit the sensor using a reversal of the removal procedure and tightening its bolt to the specified torque setting.

Throttle position sensor (TPS)

Removal

42 The throttle position sensor is located at the front of the throttle body.
43 Disconnect the battery negative lead, then disconnect the wiring plug from the sensor.
44 Remove the two sensor securing screws and recover the washers. Also recover the sensor specification plate, which is secured by the screws **(see illustration)**.
45 Carefully pull the sensor from the throttle spindle.
Caution: Do not twist or lever the throttle position sensor – it is easily damaged!

Refitting

46 Thoroughly clean the mating faces of the sensor and the housing.
47 Carefully push the sensor onto the throttle spindle, ensuring that the flat on the throttle spindle engages correctly with the sensor wiper. Push the sensor onto the throttle spindle using finger pressure only, and push only on the shaded area shown **(see illustration)** – the sensor is easily damaged.
48 Rotate the sensor ant-clockwise as necessary (**do not** rotate the sensor clockwise, and make sure that the sensor is not rotated beyond its internal stops) until the securing screw holes align with the corresponding holes in the throttle body.
49 Offer the sensor specification plate into position, then refit the sensor securing screws, ensuring that the washers are in place, and tighten the screws to the specified torque. **Do not** exceed the specified torque.
50 Reconnect the sensor wiring plug.
51 Operate the throttle lever several times, and check that the lever moves freely from the fully closed to the fully open position and back.
52 Reconnect the battery negative lead.

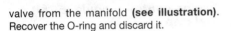

11.44 Throttle position sensor (TPS) – K8 engines

1 Sensor wiring plug
2 Securing screws
3 Specification plate

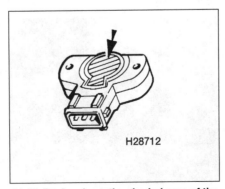

H28712

11.47 Push only on the shaded area of the throttle position sensor (TPS)

4A

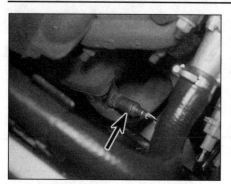

11.54 Heated oxygen sensor (HO2S) location (arrowed) – K8 engines

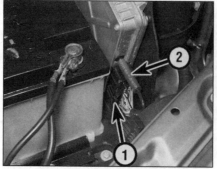

11.65 Engine control module (ECM) wiring plug (1) and vacuum pipe (2)

11.66 Engine control module (ECM) securing bolts (arrowed)

Manifold absolute pressure (MAP) sensor

53 The sensor is integral with the engine control module (ECM) and cannot be removed separately.

Heated oxygen sensor (HO₂S) – K8 engines

Removal

54 The sensor is mounted at the top of the exhaust front section **(see illustration)**.
55 Disconnect the battery negative lead.
56 Trace the wiring back from the sensor, and locate the sensor connector, at the bracket on the coolant rail, behind the distributor. Release the connector from the bracket, and separate the two halves of the connector.
57 Using an open-ended spanner, unscrew the sensor from the exhaust pipe, and recover the sealing washer.

Refitting

58 Thoroughly clean the threads on the sensor and the exhaust pipe. Examine the condition of the sealing washer, and renew if necessary.
59 Refitting is a reversal of removal, but tighten the sensor to the specified torque (a special oxygen sensor socket with a cut-out for the wiring to pass through can be obtained from motor factors or tool shops).

Heated oxygen sensor (HO₂S) – K16 engines

Removal

60 Remove the exhaust manifold, as described in Section 12.

61 Using an open-ended spanner, unscrew the sensor from the exhaust pipe, and recover the sealing washer.

Refitting

62 Proceed as described in paragraphs 58 and 59, then refit the exhaust manifold as described in Section 12.

Engine control module (ECM)

Note: *If a new engine control module is being fitted, the control unit will need to be programmed with the code from the vehicle anti-theft immobiliser system before the engine can be started. This must be carried out by a Rover dealer.*

Removal

63 The engine control module is located on the left-hand side of the engine compartment, next to the battery.
64 Disconnect the battery negative lead, then disconnect the wiring plug from the control unit.
65 Disconnect the vacuum pipe from the control unit **(see illustration)**.
66 Slacken the bolts securing the control unit to the mounting bracket (counterhold the nuts if necessary), then lift out the control unit **(see illustration)**.

Refitting

67 Refitting is a reversal of removal. Tighten the control unit securing bolts to the specified torque setting.

Engine control module (ECM) fuel trap

Removal

68 The fuel trap is located at the right-hand side of the engine compartment bulkhead, next to the fuel inertia cut-off switch **(see illustration)**.
69 Release the fuel trap from its mounting bracket, then disconnect the two vacuum pipes, noting their locations to ensure correct refitting, and remove the fuel trap.

Refitting

70 Refitting is a reversal of removal, but ensure that the vacuum pipes are correctly reconnected as noted before removal.

Engine management relay module

Removal

71 The module is located at the left-hand side of the engine compartment, next to the engine control module (ECM). The relay module incorporates the main fuel injection relay, the starter motor relay, the fuel pump relay and the heated oxygen sensor (HO₂S) relay.
72 Disconnect the battery negative lead.
73 Release the relay module from its mounting bracket, then disconnect the two wiring plugs from the bottom of the module, and remove the module **(see illustrations)**.

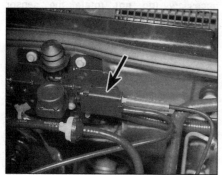

11.68 Engine control module (ECM) fuel trap location (arrowed)

11.73a Release the engine management relay module from its mounting bracket . . .

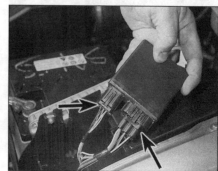

11.73b . . . then disconnect the two wiring plugs (arrowed)

11.75 Fuel inertia cut-off switch location (arrowed)

12.5 Disconnecting a breather hose from the throttle body – K8 engines

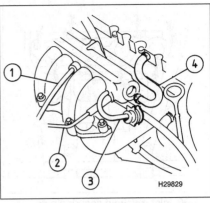

12.9 Disconnect the brake servo (1), engine control module (ECM) (2) and fuel pressure regulator (3) vacuum hoses and the breather hose (4)

Refitting

74 Refitting is a reversal of removal, but make sure that the wiring plugs are securely reconnected.

Fuel inertia cut-off switch

Removal

75 The switch is located at the right-hand side of the engine compartment bulkhead **(see illustration)**.
76 Disconnect the battery negative lead, then disconnect the wiring plug from the switch.
77 Remove the two securing screws and withdraw the switch from its mounting bracket.

Refitting

78 Refitting is a reversal of removal, but ensure that the switch is reset by pressing the button on the top of the switch.

---

12 Manifolds –
removal and refitting

Inlet manifold plenum chamber – K8 engines

Note: *Note the locations and routing of all hoses during this procedure to ensure correct refitting. A new plenum chamber-to-inlet manifold gasket will be required on refitting.*

Removal

1 Disconnect the battery negative lead.
2 Slacken the hose clip, and disconnect the air trunking from the throttle body.
3 Disconnect the wiring plug from the idle air control valve (IACV).
4 Disconnect the wiring plug from the throttle position sensor (TPS).
5 Release the hose clip(s) and disconnect the breather hose(s) from the throttle body **(see illustration)**.
6 Similarly, release the hose clip, and disconnect the charcoal canister hose from the manifold plenum chamber.
7 Slide the cable adjuster from the bracket on the inlet manifold/throttle body.
8 Slide the cable end fitting from the groove

in the throttle lever, and disconnect the cable from the lever.
9 Depress the locking collar, and disconnect the brake servo vacuum hose from the manifold plenum chamber **(see illustration)**.
10 Disconnect the engine control module (ECM) and the fuel pressure regulator vacuum hoses from the manifold plenum chamber.
11 Release the hose clip, and disconnect the breather hose from the manifold plenum chamber.
12 Release the fuel injector harness wiring connector, and the ignition coil HT lead from the brackets under the throttle body **(see illustration)**.
13 Unscrew the five bolts securing the plenum chamber to the inlet manifold, then withdraw the plenum chamber **(see illustration)**. Recover and discard the gasket.

Refitting

14 Thoroughly clean the mating faces of the plenum chamber and the inlet manifold.
15 Fit the plenum chamber, using a new gasket, and tighten the securing bolts to the specified torque setting.
16 Further refitting is a reversal of removal, but reconnect and adjust the throttle cable as described in Section 4.

Inlet manifold – K8 engines

Note: *Note the locations and routing of all hoses during this procedure to ensure correct refitting. A new inlet manifold gasket and new throttle body-to-inlet manifold and fuel feed*

pipe-to-fuel rail O-rings will be required on refitting. Silicone grease will be required to lubricate the O-rings.

Removal

17 Disconnect the battery negative lead.
18 Drain the cooling system as described in Chapter 1A.
19 Depressurise the fuel system as described in Section 7.
20 Slacken the hose clip, and disconnect the air intake trunking from the air cleaner.
21 Release the hose clip, and disconnect the breather hose from the throttle body.
22 Similarly, release the hose clip, and disconnect the charcoal canister hose from the inlet manifold.
23 Disconnect the wiring plug from the idle air control valve (IACV), then disconnect the IACV air hose.
24 Release the fuel injector harness wiring connector from the bracket under the throttle body, and separate the two halves of the connector.
25 Unscrew the four bolts securing the throttle body to the inlet manifold, then withdraw the throttle body, and lay it to one

12.12 Fuel injector harness wiring connector location (arrowed) – K8 engines

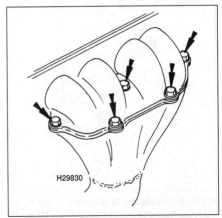

12.13 Plenum chamber-to-inlet manifold securing bolts (arrowed) – K8 engines

4A

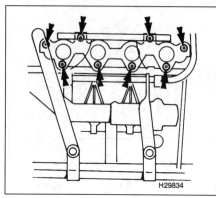

12.36 Inlet manifold securing nuts and bolts (arrowed) – K8 engines

side, clear of the manifold. Recover the O-ring and discard it.

26 Release the hose clip, and disconnect the breather hose from the inlet manifold.

27 Similarly, disconnect the breather hose from the cylinder head cover.

28 Depress the locking collar, and disconnect the brake servo vacuum hose from the inlet manifold.

29 Disconnect the engine control module (ECM) vacuum hose from the inlet manifold.

30 Place a wad of absorbent cloth around the fuel return hose connection on the fuel rail, then release the hose clip, and disconnect the fuel return hose. Be prepared for fuel spillage, and take adequate fire precautions. Plug or cover the open ends of the hose and fuel rail to prevent dirt entry and further fuel loss.

31 Release the fuel return hose from the two clips under the inlet manifold.

32 Slacken the hose clip, and disconnect the coolant hose from the inlet manifold.

33 Disconnect the wiring plug from the inlet air temperature (IAT) sensor.

34 Position a wad of absorbent cloth around the fuel feed connection to the fuel rail. Unscrew the two bolts securing the fuel feed pipe to the fuel rail, and disconnect the fuel feed pipe. Recover the O-ring and discard it. Be prepared for fuel spillage. Plug the open

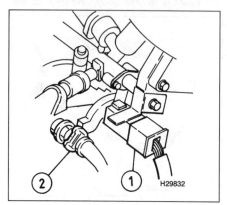

12.51 Separate the two halves of the fuel injector harness wiring connector (1) and disconnect the wiring plug (2) from the inlet air temperature (IAT) sensor

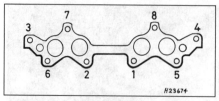

12.39 Inlet manifold securing nut and bolt tightening sequence – K8 engines

ends of the pipe and fuel rail to prevent dirt entry and further fuel spillage.

35 Unscrew the bolt securing the support bracket to the inlet manifold.

36 Working from the centre of the manifold outwards, progressively unscrew the six bolts and two nuts securing the manifold to the cylinder head **(see illustration)**.

37 Lift the manifold away from the cylinder head. Recover and discard the gasket.

Refitting

38 Thoroughly clean the mating faces of the manifold and the cylinder head.

39 Offer the manifold into position on the cylinder head, using a new gasket, then refit the securing bolts and nuts, and tighten progressively to the specified torque in the sequence shown **(see illustration)**.

40 Further refitting is a reversal of removal, bearing in mind the following points.

a) Use a new O-ring when reconnecting the fuel feed pipe to the fuel rail, and lubricate the O-ring with a little silicone grease.

b) Use a new O-ring when refitting the throttle body to the inlet manifold, and lubricate the O-ring with a little silicone grease.

c) On completion, refill the cooling system as described in Chapter 1A.

Inlet manifold – K16 engines

Note: *Note the locations and routing of all hoses during this procedure to ensure correct refitting. A new inlet manifold gasket and new throttle body-to-inlet manifold and fuel feed pipe-to-fuel rail O-rings will be required on refitting. Silicone grease will be required to lubricate the O-rings.*

Removal

41 Proceed as described in paragraphs 17 to 23.

42 Disconnect the wiring plug from the throttle position sensor (TPS).

43 Release the throttle cable from the clip on the inlet manifold.

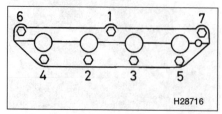

12.57 Inlet manifold securing nut and bolt tightening sequence – K16 engines

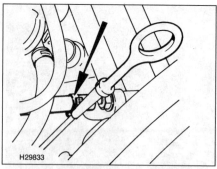

12.50 Disconnect the coolant hose (arrowed) from the inlet manifold – K16 engines

44 Unscrew the four bolts securing the throttle body to the inlet manifold, then withdraw the throttle body, and lay it to one side, clear of the manifold. Recover the O-ring and discard it.

45 Release the coil HT lead from the bracket under the inlet manifold.

46 Disconnect the breather hose from the inlet manifold.

47 Depress the locking collar, and disconnect the brake servo vacuum hose from the inlet manifold.

48 Disconnect the engine control module (ECM) vacuum hose from the inlet manifold.

49 Place a wad of absorbent cloth around the fuel return hose connection on the fuel rail, then release the hose clip, and disconnect the fuel return hose. Be prepared for fuel spillage, and take adequate fire precautions. Plug or cover the open ends of the hose and fuel rail to prevent dirt entry and further fuel loss.

50 Slacken the hose clip, and disconnect the coolant hose from the inlet manifold **(see illustration)**.

51 Release the fuel injector harness wiring connector from the bracket on the throttle body, and separate the two halves of the connector **(see illustration)**.

52 Disconnect the wiring plug from the inlet air temperature (IAT) sensor.

53 Position a wad of absorbent cloth around the fuel feed connection to the fuel rail. Unscrew the two bolts securing the fuel feed pipe to the fuel rail, and disconnect the fuel feed pipe. Recover the O-ring and discard it. Be prepared for fuel spillage. Plug the open ends of the pipe and fuel rail to prevent dirt entry and further fuel spillage.

54 Working from the centre of the manifold outwards, progressively unscrew the four bolts and three nuts securing the manifold to the cylinder head.

55 Lift the manifold away from the cylinder head. Recover and discard the gasket.

Refitting

56 Thoroughly clean the mating faces of the manifold and the cylinder head.

57 Offer the manifold into position on the cylinder head, using a new gasket, then refit the securing bolts and nuts, and tighten progressively to the specified torque in the sequence shown **(see illustration)**.

12.60 Exhaust manifold upper securing nuts (arrowed) – K8 engines

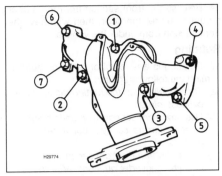

12.63 Exhaust manifold nut tightening sequence – K8 engines

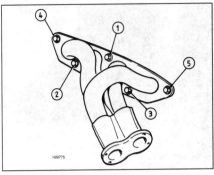

12.71 Exhaust manifold nut tightening sequence – K16 engines

58 Further refitting is a reversal of removal, bearing in mind the following points.
a) Use a new O-ring when reconnecting the fuel feed pipe to the fuel rail, and lubricate the O-ring with a little silicone grease.
b) Use a new O-ring when refitting the throttle body to the inlet manifold, and lubricate the O-ring with a little silicone grease.
c) On completion, refill the cooling system as described in Chapter 1A.

Exhaust manifold – K8 engines

Note: A new manifold gasket, and a new exhaust front section-to-manifold gasket will be required on refitting.

Removal

59 Disconnect the exhaust front section from the manifold, with reference to Section 13.
60 Unscrew the seven securing nuts, and withdraw the manifold from the cylinder head. Recover the gasket and discard it (see illustration).
61 It is possible that some of the manifold studs may be unscrewed from the cylinder head when the manifold securing nuts are unscrewed. In this event, the studs should be screwed back into the cylinder head once the manifold has been removed, using two manifold nuts locked together.

Refitting

62 Thoroughly clean the mating faces of the manifold and the cylinder head.
63 Refit the manifold using a new gasket, and progressively tighten the securing nuts to the specified torque setting in the sequence shown (see illustration).
64 Reconnect the exhaust front section to the manifold with reference to Section 13.

Exhaust manifold – K16 engines without air conditioning

Note: A new manifold gasket, and a new exhaust front section-to-manifold gasket will be required on refitting.

Removal

65 Disconnect the battery negative lead.
66 Disconnect the exhaust front section from the manifold, with reference to Section 13.

67 Trace the wiring back from the heated oxygen sensor (HO2S), and release the sensor wiring connector from its mounting bracket. Separate the two halves of the connector.
68 Unscrew the five securing nuts, and withdraw the manifold from the cylinder head. Recover the gasket and discard it.
69 It is possible that some of the manifold studs may be unscrewed from the cylinder head when the manifold securing nuts are unscrewed. In this event, the studs should be screwed back into the cylinder head once the manifold has been removed, using two manifold nuts locked together.

Refitting

70 Thoroughly clean the mating faces of the manifold and the cylinder head.
71 Refit the manifold using a new gasket, and progressively tighten the securing nuts to the specified torque setting in the sequence shown (see illustration).
72 Reconnect the oxygen sensor wiring connector, and clip the connector into position on the mounting bracket.
73 Reconnect the exhaust front section to the manifold with reference to Section 13, then reconnect the battery negative lead.

Exhaust manifold – K16 engines with air conditioning

Note: A new manifold gasket, and a new exhaust front section-to-manifold gasket will be required on refitting.

Removal

74 Remove the alternator as described in Chapter 5A.
75 Disconnect the exhaust front section from the manifold with reference to Section 13.
76 Unscrew the nut and bolts, and remove the alternator heat shield, and the alternator top mounting bracket.
77 Proceed as described in paragraphs 67 to 69.

Refitting

78 Proceed as described in paragraphs 70 to 72.
79 Refit the alternator top mounting bracket and the heat shield.

80 Reconnect the exhaust front section to the manifold with reference to Section 13.
81 Refit the alternator as described in Chapter 5A.

13 Exhaust system – general information and component renewal

General information

1 The exhaust system comprises a downpipe, a front silencer and a rear expansion box with a tailpipe.
2 The system fitted in production is of four-piece construction (including the catalytic converter). Sections may therefore be renewed individually if necessary.
3 If the complete system is to be renewed, apply the handbrake, then jack the vehicle up as high as possible and support it securely on axle stands (see "Jacking and Vehicle Support").
4 When renewing the complete system, cutting through the connecting pipes will probably make removal in sections easier than attempting to dismantle corroded joints.

Front section – K8 engines

Note: New exhaust front section-to-manifold and front section-to-catalytic converter gaskets will be required on refitting.

Removal

5 Apply the handbrake, then jack up the front of the vehicle and support securely on axle stands (see "Jacking and Vehicle Support").
6 If the exhaust front section is being renewed, remove the heated oxygen sensor (HO2S), as described in Section 11, otherwise, trace the wiring back from the oxygen sensor, and separate the two halves of the wiring connector.
7 Unscrew the two nuts securing the exhaust front section to the catalytic converter. Recover the gasket and discard it.
8 Unscrew the three nuts securing the exhaust front section to the manifold, then release the front section from the manifold

4A

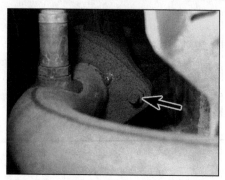

13.8 Exhaust front section-to-manifold nut (arrowed)

(see illustration). Recover the gasket and discard it.

9 Release the front section from the rubber mounting under the floor, then withdraw the front section from under the vehicle.

Refitting

10 Refitting is a reversal of removal, bearing in mind the following points.
a) *Thoroughly clean the mating faces of the exhaust joints.*
b) *Use new front section-to-manifold and front section-to-catalytic converter gaskets.*
c) *Do not tighten the front section-to-catalytic converter nuts until after the front section-to-manifold nuts have been tightened.*
d) *Where applicable, refit the oxygen sensor as described in Section 11.*

Front section – K16 engines

Note: *New exhaust front section-to-manifold and front section-to-catalytic converter gaskets will be required on refitting.*

Removal

11 Apply the handbrake, then jack up the vehicle and support it securely on axle stands (see *"Jacking and Vehicle Support"*).
12 Unscrew the three nuts securing the front section to the catalytic converter. Recover the gasket and discard it.
13 Unscrew the four nuts securing the exhaust front section to the manifold, then release the front section from the manifold. Recover the gasket and discard it.

14 Release the front section from the rubber mounting under the floor, then withdraw the front section from under the vehicle.

Refitting

15 Refitting is a reversal of removal, bearing in mind the following points.
a) *Thoroughly clean the mating faces of the exhaust joints.*
b) *Use new front section-to-manifold and front section-to-catalytic converter gaskets.*
c) *Do not tighten the front section-to-catalytic converter nuts until after the front section-to-manifold nuts have been tightened.*

Intermediate section

Note: *New exhaust intermediate section-to-catalytic converter and intermediate section-to-rear section gaskets will be required on refitting.*

Removal

16 Apply the handbrake, then jack up the vehicle and support it securely on axle stands (see *"Jacking and Vehicle Support"*).
17 Unscrew the nuts securing the exhaust intermediate section to the rear section. Recover the gasket and discard it.
18 Unscrew the nuts securing the intermediate section to the catalytic converter. Recover the gasket and discard it.
19 Release the intermediate section from the two rubber mountings under the floor, then withdraw the intermediate section from under the vehicle.

Refitting

20 Refitting is a reversal of removal, bearing in mind the following points.
a) *Thoroughly clean the mating faces of the exhaust joints.*
b) *Use new intermediate section-to-rear section and intermediate section-to-catalytic converter gaskets.*

Rear section

Note: *A new exhaust intermediate section-to-rear section gasket will be required on refitting.*

Removal

21 Apply the handbrake, then jack up the

vehicle and support it securely on axle stands (see *"Jacking and Vehicle Support"*).
22 Unscrew the nuts securing the exhaust rear section to the intermediate section. Recover the gasket and discard it.
23 Release the rear section from the three mounting rubbers under the floor, then withdraw the rear section from the vehicle.

Refitting

24 Refitting is a reversal of removal, bearing in mind the following points.
a) *Thoroughly clean the mating faces of the exhaust joints.*
b) *Use a new intermediate section-to-rear section gasket.*

Catalytic converter

Note: *New catalytic converter-to-exhaust front section and catalytic converter-to-exhaust rear section gaskets will be required on refitting.*

Removal

25 Apply the handbrake, then jack up the front of the vehicle and support it securely on axle stands (see *"Jacking and Vehicle Support"*).
26 Unscrew the nuts securing the catalytic converter to the exhaust front section. Recover and discard the gasket.
27 Ensure that the catalytic converter is adequately supported (the assembly is easily damaged if it is dropped), then unscrew the nuts securing the catalytic converter to the exhaust intermediate section, and withdraw the catalytic converter from under the vehicle. Recover the gasket and discard it.
28 If desired, on K8 engine models, the heat shields can now be unbolted from the catalytic converter.

Refitting

29 Refitting is a reversal of removal, bearing in mind the following points.
a) *Thoroughly clean the mating faces of the exhaust joints.*
b) *Use a new exhaust front section-to-catalytic converter gasket and a new intermediate section-to-catalytic converter gasket.*

Chapter 4 Part B:
Fuel and exhaust systems – diesel engines

Contents

Degrees of difficulty

Easy, suitable for novice with little experience	**Fairly easy,** suitable for beginner with some experience 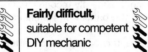	**Fairly difficult,** suitable for competent DIY mechanic	**Difficult,** suitable for experienced DIY mechanic	**Very difficult,** suitable for expert DIY or professional 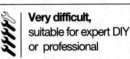

Specifications

General
System type . . . . Electronic diesel control (EDC) system indirect diesel injection system

Idle speed (not adjustable - for reference only)
Models without intercooler . . . . 850 ± 50 rpm
Models with intercooler . . . . 805 ± 50 rpm

Torque wrench settings

	Nm	lbf ft
Crankshaft position (CKP) sensor bolt	8	6
Engine control module (ECM) bolts	4	3
Engine coolant temperature (ECT) sensor	15	11
Exhaust elbow-to-turbocharger bolts	25	18
Exhaust manifold securing bolts	33	24
Exhaust manifold securing nuts	25	18
Exhaust manifold support bracket bolt	25	18
Fuel injection pump fuel feed and return pipe unions	25	18
Fuel injection pump vacuum pipe union	25	18
Fuel injection pump sprocket nut	60	44
Fuel injection pump securing nuts	25	18
Fuel injection pump mounting bracket nuts and bolts	25	18
Fuel injector clamp bolt	25	18
Fuel injector feed pipe unions	20	15
Fuel shut-off solenoid	20	15
Inlet manifold securing bolts	25	18
Intake air temperature (IAT) sensor	12	9
Intercooler-to-radiator bolts	25	18
Manifold absolute pressure (MAP) sensor bolt	9	7
Oil drain pipe-to-turbocharger nuts	10	7
Oil feed pipe-to-turbocharger nuts	20	15
Throttle position sensor nuts	4	3
Turbocharger pipe-to-cylinder head bolts	10	7
Turbocharger-to-exhaust manifold nuts	25	18

4B

1 General information and precautions

General information

The operation of the fuel injection system is described in more detail in Section 6.

Fuel is supplied from a tank mounted under the rear of the vehicle, and then passes through a filter, to the fuel injection pump, which delivers the fuel to the injectors. The injection pump is controlled by an engine control module (ECM) on the basis of information provided by various sensors.

The inducted air passes through an air cleaner, which incorporates a paper filter element to filter out potentially-harmful particles (serious internal engine damage can be caused if foreign particles enter through the air intake system).

The engine control module (ECM) controls both the fuel injection pump and the pre-heating system, integrating the two into a complete engine management system. Refer to Chapter 5C for details of the pre-heating side of the system.

The exhaust system incorporates a catalytic converter to reduce exhaust gas emissions. Further details can be found in Chapter 4C, along with details of the other emission control systems and components.

Precautions

When working on fuel system components, scrupulous cleanliness must be observed, and care must be taken not to introduce any foreign matter into fuel lines or components.

After carrying out any work involving disconnection of fuel lines, it is advisable to check the connections for leaks; pressurise the system by cranking the engine several times.

Electronic control units are very sensitive

components, and certain precautions must be taken to avoid damage to these units as follows.

When carrying out welding operations on the vehicle using electric welding equipment, the battery and alternator should be disconnected.

Although the underbonnet-mounted modules will tolerate normal underbonnet conditions, they can be adversely affected by excess heat or moisture. If using welding equipment or pressure-washing equipment in the vicinity of an electronic module, take care not to direct heat, or jets of water or steam, at the module. If this cannot be avoided, remove the module from the vehicle, and protect its wiring plug with a plastic bag.

Before disconnecting any wiring, or removing components, always ensure that the ignition is switched off.

Do not attempt to improvise fault diagnosis procedures using a test lamp or multi-meter, as irreparable damage could be caused to the module.

After working on fuel injection/engine management system components, ensure that all wiring is correctly reconnected before reconnecting the battery or switching on the ignition.

Damage to the catalytic converter may result if the following precautions are not observed:

a) *Consult an approved dealer as soon as possible in the event of misfiring, irregular engine running after a cold start, or a significant loss of engine power. If it is necessary to continue driving, do so for a short time at low engine speed, without labouring the engine.*

b) *Avoid frequent cold starts one after another.*

c) *Avoid actuation of the starter for an unnecessarily long time during starting.*

d) *Do not allow the fuel tank to become empty.*

e) *Do not attempt to start the engine by push- or tow-starting - use jump leads (see "Jump starting").*

2 Air cleaner assembly – removal and refitting

Removal

Note: *A new mass airflow sensor-to-air cleaner O-ring will be required on refitting.*

1 Remove the battery as described in Chapter 5A.

2 Release the coolant pipe from the clips on the air cleaner housing.

3 Release the two securing clips, and pull the mass airflow (MAF) sensor from the air cleaner **(see illustration)**. Recover the O-ring and discard it.

4 Unscrew the two bolts securing the air cleaner assembly to the battery tray **(see illustration)**.

5 Release the air intake tube from the bottom of the air cleaner, then remove the air cleaner assembly from the engine compartment **(see illustration)**.

Refitting

6 Refitting is a reversal of removal, but fit a new mass airflow sensor-to-air cleaner O-ring.

3 Fuel tank and fuel filler neck – removal and refitting

Fuel tank

Removal

Note: *During removal, note the locations and routing of all hoses to aid refitting.*

1 Disconnect the battery negative lead.

2 Chock the front wheels, then jack up the rear of the vehicle and support securely on axle stands (see *"Jacking and Vehicle Support"*).

3 Siphon the fuel from the tank into a clean metal container which can be sealed. Alternatively, working under the car, disconnect an accessible fuel line connection

2.3 Release the two clips securing the mass airflow (MAF) sensor to the air cleaner

2.4 Unscrew the two securing bolts . . .

2.5 . . . then remove the air cleaner assembly

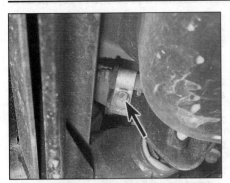

3.4 Unscrew the bolt (arrowed) securing the handbrake cable to the H-frame mounting

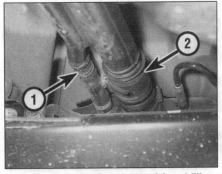

3.6 Disconnect the breather (1) and filler (2) hoses from the fuel filler neck

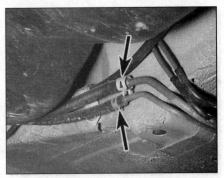

3.8 Disconnect the fuel feed and return hoses (arrowed) from the pipes

at the tank, and drain the fuel into a suitable container.

4 Unscrew the bolt securing the handbrake cable to the left-hand rear suspension H-frame mounting, and release the cable from the mounting **(see illustration)**.

5 Remove the screw securing the fuel tank filler neck to the body, noting that the screw also secures the wheel arch liner.

6 Slacken the hose clip and disconnect the breather hose from the fuel filler neck **(see illustration)**.

7 Slacken the hose clip and disconnect the filler hose from the filler neck **(see illustration 3.6)**.

8 Slacken the hose clips and disconnect the fuel feed and return hoses from the pipes under the rear of the vehicle **(see illustration)**. Plug or cover the open ends of the hoses and pipes to prevent dirt entry.

9 Place a trolley jack under the fuel tank, with a block of wood between the jack and the tank.

10 Working at the rear of the fuel tank, unscrew the locknuts, then unscrew the two fuel tank strap securing nuts **(see illustration)**.

11 Ensure that the jack is supporting the fuel tank, then release the fuel tank straps from the brackets on the body.

12 Lower the fuel tank until the fuel level gauge sender unit wiring connector can be reached, then separate the two halves of the connector, and withdraw the fuel tank from under the vehicle.

Inspection

13 If the tank contains sediment or water, it may be cleaned out using two or three rinses with paraffin. Shake vigorously using several changes of paraffin, but before doing so remove the fuel gauge sender unit (see Section 8).

14 Any repairs to the fuel tank should be carried out by a professional. Do not under any circumstances attempt to weld or solder a fuel tank.

Refitting

15 Refitting is a reversal of removal, bearing in mind the following points.

a) *Ensure that all hoses are reconnected to their correct locations as noted before removal, and use new hose clips if necessary.*

b) *On completion, prime the fuel system as described in Section 7.*

Fuel filler neck

Removal

16 Chock the front wheels, then jack up the rear of the vehicle and support securely on axle stands (see *"Jacking and Vehicle Support"*). Remove the left-hand rear roadwheel.

17 Remove the securing screws, and withdraw the rear left-hand wheel arch liner.

18 Remove the fuel filler cap, then reach up behind the filler neck and depress the three lugs securing the filler neck surround to the

body and filler neck. Pull out the filler neck surround **(see illustration)**.

19 Working under the vehicle, slacken the hose clips, and disconnect the breather hose and the filler hose from the fuel filler neck. Be prepared for fuel spillage, and have a suitable container ready to catch any fuel which may be released as the filler hose is disconnected.

20 Withdraw the filler neck assembly from under the wheel arch.

Refitting

21 Refitting is a reversal of removal.

<table>
<tr><td>4</td><td>**Throttle cable** – removal, refitting and adjustment</td><td></td></tr>
</table>

Models without intercooler

Removal

1 Unscrew the bolts securing the engine acoustic cover to the top of the cylinder head cover.

2 Remove the engine oil filler cap, then remove the seal from the acoustic cover, and remove the acoustic cover from the engine.

3 Slide the cable end fitting from the groove in the accelerator lever on the fuel injection pump, and disconnect the cable from the lever **(see illustration)**.

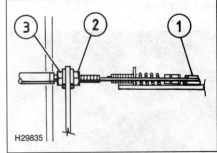

4.3 Throttle cable end fitting details – models without intercooler

1 *Cable end fitting at accelerator lever*
2 *Cable locknut*
3 *Cable adjuster nut*

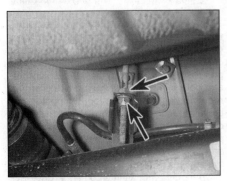

3.10 Fuel tank strap locknut and securing nut (arrowed)

3.18 Pulling out the fuel filler neck surround

4B

4.8 Depress the plastic clips (arrowed) and release the end of the throttle cable from the pedal

4 Slacken the locknut securing the cable to the support bracket, and release the cable from the bracket.

5 Release the cable from the locating clip.

6 Working at the engine compartment bulkhead, turn the collar on the throttle cable through 90°, and release the cable from the bulkhead.

7 Working in the driver's footwell, release the two securing clips, and remove the lower facia trim panel.

8 Reach up under the facia, and pull the end of the cable forwards from the pedal, then squeeze the securing lugs and remove the plastic cable securing clip from the end of the pedal. Release the end of the cable from the pedal **(see illustration)**.

9 Working in the engine compartment, pull the cable fitting from the bulkhead, then withdraw the cable from the vehicle.

Refitting

10 Refitting is a reversal of removal, but smear the bulkhead fitting with rubber grease and, before refitting the acoustic cover, check the cable adjustment as described in the following paragraphs.

Adjustment

11 With the accelerator lever on the fuel injection pump resting against its stop screw, there should be approximately 4 mm of side-to-side freeplay at the centre of the cable run between the end of the cable sheath and the accelerator lever.

5.2 Unhook the return spring (arrowed) from the pedal

4.14 Slide the throttle cable adjuster from the cable bracket (arrowed) – models with intercooler

12 If adjustment is necessary, slacken the locknut securing the cable to the bracket on the fuel injection pump, then turn the adjuster nut until the specified freeplay is obtained. Tighten the locknut when the adjustment is correct.

13 Have an assistant fully depress the throttle pedal, and check that the accelerator lever contact the maximum speed stop screw on the fuel injection pump. Release the pedal and check that the accelerator lever returns fully against its stop.

Models with intercooler

Removal

14 Working at the right-hand side of the engine compartment, slide the throttle cable adjuster from the cable bracket **(see illustration)**.

15 Slide the cable end fitting from the groove in the throttle position sensor lever.

16 Proceed as described in paragraphs 6 to 9.

Refitting

17 Refitting is a reversal of removal, but smear the bulkhead grommet with rubber grease and, on completion, check the cable adjustment as described in the following paragraphs.

Adjustment

18 Ensure that the cable is correctly routed.

19 Slide the cable adjuster from the bracket,

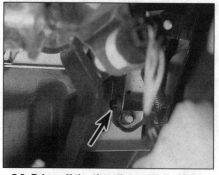

5.3 Prise off the throttle pedal securing clip (arrowed)

then position the cable adjuster against the rear of the bracket.

20 Hold the accelerator lever on the injection pump in the fully closed position, ensuring that the lever rests against its stop screw.

21 Turn the cable adjuster as necessary until all freeplay is removed from the cable, without moving the accelerator lever.

22 Slide the adjuster back into position in the bracket.

23 Have an assistant fully depress the throttle pedal, and check that the accelerator lever moves to the fully open position, and returns to the fully closed position when the pedal is released.

5 Throttle pedal – removal and refitting

Removal

1 Disconnect the end of the throttle cable from the pedal as described in Section 4.

2 Using a suitable pair of pliers, unhook the return spring from the pedal **(see illustration)**.

3 Working at the left-hand side of the pedal pivot shaft, prise off the securing clip, then slide the pedal assembly from the mounting bracket towards the right-hand side of the vehicle, until it can be removed **(see illustration)**.

Refitting

4 Refitting is a reversal of removal, but make sure that the securing clip is securely refitted.

6 Fuel injection system – general information

The system is under the overall control of the electronic diesel control (EDC) system, which also controls the pre-heating system (see Chapter 5C).

Fuel is supplied from the rear-mounted fuel tank, via a fuel filter, to the fuel injection pump. The fuel injection pump supplies the exact amount of fuel required by the engine, according to the prevailing engine operating conditions.

The engine is fitted with various sensors, which monitor the engine operating conditions, and transmit data to the engine control module (ECM). The control module processes the data from the various sensors, and determines the optimum amount of fuel required, and the injection timing for the prevailing running conditions. Additionally, the control module activates the fuel injection pump stop solenoid, the pre-heating system, and the exhaust gas recirculation (EGR) system (see Chapter 4C).

On models with an intercooler, a "drive-by-wire" throttle control system is used. The throttle pedal is not physically connected to the fuel injection pump, but instead is connected by a cable to a throttle position sensor, mounted in the engine compartment, which provides the engine control module (ECM) with a signal relating to throttle pedal movement.

The system uses the following sensors:

a) *Crankshaft position (CKP) sensor - informs the ECM of the crankshaft speed and position.*

b) *Engine coolant temperature (ECT) sensor - informs the ECM of engine temperature.*

c) *Fuel temperature sensor - informs the ECM of fuel temperature (in the injection pump).*

d) *Mass airflow (MAF) sensor – informs the ECM of the mass of air entering the intake tract.*

e) *Fuel injector needle lift sensor – informs the ECM of the start of the injection sequence.*

f) *Vehicle speed sensor – informs the ECM of the vehicle speed.*

g) *Fuel quantity servo position sensor – informs the ECM of the quantity of fuel supplied to the injectors by the fuel injection pump.*

6 Models with an intercooler are fitted with the following additional sensors:

a) *Throttle position sensor (TPS) - informs the ECM of throttle position, and the rate of throttle opening/closing.*

b) *Manifold absolute pressure (MAP) sensor - informs the ECM of the pressure of air entering the intake tract (used in conjunction with the intake air temperature sensor to calculate the volume of oxygen in the air entering the engine).*

c) *Intake air temperature (IAT) sensor - informs the ECM of the temperature of air entering the engine.*

d) *Brake pedal switch - informs the ECM when the brakes are being applied.*

The signals from the various sensors are processed by the ECM, and the optimum fuel quantity and injection timing settings are selected for the prevailing engine operating conditions.

A catalytic converter and an exhaust gas recirculation (EGR) system is fitted, to reduce harmful exhaust gas emissions. Details of this and other emissions control system equipment are given in Chapter 4C.

If certain sensors fail, and send abnormal signals to the ECM, the ECM has a back-up programme. In this event, the abnormal signals are ignored, and a pre-programmed value is substituted for the sensor signal, allowing the engine to continue running, albeit at reduced efficiency. If the ECM enters its back-up mode, the engine system warning light on the instrument panel will illuminate, and a fault code will be stored in the ECM memory. This fault code can be read using specialist Rover dedicated test equipment.

7 Fuel system – priming and bleeding

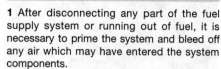

1 After disconnecting any part of the fuel supply system or running out of fuel, it is necessary to prime the system and bleed off any air which may have entered the system components.

2 All models are fitted with a hand-operated priming pump, consisting of a rubber bulb located at the rear of the engine compartment in the fuel supply line to the fuel filter, and a bleed screw on top of the fuel filter.

3 To prime the system, proceed as follows.

4 If none of the fuel system components downstream of the fuel filter (including the fuel filter itself) have been disturbed, and the vehicle has not run out of fuel, it should be possible to proceed directly to paragraph 7.

5 Place a wad of absorbent cloth around the bleed screw on top of the fuel filter, then slacken the bleed screw.

6 Switch on the ignition so that the stop solenoid is energised, then pump the rubber priming bulb until fuel free from air bubbles emerges from the bleed screw **(see illustration)**. Tighten the bleed screw.

7 If not already done, switch on the ignition, then pump the priming bulb until resistance is felt, indicating that air has been expelled from the fuel injection pump. Switch off the ignition.

8 If air has reached the injectors, the high-pressure circuit must be bled as follows.

9 Place wads of clean, absorbent cloth around the fuel feed pipe unions at the injectors, then slacken the fuel pipe unions.

10 Crank the engine on the starter motor until fuel emerges from the unions, then stop cranking the engine and tighten the unions. Mop up any spilt fuel.

11 Start the engine with the accelerator fully depressed. Additional cranking may be necessary to finally bleed the system before the engine starts.

8 Fuel gauge sender unit – removal and refitting

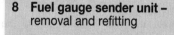

Removal

1 The fuel gauge sender unit is mounted in the top of the fuel tank, and cannot be accessed with the tank in place.

2 Remove the fuel tank as described in Section 3.

3 Release the hose clamps, and disconnect the fuel feed and return hoses from the pipes at the top of the sender unit. Plug or cover the open ends of the hoses and pipes to prevent dirt entry.

4 Unscrew the six nuts securing the sender unit to the fuel tank.

5 Carefully slide the sender unit from the fuel

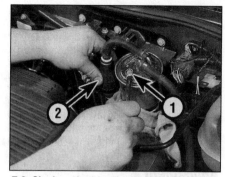

7.6 Slacken the bleed screw (1) and pump the rubber priming bulb (2)

tank, taking care not to damage the sender unit float. Recover the sealing ring **(see illustration)**.

Refitting

6 Examine the condition of the sealing ring, and renew if necessary, then thoroughly clean the mating faces of the tank and the sender unit.

7 Refitting is a reversal of removal, but if necessary, renew the fuel hose clips and, on completion, refit the fuel tank with reference to Section 3.

9 Fuel injection system – testing and adjustment

Testing

1 If a fault appears in the fuel injection system, first ensure that all the system wiring connectors are securely connected and free from corrosion. Ensure that the fault is not due to poor maintenance; ie, check that the air cleaner filter element is clean, that the cylinder compression pressures are correct (see Chapter 2B), and that the engine breather hoses are clear and undamaged (see Chapter 4C).

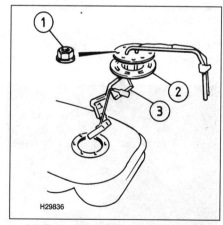

H29836

8.5 Fuel gauge sender unit mounting details

1	*Securing nuts*	3 *Sender unit*
2	*Sealing ring*	

2 If the engine will not start, check the condition of the glow plugs (see Chapter 5C).
3 If these checks fail to reveal the cause of the problem, the vehicle should be taken to a Rover dealer for testing. A wiring connector is provided on a bracket under the facia, into which a special electronic diagnostic tester can be plugged. The tester should locate the fault quickly and simply, avoiding the need to test all the system components individually, which is time-consuming, and also carries a risk of damaging the ECM.

Adjustment

4 Idle speed, maximum speed and fuel injection pump timing are all controlled by the ECM, and no manual adjustment is possible.

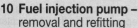
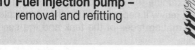

10 Fuel injection pump – removal and refitting

Models without intercooler

Note: *New vacuum pipe-to-injection pump sealing washers, fuel leak-off pipe-to-injector sealing washers, fuel feed pipe-to-pump sealing washers, and fuel return pipe-to-pump sealing washers will be required on refitting.*

Removal

1 Disconnect the battery negative lead.
2 Unscrew the bolts securing the engine acoustic cover to the top of the cylinder head cover, then remove the acoustic cover from the engine.
3 Drain the cooling system as described in Chapter 1B.
4 Slide the cable end fitting from the groove in the accelerator lever on the fuel injection pump, and disconnect the cable from the lever.
5 Slacken the locknut securing the cable to the support bracket, and release the cable from the bracket.
6 Proceed as described in paragraphs 14 to 33, but additionally, unscrew the union bolt, and disconnect the vacuum pipe from the

10.11 Unscrew the two bolts securing the EGR recirculation pipe

injection pump. Recover and discard the sealing washers.

Refitting

7 Proceed as described in paragraphs 34 to 52, but additionally, reconnect the vacuum pipe to the injection pump, using new sealing washers, and tighten the union bolt to the specified torque.
8 Further refitting is a reversal of removal, bearing in mind the following points.
  a) *Refill the cooling system as described in Chapter 1B.*
  b) *Reconnect and adjust the throttle cable as described in Section 4.*
  c) *On completion, prime the fuel system as described in Section 7.*

Models with intercooler

Note: *New vacuum pipe-to-injection pump sealing washers, fuel leak-off pipe-to-injector sealing washers, fuel feed pipe-to-pump sealing washers, fuel return pipe-to-pump sealing washers, and a new intake pipe-to-inlet manifold gasket will be required on refitting.*

Removal

9 Proceed as described in paragraphs 1 to 3.
10 Slacken the hose clip and disconnect the intercooler bottom hose from the inlet manifold intake pipe.
11 Unscrew the two bolts securing the

10.12 Unscrew the bolt securing the inlet manifold intake pipe to the cylinder head cover . . .

exhaust gas recirculation (EGR) pipe to the inlet manifold intake pipe (**see illustration**).
12 Unscrew the bolt securing the inlet manifold intake pipe to the cylinder head cover (**see illustration**).
13 Unscrew the two bolts securing the intake pipe to the inlet manifold, and remove the intake pipe. Recover and discard the gasket (**see illustrations**).
14 Slacken the hose clip and disconnect the radiator top hose from the radiator.
15 Similarly, disconnect the radiator top hose from the coolant outlet elbow and the thermostat, and remove the hose.
16 Remove the fuel injection pump drivebelt, as described in Chapter 2B.
17 Working at the front of the fuel injection pump, slacken the pump shaft clamp bolt, then remove the spacer plate from the bolt, and tighten the bolt to the 25 Nm (18 lbf ft) (**see illustration**). Take care not to lose the spacer plate.
Caution: Do not exceed the specified torque when tightening the pump shaft clamp bolt, as this may damage the pump shaft, in which case a new pump will be required at considerable expense.
18 Ensure that the locking pin is still fitted to lock the fuel injection pump sprocket in position, then unscrew the fuel injection pump sprocket securing nut, and recover the washer.
19 Remove the locking pin from the sprocket.

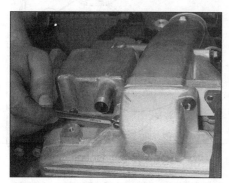

10.13a . . . then the two bolts securing the intake pipe . . .

10.13b . . . and remove the intake pipe

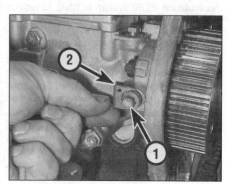

10.17 Unscrew the clamp bolt (1) and remove the spacer plate (2)

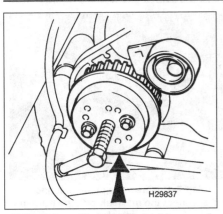

10.20 Using a Rover puller tool (arrowed) remove the fuel injection pump sprocket

20 Using a suitable puller, free the sprocket from the pump shaft taper, then remove the sprocket **(see illustration)**.

21 Unscrew the securing nut and disconnect the glow plug feed wiring from the No 2 cylinder glow plug.

22 Release the fuel injector needle lift sensor wiring connector from the fuel injection pump mounting bracket. Separate the two halves of the connector **(see illustration)**.

23 Disconnect the injection pump wiring plug(s), then release the engine wiring harness from the bracket on the pump.

24 Place a wad of absorbent cloth around the fuel feed pipe union on the pump, then slowly slacken and remove the union bolt securing the fuel feed pipe to the pump. Recover and discard the sealing washers. Plug or cover the open ends of the pipe and the pump to prevent dirt entry.

25 Similarly, unscrew the union bolt and disconnect the fuel leak-off pipe from the No 3 cylinder fuel injector. Again, recover and discard the sealing washers. Plug or cover the open ends of the pipe and the injector to prevent dirt entry.

26 Unscrew the cap nut, then disconnect the fuel return pipe from the injection pump. Recover and discard the sealing washer, and plug or cover the open ends of the pipe and the pump.

27 If not already done, release the fuel

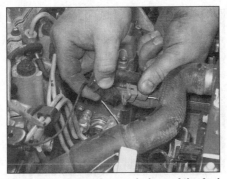

10.22 Separating the two halves of the fuel injector needle lift sensor wiring connector

10.30b . . . then remove the pipe assembly

injection pump wiring plug(s) from the mounting bracket.

28 Remove the clamp securing the four fuel injector pipes together, at the rear of the pump.

29 Place a wad of absorbent cloth around the fuel feed pipe unions on Nos 1 and 2 cylinder fuel injectors, then working on each of the two injectors in turn, slacken the union nut (counterhold the union on the injector using a second spanner), and disconnect the fuel pipe from the injector. Plug or cover the open ends of the pipes and fuel injectors to prevent dirt entry.

30 Repeat the procedure to disconnect Nos 1 and 2 cylinder fuel injector pipes from the pump, then remove the pipe assembly **(see illustrations)**.

10.30a Disconnect the fuel injector pipes from the fuel injection pump . . .

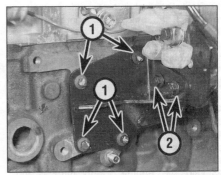

10.32a Unscrew the four bolts (1) securing the support bracket to the engine and the two nuts (2) securing the bracket to the pump . . .

31 Repeat the procedure given in paragraphs 29 and 30 to remove Nos 3 and 4 cylinder fuel injector pipes.

32 Unscrew the four bolts securing the injection pump support bracket to the engine, then unscrew the two nuts and bolts securing the bracket to the pump, and remove the bracket **(see illustrations)**.

33 Unscrew the three nuts securing the pump to the engine/transmission mounting plate, then lift the pump away from the engine **(see illustrations)**.

Refitting

34 Thoroughly clean the mating faces of the injection pump and the engine/transmission mounting plate.

4B

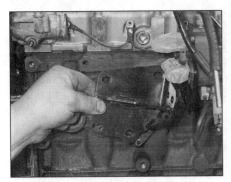

10.32b . . . then remove the bracket – engine removed for clarity

10.33a Unscrew the three securing nuts . . .

10.33b . . . and lift the pump from the engine – engine removed for clarity

35 Offer the pump into position on the engine/transmission mounting plate, then refit the securing nuts, and tighten to the specified torque.

36 Position the pump support bracket on the engine, and fit the securing bolts, but do not tighten them at this stage.

37 Refit the nuts and bolts securing the support bracket to the pump, and tighten to the specified torque.

38 Tighten the support bracket-to-engine bolts to the specified toque.

39 Reconnect the vacuum pipe to the injection pump, using new sealing washers, and tighten the union bolt to the specified torque.

40 Refit the fuel injector pipes, using a reversal of the removal procedure, then refit the injector pipe clamp.

41 Clip the injection pump wiring plug(s) into position on the mounting bracket.

42 Reconnect the fuel leak-off pipe to the No 3 cylinder fuel injector, using new sealing washers, and tighten the union bolt.

43 Similarly, reconnect the fuel feed pipe to the pump, using new sealing washers.

44 Reconnect the fuel return pipe to the pump, using new sealing washers, and tighten the cap nut.

45 Clip the engine wiring harness into position on the bracket on the pump.

46 Reconnect the fuel injector needle lift sensor wiring connector, and clip the connector into position on the pump mounting bracket.

47 Reconnect the glow plug feed wiring to No 2 cylinder glow plug, and tighten the securing nut.

48 Thoroughly clean the taper on the fuel injection pump shaft, and the pump sprocket.

49 Fit the sprocket to the pump shaft, then fit the timing pin to the sprocket, ensuring that the pin passes through the timing hole in the sprocket, until it engages with the hole in the engine/transmission mounting plate.

50 Refit the pump sprocket securing nut, ensuring that the washer is in place, then tighten the nut to the specified torque.

51 Slacken the pump shaft clamp bolt, then refit the spacer plate under the bolt head, and tighten the bolt to 10 Nm (7 lbf ft).

11.6 Unscrew the union nut and disconnect the fuel feed pipe from the injector

52 Refit the fuel injection pump drivebelt as described in Chapter 2B.

53 Further refitting is a reversal of removal, bearing in mind the following points.
a) Use a new gasket when reconnecting the intake pipe to the inlet manifold.
b) Refill the cooling system as described in Chapter 1B.
c) On completion, prime the fuel system as described in Section 7.

---

11 Fuel injectors – testing, removal and refitting

Models without intercooler

Testing

1 Injectors do deteriorate with prolonged use, and it is reasonable to expect them to need reconditioning or renewal after 60 000 miles (100 000 km) or so. Accurate testing, overhaul and calibration of the injectors must be left to a Rover dealer or a diesel fuel injection specialist. A defective injector which is causing knocking or smoking can be located without dismantling as follows.

2 Run the engine at a fast idle. Slacken each injector fuel feed pipe union in turn, placing absorbent cloth around the union to catch spilt fuel, and being careful not to expose the skin to any spray. When the union on the

11.7 Unscrew the union bolt and disconnect the fuel leak-off pipe from the injector

defective injector is slackened, the knocking or smoking will stop.

Removal

Note: *A new injector sealing washer and new fuel leak-off pipe-to-injector sealing rings will be required on refitting.*

3 Disconnect the battery negative lead.

4 Unscrew the bolts securing the engine acoustic cover to the top of the cylinder head cover, then remove the acoustic cover from the engine.

5 If No1 cylinder injector, which incorporates the needle lift sensor, is being removed, trace the wiring back from the needle lift sensor, and separate the two halves of the wiring connector.

6 Position a wad of absorbent cloth around the fuel feed pipe union on the injector, then slowly unscrew the union nut, and disconnect the pipe from the injector (counterhold the union on the injector using a second spanner) **(see illustration)**. Plug or cover the open ends of the injector and pipe to prevent dirt entry.

7 Similarly, unscrew the union bolt and disconnect the fuel leak-off pipe from the injector **(see illustration)**. Recover and discard the sealing washers.

8 Unscrew the clamp bolt, and withdraw the clamp plate securing the injector to the cylinder head **(see illustration)**.

9 Withdraw the injector from the cylinder head. Recover and discard the sealing washer **(see illustrations)**.

11.8 Withdraw the clamp plate . . .

11.9a . . . the injector . . .

11.9b . . . and recover the sealing washer – cylinder head removed

Refitting

10 Thoroughly clean the injector, and the injector seat in the cylinder head.

11 Fit a new sealing washer to the injector, with the domed surface of the washer facing the top of the injector, then fit the clamp plate to the injector.

12 Refit the injector to the cylinder head, aligning the bolt hole in the clamp plate with the corresponding hole in the cylinder head, then refit the clamp bolt and tighten to the specified torque.

13 The remainder of the refitting procedure is a reversal of removal, but use new sealing rings when reconnecting the fuel leak-off pipe. On completion, if necessary bleed the fuel system as described in Section 7.

Models with intercooler

Testing

14 Proceed as described in paragraphs 1 and 2.

Removal

Note: *The No 1 cylinder fuel injector incorporates the fuel injector needle lift sensor, and the removal and refitting procedure for this assembly is covered in Section 12. A new injector sealing washer, new fuel leak-off pipe-to-injector sealing rings, and a new intake pipe-to-inlet manifold gasket will be required on refitting.*

15 Slacken the hose clip, and disconnect the intercooler hose from the inlet manifold intake pipe.

16 Unscrew the two bolts securing the exhaust gas recirculation (EGR) pipe to the inlet manifold intake pipe.

17 Unscrew the bolt securing the inlet manifold intake pipe to the cylinder head cover.

18 Unscrew the two bolts securing the intake pipe to the inlet manifold, and remove the intake pipe. Recover and discard the gasket.

19 Proceed as described in paragraphs 7 to 10.

Refitting

20 Proceed as described in paragraphs 11 to 14, but additionally, use a new gasket when reconnecting the air intake pipe to the inlet manifold.

12 Electronic Diesel Control (EDC) system components – removal and refitting

Crankshaft position (CKP) sensor

Removal

1 Disconnect the battery negative lead.

2 The sensor is mounted at the rear of the flywheel housing (at the left-hand end of the engine) **(see illustration)**.

3 Disconnect the wiring plug from the sensor.

4 Unscrew the sensor securing bolt, then withdraw the sensor from its housing.

Refitting

5 Refitting is a reversal of removal, tightening the sensor securing bolt to the specified torque setting.

Engine coolant temperature (ECT) sensor

Note: *Suitable sealing compound will be required on refitting.*

Removal

6 Disconnect the battery negative lead.

7 The sensor is mounted in the coolant outlet elbow at the front right-hand corner of the engine **(see illustration)**.

8 Unscrew the bolts securing the engine acoustic cover to the top of the cylinder head cover.

9 Remove the engine oil filler cap, then remove the seal from the acoustic cover, and remove the acoustic cover from the engine.

10 Unscrew the bolts securing the brake servo vacuum pipe to the coolant outlet elbow and the cylinder head cover, and move the pipe to one side.

11 Disconnect the wiring plug from the coolant temperature sensor.

12 Position a container beneath the sensor to catch escaping coolant as the sensor is removed.

13 Unscrew the sensor and withdraw it from the coolant elbow.

Refitting

14 Thoroughly clean the threads on the sensor, then coat the threads with sealing compound (Loctite 577 or a suitable equivalent).

15 Screw the sensor into position, and tighten to the specified torque.

16 Further refitting is a reversal of removal, but on completion, check the coolant level as described in *"Weekly checks"*, and top up if necessary.

Fuel temperature sensor

17 The sensor is integral with the fuel injection pump, and cannot be renewed separately.

Mass airflow (MAF) sensor

Note: *A new mass airflow sensor-to-air cleaner O-ring will be required on refitting.*

Removal

18 Disconnect the battery negative lead.

19 Release the locking clip, and disconnect the wiring plug from the sensor **(see illustration)**.

20 Slacken the hose clip securing the air intake trunking to the sensor, and pull the trunking from the sensor.

21 Release the two clips securing the sensor to the air cleaner, then carefully pull the sensor from the air cleaner. Recover the O-ring and discard it.

Refitting

22 Refitting is a reversal of removal, but use a new O-ring.

Fuel injector needle lift sensor

23 The sensor is an integral part of the No 1 cylinder fuel injector, and cannot be renewed separately. Fuel injector removal and refitting is covered in Section 11.

Vehicle speed sensor

24 The engine control module receives a vehicle speed signal from the same vehicle speed sensor used to provide a signal to the speedometer. Sensor removal and refitting details can be found in Chapter 12.

4B

12.2 Crankshaft position (CKP) sensor location (arrowed) – engine removed for clarity

12.7 Engine coolant temperature (ECT) sensor location

12.19 Disconnect the wiring plug (arrowed) from the mass airflow (MAF) sensor

12.28 Throttle position sensor (TPS) mounting details

1   Throttle position sensor mounting bracket bolts
2   Throttle position sensor-to-mounting bracket bolts

Fuel quantity servo position sensor

25 The sensor is integral with the fuel injection pump, and cannot be renewed separately.

Throttle position (TPS) sensor - models with intercooler only

Removal

26 Disconnect the battery negative lead.
27 The sensor is located on the body panel at the right-hand side of the engine compartment.
28 Unscrew the two bolts securing the sensor mounting bracket to the body **(see illustration)**.
29 Slide the throttle cable adjuster from the cable bracket.
30 Slide the cable end fitting from the groove in the throttle position sensor lever.
31 Disconnect the wiring plug from the sensor, then unclip the wiring from the sensor bracket.
32 Unscrew the two nuts and bolts securing the sensor to the mounting bracket, and remove the sensor.

Refitting

33 Refitting is a reversal of removal, but reconnect and adjust the throttle cable as described in Section 4.

Manifold absolute pressure (MAP) sensor - models with intercooler only

Removal

34 Disconnect the battery negative lead.
35 The sensor is located on the right-hand side of the engine compartment bulkhead.
36 Disconnect the wiring plug from the sensor, then release the hose clip and disconnect the vacuum hose from the sensor **(see illustration)**.
37 Unscrew the bolt securing the sensor to the mounting bracket, and remove the sensor.

12.36 Manifold absolute pressure (MAP) sensor mounting details

1   Wiring plug   3   Securing bolt
2   Vacuum hose

Refitting

38 Refitting is a reversal of removal, tightening the sensor securing bolt to the specified torque setting.

Intake air temperature (IAT) sensor - models with intercooler only

Note: *Suitable sealing compound will be required on refitting.*

Removal

39 Disconnect the battery negative lead.
40 The sensor is located at the right-hand side of the inlet manifold **(see illustration)**.
41 Unscrew the bolts securing the engine acoustic cover to the top of the cylinder head cover.
42 Remove the engine oil filler cap, then remove the seal from the acoustic cover, and remove the acoustic cover from the engine.
43 Disconnect the wiring plug from the sensor.
44 Unscrew the sensor from the manifold.

Refitting

45 Thoroughly clean the threads on the sensor, then coat the threads with sealing compound (Loctite 577 or a suitable equivalent).
46 Screw the sensor into position, and tighten to the specified torque.
47 Further refitting is a reversal of removal

12.40 Intake air temperature (IAT) sensor location (arrowed)

Brake pedal switch - models with intercooler only

48 The engine control module receives a signal from the brake light switch which indicates when the brake are being applied. Brake light switch removal and refitting details can be found in Chapter 9, Section 25.

Fuel shut-off (stop) solenoid

Note: *A new solenoid O-ring will be required on refitting.*

Removal

49 Disconnect the battery negative lead.
50 The solenoid is located on the top of the fuel injection pump **(see illustration)**.
51 Unscrew the bolts securing the engine acoustic cover to the top of the cylinder head cover, then remove the acoustic cover from the engine.
52 Clean the area around the stop solenoid on the fuel injection pump.
53 Position a wad of absorbent cloth around the solenoid to absorb escaping fuel.
54 Unscrew the nut, and disconnect the wiring from the solenoid.
55 Slacken the solenoid, then unscrew the solenoid from the pump. Recover the solenoid plunger and spring. Recover and discard the O-ring.

Refitting

56 Thoroughly clean the solenoid and the plunger, then fit a new O-ring to the solenoid.
57 Fit the spring and plunger to the solenoid, then refit the assembly and tighten to the specified torque.
58 Further refitting is a reversal of removal. On completion, if necessary bleed the fuel system as described in Section 7.

Engine control module (ECM) – models without intercooler (Rover ECM)

Note: *If a new engine control module is being fitted, the control unit will need to be programmed with the code from the vehicle anti-theft immobiliser system before the engine can be started. This must be carried out by a Rover dealer.*

12.50 Stop solenoid location (arrowed) – model with intercooler (engine removed for clarity)

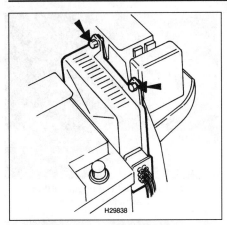

12.62 Unscrew the two bolts (arrowed) and remove the engine control module (ECM) – models without intercooler

Removal

59 Disconnect the battery negative lead.
60 The control module is located on the left-hand side of the engine compartment, next to the battery.
61 Disconnect the wiring plug from the control module.
62 Slacken the two bolts securing the control module to the mounting bracket, and remove the module **(see illustration)**.

Refitting

63 Refitting is a reversal of removal, tightening the module securing bolts to the specified torque setting.

Engine control module (ECM) – models with intercooler (Bosch ECM)

Note: *If a new engine control module is being fitted, the control unit will need to be programmed with the code from the vehicle anti-theft immobiliser system before the engine can be started. This must be carried out by a Rover dealer.*

Removal

64 Remove the battery as described in Chapter 5A.
65 Slacken the two bolts securing the control module to the battery tray, and release the

module from the battery tray **(see illustration)**.
66 Remove the screw securing the wiring plug to the module, then release the metal securing clip and disconnect the plug **(see illustration)**.
Caution: Take care, as the plug is easily damaged.
67 Remove the control module.

Refitting

68 Refitting is a reversal of removal, tightening the module securing bolts to the specified torque setting.

Engine management relay module

Removal

69 The module is located at the left-hand side of the engine compartment, next to the engine control module (ECM).
70 Disconnect the battery negative lead.
71 Release the relay module from its mounting bracket, then disconnect the two wiring plugs from the bottom of the module, and remove the module **(see illustration)**.

Refitting

72 Refitting is a reversal of removal, but make sure that the wiring plugs are securely reconnected.

13 Turbocharger – description and precautions

Description

A turbocharger is fitted to all diesel engines. It increases engine efficiency by raising the pressure in the inlet manifold above atmospheric pressure. Instead of the air simply being sucked into the cylinders, it is forced in. Additional fuel is supplied by the injection pump in proportion to the increased air intake.

Energy for the operation of the turbocharger comes from the exhaust gas. The gas flows through a specially-shaped housing (the turbine housing) and in so doing,

spins the turbine wheel. The turbine wheel is attached to a shaft, at the end of which is another vaned wheel known as the compressor wheel. The compressor wheel spins in its own housing and compresses the inducted air on the way to the inlet manifold.

On certain models, the compressed air passes through an intercooler. This is an air-to-air heat exchanger, mounted with the radiator at the front of the vehicle. The purpose of the intercooler is to remove from the inducted air some of the heat gained in being compressed. Because cooler air is denser, removal of this heat further increases engine efficiency.

Boost pressure (the pressure in the inlet manifold) is limited by a wastegate, which diverts the exhaust gas away from the turbine wheel in response to a pressure-sensitive actuator.

The turbo shaft is pressure-lubricated by an oil feed pipe from the main oil gallery. The shaft "floats" on a cushion of oil. A drain pipe returns the oil to the sump.

Precautions

The turbocharger operates at extremely high speeds and temperatures. Certain precautions must be observed to avoid premature failure of the turbo or injury to the operator.

Do not operate the turbo with any parts exposed. Foreign objects falling onto the rotating vanes could cause excessive damage and (if ejected) personal injury.

Do not race the engine immediately after start-up, especially if it is cold. Give the oil a few seconds to circulate.

Always allow the engine to return to idle speed before switching it off - do not blip the throttle and switch off, as this will leave the turbo spinning without lubrication.

Allow the engine to idle for several minutes before switching off after a high-speed run.

Observe the recommended intervals for oil and filter changing, and use a reputable oil of the specified quality. Neglect of oil changing, or use of inferior oil, can cause carbon formation on the turbo shaft and subsequent failure.

4B

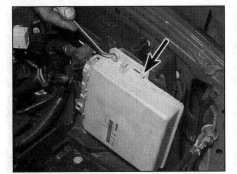

12.65 Slacken the two bolts securing the engine control module (ECM) to the battery tray . . .

12.66 . . . then disconnect the module wiring plug – model with intercooler

12.71 Removing the engine management relay module – model with intercooler

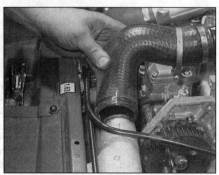

14.11 Disconnecting the top hose from the intercooler

14.12a Unscrew the bolts (arrowed) securing the turbocharger pipe to the cylinder head . . .

14.12b . . . and the engine lifting bracket . . .

14 Turbocharger –
removal and refitting

Models without intercooler

Note: *A new oil drain pipe gasket, a new exhaust front section-to-turbocharger elbow gasket, and new oil feed pipe sealing washers will be required on refitting.*

Removal

1 Disconnect the battery negative lead.
2 Apply the handbrake, then jack up the front of the vehicle and support securely on axle stands (see *"Jacking and Vehicle Support"*).
3 Unscrew the bolts securing the engine acoustic cover to the top of the cylinder head cover, then remove the acoustic cover from the engine.
4 Disconnect the exhaust front section from the turbocharger elbow, with reference to Section 18.
5 Slacken the hose clip and disconnect the air intake hose from the turbocharger.
6 Unscrew the union bolt, and disconnect the oil feed pipe from the turbocharger. Recover and discard the two sealing washers.
7 Disconnect the vacuum hose from the turbocharger wastegate actuator.
8 Proceed as described in paragraphs 17 to 20, but additionally, slacken the hose clip and disconnect the inlet manifold pipe from the turbocharger.

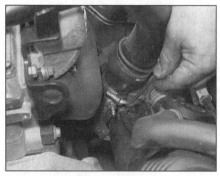

14.13 . . . then loosen the clip securing the hose to the turbocharger

Refitting

9 Proceed as described in paragraphs 21 and 22.

Models with intercooler

Note: *A new oil drain pipe gasket, a new exhaust front section-to-turbocharger elbow gasket, and new oil feed pipe sealing washers will be required on refitting.*

Removal

10 Proceed as described in paragraphs 1 to 4.
11 Loosen the hose clip, and disconnect the intercooler top hose from the intercooler **(see illustration)**.
12 Unscrew the two bolts securing the turbocharger pipe to the cylinder head and the engine lifting bracket **(see illustrations)**.

14.15 Turbocharger oil feed pipe union bolt (arrowed)

13 Loosen the hose clip securing the hose to the turbocharger, then remove the turbocharger pipe **(see illustration)**.
14 Slacken the hose clip, and disconnect the air intake hose from the turbocharger.
15 Unscrew the union bolt, and disconnect the oil feed pipe from the turbocharger **(see illustration)**. Recover and discard the two sealing washers.
16 Disconnect the manifold absolute pressure (MAP) sensor pipe from the turbocharger **(see illustration)**.
17 Unscrew the two bolts securing the oil drain pipe to the turbocharger **(see illustration)**. Recover and discard the gasket.
18 Unscrew the two bolts securing the exhaust elbow to the mounting bracket **(see illustration)**.

14.16 Disconnecting the manifold absolute pressure (MAP) sensor pipe from the turbocharger

14.17 Unscrew the two bolts (arrowed) securing the oil drain pipe to the turbocharger

14.18 Unscrew the two bolts (arrowed) securing the exhaust elbow to the mounting bracket

19 Support the turbocharger, then unscrew the three nuts securing the turbocharger to the exhaust manifold, and lift away the turbocharger, complete with the exhaust elbow **(see illustration)**.

20 If desired, the exhaust elbow can be removed from the turbocharger after unscrewing the four securing nuts.

Refitting

21 If the exhaust elbow has been removed from the turbocharger, thoroughly clean the mating faces of the elbow and the turbocharger, then refit the elbow and tighten the securing nuts to the specified torque.

22 Further refitting is a reversal of removal, bearing in mind the following points:

a) *Thoroughly clean the mating faces of the turbocharger and the manifold.*

b) *Tighten all fixings to the specified torque, where applicable.*

c) *Thoroughly clean the mating faces of the oil drain pipe and the turbocharger, and use a new gasket when reconnecting the pipe.*

d) *Reconnect the exhaust front section to the turbocharger elbow, using a new gasket, with reference to Section 18.*

e) *Use new sealing washers when reconnecting the turbocharger oil feed pipe.*

---

15 Turbocharger –
examination and overhaul

1 With the turbocharger removed, inspect the housing for cracks or other visible damage.

2 Spin the turbine or the compressor wheel to verify that the shaft is intact and to feel for excessive shake or roughness. Some play is normal since in use the shaft is 'floating' on a film of oil. Check that the wheel vanes are undamaged.

3 The wastegate and actuator are integral with the turbocharger, and cannot be checked or renewed separately. Consult a Rover dealer or other specialist if it is thought that the wastegate may be faulty.

4 If the exhaust or induction passages are oil-

14.19 Turbocharger securing nuts (arrowed)

contaminated, the turbo shaft oil seals have probably failed. (On the induction side, this will also have contaminated the intercooler, where applicable, which if necessary should be flushed with a suitable solvent.)

5 No DIY repair of the turbo is possible. A new unit may be available on an exchange basis.

---

16 Intercooler –
removal and refitting

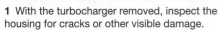

Models without air conditioning

Removal

1 Remove the air cleaner assembly as described in Section 2, and the battery as described in Chapter 5A.

2 Unscrew the radiator securing bolts, and move the radiator back from the front body panel, leaving the coolant hoses and wiring connected, with reference to Chapter 3.

3 Slacken the hose clips, and disconnect the hoses from the intercooler **(see illustration)**.

4 It is now necessary to unscrew the two nuts and bolts securing the intercooler to the radiator. Access to the bolts is tricky – the nuts are accessible from the engine compartment, but the bolts must be counterheld from the front of the assembly. The top bolt can be accessed using a cranked Torx key inserted through the hole in the top

16.3 Disconnect the intercooler lower hose (arrowed)

of the front body panel. To access the lower bolt, unbolt the plastic bonnet lock surround panel, then unscrew the front body panel/bumper upper securing nuts, and carefully pull the front body panel/bumper forwards until the remaining bolt can be reached by inserting a tool down behind the body panel/bumper **(see illustrations)**.

5 Lift the intercooler out from the front of the engine compartment, then lower the radiator back into position, taking care not to damage the radiator fins **(see illustration)**.

Refitting

6 Refitting is a reversal of removal, tightening the intercooler to the specified torque setting.

Models with air conditioning

Removal

7 Remove the front bumper, as described in Chapter 11.

8 Remove the air cleaner as described in Section 2.

9 Slacken the hose clips securing the intercooler top hose to the intercooler, and to the turbocharger pipe, then remove the intercooler top hose.

10 Release the hose clip securing the bottom hose to the intercooler, then disconnect the hose from the intercooler and position it to one side.

11 Unscrew the bolt securing the radiator top mounting bracket to the body front panel.

4B

16.4a The upper intercooler securing bolts can be counterheld using a cranked Torx key

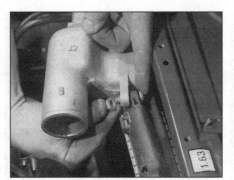

16.4b Unscrew the intercooler securing nuts

16.5 Lifting out the intercooler

12 Unscrew the bolt securing the intercooler top mounting bracket to the body front panel, and remove the bracket.

13 Unscrew the upper nut and bolt securing the intercooler to the radiator.

14 Carefully lift the radiator, taking care not to strain the coolant hoses, to gain access to the lower intercooler-to-radiator nut and bolt.

15 Unscrew the lower nut and bolt securing the intercooler to the radiator, then release the lower end of the intercooler from the radiator, and lift out the intercooler.

Refitting

16 Offer the intercooler up to the radiator, then refit the top intercooler-to-radiator nut and bolt, but do not tighten them at this stage.

17 Refit the lower intercooler-to-radiator nut and bolt, and tighten them securely, then tighten the upper nut and bolt to the specified torque.

18 The remainder of the refitting procedure is a reversal of removal, but make sure that the radiator and intercooler locate correctly in the lower mounting rubbers, and refit the front bumper with reference to Chapter 11.

17 Manifolds –
removal and refitting

1 The inlet and exhaust manifolds share a common gasket. Whenever it is desired to remove either of the manifolds, it is therefore necessary to remove both manifolds in order to renew the gasket.

Models without intercooler

Note: *A new manifold gasket, a new oil drain pipe gasket, a new exhaust front section-to-turbocharger elbow gasket, new oil feed pipe sealing washers, and a new mass airflow sensor O-ring will be required on refitting.*

Removal

2 Disconnect the battery negative lead.

3 Unscrew the bolts securing the engine acoustic cover to the top of the cylinder head cover, then remove the acoustic cover from the engine.

4 Slacken the hose clip, and disconnect the breather hose from the cylinder head cover.

5 Remove the mass airflow (MAF) sensor, as described in Section 12, then slacken the hose clip securing the air intake pipe to the turbocharger, and remove the intake pipe.

6 Disconnect the exhaust front section from the turbocharger elbow, with reference to Section 18.

7 Disconnect the vacuum hose from the turbocharger wastegate actuator.

8 Unscrew the union bolt, and disconnect the oil feed pipe from the turbocharger. Recover and discard the two sealing washers.

9 Disconnect the vacuum pipe from the exhaust gas recirculation (EGR) valve.

10 Unscrew the two bolts securing the oil drain pipe to the turbocharger. Recover and discard the gasket.

11 Unscrew the two bolts securing the exhaust elbow to the mounting bracket.

12 Slacken the six nuts and the six bolts securing the manifolds to the cylinder head, then remove the nuts and bolts, noting the locations of the washers, where applicable.

13 Carefully lift the manifolds (complete with the turbocharger) from the cylinder head. Recover and discard the gasket.

Refitting

14 Thoroughly clean the mating faces of the manifolds and the cylinder head, then position a new gasket on the cylinder head studs.

15 Manoeuvre the manifolds into position, then refit the nuts and bolts, ensuring that the washers are in place as noted before removal. Tighten the nuts and bolts to the specified torque (note that the torques for the nuts and bolts are different), in the sequence shown **(see illustration)**.

16 Further refitting is a reversal of removal, bearing in mind the following points.

a) *Tighten all fixings to the specified torque, where applicable.*

b) *Thoroughly clean the mating faces of the oil drain pipe and the turbocharger, and use a new gasket when reconnecting the pipe.*

c) *Use new sealing washers when reconnecting the turbocharger oil feed pipe.*

d) *Reconnect the exhaust front section to the turbocharger elbow, using a new gasket, with reference to Section 18.*

e) *Refit the mass airflow (MAF) sensor, using a new O-ring, with reference to Section 12.*

Models with intercooler

Note: *A new manifold gasket, a new oil drain pipe gasket, a new exhaust front section-to-turbocharger elbow gasket, new oil feed pipe sealing washers, and a new mass airflow sensor O-ring will be required on refitting.*

Removal

17 Proceed as described in paragraphs 2 to 5.

18 Slacken the clip securing the intercooler hose to the turbocharger pipe, then unscrew the two bolts securing the pipe to the cylinder head, disconnect the hose from the turbocharger, and remove the pipe/hose assembly.

19 Unscrew the union bolt, and disconnect the oil feed pipe from the turbocharger **(see illustration)**. Recover and discard the two sealing washers.

20 Disconnect the manifold absolute pressure (MAP) sensor pipe from the turbocharger.

21 Disconnect the vacuum pipe from the exhaust gas recirculation (EGR) valve.

22 Unscrew the two bolts securing the EGR pipe to the inlet manifold.

23 Unscrew the two bolts securing the EGR valve to the exhaust manifold, and withdraw the valve. Recover and discard the gasket.

24 Disconnect the exhaust front section from the turbocharger elbow, with reference to Section 18.

25 Unscrew the two bolts securing the oil drain pipe to the turbocharger. Recover and discard the gasket.

26 Unscrew the two bolts securing the exhaust elbow to the mounting bracket **(see illustration)**.

27 Slacken the six nuts and the four bolts securing the exhaust manifold to the cylinder head, then remove the nuts and bolts, noting

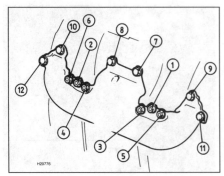

17.15 Manifold securing nut and bolt tightening sequence

17.19 Unscrew the union bolt and disconnect the oil feed pipe – engine removed for clarity

17.26 Unscrew the two bolts (arrowed) securing the exhaust elbow to the mounting bracket – engine removed for clarity

17.27 Unscrew the six bolts and four nuts (arrowed) securing the exhaust manifold to the cylinder head – engine removed for clarity

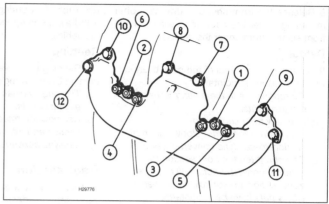

17.36 Manifold securing nut and bolt tightening sequence

the locations of the washers, where applicable **(see illustration)**.
28 Carefully lift the exhaust manifold (complete with the turbocharger) from the cylinder head.
29 Disconnect the wiring plug from the inlet air temperature (IAT) sensor.
30 Slacken the hose clip, and disconnect the intercooler hose from the inlet manifold intake pipe.
31 Unscrew the bolt securing the inlet manifold to the bracket on the cylinder head cover.
32 Unscrew the two nuts securing the inlet manifold to the cylinder head, then withdraw the manifold. Recover and discard the gasket.

Refitting

33 Thoroughly clean the mating faces of the manifolds and the cylinder head, then position a new gasket on the cylinder head studs.
34 Manoeuvre the inlet manifold into position, then refit the securing nuts, but do not fully tighten them until after the exhaust manifold has been refitted.
35 Manoeuvre the exhaust manifold into position, then refit the nuts and bolts, ensuring that the washers are in place as noted before removal.
36 Tighten the inlet and exhaust manifold securing nuts and bolts to the specified torque (note that the torques for the nuts and bolts are different), in the sequence shown **(see illustration)**.
37 Further refitting is a reversal of removal, bearing in mind the following points.
a) Tighten all fixings to the specified torque, where applicable.
b) Thoroughly clean the mating faces of the oil drain pipe and the turbocharger, and use a new gasket when reconnecting the pipe.
c) Use new sealing washers when reconnecting the turbocharger oil feed pipe.
d) Reconnect the exhaust front section to the turbocharger elbow, using a new gasket, with reference to Section 18.
e) Refit the mass airflow (MAF) sensor, using a new O-ring, with reference to Section 12.

18 Exhaust system – general information and component renewal

General information

1 The exhaust system comprises a downpipe, a front silencer and a rear expansion box with a tailpipe.
2 The system fitted in production is of four-piece construction (including the catalytic converter). Sections may therefore be renewed individually if necessary.
3 If the complete system is to be renewed, apply the handbrake, then jack the vehicle up as high as possible and support it securely on axle stands (see "Jacking and Vehicle Support").
4 When renewing the complete system, cutting through the connecting pipes will probably make removal in sections easier than attempting to dismantle corroded joints.

Front section

Note: New exhaust front section-to-turbocharger elbow and front section-to-catalytic converter gaskets will be required on refitting.

Removal

5 Apply the handbrake, then jack up the front of the vehicle and support securely on axle stands (see "Jacking and Vehicle Support").
6 Unscrew the nuts securing the exhaust front section to the catalytic converter **(see illustration)**. Recover the gasket and discard it.
7 Unscrew the three nuts securing the exhaust front section to the exhaust manifold or turbocharger elbow (as applicable), then release the front section from the manifold/turbocharger. Recover the gasket and discard it **(see illustrations)**.

4B

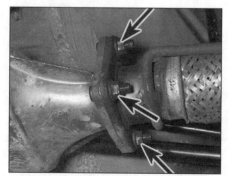

18.6 Unscrew the nuts (arrowed) and disconnect the exhaust front section from the catalytic converter – diesel engines

18.7a Unscrew the three nuts (arrowed) securing the exhaust front section to the turbocharger elbow ...

18.7b ... and recover the gasket – diesel engines

8 Release the front section from the rubber mounting under the floor, then withdraw the front section from under the vehicle.

Refitting

9 Refitting is a reversal of removal, bearing in mind the following points.
  a) *Thoroughly clean the mating faces of the exhaust joints.*
  b) *Use new front section-to-manifold/turbocharger elbow and front section-to-catalytic converter gaskets.*
  c) *Do not tighten the front section-to-catalytic converter nuts until after the front section-to-manifold/turbocharger elbow nuts have been tightened.*

Intermediate section

Note: *New exhaust intermediate section-to-catalytic converter and intermediate section-to-rear section gaskets will be required on refitting.*

Removal

10 Apply the handbrake, then jack up the vehicle and support it securely on axle stands (see *"Jacking and Vehicle Support"*).
11 Unscrew the nuts securing the exhaust intermediate section to the rear section. Recover the gasket and discard it.
12 Unscrew the nuts securing the intermediate section to the catalytic converter. Recover the gasket and discard it.
13 Release the intermediate section from the two rubber mountings under the floor, then withdraw the intermediate section from under the vehicle.

Refitting

14 Refitting is a reversal of removal, bearing in mind the following points.
  a) *Thoroughly clean the mating faces of the exhaust joints.*
  b) *Use new intermediate section-to-rear section and intermediate section-to-catalytic converter gaskets.*

Rear section

Note: *A new exhaust intermediate section-to-rear section gasket will be required on refitting.*

Removal

15 Apply the handbrake, then jack up the vehicle and support it securely on axle stands (see *"Jacking and Vehicle Support"*).
16 Unscrew the nuts securing the exhaust rear section to the intermediate section. Recover the gasket and discard it.
17 Release the rear section from the three mounting rubbers under the floor, then withdraw the rear section from the vehicle.

Refitting

18 Refitting is a reversal of removal, bearing in mind the following points.
  a) *Thoroughly clean the mating faces of the exhaust joints.*
  b) *Use a new intermediate section-to-rear section gasket.*

Catalytic converter

Note: *New catalytic converter-to-exhaust front section and catalytic converter-to-exhaust rear section gaskets will be required on refitting.*

Removal

19 Apply the handbrake, then jack up the front of the vehicle and support it securely on axle stands (see *"Jacking and Vehicle Support"*).
20 Unscrew the nuts securing the catalytic converter to the exhaust front section. Recover and discard the gasket.
21 Ensure that the catalytic converter is adequately supported (the assembly is easily damaged if it is dropped), then unscrew the nuts securing the catalytic converter to the exhaust intermediate section, and withdraw the catalytic converter from under the vehicle. Recover the gasket and discard it.

Refitting

22 Refitting is a reversal of removal, bearing in mind the following points.
  a) *Thoroughly clean the mating faces of the exhaust joints.*
  b) *Use a new exhaust front section-to-catalytic converter gasket and a new intermediate section-to-catalytic converter gasket.*

Chapter 4C
Emission control systems

Contents

Degrees of difficulty

| **Easy,** suitable for novice with little experience | | **Fairly easy,** suitable for beginner with some experience | | **Fairly difficult,** suitable for competent DIY mechanic | 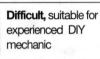 | **Difficult,** suitable for experienced DIY mechanic | | **Very difficult,** suitable for expert DIY or professional | 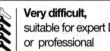 |

Specifications

Torque wrench setting	Nm	lbf ft
Exhaust gas recirculation (EGR) valve bolts (diesel engines)	25	18

1 General information

1 All petrol engine models use unleaded petrol and also have various other features built into the fuel system to help minimise harmful emissions. All models are equipped with a crankcase emission-control system, a catalytic converter, and an evaporative emission control system to keep fuel vapour and exhaust gas emissions down to a minimum.
2 The diesel engines are designed to meet strict emission requirements. All models are fitted with a crankcase emission control system, a catalytic converter and an exhaust gas recirculation (EGR) system to keep exhaust emissions down to a minimum.
3 The emission control systems function as follows.

Petrol models

Crankcase emission control

4 To reduce the emission of unburned hydrocarbons from the crankcase into the atmosphere, the engine is sealed, and the piston blow-by gases and oil vapour are drawn from inside the crankcase, through a wire mesh oil separator, into the inlet tract to be burned by the engine during normal combustion.

5 Clean air is drawn into the crankcase through a pipe connected to the air cleaner side of the throttle body. Crankcase gases and clean air are then drawn from the crankcase, via a pipe, through a filter in the cylinder head cover, into the manifold side of the throttle body. The pipe connecting the cylinder head cover to the throttle body incorporates a restrictor to prevent engine oil being drawn into the inlet manifold under conditions of high manifold depression.

Exhaust emission control

6 To minimise the amount of exhaust gas pollutants which escape into the atmosphere, all models are fitted with a catalytic converter in the exhaust system.
7 The catalytic converter consists of a canister containing a fine mesh impregnated with a catalyst material, over which the hot exhaust gases pass. The catalyst speeds up the oxidation of harmful carbon monoxide, unburned hydrocarbons and soot, effectively reducing the quantity of harmful products released into the atmosphere via the exhaust gases.
8 The system is of the closed-loop type, in which a heated oxygen sensor (HO$_2$S) mounted in the exhaust system provides the engine control module (ECM) with constant feedback, enabling the ECM to adjust the fuel/air mixture to provide the best possible conditions for the converter to operate. The oxygen sensor has a built-in heating element

which is controlled by the ECM; the heating element is used to warm the sensor when the engine is cold to bring it quickly to an efficient operating temperature.
9 The oxygen sensor's tip is sensitive to oxygen and sends the ECM a varying voltage depending on the amount of oxygen in the exhaust gases; if the intake air/fuel mixture is too rich, the exhaust gases are low in oxygen so the sensor sends a low-voltage signal, the voltage rising as the mixture weakens and the amount of oxygen rises in the exhaust gases. Peak conversion efficiency of all major pollutants occurs if the intake air/fuel mixture is maintained at the chemically-correct ratio for the complete combustion of petrol of 14.7 parts (by weight) of air to 1 part of fuel (the "stoichiometric" ratio). The sensor output voltage alters in a large step at this point, the ECM using the signal change as a reference point and correcting the intake air/fuel mixture accordingly by altering the fuel injector opening duration.

Evaporative emission control

10 To minimise the escape into the atmosphere of unburned hydrocarbons, an evaporative emissions control system is fitted to all models. The fuel tank filler cap is sealed, and a charcoal canister is mounted in the engine compartment. The canister collects the petrol vapours generated in the tank when the car is parked, and stores them until they can be cleared from the canister (under the control of the ECM), via the purge valve, into

4C

the inlet tract to be burned by the engine during normal combustion.

11 To ensure that the engine runs correctly when it is cold and/or idling, and to protect the catalytic converter from the effects of an over-rich mixture, the purge valve is not opened by the ECM until the engine has warmed up, and the engine is under load; the valve solenoid is then modulated on and off to allow the stored vapour to pass into the inlet tract.

Diesel models

Crankcase emission control

12 To reduce the emission of unburned hydrocarbons from the crankcase into the atmosphere, the engine is sealed and the piston blow-by gases and oil vapour are drawn from inside the crankcase, through a wire mesh oil separator, into the inlet tract to be burned by the engine during normal combustion.

13 The crankcase gases are drawn from the cylinder head cover, into the turbocharger intake, via a depression limiting valve (crankcase pressure limiting valve). The valve closes progressively as the engine speed increases, so limiting the maximum depression in the crankcase.

Exhaust emission control

14 To minimise the level of exhaust pollutants released into the atmosphere, all models are fitted with a catalytic converter in the exhaust system. Refer to paragraph 7 for a description of the catalytic converter.

Exhaust gas recirculation (EGR) system

15 This system is designed to recirculate small quantities of exhaust gas into the inlet tract, and therefore into the combustion process. This process reduces the level of unburnt hydrocarbons present in the exhaust gas before it reaches the catalytic converter. The system is controlled by the engine control module (ECM), using the information provided by various sensors, via the EGR valve which is fitted to the metal pipe connecting the inlet and exhaust manifolds. The EGR valve is vacuum-operated and is switched on and off by an electrical solenoid valve.

---

2 Petrol engine emission control systems - testing and component renewal

Crankcase emission control

1 The components of this system require no attention other than to check that the hose(s) are clear and undamaged at regular intervals.

Evaporative emission control system

Testing

2 If the system is thought to be faulty, disconnect the hoses from the charcoal canister and purge control valve and check that they are clear by blowing through them. Full testing of the system can only be carried out using specialist diagnostic equipment which is connected to the engine management system diagnostic wiring connector (see Chapter 4A). If the purge control valve or charcoal canister are thought to be faulty, they must be renewed.

Charcoal canister - renewal

Note: *Note the locations of the hoses on the canister before removal to ensure correct refitting.*

3 The charcoal canister is located on the left-hand side of the engine compartment.
4 Disconnect the battery negative lead.
5 Trace the outlet hose back from the canister to the inlet manifold. Release the retaining clip and disconnect the hose from the manifold **(see illustration)**.
6 Trace the inlet hose back from the canister, then release the retaining clip and disconnect the hose from the fuel tank vent pipe.
7 Pull the canister breather hose from the hole in the front suspension rear beam **(see illustration)**.
8 Disconnect the wiring connector from the purge valve (mounted on the top of the canister) **(see illustration)**.
9 Unclip the canister from its mounting, and remove the canister/hose assembly from the engine compartment.
10 Refitting is a reverse of the removal

procedure ensuring the hoses are correctly and securely reconnected, as noted before removal.

Purge valve - renewal

11 The valve is integral with the charcoal canister, and cannot be renewed separately. If the valve is faulty, the complete charcoal canister assembly must be renewed.

Exhaust emission control

Testing

12 The performance of the catalytic converter can be checked only by measuring the exhaust gases using a good-quality, accurately-calibrated exhaust gas analyser, in accordance with the manufacturer's instructions.

13 If the exhaust gas CO level is too high, the vehicle should be taken to a Rover dealer so that the engine management system, particularly the heated oxygen sensor (HO2S), can be thoroughly checked using the special diagnostic equipment. If no fault is found in the engine management system, the fault must be in the catalytic converter, which must be renewed.

Catalytic converter - renewal

14 Refer to Section 13 in Part A of this Chapter.

Oxygen sensor - renewal

15 Refer to Section 11 in Part A of this Chapter.

---

3 Diesel engine emission control systems - testing and component renewal

Crankcase emission control

Testing

1 The components of this system require no attention other than to check that the hose(s) are clear and undamaged at regular intervals. If the system is thought to be faulty, renew the crankcase pressure limiting valve.

2.5 Disconnect the charcoal canister outlet hose (arrowed) from the inlet manifold – K8 engine

2.7 Pull the charcoal canister breather hose (arrowed) from the hole in the front suspension rear beam – petrol engines

2.8 Disconnect the wiring connector (arrowed) from the purge valve – petrol engines

3.2 Crankcase pressure limiting valve location (arrowed) – diesel engines

3.9 EGR valve mounting details – diesel engines

1   Vacuum pipe
2   EGR valve-to-inlet manifold pipe bolt
3   EGR valve-to-exhaust manifold bolt

3.14 EGR solenoid valve location (arrowed) – diesel engines

Crankcase pressure limiting valve - renewal

2 Slacken the retaining clip and disconnect the breather hose from the valve **(see illustration)**.
3 Slacken the retaining clip, then ease the valve out from the intake pipe, and remove it from the engine compartment. Note the orientation of the valve to ensure correct refitting.
4 Refitting is the reverse of removal ensuring that the valve is orientated correctly, as noted before removal.

Exhaust emission control

Testing

5 The performance of the catalytic converter can be checked only by measuring the exhaust gases using a good-quality, accurately-calibrated exhaust gas analyser, in accordance with the manufacturer's instructions.
6 Before assuming that the catalytic converter is faulty, the vehicle should be taken to a Rover dealer so that the engine management system, and the fuel injectors, can be thoroughly checked using the special diagnostic equipment. If no fault is found in the engine management system or the fuel injectors, the fault must be in the catalytic converter, which must be renewed.

Catalytic converter - renewal

7 Refer to Section 18 in Part B of this Chapter.

Exhaust gas recirculation (EGR) system

Testing

8 Comprehensive testing of the system can only be carried out using specialist diagnostic equipment which is connected to the injection system diagnostic wiring connector (see Chapter 4B). If the EGR valve or solenoid valve are thought to be faulty, they must be renewed.

Exhaust gas recirculation (EGR) valve - renewal

Note: New gaskets will be required on refitting.

9 The EGR valve is bolted to the top of the exhaust manifold **(see illustration)**.
10 Disconnect the vacuum hose from the top of the EGR valve.
11 Slacken and remove the bolts securing the valve to the exhaust manifold. Recover the gasket and discard it.
12 Unscrew the bolts securing the valve to the inlet manifold pipe, and withdraw the valve. Again, recover the gasket and discard it.
13 Refitting is the reverse of removal, but use new gaskets and tighten the valve retaining bolts to the specified torque.

Exhaust gas recirculation (EGR) system solenoid valve - renewal

14 The valve is located at the right-hand side of the engine compartment bulkhead, next to the brake servo **(see illustration)**.
15 Disconnect the wiring plug from the valve, then disconnect the two hoses, noting their locations to ensure correct refitting.
16 Unscrew the two securing bolts, and withdraw the valve from its mounting bracket.
17 Refitting is a reversal of removal, but make sure that the hoses are correctly reconnected as noted before removal.

---

4 Catalytic converter - precautions

1 The catalytic converter is a reliable and simple device which needs no maintenance in itself, but there are some facts of which an owner should be aware if the converter is to function properly for its full service life.

Petrol engine

a) DO NOT use leaded petrol in a car equipped with a catalytic converter - the lead will coat the precious metals, reducing their converting efficiency and will eventually destroy the converter.

b) Always keep the ignition and fuel systems well-maintained in accordance with the manufacturer's schedule.
c) Consult an approved dealer as soon as possible in the event of misfiring, irregular engine running after a cold start, a significant loss of engine power, or any other malfunction which may indicate a fault in the ignition system. If it is necessary to continue driving, do so for a short time at low engine speed, without labouring the engine.
d) DO NOT switch off the ignition at high engine speeds.
e) DO NOT push- or tow-start the car - this will soak the catalytic converter in unburned fuel, causing it to overheat when the engine does start. Use jump leads (see "Jump starting").
f) Avoid frequent cold starts one after another.
g) DO NOT allow the fuel tank to become empty.
h) DO NOT use fuel or engine oil additives - these may contain substances harmful to the catalytic converter.
i) DO NOT continue to use the car if the engine burns oil to the extent of leaving a visible trail of blue smoke.
j) Remember that the catalytic converter operates at very high temperatures. DO NOT, therefore, park the car in dry undergrowth, over long grass or piles of dead leaves after a long run.
k) Remember that the catalytic converter is FRAGILE - do not strike it with tools during servicing work.
l) In some cases a sulphurous smell (like that of rotten eggs) may be noticed from the exhaust. This is common to many catalytic converter-equipped cars and once the car has covered a few thousand miles the problem should disappear.
m) The catalytic converter, used on a well-maintained and well-driven car, should last for between 50 000 and 100 000 miles - if the converter is no longer effective it must be renewed.

Diesel engine

2 Refer to parts e) to k) of the petrol engine information given above.

4C

Notes

Chapter 5 Part A:
Starting and charging systems

Contents

Degrees of difficulty

| Easy, suitable for novice with little experience | | Fairly easy, suitable for beginner with some experience | | Fairly difficult, suitable for competent DIY mechanic | Difficult, suitable for experienced DIY mechanic | Very difficult, suitable for expert DIY or professional |

Specifications

System type .... 12-volt, negative earth

Battery

Charge condition:
Poor .... 12.5 volts
Normal .... 12.6 volts
Good .... 12.7 volts

Torque wrench settings	Nm	lbf ft
Alternator mountings (petrol engines):		
Alternator-to-mounting bracket nut(s) and bolt(s)	45	33
Alternator-to-adjuster bracket nut and bolt	25	18
Drivebelt tensioner pulley bolt (models with air conditioning)	25	18
Upper mounting bracket-to-engine nut and bolt (models with air conditioning)	25	18
Starter motor securing bolts:		
Petrol engine models	45	33
Diesel engine models	55	41
Starter motor rear support bracket nuts (petrol engine models)	25	18
Oil pressure switch	15	11

1 General information and precautions

General information

The engine electrical system consists mainly of the charging and starting systems. Because of their engine-related functions, these components are covered separately from the body electrical devices such as the lights, instruments, etc (which are covered in Chapter 12). On petrol engine models refer to Part B for information on the ignition system, and on diesel models refer to Part C for information on the pre-heating system.

The electrical system is of the 12-volt negative earth type.

The battery is of the low maintenance or "maintenance-free" (sealed for life) type and is charged by the alternator, which is belt-driven from the crankshaft pulley.

The starter motor is of the pre-engaged type incorporating an integral solenoid. On starting, the solenoid moves the drive pinion into engagement with the flywheel ring gear before the starter motor is energised. Once the engine has started, a one-way clutch prevents the motor armature being driven by the engine until the pinion disengages from the flywheel.

Further details of the various systems are given in the relevant Sections of this Chapter. While some repair procedures are given, the usual course of action is to renew the component concerned. The owner whose interest extends beyond mere component renewal should obtain a copy of the "Automobile Electrical & Electronic Systems Manual", available from the publishers of this manual.

Precautions

It is necessary to take extra care when working on the electrical system to avoid damage to semi-conductor devices (diodes and transistors), and to avoid the risk of personal injury. In addition to the precautions given in "Safety first!" at the beginning of this manual, observe the following when working on the system:

Always remove rings, watches, etc before working on the electrical system. Even with the battery disconnected, capacitive discharge could occur if a component's live terminal is earthed through a metal object. This could cause a shock or nasty burn.

Do not reverse the battery connections. Components such as the alternator, electronic control units, or any other components having semi-conductor circuitry could be irreparably damaged.

If the engine is being started using jump leads and a slave battery, connect the batteries positive-to-positive and negative-to-negative (see "Jump starting"). This also applies when connecting a battery charger.

Never disconnect the battery terminals, the alternator, any electrical wiring or any test instruments when the engine is running.

Do not allow the engine to turn the alternator when the alternator is not connected.

Never "test" for alternator output by "flashing" the output lead to earth.

Never use an ohmmeter of the type incorporating a hand-cranked generator for circuit or continuity testing.

Always ensure that the battery negative lead is disconnected when working on the electrical system.

Before using electric-arc welding equipment on the car, disconnect the battery, alternator and components such as the fuel injection/ignition electronic control unit to protect them from the risk of damage.

The radio/cassette unit fitted as standard equipment by Rover is equipped with a built-in security code to deter thieves. If the power source to the unit is cut, the anti-theft system will activate. Even if the power source is immediately reconnected, the radio/cassette unit will not function until the correct security code has been entered. Therefore, if you do not know the correct security code for the radio/cassette unit **do not** disconnect the battery negative terminal of the battery or remove the radio/cassette unit from the vehicle. Refer to "Radio/cassette unit anti-theft system precaution" Section for further information.

2 Battery - testing and charging

Standard and low maintenance battery - testing

1 If the vehicle covers a small annual mileage, it is worthwhile checking the specific gravity of the electrolyte every three months to determine the state of charge of the battery. Use a hydrometer to make the check and compare the results with the following table. Note that the specific gravity readings assume an electrolyte temperature of 15°C (60°F); for every 10°C (18°F) below 15°C (60°F) subtract 0.007. For every 10°C (18°F) above 15°C (60°F) add 0.007.

	Ambient temperature above 25°C (77°F)	Ambient temperature below 25°C (77°F)
Fully-charged	1.210 to 1.230	1.270 to 1.290
70% charged	1.170 to 1.190	1.230 to 1.250
Fully-discharged	1.050 to 1.070	1.110 to 1.130

2 If the battery condition is suspect, first check the specific gravity of electrolyte in each cell. A variation of 0.040 or more between any cells indicates loss of electrolyte or deterioration of the internal plates.

3 If the specific gravity variation is 0.040 or more, the battery should be renewed. If the

cell variation is satisfactory but the battery is discharged, it should be charged as described later in this Section.

Maintenance-free battery - testing

4 In cases where a "sealed for life" maintenance-free battery is fitted, topping-up and testing of the electrolyte in each cell is not possible. The condition of the battery can therefore only be tested using a battery condition indicator or a voltmeter.

5 If testing the battery using a voltmeter, connect the voltmeter across the battery and compare the result with those given in the Specifications under "charge condition". The test is only accurate if the battery has not been subjected to any kind of charge for the previous six hours. If this is not the case, switch on the headlights for 30 seconds, then wait four to five minutes before testing the battery after switching off the headlights. All other electrical circuits must be switched off, so check that the doors and tailgate are fully shut when making the test.

6 If the voltage reading is less than 12.2 volts, then the battery is discharged, whilst a reading of 12.2 to 12.4 volts indicates a partially discharged condition.

7 If the battery is to be charged, remove it from the vehicle (Section 3) and charge it as described later in this Section.

Standard and low maintenance battery - charging

Note: The following is intended as a guide only. Always refer to the manufacturer's recommendations (often printed on a label attached to the battery) before charging a battery.

8 Charge the battery at a rate of 3.5 to 4 amps and continue to charge the battery at this rate until no further rise in specific gravity is noted over a four hour period.

9 Alternatively, a "trickle charger" charging at the rate of 1.5 amps can safely be used overnight.

10 Specially rapid "boost" charges which are claimed to restore the power of the battery in 1 to 2 hours are not recommended, as they can cause serious damage to the battery plates through overheating.

11 While charging the battery, note that the temperature of the electrolyte should never exceed 37.8°C (100°F).

Maintenance-free battery - charging

Note: The following is intended as a guide only. Always refer to the manufacturer's recommendations (often printed on a label attached to the battery) before charging a battery.

12 This battery type takes considerably longer to fully recharge than the standard type, the time taken being dependent on the extent of discharge, but it can take anything up to three days.

13 A constant voltage type charger is required, to be set, when connected, to 13.9 to 14.9 volts with a charger current below 25 amps. Using this method, the battery should be useable within three hours, giving a voltage reading of 12.5 volts, but this is for a partially discharged battery and, as mentioned, full charging can take considerably longer.

14 If the battery is to be charged from a fully discharged state (condition reading less than 12.2 volts), have it recharged by your Rover dealer or local automotive electrician, as the charge rate is higher and constant supervision during charging is necessary.

3.4a Unscrew the bolt (arrowed) to remove the battery retaining clamp . . .

3.4b . . . and lift the battery from the engine compartment

3 Battery - removal and refitting

Note: *If a Rover radio/cassette unit is fitted, refer to "Radio/cassette unit anti-theft system - precaution" in the Reference Section.*

Removal

1 The battery is located on the left-hand side of the engine compartment.
2 Slacken the clamp nut and disconnect the lead clamp from the battery negative (earth) terminal.
3 Lift the insulation cover and disconnect the positive terminal lead in the same way.
4 Unscrew the bolt and remove the battery retaining clamp, then lift the battery from the engine compartment **(see illustrations)**.

Refitting

5 Refitting is a reversal of removal, but smear petroleum jelly on the terminals after

reconnecting the leads, and always reconnect the positive lead first, and the negative lead last.

4 Charging system - testing

Note: *Refer to the warnings given in "Safety first!" and in Section 1 of this Chapter before starting work.*

1 If the ignition warning light fails to illuminate when the ignition is switched on, first check the alternator wiring connections for security. If satisfactory, check that the warning light bulb has not blown, and that the bulbholder is secure in its location in the instrument panel (see Chapter 12). If the light still fails to illuminate, check the continuity of the warning light feed wire from the alternator to the bulbholder. If all is satisfactory, the alternator is at fault and should be renewed or taken to an auto-electrician for testing and repair.

2 If the ignition warning light illuminates when the engine is running, stop the engine and check that the drivebelt is correctly tensioned (see Chapter 1) and that the alternator connections are secure. If all is so far satisfactory, have the alternator checked by an auto-electrician.
3 If the alternator output is suspect even though the warning light functions correctly, the regulated voltage may be checked as follows.
4 Connect a voltmeter across the battery terminals and start the engine.
5 Increase the engine speed until the voltmeter reading remains steady; the reading should be approximately 12 to 13 volts, and no more than 14 volts.
6 Switch on as many electrical accessories (eg, the headlights, heated rear window and heater blower) as possible, and check that the alternator maintains the regulated voltage at around 13 to 14 volts.
7 If the regulated voltage is not as stated, the fault may be due to worn brushes, weak brush springs, a faulty voltage regulator, a faulty diode, a severed phase winding or worn or damaged slip rings. The alternator should be renewed or taken to an auto-electrician for testing and repair.

5A

5 Alternator - removal and refitting

Petrol engine models without air conditioning

Removal

1 Disconnect the battery negative lead.
2 Where applicable, to improve access, apply the handbrake, then jack up the front of the vehicle and support securely on axle stands (see *"Jacking and Vehicle Support"*).
3 Unscrew the two securing nuts, and disconnect the two wiring leads from the rear of the alternator.
4 Unscrew the nut and bolt securing the alternator to the adjuster bracket **(see illustration)**.

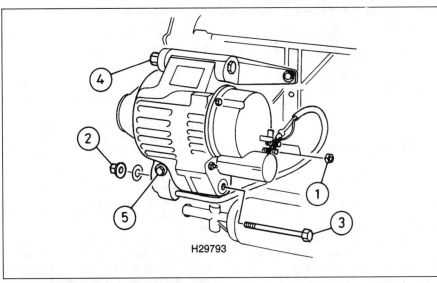

H29793

5.4 Alternator mounting details – petrol engine models without air conditioning

1 Wiring securing nuts
2 Alternator-to-adjuster bracket nut
3 Alternator-to-adjuster bracket bolt
4 Alternator top mounting nut
5 Drivebelt tension adjuster bolt

5.5 Slacken the through-bolt and nut (arrowed) securing the alternator to the mounting bracket – petrol models without air conditioning

5 Slacken the through-bolt and nut securing the top of the alternator to the mounting bracket **(see illustration)**.
6 Slacken the alternator drivebelt tension by turning the adjuster bolt anti-clockwise, then slip the drivebelt from the alternator pulley.
7 Remove the nut and bolt securing the top of the alternator to the engine, then withdraw the alternator.

Refitting

8 Refitting is a reversal of removal, but refit the drivebelt to the alternator pulley and adjust the tension as described in Chapter 1A.

Petrol engine models with air conditioning

Removal

9 Disconnect the battery negative lead.

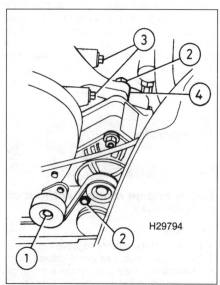

5.11 Alternator mounting details – petrol models with air conditioning

1 Drivebelt tensioner pulley securing bolt
2 Alternator mounting through-bolts
3 Upper alternator mounting bracket securing bolt and nut
4 Upper alternator mounting bracket

10 Apply the handbrake, then jack up the front of the vehicle and support securely on axle stands (see *"Jacking and Vehicle Support"*).
11 Slacken the alternator drivebelt tensioner pulley securing bolt, then relieve the tension by turning the adjuster bolt anti-clockwise **(see illustration)**. Slip the drivebelt from the alternator pulley.
12 Unscrew and remove the two through-bolts and nuts securing the alternator to the mounting brackets, and release the alternator from the mounting brackets.
13 Unscrew the upper alternator mounting bracket securing bolt, then slacken the securing nut, and pivot the mounting bracket clear of the alternator.
14 Unscrew the two securing nuts, and disconnect the two wiring leads from the rear of the alternator, then manipulate the alternator out from the engine compartment.

Refitting

15 Refitting is a reversal of removal, but refit the drivebelt to the alternator pulley and adjust the tension as described in Chapter 1A.

Diesel engine models

16 The procedure is described as part of the brake vacuum pump removal and refitting procedure in Chapter 9.

---

6 Alternator - testing and overhaul

If the alternator is thought to be suspect, it should be removed from the vehicle and taken to an auto-electrician for testing. Most auto-electricians will be able to supply and fit brushes at a reasonable cost. However, check on the cost of repairs before proceeding as it may prove more economical to obtain a new or exchange alternator. Note that no spare brushes are available from Rover dealers.

---

7 Starting system - testing

Note: *Refer to the precautions given in "Safety first!" and in Section 1 of this Chapter before starting work.*

1 If the starter motor fails to operate when the ignition key is turned to the appropriate position, the following possible causes may be to blame.
  a) The battery is faulty.
  b) The electrical connections between the switch, solenoid, battery and starter motor are somewhere failing to pass the

necessary current from the battery through the starter to earth.
  c) The solenoid is faulty.
  d) The starter motor is mechanically or electrically defective.

2 To check the battery, switch on the headlights. If they dim after a few seconds, this indicates that the battery is discharged - recharge (see Section 2) or renew the battery. If the headlights glow brightly, turn the ignition switch to the start position, and observe the lights. If they dim, then this indicates that current is reaching the starter motor, therefore the fault must lie in the starter motor. If the lights continue to glow brightly (and no clicking sound can be heard from the starter motor solenoid), this indicates that there is a fault in the circuit or solenoid - see following paragraphs. If the starter motor turns slowly when operated, but the battery is in good condition, then this indicates that either the starter motor is faulty, or there is considerable resistance somewhere in the circuit.
3 If a fault in the circuit is suspected, disconnect the battery leads (including the earth connection to the body), the starter/solenoid wiring and the engine/transmission earth strap. Thoroughly clean the connections, and reconnect the leads and wiring, then use a voltmeter or test lamp to check that full battery voltage is available at the battery positive lead connection to the solenoid, and that the earth is sound. Smear petroleum jelly around the battery terminals to prevent corrosion - corroded connections are amongst the most frequent causes of electrical system faults.
4 If the battery and all connections are in good condition, check the circuit by disconnecting the wire from the solenoid blade terminal. Connect a voltmeter or test lamp between the wire end and a good earth (such as the battery negative terminal), and check that the wire is live when the ignition switch is turned to the "start" position. If it is, then the circuit is sound - if not, the circuit wiring can be checked as described in Chapter 12.
5 The solenoid contacts can be checked by connecting a voltmeter or test lamp between the battery positive feed connection on the starter side of the solenoid, and earth. When the ignition switch is turned to the "start" position, there should be a reading or lighted bulb, as applicable. If there is no reading or lighted bulb, the solenoid is faulty and should be renewed.
6 If the circuit and solenoid are proved sound, the fault must lie in the starter motor. In this event, it may be possible to have the starter motor overhauled by a specialist, but check on the cost of spares before proceeding, as it may prove more economical to obtain a new or exchange motor.

8.5 Upper starter motor securing bolt (arrowed) – petrol models with manual transmission

8.6 Unscrew the two bolts securing the starter motor rear support bracket to the transmission – petrol models with manual transmission

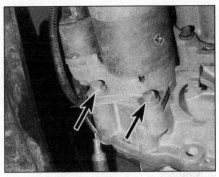

8.7 Unscrew the two lower starter motor securing bolts (arrowed) – petrol models with manual transmission

8 Starter motor - removal and refitting

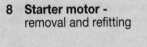

Petrol engine models with manual transmission

Removal

1 Disconnect the battery negative lead.
2 Remove the air cleaner assembly as described in Chapter 4A.
3 Apply the handbrake, then jack up the front of the vehicle and support securely on axle stands (see "Jacking and Vehicle Support").
4 Unscrew the retaining nut and disconnect the main supply lead from the solenoid, then disconnect the wiring connector from the solenoid blade terminal.
5 Unscrew the upper starter motor securing bolt, and slide the battery earth lead from the bolt (see illustration).
6 Unscrew the two bolts securing the starter motor rear support bracket to the transmission (see illustration).
7 Unscrew the two lower starter motor securing bolts, then withdraw the starter motor from the engine compartment (see illustration).

Refitting

8 Manoeuvre the starter motor into position,

and refit the two lower securing bolts. Do not fully tighten the bolts at this stage.
9 Refit the rear support bracket, and secure it to the starter motor with the two nuts.
10 Refit the upper starter motor securing bolts, ensuring that the battery earth lead is in position on the bolt, then tighten the bolt to the specified torque.
11 Tighten the two lower starter motor securing bolts to the specified torque.
12 Refit and tighten the bolt securing the starter motor rear support bracket to the bracket on the transmission to the specified torque.
13 The remainder of the refitting procedure is a reversal of removal.

Petrol engine models with automatic transmission

Removal

14 Proceed as described in paragraphs 1 and 2.
15 Unscrew the bolt securing the transmission fluid level dipstick tube to the transmission, then pull the dipstick tube from the transmission. Recover the O-ring.
16 Unscrew the retaining nut (and recover the spring washer) and disconnect the main supply lead from the solenoid, then disconnect the wiring connector from the solenoid blade terminal.

17 Unscrew the nut securing the earth cable to the end of the lower starter motor securing bolt, and release the cable from the bolt.
18 Unscrew the three bolts securing the starter motor cover plate to the transmission, and remove the cover plate (see illustration).
19 Unscrew the three now-exposed starter motor securing bolts, then manipulate the starter motor out from the engine compartment (see illustration).

Refitting

20 Refitting is a reversal of removal, bearing in mind the following points.
a) Check the condition of the main supply lead-to-solenoid spring washer, and renew if necessary.
b) Check the condition of the fluid level dipstick tube O-ring and renew if necessary. Lubricate the O-ring with a little clean transmission fluid.

Diesel engine models

Removal

21 Proceed as described in paragraphs 1 and 2.
22 Unscrew the retaining nut and disconnect the main supply lead from the solenoid, then disconnect the wiring connector from the solenoid blade terminal (see illustration).
23 Unscrew the upper starter motor securing bolt, noting that it also secures the engine

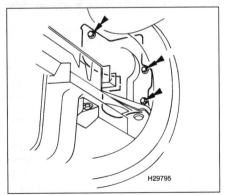

8.18 Starter motor cover plate securing bolts (arrowed) – petrol models with automatic transmission

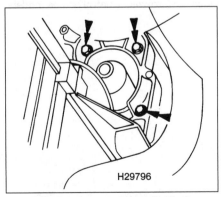

8.19 Starter motor securing bolts (arrowed) – petrol models with automatic transmission

8.22 Unscrew the main supply lead retaining nut (arrowed) – diesel engine models

5A

mounting bracing bracket, and the coolant pipe/fuel pipe assembly **(see illustration)**. It may be necessary to unscrew the nut securing the coolant pipe/fuel pipe assembly to the transmission mounting plate, to enable the pipe assembly to be moved aside sufficiently to remove the starter motor. Similarly, it may be necessary to slacken the nut securing the two parts of the engine mounting bracing bracket together.

24 Unscrew the lower starter motor mounting bolt, then manipulate the starter motor out from the engine compartment **(see illustration)**.

Refitting

25 Refitting is a reversal of removal.

9 Starter motor - testing and overhaul

If the starter motor is thought to be suspect, it should be removed from the vehicle and taken to an auto-electrician for testing. Most auto-electricians will be able to supply and fit brushes at a reasonable cost. However, check on the cost of repairs before proceeding as it may prove more economical to obtain a new or exchange motor.

10 Ignition switch - removal and refitting

The ignition switch is integral with the steering column lock. Removal and refitting of the ignition switch/steering column lock is described in Chapter 10.

11 Oil pressure warning light switch - removal and refitting

Removal

1 The switch is screwed into the oil filter housing. On petrol engines, the switch is

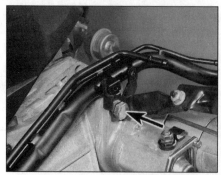
8.23 Upper starter motor securing bolt (arrowed) – diesel engine model (engine/transmission removed)

screwed into the rear of the housing (the housing is located at the front right-hand corner of the cylinder block), and on diesel engines, the switch is screwed into the top of the housing (the housing is located at the rear right-hand corner of the cylinder block) **(see illustrations)**.

2 To improve access to the switch, apply the handbrake then jack up the front of the vehicle and support securely on axle stands (see *"Jacking and Vehicle Support"*). Where necessary, remove the undershield from beneath the engine/transmission unit.

3 Disconnect the battery negative lead, then disconnect the wiring plug from the switch.

11.1a Oil pressure warning light switch location (arrowed) – petrol engine models

8.24 Removing the starter motor – diesel engine models (engine/transmission removed)

4 Position a suitable container beneath the switch to catch escaping oil, then unscrew the switch from the housing.

Refitting

5 Ensure that the switch threads are clean and dry, then refit the switch to the housing and tighten it to the specified torque.

6 Reconnect the wiring plug, then (where applicable) refit the engine/transmission undershield.

7 Lower the vehicle to the ground then reconnect the battery negative lead.

8 On completion, check and, if necessary, top up the engine oil level as described in *"Weekly checks"*.

11.1b Oil pressure warning light switch location (arrowed) – diesel engine models

Chapter 5 Part B:
Ignition system - petrol engines

Contents

Degrees of difficulty

Easy, suitable for novice with little experience	Fairly easy, suitable for beginner with some experience	Fairly difficult, suitable for competent DIY mechanic	Difficult, suitable for experienced DIY mechanic	Very difficult, suitable for expert DIY or professional

Specifications

General

System type	Rover modular engine management system (MEMS) ignition system integrated with indirect multi-point fuel injection system
Firing order	1-3-4-2 (No 1 cylinder at timing belt end)

Torque wrench settings

	Nm	lbf ft
Ignition coil securing bolts:		
M6 bolt	9	6
M10 bolts	45	33
Rotor arm retaining screw	8	6

1 General information and precautions

General information

The ignition system is controlled by the modular engine management system (MEMS) – see Chapter 4A. The MEMS controls all ignition and fuel injection functions via the engine control module (ECM).

The ignition system is responsible for igniting the air/fuel mixture in each cylinder at the correct moment in relation to engine speed and load.

The ignition system is based on feeding low tension voltage from the battery to the coil, where it is converted into high-tension voltage. The high-tension voltage is powerful enough to jump the spark plug gap in the cylinders many times a second under high compression pressures, providing that the system is in good condition.

The system functions in the following manner. Current flowing through the low-tension coil windings produces a magnetic field around the high-tension coil windings. The engine control module (ECM) produced a signal used to switch off the low-tension circuit.

The subsequent collapse of the magnetic field over the high-tension windings produces a high-tension voltage, which is then fed to the relevant spark plug, via the distributor cap and rotor arm. The low-tension circuit is automatically switched on again by the ECM, to allow the magnetic field to build up again before the firing of the next spark plug. The ignition is advanced and retarded automatically, to ensure that the spark occurs at the correct instant in relation to the engine speed and load.

The ignition timing is based on inputs provided to the ECM by various sensors supplying information on engine load, engine speed, coolant temperature and intake air temperature.

The HT voltage is supplied from the ignition coil (switched by the ECM) to the distributor cap and rotor arm, from where it is passed to the spark plugs.

Precautions

Refer to the precautions to be observed when working on models fitted with an electronic control unit, given in Chapter 4A, Section 1.

 Warning: The HT voltage generated by an electronic ignition system is extremely high and, in certain circumstances, could prove fatal. Take care to avoid receiving electric shocks from the HT side of the ignition system. Do not handle HT leads, or touch the distributor or coil, when the engine is running. If tracing faults in the HT circuit, use well-insulated tools to manipulate live leads. Persons with surgically-implanted cardiac pacemaker devices should keep well clear of the ignition circuits, components and test equipment.

Refer to the precautions given in Chapter 4A, Section 1 when carrying out work on models equipped with a catalytic converter.

5B

2 Ignition system – testing

1 The components of the electronic ignition system are normally very reliable; most faults are far more likely to be due to loose or dirty connections or to "tracking" of HT voltage due to dirt, dampness or damaged insulation, than to the failure of any of the system components. **Always** check all wiring thoroughly before condemning an electrical component, and work methodically to eliminate all other possibilities before deciding that a particular component is faulty.

2 The practice of checking for a spark by holding the live end of an HT lead a short distance away from the engine is not recommended - not only is there a high risk of a powerful electric shock, but the coil, or engine control module (ECM) may be damaged.

3 Extreme care should be taken when testing the system, as the ECM is very sensitive, and if damaged, it may prove very costly to renew.

4 If in any doubt as to test procedures, or if the correct equipment is not available, entrust testing and fault diagnosis to a Rover dealer. It is far better to pay the labour charges involved in having the vehicle checked by someone suitably qualified, than to risk damage to the system or yourself. The engine management system has a self-diagnostic function, and any system faults are stored as trouble codes, which can be read using suitable specialist diagnostic equipment. Brief details are given in Chapter 4A.

5 If a fault appears in the engine management system, first ensure that the fault is not due to a poor electrical connection or poor maintenance; ie, check that the air cleaner filter element is clean, that the spark plugs are in good condition and correctly gapped, and that the engine breather hoses are clear and undamaged. Refer to Chapter 1A for further information. Also check that the throttle cable is correctly adjusted as described in Chapter

4A. If the engine is running very roughly, check the compression pressures as described in Chapter 2A.

6 If the engine will not start, check that the fuel inertia cut-off switch has not operated (see Chapter 4A). Push the switch button to reset if necessary.

7 Check that the coil, the distributor cap and the HT leads are clean and dry. Check the leads themselves and the spark plugs (by substitution if necessary - refer to Chapter 1A for details), then check the distributor cap, carbon brush and rotor arm (see Section 4).

8 If HT voltage is not present on any particular lead, the fault will be in that lead or in the distributor cap. If HT voltage is present on all leads, the fault will be in the spark plugs; check and renew them if there is any doubt about their condition.

9 If these checks fail to reveal the cause of the problem, the vehicle should be taken to a Rover dealer for testing. A wiring connector is provided on a bracket behind the centre console, into which a special electronic diagnostic tester can be plugged. The tester should locate the fault quickly and simply, avoiding the need to test all the system components individually, which is time-consuming, and also carries a risk of damaging the ECM.

3 Ignition HT coil – removal and refitting

Removal

1 The coil is mounted on the rear of the cylinder block.

2 Disconnect the battery negative lead, then apply the handbrake, jack up the front of the vehicle and support securely on axle stands (see "Jacking and Vehicle Support").

3 Disconnect the wiring connector and HT lead from the coil.

4 Slacken and remove the three securing bolts, and remove the coil from the engine **(see illustration)**.

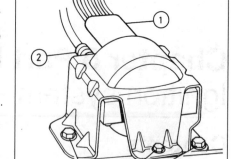

3.4 Ignition coil mounting details – viewed from underneath vehicle

1 Wiring connector
2 HT lead
3 Coil securing bolts

Refitting

5 Refitting is the reverse of removal, but tighten the securing bolts to the specified torque.

4 Distributor components – removal, inspection and refitting

Removal

Note: A new rotor arm retaining screw will be required on refitting.

1 Ensure the ignition is switched off.

2 Remove the air cleaner cover, with reference to Chapter 1A if necessary.

3 If the distributor cap is to be completely removed from the engine, check the HT leads for identification marks, and if none are present, label the leads to ensure correct refitting, then disconnect the HT leads from the distributor cap.

4 Unscrew the distributor cap securing screws, and remove the distributor cap **(see illustrations)**.

4.4a Unscrew the distributor cap securing screws . . .

4.4b . . . and remove the distributor cap – K8 engine shown

5 If desired, the distributor shield can now be removed by passing it over the rotor arm **(see illustration)**.

6 If necessary, turn the crankshaft, using a suitable spanner or socket on the pulley bolt, until the rotor arm securing screw becomes accessible **(see illustration)**.

7 Unscrew the securing screw, and withdraw the rotor arm from the camshaft. Discard the screw, a new one must be used on refitting.

Inspection

8 Check the distributor cap for corrosion of the contact segments, and for signs of tracking, indicated by a thin black line between the segments. Make sure that the carbon brush in the centre of the cap moves freely, and stands proud of the surface of the cap. Renew the cap if necessary.

9 If the metal portion of the rotor arm is badly burnt or loose, renew the rotor arm. If slightly burnt or corroded, it may be cleaned with a fine file.

Refitting

10 Refitting is a reversal of removal, but use a new rotor arm retaining screw.

4.5 The distributor shield can now be removed

4.6 Turn the crankshaft until the rotor arm securing screw (arrowed) becomes accessible

5 Ignition timing – checking and adjustment

The ignition timing is controlled by the engine control module (ECM), and is constantly being monitored and adjusted. Therefore, it is not possible for the home mechanic to check the ignition timing.

The only way in which the ignition timing can be checked is by using special electronic test equipment, connected to the engine management system diagnostic connector (see Chapter 4A). Refer to a Rover dealer for further information.

5B

Notes

Chapter 5 Part C:
Pre-heating system – diesel engines

Contents

Degrees of difficulty

Easy, suitable for novice with little experience	**Fairly easy,** suitable for beginner with some experience	**Fairly difficult,** suitable for competent DIY mechanic 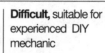	**Difficult,** suitable for experienced DIY mechanic	**Very difficult,** suitable for expert DIY or professional

Specifications

Glow plugs
Type . . . .   Beru 0100226 184

Torque wrench settings

	Nm	lbf ft
Coolant outlet elbow bolts	25	18
Glow plugs	20	15

1 General description

To assist cold starting, diesel engine models are fitted with a pre-heating system, which comprises a relay, three glow plugs (fitted to Nos 1, 2 and 3 cylinders), and a facia-mounted warning lamp. The system is controlled by the electronic diesel control (EDC) system, using information provided by the coolant temperature sensor (see Chapter 4B).

The glow plugs are miniature electric heating elements, encapsulated in a metal case with a probe at one end, and an electrical connection at the other. Each combustion chamber has one glow plug threaded into it. When the glow plug is energised, it heats up rapidly causing the temperature of the air charge drawn into each of the combustion chambers to rise. Each glow plug probe is positioned directly in line with the incoming spray of fuel from the injector. Hence the fuel passing over the glow plug probe is also heated, allowing its optimum combustion temperature to be achieved more readily. In addition, small particles of the fuel passing over the glow plugs are ignited and this helps to trigger the combustion process.

The duration of the pre-heating period is governed by the electronic diesel control (EDC) system engine control module (ECM), using information provided by the coolant temperature sensor (see Chapter 4B). The ECM alters the pre-heating time (the length for which the glow plugs are supplied with current) to suit the prevailing conditions.

A facia-mounted warning lamp informs the driver that pre-heating is taking place. The lamp extinguishes when sufficient pre-heating has taken place to allow the engine to be started, but power will still be supplied to the glow plugs for a further period until the engine is started. If no attempt is made to start the engine, the power supply to the glow plugs is switched off to prevent battery drain and glow plug burn-out.

2 Pre-heating system – testing

1 Full testing of the system can only be carried out using specialist diagnostic equipment which is connected to the engine management system diagnostic wiring connector (see Chapter 4B). If the pre-heating system is thought to be faulty, some preliminary checks of the glow plug operation may be made as described in the following paragraphs.
2 Connect a voltmeter or 12-volt test lamp between the glow plug supply cable, and a good earth point on the engine.

Caution: Make sure that the live connection is kept well clear of the engine and bodywork.
3 Have an assistant activate the pre-heating system by turning the ignition key to the second position, and check that battery voltage is applied to the glow plug electrical connection. **Note:** *The supply voltage will be less than battery voltage initially, but will rise and settle as the glow plug heats up. It will then drop to zero when the pre-heating period ends and the safety cut-out operates.*
4 If no supply voltage can be detected at the glow plug, then the glow plug relay or the supply cable may be faulty.
5 To locate a faulty glow plug, first operate the pre-heating system to allow the glow plugs to reach working temperature, then disconnect the battery negative cable and position it away from the battery terminal.
6 Refer to Section 3, and remove the supply cable from the glow plug terminal. Measure the electrical resistance between the glow plug terminal and the engine earth. A reading of anything more than a few Ohms indicates that the glow plug is defective.
7 As a final check, remove the glow plugs and inspect them visually, as described in Section 3.
8 If no problems are found, take the vehicle to a Rover dealer for testing using the appropriate diagnostic equipment.

5C

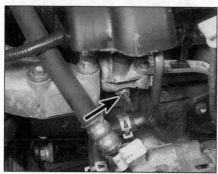

3.6 Disconnect the wiring from the temperature gauge sender (arrowed)

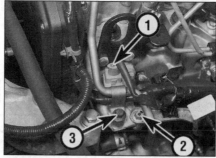

3.8 Disconnect the wiring from the coolant temperature sensor (1), unscrew the bolt (2) securing the dipstick bracket and the bolt (3) securing the vacuum pipe

3.12 Disconnect the wiring . . .

3 Glow plugs – removal, inspection and refitting

Removal

Note: *Suitable anti-seize compound, and a new coolant outlet elbow seal will be required on refitting.*

1 Disconnect the battery negative lead.

2 Unscrew the bolts securing the engine acoustic cover to the top of the cylinder head cover, then remove the acoustic cover from the engine.

3 If No 1 cylinder glow plug is to be removed, it is necessary to carry out the procedure given in paragraphs 3 to 11. If No 1 cylinder glow plug is to be left in place, proceed to paragraph 12.

4 Drain the cooling system as described in Chapter 1B.

5 On models with air conditioning, remove the alternator, as described in Part A of this Chapter.

6 Disconnect the wiring from the temperature gauge sender **(see illustration)**.

7 Slacken the hose clip, and disconnect the radiator top hose from the coolant outlet elbow.

8 Disconnect the wiring from the engine coolant temperature (ECT) sensor, located in the coolant outlet elbow, at the front right-hand corner of the engine **(see illustration)**.

9 Unscrew the bolt securing the engine oil level dipstick tube bracket to the coolant outlet elbow.

10 Similarly, unscrew the bolt securing the brake servo vacuum pipe to the coolant elbow.

11 Unscrew the four securing bolts, and remove the coolant elbow from the cylinder head. Recover the seal and discard it.

12 Unscrew the terminal nuts securing the feed wiring to the glow plugs, then disconnect the wiring, and move it to one side **(see illustration)**.

13 Unscrew the glow plugs and remove them from the cylinder head **(see illustration)**.

Inspection

14 Inspect the glow plugs for signs of damage. Burt or eroded glow plug tips can be caused by a bad injector spray pattern. Have the injectors checked if this sort of damage is found.

15 If the glow plugs are in good condition, check them electrically, as described in Section 2.

16 The glow plugs can be energised by applying 12 volts to them to verify that they heat up evenly and in the required time. Observe the following precautions:

a) *Support the glow plug by clamping it carefully in a vice or self-locking pliers. Remember it will be red hot.*

b) *Make sure that the power supply or test lead incorporates a fuse or overload trip to protect against damage from a short-circuit.*

c) *After testing, allow the glow plug to cool for several minutes before attempting to handle it.*

17 A glow plug in good condition will start to glow red at the tip after drawing current for 5 seconds or so. Any plug which takes much longer to start glowing, or which starts glowing in the middle instead of at the tip, is defective.

Refitting

18 Thoroughly clean the glow plugs, and the glow plug seating areas in the cylinder head.

19 Apply anti-seize compound to the glow plug threads, then refit the glow plugs and tighten them to the specified torque.

20 Reconnect the feed wiring to the glow plugs, noting that the main feed lead must be connected to the No 2 cylinder glow plug.

21 Further refitting is a reversal of removal, bearing in mind the following points:

a) *Thoroughly clean the mating faces of the coolant outlet elbow and the cylinder head, then refit the elbow using a new seal, and tighten the securing bolts to the specified torque.*

b) *On models with air conditioning, refit the alternator as described in Part A of this Chapter.*

c) *On completion, refill the cooling system as described in Chapter 1B.*

4 Glow plug relay – removal and refitting

Removal

1 The relay is located on a bracket attached to the left-hand suspension turret in the engine compartment. On models with three relays mounted on the suspension turret, the glow plug relay is the centre of the three relays, and on models with two relays mounted on the suspension turret, the glow plug relay is the front of the two relays **(see illustration)**.

2 Disconnect the battery negative lead.

3 Unclip the relay from its mounting bracket, and disconnect the wiring plug from the relay.

Refitting

4 Refitting is a reversal of removal.

3.13 . . . then unscrew the glow plugs – cylinder head removed for clarity

4.1 Glow plug relay location (arrowed)

Chapter 6
Clutch

Contents

Degrees of difficulty

Easy, suitable for novice with little experience	Fairly easy, suitable for beginner with some experience	Fairly difficult, suitable for competent DIY mechanic	Difficult, suitable for experienced DIY mechanic	Very difficult, suitable for expert DIY or professional 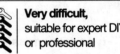

Specifications

Friction disc

Diameter:

1.1, 1.4, and 1.6 litre petrol engine models	200 mm
1.8 litre petrol engine models	215 mm
Diesel engine models:	
Models without intercooler	215 mm
Models with intercooler	228 mm
Minimum friction material thickness	1.5 mm
Minimum rivet head depth below surface of friction material	0.1 mm

Pressure plate

Maximum surface distortion	0.2 mm

Torque wrench settings

	Nm	lbf ft
Clutch cover-to-flywheel bolts:		
1.1, 1.4 and 1.6 litre petrol engine models	18	13
1.8 litre petrol engine models	26	19
Diesel engine models	26	19
Clutch release fork-to-shaft bolt ("PG1"-type transmission)	29	21

6

1 General information

The clutch is of single dry plate type, and consists of five main components: friction disc, pressure plate, diaphragm spring, cover and release bearing.

The friction disc is free to slide along the splines of the transmission input shaft. The friction disc is held in position between the flywheel and the pressure plate by the pressure exerted on the pressure plate by the diaphragm spring. Friction lining material is riveted to both sides of the friction disc.

Spring cushioning between the friction linings and the hub absorbs transmission shocks, and helps to ensure a smooth take-up of power as the clutch is engaged.

The diaphragm spring is mounted on pins, and is held in place in the cover by annular fulcrum rings.

The release bearing is located on a guide sleeve at the front of the transmission. The bearing is free to slide on the sleeve, under the action of the release arm that pivots inside the clutch bellhousing.

The release arm is operated by the clutch pedal, by means of a cable.

When the clutch pedal is depressed, the release arm is actuated by means of the cable. The release arm pushes the release

bearing forwards, to bear against the centre of the diaphragm spring, thus pushing the centre of the diaphragm spring inwards. The diaphragm spring acts against the fulcrum rings in the cover. When the centre of the spring is pushed in, the outside of the spring is pushed out, so allowing the pressure plate to move backwards away from the friction disc.

When the clutch pedal is released, the diaphragm spring forces the pressure plate into contact with the friction linings on the friction disc. This simultaneously pushes the friction disc forwards on its splines, forcing it against the flywheel. The friction disc is now firmly sandwiched between the pressure plate and the flywheel, and drive is taken up.

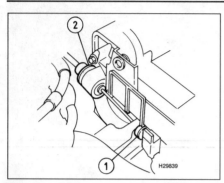

2.2 Slide the end of the clutch cable from the release lever (1) and release the cable sheath grommet from the bracket (2) on the transmission

2.7 Unhook the end of the clutch cable (arrowed) from the pedal

2.12 Push the bush on the cable fully into the bulkhead tube until the steel washer (arrowed) seats on the tube

2 Clutch cable – removal and refitting

"R65"-type transmission

Removal

1 Remove the air cleaner as described in Chapter 4A.

2 Working in the engine compartment, slide the clutch cable end fitting from the clutch release lever on the top of the transmission **(see illustration)**.

3 Release the cable sheath grommet from the bracket on the transmission **(see illustration 2.2)**.

4 On right-hand-drive models, release the cable from the support bracket.

5 Working in the driver's footwell, release the three securing clips, and remove the fusebox cover.

6 Release the securing clips, and remove the driver's side lower facia trim panel.

7 Reach up behind the facia, and unhook the end of the clutch cable from the top of the pedal **(see illustration)**.

8 Working in the engine compartment, pull the cable through the bulkhead into the engine compartment.

9 Note the cable routing, then release the

cable from any remaining clips and brackets, and withdraw it from the vehicle.

Refitting

10 Commence refitting by lubricating the cable bulkhead bush with rubber grease.

11 Route the cable through the engine compartment, and through the bulkhead, as noted before removal.

12 Working in the driver's footwell, reconnect the cable to the top of the clutch pedal, then push the rubber bush on the cable fully into the bulkhead tube until the steel washer on the cable seats on the tube **(see illustration)**.

13 Further refitting is a reversal of removal but, on completion, pull the clutch release lever on the transmission through its full range of movement, then release it to set the cable self-adjustment mechanism.

"PG1"-type transmission

Removal

14 Remove the air cleaner as described in Chapter 4.

15 Apply the handbrake, then jack up the front of the vehicle and support securely on axle stands (see *"Jacking and Vehicle Support"*).

16 Working in the engine compartment, slide the clutch cable end fitting from the clutch release lever on the transmission **(see illustration)**.

17 Release the cable sheath grommet from the bracket on the transmission **(see illustration)**.

18 On right-hand-drive models, release the cable from the clip attached to the coolant hose.

19 Proceed as described in paragraphs 5 to 9.

Refitting

20 Proceed as described in paragraphs 10 to 13.

3 Clutch pedal – removal and refitting

Removal

1 Working in the driver's footwell, release the three securing clips, and remove the fusebox cover.

2 Release the securing clips, and remove the driver's side lower facia trim panel.

3 Unhook the end of the clutch cable from the top of the pedal.

4 Unscrew the pedal retaining nut from the left-hand end of the pedal pivot shaft, then slide the pedal from the pivot shaft, releasing the return spring from the pedal as it is removed – take care as a powerful return spring is fitted **(see illustrations)**.

2.16 Slide the clutch cable end fitting from the release lever on the transmission . . .

2.17 . . . then release the cable sheath grommet from the bracket – "PG1"-type transmission

3.4a Unscrew the clutch pedal retaining nut (arrowed) . . .

3.4b . . . then release the return spring (arrowed) from the pedal

4.4a Withdraw the clutch cover . . .

4.4b . . . and the friction disc

Refitting

5 Refitting is a reversal of removal, but ensure that the pedal return spring is securely reconnected to the pedal, and tighten the pedal retaining nut securely.

4 Clutch assembly – removal, inspection and refitting

> **Warning: Dust created by clutch wear and deposited on the clutch components may contain asbestos, which is a health hazard. DO NOT blow it out with compressed air, or inhale any of it. DO NOT use petrol (or petroleum-based solvents) to clean off the dust. Brake system cleaner or methylated spirit should be used to flush the dust into a suitable receptacle. After the clutch components are wiped clean with rags, dispose of the contaminated rags and cleaner in a sealed, marked container.**

Removal

1 Remove the transmission, as described in Chapter 7A.

2 If the original clutch is to be refitted, make alignment marks between the clutch cover and the flywheel, so that the clutch can be refitted in its original position.

3 Progressively unscrew the bolts securing the clutch cover to the flywheel.

4 Withdraw the clutch cover from the flywheel. Be prepared to catch the clutch friction disc, which may drop out of the cover as it is withdrawn, and note which way round the friction disc is fitted - the side of the disc facing the flywheel is normally marked "Flywheel side" **(see illustrations).**

Inspection

5 With the clutch assembly removed, clean off all traces of dust using a dry cloth. Although most friction discs now have asbestos-free linings, some do not, and it is wise to take suitable precautions.

> **Warning: Asbestos dust is harmful, and must not be inhaled.**

6 Examine the linings of the friction disc for wear and loose rivets, and the disc for distortion, cracks, broken damping springs (where applicable) and worn splines. The surface of the friction linings may be highly glazed, but, as long as the friction material pattern can be clearly seen, this is satisfactory. If there is any sign of oil contamination, indicated by a continuous, or patchy, shiny black discolouration, the disc must be renewed. The source of the contamination must be traced and rectified before fitting new clutch components; typically, a leaking crankshaft rear oil seal or transmission input shaft oil seal - or both - will be to blame (renewal procedures are given in the relevant Part of Chapter 2, and Chapter 7A respectively). The disc must also be renewed if the lining thickness has worn down to, or just above, the level of the rivet heads.

7 Check the machined faces of the flywheel and pressure plate. If either is grooved, or heavily scored, renewal is necessary. The pressure plate must also be renewed if any cracks are apparent, or if the diaphragm spring is damaged or its pressure suspect.

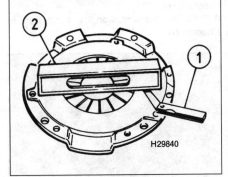

4.7 Checking the surface of the pressure plate for flatness using a straight-edge and feeler blades

1 *Feeler blades*
2 *Straight-edge*

Check the surface of the pressure plate for flatness using a straight edge and feeler blades – renew the pressure plate if the distortion exceeds the specified limit **(see illustration).**

8 With the clutch removed, it is advisable to check the condition of the release bearing, as described in Section 5.

Refitting

9 If new clutch components are to be fitted, where applicable, ensure that all anti-corrosion preservative is cleaned from the friction material on the disc, and the contact surfaces of the pressure plate.

10 It is important to ensure that no oil or grease gets onto the friction disc linings, or the pressure plate and flywheel faces. It is advisable to refit the clutch assembly with clean hands, and to wipe down the pressure plate and flywheel faces with a clean rag before assembly begins.

11 Apply a smear of molybdenum disulphide grease to the splines of the friction disc hub, then offer the disc to the flywheel, with the "Flywheel side" marking facing the flywheel **(see illustration).** Hold the friction disc against the flywheel while the cover/pressure plate assembly is offered into position.

12 Fit the clutch cover assembly, where applicable aligning the marks on the flywheel and clutch cover. Ensure that the clutch cover locates over the dowels on the flywheel **(see**

4.11 Check for markings (circled) on the friction disc which should face the flywheel

6

4.12 Ensure that the clutch cover locates over the dowels (arrowed) on the flywheel

4.14 Using a clutch alignment tool to centralise the friction disc

5.2 Removing the clutch release bearing – "R65"-type transmission shown

illustration). Insert the securing bolts and washers, and tighten them finger-tight, so that the friction disc is gripped, but can still be moved.

13 The friction disc must now be centralised, so that when the engine and transmission are mated, the transmission input shaft splines will pass through the splines in the friction disc hub.

14 Centralisation can be carried out by inserting a round bar or a long screwdriver through the hole in the centre of the friction disc, so that the end of the bar rests in the spigot bearing in the centre of the crankshaft. Where possible, use a blunt instrument, but if a screwdriver is used, wrap tape around the blade to prevent damage to the bearing surface. Moving the bar sideways or up and down as necessary, move the friction disc in whichever direction is necessary to achieve centralisation. With the bar removed, view the friction disc hub in relation to the hole in the centre of the crankshaft and the circle created by the ends of the diaphragm spring fingers. When the hub appears exactly in the centre, all is correct. Alternatively, if a suitable clutch alignment tool can be obtained, this will eliminate all the guesswork, and obviate the need for visual alignment **(see illustration)**.

15 Tighten the cover retaining bolts gradually in a diagonal sequence, to the specified torque. Remove the alignment tool.

16 Refit the transmission as described in Chapter 7A.

5 Clutch release components – removal, inspection and refitting

Release bearing

Removal

1 Remove the transmission, as described in Chapter 7A.

2 Disengage the bearing from the release fork, then pull the bearing forwards, and slide it from the guide sleeve in the transmission bellhousing **(see illustration)**.

Inspection

3 Spin the release bearing, and check it for excessive roughness. Hold the outer race, and attempt to move it laterally against the inner race. If any excessive movement or roughness is evident, renew the bearing. If a new clutch has been fitted, it is wise to renew the release bearing as a matter of course.

Refitting

4 Clean and then lightly grease the release bearing contact surfaces on the release fork. Similarly, lightly grease the guide sleeve.

5 Slide the bearing into position on the guide sleeve, then engage the bearing with the release lever.

6 Refit the transmission as described in Chapter 7A.

Release fork and lever – "R65"-type transmission

Note: A new release lever securing roll-pin will be required on refitting.

Removal

7 Remove the release bearing, as described previously in this Section.

8 Using a suitable pin-punch, drive out the roll-pin securing the release lever to the release fork shaft, then slide the release lever from the shaft **(see illustration)**.

9 Slide the release fork shaft upwards, and remove the shaft bushes from the transmission casing **(see illustration)**.

10 Withdraw the release fork shaft from the transmission.

Inspection

11 Inspect the release bearing contact faces, and the pivot faces on the release fork and shaft for wear. Renew if excessive wear is evident.

12 Examine the pivot bushes, and renew if necessary.

Refitting

13 Clean the components thoroughly, then smear the release fork shaft with a little molybdenum disulphide grease.

14 Slide the release fork shaft into position in the transmission, then fit the bushes, ensuring that the locating tags on the bushes engage with the slots in the transmission casing **(see illustration)**.

5.8 Driving out the roll-pin securing the release lever – "R65"-type transmission

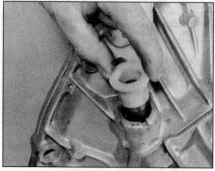

5.9 Removing a release fork shaft pivot bush – "R65"-type transmission

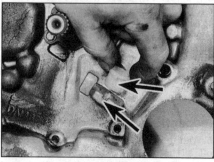

5.14 Align the pivot bush locating tags with the slots in the transmission casing (arrowed)

5.19 Removing the clutch release lever shaft – "PG1"-type transmission

5.27 Refitting the clutch release fork – "PG1"-type transmission

5.29 Refitting the clutch release bearing – "PG1"-type transmission

15 Slide the release fork shaft into position, then fit the release lever to the shaft, noting that the lever faces away from the clutch housing, and secure with a new roll-pin.

16 Refit the release bearing as described previously in this Section.

Release fork and lever – "PG1"-type transmission

Removal

17 Remove the release bearing, as described previously in this Section.

18 Unscrew the bolt (and recover the washer) securing the release fork to the release lever shaft

19 Slide the release lever shaft from the transmission, and withdraw the release fork **(see illustration)**.

Inspection

20 Inspect the release bearing contact faces, and the pivot faces on the release fork and shaft for wear. Renew if excessive wear is evident.

21 Examine the release lever shaft oil seal (located on top of the top pivot bush), and renew if necessary.

22 Examine the pivot bushes in the transmission casing for wear. If necessary the bushes can be renewed, as follows.

23 Carefully prise the lower bush from the transmission casing.

24 To remove the upper bush, carefully cut a longitudinal slot in the inner face of the bush, opposite the split in the bush, then prise the bush from the transmission casing.

25 Carefully drive the new bushes into position in the casing, using a suitable metal

tube or socket (take care not to distort the bushes during fitting).

Refitting

26 Clean the components thoroughly, then smear the release fork shaft with a little molybdenum disulphide grease.

27 Position the release fork in the transmission casing, noting that the securing bolt fits from the front, then slide the release lever shaft into position, passing it through the fork **(see illustration)**. Note that the release lever faces away from the clutch housing.

28 Align the holes in the release fork and shaft, then refit the fork securing bolt, ensuring that the washer is in place, and tighten to the specified torque.

29 Refit the release bearing as described previously in this Section **(see illustration)**.

6

Notes

Chapter 7 Part A:
Manual transmission

Contents

Degrees of difficulty

Easy, suitable for novice with little experience	**Fairly easy,** suitable for beginner with some experience	**Fairly difficult,** suitable for competent DIY mechanic	**Difficult,** suitable for experienced DIY mechanic	**Very difficult,** suitable for expert DIY or professional 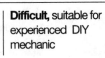

Specifications

General

Type . . . . Manual, five forward speeds and reverse. Synchromesh on all forward speeds

Designation:
  1.1, 1.4 and 1.6 litre petrol engine models . . . . Rover "R65"
  1.8 litre petrol engine models and diesel engine models . . . . Rover "PG1"

Gear ratios:
  "R65"-type transmission:
    1st 3.417:1
    2nd 1.947:1
    3rd 1.333:1
    4th 1.054:1
    5th 0.854:1
    Reverse 3.583:1
  "PG1"-type transmission:
    Petrol engine models:
      1st 3.167:1
      2nd 1.842:1
      3rd 1.308:1
      4th 1.033:1
      5th 0.765:1
      Reverse 3.000:1
    Diesel engine models:
      1st 3.250:1
      2nd 1.895:1
      3rd 1.222:1
      4th 0.848:1
      5th 0.648:1
      Reverse 3.000:1

Final drive ratio:
  1.1 litre petrol engines 4.200:1
  1.4 litre petrol engines 3.937:1
  1.6 litre petrol engines 3.765:1
  1.8 litre petrol engines 3.938:1
  Diesel engines 3.938:1

Lubrication

Recommended oil and capacity	See "Lubricants, fluids and capacities"	

Torque wrench settings	Nm	lbf ft
"R65"-type transmission		
Clutch release bearing guide sleeve bolts	5	7
Drain plug	25	18
Filler/level plug	25	18
Flywheel cover plate bolts	9	6
Gearchange selector rod rear mounting nuts	22	16
Reversing light switch	25	18
Transmission-to-engine bolts	85	63
"PG1"-type transmission		
Drain plug	45	33
Earth lead-to-transmission bolt	35	26
Filler/level plug	40	29
Flywheel front cover plate nuts and bolts (petrol engines)	80	59
Gearchange steady bar-to-transmission bolt	10	7
Reversing light switch	25	18
Transmission casing-to-differential housing bolt (for lifting bracket) . . .	27	20
Transmission-to-engine bolts	85	63

1 General information

The 5-speed transmission is contained in a casing bolted to the left-hand end of the engine.

Drive is transmitted from the crankshaft via the clutch to the input shaft, which has a splined extension to accept the clutch friction disc. The output shaft transmits the drive via the differential and driveshafts to the front wheels.

The input shaft runs in parallel with the output shaft. The input shaft and output shaft gears are in constant mesh, and selection of gears is by sliding synchromesh hubs, which lock the appropriate gears to the shafts.

Gear selection is via a floor-mounted lever and selector mechanism. The selector mechanism causes the appropriate selector fork to move its respective synchro-sleeve along the shaft, to lock the gear pinion to the synchro-hub. Since the synchro-hubs are splined to the gearshaft, this locks the pinion

to the shaft, so that drive can be transmitted. To ensure that gear-changing can be made quickly and quietly, a synchro-mesh system is fitted to all forward gears, consisting of baulk rings and spring-loaded fingers, as well as the gear pinions and synchro-hubs. The synchro-mesh cones are formed on the mating faces of the baulk rings and gear pinions.

2 Manual transmission oil – draining and refilling

Note: *New filler/level plug and drain plug sealing washers must be used when refitting the plugs.*

1 This operation is much quicker and more efficient if the car is first taken on a journey of sufficient length to warm the engine/transmission up to normal operating temperature.

2 Park the car on level ground, and switch off the ignition. To improve access during draining, apply the handbrake, then jack up the front of the car and support it securely on

axle stands (see *"Jacking and Vehicle Support"*). Note that the car must be lowered to the ground and level, to ensure accuracy, when refilling and checking the oil level.

3 Where applicable, remove the engine/transmission undershield to gain access to the filler/level and drain plugs.

4 Remove all traces of dirt from around the filler/level plug which is located on the left-hand side of the transmission, behind the driveshaft inboard joint. Unscrew the plug and recover the sealing washer **(see illustrations)**.

5 Position a suitable container under the drain plug which is also situated on the left-hand side of the transmission, below the driveshaft joint.

6 Unscrew the drain plug and allow the oil to drain into the container. If the oil is hot, take precautions against scalding. Clean both the filler/level plug and the drain plug, taking care to wipe any metallic particles off the magnetic inserts. Recover the sealing washers from the plugs, and discard them.

7 When the oil has finished draining, clean the drain plug threads in the transmission casing, fit a new sealing washer to the plug, and refit the drain plug. Tighten the plug to the specified torque. It the car was raised for the draining operation, now lower it to the ground.

8 Refilling the transmission is an awkward operation. Allow plenty of time for the oil level to settle properly before checking it. **Note:** *The car must be parked on flat level ground when checking the oil level.*

9 Using a tube inserted through the filler/level plug hole, slowly refill the transmission with the specified type of oil, until the level reaches the bottom of the filler/level plug hole. Allow plenty of time for the level to stabilise.

10 When the level is correct, refit the filler/level plug, using a new sealing washer, and tighten it to the specified torque.

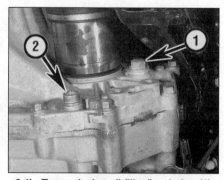

2.4a Transmission oil filler/level plug (1) and drain plug (2) locations – "R65"-type transmission

2.4b Transmission oil filler/level plug (1) and drain plug (2) locations – "PG1"-type transmission

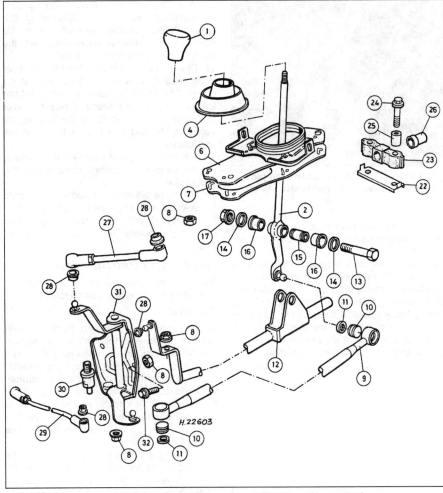

3.3 Gearchange linkage assembly – "R65"-type transmission

1 Gearchange lever knob	12 Control rod	25 Spacer
2 Gearchange lever	13 Pivot bolt	26 Bush
4 Rubber cover	14 Thrustwasher	27 Upper link rod
6 Mounting plate	15 Spacer	28 Dust cover
7 Seal	16 Bush	29 Lower link rod
8 Nut	17 Nut	30 Bucket joint
9 Selector rod	22 Mounting plate	31 Bellcrank assembly
10 Ball housing	23 Mounting rubber	32 Bolt
11 Rubber seal	24 Bolt	

3.4 Prising the gear selector rod from the balljoint on the gearchange lever

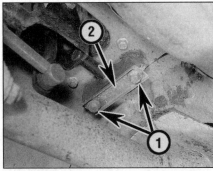

3.7 Unscrew the two bolts (1) and remove the retaining plate (2) securing the control rod mounting to the body – "R65"-type transmission

3 Gearchange linkage – removal, refitting and adjustment

"R65"-type transmission

Removal

1 Apply the handbrake, then jack up the front of the vehicle and support securely on axle stands (see *"Jacking and Vehicle Support"*).

2 Although not strictly necessary, access to the gearchange linkage can be improved if the exhaust front pipe is first removed, as described in Chapter 4A.

3 Using a large flat-bladed screwdriver, carefully prise the gear linkage rod balljoints from the gear selector levers on the transmission, taking care not to damage the balljoints or their gaiters **(see illustration)**. Make a note of the location of each linkage rod (to ensure correct refitting), note which way round they are fitted, then detach both rod balljoints from the bellcrank assembly and remove the rods from the vehicle.

4 Prise the gear selector rod from the balljoints on the gearchange lever and bellcrank assembly, and manoeuvre the selector rod out from underneath the vehicle **(see illustration)**.

5 Working inside the vehicle, remove the centre console as described in Chapter 11.

6 With the console removed, carefully peel the rubber gaiter from the base of the gearchange lever, and slide the gaiter up the lever to gain access to the control rod pivot bolt and nut. Unscrew the nut, and remove the pivot bolt and thrustwashers.

7 Working underneath the vehicle, unscrew the nut securing the front of the control rod to the bellcrank pivot, then unscrew the two bolts and remove the retaining plate securing the rear of the control rod mounting to the body **(see illustration)**. Remove the mounting assembly, taking care not to lose its spacers, then manoeuvre the control rod out from underneath the vehicle.

8 If necessary, slacken and remove the three mounting bolts and remove the bellcrank from the subframe.

9 If necessary, slacken and remove the gearchange lever housing retaining nuts and remove the seal, mounting plate and lever assembly from the vehicle.

10 Thoroughly clean all components and check them for wear or damage, renewing all worn or faulty items.

Refitting

11 Refitting is the reverse of the removal procedure, but check the linkage balljoints for wear and damage, and fit new components as necessary, and apply a smear of grease to all the linkage pivot points and balljoints.

Adjustment

12 If a stiff, sloppy or imprecise gearchange leads you to suspect that a fault exists within

7A

3.20a Remove the metal clip . . .

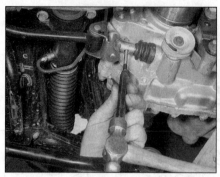

3.20b . . . then drive out the roll-pin securing the selector rod to the selector shaft

the linkage, first dismantle it completely and check for wear or damage, then reassemble it, applying a smear of the approved grease to all bearing surfaces.

13 If this does not cure the fault, the vehicle should be examined by an expert, as the fault must lie within the transmission itself. There is no adjustment as such in the linkage. While the length of the link rods can be altered, this is for initial setting-up only and is not intended to provide a form of compensation for wear.

14 If the link rods have been renewed, or the length of the originals is incorrect, adjust them as follows.

15 Ensure that the vehicle is parked on level ground, with the ignition switched off, the handbrake firmly applied and neutral selected. Remembering that the selector mechanism is spring-loaded so that the gearchange lever rests naturally between the third and fourth gear positions, have an assistant hold the gearchange lever in its normal position.

16 Working in (or under) the engine compartment, slacken the locknut at the bellcrank end of the relevant rod to be adjusted. If not already done, disconnect the rod from the transmission selector lever.

17 Check that the transmission selector lever concerned is in its neutral position, with no signs of free play or damage, then hold the link rod end socket over the selector lever ball, and alter the length of the link rod by screwing the rod end socket in or out (as applicable).

18 When the length of the link rod is correct, tighten the locknut securely whilst holding the end socket.

19 Press the link rod end socket firmly onto the selector lever and check that all gears can be selected, with the gearchange lever returning properly to its correct at-rest position.

"PG1"-type transmission

Note: *A new gear selector rod-to-selector shaft roll-pin will be required on refitting.*

Removal

20 Remove the metal clip from the gear selector rod-to-selector shaft joint to expose the roll-pin, then drive out the roll-pin using a suitable pin punch, and release the selector rod from the selector shaft **(see illustrations)**.

21 Unscrew and remove the nut and pivot bolt securing the selector rod to the base of the gearchange lever, and remove the selector rod from the vehicle **(see illustration)**.

22 Working inside the vehicle, remove the centre console as described in Chapter 11, then release the gearchange lever rubber gaiter from the housing and slide it up the lever.

23 Working underneath the vehicle, unscrew and remove the bolts and retaining plate securing the gearchange steady rod rear mounting to the body. Remove the mounting rubber from the steady rod, taking care not to lose its spacers.

24 Unscrew and remove the bolt securing the gearchange steady rod to the transmission, and recover the washers **(see illustrations)**. Manoeuvre the steady rod and

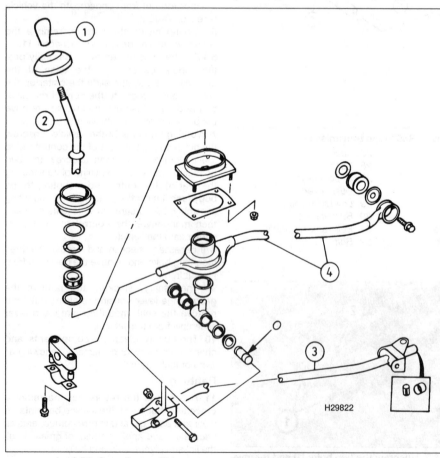

3.21 Gearchange linkage assembly – "PG1"-type transmission

1 *Gearchange lever knob*
2 *Gearchange lever*
3 *Gear selector rod*
4 *Gearchange steady rod*

3.24a Unscrew the bolt securing the gearchange steady rod to the transmission . . .

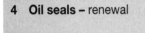

3.24b . . . and recover the washers

gearchange lever assembly out from underneath the vehicle - if necessary, the two can then be separated.

25 If necessary, slacken and remove the retaining nuts and remove the gearchange lever plate assembly and seal.

26 Thoroughly clean all components and check them for wear and damage, renewing components if necessary.

Refitting

27 Refitting is a reversal of the removal, but use a new roll-pin to secure the gear selector rod to the selector shaft, and apply a smear of grease to all the linkage pivot points.

Adjustment

28 No adjustment of the gearchange linkage is possible.

4 Oil seals – renewal

Driveshaft oil seals

Note: *Ensure that the correct type of new oil seal is obtained. Later transmissions use a modified seal, which cannot be fitted to earlier-type transmissions – refer to a Rover dealer for details.*

1 Apply the handbrake, then jack up the front of the car and support it securely on axle stands (see *"Jacking and Vehicle Support"*). Remove the appropriate front roadwheel.

2 Drain the transmission oil as described in Section 2, or be prepared for some oil loss as the driveshaft is removed.

3 Free the inboard end of the driveshaft from the transmission, as described in Chapter 8, and move it clear of the seal. Note that there is no need to disconnect the outboard end of the driveshaft from the hub. Support the driveshaft using wire or string, to avoid placing any strain on the driveshaft joints or gaiters.

4 Carefully prise the oil seal from the transmission using a large flat-bladed screwdriver **(see illustration)**.

5 Remove all traces of dirt from the area around the oil seal aperture, then apply a smear of grease to the outer lip of the new oil seal.

6 Ensure that the seal is correctly positioned, with its sealing lip facing inwards, and drive it squarely into position, using a suitable tubular drift (such as a socket) which bears only on the hard outer edge of the seal **(see illustration)**. Ensure that the seal is seated correctly in the transmission recess.

7 Reconnect the inboard end of the driveshaft as described in Chapter 8.

8 Refill/top-up the transmission with the specified type of oil, and check the oil level as described in Section 2 and/or Chapter 1, as applicable.

Input shaft oil seal

"R65"-type transmission

Note: *New release bearing guide sleeve securing bolts will be required on refitting.*

9 Remove the transmission, as described in Section 7, and remove the clutch release bearing (see Chapter 6).

10 Unscrew the three bolts securing the clutch release bearing guide sleeve to the transmission, and slide the guide sleeve off the input shaft **(see illustration)**. Discard the bolts, as they must be renewed whenever they are disturbed.

11 Carefully lever the oil seal out of the guide sleeve, using a suitable flat-bladed screwdriver.

12 Before fitting a new seal, check the seal rubbing surface on the input shaft for signs of

burrs, scratches or other damage which may have caused the seal to fail in the first place. It may be possible to polish away minor faults of this sort using fine abrasive paper, however, more serious defects will require the renewal of the input shaft.

13 Remove all traces of thread locking compound from the guide sleeve bolt holes (Rover recommend the use of Loctite Chisel and a suitable tap) then degrease thoroughly. *Caution: Do not use petrol or paraffin to clean the components.*

14 Dip the new seal in clean transmission oil, and fit it to the rear of the guide sleeve, making sure that its sealing lip is facing outwards.

15 Carefully slide the guide sleeve into position, taking care not to damage the oil seal lips on the input shaft splines. Fit the **new** retaining bolts and tighten them to the specified torque setting.

16 Refit the release bearing with reference to Chapter 6, then refit the transmission as described in Section 7.

"PG1"-type transmission

17 To renew the input shaft oil seal, the transmission must be dismantled. This task should therefore be entrusted to a Rover dealer or transmission specialist.

Gearchange selector shaft oil seal

"R65"-type transmission

Note: *A new selector lever-to-shaft roll-pin will be required on refitting.*

18 Access to the selector shaft seal is greatly improved with the transmission removed. If the transmission is fitted to the vehicle, proceed as follows. If the transmission has been removed, proceed to paragraph 22.

19 Apply the handbrake, then jack up the front of the vehicle and support securely on axle stands (see *"Jacking and Vehicle Support"*). Remove the left-hand front roadwheel.

20 Remove the left-hand engine/transmission mounting as described in Chapter 2A.

21 Using a large flat-bladed screwdriver,

7A

4.4 Levering out a driveshaft oil seal – "R65"-type transmission shown

4.6 Fitting a driveshaft oil seal using a socket – "R65"-type transmission shown

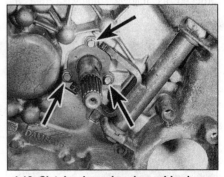

4.10 Clutch release bearing guide sleeve securing bolts (arrowed) – "R65"-type transmission

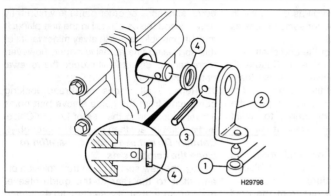

4.22 Gearchange selector shaft oil seal fitting details – "R65"-type transmission

1 Link rod   2 Selector lever   3 Roll-pin   4 Oil seal

4.32 Gearchange selector shaft oil seal renewal – "PG1"-type transmission

1 Gearchange steady bar securing bolt
3 Roll-pin
2 Metal clip
4 Selector rod

carefully prise the gear linkage rod balljoint from the gear selector lever on the transmission, taking care not to damage the balljoint or its gaiter.

22 Using a suitable punch, and if necessary extension pieces, drive out the roll-pin securing the selector lever to the shaft **(see illustration)**. Access is extremely difficult. Discard the roll-pin.

23 Lower the engine/transmission assembly slightly until the selector lever can be withdrawn from the shaft.

24 Carefully lever the seal from the transmission, taking great care not to damage the shaft or casing.

25 Before fitting a new seal, check the seal rubbing surface on the selector shaft for signs of burrs, scratches or other damage which may have caused the seal to fail in the first place. It may be possible to polish away minor faults of this sort using fine abrasive paper, however, more serious defects will require the renewal of the shaft.

26 Lubricate the new seal with a smear of clean transmission oil, then ease the seal into position. Press the seal squarely into position, using a socket which bears only on the hard outer edge of the seal, ensuring that the seal lip faces inwards.

27 Refit the selector lever to the shaft, and secure it in position with a new roll-pin.

28 If the transmission is fitted to the vehicle, proceed as follows, otherwise refit the transmission.

a) Press the gear linkage rod balljoint into position on the selector lever.
b) Refit the left-hand engine/transmission mounting as described in Chapter 2A, then refit the roadwheel and lower the vehicle to the ground.

"PG1"-type transmission

29 Apply the handbrake, then jack up the front of the vehicle and support it securely on axle stands (see *"Jacking and Vehicle Support"*).

30 Drain the transmission oil as described in Section 2, or be prepared for fluid loss as the seal is removed.

31 Unscrew the bolt securing the gearchange steady bar to the transmission. Recover the two washers.

32 Remove the metal clip from the gear selector rod-to-selector shaft joint to expose the roll-pin **(see illustration)**.

33 Drive out the roll-pin using a suitable pin punch, then release the selector rod from the selector shaft, and move the rod and the gearchange steady bar to one side.

34 If the transmission oil has not been drained, have a container ready to catch escaping oil, then slide the gaiter from the selector shaft, and carefully prise out the oil seal **(see illustrations)**.

35 Before fitting a new seal, check the seal rubbing surface on the selector shaft for signs of burrs, scratches or other damage which may have caused the seal to fail in the first place. It may be possible to polish away minor

faults of this sort using fine abrasive paper, however, more serious defects will require the renewal of the selector shaft.

36 Lubricate the new seal with clean transmission oil, and ease it over the end of the selector shaft. Press the seal squarely into the transmission housing using a tube (such as a socket) which bears only on the hard outer edge of the seal.

37 Slide the gaiter onto the shaft, ensuring that the lip on the gaiter engages with the oil seal.

38 Slide the selector rod onto the shaft, and secure using a new roll-pin. Refit the metal clip over the selector shaft and roll-pin.

39 Refit the bolt securing the gearchange steady bar to the transmission, ensuring that the washers are in place, then tighten the bolt to the specified torque.

40 Lower the vehicle to the ground, then refill/top-up the transmission with the specified type of oil and check the oil level as described in Section 2 and/or Chapter 1, as applicable.

5 Reversing light switch – testing, removal and refitting

Testing

1 The reversing light circuit is controlled by a plunger-type switch, located in the top of the transmission casing on "R65"-type transmissions, or in the side of the transmission casing on "PG1"-type transmissions. If a fault develops in the circuit, first ensure that the circuit fuse has not blown.

2 To test the switch, first disconnect the wiring connector. Use a multimeter (set to the resistance function), or a battery-and-bulb test circuit, to check that there is continuity between the switch terminals only when reverse gear is selected. If this is not the case, and there are no obvious breaks or other damage to the wires, the switch is faulty, and must be renewed.

"R65"-type transmission

Note: *A new sealing washer will be required on refitting.*

4.34a Slide the gaiter from the selector shaft . . .

4.34b . . . and carefully prise out the oil seal

Removal

3 Disconnect the battery negative lead.
4 To improve access to the switch, remove the air cleaner assembly as described in Chapter 4A.
5 Disconnect the switch wiring connector, then unscrew the switch, and remove it from the top of the transmission **(see illustration)**. Recover the sealing washer and discard it.

Refitting

6 Refitting is a reversal of removal, but use a new sealing washer, and tighten the switch to the specified torque setting.

"PG1"-type transmission

Note: *A new sealing washer will be required on refitting.*

Removal

7 The switch is located in the front of the transmission casing **(see illustration)**. Disconnect the battery negative lead.
8 Apply the handbrake, then jack up the front of the vehicle and support it securely on axle stands (see *"Jacking and Vehicle Support"*). Where necessary, remove the engine/transmission undershield to gain access to the switch.
9 Trace the wiring back from the switch, freeing it from any relevant retaining clips, and separate the two halves of the wiring connector(s).

Caution: Be prepared for possible oil loss when the switch is removed, and have ready a suitable plug to plug the aperture in the transmission whilst the switch is removed.

10 Wipe clean the area around the switch then unscrew the switch. Recover and discard the sealing washer. If necessary, plug the switch aperture to minimise oil loss.

Refitting

11 Refitting is a reversal of removal, but use a new sealing washer, and tighten the switch to the specified torque setting. If oil was lost during the removal procedure, check the transmission oil level and top up if necessary as described in Chapter 1.

5.5 Disconnecting the reversing light switch – "R65"-type transmission

6 Speedometer drive – removal and refitting

Removal

Note: *A new speedometer drive O-ring will be required on refitting.*

1 All models are fitted with an electrically-operated speedometer, which uses a signal provided by the vehicle speed sensor, mounted on the top of the transmission housing, next to the inboard end of the right-hand driveshaft **(see illustration)**.
2 Disconnect the battery negative lead.
3 To gain access to the speedometer sensor, apply the handbrake then jack up the front of the vehicle and support it securely on axle stands (see *"Jacking and Vehicle Support"*).
4 Disconnect the wiring connector from the vehicle speed sensor then unscrew the sensor securing nut, and remove the sensor from the top of the speedometer drive assembly **(see illustration)**.
5 Slacken and remove the retaining bolt, and withdraw the speedometer drive assembly from the transmission housing, along with its O-ring **(see illustration)**.

Refitting

6 Lubricate a new O-ring with a smear of clean transmission oil, then fit the O-ring to the speedometer drive housing.

5.7 Reversing light switch location – "PG1"-type transmission (transmission removed)

7 Ease the speedometer drive assembly into position in the transmission, ensuring that the drive and driven pinions are correctly engaged. Refit and tighten the retaining bolt.
8 Fit the speed sensor to the top of the drive assembly, ensuring that the sensor drive pin is correctly engaged with the pinion, and securely tighten the sensor securing nut.
9 Reconnect the wiring connector to the speed sensor then lower the vehicle to the ground, and reconnect the battery negative lead.

7 Manual transmission – removal and refitting

1.1, 1.4 and 1.6 litre petrol engine models

Removal

1 Disconnect the battery negative lead.
2 Apply the handbrake, then jack up the front of the vehicle and support it securely on axle stands (see *"Jacking and Vehicle Support"*).
3 Remove the vehicle speed sensor, with reference to Section 6.
4 Remove the starter motor as described in Chapter 5A.
5 Remove the engine control module (ECM) and the engine management relay module, as described in Chapter 4A.
6 Unscrew the two bolts securing the air

7A

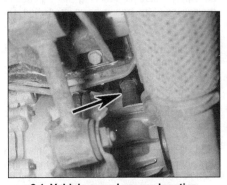
6.1 Vehicle speed sensor location (arrowed) – "R65"-type transmission

6.4 Removing the vehicle speed sensor – "PG1"-type transmission

6.5 Removing the speedometer drive assembly – "PG1"-type transmission

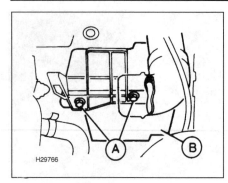

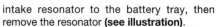

7.6 Unscrew the two bolts (A) and remove the air intake resonator (B) – 1.1, 1.4 and 1.6 l petrol models

7.14 Removing the flywheel rear cover plate – 1.1, 1.4 and 1.6 l petrol models

7.18 Unscrew the three securing bolts and remove the flywheel lower cover plate – 1.1, 1.4 and 1.6 l petrol models

intake resonator to the battery tray, then remove the resonator **(see illustration)**.

7 Remove the battery, with reference to Chapter 5A if necessary.

8 Unscrew the two bolts securing the engine compartment fusebox to the body, and move the fusebox to one side.

9 Unscrew the four upper bolts and the three lower bolts securing the battery tray, then remove the battery tray.

10 Disconnect the clutch cable from the clutch release lever, with reference to Chapter 6 if necessary, then release the cable from the transmission brackets, and move the cable to one side.

11 Disconnect the wiring plug from the reversing light switch.

12 Using a large flat-bladed screwdriver, carefully prise the gear linkage rod balljoints from the gear selector levers on the transmission, taking care not to damage the balljoints or their gaiters. Move the gear linkage rods to one side, clear of the transmission.

13 Unscrew the two bolts securing the clutch cable bracket to the transmission bellhousing, then remove the bracket.

14 Unscrew the bolt securing the flywheel rear cover plate to the bellhousing, and remove the cover plate **(see illustration)**.

15 Drain the transmission oil, as described in Section 2.

16 Disconnect the inboard ends of the driveshafts from the transmission, as

described in Chapter 8. Note that there is no need to disconnect the outboard ends of the driveshafts from the hubs. Support the driveshafts using wire or string, to avoid placing any strain on the driveshaft joints or gaiters.

17 Remove the left-hand front suspension tie-rod, as described in Chapter 10.

18 Unscrew the three securing bolts, and remove the flywheel lower cover plate **(see illustration)**.

19 Release the two clips securing the starter motor wiring to the flywheel front cover plate, then unscrew three securing bolts, and remove the front cover plate **(see illustration)**.

20 Working under the vehicle, slacken the through-bolt securing the engine/transmission steady bar to the subframe, then unscrew the bolt securing the steady bar to transmission, and move the steady bar clear of the transmission.

21 Fit a suitable lifting eye to the hole provided in the top of the transmission casing, then connect a hoist and lifting tackle to the lifting eye, and raise the hoist to just take the weight of the engine/transmission assembly **(see illustration)**.

22 Remove the left-hand engine/ transmission mounting as described in Chapter 2A.

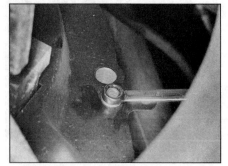

7.19 Unscrewing a flywheel front cover plate bolt – 1.1, 1.4 and 1.6 l petrol models

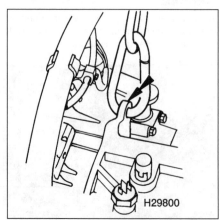

7.21 Fit a suitable lifting eye to the hole provided in the transmission casing – 1.1, 1.4 and 1.6 l petrol models

23 If not already done, position a hydraulic jack under the engine sump, with a block of wood between the jack head and sump to spread the load.

24 On models with air conditioning, unscrew the bolts securing the air conditioning refrigerant pipe to the support bracket, then unscrew the two bolts securing the support bracket to the engine and transmission.

25 Make sure that the engine and transmission are adequately supported, then unscrew the two upper engine-to-transmission bolts.

26 Unscrew the two lower engine-to-transmission bolts then, with the aid of an assistant, carefully pull the transmission from the engine (the transmission locates on dowels in the engine), ensuring that the weight of the transmission is not allowed to hang on the input shaft while it is engaged with the clutch friction disc. It may be necessary to rock the transmission gently to release it from the engine. Take care not to damage any of the surrounding components in the engine compartment.

27 Carefully lower the transmission to the ground, then disconnect the lifting tackle, and withdraw the transmission from under the front of the vehicle.

Refitting

28 Commence refitting by checking that the clutch friction disc is centralised as described in Chapter 6.

29 Apply a little high melting-point grease to the splines of the transmission input shaft. Do not apply too much, as this may contaminate the clutch.

30 Position the transmission under the front of the vehicle, then reconnect the lifting tackle, and lift the transmission into position in the engine compartment.

31 Ensure that the locating dowels are in place in the engine, then carefully offer the transmission to the engine, until the locating dowels are engaged, ensuring that the weight of the transmission is not allowed to hang on the input shaft as it is engaged with the clutch friction disc.

32 Refit the engine-to-transmission bolts, and tighten them to the specified torque.

33 Further refitting is a reversal of removal, bearing in mind the following points:

a) *Tighten all fixings to the specified torque, where applicable.*

b) *Refit the left-hand engine/transmission mounting as described in Chapter 2A.*

c) *Refit the left-hand front suspension tie-rod as described in Chapter 10.*

d) *Reconnect the driveshafts to the transmission as described in Chapter 8.*

e) *Refit the starter motor as described in Chapter 5A.*

f) *Refit the vehicle speed sensor, with reference to Section 6.*

g) *On completion, refill the transmission with oil as described in Section 2.*

1.8 litre petrol engine models

Note: *A new gear selector rod-to-selector shaft roll-pin will be required on refitting.*

Removal

34 Disconnect the battery negative lead.

35 Apply the handbrake, then jack up the front of the vehicle and support it securely on axle stands (see *"Jacking and Vehicle Support"*).

36 Proceed as described in paragraphs 4 to 8.

37 Where applicable, release the ABS fuseholder from the battery tray, then unscrew the four upper bolts and the three lower bolts securing the battery tray, and remove the battery tray.

38 Disconnect the clutch cable from the clutch release lever, with reference to Chapter 6 if necessary, then release the cable from the transmission bracket, and move the cable to one side.

39 Unscrew the bolts securing the earth lead to the transmission.

40 Trace the wiring back from the reversing light switch, locate the wiring connector(s), and separate the two halves of the wiring connector(s).

41 Disconnect the exhaust front pipe from the manifold as described in Chapter 4A.

42 Unscrew the bolt securing the gearchange steady bar to the transmission. Recover the two washers.

43 Remove the metal clip from the gear selector rod-to-selector shaft joint to expose the roll-pin **(see illustration 4.32)**.

44 Drive out the roll-pin using a suitable pin punch, then release the selector rod from the selector shaft, and suspend the rod and the gearchange steady bar clear of the working area.

45 Disconnect the inboard ends of the driveshafts from the transmission, as described in Chapter 8. Note that there is no need to disconnect the outboard ends of the driveshafts from the hubs. Support the driveshafts using wire or string, to avoid placing any strain on the driveshaft joints or gaiters.

46 Remove the left-hand front suspension tie-rod, as described in Chapter 10.

47 Disconnect the wiring plug from the vehicle speed sensor.

48 On models with air conditioning, unscrew the bolt securing the air conditioning refrigerant pipe to the bracket on the transmission.

49 If not already done, position a hydraulic jack under the engine sump, with a block of wood between the jack head and sump to spread the load.

50 Remove the left-hand engine/transmission mounting as described in Chapter 2A or 2B, as applicable.

51 Lower the engine/transmission assembly slightly, then unscrew the two bolts securing the left-hand engine/transmission mounting bracket to the transmission.

52 Unscrew the centre upper transmission casing-to-differential housing bolt, then bolt a suitable lifting bracket to the transmission, by refitting and tightening the bolt **(see illustration)**.

53 Connect a hoist and lifting tackle to the lifting eye, and raise the hoist to just take the weight of the engine/transmission assembly.

54 Make sure that the engine and transmission are adequately supported, then unscrew the two upper engine-to-transmission bolts, and remove the mounting bracket.

55 Unscrew the two lower engine-to-transmission bolts.

56 Unscrew the bolt at the rear of the engine, securing the engine to the transmission **(see illustration)**.

57 Unscrew the two nuts and bolts securing the flywheel front cover plate, then remove the cover plate and unscrew the remaining engine-to-transmission nut and bolt **(see illustration)**.

58 With the aid of an assistant, carefully pull the transmission from the engine (the transmission locates on dowels in the mounting plate), ensuring that the weight of the transmission is not allowed to hang on the input shaft while it is engaged with the clutch friction disc. It may be necessary to rock the transmission gently to release it from the engine. Take care not to damage any of the surrounding components in the engine compartment.

59 Carefully lower the transmission to the ground, then disconnect the lifting tackle, and withdraw the transmission from under the front of the vehicle.

Refitting

60 Commence refitting by checking that the clutch friction disc is centralised as described in Chapter 6.

61 Apply a little high melting-point grease to the splines of the transmission input shaft. Do not apply too much, as this may contaminate the clutch.

62 Position the transmission under the front of the vehicle, then reconnect the lifting tackle, and lift the transmission into position in the engine compartment.

63 Ensure that the locating dowels are in place in the mounting plate, then carefully offer the transmission to the engine, until the locating dowels are engaged, ensuring that the weight of the transmission is not allowed to hang on the input shaft as it is engaged with the clutch friction disc.

64 Refit the transmission-to-engine nut and bolt, and tighten to the specified torque.

65 Refit the bolt at the rear of the engine, securing the engine to the transmission, and tighten to the specified torque.

66 Fit the two lower engine-to-transmission bolts, and tighten them to the specified torque.

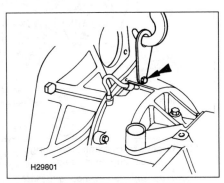

7.52 Bolt a lifting bracket to the transmission using the centre upper transmission casing-to-differential housing bolt (arrowed)

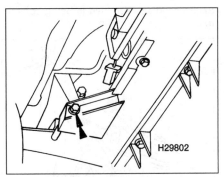

7.56 Unscrew the rear engine-to-transmission bolt (arrowed) – 1.8 l petrol models

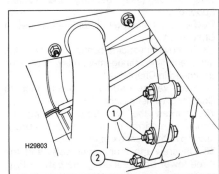

7.57 Unscrew the nuts and bolts (1) securing the flywheel front cover plate and the remaining transmission-to-engine nut and bolt (2)

7A

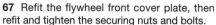

7.76 Removing the battery tray – diesel engine model

7.77 Disconnecting the clutch cable – diesel engine model

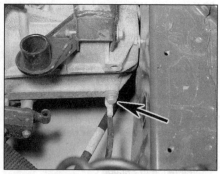

7.78 Unscrew the bolt (arrowed) securing the earth lead to the transmission

67 Refit the flywheel front cover plate, then refit and tighten the securing nuts and bolts.
68 Refit the upper engine-to-transmission bolts, and tighten to the specified torque.
69 Further refitting is a reversal of removal, bearing in mind the following points:
a) Tighten all fixings to the specified torque, where applicable.
b) Refit the left-hand engine/transmission mounting as described in Chapter 2A or 2B, as applicable.
c) Refit the left-hand front suspension tie-rod as described in Chapter 10.
d) Reconnect the driveshafts to the transmission as described in Chapter 8.
e) Use a new roll-pin when reconnecting the gear selector rod to the selector shaft.
f) Reconnect the exhaust front section to the manifold with reference to Chapter 4A.
g) Refit the starter motor as described in Chapter 5A.
h) On completion, refill the transmission with oil as described in Section 2.

Diesel engine models

Note: A new gear selector rod-to-selector shaft roll-pin will be required on refitting.

Removal

70 Disconnect the battery negative lead.
71 Apply the handbrake, then jack up the front of the vehicle and support it securely on axle stands (see "Jacking and Vehicle Support").
72 Remove the starter motor as described in Chapter 5A.
73 Remove the engine control module (ECM) and the engine management relay module, as described in Chapter 4B.
74 Remove the battery, with reference to Chapter 5A if necessary.
75 Unscrew the two bolts securing the engine compartment fusebox to the body, and move the fusebox to one side.
76 Unscrew the four upper bolts and the three lower bolts securing the battery tray, then remove the battery tray **(see illustration)**.
77 Disconnect the clutch cable from the clutch release lever, with reference to Chapter 6 if necessary, then release the cable from the

transmission brackets, and move the cable to one side **(see illustration)**.
78 Unscrew the bolt securing the earth lead to the transmission **(see illustration)**.
79 Trace the wiring back from the reversing light switch, locate the wiring connector(s), and separate the two halves of the wiring connector(s).
80 Remove the mass airflow (MAF) sensor, with reference to Chapter 4B.
81 Unscrew the nut securing the coolant pipe to the transmission mounting plate **(see illustration)**.
82 Proceed as described in paragraphs 42 to 53.
83 Unscrew the three lower bolts securing the transmission to the transmission mounting plate and the engine/transmission reinforcing bracket **(see illustration)**.
84 Unscrew the bolt at the rear of the engine, securing the transmission to the mounting plate.
85 Unscrew the two nuts and bolts securing the transmission to the mounting plate, then unscrew the remaining bolt securing the transmission to the mounting plate.
86 Carefully withdraw the transmission from the engine (the transmission locates on dowels in the mounting plate), ensuring that the weight of the transmission is not allowed to hang on the input shaft while it is engaged with the clutch friction disc.

Refitting

87 Proceed as described in paragraphs 60 to 63.

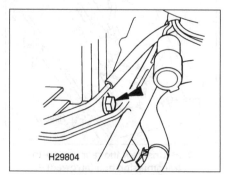

7.81 Unscrew the coolant pipe securing nut (arrowed) – diesel engine models

88 Further refitting is a reversal of removal, bearing in mind the following points:
a) Tighten all fixings to the specified torque, where applicable.
b) Refit the left-hand engine/transmission mounting as described in Chapter 2B.
c) Refit the left-hand front suspension tie-rod as described in Chapter 10.
d) Reconnect the driveshafts to the transmission as described in Chapter 8.
e) Use a new roll-pin when reconnecting the gear selector rod to the selector shaft.
f) Refit the starter motor as described in Chapter 5A.
g) On completion, refill the transmission with oil as described in Section 2.

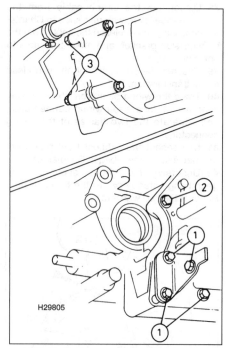

7.83 Engine-to-transmission fixings – diesel engine models

1 Lower transmission-to-mounting plate bolts
2 Rear transmission-to-mounting plate bolt
3 Transmission-to-mounting plate nuts and bolts

8 Manual transmission overhaul – general information

Overhauling a manual transmission unit is a difficult and involved job for the DIY home mechanic. In addition to dismantling and reassembling many small parts, clearances must be precisely measured and, if necessary, changed by selecting shims and spacers. Internal transmission components are also often difficult to obtain, and in many instances, extremely expensive. Because of this, if the transmission develops a fault or becomes noisy, the best course of action is to have the unit overhauled by a specialist repairer, or to obtain an exchange reconditioned unit.

Nevertheless, it is not impossible for the more experienced mechanic to overhaul the transmission, provided that the necessary special tools are available, and the job is done in a deliberate step-by-step manner, so that nothing is overlooked.

The tools necessary for an overhaul include internal and external circlip pliers, bearing pullers, a slide hammer, a set of pin punches, a dial test indicator, and possibly a hydraulic press. In addition, a large, sturdy workbench and a vice will be required.

During dismantling of the transmission, make careful notes of how each component is fitted, to make reassembly easier and more accurate.

Before dismantling the transmission, it will help if you have some idea of what area is malfunctioning. Certain problems can be closely related to specific areas in the transmission, which can make component examination and replacement easier. Refer to the *"Fault diagnosis"* Section of this manual for more information.

7A

Notes

Chapter 7 Part B:
Automatic transmission

Contents

Degrees of difficulty

Easy, suitable for novice with little experience	**Fairly easy,** suitable for beginner with some experience	**Fairly difficult,** suitable for competent DIY mechanic	**Difficult,** suitable for experienced DIY mechanic	**Very difficult,** suitable for expert DIY or professional

Specifications

General
Type . . . . Constantly Variable Transmission (CVT)

Lubrication
Recommended oil and capacity . . . . See *"Lubricants, fluids and capacities"*

Torque wrench settings

	Nm	lbf ft
Engine-to-transmission bolts	85	63
Fluid cooler pipe-to-fluid cooler union bolts	5	4
Fluid cooler pipe-to-transmission nuts	37	27
Fluid pan bolts	10	7
Flywheel rear cover plate bolts	8	6
Gear selector cable rod-to-selector lever nut	7	5
Gear selector lever-to-selector shaft nut	7	5
Mounting bracket-to-transmission bolts	80	59
Starter inhibitor/reversing light switch	12	9
Transmission drain plug	30	22
Transmission mounting bracket-to-left-hand engine/transmission mounting nut	160	118

1 General information and precautions

General information

The automatic transmission is of the Continuously Variable Transmission (CVT) type. The transmission differs from the conventional type of automatic transmission in that it provides an infinite number of gear ratios in a stepless shifting pattern.

The transmission is driven via a torsion damper bolted to the engine driveplate (flywheel). Power is transmitted to the transmission input shaft, which in turn drives a planet gear carrier. When forward or reverse gear is selected one of two multiplate wet clutch assemblies is operated, and a primary pulley rotates to transmit torque to a secondary pulley via a steel belt. The secondary pulley provides drive to the differential (integral with the transmission casing), causing the vehicle to move in the desired direction.

The primary and secondary pulleys each consist of one fixed half, and one moveable half. The moving pulley halves are located diagonally opposite each other to reduce misalignment of the steel belt as the pulley halves move. Each moving pulley half is connected to a hydraulic cylinder, controlled by hydraulic pressure generated by an integral fluid pump. By moving the pulley halves together, their effective diameter is increased, and by moving them apart the diameter is decreased - this alters the gearing of the transmission unit due to the conical shape of the pulley faces.

The steel belt is lubricated by fluid sprayed from a nozzle mounted in the transmission casing.

When the vehicle pulls away from rest a low gear ratio is required. To enable this, the primary pulley halves are moved apart, allowing the belt to sit down in the pulley, while the secondary pulley halves are moved together, forcing the belt to run on the larger diameter of the secondary pulley.

As the vehicle speed increases, a higher ratio is required. As the engine speed increases, the hydraulic fluid pressure increases (the fluid pump is driven from the crankshaft, via the transmission input shaft), and the two halves of the primary pulley are gradually forced together, increasing the effective diameter of the pulley. At the same time, the secondary pulley halves are moved apart, effectively decreasing the diameter of the pulley.

The multiplate wet clutches (one for forward and one for reverse) are hydraulically controlled so that the vehicle can move from rest smoothly, regardless of the throttle opening.

The transmission selector lever has five positions as follows:

"P" The transmission is mechanically locked by the engagement of a pawl with the secondary pulley.

"R" The reverse clutch is activated, and the forward clutch is inhibited.

"N" The transmission is in neutral. Both forward and reverse clutches are inhibited.

"D" Normal driving position. The forward clutch is activated and the reverse clutch is inhibited. The transmission ratio is varied automatically to suit prevailing speed and load.

"L" Prevents the transmission from moving into high ratios. Provides maximum acceleration and maximum engine braking.

Precautions

The following precautions must be observed to avoid damage to the transmission.

a) *Do not attempt to start the engine by pushing or towing the vehicle.*

b) *If the vehicle has to be towed for recovery, only tow the vehicle with the front wheels clear of the ground.*

c) *Only engage "P" when the vehicle is stationary.*

---

2 Selector cable – adjustment, removal and refitting

Adjustment

1 Apply the handbrake, then jack up the front of the vehicle and support securely on axle stands (see *"Jacking and Vehicle Support"*).

2 Ensure that the gear selector lever inside the vehicle is in position "P".

3 Working under the transmission, slacken the nut securing the selector cable rod to the selector lever on the transmission, then push the selector lever fully forwards **(see illustration)**.

4 Attempt to turn both the front wheels. Both wheels should be locked, indicating that the parking lock mechanism is engaged.

5 Tighten the nut securing the selector cable rod to the selector lever to the specified torque.

6 Lower the vehicle to the ground, and check that the engine can only be started with the selector lever in positions "P" and "N".

7 Check that forward drive is achieved with the lever in positions "D" and "L", and reverse drive with the lever in position "R".

Removal

8 Working inside the vehicle, remove the centre console as described in Chapter 11.

9 Move the gear selector lever to position "L".

10 Unscrew the four screws securing the selector lever housing to the body **(see illustration)**. Recover the washers.

11 Using a forked tool, or a large flat-bladed screwdriver, carefully prise the selector cable balljoint from the selector lever **(see illustration)**.

12 Prise off the C-clip securing the selector cable in position in the body aperture **(see illustration)**.

13 Apply the handbrake, then jack up the front of the vehicle and support securely on axle stands (see *"Jacking and Vehicle Support"*).

14 Working under the transmission, unscrew the nut securing the selector cable rod to the selector lever on the transmission, and release the cable from the selector.

15 Slide the rubber gaiter back from the selector cable locknut at the bracket on the transmission, then slacken the locknut **(see illustration)**.

16 Slide out the mounting rubbers, and release the cable from the bracket.

17 Release the cable from the bracket under the vehicle floor, and withdraw the cable from the vehicle.

Refitting

18 Refitting is a reversal of removal, but do not fully tighten the nut securing the selector cable rod to the selector lever on the transmission, until the selector cable has been adjusted on completion of the refitting procedure.

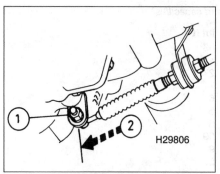

2.3 Slacken the nut (1), then push the selector lever fully forwards (2)

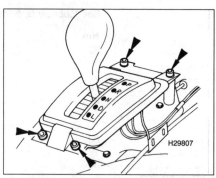

2.10 Unscrew the four screws (arrowed) securing the selector lever housing to the body

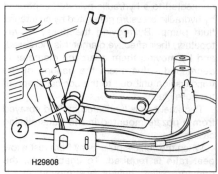

2.11 Using a forked tool (1) to disconnect the selector cable balljoint (2)

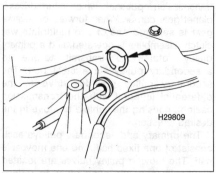

2.12 Prise off the C-clip (arrowed) securing the selector cable in position

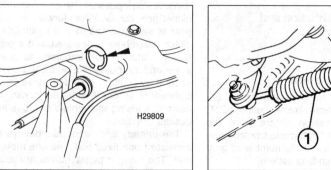

2.15 Selector cable rubber gaiter (1) and locknut (2)

3 Selector lever assembly – removal and refitting

Removal

1 Working inside the vehicle, remove the centre console as described in Chapter 11.
2 Move the gear selector lever to position "L".
3 Unscrew the four screws securing the selector lever housing to the body. Recover the washers.
4 Using a large flat-bladed screwdriver, carefully prise the selector cable balljoint from the selector lever.
5 Pull the gear selector illumination bulb holder from the housing, then remove the gear selector lever/housing assembly.

Refitting

6 Refitting is a reversal of removal, but on completion check the selector cable adjustment as described in Section 2.

4 Kickdown cable – adjustment, removal and refitting

Adjustment

1 Working at the kickdown cable bracket in the engine compartment, slacken the cable adjuster locknut and the adjuster nut **(see illustration)**.
2 Ensure that the throttle cable is correctly adjusted as described in Chapter 4.
3 Rotate the throttle lever on the throttle body and hold it in the fully-open position.
4 Have an assistant insert a 1.0 mm thick feeler blade between the kickdown cable adjuster nut, and the cable bracket.
5 Tighten the adjuster nut to remove all freeplay from the kickdown cable, ensuring

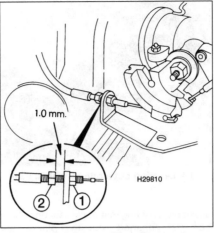

4.1 Kickdown cable adjustment

1 Locknut   2 Adjuster nut

that the throttle lever is held in the fully open position during adjustment.
6 Remove the feeler blade, and tighten the cable adjuster locknut.
7 Have the assistant release the throttle lever, and check that the lever moves freely through its full range of movement.

Removal

Note: *A new transmission fluid pan gasket will be required on refitting.*
8 Disconnect the battery negative lead.
9 Apply the handbrake, then jack up the front of the vehicle and support securely on axle stands (see *"Jacking and Vehicle Support"*).
10 Working at the kickdown cable bracket in the engine compartment, slacken the cable adjuster locknut and the adjuster nut.
11 Slide the end of the kickdown cable from the throttle lever, then release the cable from the bracket.
12 Remove the starter motor as described in Chapter 5A.
13 Remove the transmission fluid pan, as described in Section 6 (*Fluid pan gasket renewal*).
14 Working inside the transmission casing, locate the kickdown valve cam, then release the end of the cable from the cam, using a hooked length of wire as shown **(see illustration)**.
15 It is now necessary to release the cable

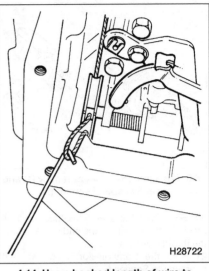

4.14 Use a hooked length of wire to release the kickdown cable from the transmission valve cam

sheath end fitting from the transmission casing. Rover tool No 18G 1650 is available for this purpose, but it should be possible to achieve the same effect using a hollow metal tube of suitable internal diameter, or a pair of pliers. Squeeze the cable sheath end fitting by pushing the tube onto the end fitting, or squeezing with the pliers to compress the slot, then pull the end fitting from the transmission casing **(see illustration)**.
16 Withdraw the cable from the vehicle, noting its routing.

Refitting

17 Working under the vehicle, push the cable sheath end fitting into position in the transmission casing, then reconnect the end of the cable to the valve cam, using a hooked length of wire as during removal.
18 Assuming that a new cable is being fitted, hold the cable as straight as possible, then working at the throttle lever end of the cable, crimp the stop block onto the inner cable the specified distance from the end face of the cable sheath **(see illustration)**.
19 Feed the cable through into the engine compartment, as noted before removal. Ensure that the cable is routed over the top of the intake air trunking connecting the air cleaner to the throttle body.

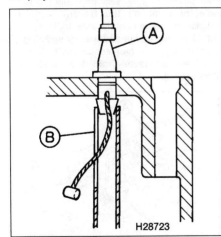

4.15 Releasing the kickdown cable sheath end fitting from the transmission casing

A   Cable sheath end fitting
B   Hollow tube

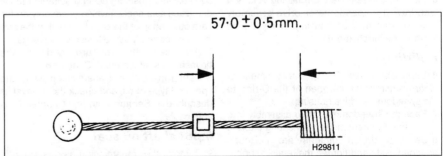

4.18 Crimp the stop block onto the inner cable as shown

57·0 ± 0·5mm.

7B

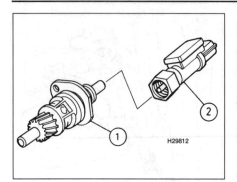

5.5 Speedometer drive assembly (1) and vehicle speed sensor (2)

6.4 Levering out a differential oil seal

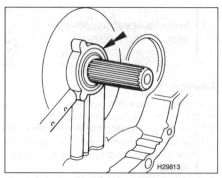

6.10 Prise out the input shaft oil seal (arrowed)

20 Slide the cable sheath into position in the bracket, and reconnect the end of the cable to the throttle lever.
21 Refit the transmission fluid pan, with reference to Section 6.
22 Refit the starter motor with reference to Chapter 5A.
23 Lower the vehicle to the ground.
24 Adjust the kickdown cable as described previously in this Section.
25 On completion, refill the transmission with fluid as described in Chapter 1.

5 Speedometer drive – removal and refitting

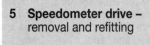

Removal

Note: *A new speedometer drive O-ring will be required on refitting.*
1 All models are fitted with an electrically-operated speedometer, which uses a signal provided by the vehicle speed sensor, mounted on the top of the transmission housing, next to the inboard end of the right-hand driveshaft.
2 Disconnect the battery negative lead.
3 To gain access to the speedometer sensor, apply the handbrake then jack up the front of the vehicle and support it securely on axle stands (see *"Jacking and Vehicle Support"*).
4 Disconnect the wiring connector from the vehicle speed sensor then unscrew the sensor securing nut, and remove the sensor from the top of the speedometer drive assembly.
5 Slacken and remove the retaining bolt, and withdraw the speedometer drive assembly from the transmission housing, along with its O-ring **(see illustration)**.

Refitting

6 Lubricate a new O-ring with a smear of clean transmission oil, then fit the O-ring to the speedometer drive housing.
7 Ease the speedometer drive assembly into position in the transmission, ensuring that the drive and driven pinions are correctly engaged. Refit and tighten the retaining bolt.
8 Fit the speed sensor to the top of the drive

assembly, ensuring that the sensor drive pin is correctly engaged with the pinion, and securely tighten the sensor securing nut.
9 Reconnect the wiring connector to the speed sensor then lower the vehicle to the ground, and reconnect the battery negative lead.

6 Oil seals – renewal

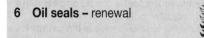

Driveshaft oil seals

1 Apply the handbrake, then jack up the front of the car and support it securely on axle stands (see *"Jacking and Vehicle Support"*). Remove the appropriate front roadwheel.
2 Drain the transmission oil as described in Chapter 1, or be prepared for some oil loss as the driveshaft is removed.
3 Free the inboard end of the driveshaft from the transmission, as described in Chapter 8, and move it clear of the seal. Note that there is no need to disconnect the outboard end of the driveshaft from the hub. Support the driveshaft using wire or string, to avoid placing any strain on the driveshaft joints or gaiters.
4 Carefully prise the oil seal from the transmission using a large flat-bladed screwdriver **(see illustration)**.
5 Remove all traces of dirt from the area around the oil seal aperture, then apply a smear of grease to the outer lip of the new oil seal.
6 Ensure that the seal is correctly positioned, with its sealing lip facing inwards, and drive it squarely into position, using a suitable tubular drift (such as a socket) which bears only on the hard outer edge of the seal. Ensure that the seal is seated correctly in the transmission recess.
7 Reconnect the inboard end of the driveshaft as described in Chapter 8.
8 Refill/top-up the transmission with the specified type of oil, and check the oil level as described in Section 2 and/or Chapter 1, as applicable.

Input shaft oil seal

9 Remove the transmission as described in Section 9.

10 Carefully prise the input shaft seal from the housing in the transmission bellhousing **(see illustration)**.
11 Thoroughly clean the oil seal housing and the input shaft.
12 Before fitting a new seal, check the seal rubbing surface on the input shaft for signs of burrs, scratches or other damage which may have caused the seal to fail in the first place. It may be possible to polish away minor faults of this sort using fine abrasive paper, however, more serious defects will require the renewal of the input shaft.
13 Dip the new seal in clean transmission oil, then slide it over the input shaft, taking care not to damage the seal. Press the seal squarely into the transmission, using a tube (such as a socket) which bears only on the hard outer edge of the seal.
14 Refit the transmission as described in Section 9.

Selector shaft oil seal

15 Remove the sump from the engine, as described in Chapter 2.
16 Ensure that the gear selector lever inside the vehicle is in position "P".
17 Working under the transmission, unscrew the nut securing the selector cable rod to the selector lever on the transmission, and release the cable from the selector lever.
18 Unscrew the nut and washer securing the selector lever to the selector shaft, then pull the selector lever from the shaft **(see illustration)**.

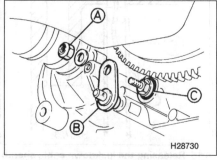

6.18 Selector shaft oil seal fitting details

A Lever securing nut   C Selector shaft
B Selector lever   oil seal

19 Carefully prise the selector shaft seal from the transmission. Be prepared for fluid spillage as the seal is removed.

20 Thoroughly clean the seal housing and the selector shaft. Before fitting a new seal, check the seal rubbing surface on the selector shaft for signs of burrs, scratches or other damage which may have caused the seal to fail in the first place. It may be possible to polish away minor faults of this sort using fine abrasive paper, however, more serious defects will require the renewal of the selector shaft.

21 Lubricate the new seal with clean transmission oil, and ease it over the end of the selector shaft. Press the seal squarely into the transmission housing using a tube (such as a socket) which bears only on the hard outer edge of the seal.

22 Fit the selector lever to the shaft, ensuring that the lever engages correctly with the shaft, then refit the washer and the securing nut, and tighten to the specified torque.

23 Reconnect the selector cable to the selector lever, and refit the securing nut, but **do not** tighten the nut at this stage.

24 Refit the sump to the engine as described in Chapter 2.

25 Lower the vehicle to the ground, then check the transmission fluid level and top up if necessary as described in Chapter 1.

26 Adjust the selector cable as described in Section 2.

Dipstick tube oil seal

27 Remove the air cleaner as described in Chapter 4.

28 Pull the transmission fluid level dipstick from the tube.

29 Clean the transmission around the base of the dipstick tube, then unscrew the bolt securing the dipstick tube bracket to the transmission, and withdraw the tube.

30 Remove the seal from the transmission.

31 Thoroughly clean the aperture in the transmission, and the dipstick tube.

32 Lubricate the new seal with a little clean transmission fluid, then fit it to the end of the dipstick tube.

33 Further refitting is a reversal of removal.

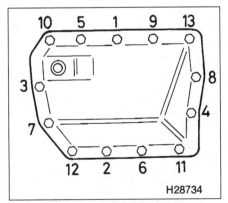

6.38 Fluid pan securing bolt tightening sequence

Fluid pan gasket

34 Apply the handbrake, then jack up the front of the vehicle and support securely on axle stands (see *"Jacking and Vehicle Support"*).

35 Drain the transmission fluid as described in Chapter 1.

36 Working in the **reverse** of the tightening sequence **(see illustration 6.38)**, progressively slacken and remove the fluid pan securing bolts, then withdraw the fluid pan. Recover and discard the gasket.

37 Thoroughly clean the mating faces of the fluid pan and the transmission, then lubricate a new gasket with a little clean transmission fluid, and fit the gasket to the fluid pan.

38 Offer the fluid pan into position on the transmission, then refit and progressively tighten the securing bolts to the specified torque setting in the order shown **(see illustration)**.

39 Lower the vehicle to the ground, then refill the transmission with fluid as described in Chapter 1.

7 Fluid cooler – removal and refitting

Removal

Note: *New fluid pipe O-rings will be required on refitting.*

1 Disconnect the battery negative lead.

2 Remove the front bumper as described in Chapter 11.

3 Position a suitable container beneath the oil cooler to catch escaping fluid.

4 Unscrew the nut and bolt securing the fluid pipe clamp to the fluid cooler **(see illustration)**.

5 Unscrew the union bolts securing the fluid feed and return pipes to the fluid cooler, then disconnect the pipes. Recover and discard the O-rings.

6 Unscrew the three securing bolts, then withdraw the fluid cooler and recover the spacer, which fits under the cooler. Drain the fluid from the cooler into the container, then withdraw the fluid cooler from the vehicle.

Refitting

7 Refitting is a reversal of removal, bearing in mind the following points.

a) Use new O-rings when reconnecting the fluid pipes to the cooler, and lubricate the O-rings with a little clean transmission fluid.

b) Refit the front bumper with reference to Chapter 11.

c) On completion, top up the transmission fluid level as described in Chapter 1.

8 Starter inhibitor/reversing light switch – removal and refitting

Removal

Note: *A new switch O-ring will be required on refitting.*

1 The switch is located in the rear of the transmission casing, below the left-hand driveshaft inboard joint.

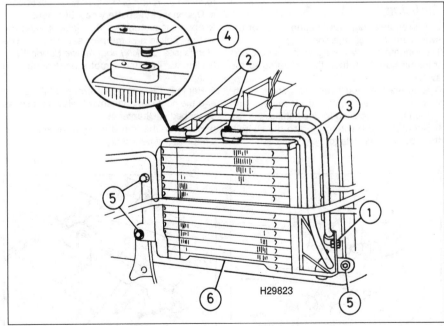

7.4 Transmission fluid cooler mounting details

1 *Fluid pipe clamp securing nut and bolt*
2 *Fluid pipe union bolts*
3 *Fluid pipes*
4 *Fluid pipe union O-ring*
5 *Fluid cooler securing bolts*
6 *Fluid cooler*

7B

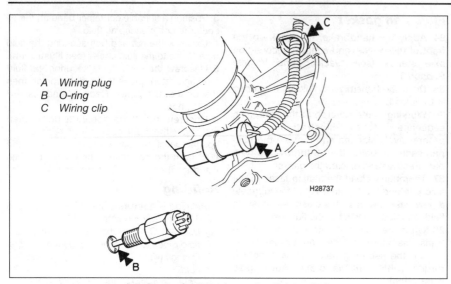

A   Wiring plug
B   O-ring
C   Wiring clip

H28737

8.5 Starter inhibitor/reversing light switch

2 Disconnect the battery negative lead.
3 Apply the handbrake, then jack up the front of the vehicle and support securely on axle stands (see "Jacking and Vehicle Support").
4 Position a suitable container beneath the switch to catch escaping fluid, and have a suitable plug ready to plug the aperture in the transmission.
5 Disconnect the wiring plug from the switch, then unscrew the switch from the transmission **(see illustration)**. Recover and discard the O-ring. Plug the aperture in the transmission to prevent dirt entry and further fluid loss.

Refitting

6 Thoroughly clean the mating faces of the switch and the transmission.
7 Lubricate a new O-ring with a little clean transmission fluid, then fit the O-ring to the switch.
8 Remove the plug from the transmission, then screw the switch into position, and tighten to the specified torque setting.
9 Reconnect the wiring plug to the switch, then lower the vehicle to the ground.

10 On completion, check and if necessary top up the transmission fluid level as described in Chapter 1.

9 Automatic transmission – removal and refitting

Removal

Note: *A new transmission mounting bracket-to-left-hand engine/transmission mounting nut, and new oil cooler pipe O-rings will be required on refitting.*

1 Disconnect the battery negative lead.
2 Apply the handbrake, then jack up the front of the vehicle and support securely on axle stands (see "Jacking and Vehicle Support").
3 Remove the starter motor as described in Chapter 5A.
4 Remove the engine control module (ECM) and the engine management relay module, as described in Chapter 4.
5 Remove the battery, with reference to Chapter 5A if necessary.

6 Unscrew the two bolts securing the engine compartment fusebox to the body, and move the fusebox to one side.
7 Unscrew the four upper bolts and the three lower bolts securing the battery tray, then remove the battery tray.
8 Disconnect the wiring plug from the vehicle speed sensor.
9 Disconnect the wiring plug from the starter inhibitor/reversing light switch, then release the clip securing the switch wiring harness to the transmission.
10 Disconnect the selector cable from the transmission, as described in Section 2.
11 Disconnect the kickdown cable from the throttle linkage, as described in Section 4.
12 Drain the transmission fluid as described in Chapter 1.
13 Remove the exhaust front section as described in Chapter 4.
14 Unscrew the union nuts, and disconnect the two transmission fluid cooler pipes from the transmission **(see illustration)**. Be prepared for some fluid spillage, and plug the open ends of the pipes and transmission to prevent dirt entry. Recover the O-rings and discard them.
15 Disconnect the inboard ends of the driveshafts from the transmission, as described in Chapter 8. Note that there is no need to disconnect the outboard ends of the driveshafts from the hubs. Support the driveshafts using wire or string, to avoid placing any strain on the driveshaft joints or gaiters.
16 Bolt a suitable lifting bracket to the transmission using a bolt screwed into the hole provided in the top of the transmission casing **(see illustration)**.
17 On models fitted with air conditioning, unscrew the bolt securing the air conditioning refrigerant pipe to the bracket on the engine/transmission assembly.
18 Unscrew the two bolts securing the flywheel rear cover plate to the bellhousing, and remove the cover plate **(see illustration)**.
19 Position a hydraulic jack under the engine sump, with a block of wood between the jack head and sump to spread the load.

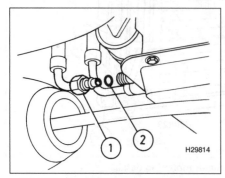

9.14 Disconnect the transmission fluid pipes (1) from the transmission and recover the O-rings (2)

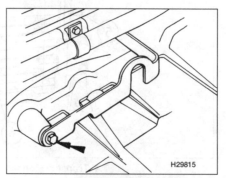

9.16 Bolt a lifting bracket to the transmission using the hole provided (arrowed)

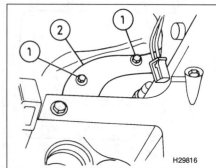

9.18 Unscrew the two securing bolts (1) and remove the flywheel rear cover plate (2)

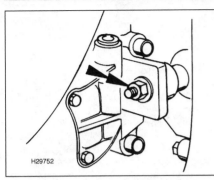

9.20 Unscrew the nut (arrowed) securing the transmission mounting bracket to the mounting

20 Unscrew and discard the nut securing the transmission mounting bracket to the left-hand engine/transmission mounting **(see illustration)**.

21 Connect a hoist and lifting tackle to the lifting bracket bolted to the transmission, then raise the hoist to just take the weight of the transmission.

22 Make sure that the engine and transmission are adequately supported, then unscrew the four engine-to-transmission bolts **(see illustrations)**. On models with air conditioning, recover the air conditioning refrigerant pipe bracket from the upper bolt.

23 With the aid of an assistant, carefully pull the transmission from the engine (the transmission locates on dowels), ensuring that the weight of the transmission is not allowed to hang on the input shaft while it is engaged with the driveplate. It may be necessary to rock the transmission gently to release it from the engine. Take care not to damage any of the surrounding components in the engine compartment.

24 Carefully lower the transmission to the ground, then disconnect the lifting tackle, and withdraw the transmission from under the front of the vehicle.

Refitting

25 Thoroughly clean the mating faces of the transmission casing and engine.

26 Position the transmission under the front of the vehicle, then reconnect the lifting tackle, and lift the transmission into position in the engine compartment.

27 Ensure that the locating dowels are in place, then carefully offer the transmission to the engine, until the locating dowels are engaged, ensuring that the weight of the transmission is not allowed to hang on the input shaft as it is engaged with the driveplate.

Caution: Do not apply grease to the transmission input shaft splines.

28 Refit the engine-to-transmission bolts, and tighten them to the specified torque. Where applicable, ensure that the air conditioning refrigerant pipe bracket is in place on the top bolt.

29 Further refitting is a reversal of removal, bearing in mind the following points:

a) Use a new nut to secure the transmission mounting bracket to the left-hand engine/transmission mounting, and tighten the nut to the specified torque.

b) Reconnect the driveshafts to the transmission as described in Chapter 8.

c) Use new O-rings when reconnecting the transmission oil cooler pipes.

d) Refit the exhaust front section with reference to Chapter 4.

e) Reconnect the kickdown cable and check the cable adjustment, as described in Section 4.

f) Reconnect the selector cable and check the adjustment, as described in Section 2.

g) Refit the starter motor with reference to Chapter 5A.

h) On completion, refill the transmission with fluid, as described in Chapter 1.

10 Automatic transmission overhaul – general information

In the event of a fault occurring with the transmission, it is first necessary to determine whether it is of an electrical, mechanical or hydraulic nature, and to do this special test equipment is required. It is therefore essential to have the work carried out by a Rover dealer if a transmission fault is suspected.

Do not remove the transmission from the vehicle for possible repair before professional fault diagnosis has been carried out, since most tests require the transmission to be in the vehicle.

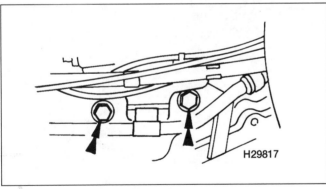

9.22a Unscrew the two upper . . .

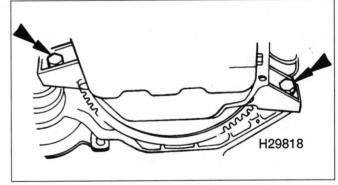

9.22b . . . and the two lower engine-to-transmission bolts (arrowed)

7B

Notes

Chapter 8
Driveshafts

Contents

Degrees of difficulty

Easy, suitable for novice with little experience	**Fairly easy,** suitable for beginner with some experience	**Fairly difficult,** suitable for competent DIY mechanic	**Difficult,** suitable for experienced DIY mechanic	**Very difficult,** suitable for expert DIY or professional

Specifications

Driveshafts

Type . . . . Unequal-length solid steel shafts, splined to inner and outer constant velocity joints, dynamic damper on both shafts

Torque wrench settings	Nm	lbf ft
Driveshaft retaining nut	180	133
Roadwheel nuts	See Chapter 10	

---

1 General information and precautions

General information

Drive is transmitted from the differential to the front wheels by means of two unequal length, solid steel driveshafts.

Both driveshafts are splined at their outer ends to accept the wheel hubs and are threaded so that each hub can be fastened by a large nut. The inner end of each driveshaft is splined to accept the differential sun gear and has a groove to accept the circlip which secures the driveshaft to the sun gear **(see illustration).**

Constant velocity (CV) joints are fitted to both ends of each driveshaft to ensure the smooth and efficient transmission of drive at all possible angles as the roadwheels move up and down with the suspension and as they turn from side to side under steering. Both inner and outer CV joints are of the ball-and-cage type.

A dynamic damper is fitted to each driveshaft to reduce harmonic vibrations and resonance.

Precautions

The driveshaft retaining nuts are extremely tight; ensure the car is securely supported when slackening and tightening them.

The only replacement parts listed are the inner CV joint/driveshaft assemblies, the outer CV joint assemblies and the rubber gaiters. The gaiters are supplied in a kit with the necessary sachets of grease and clips.

If any CV joint is worn or damaged, it cannot be reconditioned and must be renewed. In the case of the inner joints, this means that the complete joint/shaft assembly must be renewed.

2 Driveshaft rubber gaiters and constant velocity joints - inspection

1 Refer to Chapter 1 and if the checks carried out indicate wear, proceed as follows.
2 Remove the roadwheel trim. If the staking is still effective, the driveshaft nut should be correctly tightened. If in doubt, use a torque wrench to check that the nut is securely fastened and re-stake it. Refit the wheel trim.

Repeat this check on the remaining driveshaft nut.
3 Road test the vehicle and listen for a metallic clicking from the front as the vehicle is driven slowly in a circle on full lock. If a clicking noise is heard, this means that wear in the outer CV joint. This means that the joint must be renewed as reconditioning is not possible.
4 If vibration, consistent with road speed, is felt through the vehicle when accelerating, there is a possibility of wear in the inner CV joints.

3 Driveshafts - removal and refitting

Removal

1 Chock the rear wheels, firmly apply the handbrake then jack up the front of the vehicle and support it on axle stands (see "Jacking and Vehicle Support"). Remove the appropriate front roadwheel.
2 Drain the gearbox oil (see Chapter 7).
3 Using a hammer and suitable punch, tap up

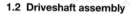

1.2 Driveshaft assembly

1 Circlip	6 Damper clip	11 Stopper ring
2 Inner joint and shaft	7 Dynamic damper	12 Circlip
assembly	8 Small gaiter retaining	13 Outer joint assembly
3 Large gaiter retaining clip	clip	14 Seal
4 Gaiter	9 Gaiter	15 Driveshaft nut
5 Small gaiter retaining clip	10 Large gaiter retaining clip	

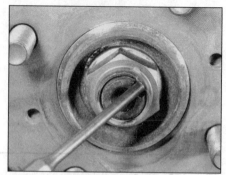

3.3 Using a hammer and punch to release driveshaft nut staking

3.6 Using a universal balljoint separator to separate balljoint shanks

the staking securing the driveshaft retaining nut to the groove in the CV joint **(see illustration)**. Note that a new driveshaft retaining nut must be obtained for reassembly.

4 Have an assistant firmly depress the brake pedal to prevent the front hub from rotating, then using a socket and extension bar, slacken and remove the driveshaft retaining nut. Discard the nut.

5 Slacken and remove the bolt and washer securing the anti-roll bar drop link to the lower suspension arm, then the two bolts securing the tie bar to the lower suspension arm.

6 Extract the split pins and undo the nuts securing the steering gear track rod end balljoint and the lower suspension arm balljoint to the swivel hub. Remove the nuts

and release the balljoint tapered shanks using a universal balljoint separator **(see illustration)**.

7 Carefully pull the swivel hub assembly outwards and withdraw the driveshaft outer CV joint from the hub assembly **(see illustration)**. If necessary, the shaft can be tapped out of the hub using a soft-faced mallet.

Caution: Take care to avoid damaging the driveshaft threads.

8 To release the inner CV joint, insert a suitable flat bar between the joint and gearbox housing, then carefully lever the joint out of position, whilst taking great care not to damage the driveshaft oil seal **(see illustration)**.

9 Support the inner CV joint whilst

withdrawing it from the gearbox, to ensure the oil seal is not damaged, then remove the driveshaft from the vehicle.

Refitting

10 Before fitting the driveshaft, examine the gearbox housing driveshaft oil seal for signs of damage or deterioration and, if necessary, renew it. Similarly, inspect the oil seal which is fitted to the outer CV joint for damage or deterioration and renew if necessary. Regardless of its apparent condition, renew the circlip which is fitted to the groove in the inner CV joint splines as a matter of course **(see illustrations)**.

11 Thoroughly clean the driveshaft splines and the apertures in the gearbox and hub assembly. Apply a thin film of grease to the oil

3.7 Pull swivel hub outwards and disengage driveshaft outer CV joint

3.8 Carefully lever driveshaft inner CV joint out of housing

3.10a Inspect outer CV joint oil seal (arrowed)

3.10b Inner CV joint circlip (arrowed) must be renewed

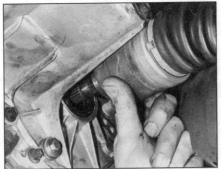

3.12 Refit driveshaft inner CV joint, taking care not to damage driveshaft oil seal . . .

3.13 . . . and engage outer CV joint with swivel hub

3.16a Fit the new driveshaft nut . . .

3.16b . . . and tighten it to the specified torque

3.16c Stake driveshaft nut firmly into CV joint groove

seal lips and to the driveshaft splines and shoulders. Check that all gaiter clips are securely fastened.

12 Ensure that the circlip fitted to the inner CV joint is located securely in its groove, then locate the joint splines with those of the differential sun gear, taking great care not to damage the oil seal. Push the joint fully into the gearbox **(see illustration)**. Check that the joint is securely retained by the circlip by pulling the shaft outwards.

13 Locate the outer CV joint splines with those of the swivel hub and slide the joint back into position in the hub **(see illustration)**.

14 Insert the lower suspension arm and track rod balljoints into their respective locations in the swivel hub and tighten the retaining nuts to the specified torque (see Chapter 10). Secure both nuts in position using new split pins.

15 Refit the bolts securing the trailing arm and anti-roll bar drop link to the lower suspension arm and tighten them to the specified torque (see Chapter 10).

16 Fit the new driveshaft retaining nut and tighten it to the specified torque setting whilst an assistant firmly depresses the brake pedal. Release the brake, check that the hub rotates freely, then stake the nut firmly into the groove on the CV joint using a suitable punch **(see illustrations)**.

17 Refit the roadwheel then lower the vehicle to the ground. Tighten the wheel nuts to the specified torque.

18 Refill the gearbox with the correct type and quantity of oil, then check that the level is correct as described in Chapter 1.

4 Driveshaft rubber gaiters - renewal

Outer joint

Removal

1 Remove the driveshaft from the vehicle.

2 Secure the driveshaft in a vice equipped with soft jaws and release the two rubber gaiter retaining clips by raising the locking tangs with a screwdriver and then raising the end of the clip with pliers. If necessary, the

gaiter retaining clips can be cut to release them **(see illustration)**.

3 Slide the rubber gaiter down the shaft to expose the outer CV joint.

4 Using a soft-faced mallet, sharply strike the inner member of the joint to drive it off the end of the shaft **(see illustration)**. The outer joint is retained on the driveshaft by a circular section circlip and striking the joint in this manner forces the circlip into its groove, so allowing the joint to slide off.

5 Once the joint assembly has been removed, remove the circlip from the groove in the driveshaft splines and discard it. A new circlip must be fitted on reassembly.

6 Withdraw the rubber gaiter from the driveshaft.

7 With the CV joint removed from the

4.2 Cutting gaiter clips to release them

4.4 Driving outer CV joint off driveshaft end

8

4.12 Ensure stopper ring and new circlip are correctly located before fitting outer CV joint

4.17 Using correct tool to tighten gaiter clip - side cutters can be used if care is exercised

4.22 Cutting inner CV joint clip to release it

driveshaft, thoroughly clean the joint using paraffin or a suitable solvent and dry it thoroughly. Inspect the joint as follows.

8 Move the inner splined driving member from side to side to expose each ball in turn at the top of its track. Examine the balls for cracks, flat spots or signs of surface pitting.

9 Inspect the ball tracks on the inner and outer members. If the tracks have widened, the balls will no longer be a tight fit. At the same time check the ball cage windows for wear or cracking between the windows.

10 If, on inspection any of the CV joint, components are found to be worn or damaged, it will be necessary to renew the complete joint assembly, since no components are available separately. If the joint is in satisfactory condition, obtain a repair kit consisting of a new gaiter, retaining clips and the correct type and quantity of grease.

Fitting

11 Tape over the splines on the end of the driveshaft, then fit the small retaining clip onto the gaiter and carefully slide the gaiter onto the shaft.

12 Remove the tape then, ensuring that the stopper ring is securely located in its groove, fit a new circlip to the groove in the driveshaft splines **(see illustration)**. Engage the help of an assistant for the following operations.

13 Position the CV joint over the splines on the driveshaft until it abuts the circlip.

14 Using two small screwdrivers placed one either side of the circlip, compress the clip

and at the same time have your assistant firmly strike the end of the joint with a soft faced mallet. This should not require an undue amount of force. If the joint does not spring into place, remove it, reposition the circlip and try again. Do not force the joint, otherwise the circlip will be damaged.

15 Check that the circlip holds the joint securely on the driveshaft end then pack the joint with the grease supplied. Work the grease well into the ball tracks whilst twisting the joint and fill the rubber gaiter with any excess.

16 Ease the gaiter over the joint and place the large retaining clip in position. Ensure that the gaiter is correctly located in the grooves on both the driveshaft and CV joint.

17 Using pliers, pull the large retaining clip and fold it over until the end locates between the two raised tangs. Hold the clip in this position and bend the tangs over to lock the clip in position. Remove any slack in the gaiter retaining clip by carefully compressing the raised section of the clip. In the absence of the special tool, a pair of side cutters may be used **(see illustration)**. Secure the small retaining clip using the same procedure.

18 Check that the CV joint moves freely in all directions, then refit the driveshaft.

Inner joint

Removal

19 Remove the outer CV joint and gaiter as described in paragraphs 1 to 5.

20 Tape over the splines on the driveshaft and carefully remove the outer CV joint rubber gaiter.

21 Release the dynamic damper retaining clip and slide the damper off the end of the driveshaft.

> **HAYNES HINT** *Use liquid soap as a lubricant if necessary to aid damper removal and clean off any rust deposits or similar using emery cloth.*

22 Release the inner joint gaiter retaining clips and slide the gaiter off the shaft **(see illustration)**.

23 Thoroughly clean the joint using paraffin, or a suitable solvent, and dry it thoroughly. Inspect the joint as described in paragraphs 8 and 9.

24 If, on inspection the CV joint components are found to be worn or damaged, it will be necessary to renew the complete joint and shaft assembly, since the joint is not available separately. If the joint is in satisfactory condition, obtain a repair kit consisting of a new gaiter, retaining clips and the correct type and quantity of grease. Although not strictly necessary, it is also recommended that the outer CV joint gaiter is renewed, regardless of its apparent condition.

Fitting

25 Pack the joint with the grease supplied in the gaiter kit. Work the grease well into the ball tracks whilst twisting the joint **(see illustration)**.

26 Clean the shaft, using emery cloth to remove any rust or sharp edges which may damage the gaiter, then slide the inner joint gaiter along the driveshaft.

27 Locate the gaiter in the grooves on the joint and shaft and fit both the large and small retaining clips. Secure the clips in position as described in paragraph 17 and check that the joint moves freely in all directions.

28 Lubricate the shaft and position a new retaining clip on the dynamic damper flange. Slide the dynamic damper onto the shaft so that its clip flange is innermost (faces the inner CV joint). Position the damper as shown **(see illustration)**, then secure it in position with the retaining clip.

29 Remove any surplus lubricant from the shaft and refit the outer CV joint.

4.25 Pack inner CV joint with grease supplied in gaiter kit

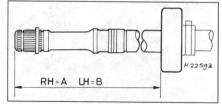

4.28 Position dynamic damper specified distance from outer end of driveshaft

Right-hand driveshaft - 405 to 411 mm
Left-hand driveshaft - 148 to 154 mm

Chapter 9
Braking system

Contents

Degrees of difficulty

Easy, suitable for novice with little experience	Fairly easy, suitable for beginner with some experience	Fairly difficult, suitable for competent DIY mechanic	Difficult, suitable for experienced DIY mechanic	Very difficult, suitable for expert DIY or professional

Specifications

Brake system

Type . . . . Dual hydraulic circuit, split diagonally on models without ABS and front to rear on models with ABS. Disc front brakes. Disc or drum rear brakes, depending on model. Vacuum servo-assistance on all models. Cable-operated handbrake, acting on rear brakes.

Front brakes

Type . . . . Disc, with single piston sliding caliper
Disc diameter . . . . 262 mm
Disc wear limit:
   Solid . . . . 11.00 mm
   Ventilated . . . . 19.00 mm
Maximum disc run-out . . . . 0.04 mm
Brake pad friction material minimum thickness . . . . 3.0 mm

Rear brakes

Models with drum brakes

Type . . . . Single drum with leading and trailing shoes
Drum diameter:
   New . . . . 203.2 mm
   Maximum diameter after machining . . . . 204 mm
Maximum drum ovality . . . . 0.012 mm
Brake shoe friction material minimum thickness . . . . 2.0 mm

Models with disc brakes

Type . . . . Disc, with single piston sliding caliper
Disc diameter . . . . 239 mm
Disc wear limit . . . . 8.0 mm
Maximum disc run-out . . . . 0.06 mm
Brake pad friction material minimum thickness . . . . 3.0 mm

General

ABS rear wheel sensor-to-reluctor ring clearance (models with drum
    brakes) . . . . 0.5 mm
Handbrake lever travel:
    Models with rear drum brakes . . . . 8 to 12 clicks
    Models with rear disc brakes . . . . 10 to 14 clicks

Torque wrench settings

	Nm	lbf ft
ABS front wheel sensor retaining screw	6	4
ABS modulator union nuts	14	10
ABS rear wheel sensor retaining screws (disc)	6	4
ABS rear wheel sensor retaining bolts (drum)	45	33
ABS wheel sensor wiring bracket bolts	10	7
Brake disc retaining screws	5	4
Brake proportioning valve union nuts	19	14
Brake proportioning valve mounting bolts	10	7
Caliper bleed screw	10	7
Front brake caliper hose union bolt	34	25
Front brake caliper guide pin bolt	27	20
Front brake caliper bracket-to-hub bolts	108	80
Handbrake cable-to-underbody retaining bolts	22	16
Handbrake lever to floorpan bolts	22	16
Handbrake warning light switch screw	5	4
Master cylinder brake pipe union nuts	19	14
Master cylinder-to-servo unit nuts	15	11
Rear brake caliper bracket-to-trailing arm bolts	108	80
Rear brake caliper guide pin bolts	27	20
Rear brake drum retaining screws	7	5
Rear wheel cylinder brake pipe union	19	14
Rear wheel cylinder-to-backplate bolts	8	6
Roadwheel nuts	See Chapter 10	
Servo to bulkhead nuts	13	10
Servo vacuum hose-to-inlet manifold union bolt	50	37
Vacuum pump-to-alternator bolts	8	6
Wheel cylinder bleed screw	7	5

1 General information and precautions

General information

The braking system is of the servo-assisted, dual circuit hydraulic type. The arrangement of the hydraulic system is such that each circuit operates one front and one rear brake from a tandem master cylinder. Under normal circumstances both circuits operate in unison. However, in the event of hydraulic failure in one circuit, full braking force will still be available in the remaining circuit **(see illustrations)**.

On models not equipped with an Anti-lock Braking System (ABS), a proportioning valve is also incorporated in the hydraulic circuit, to regulate the pressure applied to the rear brakes, reducing the possibility of the rear wheels locking under heavy braking. On models equipped with ABS, the proportioning valve is fitted, but is used for distribution only.

All models are fitted with front disc brakes, actuated by single piston, sliding-type calipers which ensure that equal pressure is applied to each disc pad. The brake discs may be solid or ventilated, depending on variant.

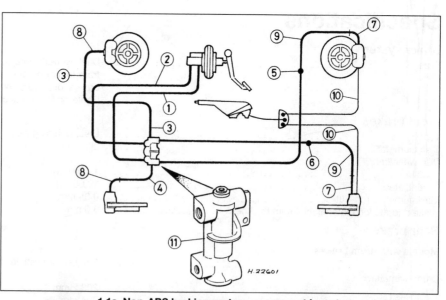

1.1a Non-ABS braking system component layout

1 Primary hydraulic circuit
2 Secondary hydraulic circuit
3 Brake pipe - pressure regulating valve to right-hand front hose
4 Brake pipe - pressure regulating valve to left-hand front hose
5 Brake pipe - pressure regulating valve to right-hand rear hose
6 Brake pipe - pressure regulating valve to left-hand rear hose
7 Brake pipe - hose to rear wheel cylinder
8 Brake flexible hose - brake pipe to front brake caliper
9 Brake flexible hose - rear wheel
10 Handbrake cable
11 Pressure regulating valve

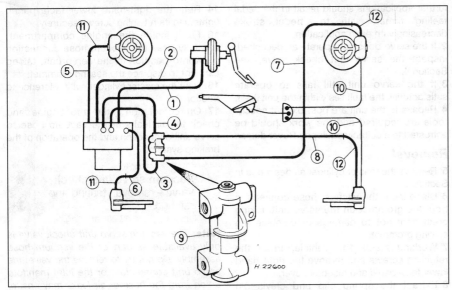

1.1b ABS braking system component layout

1   Primary hydraulic circuit
2   Secondary hydraulic circuit
3   Brake pipe - modulator to pressure regulating valve
4   Brake pipe - modulator to pressure regulating valve
5   Brake pipe - modulator to right-hand front hose
6   Brake pipe - modulator to left-hand front hose
7   Brake pipe - modulator to right-hand rear hose
8   Brake pipe - modulator to left-hand rear hose
9   Pressure regulating valve
10 Handbrake cable
11 Brake flexible hose - brake pipe to front brake caliper
12 Brake flexible hose - brake pipe to rear brake caliper

Rear drum or disc brakes may be fitted, depending on model. The drum brakes incorporate leading and trailing shoes which are actuated by twin piston wheel cylinders. A self-adjusting mechanism is incorporated, to automatically compensate for brake shoe wear. As the brake shoe linings wear, the footbrake operation automatically operates the adjuster mechanism quadrant, which effectively lengthens the shoe strut and repositions the brake shoes to remove the lining-to-drum clearance.

The rear disc brakes are actuated by a single piston sliding caliper, which incorporates a mechanical handbrake mechanism.

On all models, the handbrake is operated by a floor mounted lever and employs twin cables to provide an independent mechanical means of rear brake application. Full details of ABS system operation are as follows.

Anti-lock Braking System (ABS) - operation

ABS is available as an option on all models covered in this Manual. The system comprises a modulator block which contains an ABS Electronic Control Unit (ECU), hydraulic solenoid valves and accumulators, and an electrically-driven return pump. One sensor is fitted to each roadwheel. The purpose of the system is to prevent wheel locking during heavy braking. This is achieved

by automatic release of the brake on the relevant (locking) wheel, followed by reapplication of the brake.

The solenoid valves are controlled by the ECU which receives signals from the four roadwheel sensors, which in turn monitor the speed of rotation of each wheel. By comparing these speed signals from the four wheels, the ECU can determine the speed at which the vehicle is travelling. It can then use this speed to determine when a wheel is decelerating at an abnormal rate compared to the speed of the vehicle and therefore predict when a wheel is about to lock. During normal operation, the system functions in the same way as a non-ABS braking system.

If the ECU senses that a wheel is about to lock, the ABS system enters the 'pressure maintain' phase. The ECU operates the relevant solenoid valve in the modulator block which then isolates the brake caliper on the wheel which is about to lock from the master cylinder, effectively sealing in the hydraulic pressure.

If the speed of rotation of the wheel continues to decrease at an abnormal rate, the ABS system then enters the 'pressure decrease' phase, where the electrically-driven return pump operates and pumps the hydraulic fluid back into the master cylinder, releasing pressure on the brake caliper/wheel cylinder so that the brake is released. Once the speed of rotation of the wheel returns to

an acceptable rate, the pump stops and the solenoid valve opens thereby allowing the hydraulic master cylinder pressure to return to the caliper/wheel cylinder which then reapplies the brake. This cycle can be carried out at up to 10 times a second.

The action of the solenoid valves and return pump creates pulses in the hydraulic circuit. When the ABS system is functioning, these pulses can be felt through the brake pedal.

The solenoid valves connected to the front calipers operate independently, but the valve connected to the rear calipers, together with the proportioning valve, operates both calipers (or wheel cylinders in the case of models with rear drum brakes) simultaneously.

Operation of the ABS system is entirely dependent on electrical signals. To prevent the system responding to any inaccurate signals, a built-in safety circuit monitors all signals received by the ECU. If a spurious signal or low battery voltage is detected, the ABS system is automatically shut down and the warning lamp on the instrument panel is illuminated to inform the driver that the ABS system is not operational. Under these circumstances, the braking system operates as a conventional, non-ABS braking system.

If a fault does develop in the ABS system the vehicle must be taken to a Rover dealer for fault diagnosis and repair.

Precautions

Hydraulic fluid is poisonous. Wash off immediately and thoroughly in the case of skin contact and seek immediate medical advice if any fluid is swallowed or gets into the eyes. Certain types of hydraulic fluid are inflammable and may ignite if brought into contact with hot components.

When servicing any hydraulic system, it is safest to assume that the fluid is flammable and to take precautions against the risk of fire, as though it were petrol being handled. Hydraulic fluid is also an effective paint stripper and will attack plastics. If any is spilt, it should be washed off immediately using copious quantities of fresh water.

Hydraulic fluid is hygroscopic, that is, it absorbs moisture from the air. Brake fluid that has become contaminated with water may boil under heavy braking, causing brake fade and so must be considered unfit for further use. When topping-up or renewing fluid, always use the recommended type and ensure that it comes from a newly-opened container.

When working on brake components, take care not to disperse brake dust into the air, or to inhale it, since it may contain asbestos which is a health hazard.

When servicing any part of the system, work carefully and methodically. Also observe scrupulous cleanliness when overhauling any part of the hydraulic system. Always renew components (in axle sets, where applicable) if in doubt about their condition and use only genuine Rover replacement parts, or at least those of known good quality.

9

2.2 Extract the R-clip (arrowed) and clevis pin securing the servo unit pushrod to the brake pedal (facia removed)

2 Brake pedal - removal and refitting

Removal

1 Working inside the vehicle, undo the three screws and remove the right-hand lower facia panel. Release the stud clips and lower the felt panel to expose the pedal mountings.
2 Extract the R-clip and clevis pin securing the servo unit pushrod to the brake pedal (see illustration).
3 Using pliers, carefully unhook the brake pedal return spring from the pedal to release all the spring tension.
4 Slacken and remove the nut and washers (as applicable) from the brake pedal pivot bolt then withdraw the pivot bolt and remove the brake pedal and return spring.
5 Examine all brake pedal components for signs of wear, paying particular attention to the pedal bushes, pivot bolt and return spring, renewing as necessary.

Refitting

6 Refitting is a reverse of the removal procedure. Lubricate the bushes, pivot bolt and clevis pin with multi-purpose grease.
7 On completion, check the operation of the pedal and ensure that it returns smoothly to its at rest position under the pressure of the return spring.

3 Vacuum servo unit - testing, removal and refitting

Testing

1 To test the operation of the servo unit, depress the footbrake several times to exhaust the vacuum, then start the engine whilst keeping the pedal firmly depressed. As the engine starts, there should be a noticeable 'give' in the brake pedal as the vacuum builds up. Allow the engine to run for at least two minutes then switch it off. If the brake pedal is now depressed it should feel normal, but

further applications should result in the pedal feeling firmer, with the pedal stroke decreasing with each application.
2 If the servo does not operate as described, inspect the servo unit check valve, see Section 4.
3 If the servo unit still fails to operate satisfactorily, the fault lies within the unit itself.
4 Repairs to the unit are possible but special tools are required and the work should be entrusted to a suitably equipped Rover dealer.

Removal

5 Remove the master cylinder as described in Section 9.
6 Disconnect the vacuum hose connection from the grommet on the servo unit, taking great care not to damage or displace the sealing grommet.
7 Working inside the vehicle, undo the retaining screws and remove the right-hand lower facia panel and fusebox cover.
8 Extract the spring clip and clevis pin securing the servo unit pushrod to the brake pedal (refer to Section 2).
9 Slacken and remove the four nuts securing the servo unit to the engine compartment bulkhead then remove the unit, noting the gasket which is fitted to the rear of the unit (see illustration).

Refitting

10 Prior to refitting, check the servo unit to vacuum hose sealing grommet for signs of damage or deterioration and renew if necessary.
11 Fit a new gasket to the rear of the servo unit and reposition the unit in the engine compartment.
12 From inside the vehicle, ensure the servo unit pushrod is correctly engaged with the brake pedal then refit the servo unit mounting nuts and tighten them securely.
13 Refit the servo unit pushrod to brake pedal clevis pin and secure it in position with the R-clip.

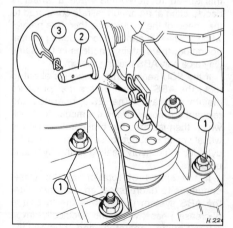

3.9 Vacuum servo unit mounting details

1 Servo unit mounting nuts
2 Pushrod clevis pin
3 R-clip

14 Refit the right-hand lower facia panel, tightening its retaining screws securely.
15 From inside the engine compartment, carefully ease the vacuum hose connection back into position in the servo unit, taking care not to displace the sealing grommet.
16 Refit the master cylinder, with reference to Section 9.
17 On completion, start the engine and check for air leaks at the vacuum hose to servo unit connection and the operation of the braking system.

4 Vacuum servo unit check valve - removal, testing and refitting

Note: *The vacuum servo unit check valve is only available as part of the vacuum hose assembly. Do not try to remove the valve, the servo unit connection, or the inlet manifold union from the hose or air leaks may ensue, necessitating renewal of the hose assembly.*

Removal

1 Carefully unplug the hose connection from the vacuum servo unit taking care not to damage the sealing grommet.
2 On petrol models, unscrew the union bolt securing the vacuum hose assembly to the inlet manifold and withdraw the hose assembly from the engine compartment. Remove the union bolt from the hose end and discard the sealing washers.
3 On diesel models, release the hose clips and disconnect the vacuum hose from the vacuum pump pipe.

Testing

4 Examine the hose for damage, splits, cracks or general deterioration. Make sure that the check valve inside the hose is working correctly by blowing through the hose from the servo unit connection end. Air should flow in this direction but not when blown through from the inlet manifold union. Renew the hose and check valve assembly if at all suspect.
5 Examine the servo unit sealing grommet for signs of damage or deterioration and renew if necessary.

Refitting

6 Position a new sealing washer on each side of the hose union and refit the hose-to-inlet manifold union bolt (petrol models). Ensure that the hose union locating pin is correctly situated between the lugs on the manifold then tighten the union bolt to the specified torque setting. On diesel models, reconnect the hose to the vacuum pump pipe and secure it in position with the clip.
7 Carefully ease the hose connection into the servo unit sealing grommet, taking care not to displace or damage the grommet.
8 On completion, start the engine and check the vacuum hose-to-servo unit connection for signs of air leaks.

5 Hydraulic fluid -
level check and renewal

Refer to "*Weekly Checks*" and Chapter 1.

6 Hydraulic system - bleeding

Warning: Refer to the '*Precautions*' given at the end of Section 1, before handling brake fluid.

Caution: Hydraulic fluid is an effective paint stripper and will attack plastics. If any is spilt onto painted components or bodywork, it should be washed off immediately with clean, warm water.

General

1 The correct operation of any hydraulic system is only possible after removal of all air from the components and circuit. This is achieved by bleeding the system.

2 During the bleeding procedure, add only clean, unused hydraulic fluid of the recommended type. Never re-use fluid that has already been bled from the system. Ensure that sufficient fluid is available before starting work.

3 If there is any possibility of incorrect fluid being already in the system, the brake components and circuit must be flushed completely with uncontaminated, correct fluid and new seals should be fitted to the various components.

4 If hydraulic fluid has been lost from the system, or air has entered because of a leak, then ensure that the fault is cured before proceeding further.

5 Park the vehicle on level ground, chock the roadwheels to prevent movement and then release the handbrake. Start the engine and allow it to idle.

6 Check that all pipes and hoses are secure, unions tight and bleed screws closed. Clean any dirt from around the bleed screws.

7 Unscrew the master cylinder reservoir cap and top the master cylinder reservoir up to the MAX level line. Refit the cap loosely and remember to maintain the fluid level at least above the MIN level line throughout the procedure or there is a risk of air being drawn into the system during the bleeding procedure.

8 There are a number of one-man, do-it-yourself brake bleeding kits currently available from motor accessory shops. It is recommended that one of these kits is used whenever possible as they greatly simplify the bleeding operation and also reduce the risk of expelled air and fluid being drawn back into the system. If such a kit is not available, then the basic (two-man) method must be used which is described in detail below.

9 If a kit is to be used, prepare the vehicle as described previously and follow the kit manufacturer's instructions as the procedure may vary slightly according to the type being used. Generally, they are as outlined below in the relevant sub-section.

10 Whichever method is used, the same sequence must be followed (paragraphs 11 and 12) to ensure the removal of all air from the system.

Bleeding sequence

11 If the system has been only partially disconnected and suitable precautions were taken to minimise fluid loss, it should be necessary only to bleed that part of the system (ie: the primary or secondary circuit).

12 If the complete system is to be bled, then it should be done working in the following sequence:

1) *Left-hand front brake.*
2) *Right-hand rear brake.*
3) *Right-hand front brake.*
4) *Left-hand rear brake.*

Bleeding - basic (two-man) method

13 Collect a clean glass jar, a suitable length of plastic or rubber tubing which is a tight fit over the bleed screw and a ring spanner to fit the screw. The help of an assistant will also be required.

14 Remove the dust cap from the first screw in the sequence. Fit the spanner and tube to the screw, place the other end of the tube in the jar and pour in sufficient fluid to cover the end of the tube.

15 Ensure that the master cylinder reservoir fluid level is maintained at least above the MIN level line throughout the procedure.

16 Have the assistant fully depress the brake pedal several times to build up pressure, then maintain it on the final stroke.

17 While pedal pressure is maintained, unscrew the bleed screw (approximately one turn) and allow the fluid and air to flow into the jar. The assistant should maintain pedal pressure, following it down to the floor if necessary and should not release it until instructed to do so. When the flow stops, tighten the bleed screw again, release the pedal slowly and recheck the reservoir fluid level.

18 Repeat the steps given in paragraphs 16 and 17 until the fluid emerging from the bleed screw is free from air bubbles. If the master cylinder has been drained and refilled and air is being bled from the first screw in the sequence, allow approximately five seconds between cycles for the master cylinder passages to refill.

19 When no more air bubbles appear, tighten the bleed screw securely, remove the tube and spanner and refit the dust cap. Do not overtighten the bleed screw.

20 Repeat the procedure on the remaining screws in the sequence until all air is removed

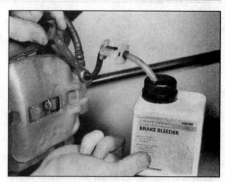
6.21 Using a one-way valve kit to bleed the braking system

from the system and the brake pedal feels firm again.

Bleeding - using a one-way valve kit

21 As their name implies, these kits consist of a length of tubing with a one-way valve fitted to prevent expelled air and fluid being drawn back into the system. Some kits include a translucent container which can be positioned so that the air bubbles can be more easily seen flowing from the end of the tube (**see illustration**).

22 The kit is connected to the bleed screw, which is then opened. The user returns to the driver's seat and depresses the brake pedal with a smooth, steady stroke and slowly releases it. This sequence is repeated until the expelled fluid is clear of air bubbles.

23 Note that these kits simplify work so much that it is easy to forget the master cylinder reservoir fluid level. Ensure that this is maintained at least above the MIN level line at all times.

Bleeding - using a pressure bleeding kit

24 These kits are usually operated by the reservoir of pressurised air contained in the spare tyre, although note that it will probably be necessary to reduce the pressure to a lower limit than normal. Refer to the instructions supplied with the kit.

25 By connecting a pressurised, fluid-filled container to the master cylinder reservoir, bleeding can be carried out simply by opening each screw in turn (in the specified sequence) and allowing the fluid to flow out until no more air bubbles can be seen in the expelled fluid.

26 This method has the advantage that the large reservoir of fluid provides an additional safeguard against air being drawn into the system during bleeding.

27 Pressure bleeding is particularly effective when bleeding 'difficult' systems or when bleeding the complete system at the time of routine fluid renewal.

All methods

28 When bleeding is complete and firm pedal feel is restored, wash off any spilt fluid, tighten the bleed screws securely and refit their dust caps.

9

8.1 Using a brake hose clamp to minimise fluid loss

8.3 Using a brake pipe spanner to unscrew a union nut

29 Check the hydraulic fluid level and top up if necessary (see "Weekly checks").
30 Discard any hydraulic fluid that has been bled from the system as it will not be fit for re-use.
31 Check the feel of the brake pedal. If it feels at all spongy, air must still be present in the system and further bleeding is required. Failure to bleed satisfactorily after a reasonable repetition of the bleeding procedure may be due to worn master cylinder seals.

7 Hydraulic pipes and hoses - inspection

Refer to Chapter 1.

8 Hydraulic pipes and hoses - renewal

1 If any pipe or hose is to be renewed, minimise fluid loss by removing the master cylinder reservoir cap and then tightening it down onto a piece of polythene (taking care not to damage the sender unit) to obtain an airtight seal. Alternatively, flexible hoses can be sealed by using a proprietary brake hose clamp, while metal brake pipe unions can be plugged (if care is taken not to allow dirt into the system) or capped immediately they are disconnected **(see illustration)**. Place a wad of rag under any union that is to be disconnected to catch any spilt fluid.
2 If a flexible hose is to be disconnected, unscrew the brake pipe union nut before removing the spring clip which secures the hose to its mounting bracket.
3 To unscrew the union nuts it is preferable to obtain a proprietary brake pipe spanner of the correct size. These spanners are available from most large motor accessory shops **(see illustration)**. Failing this, a close-fitting open-ended spanner will be required, though if the nuts are tight or corroded, their flats may be rounded-off if the spanner slips. In such a case, a self-locking wrench is often the only way to unscrew a stubborn union but it

follows that the pipe and the damaged nuts must be renewed on reassembly. Always clean a union and surrounding area before disconnecting it. If disconnecting a component with more than one union, make a careful note of the connections before disturbing any of them.
4 If a brake pipe is to be renewed, then it can be obtained from a Rover dealer, already cut to length and with the union nuts and end flares in place. All that is then necessary is to bend it to shape, following the line of the original, before fitting it to the vehicle. Alternatively, most motor accessory shops can make up brake pipes from kits but this requires very careful measurement of the original to ensure that the replacement is of the correct length. The safest answer is usually to take the original to the shop as a pattern.
5 On refitting, do not overtighten the union nuts. The specified torque wrench settings, where given, are not high and it is not necessary to exercise brute force to obtain a sound joint; brake union threads are very fine and can easily be accidentally stripped. When refitting flexible hoses, always renew any sealing washers used.
6 Ensure that the pipes and hoses are correctly routed with no kinks and that they are secured in the clips or brackets provided. After fitting, remove the polythene from the reservoir and bleed the hydraulic system. Wash off any spilt fluid and check carefully for fluid leaks.

9.2 Master cylinder brake pipe unions (arrowed) - non-ABS model shown

9 Master cylinder - removal, overhaul and refitting

> **Warning: Do not syphon brake fluid by mouth as it is poisonous.**

Note: Before attempting to overhaul the master cylinder, check the price and availability of individual components and compare this with the price of a new or reconditioned unit, as overhaul may not be viable on economic grounds alone.

Removal

1 Remove the master cylinder reservoir cap, having disconnected the sender unit wiring connector, and syphon all hydraulic fluid from the reservoir. Do not syphon the fluid by mouth as it is poisonous but use a syringe or an old poultry baster. Alternatively, open any convenient bleed screw in the system and gently pump the brake pedal to expel the fluid through a plastic tube connected to the screw.
2 Wipe clean the area around the brake pipe unions on the side of the master cylinder and place absorbent rags beneath the pipe unions to catch any surplus fluid. Unscrew the two union nuts and carefully withdraw the pipes **(see illustration)**. Plug or tape over the pipe ends and master cylinder orifices to minimise loss of brake fluid and to prevent the entry of dirt into the system. Wash off any spilt fluid immediately with clean water.
3 Slacken and remove the two nuts and spring washers securing the master cylinder to the vacuum servo unit then withdraw the unit from the engine compartment **(see illustration)**. Remove the O-ring (where fitted) from the rear of the master cylinder and discard it.

Overhaul

4 Remove the master cylinder from the vehicle as described above and clean it thoroughly.
5 Carefully prise the reservoir from the master

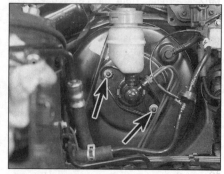

9.3 Master cylinder-to-vacuum servo unit nuts (arrowed) - non-ABS model shown

cylinder body and remove the two mounting seals **(see illustrations)**.

6 Prepare a clean working surface and proceed as follows.

Non-ABS system

7 Using a wooden dowel, press the primary piston in as far as possible and extract the secondary piston stop pin from the reservoir inlet port, then remove the retaining circlip.

8 Noting the order of removal and the direction of fitting of each component, withdraw the piston assemblies with their springs and seals, tapping the body onto a clean wooden surface to dislodge them. If necessary, clamp the master cylinder body in a vice (fitted with soft jaw covers) and use compressed air of low pressure (applied through the secondary circuit fluid port) to assist the removal of the secondary piston assembly.

9 Thoroughly clean all components using only methylated spirit, isopropyl alcohol or clean hydraulic fluid as a cleaning medium. Never use mineral-based solvents such as petrol or paraffin which will attack the hydraulic system's rubber components. Dry the components immediately using compressed air or a clean, lint-free cloth.

10 Check all components and renew any that are worn or damaged. Check particularly the cylinder bores and pistons. The complete assembly should be renewed if these are scratched, worn or corroded. If there is any doubt about the condition of the assembly or of any of its components, renew it. Check that the body's inlet and bypass ports are clear.

11 If the assembly is fit for further use, obtain a repair kit. Renew all seals and O-rings disturbed on dismantling, never re-use them. Renew also any other items included in the repair kit.

12 On reassembly, soak the pistons and new seals in clean hydraulic fluid. Smear clean fluid into the cylinder bore.

13 Fit the new seals to their pistons, using only the fingers to manipulate them into the grooves.

14 Insert the pistons into the bore by using a twisting motion to avoid trapping the seal lips. Ensure that all components are refitted in the correct order and the right way round.

15 Press the secondary piston assembly fully up into the bore using a clean wooden dowel, then refit the stop pin.

16 Refit the primary piston assembly, then secure it in position with a new circlip.

17 Press the new mounting seals into the master cylinder body and carefully refit the reservoir ensuring that it is pressed fully into position.

ABS system

18 Carefully prise out the dust cap from the rear of the master cylinder body and remove the flat washer.

19 Using a wooden dowel, press the primary piston in as far as possible and extract the

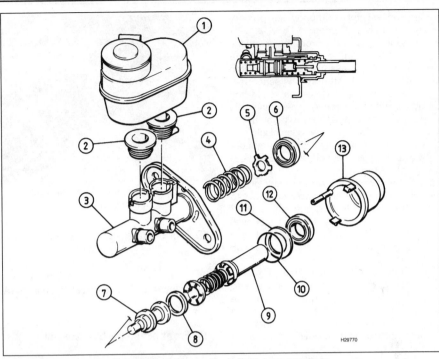

9.5a Non-ABS master cylinder components

1 Master cylinder reservoir	6 Seal	10 'O' ring
2 Seals	7 Secondary piston	11 Vacuum seal backing ring
3 Cylinder body	8 Seal	12 Vacuum seal
4 Spring	9 Primary piston	13 Transfer housing
5 Seal support	assembly	

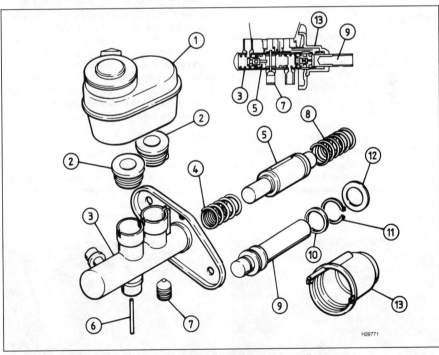

9.5b ABS master cylinder components

1 Master cylinder reservoir	5 Secondary piston assembly	9 Primary piston assembly
2 Seals	6 Secondary piston stop pin	10 Washer
3 Cylinder body	7 Stop pin screw	11 Circlip
4 Spring	8 Spring	12 Flat washer
		13 Transfer housing

9

circlip and washer. Withdraw the primary piston assembly and spring.

20 Undo the grub screw from the underside of the master cylinder body then use the wooden dowel to press the secondary piston into the body and withdraw the secondary piston retaining pin. Extract the secondary piston assembly and spring. If necessary, the piston can be dislodged by tapping the master cylinder body on a wooden block.

21 Examine and overhaul the master cylinder components as described above in paragraphs 9 to 14.

22 Fit the spring to the secondary piston assembly and use a clean wooden dowel to press the assembly fully into the master cylinder bore. Align the slot in the piston with the retaining pin hole then insert the secondary piston retaining pin. Refit the grub screw and tighten it securely.

23 Fit the spring to the primary piston assembly and press the assembly into position using the wooden dowel. Refit the washer and secure the piston assembly in position with the circlip, ensuring that it is correctly located in its groove in the master cylinder bore.

24 Fit the flat washer and refit the dust cap to the rear of the master cylinder body.

25 Align the lugs on the new mounting seals with the slots in the master cylinder body and press them into position. Carefully refit the reservoir, ensuring that it is pressed fully into the master cylinder body.

Refitting

26 Remove all traces of dirt from the master cylinder and servo unit mating surfaces, then fit a new O-ring to the groove on the master cylinder body.

27 Fit the master cylinder to the servo unit, ensuring that the servo unit pushrod enters the master cylinder bore centrally. Refit the master cylinder washers and mounting nuts and tighten them to the specified torque.

28 Wipe clean the brake pipe unions then refit them to the master cylinder ports and tighten them to the specified torque setting.

29 Refill the master cylinder reservoir with new fluid and bleed the hydraulic system, as described in Section 6.

11.2a Remove lower caliper guide pin bolt . . .

10 Front brake pads - inspection

Refer to the information given in Chapter 1A or B.

11 Front brake pads - renewal

⚠️ **Warning: Renew both sets of front brake pads at the same time. Never renew the pads on only one wheel as uneven braking may result. The dust created by pad wear may contain asbestos, which is a health hazard. Never blow it with compressed air or inhale it. An approved filtering mask should be worn when working on the brakes. DO NOT use petroleum-based solvents to clean brake parts the rubber sealing components may be damaged; use brake cleaner or methylated spirit only.**

Removal

1 Chock the rear wheels, firmly apply the handbrake then jack up the front of the vehicle and support it on axle stands (see *"Jacking and Vehicle Support"*). Remove both front roadwheels.

2 Remove the lower caliper guide pin bolt

11.2b . . . and pivot caliper away from disc

whilst, if necessary, using a slim open-ended spanner to prevent the guide pin itself from rotating. Pivot the caliper away from the disc to gain access to the brake pads and tie it to the suspension strut using a piece of wire **(see illustrations)**.

3 Remove the circular shim which is fitted to the caliper piston **(see illustration)**.

4 Remove the brake pads from the caliper mounting bracket whilst noting the correct position of the pad retainer springs and pad shims **(see illustration)**.

5 Measure the thickness of friction material remaining on each brake pad **(see illustration)**. If either pad is worn at any point to the specified minimum thickness or less, all four pads must be renewed. Also, the pads should be renewed if any are fouled with oil or grease as there is no satisfactory way of degreasing friction material once contaminated. If any of the brake pads are worn unevenly or fouled with oil or grease, trace and rectify the cause before reassembly. New brake pad kits are available from Rover dealers and include new shims and pad retainer springs.

6 If the brake pads are still serviceable, carefully clean them using a clean, fine wire brush or similar, paying particular attention to the sides and back of the metal backing. Clean out the grooves in the friction material (where applicable) and pick out any large embedded particles of dirt or debris. Carefully clean the pad retainer springs and the pad locations in the caliper body and mounting bracket.

11.3 Removing circular shim from caliper piston

11.4 Removing pads with springs and shims

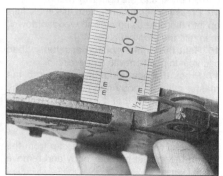

11.5 Measuring thickness of brake pad friction material

11.7 Check condition of guide pins and gaiters before refitting pads

11.8 Fit pad retainer springs to caliper bracket . . .

11.9 . . . and fit shims on pads

Fitting

7 Prior to fitting the pads, check that the guide pins are free to slide easily in the caliper bracket and check that the rubber guide pin gaiters are undamaged **(see illustration)**. Brush the dust and dirt from the caliper and piston but **do not** inhale it as it is injurious to health. Inspect the dust seal around the piston for damage and the piston for evidence of fluid leaks, corrosion or damage. Renew as necessary.

8 On refitting, first fit the pad retainer springs to the caliper mounting bracket **(see illustration)**.

9 Apply a thin smear of high-temperature brake grease (silicone- or PBC/Poly Butyl Cuprysil-based) or anti-seize compound to the sides and back of each pad's metal backing and to those surfaces of the caliper body and mounting bracket which bear on the pads. Fit the shims to the back of both pads and apply a thin smear of lubricant to the back of each shim. Do not allow the lubricant to foul the friction material **(see illustration)**.

10 Install the brake pads in the caliper mounting bracket, ensuring that the friction material is against the disc.

11 If new brake pads have been fitted, the caliper piston must be pushed back into the cylinder to make room for them. Either use a G-clamp or similar tool, or use suitable pieces of wood as levers. Provided that the master cylinder reservoir has not been overfilled with hydraulic fluid there should be no spillage but keep a careful watch on the fluid level while retracting the piston. If the fluid level rises above the MAX level line at any time, the surplus should be syphoned off or ejected via a plastic tube connected to the bleed screw.

12 Apply a thin smear of the recommended lubricant (see above) to the circular shim and fit the shim to the caliper piston. Pivot the caliper body down over the brake pads then refit the bottom guide pin bolt and tighten it to the specified torque wrench setting.

13 Check that the caliper body slides smoothly in the mounting bracket, then depress the brake pedal repeatedly until the pads are pressed into firm contact with the brake disc and normal (non-assisted) pedal pressure is restored.

14 Repeat the above procedure on the remaining front brake caliper.

15 Refit the roadwheels, then lower the vehicle to the ground and tighten the roadwheel nuts to the specified torque setting.

16 On completion, check the hydraulic fluid level (see "Weekly checks").

12 Front brake caliper - removal, overhaul and refitting

⚠️ **Warning: Brake hydraulic fluid may be under considerable pressure in a pipeline, take care not to allow hydraulic fluid to spray into the face or eyes when loosening a connection.**

Removal

1 Chock the rear wheels, firmly apply the handbrake, jack up the front of the vehicle and support on axle stands (see "Jacking and Vehicle Support"). Remove the appropriate front roadwheel.

2 Minimise fluid loss either by removing the master cylinder reservoir cap and then tightening it down onto a piece of polythene to obtain an airtight seal (taking care not to damage the sender unit), or by using a brake hose clamp, a G-clamp or a similar tool to clamp the flexible hose.

3 Clean the area around the union, then undo the brake hose union bolt and disconnect the hose from the caliper. Plug the end of the hose and the caliper orifice to prevent dirt entering the hydraulic system. Discard the sealing washers as they must be renewed whenever disturbed.

4 Unscrew the two caliper guide pin bolts whilst, if necessary, using a slim open-ended spanner to prevent the guide pins themselves from rotating **(see illustration)**.

5 Carefully lift the caliper assembly off the brake pads and remove the circular shim from

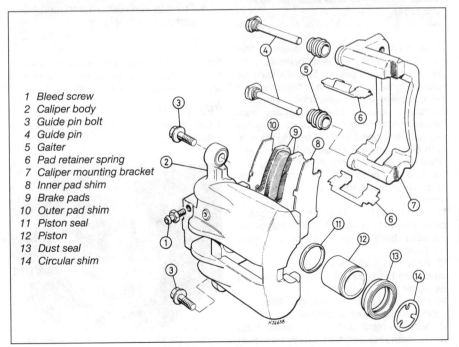

1 Bleed screw
2 Caliper body
3 Guide pin bolt
4 Guide pin
5 Gaiter
6 Pad retainer spring
7 Caliper mounting bracket
8 Inner pad shim
9 Brake pads
10 Outer pad shim
11 Piston seal
12 Piston
13 Dust seal
14 Circular shim

12.4 Front brake caliper components

the caliper piston. Note that the brake pads need not be disturbed and can be left in position in the caliper mounting bracket.

Overhaul

6 With the caliper on the bench, wipe away all traces of dust and dirt.

 Warning: Avoid inhaling the dust as it is injurious to health.

7 Withdraw the piston from the caliper body and remove the dust seal. The piston can be withdrawn by hand or if necessary, pushed out by applying compressed air to the union bolt hole. Only low pressure should be required such as is generated by a foot pump; place a block of wood at the end of the piston, to prevent it striking the caliper as it is ejected from the bore.

8 Using a small screwdriver, extract the piston hydraulic seal whilst taking great care not to damage the caliper bore.

9 Withdraw the guide pins from the caliper mounting bracket and remove the guide pin gaiters.

10 Thoroughly clean all components using only methylated spirit, isopropyl alcohol or clean hydraulic fluid as a cleaning medium.

 Warning: Never use mineral-based solvents such as petrol or paraffin which will attack the hydraulic system's rubber components.

 HAYNES HiNT *Dry the components immediately using compressed air or a clean, lint-free cloth. Use compressed air to blow clear the fluid passages.*

11 Check all components and renew any that are worn or damaged. Check particularly the cylinder bore and piston. These should be renewed (note that this means the renewal of the complete body assembly) if they are scratched, worn or corroded in any way. Similarly, check the condition of the guide pins and their bores in the mounting bracket. Both guide pins should be undamaged and (when cleaned) a reasonably tight sliding fit in the mounting bracket bores. If there is any doubt about the condition of any component, renew it.

12 If the assembly is fit for further use, obtain the appropriate repair kit. Components are available from Rover dealers in various combinations.

13 Renew all rubber seals, dust covers and caps. Also the sealing washers disturbed on dismantling.

14 On reassembly, ensure that all components are absolutely clean and dry.

15 Soak the piston and the new piston (fluid) seal in clean hydraulic fluid. Smear clean fluid on the cylinder bore surface.

16 Fit the new piston (fluid) seal using only the fingers to manipulate it into the cylinder bore groove. Fit the new dust seal to the piston and refit it to the cylinder bore using a twisting motion, ensuring that the piston enters squarely into the bore. Press the piston fully into the bore, then secure the dust seal to the caliper body.

17 Apply the grease supplied in the repair kit, or a good quality high-temperature brake grease (silicone- or PBC/Poly Butyl Cuprysil-based) or anti-seize compound, to the guide pins and fit the new gaiters. Fit the guide pins to the caliper mounting bracket, ensuring that the gaiters are correctly located in the grooves on both the guide pin and mounting bracket.

Refitting

18 Refit the circular shim to the piston and carefully slide the caliper into position over the brake pads. Refit the caliper guide pin bolts and tighten them to the specified torque setting.

19 Position a new sealing washer on each side of the hose union and refit the brake hose union bolt. Ensure that the brake hose union is correctly positioned between the lugs on the caliper then tighten the union bolt to the specified torque setting.

20 Remove the brake hose clamp, where fitted, and bleed the hydraulic system. Providing the precautions described were taken to minimise brake fluid loss, it should only be necessary to bleed the relevant front brake.

21 Refit the roadwheel then lower the vehicle to the ground and tighten the roadwheel nuts to the specified torque.

---

13 Front brake disc - inspection, removal and refitting

Note: *If either brake disc requires renewal, both should be renewed at the same time to ensure even and consistent braking.*

Inspection

1 Chock the rear wheels, firmly apply the handbrake, jack up the front of the vehicle and support on axle stands (see "*Jacking and Vehicle Support*"). Remove the appropriate front roadwheel.

2 Slowly rotate the brake disc so that the full area of both sides can be checked. Remove the brake pads if better access is required to the inboard surface. Light scoring is normal in the area swept by the brake pads but if heavy scoring is found, then the disc must be renewed. The only alternative to this is to have the disc surface-ground until it is flat again, but this must not reduce the disc to less than the minimum thickness specified.

3 It is normal to find a lip of rust and brake dust around the disc's perimeter. This can be scraped off if required. If, however, a lip has formed due to excessive wear of the brake pad swept area, particularly on the outer edge of the disc, then the disc's thickness must be measured by using a micrometer **(see illustration)**. Take measurements at several places around the disc at the inside and outside of the pad swept area. If the disc has worn at any point to the specified minimum thickness or less, then it must be renewed. Note that a large variation in the thickness of the disc around its circumference may be caused by poor disc seating and can cause brake judder.

4 If the disc is thought to be warped, it can be checked for run-out (at a point 6.0 mm in from the disc's outer edge) by either using a dial gauge mounted on any convenient fixed point, while the disc is slowly rotated, or by using feeler blades to measure (at several points all around the disc) the clearance between the disc and a fixed point, such as the caliper mounting bracket **(see illustration)**. If the measurements obtained are at the specified maximum or beyond, the disc is excessively warped and must be renewed. However, it is worth checking first that the hub bearing is in good condition. Also, try the effect of removing the disc, cleaning the hub and disc mating surfaces and turning the disc through 180° to reposition it on the hub. If run-out is still excessive, the disc must be renewed.

5 Check the disc for cracks, especially around the stud holes, and any other wear or damage. Renew it if any of these are found.

13.3 Using a micrometer to measure brake disc thickness

13.4 Using a dial gauge to check brake disc run-out

13.6 Removing caliper assembly

13.7a Removing disc retaining screws (jacking holes arrowed)

13.7b Drawing off a disc using two 8 mm bolts

Removal

6 Unscrew the two bolts securing the caliper mounting bracket to the swivel hub and slide the caliper assembly off the disc **(see illustration)**. Using a piece of wire or string, tie the caliper to the front suspension coil spring to avoid placing any strain on the hydraulic brake hose.

7 Use chalk or paint to mark the relationship of the disc to the hub, then remove the two screws securing the brake disc to the hub and remove the disc. If the disc is a tight fit on the hub it can be drawn off by screwing two bolts into the jacking holes provided **(see illustrations)**.

Refitting

8 Thoroughly clean the mating surfaces of the hub and brake disc, using a wire brush or fine grade emery paper. Remove all traces of brake dust and corrosion to ensure that the disc seats correctly.

9 The remainder of the refitting procedure is the reverse of the removal procedure, noting the following:

a) Where applicable, observe the disc alignment markings made during removal.

b) If a new disc is being fitted, use a suitable solvent to wipe any preservative coating from the disc before fitting it.

c) Fit and tighten the brake disc screws to their specified torque, then fit the brake caliper and mounting bracket using only

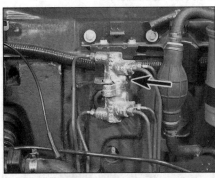

14.2 Brake proportioning valve plug (arrowed) - diesel-engined, non-ABS model shown

the upper mounting bolt. Check the disc run-out, as described earlier in this Section, before proceeding.

d) Tighten the caliper mounting bracket bolts and roadwheel nuts to their specified torque wrench settings.

14 Brake proportioning valve - testing, removal and refitting

Testing

1 The valve is mounted on the right-hand side of the engine compartment bulkhead.

2 Specialist equipment is required to check valve performance. If the valve is thought to be faulty, the vehicle should be taken to a suitably equipped Rover dealer for testing. However, in the event of an internal failure, brake fluid will seep from the plug on the front face of the valve which is situated directly below the upper two hose unions **(see illustration)**. Repairs are not possible; if the valve is thought to be faulty, it must be renewed.

Removal

3 Disconnect the sender unit wiring connector and unscrew the master cylinder reservoir filler cap. Place a piece of polythene over the filler neck and securely refit the cap (taking care not to damage the sender unit). This will minimise brake fluid loss during subsequent operations. As an added precaution, place absorbent rags beneath the proportioning valve brake pipe unions.

4 Wipe clean the area around the brake pipe unions on the proportioning valve, then make a note of how the pipes are arranged for reference on refitting. Unscrew the union nuts and carefully withdraw the pipes. Plug or tape over the pipe ends and valve orifices to minimise the loss of brake fluid and to prevent the entry of dirt into the system. Wash off any spilt fluid immediately with cold water.

5 Slacken the two bolts which secure the valve to the bulkhead and remove it from the engine compartment.

Refitting

6 Refit the proportioning valve to the bulkhead and tighten its mounting bolts to the specified torque.

7 Wipe the brake pipe unions clean and refit them to the valve, using the notes made on dismantling to ensure they are correctly positioned. Tighten the union nuts to the specified torque.

8 Remove the polythene from the master cylinder reservoir filler neck and bleed the complete hydraulic system.

15 Rear brake shoes - inspection

Refer to the information given in Chapter 1A or B as applicable.

16 Rear brake shoes - renewal

Warning: Brake shoes must be renewed on both rear wheels at the same time. Never renew the shoes on only one wheel as uneven braking may result.

Removal

1 Remove the brake drum (see Section 17).

2 Working carefully and noting all precautions, remove all traces of brake dust from the brake drum, backplate and shoes.

3 Measure the thickness of friction material remaining on each brake shoe at several points. If either shoe is worn at any point to the specified minimum thickness or less, all four shoes must be renewed as a set. Also, the shoes should be renewed if any are fouled with oil or grease as there is no satisfactory way of degreasing friction material once it is contaminated.

4 If any of the brake shoes are worn unevenly or fouled with oil or grease, trace and rectify the cause before reassembly.

5 To remove the brake shoes, first remove the shoe retainer springs and pins, using a pair of

9

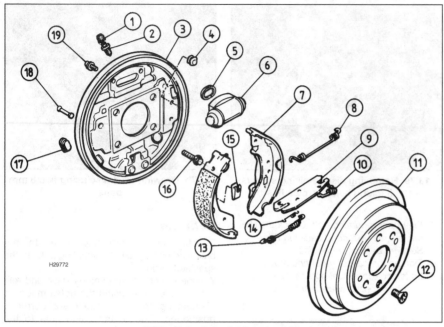

16.5a Rear drum brake assembly

1 Dust cap
2 Bleed screw
3 Backplate
4 Plug for brake shoe release access hole
5 Seal
6 Wheel cylinder
7 Brake shoes
8 Upper shoe return spring
9 Adjuster strut assembly
10 Strut return spring
11 Brake drum
12 Drum securing screw
13 Lower shoe return spring
14 Strut quadrant spring
15 Shoe retaining pin spring clip
16 Backplate securing screw
17 Shoe lining inspection hole
18 Shoe retaining pin
19 Wheel cylinder securing screw

pliers to press in each retainer clip until it can be rotated through 90° and released. Ease the shoes out one at a time from the lower pivot point to release the tension of the return spring, then disconnect the lower return spring from the leading shoe. Ease the upper end of both shoes out from their wheel cylinder locations, and disconnect the handbrake cable from the trailing shoe. The brake shoe and adjuster strut assembly can now be manoeuvred out of position and away from the backplate **(see illustrations)**. Do not depress the brake pedal until the brakes are reassembled. Wrap a strong elastic band around the wheel cylinder pistons to retain them.

Caution: Take great care to avoid damaging the wheel cylinder seals when removing the brake shoes.

6 With the brake shoe assembly on the worksurface, make a note of the fitted positions of the adjuster strut and springs to use as guide on reassembly **(see illustration)**. Carefully ease the adjuster strut from its slot in the trailing shoe and remove the short spring which secures the two components together. Detach the upper return spring and separate the shoes and strut.

7 Examine the adjuster strut assembly for signs of wear or damage, paying particular attention to the adjuster quadrant and knurled wheel. If damaged, the strut assembly must be renewed. Renew all the brake shoe return springs regardless of their apparent condition.

8 Peel back the rubber protective caps and check the wheel cylinder for fluid leaks or other damage. Check that both cylinder pistons are free to move easily.

Fitting

9 Prior to fitting, clean the backplate and apply a thin smear of high-temperature brake grease (silicone- or PBC/Poly Butyl Cuprysil-based) or anti-seize compound to all those surfaces of the backplate which bear on the shoes, particularly the adjuster and the wheel cylinder pistons.

Caution: Do not allow lubricant to foul the friction material.

10 Ensure the handbrake lever stop on the trailing shoe is correctly engaged with the lever and is pressed tight against the brake shoe **(see illustration)**.

16.5b Remove brake shoe retainer springs . . .

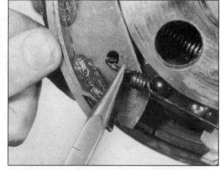

16.5c . . . unhook lower return spring . . .

16.5d . . . and manoeuvre shoe and adjuster strut assembly away from backplate

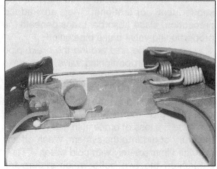

16.6 Correct fitted positions of adjuster strut and springs

16.10 Ensure handbrake stop lever is correctly located

11 Fully extend the adjuster strut quadrant and fit the leading brake shoe into the adjuster strut slot, ensuring that the strut spring and knurled wheel are situated on the underside of the strut assembly. Using a screwdriver, move the quadrant away from the knurled wheel and set it in the minimum adjustment position.

12 Fit the upper return spring to its respective location on the leading shoe. Fit the trailing shoe to the upper return spring and carefully ease the shoe into position in the adjuster strut slot. Once in position, fit the small spring which secures the trailing shoe to the strut assembly.

13 Remove the elastic band fitted to the wheel cylinder and manoeuvre the shoe and strut assembly into position on the backplate. Locate the upper end of both shoes with the wheel cylinder pistons and fit the handbrake cable to the trailing shoe operating lever. Fit the lower return spring to both shoes and ease the shoes into position on the lower pivot point.

14 Tap the shoes to centralise them with the backplate, then refit the shoe retainer pins and springs and secure them in position with the retainer clips. Check that the adjuster quadrant is still in the minimum adjuster position and if necessary, reset as follows. Place a block of wood between the trailing shoe and hub, to prevent the shoe moving forwards, then lever the leading shoe away from the hub to release the brake shoe return spring pressure on the adjuster quadrant. With the shoe held in this position, reset the quadrant to the minimum adjustment setting **(see illustration)**. Once the adjuster strut is correctly set, ease the leading shoe back into position then remove the block of wood and check that the shoes are still central.

15 Refit the brake drum and repeat the above operation on the remaining rear brake assembly.

16 On completion, apply the footbrake repeatedly to set the shoe-to-drum clearance, until normal (non-assisted) brake pedal operation returns.

17 Check handbrake cable operation and, if necessary, adjust as described in Chapter 1.

18 Refit the roadwheels then lower the

17.4a Location of shoe release access hole and plug (arrowed)

16.14 Reset adjuster strut prior to refitting drum

vehicle to the ground and tighten the roadwheel nuts to the specified torque.

19 Check and if necessary top up the hydraulic fluid level (see "*Weekly checks*").

17 Rear brake drum - removal, inspection and refitting

Note: *If either brake drum requires renewal, both should be renewed at the same time to ensure even and consistent braking.*

Removal

1 Chock the front wheels then jack up the rear of the vehicle and support it on axle stands (see "*Jacking and Vehicle Support*"). Remove the appropriate rear wheel.

2 Use chalk or paint to mark the relationship of the drum to the hub.

3 With the handbrake firmly applied to prevent drum rotation, unscrew the drum retaining screws **(see illustration)**. Fully release the handbrake cable and withdraw the drum.

4 If the drum will not pull away, first check that the handbrake is fully released. If the drum will still not come away, remove the grommet from the rear of the backplate and,

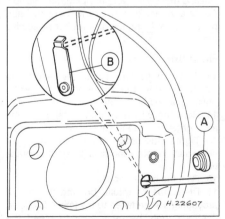

17.4b Releasing handbrake mechanism stop lever

Remove rubber grommet (A) and use small screwdriver to depress handbrake lever stop (B)

17.3 Removing brake drum retaining screws (jacking holes arrowed)

using a small screwdriver, disengage the handbrake lever stop from behind the lever to increase the shoe to drum clearance. If removal is still difficult, slacken the handbrake cable adjusting nut (see Section 24). If the drum is still held firm, it can be drawn off the shoes by screwing two bolts into the jacking holes provided **(see illustrations)**.

Inspection

5 Working carefully, remove all traces of brake dust from the drum.

> ⚠ *Warning: Avoid inhaling the dust as it is injurious to health.*

6 Scrub clean the outside of the drum and check it for obvious signs of wear or damage such as cracks around the roadwheel stud holes. Renew the drum if necessary.

7 Examine carefully the inside of the drum. Light scoring of the friction surface is normal but if heavy scoring is found, the drum must be renewed. It is usual to find a lip on the drum's inboard edge which consists of a mixture of rust and brake dust. This should be scraped away to leave a smooth surface which can be polished with fine (120 to 150 grade) emery paper. If, however, the lip is due to the friction surface being recessed by excessive wear, then the drum must be renewed.

8 If the drum is thought to be excessively worn or oval, its internal diameter must be measured at several points by using an

17.4c Brake drum can be drawn off hub by using two 8 mm bolts

9

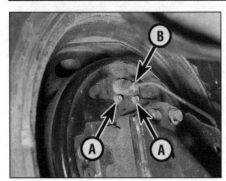

18.3 Wheel cylinder retaining bolts (A) and brake pipe union nut (B)

internal micrometer. Take measurements in pairs, the second at right angles to the first, and compare the two to check for signs of ovality. Provided that it does not enlarge the drum to beyond the specified maximum diameter, it may be possible to have the drum refinished by skimming or grinding but if this is not possible, the drums on both sides must be renewed.

Refitting

9 Refitting is the reverse of the removal procedure, noting the following:
a) On fitting a new brake drum, use a suitable solvent to remove any preservative coating that may have been applied to its interior.
b) If the existing drum is to be refitted, use a clean wire brush to remove all traces of dirt, brake dust and corrosion from the mating surfaces of the drum and the hub flange.
c) Align the marks made on removal (where applicable).
d) Tighten the drum retaining screws and the roadwheel nuts to their specified torque wrench settings.

18 Rear wheel cylinder - removal, overhaul and refitting

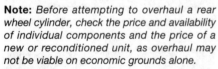

Note: Before attempting to overhaul a rear wheel cylinder, check the price and availability of individual components and the price of a new or reconditioned unit, as overhaul may not be viable on economic grounds alone.

Removal

1 Remove the brake shoes.
2 Minimise fluid loss by removing the master cylinder reservoir cap and then tightening it down onto a piece of polythene to obtain an airtight seal (taking care not to damage the sender unit), or by using a brake hose clamp, a G-clamp or a similar tool to clamp the flexible hose.
3 Wipe away all traces of dirt around the brake pipe union at the rear of the wheel cylinder and unscrew the union nut. Carefully ease the pipe out of the wheel cylinder and

plug or tape over its end to prevent dirt entry **(see illustration)**.
4 Unscrew the two wheel cylinder retaining bolts from the rear of the backplate and remove the cylinder, noting the rubber sealing ring which is fitted between the cylinder and backplate.

Overhaul

5 Remove the wheel cylinder from the vehicle and clean it thoroughly.
6 Mount the wheel cylinder in a soft-jawed vice and remove the rubber protective caps. Extract the piston assemblies.
7 Thoroughly clean all components using only methylated spirit, isopropyl alcohol or clean hydraulic fluid as a cleaning medium. **Caution: Never use mineral-based solvents such as petrol or paraffin which will attack the hydraulic system's rubber components. Dry the components immediately using compressed air or a clean, lint-free cloth.**
8 Check all components and renew any that are worn or damaged. Check particularly the cylinder bore and pistons. The complete assembly must be renewed if these are scratched, worn or corroded. If there is any doubt about the condition of the assembly or of any of its components, renew it. Remove the bleed screw and check that the fluid entry port and bleed screw passages are clear.
9 If the assembly is fit for further use, obtain a repair kit. Renew the rubber protective caps, dust caps and seals disturbed on dismantling, these should never be re-used. Renew also any other items included in the repair kit.
10 On reassembly, soak the pistons and the new seals in clean hydraulic fluid. Smear clean fluid on the cylinder bore surface.
11 Fit the new seals to their pistons using only the fingers to manipulate them into the grooves. Ensure that all components are refitted in the correct order and the right way round.
12 Insert the pistons into the bore using a twisting motion to avoid trapping the seal lips. Apply a smear of rubber lubricant to each piston before fitting the new rubber protective caps.

Refitting

13 Fit a new sealing ring to the rear of the wheel cylinder and place the cylinder in position on the backplate.
14 Refit the wheel cylinder retaining bolts and tighten them to the specified torque.
15 Tighten the brake pipe union nut and, if necessary, remove the clamp from the brake hose.
16 Refit the brake shoes.
17 Bleed the hydraulic braking system. If precautions were taken to minimise fluid loss, it should only be necessary to bleed the relevant rear brake. On completion, check that both footbrake and handbrake function correctly before taking the vehicle on the road.

19 Rear brake pads - inspection

Refer to Chapter 1.

20 Rear brake pads - renewal

⚠️ **Warning: Renew both sets of rear brake pads at the same time. Never renew the pads on only one wheel as uneven braking may result.**

Removal

1 Chock the front wheels then jack up the rear of the vehicle and support on axle stands (see "Jacking and Vehicle Support"). Remove the rear roadwheels.
2 Undo the two bolts securing the caliper shield in position and remove the shield from the rear of the caliper.
3 Remove both caliper guide pin bolts whilst, if necessary, using a slim open-ended spanner to prevent the guide pins from rotating. Lift the caliper away from the disc, noting the upper pad spring which is fitted to the roof of the caliper. Tie the caliper to the suspension strut using a piece of wire to avoid straining the hydraulic hose **(see illustration)**.
4 Remove the brake pads from the caliper mounting bracket whilst noting the correct fitted positions of the brake pads, pad retainer springs and pad shims.
5 Inspect the pads as described for the front brake pads and, if necessary, renew as a complete axle set.

Fitting

6 Fit the pad retainer springs to the caliper mounting bracket.
7 Apply a thin smear of Molykote M77 compound to the sides and back of each pad's metal backing and to those surfaces of the caliper body and mounting bracket which bear on the pads. In the absence of the specified lubricant, a good quality high-temperature brake grease (silicone- or PBC/Poly Butyl Cuprysil-based) or anti-seize compound may be used. Fit the shims to the back of both pads, noting that the smaller shim must be fitted to the piston side pad, and apply a thin smear of lubricant to the back of each shim.
Caution: Do not allow lubricant to foul the friction material.
8 Install the brake pads in the caliper mounting bracket, ensuring that the friction material is against the disc and the pad with the smaller shim attached is fitted on the inside.
9 If new pads have been fitted, it will be necessary to retract the piston fully into the caliper bore by rotating it in a clockwise

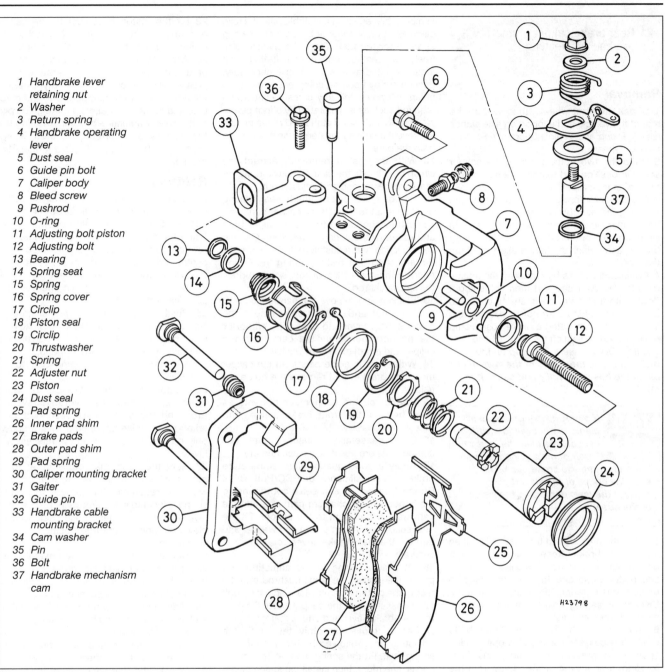

1 Handbrake lever
   retaining nut
2 Washer
3 Return spring
4 Handbrake operating
   lever
5 Dust seal
6 Guide pin bolt
7 Caliper body
8 Bleed screw
9 Pushrod
10 O-ring
11 Adjusting bolt piston
12 Adjusting bolt
13 Bearing
14 Spring seat
15 Spring
16 Spring cover
17 Circlip
18 Piston seal
19 Circlip
20 Thrustwasher
21 Spring
22 Adjuster nut
23 Piston
24 Dust seal
25 Pad spring
26 Inner pad shim
27 Brake pads
28 Outer pad shim
29 Pad spring
30 Caliper mounting bracket
31 Gaiter
32 Guide pin
33 Handbrake cable
   mounting bracket
34 Cam washer
35 Pin
36 Bolt
37 Handbrake mechanism
   cam

H23798

20.3 Rear brake caliper components

direction. This can be achieved by using a suitable pair of circlip pliers as a peg spanner or by fabricating a peg spanner for the task. Provided that the master cylinder reservoir has not been overfilled with hydraulic fluid, there should be no spillage, but keep a careful watch on the fluid level while retracting the piston. If the fluid level rises above the MAX level line at any time, the surplus should be syphoned off or ejected via a plastic tube connected to the bleed screw.

10 Ensure the upper pad spring is still in position in the caliper then slide the caliper into

position in its mounting bracket. When fitting the caliper, ensure that the lug on the rear of the piston side pad is located in one of the piston slots. Refit the caliper guide pin bolts and tighten them to the specified torque setting.

11 Depress the footbrake to bring the piston into contact with the pads then check that the lug on the piston side pad is located in one of the piston slots. If necessary, remove the caliper and adjust the piston position as described above. Refit the shield to the rear of the caliper.

12 Repeat the above procedure on the remaining rear brake caliper.

13 Once both calipers have been done, repeatedly depress the brake pedal until normal (non-assisted) pedal operation returns, then repeatedly apply the handbrake to set handbrake adjustment. Check the operation of the handbrake and, if necessary, adjust the cable as described in Chapter 1.

14 Refit the roadwheels, then lower the vehicle to the ground and tighten the roadwheel nuts to the specified torque.

15 Check the hydraulic fluid level (see "Weekly checks").

9

21 Rear brake caliper - removal, overhaul and refitting

Removal

1 Chock the front wheels, then jack up the rear of the vehicle and support on axle stands (see "*Jacking and Vehicle Support*"). Remove the rear wheel.

2 Undo the two bolts securing the caliper shield in position and remove the shield from the rear of the caliper.

3 Extract the spring clip and clevis pin securing the handbrake cable to the caliper handbrake lever, then remove the clip securing the outer cable to its mounting bracket and detach the handbrake cable from the caliper.

4 Minimise fluid loss by removing the master cylinder reservoir cap and then tightening it down onto a piece of polythene to obtain an airtight seal (taking care not to damage the sender unit), or by using a brake hose clamp or similar tool to seal off the flexible hose. *Caution: Do not use a G-clamp on the brake hose, as the edges of the jaws may pinch the hose internally and cause it to fail.*

 If a proprietary brake hose clamp is not available, fit two old sockets over the jaws of a pair of mole grips then use them to clamp the brake hose. The rounded edges of the socket will prevent the jaws damaging the inside of the hose.

5 Clean the area around the hose union, then undo the brake hose union bolt and disconnect the hose from the caliper. Plug the end of the hose and the caliper orifice to prevent dirt entering the hydraulic system. Discard the sealing washers as they must be renewed whenever disturbed.

6 Remove both the caliper guide pin bolts whilst, if necessary, using a slim open-ended spanner to prevent the guide pins from rotating, then lift the caliper away from the disc, noting the upper pad spring which is fitted to the roof of the caliper. Note that the brake pads need not be disturbed and can be left in position in the caliper mounting bracket.

Overhaul

7 With the caliper on the bench, wipe away all traces of dust and dirt.

 Warning: Avoid inhaling the dust as it is injurious to health.

8 Using a small screwdriver, carefully prise out the dust seal from the caliper bore.

9 Remove the piston from the caliper bore by rotating it in an anti-clockwise direction. This can be achieved using a suitable pair of circlip pliers as a peg spanner or by fabricating a peg spanner for the task. Once the piston turns freely but does not come out any further, then it can be withdrawn by hand, or if necessary, pushed out by applying compressed air to the union bolt hole. Only low pressure should be required such as is generated by a foot pump; place a block of wood at the end of the piston, to prevent it striking the caliper as it is ejected from the bore.

10 With the piston removed, extract the circlip from inside the piston and withdraw the thrustwasher, spring and adjuster nut.

11 Remove the piston (fluid) seal, taking great care not to scratch the caliper bore.

12 Extract the circlip from the caliper bore and withdraw the spring cover, spring, spring seat, bearing and adjusting bolt. Now remove the adjusting bolt piston, noting the O-ring fitted to the rear of the piston, and withdraw the small pushrod.

13 Slacken and remove the handbrake lever retaining nut and washer and remove the return spring, lever and dust seal. Withdraw the handbrake mechanism cam from the caliper and remove the cam washer.

14 Withdraw the guide pins from the caliper mounting bracket and remove the guide pin gaiters.

15 Inspect all the caliper components as described for the front brake caliper and renew as necessary.

16 On reassembly ensure that all components are absolutely clean and dry.

17 Apply a good quality high-temperature brake grease (silicone- or PBC/Poly Butyl Cuprysil-based) or anti-seize compound to the handbrake mechanism cam and refit the cam washer and cam to the caliper. Fit the dust seal, lever, return spring and washer and tighten the handbrake lever retaining nut securely.

18 Fit a new O-ring to the adjusting bolt piston then insert the small pushrod into the rear of the piston and install the adjusting bolt piston assembly in the caliper bore. Operate the handbrake lever and check that the piston is free to move smoothly then refit the adjusting bolt, followed by the bearing and spring seat. Fit the spring, so that its tapered end is innermost, then install the spring cover. Secure all the above components in position with the circlip, ensuring that it is correctly seated in the groove in the caliper bore.

19 Locate the adjusting nut with the cutout on the inside of the caliper piston and refit the spring, thrustwasher and circlip. Ensure the circlip is correctly located in its groove.

20 Soak the piston and the new piston fluid seal in clean hydraulic fluid. Smear clean fluid on the cylinder bore surface.

21 Fit the new piston fluid seal into the cylinder bore groove by hand (do not use any tools), then refit the piston assembly. Turn the piston in a clockwise direction, using the method employed on dismantling, until it is fully retracted into the caliper bore.

22 Fit the piston dust seal to the caliper ensuring that it is correctly located in the caliper and also the groove on the piston.

23 Apply the grease supplied in the repair kit, or a good quality high-temperature brake grease (silicone- or PBC/Poly Butyl Cuprysil-based) or anti-seize compound to the guide pins and fit the new gaiters. Fit the guide pins to the caliper mounting bracket, ensuring that the gaiters are correctly located in the grooves on both the guide pin and mounting bracket.

Refitting

24 Ensure the upper pad spring is still in position in the caliper then slide the caliper into position in its mounting bracket. When fitting the caliper, ensure that the lug on the rear of the piston side pad is located in the centre of the caliper piston at the point where the two piston slots cross. Refit the caliper guide pin bolts and tighten them to the specified torque setting.

25 Position a new sealing washer on each side of the hose union and refit the brake hose union bolt. Ensure that the brake hose union is correctly positioned between the lugs on the caliper then tighten the union bolt to the specified torque setting.

26 Remove the brake hose clamp, where fitted, and bleed the hydraulic system. Providing the precautions described were taken to minimise brake fluid loss, it should only be necessary to bleed the relevant rear brake.

27 Refit the handbrake cable outer to its mounting bracket and secure it in position with the retaining clip. Ensure the return spring is located in the groove in the operating lever then refit the handbrake cable to lever clevis pin and secure it in position with the spring clip.

28 Depress the brake pedal several times until normal (non-assisted) operation returns then check and, if necessary, adjust the handbrake cable as described in Chapter 1.

29 Refit the shield to the rear of the caliper and tighten its retaining bolts securely.

30 Refit the roadwheel, then lower the vehicle to the ground and tighten the roadwheel nuts to the specified torque.

31 Check the hydraulic fluid level (see "*Weekly checks*").

22 Rear brake disc - inspection, removal and refitting

Note: *If either rear brake disc requires renewal, both should be renewed at the same time to ensure even and consistent braking.*

Inspection

1 Chock the front wheels, then jack up the rear of the vehicle and support on axle stands (see "*Jacking and Vehicle Support*"). Remove the appropriate rear roadwheel.

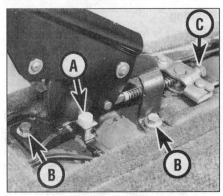

23.3 Handbrake lever switch (A), mounting bolts (B) and adjusting nut (C)

2 Inspect the disc as described for the front brake disc.

Removal

3 Undo the two caliper shield retaining bolts and remove the shield from the rear of the caliper.

4 Undo the two bolts securing the caliper mounting bracket to the trailing arm assembly and slide the caliper assembly off the disc. Using a piece of wire or string, tie the caliper to the coils of the rear suspension strut to avoid placing any strain on the hydraulic brake hose.

5 Use chalk or paint to mark the relationship of the disc to the hub, then remove the two screws securing the brake disc to the hub and remove the disc. If the disc is a tight fit on the hub, it can be drawn off by screwing two bolts into the jacking holes provided.

Refitting

6 Refitting is the reverse of the removal procedure, noting the following:
  a) Ensure that the mating surfaces of the disc and hub are clean and flat.
  b) Align (if applicable) the marks made on removal.
  c) If a new disc has been fitted, use a suitable solvent to wipe any preservative coating from the disc before refitting the caliper.
  d) Tighten the disc retaining screws, caliper bracket bolts and roadwheel nuts to their specified torque wrench settings.

23 Handbrake lever - removal and refitting

Removal

1 With the vehicle parked on level ground, chock the roadwheels so that the vehicle cannot move.

2 From inside the vehicle, prise out the cover from the top of the rear centre console section to gain access to the two retaining screws. Undo the two screws and remove the rear console section.

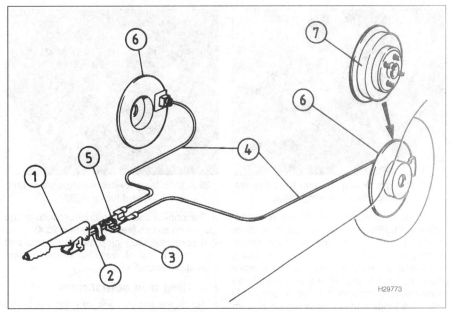

23.4 Handbrake mechanism layout

1	Handbrake lever	4	Rear cables
2	Intermediate rod	5	Adjusting nut
3	Compensator		
		6	Rear disc brake
		7	Rear drum brake

3 Remove the handbrake lever rubber gaiter and disconnect the wiring connector from the lever warning lamp switch **(see illustration)**.

4 Slacken and remove the handbrake cable adjusting nut from the rear of the lever and undo the bolts securing the handbrake lever assembly to the floorpan **(see illustration)**.

5 Lift the handbrake assembly out of position, noting the spring which is fitted to the lever adjusting rod.

Refitting

6 Refitting is a reverse of the removal procedure. Prior to refitting the handbrake lever rubber gaiter, adjust the handbrake cable as described in Chapter 1.

24 Handbrake cables - removal and refitting

Removal

1 Firmly chock the front wheels then jack up the rear of the vehicle and support it on axle stands (see "Jacking and Vehicle Support"). The handbrake cable consists of two sections (right and left-hand), which are linked to the lever assembly by an equalizer plate. Each section can be removed individually.

2 From inside the vehicle, prise out the cover from the top of the rear centre console section to gain access to the two retaining screws. Undo the two screws and remove the rear console section.

3 Slacken and remove the handbrake cable adjusting nut from the rear of the lever and disconnect the equalizer plate, noting the

spring which is fitted to the lever adjusting rod.

4 Undo the two bolts securing the cable outer retaining plate to the floor pan **(see illustration)**. Remove the retaining plate then detach the relevant cable inner from the equalizer plate and release the cable grommet from the floorpan.

5 On models equipped with rear disc brakes, working from underneath the vehicle, remove the two brake caliper shield retaining bolts and remove the shield from the caliper. Extract the spring clip and clevis pin securing the handbrake cable to the caliper handbrake lever then remove the clip securing the cable outer to its mounting bracket and detach the handbrake cable from the caliper.

6 On models equipped with rear drum brakes, remove the relevant rear brake drum. Remove the trailing shoe retainer spring and pin, using a pair of pliers to press in the retainer clip until

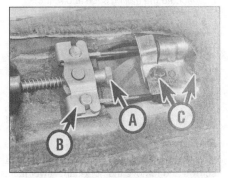

24.4 Handbrake cable adjusting nut (A), equalizer plate (B) and cable outer retaining plate bolts (C)

24.6 Using a 12 mm spanner to compress cable outer retaining tangs

it can be rotated through 90° and released. Ease the trailing shoe out of the lower pivot point to release the tension of the return spring, then disconnect the lower return spring from both shoes. Disconnect the handbrake cable from the trailing shoe then use a 12 mm spanner to compress the handbrake cable retaining tangs and withdraw the cable from the rear of the backplate (see illustration).

7 On all models, release the main silencer from its three rubber mountings and carefully lower the tailpipe section to gain access to the heat shield. Undo the three heat shield retaining bolts and remove the shield from the vehicle underbody.

8 Work along the length of the cable section and remove all bolts securing the cable outer to the vehicle underbody and trailing arm. Once free, withdraw the cable from underneath the vehicle and, if necessary, repeat the procedure for the remaining cable section.

Refitting

9 Refitting is a reversal of the removal sequence noting the following:

a) Lubricate all exposed linkages and cable pivots with a good quality multi-purpose grease.

b) Ensure the cable outer grommet is correctly located in the floorpan and that all retaining bolts are tightened to the specified torque.

c) On models with rear drum brakes, relocate the trailing shoe and refit the brake drum.

d) Prior to refitting the rear centre console section, adjust the handbrake cable as described in Chapter 1.

25 Stop lamp switch - removal, refitting and adjustment

Removal

1 Working inside the vehicle, undo the five screws and remove the right-hand lower facia panel.

2 Remove the screws and lower the fuse panel away from its mounting bracket.

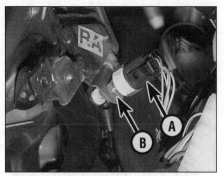

25.4 Stop lamp switch wiring connector (A) and locknut (B)

3 Disconnect the wiring connector from the stop lamp switch (see illustration 25.4).

4 Slacken the stop lamp switch locknut and unscrew the switch from the pedal bracket (see illustration).

Refitting and adjustment

5 Screw the switch back into position in the mounting bracket.

6 Connect an ohmmeter across the stop lamp switch terminals and screw the switch in until an open circuit is present between the switch terminals. Depress the pedal and check that continuity exists between the switch terminals as soon as the pedal is depressed. If necessary, reposition the switch until it operates as specified.

7 Once the stop lamp switch is correctly adjusted, hold the switch stationary and tighten the locknut securely.

8 Connect the wiring connector to the switch and refit the fuse panel lower facia panel.

26 Anti-lock Braking System (ABS) - component removal and refitting

> **Warning: After disturbing any of the ABS components, the operation of the system must be verified by a Rover dealer using dedicated electronic test equipment.**

ABS ECU

Removal

1 Disconnect the battery negative terminal then undo the screw and remove the modulator relay cover.

2 Disconnect the wiring connectors from the modulator and free the wiring from its retaining clip on the unit.

3 Slacken and remove the retaining nuts, then lift the ABS modulator together with the ABS ECU from the mounting bracket.

4 Slide the rubber mounting from the stud at the base of the ECU casing, then unscrew the stud from the casing.

5 Slacken and withdraw the screws, then separate the ECU from the modulator block.

Refitting

6 Refitting is a reversal of removal. Ensure that the ECU wiring connector is securely refitted.

ABS hydraulic modulator

Removal (models up to 1998)

7 Disconnect the battery negative cable and position it away from the terminal.

8 With reference to Chapter 3, unbolt the coolant expansion tank from its mountings and move it to one side; there is no need to disconnect the coolant hoses from it.

9 Disconnect the sender unit wiring connector and unscrew the master cylinder reservoir filler cap. Place a piece of polythene over the filler neck and securely refit the cap (taking care not to damage the sender unit). This will minimise brake fluid loss during subsequent operations. As an added precaution, place absorbent rags beneath the modulator brake pipe unions.

10 Release the clip and detach the ABS ECU wiring harness from the mounting bracket.

11 Release the locking clip and unplug the wiring harness connector from the ECU.

12 Slacken and remove the securing nut, then disconnect the earthing lead from the front of the modulator body.

13 Wipe clean the area around the six brake pipe unions then make a note of how the pipes are arranged for reference when refitting. Unscrew the union nuts and carefully withdraw the pipes. Plug or tape over the pipe ends and valve orifices to minimise the loss of brake fluid and to prevent the entry of dirt into the system. Wash off any spilt fluid immediately with cold water.

14 Refer to the previous sub-section and separate the ECU from the modulator body.

15 Remove the modulator assembly from the engine compartment. Do not attempt to dismantle the modulator block assembly. Overhaul of the unit is a complex job and should be entrusted to a Rover dealer.

Refitting

16 Refitting is the reverse of the removal procedure, noting the following:

a) Tighten the modulator block mounting nuts to the specified torque.

b) Refit the brake pipes to their respective unions and tighten the union nuts to the specified torque.

c) On completion, bleed the braking system as described in Section 6.

d) After disturbing any of the ABS components, the operation of the system must be verified by a Rover dealer using dedicated electronic test equipment.

Removal (models from 1998-on)

17 Disconnect the battery negative cable and position it away from the terminal. Jack up the front of the car, rest it securely on axle stands (see "Jacking and Vehicle Support") and remove the front right-hand roadwheel.

18 With reference to Section 6, connect a suitable length of tubing to the bleed screw on the front right-hand brake caliper. Place the other end of the tube in a container. Open the caliper bleed screw, then pump the brake pedal to expel the brake fluid from the master cylinder. Tighten the caliper bleed screw on completion.

19 Repeat the operation described in previous paragraph at the front left-hand caliper.

20 Slide the locking bar towards the front of the car, then unplug the wiring connector from the side of the modulator unit.

21 Wipe clean the area around the six brake pipe unions then make a note of how the pipes are arranged for reference when refitting. Unscrew the union nuts and carefully withdraw the pipes. Plug or tape over the pipe ends and valve orifices to minimise the loss of brake fluid and to prevent the entry of dirt into the system. Wash off any spilt fluid immediately with cold water.

22 Slacken the securing nuts and detach the modulator from its mounting bracket.

23 Remove the modulator assembly from the engine compartment. Do not attempt to dismantle the modulator block assembly. Overhaul of the unit is a complex job and should be entrusted to a Rover dealer.

Refitting

24 Refitting is the reverse of the removal procedure, noting the following:
a) Tighten the modulator block mounting nuts to the specified torque.
b) Refit the brake pipes to their respective unions and tighten the union nuts to the specified torque.
c) On completion, bleed the braking system as described in Section 6.
d) After disturbing any of the ABS components, the operation of the system must be verified by a Rover dealer using dedicated electronic test equipment.

Front wheel sensor

Removal

25 Chock the rear wheels, firmly apply the handbrake, jack up the front of the vehicle and support on axle stands (see "Jacking and Vehicle Support"). Remove the appropriate front roadwheel.

26 From inside the engine compartment, disconnect the relevant sensor wiring connector and displace the sensor wiring grommet.

27 From underneath the vehicle, pull the sensor wiring lead through the wing valance then undo the sensor lead bracket retaining bolts and remove the brackets.

28 Slacken and remove the two bolts securing the sensor unit to the wheel hub then remove the sensor and lead assembly.

Refitting

29 Refitting is the reverse of the removal procedure, noting the following:

a) Ensure that the sensor and hub sealing faces are clean then refit the sensor and tighten its retaining bolts to the specified torque.
b) Ensure the sensor wiring is correctly routed and all bracket retaining bolts are tightened to the specified torque.

Rear wheel sensor - models with disc brakes

Removal

30 Chock the front wheels then jack up the rear of the vehicle and support it on axle stands (see "Jacking and Vehicle Support"). Remove the appropriate roadwheel.

31 Trace the wiring back from the sensor to the wiring connector then free the connector from its retaining clips and disconnect it.

32 Undo the sensor lead bracket retaining bolts and remove the brackets.

33 Slacken and remove the bolt securing the strap to the sensor cover then undo the sensor cover retaining bolts and remove the cover.

34 Undo the two screws securing the sensor to the rear hub assembly and remove it from the vehicle, along with the shim which is fitted behind it.

Refitting

35 Refitting is the reverse of the removal procedure, noting the following:
a) Ensure the sensor and hub sealing faces are clean, then install the sensor and shim and tighten the sensor retaining screws to the specified torque.
b) Refit the sensor cover, cover strap retaining bolt and sensor lead brackets, then tighten all retaining bolts to the specified torque.
c) Reconnect the sensor lead wiring connector and refit the connector to its retaining clip.

Rear wheel sensor - models with drum brakes

Removal

36 With reference to Sections 16 and 17, remove the relevant brake drum and both brake shoes from the backplate.

37 Work along the length of the ABS sensor wiring and release it from the clips on the rear suspension components. Locate the wiring connector, to the rear of the axle beam mounting. Prise the connector from its retaining clip and unplug it.

38 Slacken and withdraw the two mounting bolts, then lift the sensor and adapter assembly from the brake backplate.

39 Prise the sensor wiring grommet from the backplate, then withdraw the sensor and adapter assembly through the backplate aperture.

40 Loosen the lockscrew and slide sensor body from the adapter.

Refitting

41 Fit the new sensor to the adapter, then pass the assembly through the backplate aperture and press the wiring grommet into place. Fit and tighten the two retaining bolts to the specified torque.

42 Loosen the adapter lockscrew, then using a feeler blade, adjust the position of the sensor in the adapter so that the clearance between the tip of the sensor and the reluctor ring is as listed in the Specifications. On completion, tighten the adapter lockscrew.

43 The remainder of the refitting procedure is a reversal of removal, noting the following points:
a) Ensure that the sensor wiring connector is securely refitted.
b) Press the sensor wiring and connector firmly into their retaining clips.
c) Refit the brake shoes and drum with reference to Sections 16 and 17 respectively.

Reluctor rings

44 The reluctor rings are not available as separate items. The front rings are available only as an integral part of the outer constant velocity joint assembly and the rear rings are available only as an integral part of the rear hub.

Relays

45 Both the solenoid relay and return pump relay are located in the modulator block assembly. To gain access to them, undo the relay cover retaining screw and lift off the cover. Either relay can then be simply pulled out of position. Refer to Chapter 12 for further information on relays.

27 Brake servo vacuum pump (diesel models) - removal and refitting

Removal

1 Disconnect the battery negative cable and position it away from the terminal.

2 Raise the front of the car, support it securely on axle stands (see "Jacking and Vehicle Support") and remove the right-hand front roadwheel.

3 Remove the fixings and lower the undertray away from the underside of the engine compartment.

4 Remove the auxiliary drivebelt with reference to Chapter 10, Section 21.

5 Position a trolley jack under the engine and place a wooden block in the jack head. Raise the jack so that it is just supporting the weight of the engine.

6 Refer to Chapter 2B and remove the right-hand engine mounting bracket.

7 Unplug the multiway wiring connector from the rear of the alternator, then remove the nut and disconnect the main battery cable from the alternator stud terminal.

8 Release the clip and disconnect the vacuum hose from the pump port.

9

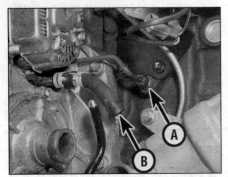

27.10 Vacuum pump oil supply pipe (A) and return hose (B)

27.11a Alternator/vacuum pump upper mounting bolt

27.11b Alternator/vacuum pump upper mounting nut and bolt (arrowed)

9 Slacken the clip and disconnect the vacuum pump oil return hose from the sump pipe.
Caution: Be prepared for some oil spillage; position a drain container under the union and pad the surrounding area with absorbent rags.
10 Undo the union and disconnect the vacuum pump oil supply pipe from the cylinder block. Again, be prepared for some oil spillage **(see illustration)**.
11 Lift the right-hand end of the engine slightly, by raising the trolley jack to gain access to the alternator mounting bolts. Slacken and withdraw the bolts and remove the alternator from its mounting bracket **(see illustrations)**.
12 Remove the alternator from the engine bay.

13 Remove the four securing bolts and detach the vacuum pump from the front of the alternator **(see illustration)**.

Refitting

14 Refitting is a reversal of removal, noting the following points:
a) *Ensure that the vacuum pump to alternator bolts are tightened to the specified torque.*
b) *Tighten the alternator mounting bolts to the specified torque (see Chapter 5A).*
c) *Ensure that all oil supply and return unions are clean before reconnection, and tighten the union nuts securely.*
d) *Refit the right-hand engine mountings with reference to Chapter 2B.*
e) *Refit the auxiliary drivebelt with reference to Chapter 1B.*

27.13 Remove the four securing bolts (arrowed) and detach the vacuum pump from the front of the alternator

Chapter 10
Suspension and steering

Contents

Degrees of difficulty

Easy, suitable for novice with little experience	Fairly easy, suitable for beginner with some experience	Fairly difficult, suitable for competent DIY mechanic	Difficult, suitable for experienced DIY mechanic	Very difficult, suitable for expert DIY or professional

Specifications

Front suspension

Type . . . . Fully independent with coil-over-shock absorber struts, transverse lower arms and tie rods. Anti-roll bar connected to lower arms via drop links.

Rear suspension

Type . . . . Torsion beam assembly with trailing arms and coil-over-shock absorber struts, angled rubber pivot mountings on trailing arms giving 'in phase, passive rear steer' effect, anti-roll bar on diesel and 1.8 litre models.

Steering

Type . . . . Rack and pinion, power-assisted steering available as standard or optional extra.

Turns lock-to-lock:
Manual 4.0
Power-assisted 3.4

Wheel alignment and steering angles

All measurements are with vehicle at kerb weight
Toe-out (on turns) . . . . Inside roadwheel 20°, outside roadwheel 18° 30'
Camber angle, front and rear . . . . 0° 20' negative ± 0° 10'
Front castor angle . . . . 2° positive ± 0° 30'
Steering axis inclination (SAI) or kingpin inclination (KPI) . . . . 12° 7' ± 0° 30'
Toe setting:
Front . . . . 0° 5' ± 0° 7' 30'' toe-out per side
Rear . . . . 0° 8' ± 10' toe-in per side

Roadwheels

Type . . . . Steel (alloy optional)
Size:
1.1, 1.4 and 1.6 litre petrol and 2.0 litre diesel models:
    Standard . . . . 5Jx14 (steel)
    Optional . . . . 5.5Jx15 (alloy)
1.8 litre petrol models . . . . 5.5Jx15 (alloy)

Tyres

Type . . . . Tubeless, steel-braced radial
Size:
1.1 litre petrol models . . . . 175/65 - R14 82T
1.4 litre petrol models:
    Steel wheels . . . . 175/65 - R14 82T
    Alloy wheels . . . . 185/55 - R15 81V
1.6 litre petrol models:
    Steel wheels . . . . 175/65 - R14 82H
    Alloy wheels . . . . 185/55 - R15 81V
1.8 litre petrol models . . . . 185/55 - R15 81V
2.0 litre diesel (86 PS) models:
    Steel wheels . . . . 175/65 - R14 82T
    Alloy wheels . . . . 185/55 - R15 81V
2.0 litre diesel (105 PS) models:
    Steel wheels . . . . 175/65 - R14 82H
    Alloy wheels . . . . 185/55 - R15 81V
Tyre pressures . . . . See end of "*Weekly checks*"

Torque wrench settings

	Nm	lbf ft
Front suspension		
Driveshaft retaining nut	180	133
Swivel hub brake shield screws	9	7
Front suspension strut:		
Damper rod nut	40	30
Upper mounting nuts	30	22
Swivel hub pinch-bolt	80	59
Brake hose clamp bolt	25	18
Anti-roll bar:		
Mounting clamp bolts	22	16
Drop link to anti-roll bar bolts	45	33
Drop link to lower arm bolts	60	44
Tie bar:		
Lower suspension arm bolts	80	59
Retaining nut	45	33
Lower arm:		
Balljoint retaining nut	55	41
Body pivot bolt	45	33
Front beam securing bolts	100	74
Rear beam securing bolts	100	74
Rear suspension		
Rear hub nut	180	133
Brake hose bracket to trailing arm bolts	15	11
Handbrake cable to trailing arm bolts	22	16
Stub axle to beam axle retaining bolts	45	33
Stub axle backplate retaining bolts	45	33
Rear suspension strut:		
Damper rod nut	29	21
Lower mounting bolt	80	59
Upper mounting nuts	38	28
Beam axle mounting bracket-to-body	100	74
Beam axle pivot bolts	100	74
Anti-roll bar to beam axle nuts	100	74
Steering		
Steering wheel nut	50	37
Steering column:		
Lower mounting bolt and nut	22	16
Upper mounting bolts and nuts	15	11
Universal joint pinch-bolts	30	22
Steering gear-to-mounting bracket bolts	38	28

Torque wrench settings

	Nm	lbf ft
Steering (continued)		
Steering gear-to-suspension rear beam flange bolts	58	43
Power-assisted steering gear:		
Feed pipe union nut	37	27
Return pipe union nut	28	20
Track rod balljoint:		
Balljoint-to-hub carrier nut	45	33
Locknut	45	33
Power steering pump (petrol models):		
Mounting bolts	48	35
Outlet pipe union nut	55	41
Pulley retaining bolts	9	7
Power steering pump (diesel models):		
Mounting bolts	25	18
Outlet pipe union	20	15
Pulley retaining bolts	10	7
Pump drivebelt tensioner pulley bolt (manual tensioner)	25	18
Roadwheels		
Roadwheel nuts	110	81

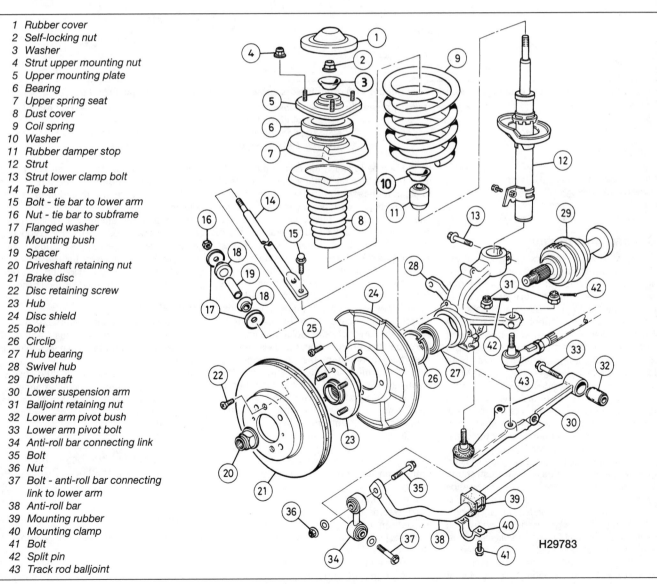

1 Rubber cover
2 Self-locking nut
3 Washer
4 Strut upper mounting nut
5 Upper mounting plate
6 Bearing
7 Upper spring seat
8 Dust cover
9 Coil spring
10 Washer
11 Rubber damper stop
12 Strut
13 Strut lower clamp bolt
14 Tie bar
15 Bolt - tie bar to lower arm
16 Nut - tie bar to subframe
17 Flanged washer
18 Mounting bush
19 Spacer
20 Driveshaft retaining nut
21 Brake disc
22 Disc retaining screw
23 Hub
24 Disc shield
25 Bolt
26 Circlip
27 Hub bearing
28 Swivel hub
29 Driveshaft
30 Lower suspension arm
31 Balljoint retaining nut
32 Lower arm pivot bush
33 Lower arm pivot bolt
34 Anti-roll bar connecting link
35 Bolt
36 Nut
37 Bolt - anti-roll bar connecting
   link to lower arm
38 Anti-roll bar
39 Mounting rubber
40 Mounting clamp
41 Bolt
42 Split pin
43 Track rod balljoint

H29783

1.1 Front suspension components

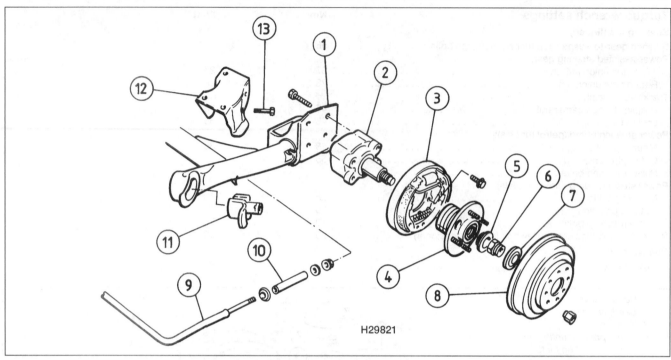

1.2 Rear suspension components (model with drum brakes shown - models with disc brakes similar)

1 Beam axle	4 Hub and bearing assembly	8 Brake drum
2 Stub axle	5 Spacer	9 Anti-roll bar
3 Brake shoe and backplate assembly	6 Hub nut	10 Anti-roll bar collar
	7 Dust cap	11 Beam axle pivot bush

12 Beam axle pivot mounting bracket
13 Beam axle pivot mounting bolt

1 General information and precautions

General information

The independent front suspension is of the MacPherson strut type, incorporating coil springs and integral telescopic shock absorbers **(see illustration on previous page)**. The MacPherson struts are located by transverse lower suspension arms, which utilize rubber inner mounting bushes and incorporate a balljoint at the outer ends, and forward facing longitudinal tie bars. Both lower suspension arms are connected to an anti-roll bar via a short drop link. The front swivel hubs, which carry the wheel bearings, brake calipers and the hub/disc assemblies, are bolted to the MacPherson struts and connected to the lower arms via the balljoints.

The rear suspension is of the torsion beam type, utilising tubular steel trailing arms linked via a single twist beam axle **(see illustration)**. The roadwheel stub axles are bolted to the ends of the trailing arms. Each trailing arm is mounted on the vehicle underbody at an angle by means of a large rubber bush, which incorporates a combination of voids and steel interleaving. This construction allows the entire trailing arm and torsion beam assembly to rotate about one mounting slightly during cornering; the amount of rotation is governed

by the degree to which the rear of the vehicle rolls. The net effect is that the rear wheels tend to steer in phase with the front wheels during hard cornering, thus improving the vehicles grip and handling. The rear suspension struts incorporate coil springs and integral telescopic shock absorbers and are mounted onto the rear lower lateral link via a rubber mounting bush.

The steering wheel is of the energy-absorbing type (to protect the driver in the event of an accident) and is attached by a deeply-recessed nut to the steering column which is also collapsible. In the event of an impact, the lower steering column clamp and the upper column mounting, fitted with energy absorbing bending plates, is designed to allow the column to slide downwards. The downwards movement of the column bends the mounting plates which absorb some of the energy, so lessening the force transmitted to the driver via the steering wheel.

A driver's airbag is fitted to all models as standard, with seat belt pre-tensioners and a front seat passenger airbag available as options on all models; See Chapter 12 for further details.

The steering column has a universal joint fitted towards the lower end of its length and its bottom end is clamped to a second universal joint, which is in turn clamped to the steering gear pinion.

The steering gear is mounted onto the engine compartment bulkhead and is connected by two track rods, with balljoints at

their outer ends, to the steering arms projecting rearwards from the hub carriers. The track rod ends are threaded to facilitate adjustment.

Power-assisted steering is available as an option on certain models. The main components being a rack and pinion steering gear unit, a hydraulic pump which is belt-driven off the crankshaft and the hydraulic feed and return lines between the pump and steering gear.

Precautions

The driveshaft hub and stub axle nuts are tightened to a very high torque - ensure the car is securely supported when loosening and tightening them.

A number of precautions must be observed when working on the steering components of vehicles equipped with a Supplementary Restraint System (SRS); these are listed in Chapter 12.

2 Front swivel hub assembly - removal and refitting

Removal

1 Chock the rear wheels, firmly apply the handbrake then jack up the front of the vehicle and support it on axle stands (see *"Jacking and Vehicle Support"*). Remove the appropriate front roadwheel.

2.8 Removing the swivel hub assembly

2 Using a hammer and suitable chisel nosed tool, tap up the staking securing the driveshaft retaining nut to the groove in the CV joint (refer to Chapter 8 for details).

3 Have an assistant firmly depress the footbrake, then using a socket and extension bar, slacken and remove the driveshaft retaining nut. Discard the nut; a new nut must be obtained for reassembly.

4 Remove the securing bolt and detach the brake hose mounting bracket from the base of the suspension strut. If the hub bearings are to be disturbed, remove the brake disc. If not, undo the two bolts securing the caliper mounting bracket to the hub and slide the caliper off the disc. Tie the caliper to the suspension strut to avoid placing any strain on the brake hose.

5 On models equipped with ABS, remove the front wheel sensor.

6 Slacken and remove the bolt and washer securing the anti-roll bar drop link to the lower suspension arm and undo the two bolts securing the tie bar to the lower suspension arm.

7 Extract the split pins and undo the nuts securing the steering gear track rod and lower suspension arm balljoints to the swivel hub. Release both the balljoints from the swivel hub by using a suitable balljoint separator, taking great care not to damage the balljoint gaiters.

8 Slacken the swivel hub-to-suspension strut clamp bolt then carefully ease the hub off the

strut. Once free, pull the hub outwards to free it from the constant velocity joint splines, then remove it from the vehicle **(see illustration)**. Whilst the hub is removed, support the driveshaft by tying it to the suspension strut to avoid damaging the inner constant velocity joint or gaiter.

Refitting

9 Refitting is reversal of the removal procedure noting the following:
a) *Ensure that the lug on the base of the suspension strut correctly engages with the slot in the swivel hub assembly clamp.*
b) *Tighten all nuts and bolts to the specified torque.*
c) *Where necessary, refit the brake disc and/or ABS wheel sensor as described in Chapter 9.*
d) *Use new split pins to secure the track rod and lower suspension arm balljoint retaining nuts in position.*
e) *When fitting the new driveshaft retaining nut, tighten it to the specified torque then stake it firmly into the groove in the CV joint by using a suitable punch.*

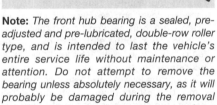

3 Front hub bearings - removal and refitting

Note: *The front hub bearing is a sealed, pre-adjusted and pre-lubricated, double-row roller type, and is intended to last the vehicle's entire service life without maintenance or attention. Do not attempt to remove the bearing unless absolutely necessary, as it will probably be damaged during the removal operation. Never overtighten the driveshaft nut beyond the specified torque wrench setting in an attempt to 'adjust' the bearing.*
Note: *A press will be required to dismantle and rebuild the hub assembly. If such a tool is not available, a large bench vice and suitable spacers (such as large sockets) will serve as an adequate substitute. The service tool numbers for the special Rover mandrels are given in the accompanying illustrations. The bearing's inner races are an interference fit on*

the hub. If the outboard inner race remains on the hub when it is pressed out of the hub carrier, a proprietary knife-edged bearing puller will be required to remove it.

Removal

1 Remove the swivel hub assembly as described in Section 2, then undo the brake disc shield retaining screws and remove the shield from the hub.

2 Press the hub out of the swivel hub using a tubular spacer **(see illustration)**. If the bearing's outboard inner race remains on the hub, remove it using a suitable bearing puller.

3 Extract both circlips from the swivel hub and discard them as they should be renewed whenever disturbed.

4 Press the bearing out of the swivel hub by using a suitable tubular spacer **(see illustration)**.

5 Thoroughly clean the hub and swivel hub, removing all traces of dirt and grease. Polish away any burrs or raised edges which might hinder reassembly. Check both for cracks or any other signs of wear or damage and renew the hub if necessary. The bearing and its circlips must be renewed whenever they are disturbed. A replacement bearing kit is available from Rover dealers which consists of the bearing and both circlips.

6 Check the condition of the roadwheel studs in the hub flange. If any are sheared off, stretched or have damaged threads, they can be pressed out of the hub providing that its flange is fully supported. On refitting, support the hub flange and press in the new stud until it seats fully.

Refitting

7 On reassembly, check (if possible) that the new bearing is packed with grease and fit the new circlip to the swivel hub outboard groove. Apply a light film of oil to the bearing inner and outer races and to the matching surfaces in the hub and swivel hub to aid fitting of the bearing.

8 Support the swivel hub outboard face and, using a suitable tubular spacer which bears only on the bearing's outer race, press in the new bearing until it seats against the circlip **(see illustration)**. Secure the bearing in

10

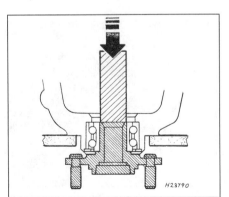

3.2 Pressing out hub from swivel hub

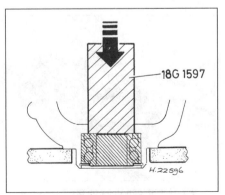

3.4 Pressing hub bearing out of swivel hub

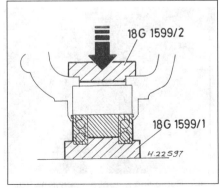

3.8 Pressing new hub bearing into swivel hub

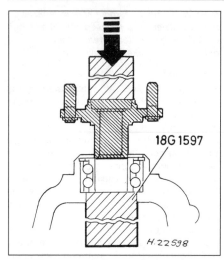

3.9 Pressing hub into swivel hub - note support for bearing inner race

position by fitting the second new circlip to the swivel hub's inboard groove.

9 Fully supporting the bearing inner race, press the hub into the bearing and swivel hub until the hub shoulder seats against the bearing's inner race **(see illustration)**. Wipe off any surplus oil or grease.

10 Refit the brake disc shield to the swivel hub and tighten its retaining screws securely.

11 Refit the swivel hub assembly.

4 Front suspension strut - removal, overhaul and refitting

Caution: If renewing the strut damper during overhaul, both the left- and right-hand dampers should be renewed as a pair, to preserve the handling characteristics of the vehicle.
Note: *Before attempting to dismantle the front suspension strut, a suitable tool to hold the coil spring in compression must be obtained. Adjustable coil spring compressors are readily available and are recommended for this operation. Any attempt to dismantle the strut*

4.3 Removing the bolt securing the brake hose to suspension strut

without such a tool is likely to result in damage or personal injury. In addition, a suitable crows-foot adapter will be needed to allow the strut top mounting nut to be tightened to the correct torque during reassembly.

Removal

1 Chock the rear wheels, firmly apply the handbrake, then jack up the front of the vehicle and support on axle stands (see *"Jacking and Vehicle Support"*). Remove the appropriate roadwheel.

2 Slacken and remove the bolt and washer securing the anti-roll bar drop link to the suspension lower arm (see Section 6 for details).

3 Undo the bolt securing the brake hose retaining clamp to the strut, then remove the clamp and free the flexible hose **(see illustration)**.

4 Slacken the swivel hub-to-suspension strut clamp bolt, then insert a stout pry bar between the clamp bolt flanges at the rear of the swivel hub. Use the bar to prise the flanges apart slightly, so that the base of the strut is released from the swivel hub.

5 Carefully ease the swivel hub assembly off the lower end of the strut by pressing down on the suspension lower arm and pivoting the top of the swivel hub towards you. Avoid straining the driveshaft CV joint as you do this.

6 Working in the engine compartment, remove the strut rubber dust cover. Use chalk

4.6 Remove the rubber cover and strut upper mounting nuts (arrowed)

or a marker pen to mark the relative positions of the suspension strut upper mounting and bodywork **(see illustration)**.

7 Support the strut inside the wheelarch, then undo the three upper mounting nuts - DO NOT slacken or remove the strut centre nut at this stage. Lower the strut assembly away from the bodywork and out of the wheelarch. Note the seal which is fitted between the upper mounting plate and vehicle body **(see illustration)**.
Caution: Do not attempt to slacken or remove the strut centre nut until the coil spring is compressed using suitable compressors.

Overhaul

8 With the strut removed from the vehicle, clean away all external dirt then mount it upright in a bench vice, with the lower end of the strut clamped in the vice jaws.

9 Fit the spring compressor and compress the coil spring until all tension is relieved from the upper mounting plate **(see illustration)**.

10 Slacken the upper mounting retaining nut with a ring spanner; counterhold the damper rod, using a suitable Allen key or hex bit, as the nut is unscrewed - do not allow the rod to rotate inside the damper, as this may damage the piston seal **(see illustration)**.

11 Remove the nut and upper cup washer, followed by the mounting plate/bearing, upper spring seat and lower cup washer. Slide the

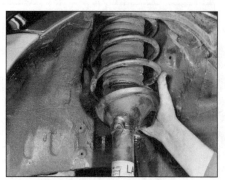

4.7 Removing a front suspension strut

4.9 Compress the coil spring with a suitable pair of spring compressors . . .

4.10 . . . and remove the upper mounting nut whilst retaining the piston with an Allen key

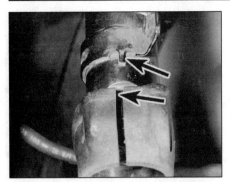

4.21 Align the suspension strut lug with the slot in the swivel hub (arrowed)

bump stop rubber off the damper piston rod, then lift off the coil spring together with the piston dust cover and separate the two components. Make a careful note of the order of removal to aid reassembly.

12 With the strut assembly completely dismantled, examine all components for wear, damage or corrosion, and check the mounting plate/bearing for smoothness of rotation. Renew any component displaying signs of deterioration.

13 Examine the damper for signs of fluid leakage. Check the piston rod for signs of pitting along its entire length and check the strut body for signs of damage or corrosion. Test the operation of the strut, while holding it in an upright position, by moving the piston through several full-length strokes; the resistance felt should be smooth and continuous. Now operate the piston rod through short strokes of 50 to 100 mm. If fluid has leaked from the damper, the piston will have an amount of undamped 'freeplay' at the end of its travel. If this is the case, or if there are any visible signs of wear, damage or corrosion, renewal of the strut will be necessary.

14 If any doubt exists about the condition of the coil spring, carefully remove the spring compressors and check the spring for distortion, cracking or excessive corrosion. Since no minimum free length is specified by Rover, the only way to check the tension of the spring is to compare it to a new

component. Renew the spring if it is damaged or distorted or there is any doubt as to its condition.

15 Inspect all other components for signs of damage or deterioration and renew any that are suspect.

16 If new damper strut insert is being fitted, prime the damper with reference to the (manufacturer's instructions) by operating the piston rod through several full-length strokes.

17 Pass the compressed coil spring over the top of the damper piston rod and place it in position on the lower spring seat, ensuring that the end of the spring is correctly located in the lower spring seat recess. Fit the damper dust cover over the top of the coil spring.

18 Slide the bump stop rubber over the end of the damper piston rod. Fit the lower cup washer, followed by the upper spring seat, the mounting plate/bearing and the upper cup washer. Ensure that the upper end of the coil spring is correctly located in the recess in the upper spring seat, then fit the new damper rod top nut and tighten it to the specified torque setting. Note that you will need to fit a crow's-foot adapter to the torque wrench to allow the damper rod nut to be tightened to the correct torque. Counterhold the damper rod, using a suitable Allen key or hex bit, as the nut is tightened.

Caution: Do not allow the rod to rotate inside the damper, as this may damage the piston seal.

Refitting

19 Manoeuvre the strut assembly into position under the wheel arch, passing the three mounting plate studs through the holes in the suspension turret. Use the markings made during removal to ensure that the strut to bodywork alignment is correct.

20 Fit the three top mounting nuts loosely - do not tighten them at this stage.

21 Engage the lower end of the strut with the hub carrier, ensuring that the locating lug at the base of the strut slots between the clamp bolt flanges at the rear of the swivel hub **(see illustration)**. Insert the clamp bolt, then fit the nut and tighten it to the specified torque.

22 Tighten the three strut upper mounting nuts to the specified torque, then press the dust cover into position.

23 Refit the brake hydraulic line bracket to the base of the strut and tighten the securing bolt to the specified torque.

24 Refit the anti-roll bar drop link to the suspension lower arm, with reference to Section 6.

25 Refit the roadwheel, lower the vehicle to the ground and tighten the roadwheel nuts to the specified torque.

26 Have the front wheel alignment checked (and if necessary, adjusted) by a Rover dealer or a tyre specialist at the earliest opportunity.

5 Anti-roll bars - removal and refitting

Front anti-roll bar

Removal

1 Chock the rear wheels, firmly apply the handbrake then jack up the front of the vehicle and support it on axle stands (see *"Jacking and Vehicle Support"*).

2 Slacken and remove the nuts and washers securing each end of the anti-roll bar to the drop links and remove the bolts **(see illustration)**.

3 Mark the location of the clamp bushes on the bar to aid refitting, then undo the mounting clamp retaining bolts. Lower the clamps away from the anti-roll bar. Make a note of the fitted position of the rubber bush splits to ensure that they are positioned correctly on refitting **(see illustration)**. Manoeuvre the anti-roll bar away from the underside of the vehicle.

4 Carefully examine the anti-roll bar components for signs of wear, damage or deterioration, paying particular attention to the mounting rubbers. Renew worn components as necessary.

Refitting

5 Manoeuvre the anti-roll bar into position under the vehicle and refit the drop link bolts. Refit the washers and tighten the nuts, finger-tight only.

6 Lubricate the mounting clamp bushes with a solution of soapy water then lever the bar down and slide them into position on the anti-roll bar. Ensure that the bush splits are facing the rear of the vehicle, then align them with the marks made during removal.

7 Refit the anti-roll bar mounting clamps and tighten the retaining bolts to the specified torque setting, then tighten the anti-roll bar-to-drop link bolts to the specified torque.

8 Lower the car to the ground, then rock it from side to side to settle the anti-roll bar in its mountings.

5.2 Remove the anti-roll bar-to-drop link bolts

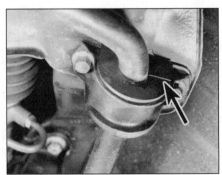

5.3 Correct position of the anti-roll bar mounting bush split (arrowed)

10

5.10 Remove the nuts (arrowed) and washers securing each end of the anti-roll bar to the rear axle assembly

6.2 Anti-roll bar drop link

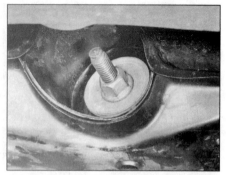

7.2 Tie bar retaining nut is accessed from front of subframe

Rear anti-roll bar

Removal

9 Chock the front wheels, then jack up the rear of the vehicle and support it on axle stands (see "*Jacking and Vehicle Support*").

10 Remove the nuts and washers securing each end of the anti-roll bar to the rear axle assembly **(see illustration)**.

11 Pull the anti-roll bar towards the front of the vehicle to release it from the beam axle. Manoeuvre the anti-roll bar away from the underside of the vehicle.

12 Carefully examine the anti-roll bar components for signs of wear, damage or deterioration, paying particular attention to the mounting rubbers and tubular collar. Renew worn components as necessary.

Refitting

13 Fit the tubular collars into the mounting holes at the base of the trailing arms.

14 Fit the washers to the anti-roll bar, then manoeuvre the anti-roll bar into position under the vehicle. Apply a light coating of grease to the anti-roll bar spigots and pass the spigots through the spacers. Refit the washers, then fit the retaining nuts and tighten them to the specified torque.

15 Lower the car to the ground, then rock it from side to side to settle the anti-roll bar in its mountings.

6 Front anti-roll bar drop link - removal and refitting

Removal

1 Chock the rear wheels, firmly apply the handbrake, jack up the front of the vehicle and support on axle stands (see "*Jacking and Vehicle Support*"). Remove the appropriate front roadwheel.

2 From underneath the vehicle, remove the bolt and washer securing the drop link to the lower suspension arm **(see illustration)**.

3 Remove the nut and washer securing the drop link to the anti-roll bar, then withdraw the bolt and remove the drop link from under the vehicle.

Refitting

4 Refitting is the reverse of the removal sequence. Tighten both the drop link bolts to the specified torque setting.

7 Front suspension tie bar - removal and refitting

Removal

1 Chock the rear wheels, firmly apply the

handbrake, jack up the front of the vehicle and support on axle stands (see "*Jacking and Vehicle Support*"). Remove the appropriate front roadwheel.

2 Undo the nut securing the front of the tie bar to the front suspension beam then remove the flanged washer and mounting bush, noting the direction the flange faces **(see illustration)**.

3 Undo the two bolts securing the tie bar to the lower suspension arm, then remove the rod from the vehicle and slide the spacer, mounting bush and flanged washer off the tie bar **(see illustration)**.

4 Examine all the components for signs of wear or damage, paying particular attention to the mounting bushes and tie bar threads. Renew components as necessary **(see illustration)**.

Refitting

5 Slide the flange washer, mounting bush and spacer onto the tie bar threads. Ensure that the flange of the washer is facing away from the mounting bush and that the rounded surface of the bush is facing the washer **(see illustration)**.

6 Refit the tie bar to the front suspension beam and fit the second mounting bush and flanged washer. Ensure the flat surface of the mounting bush is facing the subframe and that the flange of the washer is facing away from the mounting bush, then refit the tie

7.3 Tie bar-to-lower suspension arm bolts (arrowed)

7.4 Renew tie bar mounting bushes (arrowed) if damaged

7.5 Fit flange washer, spacer and mounting bush onto tie bar . . .

7.6 . . . then refit tie bar to subframe and install second mounting bush and flange washer

8.4a Release the balljoint from the swivel hub assembly . . .

8.4b . . . then remove the pivot bolt (arrowed) and withdraw the lower suspension arm

bar nut, tightening it finger-tight **(see illustration)**.

7 Refit the tie bar-to-lower suspension arm bolts and tighten them to the specified torque, then tighten the tie bar retaining nut to the specified torque setting.

8 Refit the roadwheel, then lower the vehicle to the ground and tighten the roadwheel nuts to the specified torque.

8 Front suspension lower arm - removal, overhaul and refitting

Note: *The lower arm balljoint is an integral part of the lower arm assembly and is not available separately. If renewal of the balljoint is necessary, then the complete lower arm assembly must be renewed.*

Removal

1 Chock the rear wheels, firmly apply the handbrake, jack up the front of the vehicle and support on axle stands (see *"Jacking and Vehicle Support"*). Remove the appropriate front roadwheel.

2 Slacken and remove the bolt and washer securing the anti-roll bar drop link to the lower suspension arm (see Section 6) and undo the two bolts securing the tie bar to the lower suspension arm (see Section 7).

3 Extract the split pin and undo the nut securing the lower arm balljoint to the swivel hub. Release the balljoint shank by using a suitable balljoint separator tool whilst taking care not to damage the balljoint gaiter.

4 Undo the lower suspension arm-to-rear suspension beam pivot bolt and withdraw the lower arm from the vehicle **(see illustrations)**.

Overhaul

5 Thoroughly clean the lower arm and the area around the arm mountings, removing all traces of dirt and underseal if necessary, then check carefully for cracks, distortion or any other signs of wear or damage. Check that the lower arm balljoint moves freely without any sign of roughness and that the balljoint gaiter shows no sign of deterioration and is free from cracks and splits. Examine the shank of the pivot bolt for signs of wear or scoring. Renew worn components, as necessary.

6 Check the lower arm inner pivot bush and

renew it if worn, cracked, split or perished. Bush renewal is best left to a Rover dealer as a press, a special bush removal/refitting mandrel and a support are required (Rover Service Tool Numbers 18G 1600/2 and 18G 1600/1 respectively). While the old bush can be extracted using a strong bench vice and suitable sockets, it is unlikely that new bushes can be installed successfully without the shaped mandrel **(see illustration)**.

Refitting

7 Offer up the lower arm and fit the arm to rear beam pivot bolt. Tighten the bolt by hand only at this stage.

8 Insert the lower arm balljoint shank into the swivel hub and tighten its retaining bolt to the specified torque. Secure the balljoint nut in position with a new split pin.

9 Refit the tie bar and anti-roll bar drop link to lower arm bolts and tighten them to the specified torque.

10 Refit the roadwheel, then lower the vehicle to the ground and tighten the roadwheel nuts to the specified torque.

11 With the vehicle standing on its wheels, rock the suspension to settle the lower arm bush in position then tighten the lower arm-to-rear suspension beam pivot bolt to the specified torque setting.

12 Have the front wheel alignment checked and, if necessary adjusted, at the earliest opportunity.

9 Front suspension front beam - removal and refitting

Removal

1 Chock the rear wheels, firmly apply the handbrake, jack up the front of the vehicle and support on axle stands (see *"Jacking and Vehicle Support"*). Remove both front roadwheels to improve access.

2 On diesel-engined models, remove the screws and lower the undertray away from the engine compartment.

3 With reference to Section 7, remove the

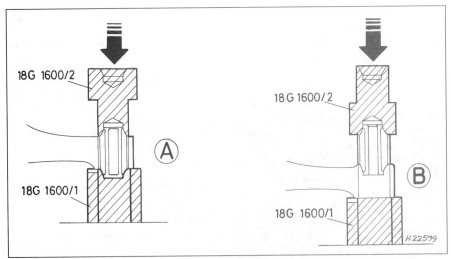

8.6 Using special Rover mandrels to renew the lower suspension arm bush

A Removing old bush   B Fitting new bush

10

9.3a Remove the tie bar securing nut . . .

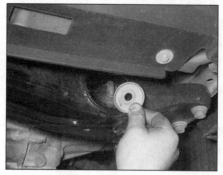

9.3b . . . washers . . .

9.3c . . . and bushes

nuts, bushes and cupped washers from the ends of both tie bars **(see illustrations)**.

4 Slacken and withraw the four securing bolts (two at either end of the beam), then lower the beam away from the underside of the vehicle **(see illustrations)**.

Refitting

5 Refitting is a reversal of removal, noting the following points:

a) *Thoroughly clean the mating surface between the suspension beam and the vehicle's bodywork.*

b) *Tighten the suspension beam securing bolts to the specified torque.*

c) *Refit the tie bars to the front suspension beam with reference to Section 7.*

10 Front suspension rear beam - removal and refitting

Removal

1 Chock the rear wheels, firmly apply the handbrake, jack up the front of the vehicle and support on axle stands (see "*Jacking and Vehicle Support*"). Remove both front roadwheels to improve access.

2 Disconnect the exhaust system downpipe from the exhaust manifold, with reference to the relevant part of Chapter 4.

3 Remove the steering gear from the vehicle (see Section 20).

9.4a Slacken and withdraw the four securing bolts . . .

4 Unbolt both suspension lower arms from the rear beam (see Section 8).

5 Unbolt the drop links from both ends of the anti-roll bar (see Section 6).

6 Slacken and withdraw the bolts securing the PAS fluid pipe and (where applicable) the clutch cable bracket to the suspension rear beam.

7 On petrol-engined models, release the evaporative emission canister vent hose from the grommet in the suspension rear beam.

8 On models with power assisted steering, slacken the four securing bolts (two at either end of the beam), and lower the beam away from the underside of the vehicle slightly. Remove the remaining power steering pipe securing bolts as they become accessible.

9 Position a trolley jack underneath the beam and raise it until the jack just takes the weight of the beam. Remove the four beam securing bolts, then disengage the suspension lower arms from the beam and use the jack to lower the beam to the ground.

Refitting

10 Position the beam on the head of a trolley jack and use the jack to lift the beam into position. Insert the beam securing bolts and rotate them through one or two turns, but do not tighten them at this stage.

11 Engage the suspension lower arms with the beam and insert the pivot bolts. Thread the nuts onto the ends of the pivot bolts, but do not tighten them at this stage.

12 On models with power steering, place the

9.4b . . . then lower the beam away from the underside of the vehicle

fluid pipe bracket in position on the beam, then insert and tighten the bracket retaining bolt.

13 Tighten the four beam securing bolts to the specified torque.

14 On petrol engined models, press the evaporative loss canister vent hose into the grommet on the suspension beam.

15 Refit the bolts that secure the clutch cable bracket and the remaining power steering fluid hose bracket to the beam, and tighten them securely.

16 Refit the drop links to each end of the anti-roll bar, with reference to Section 7.

17 Tighten the suspension lower arm pivot bolt nuts to the specified torque, with reference to Section 8.

18 Refit the steering gear with reference to Section 20.

19 Refer to the relevant Part of Chapter 4 and refit the exhaust system downpipe to the exhaust manifold.

20 Refit the roadwheels, lower the vehicle to the ground and tighten the nuts to the specified torque.

11 Rear hub and bearings - removal and refitting

Note: *The bearing is a sealed, pre-adjusted and pre-lubricated, double-row tapered-roller type and is intended to last the vehicle's entire service life without maintenance or attention. Never overtighten the hub nut beyond the specified torque wrench setting in an attempt to 'adjust' the bearings.*

Note: *The bearing is an integral part of the hub and can not be purchased separately. If renewal of the bearing is necessary, the complete hub assembly must be renewed as a unit. The only component which is available separately are roadwheel studs.*

Removal

1 Chock the front wheels, then jack up the rear of the vehicle and support it on axle stands (see "*Jacking and Vehicle Support*"). Remove the appropriate rear roadwheel.

2 Prise out the cap from the centre of the hub

11.5a Removing the hub and bearing assembly from the stub axle

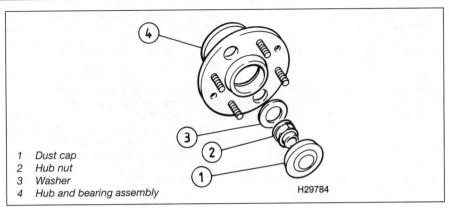

1 Dust cap
2 Hub nut
3 Washer
4 Hub and bearing assembly

H29784

11.5b Rear hub and bearing components

assembly and, using a hammer and suitable chisel-nosed tool, tap up the staking securing the hub retaining nut to the groove in the stub axle.

3 Using a socket and extension bar, slacken and remove the hub retaining nut, followed by the washer.

Note: *The **left hand** hub nut has a **left-handed** thread.*

4 Remove the brake drum or caliper and disc, as applicable. On models with drum brakes and ABS, also remove both brake shoes.

5 Once the brake drum/disc has been removed, the hub assembly can be pulled off the stub axle **(see illustrations)**. If necessary, the hub can be drawn off the stub axle using a three-legged puller. Discard the nut, noting that a new hub retaining nut must be obtained for reassembly.

6 Check that there is no sign of free play in the hub bearing and that the bearing inner race rotates smoothly and easily without any sign of roughness. If there is any sign of wear or damage to the hub assembly or bearing, the complete hub assembly must be renewed as a unit.

7 Check the condition of the roadwheel studs in the hub flange. If any are sheared off, stretched or have damaged threads, they can be pressed out of the hub providing that its flange is fully supported from the opposite side. On refitting, support the hub flange using the same method employed during removal, pressing in the new stud until it seats fully.

Refitting

8 Prior to refitting the hub, inspect the stub axle for signs of wear or scoring and, if necessary, renew it.

9 Apply a thin smear of grease to the hub bearing seal and refit the hub assembly. Refit the toothed washer, ensuring that its tooth locates with the groove in the stub axle. Install the new hub nut and tighten it to the specified torque.

10 Check that the hub rotates smoothly, then stake the hub retaining nut fully into the stub axle groove. Refit the hub centre cap.

11 On models with drum brakes and ABS, refer to Chapter 9 and set the clearance

between the hub rotor and the wheel sensor. On completion, refit the brake shoes.

12 Refit the brake drum or disc and caliper (as applicable) with reference to Chapter 9.

13 Refit the roadwheel, then lower the vehicle to the ground and tighten the roadwheel nuts to the specified torque.

14 Check the operation of the braking system thoroughly before using the vehicle on the road. On models with ABS, the operation of the ABS system should be verified by a Rover dealer using the appropriate diagnostic equipment.

12 Rear stub axle - removal and refitting

Models with rear drum brakes

Removal

1 Chock the front wheels, jack up the rear of the vehicle, support it securely on axle stands (see *"Jacking and Vehicle Support"*) and remove the appropriate rear roadwheel. Carry out the following preliminary operations:

a) Remove the brake drum and shoes (Chapter 9)

b) Remove the rear hub from the stub axle (Section 11)

2 Undo the bolts securing the handbrake cable to the beam axle assembly, then use a 12 mm ring spanner to compress the handbrake cable retaining clip and withdraw the cable from the brake backplate.

3 Clamp the flexible section of the brake hose leading to the wheel cylinder, using a proprietary brake hose clamp. Slacken the union and disconnect the brake pipe from the wheel cylinder (see Chapter 9). Plug the end of the brake pipe to minimise fluid loss and to prevent the ingress of dirt.

4 Release the ABS wheel sensor connector from the securing clip on the underside of the car. Unplug the connector and release the remainder of the harness from the clips on the beam axle assembly.

5 Slacken and withdraw the four stub axle

securing bolts, then lift the stub axle and backplate away from the beam axle.

6 Examine the stub axle spindle and mounting plate for signs of wear or damage such as scoring or cracking. If damaged, the stub axle must be renewed.

Refitting

7 Unbolt the backplate from the existing stub axle and transfer it, together with the wheel cylinder and ABS wheel sensor (where applicable), to the new stub axle. Tighten the retaining bolts to the specified torque.

8 Offer the stub axle up to the beam axle mounting plate, then insert the securing bolts and tighten them to the specified torque.

9 Reconnect the brake pipe to the rear of the wheel cylinder and tighten the union to the specified torque (see Chapter 9).

10 Reconnect the ABS wheel sensor wiring, and fit the connector body and wiring harness into the securing clips.

11 Refit the hub, with reference to Section 11, then tighten the hub retaining nut to the specified torque.

12 Check that the hub rotates smoothly, then stake the hub retaining nut fully into the stub axle groove. Refit the hub centre cap.

13 On models with ABS, refer to Chapter 9 and set the wheel sensor to reluctor ring clearance using a feeler blade.

14 Refit the handbrake cable, brake shoes and brake drum, with reference to Chapter 9, then bleed the braking system.

15 Refit the roadwheel, then lower the vehicle to the ground and tighten the roadwheel nuts to the specified torque.

16 Check the operation of the braking system thoroughly before using the vehicle on the road. On models with ABS, the operation of the ABS system should be verified by a Rover dealer using the appropriate diagnostic equipment.

Models with rear disc brakes

Removal

17 Jack up the rear of the vehicle, support it securely on axle stands (see *"Jacking and Vehicle Support"*) and remove the appropriate

10

rear roadwheel. Carry out the following preliminary operations:

a) *Remove the brake caliper (Chapter 9)*
b) *Remove the brake disc (Chapter 9)*
c) *Remove the rear hub from the stub axle (Section 11)*
d) *Remove the ABS wheel sensor (Chapter 9)*

18 Slacken and withdraw the four stub axle securing bolts, then lift the stub axle and backplate away from the beam axle.

Refitting

19 Examine the stub axle spindle and mounting plate for signs of wear or damage such as scoring or cracking. If damaged, the stub axle must be renewed.

20 If a new stub axle is to be fitted, unbolt the

ABS wheel sensor mounting bracket and the brake backplate from the existing stub axle and transfer it to the new one. Tighten the securing bolts to the specified torque.

21 Offer the stub axle up to the beam axle mounting plate, then insert the securing bolts and tighten them to the specified torque.

22 Refit the hub with reference to Section 11 and tighten the hub retaining nut to the specified torque. Check that the hub rotates smoothly, then stake the hub retaining nut fully into the stub axle groove. Refit the hub centre cap.

23 Refit the brake disc and caliper with reference to Chapter 9.

24 Refit the ABS wheel sensor with reference to Chapter 9.

25 Refit the roadwheel, then lower the vehicle to the ground and tighten the roadwheel nuts to the specified torque.

26 Check the operation of the braking system thoroughly before using the vehicle on the road. On models with ABS, the operation of the ABS system should be verified by a Rover dealer using the appropriate diagnostic equipment.

---

13 Rear suspension strut - removal, overhaul and refitting

Caution: If renewing the strut damper during overhaul, both the left- and right-hand dampers should be renewed as a pair, to preserve the handling characteristics of the vehicle.

Removal

1 Chock the front wheels, then jack up the rear of the vehicle and support it on axle stands (see *"Jacking and Vehicle Support"*). Remove the appropriate rear roadwheel.

2 Position a trolley jack directly under the strut lower mounting bolt and raise the jack head until it is just supporting the trailing arm.

3 Slacken and remove the strut lower mounting bolt **(see illustration)**. If the bolt is difficult to remove, relieve the strain on it by adjusting the height of the trailing arm using the trolley jack.

4 Open the tailgate, then remove the trim securing screws and fold the carpet panel away from the side of the load space. Lift the rubber cover from the strut upper mounting **(see illustrations)**.

5 Use chalk or a marker pen to mark the position of the suspension strut upper mounting in relation to the bodywork. Slacken and remove the two strut upper mounting nuts. DO NOT slacken the damper rod nut, at the centre of the strut **(see illustration)**.

6 Lower the trolley jack and manoeuvre the strut out from under the wheelarch, noting the seal (where applicable) fitted between the upper mounting plate and vehicle body **(see illustration)**.

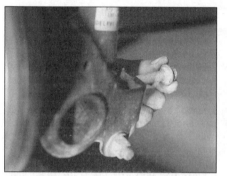

13.3 Support the trailing arm, then slacken and remove the strut lower mounting bolt

13.4a Remove the upper . . .

13.4b . . . and lower trim securing screws . . .

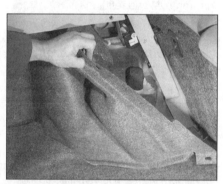

13.4c . . . and fold the carpet panel away from the side of the load space . . .

13.4d . . . then lift the rubber cover from the strut upper mounting

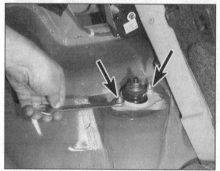

13.5 Remove the two strut upper mounting nuts (arrowed) - do not slacken the centre nut

13.6 Remove the strut from the wheelarch

13.8 Fit the spring compressor and compress the spring until all tension is relieved from the upper mounting plate

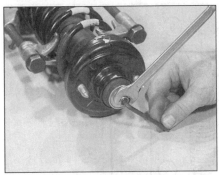

13.9 Slacken the damper rod nut with a spanner, using an Allen key to prevent the rod from rotating

13.10a Remove the nut . . .

Overhaul

Note: *Before attempting to dismantle the rear suspension strut, a suitable tool to hold the coil spring in compression must be obtained. Adjustable coil spring compressors are readily available and are recommended for this operation. Any attempt to dismantle the strut without such a tool is likely to result in damage or personal injury.*

7 With the strut removed from the vehicle, clean away all external dirt. If desired, the strut can be mounted upright in the jaws of a bench vice.

8 Fit the spring compressor and compress the coil spring until all tension is relieved from the upper mounting plate **(see illustration)**.

9 Slacken the damper rod nut with a spanner, using an Allen key to prevent the damper rod from rotating as the nut is slackened **(see illustration)**.

10 Remove the nut and washer followed by the upper spring seat/mounting plate assembly, noting the correct fitted position of the mounting rubber. Remove the coil spring and lower spring seat rubber. Lift the dust seal and cover off the damper and slide the bump stop plate and rubber bump stop off the damper piston **(see illustrations)**.

11 With the strut assembly completely dismantled, examine all components for wear, damage or corrosion. Renew any component

13.10b . . . and washer (noting its orientation) . . .

13.10c . . . followed by the upper spring seat/mounting plate assembly . . .

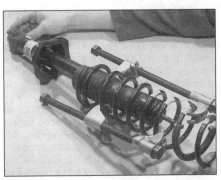

13.10d . . . then remove the coil spring . . .

13.10e . . . and the lower spring seat rubber . . .

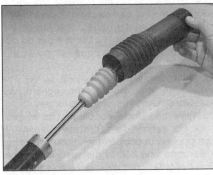

13.10f . . . lift the dust seal and cover off the damper . . .

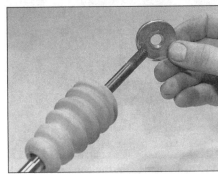

13.10g . . . and slide the bump stop plate . . .

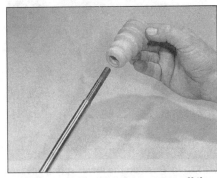

13.10h . . . and rubber bump stop off the damper piston

10

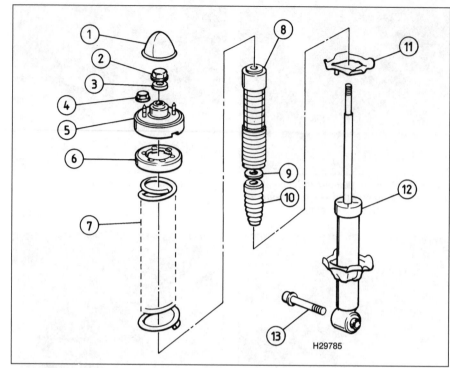

13.11 Rear suspension strut components

1 Rubber cap
2 Damper rod nut
3 Washer
4 Strut upper mounting nuts
5 Upper spring seat/mounting plate assembly
6 Upper spring seat rubber
7 Coil spring
8 Dust seal and cover
9 Bump stop plate
10 Bump stop rubber
11 Lower spring seat rubber
12 Damper unit
13 Strut lower mounting bolt

displaying signs of deterioration **(see illustration)**.

12 Examine the damper for signs of fluid leakage. Check the piston rod for signs of pitting along its entire length and check the strut body for signs of damage or corrosion. Test the operation of the strut, while holding it in an upright position, by moving the piston through several full-length strokes; the resistance felt should be smooth and continuous. Now operate the piston rod through short strokes of 50 to 100 mm. If fluid has leaked from the damper, the piston will

have an amount of undamped 'freeplay' at the end of its travel. If this is the case, or if there are any visible signs of wear, damage or corrosion, renewal of the strut will be necessary.

13 If any doubt exists about the condition of the coil spring, carefully remove the spring compressors and check the spring for distortion, cracking or excessive corrosion. Since no minimum free length is specified by Rover, the only way to check the tension of the spring is to compare it to a new component. Renew the spring if it is damaged

or distorted or there is any doubt as to its condition.

14 Inspect all other components for signs of damage or deterioration and renew any that are suspect.

15 If new damper strut insert is being fitted, prime the damper (with reference to the manufacturer's instructions) by operating the piston rod through several full-length strokes.

16 Slide the bump stop rubber, bump stop plate and dust cover over the end of the damper piston rod.

17 Place the lower spring seat rubber in position and orientate it such that the orientation peg fits into the hole in the spring seat. Pass the compressed coil spring over the top of the damper piston rod and place it in position on the lower spring seat, ensuring that the end of the spring is correctly located in the lower spring seat recess **(see illustrations)**.

18 Fit the upper spring seat rubber followed by the upper spring seat/mounting plate, ensuring that the upper end of the coil spring is correctly located in the corresponding mounting plate recess and that the mounting plate studs are vertical. Fit the washer (with the lip facing upwards) and then fit the new damper rod nut.

19 Tighten the damper rod nut to the specified torque setting. Note that you will need to fit a crow's-foot adapter to the torque wrench, to allow the damper rod nut to be tightened to the correct torque. Counterhold the damper rod, using a suitable Allen key or hex bit, as the nut is tightened.

Caution: Do not allow the rod to rotate inside the damper, as this may damage the piston seal.

Refitting

20 Ensure the rubber seal (where applicable) is in position between the upper mounting plate and the bodywork then refit the suspension strut, using the alignment marks made during removal (where necessary). Refit the strut upper mounting nuts, but do not tighten them to the final torque setting at this stage.

21 Raise the trailing arm using the trolley jack, as described in the *Removal* procedure. Align the trailing arm mounting hole with the strut lower mounting bush, then insert the lower mounting bolt. Fit the nut but do not tighten it to the final torque setting at this stage.

22 Refit the roadwheel, then lower the vehicle to the ground and tighten the roadwheel nuts to the specified torque.

23 With the vehicle standing on its wheels, rock the vehicle to settle the suspension components in position then tighten the strut lower mounting bolt to the specified torque. Finally, tighten both strut upper mounting nuts to the specified torque and refit the protective plastic cap.

13.17a Position the lower spring seat rubber such that its orientation peg fits into the hole in the spring seat (arrowed) . . .

13.17b . . . and place the compressed coil spring in position (lower spring seat recess arrowed)

14 Rear suspension beam axle - removal and refitting

Removal

1 Chock the front wheels, jack up the rear of the vehicle and support it securely on axle stands (see "*Jacking and Vehicle Support*").
2 With reference to Chapter 9, carry out the following:
a) *Disconnect the handbrake cables from the rear brake drums/calipers (as applicable).*
b) *On models with disc brakes, remove the brake calipers (together with their mounting brackets) from the stub axles.*
c) *On models with drum brakes, slacken the unions and disconnect the brake pipes from the rear of both wheel cylinders.*
3 Withdraw the metal clips and detach the brake hose unions from the mounting brackets on both trailing arms. Where applicable, release the ABS wheel sensor wiring harness from the retaining clips on each trailing arm.
4 Unscrew the retaining bolts and release both handbrake cable mounting brackets from the beam axle mountings.
5 Using the information given in Section 13, position a trolley jack under each trailing arm then slacken and withdraw both rear strut lower mounting bolts, to separate the rear struts from the beam axle. On completion, carefully lower the beam axle trailing arms to the ground.
6 Reposition the trolley jack so that it now supports the centre of the leading edge of the beam axle assembly. Slacken and withdraw both pivot mounting bolts **(see illustration)**. Check that nothing remains connected to the beam axle assembly, then carefully lower it to the ground.
7 If a new beam axle assembly is to be fitted, remove the stub axle assemblies (as described in Section 11) and transfer them to the new beam axle.

Refitting

8 Position the axle assembly under the car on a trolley jack, then lift the assembly up to its mountings by raising the trolley jack.
9 Insert the beam axle pivot mounting bolts, but do not tighten them at this stage.
10 Reposition the trolley jack, then raise the rear of the beam axle using the jack so that the trailing arms engage with the suspension strut lower bushes. Insert the suspension strut lower mounting bolts, but do not tighten them at this stage.
11 Tighten the beam axle pivot mounting bolts to the specified torque.
12 Refit the handbrake cable mounting brackets to the beam axle mountings and tighten the bolts securely.
13 Press the brake hose union grommets into the brackets on the beam axle and fit the

14.6 Remove the beam axle pivot mounting bolt (arrowed)

metal retaining clips. Similarly, press the ABS wiring grommets into the brackets on the beam axle.
14 Refer to Chapter 9 and carry out the following:
a) *Refit the brake calipers and mounting brackets (models with rear disc brakes).*
b) *Refit the brake pipes to the rear of the wheel cylinder and tighten the union to the specified torque (models with rear disc brakes).*
c) *Refit the handbrake cables.*
15 Refit the roadwheel, then lower the vehicle to the ground and tighten the roadwheel nuts to the specified torque.
16 With the vehicle standing on its wheels, rock the vehicle to settle the suspension components in position then tighten the suspension strut lower mounting bolts to the specified torque (see Section 13).
17 Refer to Chapter 9 and bleed the brake hydraulic system. On completion, adjust the operation of the handbrake.

15 Rear suspension beam axle bush renewal - general information

Bush renewal is best left to a Rover dealer, as a press, special bush removal/refitting mandrel, extraction tool and support are required (Rover Service Tool Numbers 18G

16.3 Detach the horn button and remote audio control button wiring multiplug from the rotary coupler

1756/3, 18G 1756/12 and IG 1756/5 respectively). While the old bush can be extracted using a strong bench vice and suitable selection of sockets, it is unlikely that new bushes can be installed successfully without the specially shaped mandrel.

16 Steering wheel - removal and refitting

Removal

1 Remove the ignition key and wait at least ten minutes to allow the SRS system backup circuit to fully discharge. Disconnect BOTH battery leads, earth lead first, to avoid accidental detonation of the airbag.
2 Remove the airbag unit from the centre of the steering wheel (see Chapter 12).
3 With further reference to Chapter 12, detach the horn button (and where applicable, the remote audio control button) wiring multiplug from the rotary coupler **(see illustration)**.
4 Set the steering in the straight-ahead position and, using a socket, unscrew the steering wheel retaining nut until its top is flush with the end of the column shaft. Do not use the steering column lock to brace the steering wheel as this may damage it.
5 Mark the steering wheel and steering column shaft in relation to each other then lift the steering wheel off the column splines. If it is tight, tap it up near the centre, using the palm of your hand, to release it from the shaft splines.
6 Remove and discard the steering wheel retaining nut. A new self-locking nut must be obtained for reassembly.
7 Remove the steering wheel from the column **(see illustration)**. Tape the inner and outer sections of the rotary coupler together, so that the coupler's alignment with the steering column shaft is preserved.
Caution: Do not allow the rotary coupler to rotate until the steering wheel is refitted.

16.7 Remove the steering wheel from the steering column

10

16.8a Fit a new self-locking steering wheel nut . . .

16.8b . . . and tighten it to the specified torque

17.5 Remove the fusebox cover panel from the underside of the facia

Refitting

8 Refit the steering wheel by reversing the removal procedure, noting the following **(see illustrations)**:

a) *Before refitting, check that the steering column splines are clean.*

b) *Enter the cut-outs on the lower surface of the wheel with the direction indicator cancelling cam tabs and align the marks made on dismantling. This should leave the wheel in the same position as before removal.*

c) *Ensure that the rotary coupler wiring is reconnected and take care to ensure that wiring harness is not trapped beneath the steering wheel.*

d) *Fit a new wheel retaining nut and tighten*

it to the specified torque wrench setting.

e) *Refit the driver's airbag unit with reference to Chapter 12.*

f) *When reconnecting the battery leads, fit the negative lead last.*

17 Steering column - removal and refitting

Removal

1 Remove the ignition key and wait at least ten minutes to allow the SRS system backup circuit to fully discharge. Disconnect both battery leads, earth lead first, to avoid accidental detonation of the airbag.

2 Set the steering in the straight-ahead position then lock the steering column in its lowest position.

3 Remove the airbag unit (see Chapter 12).

4 Remove the steering wheel, with reference to Section 16.

5 Release the stud fasteners and remove the fusebox cover panel from the underside of the facia **(see illustration)**.

6 Slacken and withdraw the three screws, then remove the lower part of the plastic shroud from the underside of the steering column. Carefully disengage the upper part of the steering column shroud from the lower edge of the instrument panel and lift it out over the combination switch stalks **(see illustrations)**.

7 Refer to Chapter 12 and remove the SRS rotary coupler from the steering column. Place a strip of masking tape around the rotary coupler to preserve its alignment.

8 Remove the steering column combination switch together with the direction indicator cancelling cam (see Chapter 12).

9 On later models, follow the wiring harness from the ignition switch sensor coil to the multi-way connector and unplug it.

10 Trace the ignition switch wiring harness back to the fusebox and main wiring harness, then unplug the two multi-way wiring connectors. Release the cable ties securing the wiring harness to the steering column **(see illustrations)**.

17.6a Remove the securing screws . . .

17.6b . . . and remove the lower . . .

17.6c . . . and upper sections of the steering column shroud

17.10a Unplug the steering column wiring from the main harness connector. . .

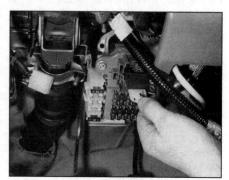

17.10b . . . and the fusebox

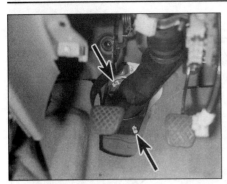

17.11a Remove the two plastic clips (arrowed) securing the lower column cover to the floor

17.11b . . . the two metal spring clips . . .

17.11c . . . and withdraw the lower column cover

11 Pull back the driver's footwell carpet and remove the two plastic clips securing the lower column cover to the floor. Remove the two retaining clips from the upper end of the cover and withdraw the cover **(see illustrations)**.

12 Using a hammer and punch, white paint or similar, mark the exact relationship between the steering column shaft and shaft-to-steering gear universal joint, then slacken and remove the pinch-bolt securing the joint to the column shaft **(see illustration)**.

13 Undo the nut and bolt securing the lower steering column mounting clamp to the swivel bracket and remove the clamp **(see illustration)**.

14 Slacken and remove the two nuts and two bolts securing the upper mounting assembly to the vehicle **(see illustrations)**.

15 Disengage the column from its mounting studs and the universal joint, then remove it from the vehicle.

Refitting

16 Before refitting the steering column, closely examine the upper mounting assembly for damage or misalignment.

17 Align the marks made on dismantling and engage the steering column shaft splines with those of the universal joint.

18 Locate the upper mounting bracket assembly over its mounting studs and refit the upper mounting nuts and bolts. Refit the lower mounting clamp and tighten its retaining nut

17.12 Remove the pinch-bolt (arrowed) from the steering column shaft-to-steering gear universal joint

and bolt to the specified torque setting, then tighten the upper mounting nuts and bolts to their specified torque setting.

19 Refit the universal joint to steering column pinch-bolt and tighten it to the specified torque. Refit the universal joint cover and secure it in position with the clips and studs.

20 Reconnect the combination switch and ignition switch multiplugs, then secure the wiring harness to the steering column.

21 Refit the steering column combination switch, direction indicator cancelling cam and SRS rotary coupler (see Chapter 12). Reconnect the ignition switch sensor coil wiring.

22 Refit the steering column shroud panels

17.13 Lower steering column mounting clamp-to-swivel bracket bolt (arrowed)

and fusebox cover, securing them in place with the screws and stud fixings.

23 Refit the steering wheel (Section 16) then refit the airbag unit, see Chapter 12.

18 Steering lock/ignition switch - removal and refitting

> ⚠ **Warning: Before attempting removal of the ignition switch, read carefully the precautions listed in Chapter 12, appertaining to vehicles equipped with airbags (SRS).**

Note: *The steering lock/ignition switch is secured by two shear-head bolts. Although new bolts are supplied with replacement steering lock assemblies, always ensure that the bolts themselves are available before beginning work.*

Removal

1 Remove the steering column (see Section 17).

2 Securely clamp the column assembly in a vice equipped with soft jaws, taking great care not to overtighten the vice and distort the steering column.

3 Centre-punch the two steering lock shear bolts then drill off the heads of the bolts **(see**

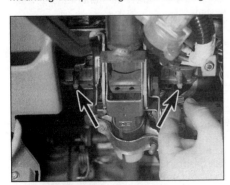

17.14a Remove the steering column mounting nuts from the studs (arrowed) . . .

17.14b . . . then remove the two mounting bolts (arrowed)

10

18.3 Ignition switch shear bolt heads (arrowed)

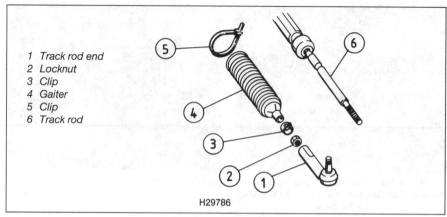

1 Track rod end
2 Locknut
3 Clip
4 Gaiter
5 Clip
6 Track rod

H29786

19.2 Track rod end assembly

illustration). Note that new shear bolts must be obtained for refitting.
4 Withdraw the steering lock/ignition switch, then unscrew the remains of the shear bolts by using a self-locking wrench or similar on the exposed ends.

Refitting

5 On refitting, carefully align the assembly on the steering column, lightly tighten the bolts and check that the steering lock works smoothly.
6 Tighten the shear bolts evenly until their heads shear off.
7 Refit the steering column (see Section 17).

19 Steering gear rubber gaiters - renewal

1 Remove the track rod balljoint (see Section 24) and unscrew the locknut from the track rod end.
2 Using a pair of pliers, release the outer steering gear gaiter retaining clip and slide it off the track rod end. Remove the inner gaiter retaining clip by cutting it, then slide the gaiter off the end of the track rod **(see illustration)**.
3 Thoroughly clean the track rod and the steering gear housing, using fine abrasive paper to polish off any corrosion, burrs or sharp edges which might damage the new gaiter's sealing lips on fitting. Repair kits

which consist of new gaiters and retaining clips are available from Rover dealers.
4 Fit the new rubber gaiter, ensuring that it is correctly seated in the grooves in the steering gear housing and track rod.
5 Check that the gaiter is not twisted or dented then secure it in position using new retaining clips.
6 Refit the locknut and balljoint onto the track rod end.

20 Steering gear - removal and refitting

Removal

1 Chock the rear wheels, firmly apply the handbrake, jack up the front of the vehicle and support on axle stands (see "Jacking and Vehicle Support"). Remove the appropriate front roadwheel.
2 Working inside the vehicle, peel back the driver's footwell carpet and remove the studs securing the lower steering column cover to the floor. Remove the two retaining clips from the upper end of the cover and withdraw the cover (see Section 17 for details).
3 Mark the relative positions of the steering gear pinion and joint to use as a guide when refitting, then slacken and remove the two universal joint pinch-bolts **(see illustration)**.

Slide the universal joint up the steering column shaft splines until it is free from the steering gear pinion.
4 Extract the split pins and undo the nuts securing the steering gear track rod balljoints to the swivel hubs (see Section 24). Release the balljoint shanks by using a suitable balljoint separator tool whilst taking care not to damage the balljoint gaiters.
5 From underneath the vehicle, slacken and remove the bolt securing the rear engine/gearbox unit mounting connecting link to the front suspension rear beam bracket, then remove the three retaining bolts and remove the bracket. Undo the two bolts securing the connecting link and bracket assembly to the gearbox housing and remove the assembly from the vehicle.
6 On models with manual steering gear, carefully lever the gear change and selector linkage balljoints off the bellcrank assembly. In the absence of the special gearchange linkage balljoint separator (Rover service tool Number 18G 1592), use a suitable pair of flat-bladed screwdrivers as levers. Apply equal leverage to either side of the balljoint, or the joint may be damaged.
7 On diesel-engined models, undo the three front exhaust pipe to manifold retaining nuts and the two bolts securing the front pipe mounting bracket to the vehicle. Release the intermediate exhaust section from its mountings and lower the front of the exhaust system.
8 On diesel-engined models, refer to Chapter 7 and carry out the following:
 a) *Unbolt the gear change steady bar from the transmission casing.*
 b) *Remove the clip, drive out the selector rod roll pin using a hammer punch and then disconnect the selector rod from the selector shaft.*
9 On models equipped with power-assisted steering, remove the bolt securing the feed and return pipe mounting bracket to the suspension rear beam. Mark the pipe union bolts to ensure they are correctly positioned on reassembly, then unscrew the pipe to steering gear union nuts **(see illustration)**. Be prepared for fluid

20.3 Steering column universal joint pinch-bolts (arrowed)

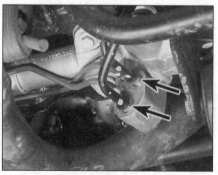

20.9 Unscrew the fluid feed and return pipe union nuts (arrowed) at the steering gear

spillage and position a suitable container beneath the pipes whilst unscrewing the union nuts. This fluid must be disposed of and new fluid of the specified type used when refilling. Plug the pipe ends and steering gear orifices to prevent excessive fluid leakage and entry of dirt into the hydraulic system.

10 Undo the two left-hand steering gear mounting bolts, then remove the mounting bracket and collect the rubber mounting. Undo the two right-hand mounting bolts, noting the mounting bushes and spacers, and free the steering gear pinion from its cutout **(see illustrations)**.

11 Manoeuvre the assembly out from the left-hand side of the vehicle. Remove the washers from the steering gear pinion (where applicable) **(see illustrations)**.

Refitting

12 Refit the washers to the pinion and, with the left-hand track rod fully extended, manoeuvre the steering gear into position from the left-hand side of the vehicle.

13 Refit the steering gear mounting rubbers, clamps and bolts, ensuring that rubbers and spacers are correctly positioned. Tighten the mounting bolts to the specified torque.

14 Centralise the steering gear rack so that both track rods are protruding by an equal distance.

15 On models equipped with power-assisted steering, wipe clean the feed and return pipe unions then refit them to their respective positions on the steering gear and tighten the union nuts to the specified torque. Refit the bolt securing the pipe retaining bracket to the subframe and tighten securely.

16 The remainder of the refitting procedure is direct reversal of removal, noting the following:

a) *Tighten all nuts and bolts to the specified torque settings.*

b) *Secure the track rod balljoint retaining nuts in position with new split pins.*

c) *When refitting the universal joint to the steering gear pinion splines, ensure that the front wheels are pointing in the straight-ahead direction then, if necessary, align the marks made on dismantling and check that the steering wheel spokes are horizontal.*

d) *On completion, check and, if necessary, adjust front wheel alignment.*

e) *On models equipped with power-assisted steering, bleed the hydraulic system (see Section 23).*

21 Power steering pump drivebelt - renewal

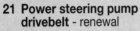

Petrol models with automatic tensioner

Removal

1 Park the vehicle on a level surface and turn the steering wheel to full left-hand lock.

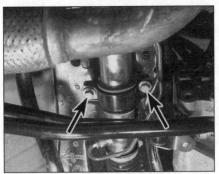

20.10a Undo the two left-hand steering gear mounting bolts (arrowed)

20.10b Steering gear right-hand mounting bolts (arrowed)

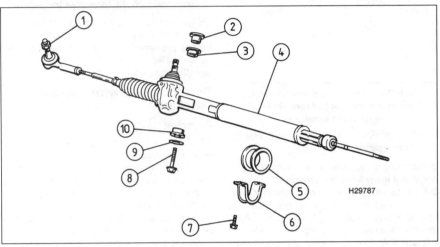

20.11a Manual steering gear components

1 *Track rod end balljoint*	5 *Mounting rubber*	8 *Right-hand mounting bolt*
2 *Collar*	6 *Clamp*	9 *Washer*
3 *Bush*	7 *Left-hand mounting bolt*	10 *Bush*
4 *Steering gear*		

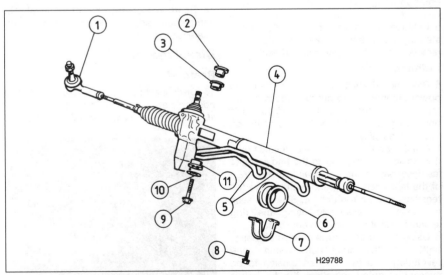

20.11b Power assisted steering gear components

1 *Track rod end balljoint*	5 *Fluid pipes*	9 *Right-hand mounting bolt*
2 *Collar*	6 *Mounting rubber*	10 *Washer*
3 *Bush*	7 *Clamp*	11 *Bush*
4 *Steering gear*	8 *Left-hand mounting bolt*	

10

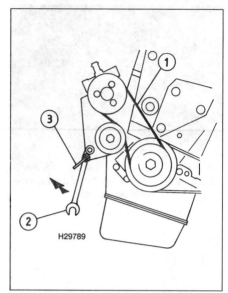

21.4 Power steering pump drivebelt arrangement - petrol models with automatic tensioner

1 Drivebelt
2 13mm spanner
3 4mm diameter rod

2 Disconnect the battery negative cable and position it away from the terminal.

3 Fit a 13mm spanner to the tensioner pivot bolt and use it rotate the whole tensioner assembly down and away from the engine, so that the tension on the drivebelt is relieved.

4 Insert a 4mm rod, or twist drill bit, through the centre of the pivot bolt and engage it with the corresponding hole in the tensioner assembly backplate **(see illustration)**. This will lock the tensioner in the 'slackened' position allowing the spanner to be removed. Ensure that the rod/drill bit is fully inserted before removing the spanner.

5 Release the drivebelt from the power steering pump and crankshaft pulleys and remove it from the engine compartment.

Refitting

6 Pass the drivebelt over the crankshaft and power steering pump pulleys, ensuring that the 'vee' pattern on the drive surface of the belt engages correctly with the grooves on each of the pulleys.

7 Manoeuvre the flat surface of the belt over the tensioner pulley. Using the ring spanner (as described during *Removal*) take the strain of the tensioner spring and then remove the tensioner locking rod/drill bit. Slowly release the tensioner assembly using the ring spanner, until it contacts the drivebelt.

8 Using a spanner on the crankshaft pulley bolt, turn the crankshaft through one revolution to allow the belt tension to be evenly distributed and check that the belt is correctly engaged with both pulleys.

9 Check that the indicator marking on the tensioner assembly falls within the 'gauge' recessed into the tensioner backplate **(see illustration)**. If the indicator falls outside of

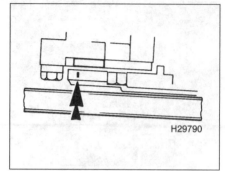

21.9 Check that marking (arrowed) on tensioner assembly falls within the 'gauge' recessed into the tensioner backplate

the gauge markings, the wrong belt may have been fitted - check with your parts supplier before proceeding. Note that the recessed gauge is also used to indicate drivebelt wear - see Chapter 1A for details.

Petrol models with manual tensioner

Removal

10 Disconnect the battery negative cable and position it away from the terminal.

11 Chock the rear wheels, raise the front of the vehicle and support it securely on axle stands (see "*Jacking and Vehicle Support*").

12 Slacken the drivebelt tensioner pulley spindle nut and bolt, then rotate the adjuster bolt (situated on the underside of the pulley assembly) to relieve all tension from the drivebelt **(see illustration)**.

13 Release the drivebelt from the power steering pump and crankshaft pulleys and remove it from the engine compartment.

Refitting

14 Refitting is a reversal of removal. On completion, adjust the belt tension with reference to Chapter 1A.

Diesel models

Removal

15 Disconnect the battery negative cable and position it away from the terminal.

16 Chock the front wheels, raise the front of

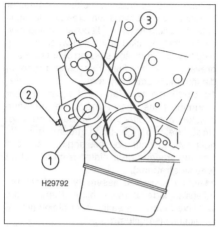

21.12 Power steering pump drivebelt arrangement - petrol models with manual tensioner

1 Tensioner pulley spindle bolt
2 Adjuster bolt
3 Drivebelt

the vehicle and support it securely on axle stands (see "*Jacking and Vehicle Support*"). Remove the right-hand front roadwheel, then undo the screws and remove the plastic wheel arch liner.

17 Working through the right-hand wheel arch, fit a 15mm spanner to the tensioner pulley bolt and use it to rotate the whole tensioner assembly clockwise, so that the tension on the drivebelt is relieved **(see illustration)**.

18 Hold the tensioner in this position and then release the drivebelt from the power steering pump, crankshaft, alternator (and where applicable, air conditioning compressor) pulleys **(see illustration)**.

19 Slowly release the tensioner and remove the drivebelt from the engine compartment.

Refitting

20 Fit a spanner to the tensioner pulley bolt (as described in *Removal*) and use it rotate the whole tensioner assembly clockwise to the limit of its travel.

21 Whilst holding the tensioner in the fully-rotated position, pass the drivebelt over the

21.17 Tensioner pulley bolt (arrowed) - diesel models with automatic tensioner (engine removed for clarity)

21.18 Using the spanner, hold the tensioner in the 'slackened' position, then release the drivebelt from the pulleys

crankshaft, power steering pump, alternator (and where applicable, air conditioning compressor) pulleys, ensuring that the 'vee' pattern on the drive surface of the belt engages correctly with the grooves on each of the pulleys.

22 Manoeuvre the flat surface of the belt under the tensioner pulley. Using the ring spanner, slowly release the tensioner assembly, until it contacts the drivebelt.

23 Using a spanner on the crankshaft pulley bolt, turn the crankshaft through one revolution to allow the belt tension to be evenly distributed and check that the belt is correctly engaged with both pulleys.

24 Check that the indicator marking on the tensioner assembly falls within the 'gauge' recessed into the tensioner backplate **(refer to illustration 21.9)**. If the indicator falls outside of the gauge markings, the wrong belt may have been fitted - check with your parts supplier before proceeding. Note that the recessed gauge is also used to indicate drivebelt wear - see Chapter 1B for details.

22 Power steering pump - removal and refitting

Petrol models

Removal

1 Disconnect the battery negative cable and position it away from the terminal.

2 Chock the rear wheels, raise the front of the vehicle and rest it securely on axle stands (see "*Jacking and Vehicle Support*").

3 Working underneath the front of the car, loosen the bolt securing the engine steady bar to the front suspension rear beam. Unbolt the steady bar from the transmission bracket.

4 Support the engine and transmission using a lifting beam or trolley jack, then unbolt and remove the right-hand engine mounting, with reference to Chapter 2A.

5 Raise the engine slightly using the lifting beam or trolley jack to allow access to the power steering pump pulley retaining bolts.

6 Slacken, but do not remove, the three power steering pump pulley retaining bolts, then remove the power steering pump drivebelt.

7 Unscrew the pump pulley retaining bolts and remove the pulley. Check that the front face of the pulley is marked FRONT and if not, mark it by using a dab of white paint. This mark can then be used to ensure that the pulley is correctly refitted.

8 Position a suitable container beneath the power steering pump to catch any spilt fluid, then slacken the inlet hose retaining clip and disconnect the hose from the top of the steering pump. Undo the bolt securing the outlet pipe retaining bracket to the pump, then unscrew the outlet pipe union nut and disconnect the pipe from the pump, noting the O-ring which is fitted to the union **(see illustration)**. Plug the hose ends and pump unions to prevent excessive fluid loss and the possible entry of dirt into the system.

9 Undo the three bolts securing the power steering pump to the mounting bracket and remove the pump from the engine **(see illustration)**.

Refitting

10 Refitting is a reverse of the removal procedure, noting the following:

 a) *Tighten the pump mounting bolts to the specified torque.*

 b) *Fit a new O-ring to the pump outlet pipe union and tighten the union nut to the specified torque.*

 c) *Ensure the pulley is correctly installed and lightly tighten its mounting bolts.*

 d) *Refit and adjust the drivebelt, then tighten the pulley mounting bolts to the specified torque.*

 e) *On completion, bleed the hydraulic system (see Section 23).*

Diesel models

Removal - models without air conditioning

11 Disconnect the battery negative cable and position it away from the terminal.

12 Chock the rear wheels, raise the front of the vehicle and rest it securely on axle stands (see "*Jacking and Vehicle Support*").

13 Refer to Chapter 5A and remove the alternator.

14 Refer to Section 9 and remove the front suspension front beam.

15 Position a suitable container beneath the power steering pump to catch any spilt fluid, then slacken the union securing the high pressure delivery hose to the power steering pump. Counterhold the base of the union with a spanner to prevent it from rotating in the pump casing.

16 Remove the O-ring seal and discard it - a new one must be used on refitting.

17 Release the hose clip and disconnect the low pressure fluid supply hose from the power steering pump.

18 Plug the hose ends and pump unions to prevent excessive fluid loss and the possible entry of dirt into the hydraulic system.

19 Remove the five bolts securing the power steering pump to the support bracket and coolant pump. Note that the bolts are of different lengths - make a note of their fitted positions to aid correct reassembly later.

20 Lift the power steering pump out of the engine bay.

Removal - models with air conditioning

21 Disconnect the battery negative cable and position it away from the terminal.

22 Chock the rear wheels, raise the front of the vehicle and rest it securely on axle stands (see "*Jacking and Vehicle Support*").

23 Working underneath the front of the car, remove the fixings and lower the undertray away from the engine compartment.

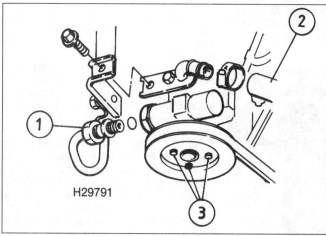

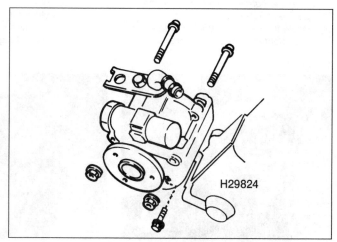

22.8 Power steering pump fluid delivery pipe (1), supply hose (2) and pulley mounting bolts (3) - petrol models

22.9 Power steering pump mountings - petrol models

10

24 Support the engine and transmission using a lifting beam or trolley jack, then unbolt and remove the right-hand engine mounting components, with reference to Chapter 2A.

25 Raise the engine slightly using the lifting beam or trolley jack to allow access to the power steering pump pulley retaining screws.

26 Slacken, but do not remove, the three power steering pump pulley retaining screws, then remove the power steering pump drivebelt.

27 Unscrew the pump pulley retaining bolts and remove the pulley. Check that the front face of the pulley is marked FRONT and if not, mark it by using a dab of white paint. This mark can then be used to ensure that the pulley is correctly refitted.

28 Position a suitable container beneath the power steering pump to catch any spilt fluid, then slacken the inlet hose retaining clip and disconnect the hose from the top of the steering pump. Undo the bolt securing the outlet pipe retaining bracket to the pump, then unscrew the outlet pipe union nut and disconnect the pipe from the pump, noting the O-ring which is fitted to the union. Plug the hose ends and pump unions to prevent excessive fluid loss and the possible entry of dirt into the system.

29 Undo the five bolts securing the power steering pump to the mounting bracket and remove the pump from the engine. Note that the securing bolts are of different lengths - make a note of their fitted positions to aid correct reassembly later.

Refitting

30 Offer up the power steering pump to the coolant pump housing and align the drive lugs with those on the rear of the coolant pump shaft.

31 The remainder of the refitting procedure is a reversal of removal, noting the following points:

a) *Tighten the pump mounting bolts to the specified torque.*

b) *Fit a new O-ring to the pump outlet pipe union and tighten the union nut to the specified torque.*

c) *Ensure the pulley is correctly installed and lightly tighten its mounting bolts.*

d) *Refit and adjust the drivebelt, then tighten the pulley mounting bolts to the specified torque.*

e) *On completion, bleed the hydraulic system (see Section 23).*

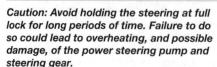

23 Power steering system - bleeding

Caution: Avoid holding the steering at full lock for long periods of time. Failure to do so could lead to overheating, and possible damage, of the power steering pump and steering gear.

1 Remove the cap from the power steering fluid reservoir and fill the reservoir with the specified fluid (see *"Lubricants, fluids and capacities"*).

2 On petrol models, disconnect the HT wiring from the distributor (see Chapter 5B) to prevent the engine from starting. On diesel models, this can be achieved by disconnecting the wiring from the fuel injection pump fuel cut-off solenoid (see Chapter 4B).

3 Crank the engine for approximately 5 seconds to prime the power steering pump.

4 Reconnect the distributor/fuel cut-off solenoid wiring, then check the reservoir fluid level is between the MAX and MIN level markings on the side of the reservoir, topping up if necessary.

5 Start the engine and allow it to idle for approximately 30 seconds with the front wheels pointing in the straight-ahead position. After 30 seconds, turn the steering onto full lock in one direction, hold it there for a few seconds, then turn it onto full lock in the opposite direction and hold it there for a few seconds. Return the front wheels to the straight-ahead position. Repeat this procedure until air bubbles cease to appear in the fluid reservoir.

6 If, when turning the steering, an abnormal noise is heard from the fluid lines, it indicates that there is still air in the system. Check this by turning the wheels to the straight-ahead position and switching off the engine. If the fluid level in the reservoir rises, then air is present in the system and further bleeding is necessary.

7 Once all traces of air have been removed from the power steering hydraulic system, turn the engine off and allow the system to cool. Once cool, check that the fluid level is up to the MAX mark on the power steering fluid reservoir. Top up if necessary.

24 Track rod balljoint - removal and refitting

Removal

1 Apply the handbrake, then jack up the front of the vehicle and support it on axle stands (see *"Jacking and Vehicle Support"*). Remove the appropriate front roadwheel.

2 If the balljoint is to be re-used, use a straight-edge and a scriber, or similar, to mark its relationship to the track rod.

3 Holding the balljoint, unscrew its locknut by one quarter of a turn only.

4 Extract the split pin and undo the nut securing the steering gear track rod balljoint to the swivel hub. Release the balljoint shank by using a suitable balljoint separator tool whilst taking care not to damage the balljoint gaiter **(see illustration)**.

5 Unscrew the balljoint from the track rod, counting the exact number of turns necessary to do so. If the locknut is to be removed, mark its position on the track rod and count the number of turns required to remove it so that it can be returned exactly to its original position on reassembly.

6 Carefully clean the balljoint and the threads. Renew the balljoint if its movement is sloppy or too stiff, if it is excessively worn, or if it is damaged in any way. Carefully check the stud taper and threads. No grease leakage should be visible.

Refitting

7 If necessary, screw the locknut onto the track rod by the number of turns noted on removal. This should align the locknut with the mark made on dismantling.

8 Screw the balljoint onto the track rod by the number of turns noted on removal. This should bring the balljoint to within a quarter of a turn from the locknut, with the alignment marks that were made (if applicable) on removal lined up.

9 Refit the balljoint shank to the swivel hub and tighten its retaining nut to the specified torque setting. Use a new split pin to secure the retaining nut in position **(see illustration)**.

10 Refit the roadwheel, then lower the vehicle to the ground and tighten the roadwheel nuts to the specified torque setting.

11 Check and, if necessary, adjust front wheel alignment.

24.4 Using a universal balljoint separator to free track rod balljoint from swivel hub

24.9 Secure balljoint retaining nut in position with new split pin

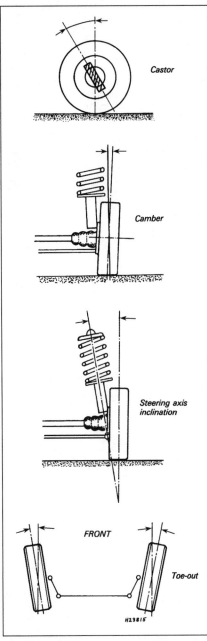

25.1 Wheel alignment and steering angles

25 Wheel alignment and steering angles

1 A vehicle's steering and suspension geometry is defined in five basic settings. All angles are expressed in degrees and the steering axis is defined as an imaginary line drawn through the centres of the front suspension upper and lower balljoints, extended where necessary to contact the ground **(see illustration)**.

Camber

2 Camber is the angle between each roadwheel and a vertical line drawn through its centre and tyre contact patch when viewed from the front or rear of the vehicle. Positive camber is when the roadwheels are tilted outwards from the vertical at the top. Negative camber is when they are tilted inwards.

3 Camber is not adjustable and given for reference only. While it can be checked using a camber checking gauge, if the figure obtained is significantly different from that specified, then the vehicle must be taken for careful checking by a professional, as the fault can only be caused by wear or damage to the body or suspension components.

Castor

4 Castor is the angle between the steering axis and a vertical line drawn through each roadwheel's centre and tyre contact patch when viewed from the side of the vehicle. Positive castor is when the steering axis is tilted so that it contacts the ground ahead of the vertical. Negative castor is when it contacts the ground behind the vertical.

5 Castor is not adjustable and is given for reference only. While it can be checked using a castor checking gauge, if the figure obtained is significantly different from that specified, then the vehicle must be taken for careful checking by a professional, as the fault can only be caused by wear or damage to the body or suspension components.

Steering axis inclination/SAI

6 Also known as kingpin inclination/KPI, this is the angle between the steering axis and a vertical line drawn through each roadwheel's centre and tyre contact patch when viewed from the front or rear of the vehicle.

7 SAI/KPI is not adjustable and is given for reference only.

Toe

8 Toe is the difference, viewed from above, between lines drawn through the roadwheel centres and the vehicle's centre-line. Toe-in is when the roadwheels point inwards, towards each other at the front. Toe-out is when they splay outwards from each other at the front.

9 At the front, toe setting is adjusted by screwing the track rods in or out of their balljoints to alter the effective length of the track rod assemblies.

10 At the rear, toe setting is adjusted by slackening the bolts securing the beam axle assembly mounting brackets and moving the brackets in relation to the chassis.

Toe-out on turns

11 Also known as turning angles or Ackermann angles, this is the difference, viewed from above, between the angles of rotation of the inside and outside front roadwheels when they have been turned through a given angle.

12 Toe-out on turns is set in production and is not adjustable as such, but can be upset by altering the length of the track rods unequally. It is essential, therefore, to ensure that the track rod lengths are exactly the same and that they are turned by the same amount whenever the toe setting is altered.

Checking and adjustment

13 Due to the special measuring equipment necessary to check wheel alignment and the skill required to use it properly, checking and adjustment of the aforementioned settings is best left to a Rover dealer or similar expert. Note that most tyre-fitting shops now possess sophisticated checking equipment.

10

Notes

Chapter 11
Bodywork and fittings

Contents

Degrees of difficulty

Easy, suitable for novice with little experience	**Fairly easy,** suitable for beginner with some experience	**Fairly difficult,** suitable for competent DIY mechanic	**Difficult,** suitable for experienced DIY mechanic	**Very difficult,** suitable for expert DIY or professional

Specifications

Torque wrench settings	Nm	lbf ft
Bonnet hinge bolts	10	7
Bonnet lock bolts	10	7
Bumper mounting bolts	6	4
Facia mounting bolts/nuts	9	7
Quarterlight hinge bolts	9	7
Quarterlight mounting bolts	4	3
Rear door window glass channel nuts	10	7
Rear seat belt stalk bolt	50	37
Rear seat cushion bolts	10	7
Seat belt mounting bolts	50	37
Seat runner-to-floor bolts	34	25
Tailgate hinge bolts	22	16
Tailgate striker bolts	10	7
Window glass-to-regulator bolts	10	7
Window regulator bolts	10	7

1 General information and precautions

General information

The vehicle bodyshell is made of pressed-steel sections in three and five-door hatchback versions. Most components are welded together but some use is made of structural adhesives. The front wings are bolted on.

The bonnet, door, tailgate and some other vulnerable panels are made of zinc-coated metal. Once assembled, the entire body is given an eight-stage pre-treatment process including a high-pressure wash before painting. The first coat of primer is applied by cathodic electro-deposition, followed by four coats of paint and two of lacquer. An anti-stone chip coating (finished in matt black,

where exposed) is applied to the outer faces of the sills and the corresponding surfaces of the front and rear wings. A PVC coating is applied to the underbody, followed by a coating of protective wax. All chassis members, box-sections and sills are injected with liquid cavity wax.

Several of the body cavities are filled with 'expand-in-place' foam. This process features a two-part liquid silicon foam and hardener mix which is injected into the cavities after the

11

body has been painted and wax treated. The foam improves the noise insulation of the vehicle and is flame retardant. The foam is also hydrophobic, that is, it repels water.

Extensive use is made of plastic materials, mainly on the interior but also in exterior components such as the wheelarch liners to improve the body's resistance to corrosion.

Precautions

Supplementary Restraint System (SRS) components

Refer to the *Precautions* listed in Section 1 of Chapter 12.

2 Vehicle exterior and interior - maintenance and inspection

Vehicle exterior

The general condition of a vehicle's bodywork is the one thing that significantly affects its value. Maintenance is easy but needs to be regular. Neglect, particularly after minor damage, can lead quickly to further deterioration and costly repair bills. It is important also to keep watch on those parts of the vehicle not immediately visible, for instance the underbody, inside all the wheelarches and the lower part of the engine compartment.

The basic maintenance routine for the bodywork is washing - preferably with a lot of water, from a hose. This will remove all the loose solids which may have stuck to the vehicle. It is important to flush these off in such a way as to prevent grit from scratching the finish. The wheelarches and underbody need washing in the same way to remove any accumulated mud which will retain moisture and tend to encourage rust, particularly in winter when it is essential that any salt (from that put down on the roads) is washed off. Paradoxically enough, the best time to clean the underbody and wheelarches is in wet weather when the mud is thoroughly wet and soft. In very wet weather the underbody is usually cleaned automatically of large accumulations; this is therefore a good time for inspection.

If the vehicle is very dirty, especially underneath or in the engine compartment, it is tempting to use one of the pressure washers or steam cleaners available on garage forecourts. Whilst these are quick and effective, especially for the removal of the accumulation of oily grime which sometimes is allowed to become thick in certain areas, their usage does have some disadvantages. If caked-on dirt is simply blasted off the paintwork, its finish soon becomes scratched and dull and the pressure can allow water to penetrate door and window seals and the lock mechanisms. If the full force of such a jet is directed at the vehicle's underbody, the wax-

based protective coating can easily be damaged and water (with whatever cleaning solvent is used) could be forced into crevices or components that it would not normally reach. Similarly, if such equipment is used to clean the engine compartment, water can be forced into the components of the fuel and electrical systems and the protective coating can be removed that is applied to many small components during manufacture; this may therefore actually promote corrosion (especially inside electrical connectors) and initiate engine problems or other electrical faults. Also, if the jet is pointed directly at any of the oil seals, water can be forced past the seal lips and into the engine or transmission. Great care is required, therefore, if such equipment is used and, in general, regular cleaning by such methods should be avoided.

A much better solution in the long term is just to flush away as much loose dirt as possible using a hose alone, even if this leaves the engine compartment looking dirty. If an oil leak has developed, or if any other accumulation of oil or grease is to be removed, there are one or two excellent grease solvents available, which can be brush applied. The dirt can then be simply hosed off. Take care to replace the wax-based protective coat, if this was affected by the solvent.

Normal washing of the bodywork is best carried out using cold or warm water with a proprietary car shampoo. Tar spots can be removed by using white spirit, followed by soapy water to remove all traces of spirit. Try to keep water out of the bonnet air intakes and check afterwards that the heater air inlet box drain tube is clear so that any water has drained out of the box.

After washing the paintwork, wipe off with a chamois leather to give an unspotted clear finish. A coat of clear protective wax polish will give added protection against chemical pollutants in the air. If the paintwork sheen has dulled or oxidised, use a cleaner/polisher combination to restore the brilliance of the shine. This requires a little effort, but such dulling is usually caused because regular washing has been neglected. Care needs to be taken with metallic paintwork, as special non-abrasive cleaner/polisher is required to avoid damage to the finish.

Brightwork should be treated in the same way as paintwork.

Windscreens and windows can be kept clear of the smeary film which often appears, by the use of proprietary glass cleaner. Never use any form of wax or other body or chromium polish on glass.

Vehicle interior

Mats and carpets should be brushed or vacuum cleaned regularly to keep them free of grit. If they are badly stained remove them from the vehicle for scrubbing or sponging and make quite sure they are dry before refitting.

Where leather upholstery is fitted it should be cleaned only if necessary, using either a mild soap (such as saddle soap) or a proprietary leather cleaner; do not use strong soaps, detergents or chemical cleaners. If the leather is very stained, seek the advice of a Rover dealer. Fabric-trimmed seats and interior trim panels can be kept clean by wiping with a damp cloth and a suitable cleaner. If they do become stained (which can be more apparent on light coloured upholstery) use a little liquid detergent and a soft nail brush to scour the grime out of the grain of the material. Do not forget to keep the headlining clean in the same way as the (fabric) upholstery.

When using liquid cleaners of any sort inside the vehicle, do not over-wet the surfaces being cleaned. Excessive damp could get into the seams and padded interior causing stains, offensive odours or even rot. If the inside of the vehicle gets wet accidentally it is worthwhile taking some trouble to dry it out properly, particularly where carpets are involved. Do not leave oil or electric heaters inside the vehicle for this purpose.

Do not allow the airbag unit in the centre of the steering wheel to become flooded with detergents or water and do not clean with petrol or furniture cream and polishes. Clean the unit sparingly with a damp cloth and upholstery cleaner. Failure to observe these precautions may result in the airbag inflating, with the subsequent risk of personal injury.

3 Minor body damage - repair

Repairs of minor scratches in bodywork

If the scratch is very superficial, and does not penetrate to the metal of the bodywork, repair is very simple. Lightly rub the area of the scratch with a paintwork renovator, or a very fine cutting paste, to remove loose paint from the scratch, and to clear the surrounding bodywork of wax polish. Rinse the area with clean water.

Apply touch-up paint to the scratch using a fine paint brush; continue to apply fine layers of paint until the surface of the paint in the scratch is level with the surrounding paintwork. Allow the new paint at least two weeks to harden, then blend it into the surrounding paintwork by rubbing the scratch area with a paintwork renovator or a very fine cutting paste. Finally, apply wax polish.

Where the scratch has penetrated right through to the metal of the bodywork, causing the metal to rust, a different repair technique is required. Remove any loose rust from the bottom of the scratch with a penknife, then apply rust-inhibiting paint to prevent the formation of rust in the future. Using a rubber or nylon applicator, fill the scratch with bodystopper paste. If required, this paste can be mixed with cellulose thinners to provide a very thin paste which is ideal for filling narrow scratches. Before the stopper-paste in the scratch hardens, wrap a piece of smooth cotton rag around the top of a finger. Dip the finger in cellulose thinners, and quickly sweep it across the surface of the stopper-paste in the scratch; this will ensure that the surface of the stopper-paste is slightly hollowed. The scratch can now be painted over as described earlier in this Section.

Repairs of dents in bodywork

When deep denting of the vehicle's bodywork has taken place, the first task is to pull the dent out, until the affected bodywork almost attains its original shape. There is little point in trying to restore the original shape completely, as the metal in the damaged area will have stretched on impact, and cannot be reshaped fully to its original contour. It is better to bring the level of the dent up to a point which is about 3 mm below the level of the surrounding bodywork. In cases where the dent is very shallow anyway, it is not worth trying to pull it out at all. If the underside of the dent is accessible, it can be hammered out gently from behind, using a mallet with a wooden or plastic head. Whilst doing this, hold a suitable block of wood firmly against the outside of the panel, to absorb the impact from the hammer blows and thus prevent a large area of the bodywork from being "belled-out".

Should the dent be in a section of the bodywork which has a double skin, or some other factor making it inaccessible from behind, a different technique is called for. Drill several small holes through the metal inside the area - particularly in the deeper section. Then screw long self-tapping screws into the holes, just sufficiently for them to gain a good purchase in the metal. Now the dent can be pulled out by pulling on the protruding heads of the screws with a pair of pliers.

The next stage of the repair is the removal of the paint from the damaged area, and from an inch or so of the surrounding "sound" bodywork. This is accomplished most easily by using a wire brush or abrasive pad on a power drill, although it can be done just as effectively by hand, using sheets of abrasive paper. To complete the preparation for filling, score the surface of the bare metal with a screwdriver or the tang of a file, or alternatively, drill small holes in the affected area. This will provide a really good "key" for the filler paste.

To complete the repair, see the Section on filling and respraying.

Repairs of rust holes or gashes in bodywork

Remove all paint from the affected area, and from an inch or so of the surrounding "sound" bodywork, using an abrasive pad or a wire brush on a power drill. If these are not available, a few sheets of abrasive paper will do the job most effectively. With the paint removed, you will be able to judge the severity of the corrosion, and therefore decide whether to renew the whole panel (if this is possible) or to repair the affected area. New body panels are not as expensive as most people think, and it is often quicker and more satisfactory to fit a new panel than to attempt to repair large areas of corrosion.

Remove all fittings from the affected area, except those which will act as a guide to the original shape of the damaged bodywork (eg headlight shells etc). Then, using tin snips or a hacksaw blade, remove all loose metal and any other metal badly affected by corrosion. Hammer the edges of the hole inwards, in order to create a slight depression for the filler paste.

Wire-brush the affected area to remove the powdery rust from the surface of the remaining metal. Paint the affected area with rust-inhibiting paint, if the back of the rusted area is accessible, treat this also.

Before filling can take place, it will be necessary to block the hole in some way. This can be achieved by the use of aluminium or plastic mesh, or aluminium tape.

Aluminium or plastic mesh, or glass-fibre matting, is probably the best material to use for a large hole. Cut a piece to the approximate size and shape of the hole to be filled, then position it in the hole so that its edges are below the level of the surrounding bodywork. It can be retained in position by several blobs of filler paste around its periphery.

Aluminium tape should be used for small or very narrow holes. Pull a piece off the roll, trim it to the approximate size and shape required, then pull off the backing paper (if used) and stick the tape over the hole; it can be overlapped if the thickness of one piece is insufficient. Burnish down the edges of the tape with the handle of a screwdriver or similar, to ensure that the tape is securely attached to the metal underneath.

Bodywork repairs - filling and respraying

Before using this Section, see the Sections on dent, deep scratch, rust holes and gash repairs.

Many types of bodyfiller are available, but generally speaking, those proprietary kits which contain a tin of filler paste and a tube of resin hardener are best for this type of repair. A wide, flexible plastic or nylon applicator will be found invaluable for imparting a smooth and well-contoured finish to the surface of the filler.

Mix up a little filler on a clean piece of card or board - measure the hardener carefully (follow the maker's instructions on the pack), otherwise the filler will set too rapidly or too slowly. Using the applicator, apply the filler paste to the prepared area; draw the applicator across the surface of the filler to achieve the correct contour and to level the surface. As soon as a contour that approximates to the correct one is achieved, stop working the paste - if you carry on too long, the paste will become sticky and begin to "pick-up" on the applicator. Continue to add thin layers of filler paste at 20-minute intervals, until the level of the filler is just proud of the surrounding bodywork.

Once the filler has hardened, the excess can be removed using a metal plane or file. From then on, progressively-finer grades of abrasive paper should be used, starting with a 40-grade production paper, and finishing with a 400-grade wet-and-dry paper. Always wrap the abrasive paper around a flat rubber, cork, or wooden block - otherwise the surface of the filler will not be completely flat. During the smoothing of the filler surface, the wet-and-dry paper should be periodically rinsed in water. This will ensure that a very smooth finish is imparted to the filler at the final stage.

At this stage, the "dent" should be surrounded by a ring of bare metal, which in turn should be encircled by the finely "feathered" edge of the good paintwork. Rinse the repair area with clean water, until all of the dust produced by the rubbing-down operation has gone.

Spray the whole area with a light coat of primer - this will show up any imperfections in the surface of the filler. Repair these imperfections with fresh filler paste or bodystopper, and once more smooth the surface with abrasive paper. Repeat this spray-and-repair procedure until you are satisfied that the surface of the filler, and the feathered edge of the paintwork, are perfect. Clean the repair area with clean water, and allow to dry fully. If bodystopper is used, it can be mixed with cellulose thinners to form a really thin paste which is ideal for filling small holes.

The repair area is now ready for final spraying. Paint spraying must be carried out in a warm, dry, windless and dust-free atmosphere. This condition can be created artificially if you have access to a large indoor working area, but if you are forced to work in the open, you will have to pick your day very carefully. If you are working indoors, dousing the floor in the work area with water will help to settle the dust which would otherwise be in the atmosphere. If the repair area is confined to one body panel, mask off the surrounding panels; this will help to minimise the effects of a slight mis-match in paint colours. Bodywork fittings (eg chrome strips, door handles etc) will also need to be masked off. Use genuine masking tape, and several thicknesses of newspaper, for the masking operations.

Before commencing to spray, agitate the aerosol can thoroughly, then spray a test area (an old tin, or similar) until the technique is mastered. Cover the repair area with a thick coat of primer; the thickness should be built up using several thin layers of paint, rather than one thick one. Using 400-grade wet-and-

11

dry paper, rub down the surface of the primer until it is really smooth. While doing this, the work area should be thoroughly doused with water, and the wet-and-dry paper periodically rinsed in water. Allow to dry before spraying on more paint.

Spray on the top coat, again building up the thickness by using several thin layers of paint. Start spraying at one edge of the repair area, and then, using a side-to-side motion, work until the whole repair area and about 2 inches of the surrounding original paintwork is covered. Remove all masking material 10 to 15 minutes after spraying on the final coat of paint.

Allow the new paint at least two weeks to harden, then, using a paintwork renovator, or a very fine cutting paste, blend the edges of the paint into the existing paintwork. Finally, apply wax polish.

Plastic components

With the use of more and more plastic body components by the vehicle manufacturers (eg bumpers. spoilers, and in some cases major body panels), rectification of more serious damage to such items has become a matter of either entrusting repair work to a specialist in this field, or renewing complete components. Repair of such damage by the DIY owner is not really feasible, owing to the cost of the equipment and materials required for effecting such repairs. The basic technique involves making a groove along the line of the crack in the plastic, using a rotary burr in a power drill. The damaged part is then welded back together, using a hot-air gun to heat up and fuse a plastic filler rod into the groove. Any excess plastic is then removed, and the area rubbed down to a smooth finish. It is important that a filler rod of the correct plastic is used, as body components can be made of a variety of different types (eg polycarbonate, ABS, polypropylene).

Damage of a less serious nature (abrasions, minor cracks etc) can be repaired by the DIY owner using a two-part epoxy filler repair material. Once mixed in equal proportions, this is used in similar fashion to the bodywork filler used on metal panels. The filler is usually cured in twenty to thirty minutes, ready for sanding and painting.

If the owner is renewing a complete component himself, or if he has repaired it with epoxy filler, he will be left with the problem of finding a suitable paint for finishing which is compatible with the type of plastic used. At one time, the use of a universal paint was not possible, owing to the complex range of plastics encountered in body component applications. Standard paints, generally speaking, will not bond to plastic or rubber satisfactorily. However, it is now possible to obtain a plastic body parts finishing kit which consists of a pre-primer treatment, a primer and coloured top coat. Full instructions are normally supplied with a kit, but basically, the method of use is to first apply the pre-primer

6.1a Remove the four nuts securing the upper edge of the bumper to bonnet lock platform . . .

to the component concerned, and allow it to dry for up to 30 minutes. Then the primer is applied, and left to dry for about an hour before finally applying the special-coloured top coat. The result is a correctly-coloured component, where the paint will flex with the plastic or rubber, a property that standard paint does not normally possess.

4 Major body damage - repair

Note: *Where serious damage has occurred to a vehicle, any repair is best left to a professional or a Rover agent with specialist equipment.*

Where serious damage has occurred, or large areas need renewal due to neglect, it means that complete new panels will need welding in. This is best left to professionals. If the damage is due to impact, it will also be necessary to check completely the alignment of the bodyshell. This can only be carried out accurately by a Rover dealer using special jigs. If the body is left misaligned, it is primarily dangerous as the vehicle will not handle properly and secondly, uneven stresses will be imposed on the steering, suspension and possibly transmission, causing abnormal wear or complete failure, particularly to items such as the tyres.

6.2 Remove the screws securing the lower edge of the bumper to the wheel arch liners

6.1b . . . then remove the plastic cover panel

5 Body exterior trim panels - renewal

The exterior body and door trim strips are held in position with a special adhesive tape. Removal requires the trim to be heated, to soften the adhesive, and then cut away from the door surface. Due to the high risk of damage to the vehicle's paintwork during this operation, it is recommended that work is entrusted to a Rover dealer.

6 Bumpers - removal and refitting

Front bumper

Removal

1 Remove the four nuts securing the upper edge of the bumper to bonnet lock platform, then remove the plastic cover panel **(see illustrations)**.
2 Slacken and withdraw the six screws (three on each side) securing the lower edge of the bumper to both wheel arch liners **(see illustration)**.
3 Pull the front edge of the wheel arch liner away from the bodywork slightly, and undo the bolts securing the trailing edge of the bumper to the bodywork **(see illustration)**.

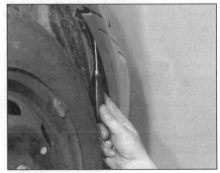

6.3 Undo the bolts securing the trailing edge of the bumper to the bodywork

6.4 Remove the screws securing the lower edge of the bumper to the front valence

6.5 Remove the number plate then undo the single bumper securing screw

6.6 Carefully pull the bumper assembly away from the front of the car

4 At the centre of the lower edge of the bumper, remove the three screws that secure the bumper to the front valence **(see illustration)**.

5 Remove the number plate by slicing through the adhesive backing with a suitable blade, then undo the single screw securing the front of the bumper to the bodywork **(see illustration)**.

6 Carefully pull the bumper assembly away from the front of the car, ensuring that the trailing edges of the assembly do not scratch the bodywork **(see illustration)**.

7 If necessary, the mounting rail and brackets can be removed from the bodywork, by slackening and withdrawing the four mounting screws.

Refitting

8 Refitting is a reverse of the removal sequence. Ensure that the mounting nuts and bolts are tightened to the specified torque. Use new adhesive pads when refitting the number plate.

Rear bumper

Removal

9 Open the tailgate, then remove the five screw plug fixings, securing the upper edge of the bumper to the bodywork. This kind of fixing is removed by first undoing the screw, then prising out the plug beneath using a forked implement **(see illustrations)**.

10 Working at the lower corners of the

bumper assembly, remove the two screws (one each side) that secure the bumper to the wheel arch liners **(see illustration)**.

11 Pull the wheel arch liners away from the bodywork slightly, then unscrew the bolts securing the upper corners of the bumper assembly to the bodywork **(see illustration)**.

12 Undo the screw securing the centre of the lower edge of the bumper to the bodywork **(see illustration)**.

13 Carefully pull the bumper assembly away from the rear of the car, ensuring that the edges of the assembly do not scratch the bodywork **(see illustration)**.

Refitting

14 Refitting is a reverse of the removal

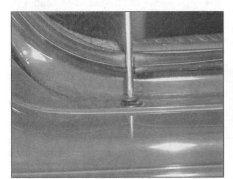

6.9a Remove the fixings securing the upper edge of the bumper to the bodywork by first undoing the centre screw . . .

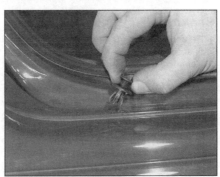

6.9b . . . then prising out the plug beneath

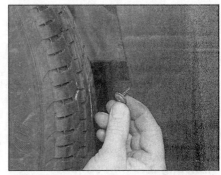

6.10 Remove the screws that secure the lower edge of the bumper to the wheel arch liners

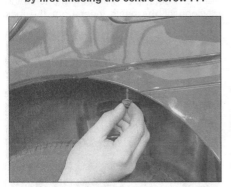

6.11 Unscrew the bolts securing the upper corners of the bumper assembly to the bodywork

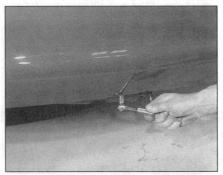

6.12 Undo the screw securing the centre of the lower edge of the bumper to the bodywork

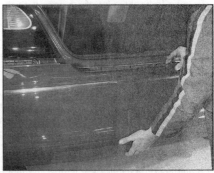

6.13 Carefully pull the bumper assembly away from the rear of the car

11

sequence. Ensure that the bumper mounting nuts and bolts are tightened to their specified torque setting.

7 Radiator grille - removal and refitting

Removal

1 Remove the front bumper as described in Section 6.
2 Remove the ten screws and detach the grille from the bumper assembly.

Refitting

3 Refitting is a reversal of removal. Tighten the grille retaining screws securely, then refit the bumper with reference to Section 6.

8 Bonnet - removal, refitting and adjustment

Removal

1 Open the bonnet and have an assistant support it. Mark the outline of each bonnet hinge to use as a guide when refitting.
2 Disconnect the windscreen washer supply pipe from the T-piece, and catch any fluid that spills out in a suitable container **(see illustration)**.
3 On models with heated washer jets, unplug the electrical wiring from the jets at the multi-way connectors, then remove the bonnet sound insulation panel and release the washer jet wiring harness from the clips.
4 Undo the bonnet retaining bolts, and with the help of an assistant, carefully lift the bonnet away from the engine compartment. Note any shims which may be fitted between the bonnet and hinge **(see illustration)**. Store the bonnet out of the way in a safe place.

Refitting and adjustment

5 Offer up the bonnet to the vehicle, position the shims (where fitted) between the bonnet and hinges, then fit and finger-tighten the retaining bolts, aligning the hinges with the marks made on removal (where applicable).
6 Reconnect the windscreen washer supply pipe. On models with heated washer jets, secure the harness to the bonnet with the securing clips, then refit the sound insulation panel.
7 Close the bonnet so that only the safety catch engages and check for the alignment of the bonnet by observing the gap between each edge of the bonnet and the surrounding body panels. If necessary, slacken the hinge bolts and realign the bonnet to suit. Once the bonnet is correctly aligned, tighten the hinge bolts to the specified torque.
8 Check that the bonnet height is correct as compared with that of the front wings. If

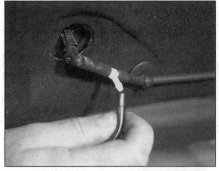

8.2 Disconnect the windscreen washer supply pipe from the T-piece

necessary, adjust by slackening the locknut and rotating the relevant bonnet rubber stop, to alter its height.
9 Once the bonnet is correctly aligned, check that the bonnet fastens and releases in a satisfactory manner. If adjustment is necessary, remove the plastic lock cover then slacken the bonnet lock retaining bolts and adjust the position of the lock to suit. Once the lock is operating correctly, tighten its retaining bolts to the specified torque and refit the lock cover.

9 Bonnet release cable - removal and refitting

Removal

1 Refer to Section 10 and remove the bonnet lock assembly.
2 Refer to Section 6 and remove the nuts that secure the upper edge of the bumper assembly to the lock mounting platform. Carefully prise the edge of the bumper away from the mounting platform, then free the bonnet release cable from its securing clips as they become accessible. Withdraw the cable from the mounting platform.
3 Work along the length of the cable and release it from any remaining retaining clips in the engine compartment.
4 Release the securing studs and remove the cover from the fusebox, located on the underside of the driver's side of the facia.

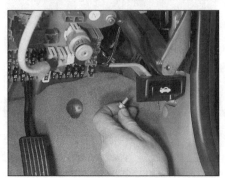

9.5a Slacken and withdraw the securing bolts . . .

8.4 Undo the bonnet retaining bolts

Release the clips and lower the felt panel from the space above the driver's footwell.
5 Slacken and withdraw the securing bolts, then detach the bonnet release knob mounting bracket from the bodywork. Remove the cable from the mounting bracket **(see illustrations)**.
6 Release the cable sealing grommet from the bulkhead. Pull the cable through from inside the vehicle and remove it from the vehicle.

Refitting

7 Refitting is a reversal of removal. Ensure that the cable is routed correctly and is not kinked or twisted. Refit the lock mechanism with reference to Section 10, then check that the operation of the release cable is satisfactory before securing the bumper in place.

10 Bonnet lock - removal, refitting and adjustment

Removal

1 Remove the two nuts securing the plastic cover to the lock mechanism. Lift off the plastic cover from the lock then mark the outline of the bonnet lock on the body to use as a guide when refitting.
2 Slacken and remove the three bonnet lock retaining bolts then withdraw the lock and disconnect the cable inner from the lock

9.5b . . . then detach the bonnet release knob mounting bracket from the bodywork

10.2 Bonnet lock mounting bolts

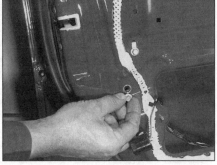

11.4a Remove the bolts that secure the window glass rear guide channel to the door . . .

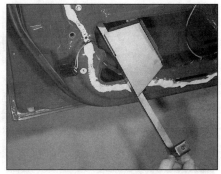

11.4b . . . and the guide channel from the door to give access to the lock mechanism

operating mechanism. Release the cable outer from the lock bracket and remove the lock from the vehicle **(see illustration)**.

Refitting and adjustment

3 Refit the release cable to the lock operating mechanism then align the lock with the marks made on removal and tighten the lock retaining bolts to the specified torque.

4 Check that the bonnet fastens and releases in a satisfactory manner. If adjustment is necessary, slacken the bonnet lock retaining bolts and adjust the position of the lock to suit. Once the lock is operating correctly, tighten its retaining bolts to the specified torque and refit the lock cover.

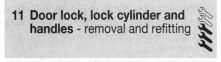

11 Door lock, lock cylinder and handles - removal and refitting

Removal

Front door lock mechanism

1 Disconnect the battery negative cable and position it away from the terminal. Refer to the relevant sub-Section and remove the exterior door handle.

2 Release the clip and detach the outside door handle control rod from the lock mechanism. Where applicable, detach the

lock cylinder control rod from the lock mechanism in the same manner.

3 Refer to the relevant sub-Section and remove the interior door handle. Detach the control rod from the rear of the handle assembly.

4 Slacken and remove the bolts that secure the window glass rear guide channel to the door. Remove the guide channel from the door to give access to the lock mechanism **(see illustrations)**.

5 Undo the lock mechanism securing screws and detach the mechanism from the door. On models with central locking, unplug the wiring harness from the lock mechanism at the multiway connector **(see illustrations)**.

11.5a Undo the lock mechanism securing screws and detach the mechanism from the door . . .

6 Release the interior handle and locking knob control rods from the lock mechanism, then manoeuvre the lock mechanism from the door, guiding the remaining control rods through the aperture **(see illustrations)**.

Rear door lock mechanism

7 Disconnect the battery negative cable and position it away from the terminal. Refer to the relevant sub-Section and remove the exterior door handle.

8 Release the clip and detach the interior door handle control rod from the lock mechanism. Detach the locking knob control rod from the lock mechanism in the same manner **(see illustration)**.

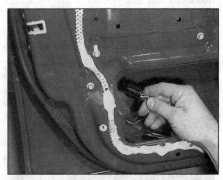

11.5b . . . and unplug the wiring harness at the multiway connector (models with central locking)

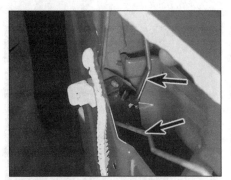

11.6a Release the interior handle and locking knob control rods from the lock mechanism . . .

11.6b . . . then manoeuvre the lock mechanism from the door, guiding the remaining control rods through the aperture

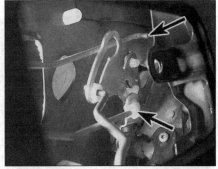

11.8 Detach the interior door handle and locking knob control rods (arrowed) from the lock mechanism

11

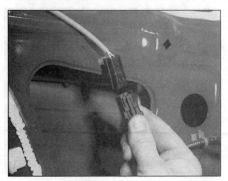

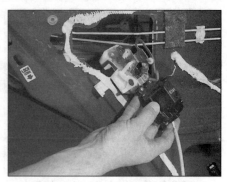

11.9 On models with central locking, unplug the harness from the lock mechanism at the multiway connector

11.10 Undo the lock mechanism securing screws . . .

11.11 . . . and manoeuvre the lock mechanism from the door

9 On models with central locking, release the wiring harness from the securing clip, then unplug the harness from the lock mechanism at the multiway connector **(see illustration)**.

10 Undo the lock mechanism securing screws and detach the mechanism from the door **(see illustration)**.

11 Manoeuvre the lock mechanism from the door **(see illustration)**.

Front door lock cylinder

12 Ensure the window glass is fully up then remove the door inner trim panel and waterproof membrane. Disconnect the battery negative cable and position it away from the terminal.

13 Slacken and withdraw the lock cylinder retaining bolt.

14 Release the clip and detach the lock mechanism control rod from the lever at the rear of the lock cylinder.

15 Manoeuvre the lock cylinder from the door.

Interior door handle

16 Remove the inner trim panel and the waterproof membrane.

17 Undo the screws securing the interior handle to the door, then disconnect the handle from its operating rod and remove it from the vehicle **(see illustration)**.

Front door exterior handle

18 Remove the inner trim panel and partially

peel back the waterproof membrane, to gain access to the rear of the exterior handle retaining bolts. Ensure that the window glass is fully raised. Disconnect the battery negative cable and position it away from the terminal.

19 Undo the two retaining bolts and detach the handle from the door **(see illustration)**.

20 Release the clips and disconnect the lock mechanism control rod from the handle **(see illustration)**.

Rear door exterior handle

21 Remove the inner trim panel and partially peel back the waterproof membrane, to gain access to the rear of the exterior handle retaining bolts.

22 Undo the two retaining bolts and withdraw the handle from the door. Release the clip and disconnect the lock mechanism control rod from the handle **(see illustrations)**.

23 Remove the handle from the door aperture.

Refitting

24 Refitting is the reverse of the removal sequence, noting the following:
  a) *Tighten all retaining bolts to the specified torque settings.*
  b) *Ensure that all operating rods are securely held in position by the retaining clips.*
  c) *Apply grease to all lock and operating rod pivot points.*

11.17 Interior door handle securing screws (arrowed)

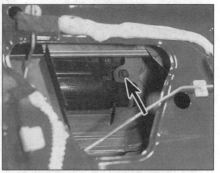

11.19 Front door exterior handle securing bolts (one hidden from view)

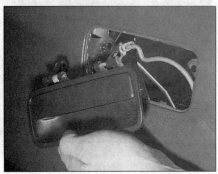

11.20 Release the clips and disconnect the lock mechanism control rod from the handle

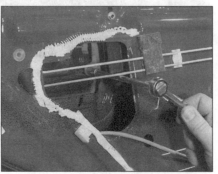

11.22a Undo the two retaining bolts and withdraw the handle from the door . . .

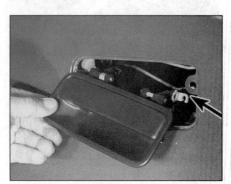

11.22b . . . release the clip and disconnect the lock mechanism control rod (arrowed) from the handle

d) *Before fitting the inner trim panel, thoroughly check the operation of all the door lock handles and, where necessary, the central locking system. Ensure that the water membrane is securely stuck to the door.*

12 Doors - removal, refitting and adjustment

Note: *If there is insufficient slack in the wiring to be able to withdraw the wiring connectors from the door panel, then it will be necessary to remove the inner trim panel and peel back the waterproof membrane to gain further access.*

Removal

1 Open the door and peel back the wiring gaiter, or displace the wiring grommet from the front edge of the door panel. Carefully withdraw the wiring from the door until the wiring connector(s) emerge. Disconnect the block connector(s) and tape the door side of the connectors to the door frame to prevent them falling back into the door panel **(see illustration)**.

2 Mark the outline position of each door hinge to use as a guide when refitting.

3 Remove the retaining clip (where fitted) and extract the pin securing the door check link to the door pillar **(see illustration)**.

4 Have an assistant support the door and undo the nuts which secure the upper and lower hinges to the door, then remove the door from the vehicle.

5 If necessary, the hinges can now be unbolted and removed from the door pillar, having first marked the position of the hinge on the pillar. To gain access to the front door hinge bolts, it will first be necessary to remove the wheelarch liner.

Refitting and adjustment

6 The door is refitted by a reversal of the removal procedure. Align the hinges with the marks made on removal and tighten the bolts securely.

7 On completion, shut the door carefully and check that the door is correctly aligned with all surrounding bodywork with an equal clearance all around. If necessary, adjustment can be made by slackening the hinge bolts and moving the door. Once the door is positioned correctly, tighten the hinge bolts securely.

8 With the door correctly aligned, check that it closes easily, is flush with the adjacent panels and does not rattle when closed. If not, slacken the door striker retaining screws and reposition the striker. Once door operation is satisfactory, tighten the striker retaining screws securely.

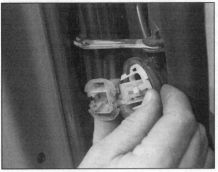

12.1 Unplug the door wiring from the block connectors

13 Door inner trim panel - removal and refitting

Removal

Front door

1 Carefully prise the escutcheon from the door pull handle. Slacken and withdraw the two pull handle screws and remove the handle from the door panel **(see illustrations)**.

2 On models equipped with manually-operated windows, remove the window

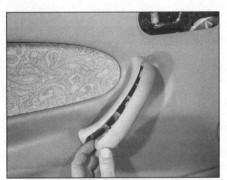

13.1a Carefully prise the escutcheon from the door pull handle . . .

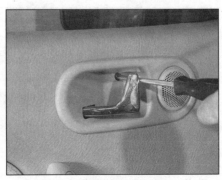

13.3a Undo the securing screw . . .

12.3 Extract the pin (arrowed) securing the door check link to the door pillar

regulator handle horseshoe clip **(refer to illustrations 13.8a)** by hooking it out with a screwdriver or bent piece of wire, then pull the handle off the spindle. Remove the regulator escutcheon.

3 Hold the door interior handle in the 'open' position, undo the securing screw and remove the escutcheon **(see illustrations)**. Unplug the wiring from the speaker as the connectors become accessible (where applicable).

4 Work around the periphery of the trim panel and remove the securing screws. Note that two of the screws also secure the door storage bin. Note also that some of the screws may be hidden behind trim caps;

13.1b . . . withdraw the two pull handle screws and remove the handle from the door panel

13.3b . . . and remove the door interior handle escutcheon

11

13.5a Prise out the locking knob trim and remove it from the door panel . . .

13.5b . . . and lift the whole panel upwards over the locking knob and away from the door

13.7 Carefully peel the waterproof plastic membrane away from the door

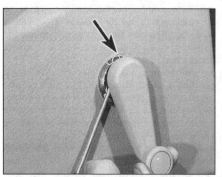

13.8a Remove the regulator handle horseshoe clip (arrowed) by hooking it out with a screwdriver . . .

13.8b . . . then pull the handle off the spindle

these can be prised off using a small, flat bladed screwdriver.

5 At the rear and lower edges of the door trim panel, release the panel from the press stud fixings by levering between the panel and door using a flat forked instrument. Prise out the locking knob trim and remove it from the door panel. Lift the whole panel upwards over the locking knob and away from the door **(see illustrations)**.

6 If the waterproof membrane is to be removed, first remove the front door speaker as described in Chapter 12.

7 Extract the plastic membrane locating dowel(s), then carefully peel the membrane from the door **(see illustration)**.

Rear door

8 Remove the window regulator handle horseshoe clip by hooking it out with a screwdriver or bent piece of wire, then pull the handle off the spindle **(see illustrations)**.

9 Remove the window regulator escutcheon from the spindle.

10 Hold the door interior handle in the 'open' position, undo the securing screw and remove the escutcheon **(see illustrations)**.

11 Carefully prise the escutcheon from the door pull handle. Slacken and withdraw the two pull handle screws and remove the handle from the door panel **(see illustrations)**.

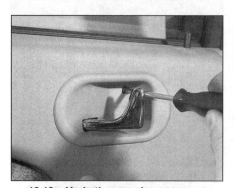

13.10a Undo the securing screw . . .

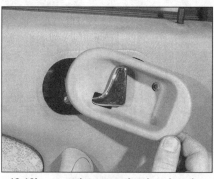

13.10b . . . and remove the door interior handle escutcheon

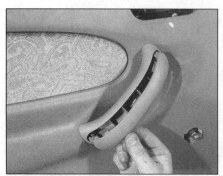

13.11a Carefully prise the escutcheon from the door pull handle . . .

13.11b . . . slacken and withdraw the two pull handle screws

13.11c . . . and remove the handle from the door panel

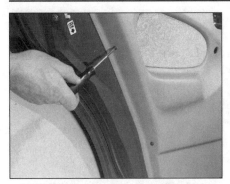

13.12 Work around the periphery of the trim panel and remove the securing screws

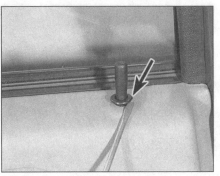

13.13a Prise out and remove the locking knob trim . . .

13.13b . . . then lift the whole door panel upwards and away from the door

12 Work around the periphery of the trim panel and remove the securing screws **(see illustration)**. Note that some of the screws may be hidden behind trim caps; these can be prised off using a small, flat bladed screwdriver.

13 At the lower edges of the door trim panel, release the panel from the press stud fixings by levering between the panel and door using a flat forked instrument. Prise out and remove the locking knob trim, then lift the whole door panel upwards over the locking knob and away from the door **(see illustrations)**.

14 If the waterproof membrane is to be removed, extract the two plastic membrane locating dowels, then carefully peel the membrane from the door **(see illustration)**.

Refitting

15 Refitting the trim panel is the reverse of removal, noting the following:
 a) *Check the trim panel retaining studs for breakage and renew as necessary.*
 b) *When refitting the window regulator handle (where fitted), fit the clip to the handle first then push the handle onto the regulator spindle.*

---

14 Door window glass and regulator -
removal and refitting

Front door window glass and regulator

Removal

1 Remove the front door inner trim panel and waterproof membrane (see Section 13).

2 On models equipped with electrically-operated windows, temporarily reconnect the window switch wiring connector(s) and position the glass so that access can be

13.14 Carefully peel the waterproof membrane from the door

gained to both glass retaining bolts via the cutaway in the door panel.

3 On models equipped with manually-operated windows, temporarily refit the regulator handle and position the glass so that its retaining bolts can be accessed through the cutaway in the door.

4 Undo the two bolts securing the window glass to the regulator, then lift up the glass and manoeuvre it out of the door **(see illustrations)**.

5 On models with electric windows, unplug the wiring connector from the regulator motor and release the wiring harness from its securing clips **(see illustration)**.

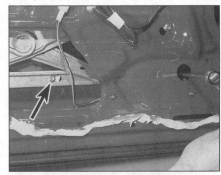

14.4a Undo the two bolts securing the window glass to the regulator . . .

14.4b . . . then lift up the glass and manoeuvre it out of the door

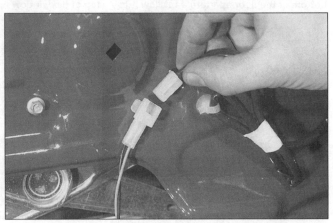

14.5 On models with electric windows, unplug the wiring connector from the regulator motor

11

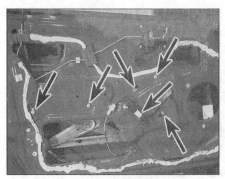

14.6a Slacken and withdraw the regulator assembly retaining bolts . . .

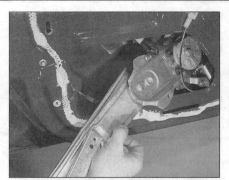

14.6b . . . then manoeuvre the assembly out through the door panel aperture

14.17a Slacken the securing bolts and detach the glass from the regulator . . .

6 Mark the position of the two regulator roller guide retaining bolts, in relation to the door. Slacken and withdraw all six regulator assembly retaining bolts, then manoeuvre the assembly out through the door panel aperture **(see illustrations)**.

7 The window regulator motor can be removed as follows: mark the relationship between the regulator and the geared segment using a marker pen or similar, then undo the three securing screws and withdraw the motor from the regulator.

Refitting

8 Apply a small amount of general purpose grease to the motor gear, then refit the motor

to the regulator assembly using the alignment marks made during removal. Insert the securing screws and tighten them to the specified torque.

9 Lubricate the regulator joints and pivot points using a multi-purpose grease.

10 Refit the regulator to the door panel and lightly tighten its retaining bolts. Position the roller guide according to the alignment marks made during removal, then tighten the retaining bolts to the specified torque.

11 On models with electric windows, reconnect the wiring harness multiway plug.

12 Install the window glass and tighten the glass to regulator bolts to the specified torque.

13 Operate the regulator mechanism a few times to check that the window travels up and down smoothly.

14 Refit the waterproof membrane to the door ensuring that it is securely stuck down around the edges. The remainder of refitting is a reversal of the removal procedure.

Rear door window glass and regulator

Removal

15 Remove the rear door inner trim panel and waterproof membrane.

16 Temporarily refit the regulator handle and position the window glass such that its retaining bolts can be accessed through the cutaway in the door panel.

17 Line the bottom of the door aperture with a thick wad of rags or newspapers, to act as padding. Slacken the securing bolts and detach the glass from the regulator. Manoeuvre the glass to the bottom of the door aperture and allow it to rest on the padding **(see illustrations)**.

18 Carefully peel the rubber seal at the top of the window aperture away from the rear glass channel **(see illustration)**.

19 Slacken and remove the securing nuts and detach the rear glass channel from the door **(see illustration)**.

20 Manoeuvre the glass panel past the regulator and lift it out of the door aperture **(see illustration)**.

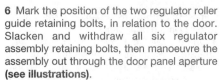

14.17b . . . manoeuvre the glass to the bottom of the door aperture and allow it to rest on the padding

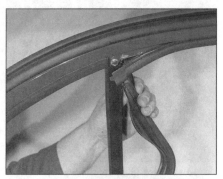

14.18 Carefully peel the rubber seal at the top of the window aperture away from the rear glass channel

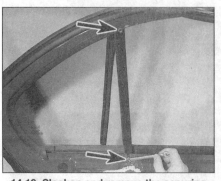

14.19 Slacken and remove the securing nuts (arrowed) and detach the rear glass channel from the door

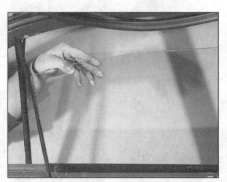

14.20 Manoeuvre the glass panel past the regulator and lift it out of the door aperture

14.21a Undo the four regulator securing bolts . . .

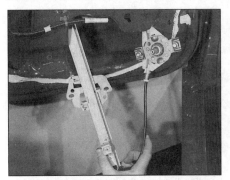

14.21b ... and manoeuvre the regulator assembly from the door

15.1 Unclip the mirror glass from the mirror assembly (models with manually-operated mirrors)

15.2 Carefully prise the interior trim panel from the rear of the mirror assembly

21 Undo the four regulator securing bolts and manoeuvre the regulator assembly from the door **(see illustrations)**.

Refitting

22 Refitting is a reversal of removal. Before the door inner trim panel is refitted, operate the regulator mechanism a few times to check that the window travels up and down smoothly, before tightening the rear glass channel securing nuts to their specified torque.

15 Exterior mirror - removal and refitting

Removal
Mirror glass

1 On models with manually-operated mirrors, the mirror glass can be simply unclipped from the mirror assembly **(see illustration)**. On other models, angle the mirror so that access can be gained to the rear, outer edge of the glass. Using a piece of welding rod or other suitable wire, bend the end of the rod into a small diameter hook. Locate the hook with the spring clip on the rear of the mirror glass and pull the clip outwards to release the mirror. On models with electrically-heated mirrors, disconnect the wiring from the mirror heating element and remove the glass from the vehicle.

Mirror assembly (manually-operated)

2 Refer to Section 13 and remove the door trim panel. Carefully prise the interior trim panel from the rear of the mirror assembly and lift it off over the remote control lever **(see illustration)**.

3 Lever the moulded cap from the remote control lever, then release the internal clip and remove the lever from the control shaft **(see illustrations)**.

4 Slide the grommet off the control shaft, then slacken and remove the shaft nut **(see illustrations)**.

5 Support the mirror assembly, then slacken and withdraw the two securing screws and remove the assembly from the door, together with the exterior trim panel **(see illustrations)**.

15.3a Lever the moulded cap from the remote control lever ...

15.3b ... then remove the lever from the control shaft

15.4a Slide the grommet off the control shaft ...

15.4b ... then slacken and remove the shaft nut

15.5a Slacken and withdraw the mirror assembly securing screws ...

15.5b ... and remove the assembly from the door ...

11

15.5c ... together with the exterior trim panel

6 If a new mirror assembly is to be fitted, unclip the exterior trim panel from the existing assembly and transfer it to the new one.

Mirror assembly (electrically-operated)

7 Refer to Section 13 and remove the door inner trim panel. Disconnect the battery negative cable and position it away from the terminal.

8 Reach inside the door aperture and unplug the door mirror wiring at the multiway connector. It may be necessary to peel off the anti-rattle foam padding first.

9 Support the mirror assembly, then slacken and withdraw the two securing screws. Feed the wiring and connector through the opening and remove the mirror assembly from the door, together with the exterior trim panel.

10 If a new mirror assembly is to be fitted, unclip the exterior trim panel from the existing assembly and transfer it to the new one.

Refitting

Mirror glass

11 On models equipped with electrically-operated mirrors, connect the wiring connectors to the heating element terminals.

12 Where applicable, align the mirror spring clip with the motor mounting point. Press the mirror glass firmly onto the motor and check that it is securely retained by the spring clip. Finally, adjust the mirror to the required position.

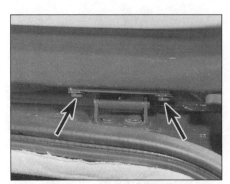

16.6 Tailgate hinge retaining bolts (arrowed)

16.3 Displace the grommet from the tailgate and withdraw the wiring

Mirror assembly

13 Refitting is a reverse of the removal procedure. On models with electrically-operated mirrors, ensure that the wiring is reconnected before refitting the door inner trim panel.

16 Tailgate - removal, refitting and adjustment

Removal

1 Open the tailgate and undo the screws (two each side) securing both tailgate side trim panels in place.

2 Using a large, flat-bladed screwdriver, work around the outside of each side trim panel and carefully prise it away from the tailgate, to free the retaining clips. Once all the retaining clips have been freed, remove the side trim panels. Prise the upper trim panel away from the tailgate in the same manner.

3 Disconnect the two wiring block connectors, situated on the right-hand side of the tailgate, which connect the tailgate electrical components to the main wiring loom. Tie a piece of string around the wiring side of the block connector, then displace the grommet from the upper right-hand corner of the tailgate and withdraw the wiring (see illustration). Once free, untie the string from the end of the wiring and leave it in place in

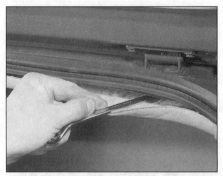

16.11 Slacken the bolts and reposition the tailgate hinges to achieve correct tailgate-to-body alignment

the tailgate. The string can then be used to draw the wiring back into position when refitting.

4 Disconnect the washer hose from the tailgate grommet.

5 Mark the positions of the hinges on the tailgate.

6 Have an assistant support the tailgate then raise the spring clips and pull the support struts off their balljoint studs on the tailgate (see Section 17). Undo the four hinge retaining bolts and remove the tailgate from the vehicle, noting the positions of any shims which may be fitted between the hinge and tailgate (see illustration).

Refitting and adjustment

7 Offer up the tailgate, positioning any shims necessary between the hinge and tailgate. Refit the hinge bolts. Press the support struts firmly onto the balljoint mountings and clip the spring clips back into position. Align the hinges with the marks made on removal, or centralise the hinges, and tighten the retaining bolts securely.

8 Tie the string around the end of the tailgate wiring and draw the wiring back into position. Untie the string, then reconnect the wiring harness plugs and relocate the grommet in the tailgate.

9 Renew any broken retaining clips, then refit the upper and side trim panels to the tailgate. Ensure both side panels are securely clipped in position then refit and tighten the retaining screws. Reconnect the washer hose to the tailgate grommet.

10 On completion, shut the tailgate and check that it is correctly aligned with the surrounding bodywork. If adjustment is necessary, slacken the hinge bolts and reposition the tailgate as necessary. Once alignment is correct, tighten the hinge bolts to the specified torque.

11 If correct alignment is not possible by repositioning the tailgate, it will be necessary to alter the hinge-to-body position. To do this, release the rubber tailgate sealing strip from the top edge of the body aperture and extract the stud fixings securing the headlining in position. Peel the sealant away from the joint between the hinge and the bodywork. Slacken the hinge bolts and reposition the tailgate to suit (see illustration). On completion, tighten the hinge retaining bolts to the specified torque. Finally, relocate the headlining and tailgate sealing strip, then apply a bead of silicone sealant to the joint between the hinge and bodywork.

12 Adjust the height of the tailgate by screwing the rubber stop in or out, as necessary, then check that the tailgate closes easily and does not rattle when closed. If adjustment is necessary, slacken the tailgate striker retaining screws and reposition the striker. Once the tailgate operation is satisfactory, tighten the striker retaining bolts securely.

17.2 Raise the balljoint spring clip and pull the support strut off the tailgate mounting

17 Tailgate support strut - removal and refitting

Removal

1 Support the tailgate in the open position by using a stout piece of wood, or with the help of an assistant.

2 Raise the spring clip and pull the support strut off its balljoint mounting on the tailgate **(see illustration)**. The strut may extend suddenly when released from its upper mounting, so keep it compressed by hand and allow the spring pressure to release slowly.

3 Detach the lower of the strut from the

18.2 Removing the interior trim panel from the tailgate

bodywork mounting in a similar manner, then remove the strut from the vehicle.

Refitting

4 Refitting is the reverse sequence of removal. Ensure that the strut is pressed firmly onto each of its balljoints and the spring clips are correctly positioned.

18 Tailgate lock and lock cylinder - removal and refitting

Tailgate lock

Removal

1 Open the tailgate and undo the two screws

securing the tailgate inner trim panel to the tailgate, then carefully prise out the screw retaining plugs.

2 Using a large flat-bladed screwdriver, work around the outside of the trim panel and carefully prise it away from the tailgate to free all the retaining clips **(see illustration)**. Once all the clips have been freed, remove the trim panel.

3 Disconnect the release cable from the latch mechanism, then on models with central locking, disconnect the motor link rod from the lock mechanism lever **(see illustration)**.

4 Slacken and withdraw the securing screws, then lift the lock assembly from the tailgate **(see illustrations)**.

5 Where applicable, unplug the wiring at the connector, then remove the two retaining screws and withdraw the lock motor from the tailgate **(see illustrations)**.

Refitting

6 Refitting is a reverse of the removal sequence.

Tailgate latch

Removal

7 Open the tailgate and remove the lower trim panel, as described in the previous sub-Section.

8 Unclip the moulded cover from the latch mechanism, then slacken and remove the latch retaining bolts **(see illustrations)**.

18.3 On models with central locking, disconnect the motor link rod (arrowed) from the lock mechanism lever

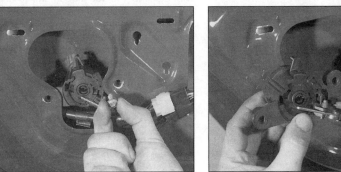

18.4a Slacken and withdraw the securing screws . . .

18.4b . . . then lift the lock assembly from the tailgate

18.5a Unplug the lock motor wiring at the connector . . .

18.5b . . . then remove the two retaining screws and withdraw the lock motor from the tailgate

18.8a Unclip the moulded cover from the latch mechanism . . .

11

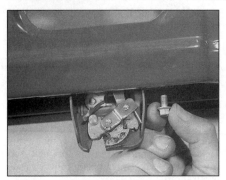

18.8b . . . then slacken and remove the latch retaining bolts

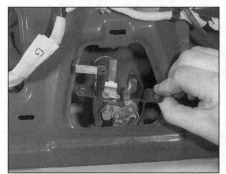

18.9 Lift the latch mechanism away from the tailgate

18.10 Unplug the switch wiring from the latch at the connectors

9 Lift the latch mechanism away from the tailgate, then detach the release cable from the operating lever **(see illustration)**.

10 Unplug the switch wiring from the latch at the connectors, then remove the latch from the vehicle **(see illustration)**.

Refitting

11 Refitting is a reverse of the removal procedure.

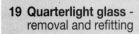

19 Quarterlight glass - removal and refitting

Removal

5-door models

1 Refer to Section 14 and remove the rear door window glass.

2 Pull the quarterlight from the door, together with the sealing strip **(see illustration)**.

3-door models

3 Remove the rear window parcel shelf, then remove the rear seat back and cushion, as described in Section 22.

4 Refer to Section 24 and unbolt the relevant, rear passenger lower seat belt anchorage from the floorpan. Unclip the seat belt aperture trim from the parcel shelf support panel.

5 At the underside of the parcel shelf support

19.2 Pull the quarterlight from the door, together with the sealing strip (5-door model shown)

panel, disconnect the wiring from the luggage compartment light and the rear speakers.

6 Remove the screws and stud fixings, then disengage the clip at the front of the parcel shelf support panel and lift it away from the bodywork.

7 Open the front door, then prise enough of the rubber seal away from the rear of the door aperture to reveal the edge of the rear quarter lower trim panel.

8 Open the quarterlight and prise the rubber seal away from the lower edge of the quarterlight aperture, to reveal the upper edge of the rear quarter lower trim panel.

9 Remove the three screws securing the rear quarter lower trim panel in position, then carefully prise the panel away from the body with a suitable forked instrument, to release the remaining press-stud fixings. Once all the fixings have been released, remove the trim panel from the vehicle.

10 Extract the screw-stud fixing and remove the door B-pillar trim panel. Similarly, extract the screw stud fixing and remove the tailgate D-pillar trim panel. Prise the alarm system volumetric sensor from the B-pillar trim panel and unplug the wiring from it at the connector.

11 Refer to Section 24 and unbolt the front seat belt upper mounting from the anchorage. Note that the securing bolt must be renewed.

12 Open the tailgate and prise the rubber seal away from the side of the tailgate aperture, to reveal the rear edge of the rear quarter upper trim panel.

13 Working around the edge of the rear quarter upper trim panel, use a suitable forked instrument to release all of the press-stud fixings in turn and then detach the trim panel from the bodywork.

14 Mark the position of the quarterlight rear catch on the body, then remove the three hinge retaining screws.

15 Support the window glass, undo the two front hinge retaining nuts, then release the glass from the clip at its leading edge and remove it from the vehicle.

Refitting

5-door models

16 Refitting is a reversal of removal.

3-door models

17 Refitting is a reverse of the removal sequence, noting the following:

a) *Align the rear window catch with the marks made on dismantling and lightly tighten the retaining screws.*

b) *Close the window and check that it is correctly aligned with the surrounding bodywork. Adjust, if necessary, by repositioning the hinge, then tighten all the hinge retaining screws to the specified torque setting.*

c) *Where possible, renew any broken trim panel retaining clips.*

d) *Tighten the new seat belt upper mounting nut to the specified torque, with reference to the relevant Section in this Chapter.*

e) *On completion, ensure all trim panels are securely retained and the door/window/tailgate seals are correctly located.*

20 Windscreen and tailgate glass - general information

These areas of glass are bonded directly the body aperture. The process of removing and refitting areas of glass that are secured in this manner can be difficult, messy and time-consuming, particularly for the inexperienced. Without plenty of practice, it is very difficult to obtain a secure, waterproof fit. Furthermore, the task carries a high risk of breakage; this applies especially to the laminated glass windscreen. In view of this, owners are strongly advised to have work of this nature carried out by one of the many specialist windscreen fitters.

21 Sunroof - repair

1 An electrically-operated sunroof is available as an option (or standard fit) on all models. Due to the complexity of the sunroof mechanism, considerable expertise is needed to repair or replace sunroof components

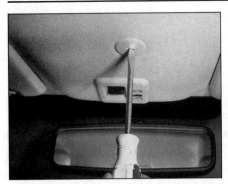

21.2a Unscrew the circular access cover in the panel in the headlining, between the sun visors . . .

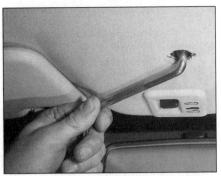

21.2b . . . and insert the wrench into the drive spindle. Rotate the key to move the sunroof to the required position

22.2 Remove the Torx bolts securing the rear of the seat runners to the floor

successfully. Removal of the sunroof requires the headlining to be removed, which is a complex and tedious operation and not a task to be undertaken lightly. Any problems with the sunroof should therefore be referred to a Rover dealer.

2 If the sunroof motor fails to operate, first check the relevant fuse. If the fault cannot be traced and rectified, then the sunroof can be opened and closed manually by using a suitable cranked screwdriver. Use a screwdriver or coin to unscrew the circular access cover in the panel in the headlining, situated between the sun visors, and insert the wrench into the drive spindle. Rotate the key to move the sunroof to the required position **(see illustrations)**. A suitable wrench is supplied with the vehicle and should be in the luggage compartment where it is stowed next to the wheel trim remover.

22 Seats -
    removal and refitting

Front seats

 Warning: All models are fitted with front seat belt pretensioners. Before removing the front seat(s), read the Supplementary Restraint System (SRS) safety information given in Chapter 12. Failure to observe the precautions could result in accidental detonation of the seat belt pre-tensioners.

Removal

1 Remove the ignition key and wait **AT LEAST TEN MINUTES** to allow the system backup circuit to fully discharge. Disconnect **BOTH** battery leads (negative lead first) from the battery and position them well away from the battery terminals. Failure to observe this procedure could cause accidental detonation of the airbag and/or seat belt pre-tensioners.
2 Slide the seat fully forwards, then slacken and remove the two Torx bolts securing the rear of the seat runners to the floor **(see illustration)**.

3 Slide the seat fully rearwards, then undo the two Torx bolts securing the front of the seat runners to the floor **(see illustration)**.
4 Where applicable, reach underneath the seat and unplug the wiring from the seat belt pretensioner at the multiway connector **(see illustration)**.
5 Lift the seat, together with its runners, away from the floorpan and remove it from the vehicle.

Refitting

6 Refitting is a reversal of removal.

Rear seat cushion

Removal

7 Press down the rear edge of the cushion to

expose the three cushion securing bolts. Slacken and withdraw the bolts, then pivot the cushion forward and unhook the leading edge from the floorpan **(see illustrations)**.

Refitting

8 Refitting is a reversal of removal.

Rear seat back

Removal

9 Remove the rear seat cushion, as described in the previous sub-Section.
10 Refer to Section 24 and unbolt each of the rear seat belt lower anchorage brackets from the floorpan.
11 Working at the rear of the seat back, rotate the centre hinge clamp bolt clockwise,

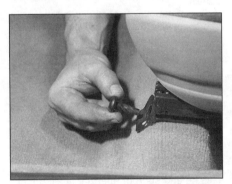

22.3 Undo the Torx bolts securing the front of the seat runners to the floor

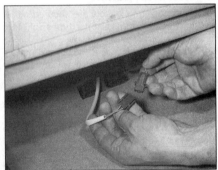

22.4 Unplug the wiring from the seat belt pretensioner at the multiway connector

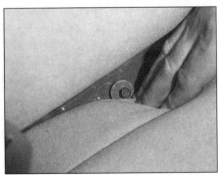

22.7a Press down on the rear seat cushion to expose the securing bolts . . .

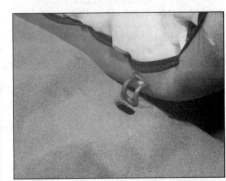

22.7b . . . pivot the cushion forward and unhook the leading edge from the floorpan

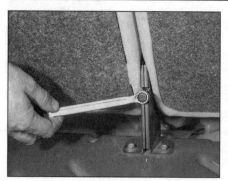

22.11a Rotate the centre hinge clamp bolt clockwise . . .

22.11b . . . until the hinge pin can be withdrawn from the bracket

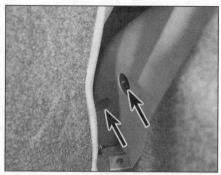

22.12 Release the pins from the outer seat back hinges (arrowed)

until the hinge pin can be withdrawn from the bracket **(see illustrations)**. There is no need to remove the clamp bolt completely.

12 Release the pins from the outer seat back hinges and then lift the seat back out of the vehicle **(see illustration)**.

Refitting

13 Refitting is a reversal of removal. Tighten the seat belt lower anchorage bracket bolts to the correct torque.

23 Interior trim - removal and refitting

Interior trim panels

1 The interior trim panels are secured either by screws or by various types of trim fasteners, usually studs or clips.

2 Check that there are no other panels overlapping the one to be removed. Usually there is a sequence that has to be followed that will become obvious on close inspection.

3 Remove all obvious fasteners, such as screws. If the panel will not come free then it is held by hidden clips or fasteners. These are usually situated around the edge of the panel and can be prised up to release them. Note, however, that they can break quite easily, so care should be exercised. The best way of releasing such clips in the absence of the correct type of tool, is to use a large flat-bladed screwdriver. Pad the screwdriver blade by wrapping insulating tape around it, to avoid scratching paintwork. Note that in many cases, rubber sealing strips (such as those fitted to door or tailgate apertures) may need to be prised back when releasing a panel.

4 When removing a panel, never use excessive force or the panel may be damaged. Always check carefully that all fasteners have been removed or released before attempting to withdraw a panel.

5 When refitting a panel, secure the fasteners by pressing them firmly into place and ensure that all disturbed components are correctly secured to prevent rattles. Use a suitable trim

adhesive (a Rover dealer should be able to recommend a proprietary product) on reassembly.

> **HAYNES HiNT** *If adhesives were found at any point on removal, use white spirit to remove all traces of old adhesive, then wash off all traces of spirit using soapy water.*

Carpets

6 The passenger compartment floor carpet is in one piece and is secured at its edges by screws or clips, usually the same fasteners used to secure the various adjoining trim panels.

7 Carpet removal and refitting is reasonably straightforward but very time-consuming due to the fact that all adjoining trim panels must be removed first, as must components such as the seats, the centre console and seat belt lower anchorages.

Headlining

8 The headlining is clipped to the roof and can be withdrawn once all fittings such as the grab handles, sun visors, sunroof (if fitted), windscreen and rear quarterlights and related trim panels have been removed and the door, tailgate and sunroof aperture sealing strips have been prised clear.

9 Note that headlining removal and refitting

requires considerable skill and experience if it is to be carried out without damage and is therefore best entrusted to an expert.

24 Seat belts - removal and refitting

Removal

> ⚠ **Warning: All models are fitted with front seat belt pre-tensioners. Before disturbing the front seat belt(s), read the Supplementary Restraint System (SRS) safety information given in Chapter 12. Failure to observe the precautions could result in accidental detonation of the seat belt pre-tensioners.**

Front seat belt - 5-door models

1 Carefully prise the rubber seal from the rear edge of the front door aperture, then release the clips and remove the B-pillar lower trim panel **(see illustrations)**.

2 Remove the bolt cover at the belt upper mounting, undo the seat belt retaining bolt and detach the belt **(see illustrations)**.

3 Remove the cap from the seat belt lower mounting bolt then undo the Torx bolt and detach the belt from the bodywork **(see illustration)**.

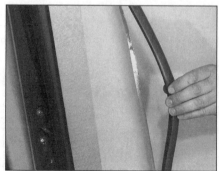

24.1a Carefully prise the rubber seal from the rear edge of the front door aperture . . .

24.1b . . . then release the clips and remove the B-pillar lower trim panel

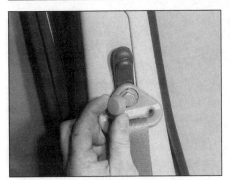

24.2a Remove the bolt cover at the belt upper mounting . . .

24.2b . . . and undo the seat belt retaining bolt and detach the belt

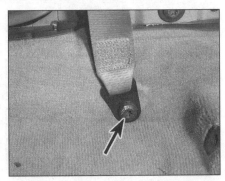

24.3 Undo the Torx bolt and detach the seat belt lower mounting from the bodywork

4 Undo the bolt securing the inertia reel unit to the base of the door B-pillar and remove the reel and seat belt assembly from the vehicle (see illustration).

Front seat belt - 3-door models

5 Remove the rear window parcel shelf, then remove the rear seat back and cushion, as described in Section 22. Unclip the rear side seat belt aperture trim from the parcel shelf support panel.

6 At the underside of the parcel shelf support panel, disconnect the wiring from the luggage compartment light and the rear speakers.

7 Remove the screws and stud fixings, then disengage the clip at the front of the parcel shelf support panel and lift it away from the bodywork.

8 Open the front door, then prise enough of the rubber seal away from the rear of the door aperture to reveal the edge of the rear quarter lower trim panel.

9 Open the rear quarterlight and prise the rubber seal away from the lower edge of the quarterlight aperture, to reveal the upper edge of the rear quarter lower trim panel.

10 Remove the three screws securing the rear quarter lower trim panel in position, then carefully prise the panel away from the body with a suitable forked instrument, to release the remaining press-stud fixings. Once all the fixings have been released, remove the trim panel from the vehicle.

11 Remove the bolt cover at the belt upper mounting, then undo the seat belt retaining

bolt and detach the belt from the door B-pillar.

12 Unbolt the front of the seat belt lower guide rail from the bodywork. Slide the seat belt off the end of the guide rail.

13 Undo the bolt securing the inertia reel unit to the base of the door B-pillar, then remove the reel and seat belt assembly from the vehicle.

Front seat belt stalk and pre-tensioner - all models

14 Refer to the information given in Chapter 12.

Rear seat side belt - 3-door models

15 Remove the rear quarter lower trim panel, as described in paragraphs 5 to 10.

16 Unbolt the seat belt lower anchorage bracket from the bodywork.

24.4 Undo the bolt securing the inertia reel unit to the base of the door B-pillar

17 Slacken and withdraw the securing bolt and detach the seat belt stalk from the bodywork.

18 Undo the two securing bolts and remove the inertia reel unit from the seat back support bracket. Remove the seat belt assembly from the vehicle.

Rear seat side belt - 5-door models

19 Remove the rear parcel shelf support panel, as described in paragraphs 5 to 7 (see illustrations).

20 Open the rear door and prise the rubber seal away from the rear of the door aperture to expose the front edge of the rear quarter lower trim panel (see illustration).

21 Remove the securing screws and lift the rear quarter lower trim panel away from the bodywork (see illustration).

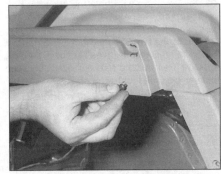

24.19a Slacken and withdraw the screws . . .

24.19b . . . and remove the rear parcel shelf support panel (5-door model shown)

24.20 Prise the rubber seal away from the rear of the door aperture

24.21 Remove the securing screws and lift the rear quarter lower trim panel away from the bodywork

11

24.22 Unbolt the seat belt lower anchorage bracket from the bodywork

24.23 Withdraw the securing bolt and detach the seat belt stalk from the bodywork

24.24a Inertia reel unit upper . . .

24.24b . . . and lower mounting bolts

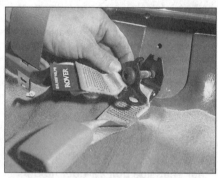

24.26 Unbolt the seat belt lower anchorage bracket from the bodywork

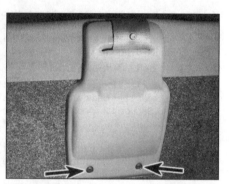

24.29 Remove the screws and lift off the seat belt inertia reel cover panel

22 Unbolt the seat belt lower anchorage bracket from the bodywork **(see illustration)**.
23 Slacken and withdraw the securing bolt and detach the seat belt stalk from the bodywork **(see illustration)**.
24 Undo the two securing bolts and remove the inertia reel unit from the seat back support bracket. Remove the seat belt assembly from the vehicle **(see illustrations)**.

Rear seat centre belt - all models

25 Refer to Section 22 and remove the rear seat cushion.
26 Unbolt the seat belt lower anchorage bracket from the bodywork **(see illustration)**.
27 Slacken and withdraw the securing bolt and detach the seat belt stalk from the bodywork.

28 Open the tailgate and remove the parcel shelf.
29 Undo the screws and lift off the seat belt inertia reel cover panel **(see illustration)**. Slacken and remove the securing nut then withdraw the inertia reel unit from the seat back.

Refitting

30 Refitting is the reversal of removal, noting the following:
  a) *Tighten all the seat belt, seat belt guide, seat belt stalk and inertia reel mounting nuts and bolts (as applicable) to the specified torque setting.*
  b) *Where possible, renew any broken trim panel retaining clips.*

  c) *On completion, ensure all trim panels are securely held by their retaining clips and, if disturbed, the door sealing strips are correctly located.*

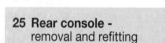

25 Rear console - removal and refitting

Removal

1 Unclip the rear ashtray from its housing **(see illustration)**.
2 Carefully prise up and remove the cover panel from the front edge of the console. Slacken and remove the two exposed securing screws beneath **(see illustrations)**.

25.1 Unclip the rear ashtray from its housing

25.2a Carefully prise up and remove the cover panel from the front edge of the console . . .

25.2b . . . slacken and remove the two exposed securing screws

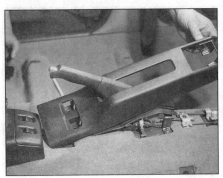

25.3 Lift the console up over the handbrake lever and remove it from the vehicle

26.3 Unscrew the gear knob and remove it from the lever

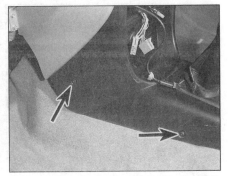

26.4 Remove the centre console retaining screws

3 Lift the console up over the handbrake lever and remove it from the vehicle **(see illustration)**.

Refitting

4 Refitting is a reversal of removal.

26 Centre console - removal and refitting

Removal

1 Refer to Section 25 and remove the rear console.

2 Remove the radio unit as described in Chapter 12.

3 Release the gear change lever gaiter from the base of the knob, then unscrew the knob and remove it from the lever **(see illustration)**.

4 Remove the four centre console section retaining screws, then pull the assembly away from the facia slightly **(see illustration)**.

5 Unplug the wiring harness connectors from the bank of switches at the top of the centre console **(see illustration)**. Label each connector carefully, to avoid confusion on refitting. Similarly, unplug the wiring from the rear of the cigar lighter.

6 Check that nothing remains connected to the rear of the centre console, then remove it from the vehicle **(see illustration)**. Note that the heater control panel remains in position on the facia.

Refitting

7 Refitting is a reversal of the removal procedure.

27 Facia - removal and refitting

Warning: All models are fitted with a Supplementary Restraint System (SRS). Before disturbing the front seat belt(s), read the safety information given in Chapter 12. Failure to observe the precautions could result in accidental detonation of the seat belt pre-tensioners.

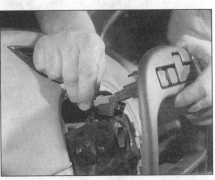

26.5 Unplug the wiring harness connectors from the bank of switches at the top of the centre console

26.6 Withdraw the centre console from the facia

Removal

1 Disconnect both battery cables from the terminals (negative first).

2 Refer to Section 26 and remove the centre console.

3 Release the stud fixings, then remove the lower cover panel from the passenger's side of the facia **(see illustration)**.

4 Remove the two securing screws and withdraw the glovebox from the facia **(see illustrations)**.

5 Where applicable, remove the passenger airbag unit as described in Chapter 12.

6 Refer to Chapter 3 and remove the heater control panel.

27.3 Remove the lower cover panel from the passenger's side of the facia

27.4a Remove the two securing screws . . .

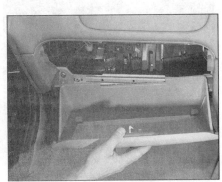

27.4b . . . and withdraw the glovebox from the facia

11

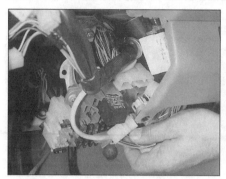

27.8 Unplug the facia wiring harness from the fusebox at the two multiway connectors

27.9 Slacken and remove the exposed facia securing nut (arrowed)

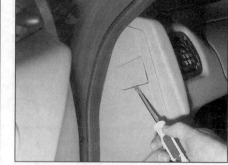

27.10a Prise the cover panels from the ends of the facia assembly . . .

7 Refer to Chapter 10 and remove the steering column.

8 Unplug the facia wiring harness from the fusebox at the two multiway connectors **(see illustration)**.

9 Carefully prise the trim panel from the clock display (see Chapter 12), then slacken and remove the exposed facia securing nut **(see illustration)**.

10 Open the front doors and prise the cover panels from the ends of the facia assembly,

then slacken and remove the exposed facia securing bolts **(see illustrations)**.

11 Remove the bolts securing the lower edge of the facia to the mounting brackets at the base of the door A-pillars **(see illustrations)**.

12 Remove the two bolts securing the centre, lower edge of the facia to the mounting bracket at the top of the transmission linkage tunnel **(see illustration)**.

13 Carefully manoeuvre the facia assembly away from the bulkhead. Disconnect the

heater/ventilation ducts from the rear of their respective vents as they become accessible. Release the remaining sections of the wiring harness from any retaining clips. With the front seats fully retracted, lift the facia assembly out of the vehicle **(see illustration)**.

Refitting

14 Offer up the facia, reconnect the heater/ventilation ducting and secure the wiring harness in position with the retaining clips.

15 Manoeuvre the facia into position on the bulkhead then refit the facia mounting bolts and tighten them to the specified torque.

16 The remainder of the refitting procedure is a reversal of removal, noting the following:

a) Refit the steering column with reference to Chapter 10.

b) Ensure that all SRS component wiring (including the control unit earth lead) is properly located and securely reconnected - refer to Chapter 12 for guidance and observe the safety precautions given.

c) Refit the heater control panel with reference to Chapter 3.

d) On completion, reconnect the battery and check that all electrical components and switches function correctly.

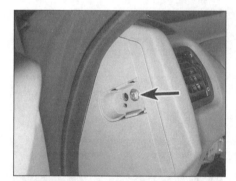

27.10b . . . then slacken and remove the exposed facia securing bolts

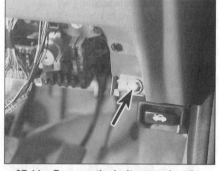

27.11a Remove the bolts securing the lower edge of the facia to the mounting brackets (right-hand side) . . .

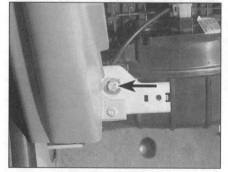

27.11b . . . (left-hand side)

27.12 Remove the two bolts securing the centre, lower edge of the facia to its mounting bracket

27.13 Withdraw the facia assembly from the bulkhead and lift it out of the vehicle

Chapter 12
Body electrical systems

Contents

Degrees of difficulty

Easy, suitable for novice with little experience 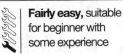	**Fairly easy,** suitable for beginner with some experience	**Fairly difficult,** suitable for competent DIY mechanic 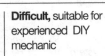	**Difficult,** suitable for experienced DIY mechanic	**Very difficult,** suitable for expert DIY or professional

Specifications

Fuses .... See Wiring diagrams

Bulbs

	Fitting	Wattage
Headlamp dip/main beam bulb	H4	55/60
Front foglamps	H1	55
Front sidelamps	Capless	5
Direction indicator lamps	Bayonet	21
Direction indicator side repeater lamps	Capless	5
Interior lamp	Festoon	10
Instrument panel illumination lamps	Integral with holder	14V, 3.4W
High level brake lamp	Capless	3
Glovebox lamp	Festoon	5
Luggage compartment lamp	Bayonet	10
Reversing lamps	Bayonet	21
Tail lamps	Bayonet	10
Stop lamps	Bayonet	21
Rear foglamps	Bayonet	21
Number plate lamps	Festoon	5

Torque wrench settings	Nm	lbf ft
Airbag control unit screws	9	6
Driver's airbag screws	9	6
Passenger's airbag screws	9	6
Seat belt pre-tensioner bolts	30	22
Tailgate wiper motor bolts	8	6
Vehicle speed sensor bolt	9	6
Windscreen wiper linkage assembly bolts	10	7
Wiper arm spindle nut	10	7
Wiper motor mounting bracket bolts	10	7
Wiper motor-to-bracket bolts	5	4

1 General information and precautions

General information

The electrical system is of the 12-volt negative earth type and comprises a 12-volt battery, an alternator with integral voltage regulator, a starter motor and related electrical accessories, components and wiring. The battery is of the maintenance-free (sealed for life) type and is charged by the alternator, which is belt-driven from a crankshaft-mounted pulley.

While some repair procedures are given, the usual course of action is to renew a defective component. The owner whose interest extends beyond mere component renewal should obtain a copy of the *Automobile Electrical & Electronic Systems Manual*, available from the publishers of this Manual.

Precautions

It is necessary to take extra care when working on the electrical system to avoid the risk of personal injury and to avoid damage to components. In addition to the precautions given in *"Safety first!"* at the beginning of this Manual, observe the following when working on the system:

a) Always remove rings, watches, etc. before working on the electrical system. Even with the battery disconnected, capacitive discharge could occur if a component's live terminal is earthed through a metal object. This could cause a shock or nasty burn.

b) Do not reverse the battery connections. Components such as the alternator, fuel injection/ignition system ECU, or any other having semi-conductor circuitry could be irreparably damaged.

c) If the engine is being started using jump leads and a slave battery, connect the batteries positive-to-positive and negative-to-negative. This also applies when connecting a battery charger.

d) Never disconnect the battery terminals, the alternator, any electrical wiring or any test instruments when the engine is running.

e) Do not allow the engine to turn the alternator when the alternator is not connected.

f) Never test for alternator output by 'flashing' the output lead to earth.

g) Always ensure that the battery negative lead is disconnected when working on the electrical system.

Electronic Control Units (ECUs) contain semiconductor components that are sensitive to static electricity. Once the multiway harness connector has been unplugged, the exposed ECU connector pins can freely conduct stray static electricity to these components, damaging or even destroying them - the damage will be invisible and may not manifest itself immediately. Expensive repairs can be avoided by observing the following basic handling rules:

a) Handle a disconnected ECU by its case only; do not allow fingers or tools to come into contact with the pins.

b) When carrying an ECU around, "ground" yourself from time to time, by touching a metal object such as an unpainted water pipe, this will discharge any potentially damaging static that may have built up during normal activity.

c) Do not leave the ECU unplugged from its connector for any longer than is absolutely necessary.

d) Never use an ohmmeter of the type incorporating a hand-cranked generator for sensor or actuator testing.

e) Before using electric-arc welding equipment on the vehicle, disconnect the battery, alternator and the engine management system ECU.

A number of additional precautions must be observed when working on vehicles equipped with a Supplementary Restraint System (SRS); these are as follows:

a) When cleaning the interior of the vehicle, do not allow the airbag or seat belt pre-tensioner units to become flooded with detergents or water and do not clean with petrol or furniture cream and polishes. Clean the unit sparingly with a damp cloth and upholstery cleaner.

b) Before working on any part of the system, remove the ignition key and wait at least ten minutes to allow the system backup circuit to fully discharge. Disconnect both battery leads, earth lead first, to avoid accidental detonation of the airbag or seat belt pre-tensioner components.

c) Make no attempt to splice into any of the electric cables in the SRS wiring harness as this may affect the operation of the SRS. Never fit electronic equipment such as mobile telephones, radios, etc. into the harness and ensure that the harness is routed so that it cannot be trapped.

d) Avoid hammering or causing any harsh vibration at the front of the vehicle, particularly in the engine bay, as this may trigger the crash sensors and activate the SRS.

e) Do not use ohmmeters, continuity testers or any other device capable of supplying current on any of the SRS components, as this may cause accidental detonation.

f) Always use new replacement parts. Never fit parts that are from another vehicle or show signs of damage through being dropped or improperly handled.

g) Airbags are classed as pyrotechnical devices and must be stored and handled according to the relevant laws in the country concerned. In general, do not leave these components disconnected from their electrical cabling any longer than is absolutely necessary as in this state they are unstable and the risk of accidental detonation is introduced. Rest a disconnected airbag unit with the pad surface facing upwards and never rest anything on the pad. Store it on a secure flat surface, away from flammable materials, high heat sources, oils, grease, detergents or water, and never leave it unattended.

h) The SRS indicator light should extinguish 3 seconds after the ignition switch is turned to position "II". If this is not the case, check the electrical system connections as soon as possible.

i) The SRS control unit and slip ring are non-serviceable components and no attempt should be made to carry out repairs or modifications to them.

j) Only use the recommended special bolts when fitting the airbag assembly. Do not use any other type of bolt.

k) Never invert the airbag unit.

l) Renew the airbag unit and slip ring every ten years, regardless of condition.

m) Return disused airbag and seat belt pre-tensioner units to your Rover dealer for safe disposal. Do not endanger others by careless disposal.

2 Electrical fault finding - general information

A typical electrical circuit consists of an electrical component, any switches, relays, motors, fuses, fusible links or circuit breakers related to that component and the wiring and connectors that link the component to both the battery and the chassis. To help you pinpoint an electrical circuit problem, wiring diagrams are included at the end of this Chapter.

Before tackling any troublesome electrical circuit, first study the appropriate wiring diagrams to get a complete understanding of what components are included in that individual circuit. Trouble spots can be identified by noting if other components related to the circuit are operating properly. If several components or circuits fail at one time, then the problem is probably in a fuse or earth connection, because several circuits are often routed through the same fuse and earth connections.

Electrical problems usually stem from simple causes, such as loose or corroded connections, a blown fuse, a melted fusible link or a faulty relay. Inspect the condition of all fuses, wires and connections in a problem circuit before testing the components. Use the diagrams to note which terminal connections will need to be checked in order to pinpoint the trouble spot.

The basic tools needed for electrical fault finding include a circuit tester or voltmeter (a 12-volt bulb with a set of test leads can also be used), a continuity tester, a battery and set of test leads, and a jumper wire, preferably with a circuit breaker incorporated, which can be used to bypass electrical components. Before attempting to locate a problem with test instruments, use the wiring diagram to decide where to make the connections.

Voltage checks

Voltage checks should be performed if a circuit is not functioning properly. Connect one lead of a circuit tester to either the negative battery terminal or a known good earth. Connect the other lead to a connector in the circuit being tested, preferably nearest to the battery or fuse. If the bulb of the tester lights then voltage is present, which means that the part of the circuit between the connector and the battery is problem free. Continue checking the rest of the circuit in the same fashion. When you reach a point at which no voltage is present, the problem lies between that point and the last test point with voltage. Most problems can be traced to a loose connection. Bear in mind that some circuits are only live when the ignition switch is switched to a particular position.

Finding a short circuit

One method of finding a short circuit is to remove the fuse and connect a test light or voltmeter to the fuse terminals with all the relevant electrical components switched off. There should be no voltage present in the circuit. Move the wiring from side to side while watching the test light. If the bulb lights up, there is a short to earth somewhere in that area, probably where the insulation has rubbed through. The same test can be performed on each component in the circuit, even a switch.

Earth check

On vehicles with a negative-earth electrical system, current is supplied by the battery to electrical components via the wiring harness and is returned to the battery via common earth points on the vehicle's bodywork. Performing an earth check tests whether a component has a good earth point.

Disconnect the battery and connect one lead of a self-powered test light, known as a continuity tester, to a known good earth point. Connect the other lead to the wire or earth connection being tested. If the bulb lights up, the earth is good. If not, the earth is faulty.

If an earth connection is thought to be faulty, dismantle the connection and clean back to bare metal both the bodyshell and the wire terminal or the component's earth connection mating surface. Be careful to remove all traces of dirt and corrosion, then use a knife to trim away any paint, so that a clean metal-to-metal joint is made. On reassembly, tighten the joint fasteners securely; if a wire terminal is being refitted, use serrated washers between the terminal and the bodyshell to ensure a clean and secure connection. When the connection is remade, prevent the onset of corrosion in the future by applying a coat of petroleum jelly or silicone-based grease or by spraying on a proprietary ignition sealer or a water dispersant lubricant at regular intervals.

Continuity check

A continuity check is necessary to determine if there are any breaks in a circuit. With the circuit off (ie: no power in the circuit), a self-powered continuity tester can be used to check the circuit. Connect the test leads to both ends of the circuit, or to the positive end and a good earth. If the test light comes on, the circuit is passing current properly. If the light does not come on, there is a break somewhere in the circuit. The same procedure can be used to test a switch, by connecting the continuity tester to the switch terminals. With the switch turned on, the test light should come on.

Finding an open circuit

When checking for possible open circuits, it is often difficult to locate them by sight because oxidation or terminal misalignment may be hidden by the connectors. Merely moving a connector on a sensor or in the wiring harness may correct the open circuit condition. Remember this when an open circuit is indicated when fault finding in a circuit. Intermittent problems may also be caused by oxidized or loose connections. Bear in mind that a circuit carrying a heavy load (i.e. passing a lot of current) may 'break down' under load. For example, a poor connection in the wiring supplying a starter motor may not be detectable with a simple continuity tester, but under cranking conditions the volt drop caused by the poor connection may be severe enough to prevent the starter motor turning properly. If you have doubts about the condition of a particular

wiring connection, it's best to separate it and clean the connection surfaces (as described in *Earth Check*) to be on the safe side.

General

Electrical fault finding is simple if you keep in mind that all electrical circuits are basically electricity flowing from the battery, through the wires, switches, relays, fuses and fusible links to each electrical component (light bulb, motor, etc.) and to earth, from which it is passed back to the battery. Any electrical problem is an interruption or restriction in the flow of electricity to and from the battery.

3 Fuses, fusible links and relays - location and renewal

Fuses

1 Most of the fuses are located behind a panel at the lower right-hand side of the facia. A number of additional fuses are located in an auxiliary fusebox, mounted at the left-hand side of the engine compartment **(see illustration)**. The Anti-lock Braking System (ABS) fuse is mounted separately, next to the battery tray.

2 Access to the main fusebox is gained by removing the plastic cover panel. Symbols on the reverse of the lid/cover indicate the circuits protected by the fuses and a number of spare fuses are supplied, together with plastic extractor to remove and fit them **(see illustrations)**.

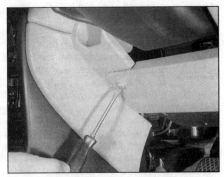

3.1 The auxiliary fusebox is mounted at the left-hand side of the engine bay

3.2a Release the fixings by turning them through a quarter of a turn . . .

3.2b . . . remove the plastic cover panel

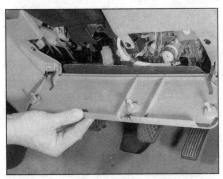

3.2c . . . then release the clips and lower the felt panel away from the underside of the fusebox

12

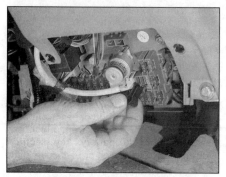

3.4a Withdraw the integral plastic extractor from its slot . . .

3.4b . . . and use it to remove the fuse

3.5 Push the new fuse firmly into place

3 On vehicles equipped with airbags, the fuse protecting the Supplementary Restraint System (SRS) circuit is located on the side of the main fusebox and is indicated by a yellow plastic collar.

Caution: Under no circumstances should this fuse be removed as this may cause accidental inflation of the airbag. Refer to your Rover dealer if you think renewal of this fuse may be necessary.

4 To remove a fuse, first switch off the circuit concerned (or the ignition), then fit the tweezers and pull the fuse out of its terminals. Slide the fuse sideways from the tweezers. The wire within the fuse is clearly visible. If the fuse is blown, the wire will be broken or melted **(see illustrations)**.

5 Always renew a fuse with one of an identical rating **(see illustration)**. The fuse rating is stamped on top of the fuse. Fuses are also colour-coded for easy recognition.

 Warning: Never use a fuse with a different rating from the original or substitute anything else in its place - it could cause a fire in the wiring harness.

6 If a new fuse blows immediately, find the cause before renewing it again. A short to earth as a result of faulty insulation is the most likely cause. Where a fuse protects more than one circuit, try to isolate the defect by switching on each circuit in turn (if possible) until the fuse blows again.

7 If any of the spare fuses are used, always

replace them so that a spare of each rating is available.

Fusible links

8 The fusible links are located in the rear of the fusebox, situated on the left-hand side of the engine compartment (refer to illustration 3.1). Unclip the lid to gain access to them. All links are numbered on the rear of the fusebox lid.

9 To remove a fusible link, first ensure that the circuit concerned is switched off then prise off the plastic cover. Slacken the two link retaining screws then lift the fusible link out of the fusebox. The wire within the fusible link is clearly visible. If the fuse is blown, it will be broken or melted. A blown fusible link indicates a serious wiring or system fault which must be diagnosed before the link is renewed.

10 Always renew a fusible link with one of an identical rating. Never use a link with a different rating from the original or substitute anything else. On refitting, tighten the link retaining screws securely and refit the link cover.

Relays

11 Refer to the relevant wiring diagram for relay locations and wiring connections.

12 If a circuit or system controlled by a relay develops a fault and the relay is suspect, operate the system. If the relay is functioning, it should be possible to hear it click as it is energized. If this is the case, the fault lies with

the components or wiring of the system. If the relay is not being energized, then either the relay is not receiving a main supply or a switching voltage, or the relay itself is faulty. Testing is by the substitution of a known good unit but be careful as some relays are identical in appearance, but perform different functions and have different electrical specifications.

13 To renew a relay, ensure that the ignition switch is off, then pull the unit from the socket and press in replacement. Note that heavy duty relays may be secured to their bases with one or more screws.

---

4 Switches -
 removal and refitting

Note: *Disconnect the battery negative lead before removing any switch and after refitting the switch, reconnect the lead.*

Ignition switch

1 Refer to Chapter 10 for details of steering lock/ignition switch removal and refitting.

Steering column combination switch

Removal

2 Remove the ignition key and wait at least ten minutes to allow the SRS system backup circuit to fully discharge. Disconnect both battery leads, earth lead first, to avoid accidental detonation of the airbag.

3 Set the steering in the straight-ahead position then lock the steering column in its lowest position.

4 Remove the driver's airbag unit, as described in Section 14.

5 Remove the steering wheel, as described in Chapter 10.

6 Remove the airbag rotary coupler, as described in Section 14.

7 Withdraw the indicator cancelling cam from the steering column **(see illustration)**.

8 To remove the complete combination switch assembly, slacken and remove the two retaining screws and slide the switch off the steering column **(see illustration)**.

4.7 Withdraw the indicator cancelling cam from the steering column

4.8 Remove the two retaining screws and slide the switch off the steering column

4.9a Disconnect the multiplugs from the combination switch . . .

4.9b . . . followed by the SRS wiring connector

4.14a Prise the switch unit out using a suitable flat-bladed screwdriver . . .

9 Disconnect the multiplugs from the combination switch, followed by the SRS wiring connector **(see illustrations)**.

10 Each individual switch can be removed by unscrewing its two retaining screws and sliding the switch out of the housing.

Refitting

11 Refitting is the reverse of the removal procedure.

12 Upon completion of refitting the airbag unit, reconnect both battery leads, negative lead last, and turn the ignition switch to the "II" position. Check the condition of the system by observing the SRS warning light located in the steering wheel centre pad. The light should stay illuminated for 3 seconds whilst the system performs a self-diagnosis test. If the test is satisfactory, the light will extinguish. If the test is unsatisfactory, the light will remain on or fail to illuminate at all, denoting that the system must be serviced as soon as possible.

Instrument panel and facia switches

13 Ensure that the ignition switch and the switch to be removed are both in the off position.

14 Taking great care not to scratch or damage the switch or its surround, prise the switch unit out using a suitable flat-bladed screwdriver; pad the blade with insulating

tape to prevent damage. Withdraw the switch until the connector plug appears then unplug the wiring connector and remove the switch **(see illustrations)**. Tie a piece of string to the wiring connector to prevent it from falling behind the facia panel.

15 On refitting, connect the wiring connector to the switch and press the switch into position until the retaining clips click into place.

Electrically-operated window switches

Removal

16 Carefully prise the switch panel from the rear of the centre console front section.

17 Unplug the wiring connector from the relevant switch unit **(see illustration)**.

18 Remove the screws and detach the switch unit from the panel.

Refitting

19 Refitting is a reversal of removal.

Courtesy lamp door switches

Removal

20 With the door open, undo the screw securing the switch to the body. Pull out the switch and tie a piece of string to the wiring to prevent it dropping into the body.

21 Disconnect the wiring from the switch and remove it from the vehicle.

Refitting

22 Refitting is a reverse of removal.

Handbrake warning lamp switch

Removal

23 From inside the vehicle, carefully prise out the cover from the top of the centre console rear section to gain access to the two retaining screws. Undo the two screws and remove the rear centre console section.

24 Unplug the wiring connector from the handbrake lever switch, then slacken and remove the retaining screw and remove the switch from the handbrake lever quadrant **(see illustration)**.

Refitting

25 Refitting is a reverse of the removal procedure.

Horn push switch

Removal

26 Remove the driver's airbag unit from the steering wheel, as described in Section 14.

27 Detach the earth wire from the steering wheel **(see illustration 4.30)**.

28 Unplug the multiway connector from the steering wheel rotary coupler **(see illustration 4.30)**.

29 Remove each horn button by carefully using the flat blade of a small screwdriver to lever it from position. Pad the blade of the

4.14b . . . and unplug the wiring connector from the rear of the switch

4.17 Unplug the wiring connector from the electric window switch unit

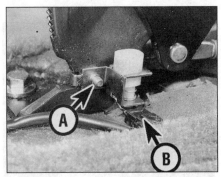

4.24 Handbrake warning lamp switch retaining screw (A) and wiring connector (B)

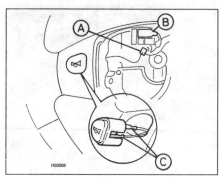

4.30 Disconnect the earth wire (A) and rotary coupler connector (B), then lever out the switch and unplug the contact wiring (C)

5.2 Unclip the circular plastic cover and remove it from the rear of the headlamp unit

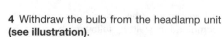

5.3a Unplug the wiring connector ...

screwdriver with insulation tape to prevent damage.

30 Unplug the two electrical connectors from the button and remove it **(see illustration)**.

Refitting

31 Refitting is the reversal of removal, noting the following:

a) Take care to ensure that wiring is not trapped between mating surfaces.

b) Refit the airbag unit as described in Section 14 and carry out the system check.

c) Test the horn after refitting each button.

5.3b ... then unhook the bulb retaining clip and pivot it away from the rear of the lamp

5 Bulbs (exterior lamps) - renewal

General

1 Whenever a bulb is to be renewed, note the following:

a) Disconnect the battery negative lead before starting work.

b) Remember that if the lamp has just been in use, the bulb may be extremely hot.

c) Always check the bulb contacts and holder, ensuring that there is clean metal-to-metal contact between the bulb and its live contacts and earth. Clean off any corrosion or dirt before fitting a new bulb.

d) Wherever bayonet-type bulbs are fitted, ensure that the live contacts bear firmly against the bulb contact.

e) Always ensure that the new bulb is of the correct rating and that it is completely clean before fitting. This applies particularly to headlamp bulbs.

Headlamp

2 Working in the engine compartment, unclip the relevant circular plastic cover and remove it from the rear of the headlamp unit **(see illustration)**.

3 Unplug the wiring connector, then unhook the bulb retaining clip and pivot it away from the rear of the lamp **(see illustrations)**.

4 Withdraw the bulb from the headlamp unit **(see illustration)**.

5 When handling a new bulb, use a tissue or clean cloth to avoid touching the glass with the fingers. Moisture and grease from the skin can cause blackening and rapid failure of Halogen bulbs.

> **HAYNES HiNT** *If the glass of a headlamp bulb is accidentally touched, wipe it clean using methylated spirit.*

6 Refitting is the reverse of the removal procedure. Ensure that the new bulb locating tabs are correctly located in the lamp cutouts.

Front sidelamp

7 Working in the engine compartment, unclip the relevant circular plastic cover and remove it from the rear of the headlamp unit **(see illustration 5.2)**.

8 Pull the bulbholder from the rear of the headlamp reflector **(see illustration)**.

9 Pull the capless (push fit) bulb from its socket **(see illustration)**.

10 Refitting is the reverse of the removal procedure.

Front direction indicator

Note: *On some models, it will be necessary to remove the power steering fluid reservoir from its mounting bracket, to give adequate access*

5.4 Withdraw the bulb from the headlamp unit (headlamp unit removed for clarity)

5.8 Pull the bulbholder from the rear of the headlamp reflector

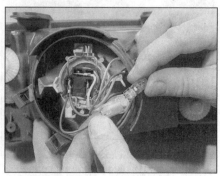

5.9 Pull the capless (push fit) bulb from its socket (headlamp unit removed for clarity)

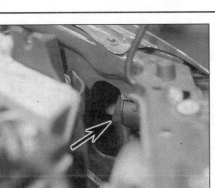

5.11a Grasp the bulbholder protruding from the rear of the direction indicator lamp unit (arrowed) . . .

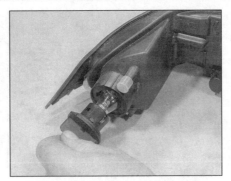

5.11b . . . and rotate it anticlockwise through one quarter of a turn (headlamp unit removed for clarity)

5.12 Remove the front direction indicator bulb from its holder

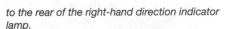

to the rear of the right-hand direction indicator lamp.

11 Working in the engine compartment, grasp the bulbholder protruding from the rear of the direction indicator lamp unit and rotate it anticlockwise through one quarter of a turn **(see illustrations)**.

12 The bulb is a bayonet fit in the holder and can be removed by pressing it in slightly and twisting in an anti-clockwise direction **(see illustration)**.

Caution: Do not press too hard on the bulb, as the glass may shatter - use a soft cloth to protect your hands.

13 Refitting is a reverse of the removal procedure.

Front direction indicator side repeater

14 Push the lamp unit towards the right to free its retaining clips then withdraw it from the wing **(see illustrations)**.

15 Pull the bulbholder out of the lamp unit then pull the capless (push fit) bulb from its holder **(see illustrations)**.

16 Refitting is a reverse of the removal procedure.

Rear lamp cluster

17 From inside the luggage compartment, release the two-piece stud fixings and remove the trim panel from the rear of the relevant lamp cluster.

18 Depress the catch at the centre of the unit and withdraw the bulb panel from the lens unit **(see illustration)**.

19 The relevant bulb can then be removed from the panel. All bulbs are a bayonet fit in the panel and can be removed by pressing them in slightly and twisting in an anti-clockwise direction **(see illustration)**.

Caution: Do not press too hard on the bulb, as the glass may shatter - use a soft cloth to protect your hands.

20 Refitting is the reverse of the removal sequence. Note that the bulb panel rubber seal must be renewed if damaged.

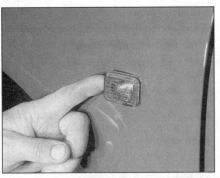

5.14a Push the lamp unit towards the right to free its retaining clips . . .

5.14b . . . then withdraw it from the wing

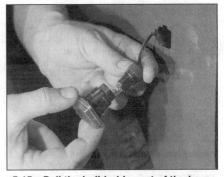

5.15a Pull the bulbholder out of the lamp unit . . .

5.15b . . . then pull the capless (push fit) bulb from its holder

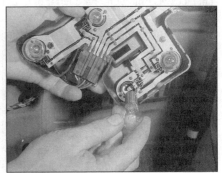

5.18 Depress the catch at the centre of the unit and withdraw the bulb panel from the lens unit

5.19 Rear lamp cluster bulb removal

12

5.21 Undo the two mounting screws and remove the combined number plate lamp lens and bulbholder

5.22 The festoon-type bulb can be pulled from the terminal clips

5.29a Slacken and withdraw the securing screws . . .

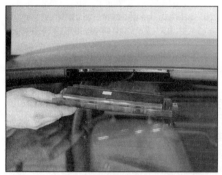

5.29b . . . then remove the high level brake light unit from the tailgate spoiler

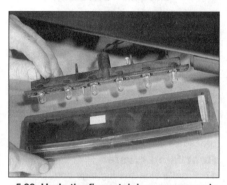

5.30 Undo the five retaining screws and detach the lens from the front of the light unit

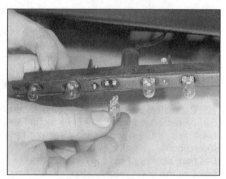

5.31 The capless bulbs are a push fit in the holder

Number plate lamps

21 Undo the two mounting screws and remove the combined number plate lamp lens and bulbholder **(see illustration)**.
22 The festoon bulb can be pulled from the terminal clips **(see illustration)**.
23 Refitting is a reverse of the removal procedure.

Front foglamps

24 Using a flat bladed screwdriver, carefully lever off the foglamp surround panel.
25 Slacken and remove the three foglamp securing screws, then withdraw the lamp unit from the valence.
26 Grasp the bulbholder, rotate it anticlockwise through one quarter of a turn

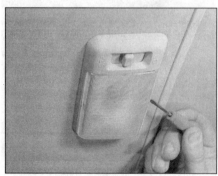

6.2a Carefully prise the lens off the lamp unit . . .

and then withdraw it from the rear of the lamp unit.
27 The bulb is a push-fit in the holder. When handling a new bulb, use a tissue or clean cloth to avoid touching the glass with the fingers. Moisture and grease from the skin can cause blackening and rapid failure of Halogen bulbs.

> **HAYNES HiNT**
> *If the glass of a headlamp bulb is accidentally touched, wipe it clean using methylated spirit before fitting it.*

28 Refitting is the reverse of the removal

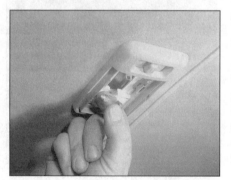

6.2b . . . then remove the festoon bulb from its terminal clips

procedure. Ensure that the bulbholder locks securely into the rear of the foglamp unit.

High level brake lamp

29 Slacken and withdraw the securing screws, then remove the high level brake light unit from the tailgate spoiler **(see illustrations)**.
30 Undo the five retaining screws and detach the lens from the front of the light unit **(see illustration)**.
31 The capless bulbs are a push fit in the holder **(see illustration)**.
32 Refitting is a reversal of removal.

---

6 Bulbs (interior lamps) - renewal

General

1 Refer to the information given in Section 5.

Courtesy lamps

2 Carefully prise the lens off the lamp unit then remove the festoon bulb from its terminal clips **(see illustrations)**.
3 Fit the new bulb using a reversal of the removal procedure. Check the tension of the spring contacts and if necessary, bend them so that they firmly contact the bulb end caps.

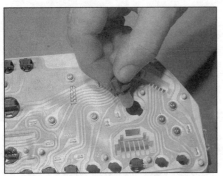

6.11a Twist the relevant bulbholder anti-clockwise and withdraw it from the rear of the instrument panel

6.11b The bulbs are a push fit in the holders

6.19 Unscrew the capped bulb from the side of the switch body

Glovebox lamp

4 Open up the glovebox and then using a flat-bladed screwdriver, carefully prise the lamp unit from the facia.
5 Release the festoon bulb from its contacts and remove it from the light unit.
6 Fit the new bulb using a reversal of the removal procedure. Check the tension of the spring contacts and if necessary, bend them so that they firmly grip the bulb end caps.

Luggage compartment lamp

7 Slide the lamp unit/bulbholder to the left and release it from the parcel shelf support panel.
8 The bulb is a bayonet fit and can be removed by pressing it in and twisting anti-clockwise.
9 Refitting is a reverse of the removal procedure.

Instrument panel illumination and warning lamps

10 Remove the instrument panel, as described in Section 10.
11 Twist the relevant bulbholder anti-clockwise and withdraw it from the rear of the panel. The bulbs are a push fit in the holders **(see illustrations)**.

12 Refitting is the reverse of the removal procedure. Be very careful to ensure that the new bulbs are of the same rating as those removed. This is especially important in the case of the ignition/battery charging warning lamp.

Heater control panel illumination bulbs

13 Working as described in Chapter 3, remove the heater control panel from the facia.
14 Detach the knobs from the heater controls.
15 Remove the two securing screws, then release the clips and detach the face plate from the front of the control panel.
16 Twist the relevant bulbholder anti-clockwise and withdraw it from the rear of the face plate.
17 Refitting is the reverse of the removal procedure. Be very careful to ensure that the new bulbs are of the same rating as those removed.

Switch illumination bulbs

18 All of the facia panel switches are fitted with illuminating bulbs. Some are also fitted with a bulb to show when the circuit concerned is operating.

19 Remove the relevant switch (see Section 4), then unscrew the capped bulb from the side of the switch body **(see illustration)**.

Clock illumination bulb

20 Remove the clock unit as described in Section 11.
21 Unscrew the capped bulb from the rear of the clock body and remove it **(see illustrations)**.

7 Exterior lamp units - removal and refitting

Note: *Disconnect the battery negative lead before removing any lamp unit, and reconnect the lead after refitting the lamp.*

Headlamp

Removal

1 Refer to Chapter 11 and remove the front bumper from the vehicle.
2 Unplug the multiway wiring connector from the rear of the headlamp unit. Where applicable, unplug the wiring from the headlamp levelling motor at the multiway connector.

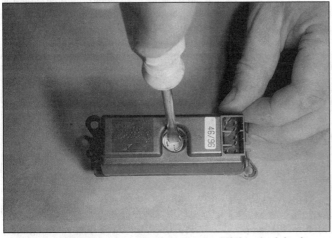

6.21a Unscrew the capped bulb at the rear of the clock body . . .

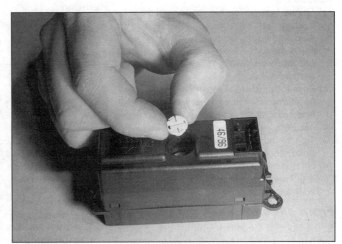

6.21b . . . and remove it

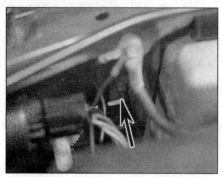

7.3a Undo the retaining nut from the rear of the headlamp unit (arrowed) . . .

7.3b . . . then remove the two bolts securing the upper edge of the headlamp unit to the bodywork . . .

7.3c . . . and remove the headlamp unit from the vehicle

7.4a Front lower edge of the headlight unit must engage with retaining strip (arrowed) on bodywork . . .

7.4b . . . press the clip (arrowed) at the rear outer edge of the headlamp unit into the socket on the bodywork . . .

7.4c . . . pass the stud at the rear inner edge of the headlamp unit through the hole in the bodywork

3 Undo the retaining nut from the rear of the headlamp unit, then remove the two bolts securing the upper edge of the headlamp unit to the bodywork. Release the press-stud clip at the rear outer edge of the headlamp unit, then lift the unit up over the retaining strip and remove it from the vehicle **(see illustrations)**.

Refitting

4 Refitting is a reversal of the removal procedure, noting the following points **(see illustrations)**:

a) *Ensure that the front lower edge of the headlight unit engages with the retaining strip on the bodywork.*

b) *Press the clip at the rear outer edge of the headlamp unit into the socket on the bodywork.*

c) *Pass the stud at the rear inner edge of the headlamp unit through the hole in the bodywork, fit the retaining nut and tighten securely.*

d) *Tighten the headlamp unit upper securing bolts securely.*

e) *On completion have the headlamp beam alignment checked and if necessary adjusted (see Section 8).*

Front direction indicator

5 The front direction indicator is integral with the headlamp unit; refer to the previous sub-Section for details.

Front direction indicator side repeater

Removal

6 Push the lamp unit towards the right to free its retaining clips then withdraw it from the wing (refer to the illustrations in Section 6 for greater detail).

7 Pull the bulbholder out and remove the lamp from the vehicle. Recover the O-ring seal.

Refitting

8 Refitting is a reverse of the removal procedure.

7.10 Unplug the wiring from the lamp cluster at the multiway connector

Rear lamp cluster

Removal

9 Open the tailgate, then release the two-piece stud fixings and move the carpet trim to one side, to gain access to the rear of the lamp cluster.

10 Unplug the wiring from the lamp cluster at the multiway connector **(see illustration)**.

11 Undo the three nuts securing the lamp unit to the body and remove the unit from the vehicle. Note the sealing material which is fitted between the lamp unit and body **(see illustrations)**.

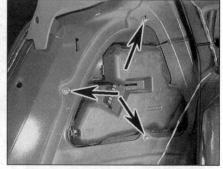

7.11a Undo the three nuts securing the lamp unit to the body . . .

7.11b . . . and remove the unit from the vehicle

Refitting

12 Refitting is a reversal of the removal procedure. The sealing material must be renewed if damaged.

Number plate lamps

Removal

13 Undo the two mounting screws and remove the number plate lamp lens/bulbholder and seal.
14 Withdraw the lamp unit until the wiring connector appears then disconnect the connector and remove the unit from the vehicle.

Refitting

15 Refitting is the reverse of the removal procedure. The seal must be renewed if damaged.

Front foglamps

Removal

16 Carefully unclip the surround panel from the front of the foglamp unit.
17 Remove the three screws and withdraw the foglamp from the valence. Unplug the wiring connector as it becomes accessible.

Refitting

18 Refitting is a reversal of removal. Check

10.2a Remove the instrument panel shroud lower . . .

the foglamp beam alignment and adjust if necessary to avoid dazzling other road users.

8 Headlamp beam alignment - general information

Accurate adjustment of the headlight beam is only possible using optical beam-setting equipment, and this work should therefore be carried out by a Rover dealer or service station with the necessary facilities. In an emergency, however, the following procedure will provide an acceptable light pattern.

Position the car on a level surface with tyres correctly inflated, approximately 10 metres in front of, and at right-angles to, a wall or garage door.

Draw a horizontal line on the wall or door at headlamp centre height. Draw a vertical line corresponding to the centre line of the car, then measure off a point either side of this, on the horizontal line, corresponding with the headlamp centres.

Switch on the main beam and check that the areas of maximum illumination coincide with the headlamp centre marks on the wall. If not, turn the adjustment screws located on the rear and upper surfaces of the headlight

unit (depending on model) to adjust the beam horizontally, and vertically . On models with electric headlight adjustment, make sure that the control is set at its basic setting before making the adjustment.

Have the headlamp beam alignment checked accurately at the earliest opportunity.

9 Dim-dip headlamp system - operation

This system comprises the dim-dip unit (mounted behind the right-hand lower facia panel) and a resistor (situated behind the left-hand headlamp assembly).

The dim-dip unit is supplied with current from the sidelamp circuit and energised by a feed from the ignition switch. When energised, the unit allows battery voltage to pass through the resistor to the headlamp dipped-beam circuits. This lights the headlamps with approximately one-sixth of their normal power so that the vehicle cannot be driven using sidelamps alone.

10 Instrument panel - removal and refitting

Removal

1 Disconnect the battery negative lead and position it away from the terminal.
2 Position the steering column in its lowest possible height setting, then remove the four instrument panel shroud retaining screws and remove the shroud from the facia **(see illustrations)**.
3 Undo the four screws securing the instrument panel to the facia and carefully withdraw the panel until access to the rear of the panel can be gained. Disconnect the two multiway wiring connectors from the rear of

10.2b . . . and upper screws

10.2c . . . and remove the shroud from the instrument panel

10.3a Undo the four screws (arrowed) securing the instrument panel . . .

10.3b . . . and carefully withdraw the panel from the facia

10.3c . . . then disconnect the two multiway wiring connectors from the rear of the panel

the panel, as they become accessible **(see illustrations)**.

4 Remove the instrument panel from the facia **(see illustration)**.

5 To renew individual components within the instrument panel, first undo the screws and remove the support brackets from the sides of the panel. Release the clips and detach the window from the front of the panel.

6 The speedometer/odometer/tripmeter, tachometer, temperature gauge and fuel gauge units are each secured to the rear of the instrument panel with self-tapping screws and may be removed individually as required.

Refitting

7 Refitting is a reverse of the removal procedure. Ensure that the instrument panel wiring connectors are securely refitted. On completion, check the operation of all gauges and warning lamps.

11 Clock -
removal and refitting

Removal

1 Disconnect the battery negative lead.

2 Using a suitable flat-bladed instrument, carefully release the clips at the base of the clock mounting trim strip from the facia. Withdraw the trim from the facia **(see illustrations)**.

3 Undo the two clock retaining screws and remove the clock from the facia. Disconnect the wiring connector from the rear of the clock. Tie a piece of string around the connector to prevent it from falling back inside the facia **(see illustrations)**.

Refitting

4 Refitting is a reversal of the removal procedure.

12 Multi-function unit -
operation, removal and refitting

Operation

1 The multi-function unit (MFU) is mounted onto the rear of the fusebox, which is located behind the right-hand lower facia panel. The unit controls the following functions:

  a) Front and rear wiper system delay intervals.
  b) Heated rear window timer
  c) Courtesy lamp delay
  d) Lamps-on warning bleeper
  e) Horn
  f) Dim-dip headlamp operation
  g) Rear fog lamps
  h) Engine immobilisation
  i) Catalyst overheat detection
  j) Electric windows
  k) Electric sunroof operation

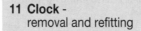

10.4 View of the rear of the instrument panel

11.2a Using a flat-bladed instrument, release the clips at the base of the clock mounting trim

11.2b . . . and remove the clock trim from the facia

11.3a Undo the two clock retaining screws . . .

11.3b . . . then remove the clock from the facia and unplug the wiring connector

Removal

2 Disconnect the battery negative terminal.

3 Undo the quick-release screw fixings and remove the right-hand lower facia panel.

4 Remove the two fusebox retaining nuts then partially withdraw the fusebox until the upper wiring block connector(s) can be disconnected.

5 Carefully turn the fusebox assembly around and unplug both multiway connectors from the MFU. Release the MFU from the rear of the fusebox and remove it from the vehicle.

Refitting

6 Refitting is a reversal of the removal procedure. Ensure that all wiring connectors are correctly refitted. On completion, reconnect the battery terminal and check that all electrical circuits function correctly.

13 Supplementary Restraint System (SRS) - operation

The Supplementary Restraint System (SRS) components comprise: a driver's airbag (mounted at the centre of the steering wheel), a front seat passenger's airbag (where fitted, mounted above the glovebox in the facia), a diagnostic control unit located behind the facia, two seat belt pre-tensioner units (one per front seat), an instrument panel-mounted warning light, a steering wheel rotary coupler and a dedicated wiring harness. System operation is as follows:

If the vehicle suffers a direct or oblique frontal impact of sufficient force, a sensor inside the diagnostic control unit triggers the SRS. A secondary sensor (fitted to discriminate between an actual crash and false triggering) confirms the impact and a detonation current, supplied from the battery or a backup circuit, activates the airbag(s) and seat belt pre-tensioners.

Explosive materials in the airbag(s) rapidly produce large volumes of inert gas, causing the airbags to inflate fully within 30 milliseconds. As the driver (or passenger) is thrown forward, airbag deflates progressively through built-in

vents, cushioning the impact and reducing the risk of injury from contact with the steering wheel, facia or windscreen. The total time from impact to complete airbag inflation is approximately one tenth of a second.

At the same time, explosive materials in the seat belt pre-tensioners produce gas which causes the retraction of a piston mechanism, connected to the seat belt stalk. This the effect of taking up all the slack in the seat belts, pulling the occupants back into their seats. Their forward movement towards the facia, windscreen, steering wheel and column is greatly reduced and this helps to minimise the risk of impact injuries.

At vehicle start-up, a warning light located in the instrument panel will illuminate when the system electrical circuits are activated by turning the ignition switch to position "II" and will stay illuminated for a short period of time whilst the system performs a self-diagnostic test. If this test is satisfactory, the light will extinguish. If the test is unsatisfactory, the light will remain on or fail to illuminate at all indicating that the system must be serviced as soon as possible.

14 Supplementary Restraint System (SRS) - component removal and refitting

Note: *For safety reasons, owners are strongly advised against attempting to diagnose problems with the SRS using standard workshop equipment. The information in this Section is therefore limited to those components in the SRS which must be removed to gain access to other components on the vehicle. Read carefully the precautions given in Section 1 of this Chapter before commencing work on any part of the system.*

Note: *All SRS system wiring can be identified by its yellow, or yellow and black insulation.*

Driver's airbag unit

Removal

1 Remove the ignition key and wait **AT LEAST TEN MINUTES** to allow the system backup circuit to fully discharge. Disconnect

BOTH battery leads (negative lead last) from the battery and position them well away from the battery terminals. Failure to observe this procedure could cause accidental detonation of the airbag and/or seat belt pre-tensioners.

2 Remove the two airbag unit retaining screws which are accessed from behind the steering wheel **(see illustration)**.

3 Carefully release the airbag unit from the steering wheel **(see illustration)** and withdraw it just enough to gain access to its wiring behind. Do not allow the unit to hang from its wiring.

4 Unplug the wiring connector from the rear of the airbag unit **(see illustration)** and carefully remove the unit from the vehicle, placing it in safe storage.

Refitting

5 Refit the airbag unit by reversing the removal procedure, noting the following:

a) *The cable connector must face uppermost when refitted to the airbag unit.*

b) *Observe the specified torque wrench setting when tightening the airbag retaining screws (Torx type) and take care not to cross-thread them. Note that special screws are used to secure the airbag in place - do substitute them for any other kind of screw.*

c) *Reconnect both battery leads, negative lead last, and turn the ignition switch to the "II" position. Check the condition of the system by observing the SRS warning light located in the steering wheel centre pad. The light should stay illuminated for 3 seconds whilst the system performs a self-diagnosis test. If the test is satisfactory, the light will extinguish. If the test is unsatisfactory, the light will remain on or fail to illuminate at all, denoting that the system must be serviced as soon as possible.*

Passenger airbag unit

Removal

6 Remove the ignition key and wait **AT LEAST TEN MINUTES** to allow the system backup circuit to fully discharge. Disconnect **BOTH** battery leads (negative lead first) from the battery and position them well away from

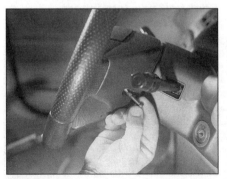

14.2 Remove the two airbag unit retaining screws accessed from behind the steering wheel

14.3 Carefully release the airbag unit from the steering wheel

14.4 Unplug the wiring connector from the rear of the airbag unit

the battery terminals. Failure to observe this procedure could cause accidental detonation of the airbag and/or seat belt pre-tensioners.

7 Refer to Chapter 11 and remove the glovebox.

8 Remove the two screws that secure the airbag unit to its support panel.

9 Withdraw the airbag unit from the facia slightly. Unplug the two multiway wiring connectors from the unit as they become accessible.

10 Carefully remove the passenger airbag unit from the vehicle, placing it in safe storage.

Refitting

11 Refit the airbag unit by reversing the removal procedure, noting the following:

a) *Observe the specified torque wrench setting when tightening the airbag retaining screws (Torx type) and take care not to cross-thread them. Note that special screws are used to secure the airbag in place - do substitute them for any other kind of screw.*

b) *Reconnect both battery leads, negative lead last, and turn the ignition switch to the "II" position. Check the condition of the system by observing the SRS warning light located in the steering wheel centre pad. The light should stay illuminated for 3 seconds whilst the system performs a self-diagnosis test. If the test is satisfactory, the light will extinguish. If the test is unsatisfactory, the light will remain on or fail to illuminate at all, denoting that the system must be serviced as soon as possible.*

Airbag control unit

Removal

12 Remove the ignition key and wait **AT LEAST TEN MINUTES** to allow the system backup circuit to fully discharge. Disconnect **BOTH** battery leads (negative lead first) from the battery and position them well away from the battery terminals. Failure to observe this procedure could cause accidental detonation

of the airbag and/or seat belt pre-tensioners.

13 The control unit is mounted beneath the facia, on the top of the gearchange linkage tunnel. Extract the screw-stud fixings and remove the cover panel from the top of the control unit.

14 Unplug the wiring harness from the control unit at the multiway connector, then undo the bolt and disconnect the earth lead from the side of the control unit casing.

15 Slacken and withdraw the three screws securing the control unit to the floorpan, then remove the unit from the vehicle. Discard the screws, as new ones must be used on refitting.

Refitting

16 Refit the control unit by reversing the removal procedure, noting the following:

a) *Ensure that the mating surface between the control unit and the floorpan is completely clean and free from burrs. A poor mounting surface could cause the SRS to malfunction.*

b) *Take care to ensure that wiring is not trapped between mating surfaces.*

c) *Use new control unit securing screws (Torx type) and observe the specified torque wrench setting when tightening them.*

d) *Reconnect both battery leads, negative lead last, and turn the ignition switch to the "II" position. Check the condition of the system by observing the SRS warning light located in the steering wheel centre pad. The light should stay illuminated for 3 seconds whilst the system performs a self-diagnosis test. If the test is satisfactory, the light will extinguish. If the test is unsatisfactory, the light will remain on or fail to illuminate at all, denoting that the system must be serviced as soon as possible.*

Steering wheel rotary coupler

Removal

17 Set the steering in the straight-ahead position.

18 Remove the ignition key and wait **AT LEAST TEN MINUTES** to allow the system backup circuit to fully discharge. Disconnect **BOTH** battery leads (negative lead first) from the battery and position them well away from the battery terminals. Failure to observe this procedure could cause accidental detonation of the airbag and/or seat belt pre-tensioners.

19 Remove the driver's airbag unit as described earlier in this Section.

20 Unplug the wiring from the rotary coupler at the multiway connector.

21 With reference to Chapter 10, remove the steering wheel, followed by the steering column upper and lower shroud panels.

22 Apply a length of self-adhesive tape to the rotary coupler, to prevent rotation after removal **(see illustration 14.23b)**.

23 Remove the four screws securing the rotary coupler to the column switch assembly and remove the unit from the vehicle **(see illustrations)**.

Refitting

24 Refit the rotary coupler by reversing the removal procedure, noting the following:

a) *Remove the self-adhesive tape after securing the rotary coupler in place with its retaining screws.*

b) *Take care to ensure that wiring harness is not trapped between mating surfaces.*

c) *Refit the steering wheel and column shroud panels with reference to Chapter 10.*

d) *Refit the driver's airbag unit, as described earlier in this Section.*

e) *Reconnect both battery leads, negative lead last, and turn the ignition switch to the "II" position. Check the condition of the system by observing the SRS warning light located in the steering wheel centre pad. The light should stay illuminated for 3 seconds whilst the system performs a self-diagnosis test. If the test is satisfactory, the light will extinguish. If the test is unsatisfactory, the light will remain on or fail to illuminate at all, denoting that the system must be serviced as soon as possible.*

Seat belt pre-tensioners

Removal

25 Remove the ignition key and wait **AT LEAST TEN MINUTES** to allow the system backup circuit to fully discharge. Disconnect **BOTH** battery leads (negative lead first) from the battery and position them well away from the battery terminals. Failure to observe this procedure could cause accidental detonation of the airbag and/or seat belt pre-tensioners.

26 Refer to Chapter 11 and remove the relevant front seat.

27 Release the pre-tensioner wiring harness from the clip on the underside of the seat cushion.

28 Slacken and withdraw the securing bolt,

14.23a Remove the four screws (arrowed) securing the rotary coupler . . .

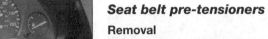

14.23b . . . and remove the coupler from the column switch assembly. Self-adhesive tape (arrowed) applied to the coupler to prevent rotation

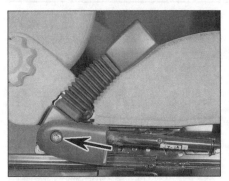

14.28 Seat belt pre-tensioner unit securing bolt (arrowed)

then remove the pre-tensioner unit from the seat **(see illustration)**.

Refitting

29 Refitting is a reversal of removal. Tighten the pre-tensioner securing bolt to the specified torque wrench setting.

15 Vehicle speed sensor - removal and refitting

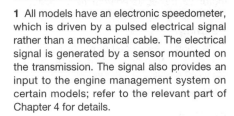

1 All models have an electronic speedometer, which is driven by a pulsed electrical signal rather than a mechanical cable. The electrical signal is generated by a sensor mounted on the transmission. The signal also provides an input to the engine management system on certain models; refer to the relevant part of Chapter 4 for details.

Removal

2 Disconnect the negative cable from the battery and position it away from the terminal.
3 Raise the front of the vehicle and rest it securely on axle stands (see *"Jacking and Vehicle Support"*).
4 The sensor is located at the rear of the transmission, on the differential casing. Unplug the wiring connector from the top of the sensor.
5 Slacken the nut and separate the speed sensor from the drive pinion. Recover the O-ring seal from the base of the drive pinion **(see illustration)**.
6 Slacken and remove the securing bolt, then withdraw the drive pinion from the transmission **(see illustration)**. Be prepared for a small amount of transmission oil loss - position a container underneath the transducer to catch any spillage.
7 Examine the teeth of the drive pinion for signs of wear or damage; renew if necessary.

Refitting

8 Refitting is a reversal of removal. Ensure that the drive pinion O-ring seal is correctly seated and tighten the sensor securing bolt to the specified torque.

15.5 Slacken the nut and separate the speed sensor from the drive pinion

16 Horn - removal and refitting

Removal

1 Disconnect the battery negative cable and position it away from the terminal.
2 Remove the front bumper, as described in Chapter 11.
3 Disconnect the horn wiring connectors and unbolt the horn(s) from the mounting bracket **(see illustration)**.

Refitting

4 Refitting is a reversal of the removal procedure.

17 Windscreen/tailgate washer system components - removal and refitting

1 The windscreen washer reservoir is situated at the front right-hand corner of the engine compartment, with the washer system pump being mounted on the side of the reservoir. The reservoir is also used to supply the tailgate washer system via a second pump.

Washer fluid reservoir and pumps

Removal

2 Refer to Chapter 11 and remove the front

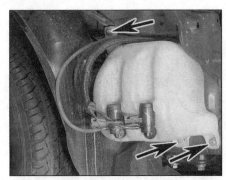

17.5 Washer fluid reservoir mounting screws (arrowed)

15.6 Slacken and remove the securing bolt, then withdraw the drive pinion from the transmission

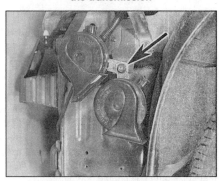

16.3 Horn mounting bolt (arrowed)

bumper. Position a container underneath the reservoir to catch any spilt washer fluid.
3 Unplug the wiring connectors from the pumps, then disconnect the plastic tubing from the reservoir.
4 Slacken and remove the screw securing the filler neck to the bodywork. Extract the filler neck from the top of the reservoir.
5 Undo the three screws and remove the reservoir from the bodywork **(see illustration)**.
6 Empty the reservoir of any remaining fluid then if required, carefully separate the pumps from the reservoir and recover the rubber seals.

Refitting

7 Refitting is a reversal of removal. Lubricate the pump seals with soapy water before fitting them to the reservoir **(see illustration)**.

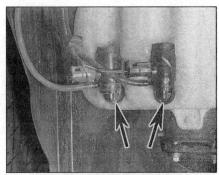

17.7 Ensure that the washer pump seals (arrowed) are securely seated

17.13 Flip up the protective plastic cap and pull it off the wiper arm spindle

18.4 Slacken and withdraw the motor mounting bracket bolts

18.5a Pull the motor and bracket assembly away from the bulkhead to gain access to the linkage nut (arrowed) . . .

Ensure that the washer tubes are not trapped when refitting the reservoir and note that the pump wiring connectors are colour-coded to aid correct reconnection.

Windscreen washer jets

Removal

8 Open the bonnet and disconnect the windscreen washer supply pipe from the underside of the relevant jet. Catch any fluid that spills out in a suitable container.
9 On models with heated washer jets, unplug the electrical wiring from the jet at the multi-way connectors.
10 Depress the catch at the side of the jet body and carefully prise it from the bonnet aperture.

Refitting

11 Refitting is a reversal of removal. To adjust the aim of the jet, carefully push a pin into the spherical insert at the centre of the jet and swivel it to alter the direction of the jet of washer fluid.

Tailgate washer jet

Removal

12 The tailgate washer jet is located at the end of the tailgate wiper arm spindle.
13 Flip up the protective plastic cap (which

contains the jet and its seal) and pull it off the wiper arm spindle **(see illustration)**.

Refitting

14 Refitting is a reversal of removal. If trouble is experienced at any time with the flow to the tailgate washer, check that the non-return valve is not blocked. The valve is fitted in the tube next to the reservoir and should allow fluid to pass only outwards to the jet.

18 Windscreen wiper motor and linkage - removal and refitting

Windscreen wiper motor

Removal

1 Operate the wiper motor then switch it off so that the wiper blades return to the rest position.
2 Stick a piece of masking tape on the windscreen alongside the edge of each wiper blade to use as an alignment aid on refitting, then open the bonnet.
3 Disconnect the battery negative cable and position it away from the terminal.
4 Slacken and withdraw the motor mounting bracket bolts **(see illustration)**. Recover the mounting rubbers, if they are loose.
5 Pull the motor and bracket assembly away

from the bulkhead slightly, to gain access to the linkage, then undo the nut (recover the washer) and detach the wiper linkage from the motor spindle **(see illustrations)**.
6 Release the wiring harness from the clip on the wiper motor mounting bracket. Unplug the wiring connector from the wiper motor harness **(see illustration)**.
7 Remove the motor and bracket assembly from the engine compartment. If required, the motor can be separated from the bracket after removing the three securing screws.

Refitting

8 Refitting is a reversal of removal. Tighten the linkage-to-motor spindle nut to the specified torque.

Wiper linkage

Removal

9 Slacken and remove the wiper arm spindle nuts and pull the arms off their spindles (see Section 19). If necessary, the arms can be levered off their spindles by using a large flat-bladed screwdriver.
10 Carefully prise out the seven trim caps from the ventilation grille to gain access to the grille retaining screws. Slacken and remove all the retaining screws then release the eight retaining clips situated along the front edge of the grille and remove the grille from the vehicle **(see illustrations)**.

18.5b . . . undo the nut and detach the wiper linkage from the motor spindle

18.6 Unplug the wiring connector from the wiper motor harness

18.10a Carefully prise out the seven trim caps from the ventilation grille . . .

18.10b . . . slacken and remove all the retaining screws . . .

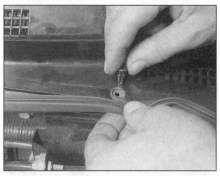

18.10c . . . then release the eight retaining clips situated along the front edge of the grille . . .

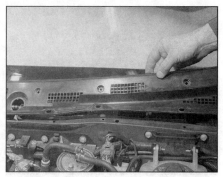

18.10d . . . and remove the grille from the vehicle

11 With reference to the previous sub-Section, disconnect the linkage from the wiper motor spindle **(see illustration)**.

12 Slacken and remove the six securing bolts, then remove the linkage assembly from the bulkhead **(see illustration)**.

Refitting

13 Refitting is a reversal of removal.

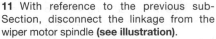

19 Windscreen/tailgate wiper arms - removal and refitting

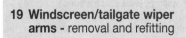

Removal

1 Operate the wiper motor then switch it off so that the wiper blades return to the rest position.

2 Stick a piece of masking tape on the windscreen alongside the edge of each wiper blade to use as an alignment aid on refitting, then open the bonnet.

3 Where applicable, remove the plastic cap from the spindle nut. Slacken the nut with a ring spanner, then remove it from the spindle. Note that on the tailgate wiper arm, the washer jet is integrated into the wiper arm spindle **(see illustrations)**.

4 Lift the wiper arm from the spindle **(see illustrations)**.

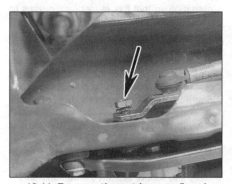

18.11 Remove the nut (arrowed) and disconnect the linkage from the wiper motor spindle

18.12 Wiper linkage securing bolts (left-hand side shown)

19.3a Remove the plastic cap/washer jet from the spindle nut . . .

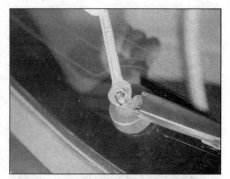

19.3b . . . and slacken the nut with a ring spanner, then remove it from the spindle (tailgate wiper)

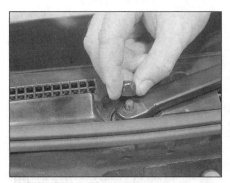

19.3c Removing the wiper spindle nut (windscreen wiper)

19.4a Removing the windscreen wiper arm

19.4b Removing the tailgate wiper arm

20.4a Prise off the spindle nut cover . . .

20.4b . . . then undo the spindle retaining nut . . .

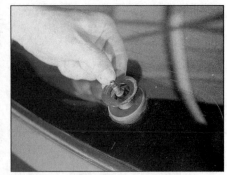

20.4c . . . and remove the washer . . .

Refitting

5 Refitting is a reversal of removal, tightening the spindle nut to the specified torque. Align the wiper arm so that the edge of the wiper lies on the alignment mark made during removal. Operate the wipers, then switch them off and check that the wiper arm stops in the correct rest position on the screen.

20 Tailgate wiper motor - removal and refitting

Removal

1 Operate the tailgate wiper motor, then switch it off so that the wiper blade returns to the rest position.
2 Stick a piece of masking tape alongside the edge of the wiper blade to use as an alignment aid on refitting.
3 Prise off the spindle nut cover/washer jet then undo the wiper arm spindle nut and pull the arm off its spindle- see the previous sub-Section for details. If necessary, the arm can be levered off using a large flat-bladed screwdriver.
4 Prise off the spindle nut cover, then undo the spindle retaining nut and remove the washer and rubber seal **(see illustrations)**.
5 Open up the tailgate and undo the two screws securing the tailgate lower trim panel **(see illustration)**.

6 Using a large flat-bladed screwdriver (pad the blade with insulating tape to prevent damage), work around the outside of the trim panel and carefully prise it away from the tailgate to release the press stud fixings. Remove the trim panel from the tailgate when all of the fixings have been released.
7 Disconnect the washer fluid supply pipe, then unplug the wiring connector from the wiper motor - be prepared for a small amount of fluid spillage **(see illustrations)**.
8 Undo the bolts securing the wiper motor to the tailgate. Remove the motor from the tailgate, noting the motor mounting rubbers and the washer and rubber seal fitted to the wiper spindle **(see illustrations)**.

20.4d . . . and rubber seal

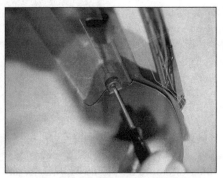

20.5 Undo the two screws securing the tailgate lower trim panel

20.7a Disconnect the washer fluid supply pipe - be prepared for a small amount of fluid spillage . . .

20.7b . . . and unplug the wiring connector from the wiper motor

20.8a Undo the securing bolts . . .

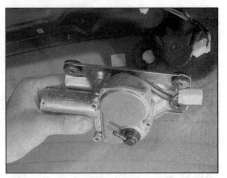

20.8b . . . and remove the motor from the tailgate

21.3a Removing the radio/cassette unit using the special extraction tools . . .

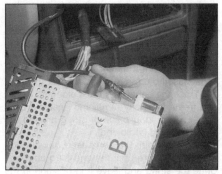

21.3b . . . and disconnecting the aerial co-axial cable from the rear of the unit

22.2a Undo the three speaker retaining screws then withdraw the speaker from the front door . . .

Refitting

9 Refitting is a reverse of the removal procedure, noting the following:

a) Examine the wiper motor mounting rubbers and spindle seals for signs of damage and deterioration and renew if necessary.

b) Tighten the wiper motor mounting bolts to the specified torque.

c) Ensure the wiper arm spindle is clean, then align the wiper blade with the tape fitted on removal and press the arm firmly onto the spindle. Tighten the wiper arm spindle nut to the specified torque and refit the nut cover.

21 Radio/cassette player - removal and refitting

Note: The following removal and refitting procedure is for the range of radio/cassette units which Rover fit as standard equipment. Removal and refitting procedures of non-standard units may differ slightly.

Removal

1 Referring to the instructions supplied with the radio/cassette unit, temporarily de-activate the security code.

2 Disconnect the battery negative lead.

3 To remove the unit, two standard DIN extraction tools are required. These are two U-shaped rods which are inserted into the four small holes in the front of the unit to release the unit retaining clips. The tools may possibly be obtained from a Rover dealer or any audio accessory outlet, or can be made out of 3.0 mm wire rod, such as a welding rod. Using the tools, push back the clamps on the left and right-hand sides, withdraw the unit and disconnect the wiring plugs and aerial **(see illustrations)**.

Refitting

4 Refitting is the reverse of the removal procedure. On completion, connect the battery negative terminal and reactivate the unit by entering the security code.

22 Speakers - removal and refitting

Removal

Front door mounted woofer

1 Remove the front door inner trim panel, as described in Chapter 11.

2 Undo the three speaker retaining screws then withdraw the speaker. Disconnect the speaker wiring connectors and remove the speaker from the door **(see illustrations)**.

Front door mounted tweeter

3 The speaker is integrated into the interior door handle trim panel. Refer to Chapter 11 for details of its removal.

Rear speaker

4 Disconnect the wiring from the speaker at the multiway connector **(see illustration)**.

5 Undo the four speaker retaining screws, then detach the speaker from the underside of the parcel shelf support panel and remove it from the vehicle **(see illustration)**.

Refitting

6 Refitting is a reverse of the removal procedure.

23 Radio aerial and co-axial cable - removal and refitting

Removal

Note: The aerial whip can be unscrewed from the aerial base and renewed as separate item.

1 Remove the radio/cassette player and unplug the co-axial cable from the rear of the unit.

2 Refer to Chapter 11 and remove the glovebox from the facia. Reach inside the facia and release the co-axial cable from the clips on the heater/blower unit.

3 Release the rubber sealing strip from the

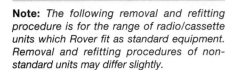

22.2b . . . and disconnect the speaker wiring connectors

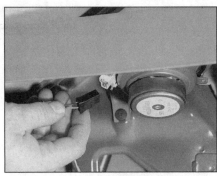

22.4 Disconnect the wiring from the rear speaker at the connectors

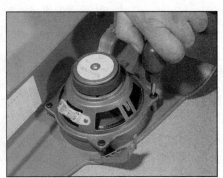

22.5 Undo the retaining screws, then detach the speaker from the parcel shelf support panel (panel removed)

passenger's door aperture, then unclip the trim panel from the A-pillar.

4 Slacken and withdraw the securing screws and remove all four sun visor hinge brackets from the roof.

5 Carefully prise out the press stud fixings that secure the front edge of the headlining to the roof.

6 On models fitted with a sunroof, unclip the sunroof switch trim panel from the headlining.

7 Lower the headlining away from the roof slightly to gain access to the underside of the aerial base.

8 On models fitted with a sunroof, remove the two securing screws and detach the sunroof

switch assembly from the roof. Allow the assembly to rest on the headlining.

9 Remove the plastic cap from the stud terminal on the underside of the aerial base, then remove the nut and disconnect the co-axial cable from the aerial base. Remove the aerial base from the roof and recover the seal.

10 Trace the aerial lead back along its length and free it from any remaining retaining clips or ties. Tie a long piece of string around the aerial end plug (radio end).

11 Carefully pull the aerial lead out through the roof aperture until the end plug appears. Untie the string and leave it in position in the vehicle.

Refitting

12 Securely tie the string around the aerial lead plug and fit the rubber seal to the aerial.

13 From inside the vehicle, gently pull the string through the facia and out of the radio aperture, whilst feeding the aerial lead in through the roof aperture. When the aerial lead plug emerges on the inside of the vehicle, untie the string.

14 The remainder of the refitting procedure is a reversal of the removal procedure. Ensure that the co-axial cable is retained by its securing clips, so that it does not interfere with the operation of the heater controls.

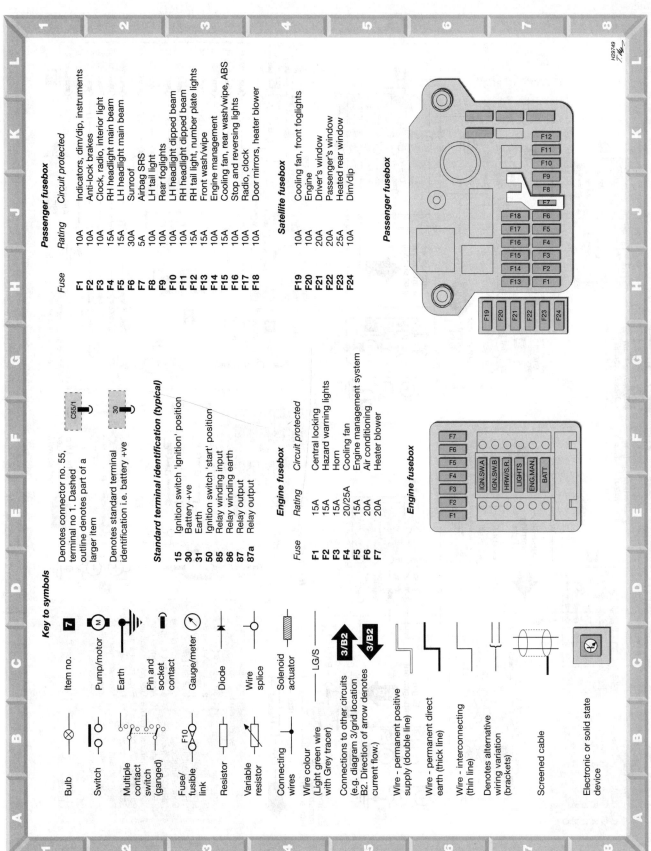

Key to symbols

	Bulb
	Switch
	Multiple contact switch (ganged)
	Fuse/ fusible link
	Resistor
	Variable resistor
	Connecting wires
LG/S	Wire colour (Light green wire with Grey tracer)
3/B2	Connections to other circuits (e.g. diagram 3/grid location B2. Direction of arrow denotes current flow.)
	Wire - permanent positive supply (double line)
	Wire - permanent direct earth (thick line)
	Wire - interconnecting (thin line)
	Denotes alternative wiring variation (brackets)
	Screened cable
	Electronic or solid state device

7	Item no.
M	Pump/motor
	Earth
	Pin and socket contact
	Gauge/meter
	Diode
	Wire splice
	Solenoid actuator

Denotes connector no. 55, terminal no 1. Dashed outline denotes part of a larger item

Denotes standard terminal identification i.e. battery +ve

Standard terminal identification (typical)

15	Ignition switch 'ignition' position
30	Battery +ve
31	Earth
50	Ignition switch 'start' position
85	Relay winding input
86	Relay winding earth
87	Relay output
87a	Relay output

Engine fusebox

Fuse	Rating	Circuit protected
F1	15A	Central locking
F2	15A	Hazard warning lights
F3	15A	Horn
F4	20/25A	Cooling fan
F5	15A	Engine management system
F6	20A	Air conditioning
F7	20A	Heater blower

Engine fusebox

Passenger fusebox

Fuse	Rating	Circuit protected
F1	10A	Indicators, dim/dip, instruments
F2	10A	Anti-lock brakes
F3	10A	Clock, radio, interior light
F4	15A	RH headlight main beam
F5	15A	LH headlight main beam
F6	30A	Sunroof
F7	5A	Airbag SRS
F8	10A	LH tail light
F9	10A	Rear foglights
F10	10A	LH headlight dipped beam
F11	10A	RH headlight dipped beam
F12	15A	RH tail light, number plate lights
F13	15A	Front wash/wipe
F14	10A	Engine management
F15	15A	Cooling fan, rear wash/wipe, ABS
F16	10A	Stop and reversing lights
F17	10A	Radio, clock
F18	10A	Door mirrors, heater blower

Satellite fusebox

Fuse	Rating	Circuit protected
F19	10A	Cooling fan, front foglights
F20	10A	Engine
F21	20A	Driver's window
F22	20A	Passenger's window
F23	25A	Heated rear window
F24	10A	Dim/dip

Passenger fusebox

Diagram 1 : Information for wiring diagrams

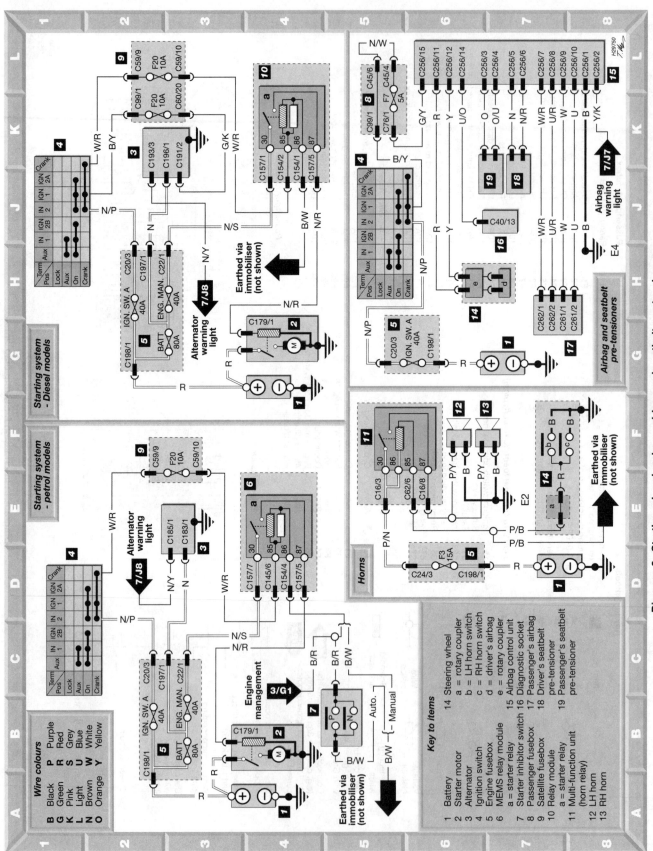

Diagram 2 : Starting, charging, horn, airbag and seatbelt pre-tensioners

Wire colours

B Black	**P** Purple
G Green	**R** Red
K Pink	**S** Grey
L Light	**U** Blue
N Brown	**W** White
O Orange	**Y** Yellow

Key to items

1 Battery
2 Starter motor
3 Alternator
4 Ignition switch
5 Engine fusebox
6 MEMS relay module
  a = starter relay
7 Starter inhibitor switch
8 Passenger fusebox
9 Satellite fusebox
10 Relay module
  a = starter relay
11 Multi-function unit
  (horn relay)
12 LH horn
13 RH horn

14 Steering wheel
  a = rotary coupler
  b = LH horn switch
  c = RH horn switch
  d = driver's airbag
  e = rotary coupler
15 Airbag control unit
16 Diagnostic socket
17 Passenger's airbag
18 Driver's seatbelt
  pre-tensioner
19 Passenger's seatbelt
  pre-tensioner

Starting system - Diesel models

Starting system - petrol models

Horns

Airbag and seatbelt pre-tensioners

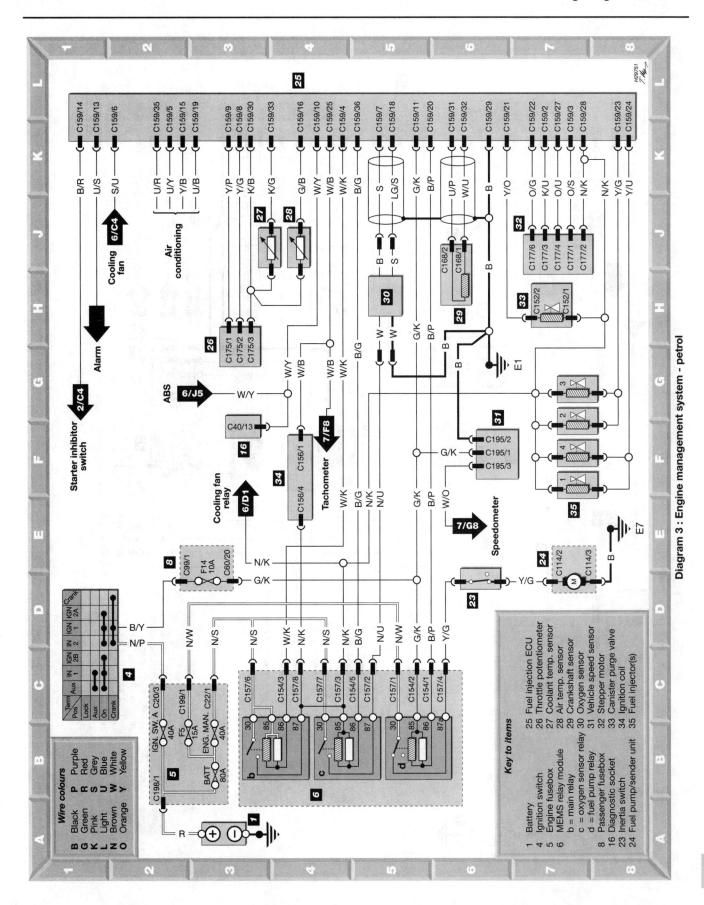

Diagram 3 : Engine management system - petrol

Key to items

1 Battery	25 Fuel injection ECU
4 Ignition switch	26 Throttle potentiometer
5 Engine fusebox	27 Coolant temp. sensor
6 MEMS relay module	28 Air temp. sensor
b = main relay	29 Crankshaft sensor
c = oxygen sensor relay	30 Oxygen sensor
d = fuel pump relay	31 Vehicle speed sensor
8 Passenger fusebox	32 Stepper motor
16 Diagnostic socket	33 Canister purge valve
23 Inertia switch	34 Ignition coil
24 Fuel pump/sender unit	35 Fuel injector(s)

Wire colours

B	Black	P	Purple
G	Green	R	Red
K	Pink	S	Grey
L	Light	U	Blue
N	Brown	W	White
O	Orange	Y	Yellow

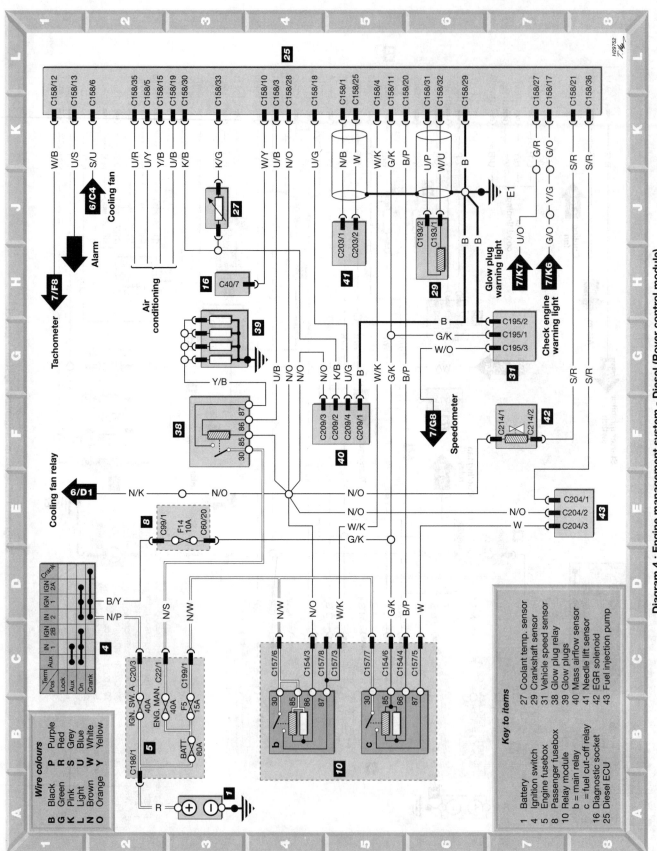

Diagram 4 : Engine management system – Diesel (Rover control module)

Wire colours

B	Black	P	Purple
G	Green	R	Red
K	Pink	S	Grey
L	Light	U	Blue
N	Brown	W	White
O	Orange	Y	Yellow

Key to items

1 Battery
4 Ignition switch
5 Engine fusebox
10 Relay module
16 Passenger fusebox
25 Diesel ECU

b = main relay
c = fuel cut-off relay

27 Coolant temp. sensor
29 Crankshaft sensor
31 Vehicle speed sensor
38 Glow plug relay
39 Glow plugs
40 Mass airflow sensor
41 Needle lift sensor
42 EGR solenoid
43 Fuel injection pump

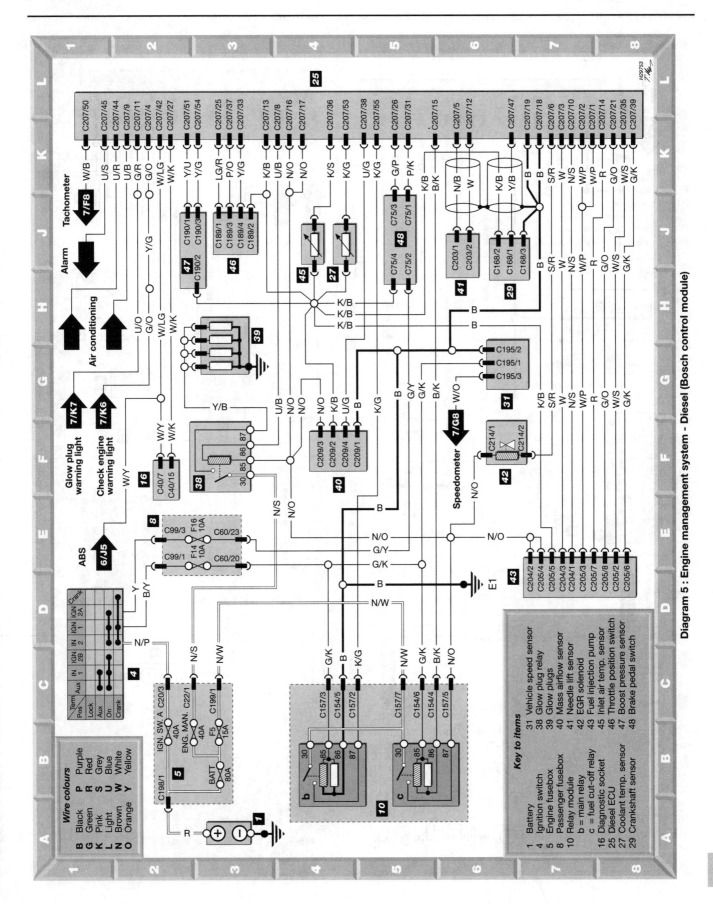

Diagram 5 : Engine management system - Diesel (Bosch control module)

Wire colours

B	Black	**P**	Purple
G	Green	**R**	Red
K	Pink	**S**	Grey
L	Light	**U**	Blue
N	Brown	**W**	White
O	Orange	**Y**	Yellow

Key to items

1	Battery
4	Ignition switch
5	Engine fusebox
8	Passenger fusebox
10	Relay module
	b = main relay
	c = fuel cut-off relay
16	Diagnostic socket
25	Diesel ECU
27	Coolant temp. sensor
29	Crankshaft sensor
31	Vehicle speed sensor
38	Glow plug relay
39	Engine fusebox
40	Mass airflow sensor
41	Needle lift sensor
42	EGR solenoid
43	Fuel injection pump
45	Inlet air temp. sensor
46	Throttle position switch
47	Boost pressure sensor
48	Brake pedal switch

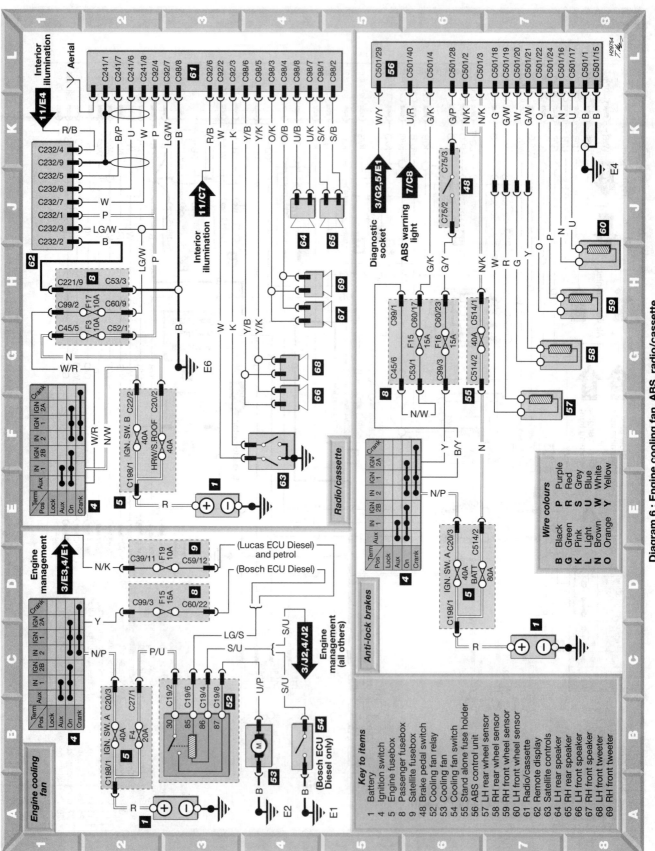

Diagram 6 : Engine cooling fan, ABS, radio/cassette

Wire colours

B Black	P Purple
G Green	R Red
K Pink	S Grey
L Light	U Blue
N Brown	W White
O Orange	Y Yellow

Key to items

1 Battery
4 Ignition switch
5 Engine fusebox
8 Passenger fusebox
9 Satellite fusebox
48 Brake pedal switch
52 Cooling fan relay
53 Cooling fan
54 Cooling fan switch
55 Stand alone fuse holder
56 ABS control unit
57 LH rear wheel sensor
58 RH rear wheel sensor
59 RH front wheel sensor
60 LH front wheel sensor
61 Radio/cassette
62 Remote display
63 Satellite controls
64 LH rear speaker
65 RH rear speaker
66 LH front speaker
67 RH front speaker
68 LH front tweeter
69 RH front tweeter

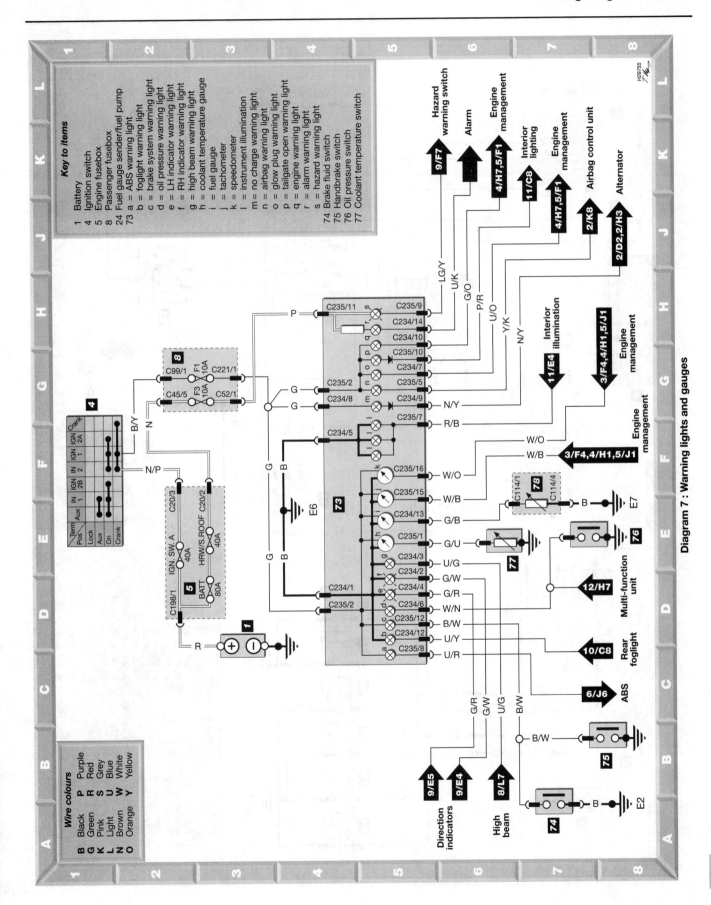

Key to items

1 Battery
4 Ignition switch
5 Engine fusebox
8 Passenger fusebox
24 Fuel gauge sender/fuel pump
73 a = ABS warning light
b = foglight warning light
c = brake system warning light
d = oil pressure warning light
e = LH indicator warning light
f = RH indicator warning light
g = high beam warning light
h = coolant temperature gauge
i = fuel gauge
j = tachometer
k = speedometer
l = instrument illumination
m = no charge warning light
n = airbag warning light
o = glow plug warning light
p = tailgate open warning light
q = engine warning light
r = alarm warning light
s = hazard warning light
74 Brake fluid switch
75 Handbrake switch
76 Oil pressure switch
77 Coolant temperature switch

Wire colours

B Black   P Purple
G Green   R Red
K Pink   S Grey
L Light   U Blue
N Brown   W White
O Orange Y Yellow

Hazard warning switch 9/F7
Alarm
Engine management 4/H7,5/F1
Interior lighting 11/C8
Engine management 4/H7,5/F1
Airbag control unit 2/K8
Alternator 2/D2,2/H3

Interior illumination 11/E4
Engine management 3/F4,4/H1,5/J1
Engine management 3/F4,4/H1,5/J1

Multi-function unit 12/H7
Rear foglight 10/C8
ABS 6/J6

Direction indicators 9/E5 9/E4
High beam 8/L7

Diagram 7 : Warning lights and gauges

12

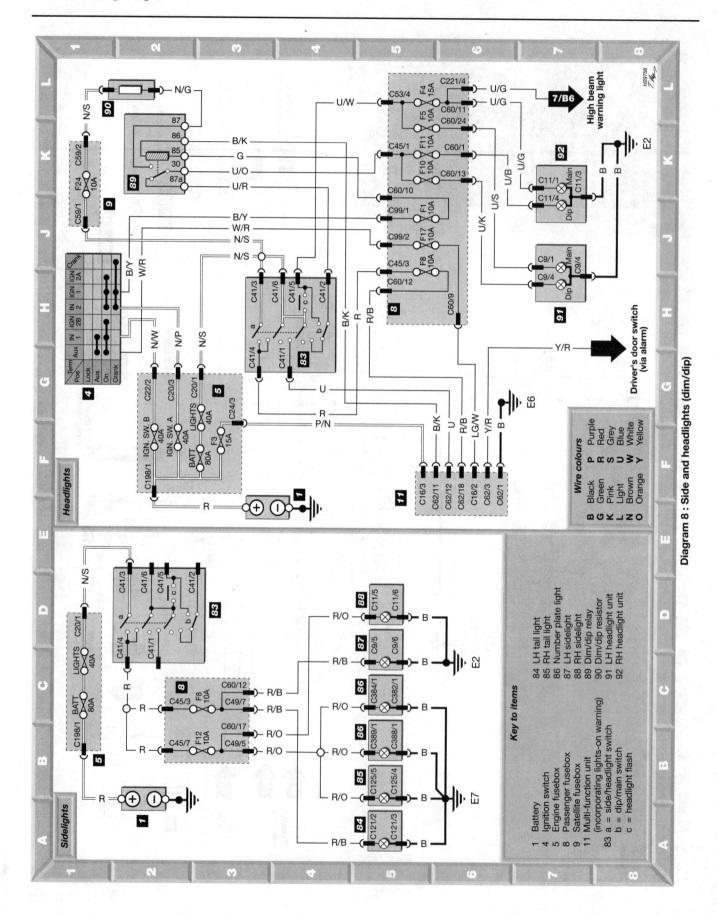

Diagram 8 : Side and headlights (dim/dip)

Wire colours

B	Black	**P**	Purple
G	Green	**R**	Red
K	Pink	**S**	Grey
L	Light	**U**	Blue
N	Brown	**W**	White
O	Orange	**Y**	Yellow

Key to items

1 Battery
4 Ignition switch
5 Engine fusebox
8 Passenger fusebox
9 Satellite fusebox
11 Multi-function unit
(incorporating lights-on warning)
83 a = side/headlight switch
b = dip/main switch
c = headlight flash

84 LH tail light
85 RH tail light
86 Number plate light
87 LH sidelight
88 RH sidelight
89 Dim/dip relay
90 Dim/dip resistor
91 LH headlight unit
92 RH headlight unit

High beam warning light

7/B6

Driver's door switch
(via alarm)

Headlights

Sidelights

H29756

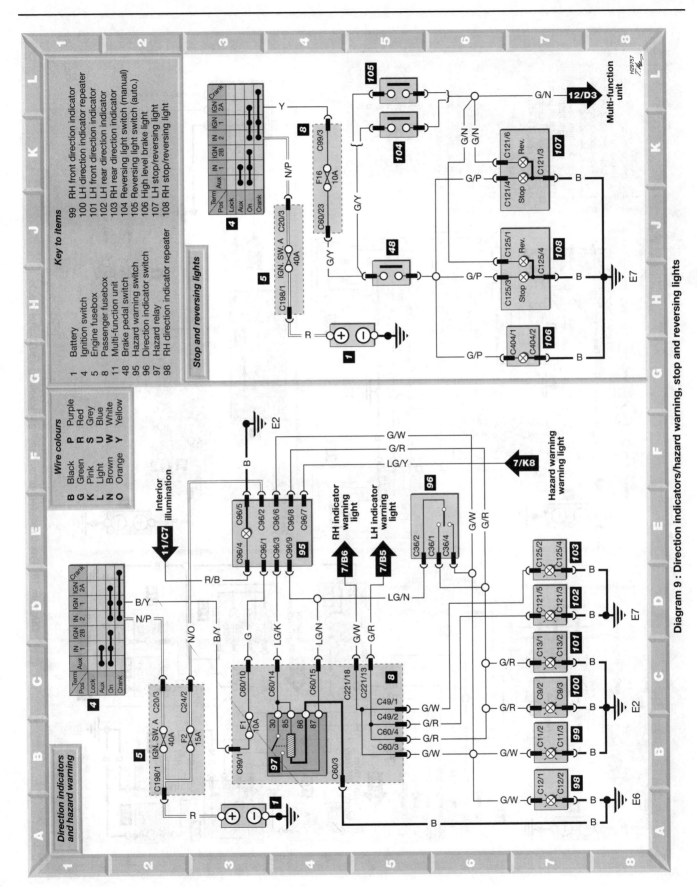

Key to items

1	Battery
4	Ignition switch
5	Engine fusebox
8	Passenger fusebox
11	Multi-function unit
48	Brake pedal switch
95	Hazard warning switch
96	Direction indicator switch
97	Hazard relay
98	RH direction indicator repeater
99	RH front direction indicator
100	LH direction indicator repeater
101	LH front direction indicator
102	LH rear direction indicator
103	RH rear direction indicator
104	Reversing light switch (manual)
105	Reversing light switch (auto.)
106	High level brake light
107	LH stop/reversing light
108	RH stop/reversing light

Stop and reversing lights

Wire colours

B	Black	K	Purple
G	Green	R	Red
K	Pink	S	Grey
L	Light	U	Blue
N	Brown	W	White
O	Orange	Y	Yellow

Direction indicators and hazard warning

Diagram 9 : Direction indicators/hazard warning, stop and reversing lights

12

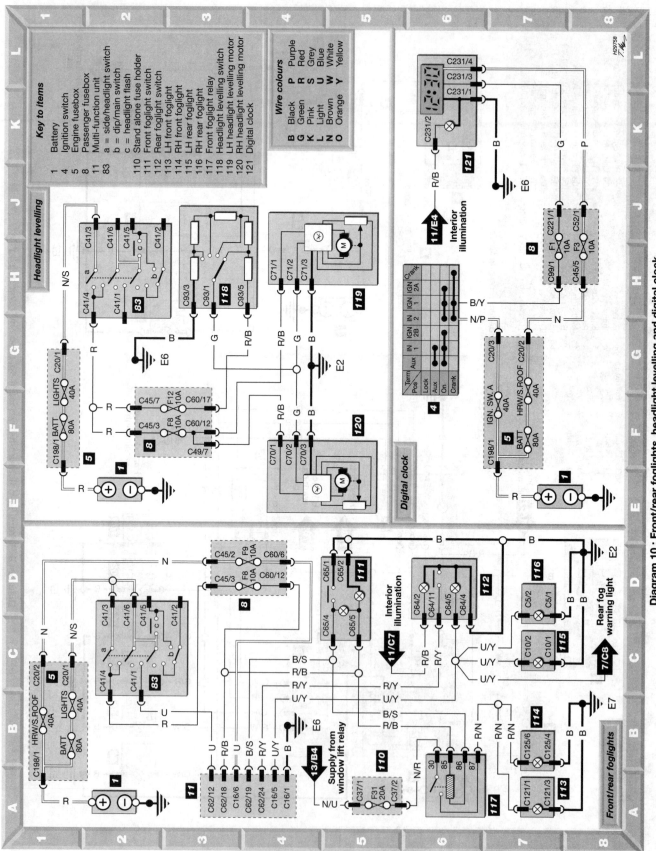

Diagram 10 : Front/rear foglights, headlight levelling and digital clock

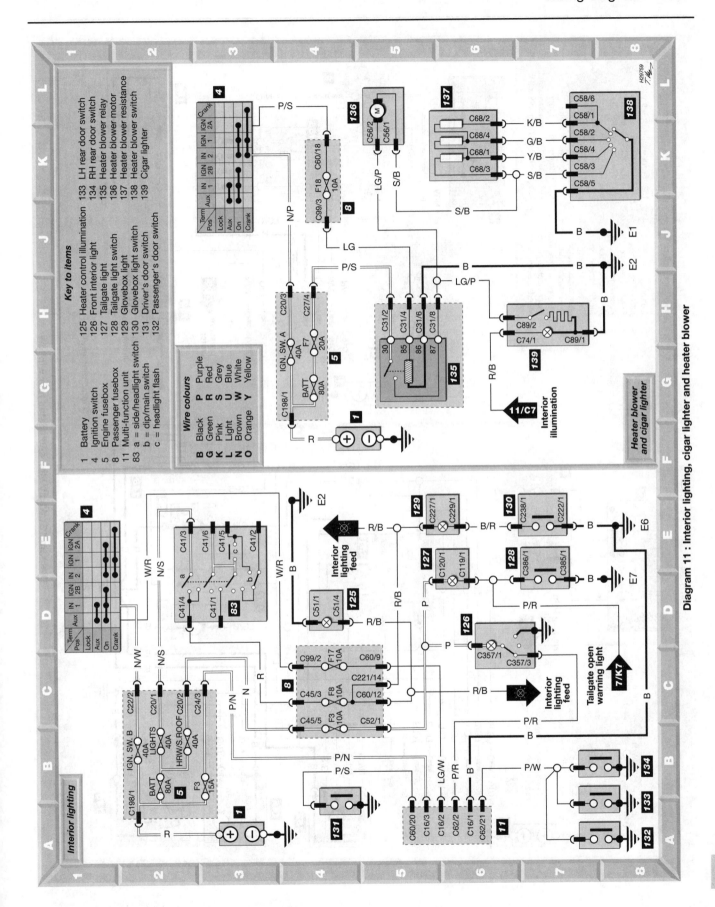

Key to items

1	Battery
4	Ignition switch
5	Engine fusebox
8	Passenger fusebox
11	Multi-function unit
83	a = side/headlight switch
	b = dip/main switch
	c = headlight flash
125	Heater control illumination
126	Front interior light
127	Tailgate light
128	Tailgate light switch
129	Glovebox light
130	Glovebox light switch
131	Driver's door switch
132	Passenger's door switch
133	LH rear door switch
134	RH rear door switch
135	Heater blower relay
136	Heater blower motor
137	Heater blower resistance
138	Heater blower switch
139	Cigar lighter

Wire colours

B	Black	P	Purple
G	Green	R	Red
K	Pink	S	Grey
L	Light	U	Blue
N	Brown	W	White
O	Orange	Y	Yellow

Interior illumination

Heater blower and cigar lighter

Interior lighting

Diagram 11 : Interior lighting, cigar lighter and heater blower

12

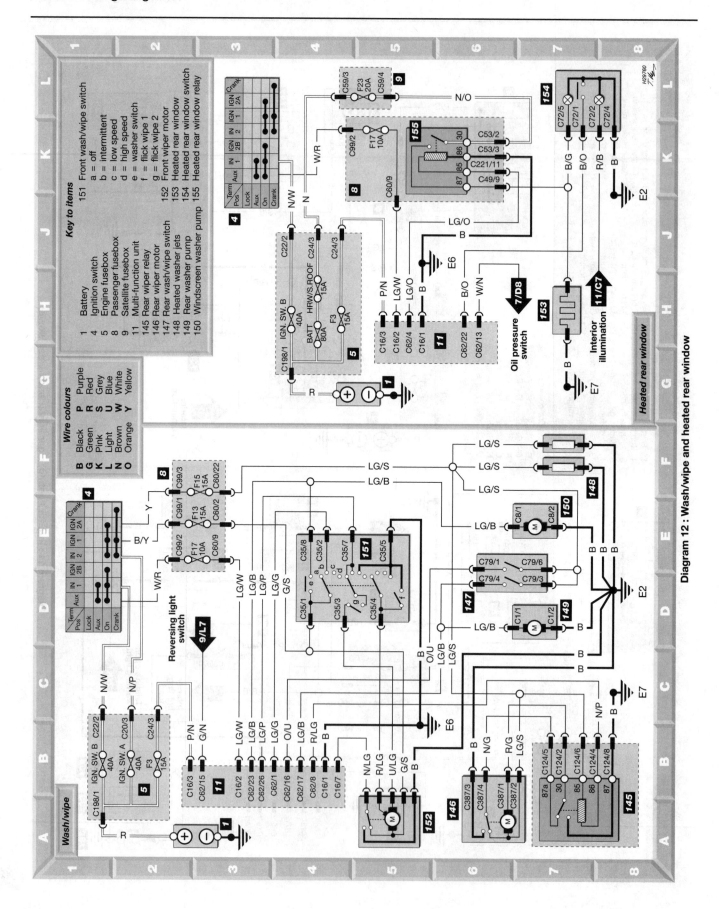

Diagram 12 : Wash/wipe and heated rear window

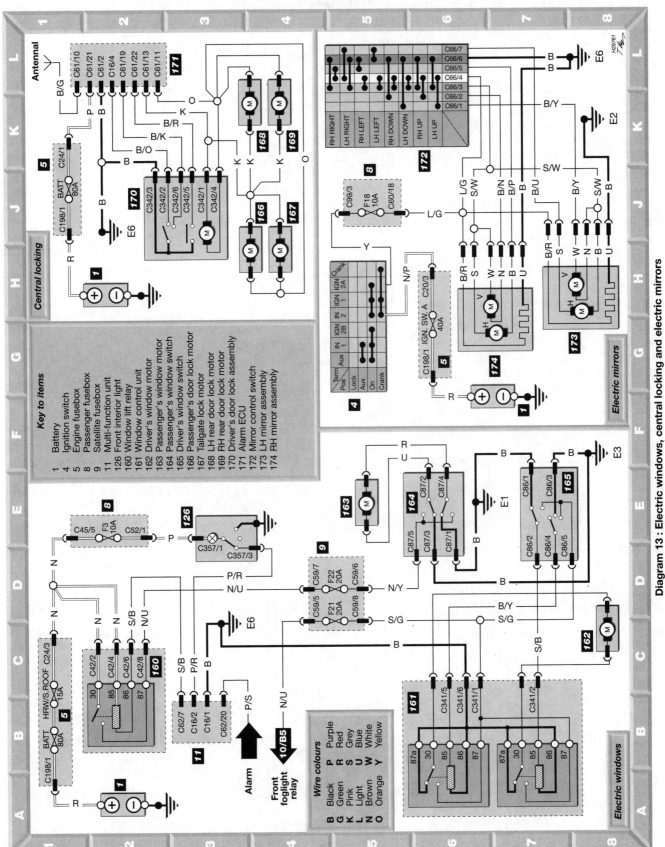

Diagram 13 : Electric windows, central locking and electric mirrors

Key to items

1 Battery
4 Ignition switch
5 Engine fusebox
8 Passenger fusebox
9 Satellite fusebox
11 Multi-function unit
126 Front interior light
160 Window lift relay
161 Window control unit
162 Driver's window motor
163 Passenger's window motor
164 Passenger's window switch
165 Driver's window switch
166 Passenger's door lock motor
167 Tailgate lock motor
168 LH rear door lock motor
169 RH rear door lock motor
170 Driver's door lock assembly
171 Alarm ECU
172 Mirror control switch
173 LH mirror assembly
174 RH mirror assembly

Wire colours

B Black
G Green
K Pink
L Light
N Brown
O Orange
P Purple
R Red
S Grey
U Blue
W White
Y Yellow

Central locking

Electric mirrors

Electric windows

12

Notes

Dimensions and weights

Dimensions

Overall length . . . . 3.973 m
Overall width (including mirrors) . . . . 1.890 m
Overall height (at kerb weight) . . . . 1.419 m
Wheelbase . . . . 2.502 m
Turning circle (kerb to kerb) . . . . 10.31 m
Ground clearance . . . . 120 mm

Weights

Kerb weight:*
214i 3-door . . . . 985 kg
214 Si - 5-door . . . . 1030 kg
216 SLi - 5-door automatic . . . . 1085 kg
220D 3-door . . . . 1105 kg
220SDi 5-door . . . . 1150 kg
Maximum rear axle load . . . . 750 kg

Maximum rear axle load when towing . . . . 860 kg
Maximum gross vehicle weight:
214i 3-door . . . . 1460 kg
214 Si - 5-door . . . . 1480 kg
216 SLi - 5-door automatic . . . . 1550 kg
220D 3-door . . . . 1600 kg
220SDi 5-door . . . . 1620 kg
Maximum roof rack load (including weight of rack) . . . . 65 kg
Maximum towing weight with braked trailer **:
214i models . . . . 900 kg
All other models . . . . 1000 kg
Towing hitch downward load . . . . 70 kg

*Vehicle unladen, excluding options, with full fuel tank, coolant and all fluids, tools and spare wheel. Add 5 kg if catalytic converter is fitted
**Allows vehicle to restart from rest efficiently on 12% (1 in 8) gradient with two occupants. The weight of additional passengers or luggage must be deducted from the figure given.

Conversion factors

Length (distance)

Inches (in)	x 25.4	= Millimetres (mm)	x 0.0394	= Inches (in)
Feet (ft)	x 0.305	= Metres (m)	x 3.281	= Feet (ft)
Miles	x 1.609	= Kilometres (km)	x 0.621	= Miles

Volume (capacity)

Cubic inches (cu in; in³)	x 16.387	= Cubic centimetres (cc; cm³)	x 0.061	= Cubic inches (cu in; in³)
Imperial pints (Imp pt)	x 0.568	= Litres (l)	x 1.76	= Imperial pints (Imp pt)
Imperial quarts (Imp qt)	x 1.137	= Litres (l)	x 0.88	= Imperial quarts (Imp qt)
Imperial quarts (Imp qt)	x 1.201	= US quarts (US qt)	x 0.833	= Imperial quarts (Imp qt)
US quarts (US qt)	x 0.946	= Litres (l)	x 1.057	= US quarts (US qt)
Imperial gallons (Imp gal)	x 4.546	= Litres (l)	x 0.22	= Imperial gallons (Imp gal)
Imperial gallons (Imp gal)	x 1.201	= US gallons (US gal)	x 0.833	= Imperial gallons (Imp gal)
US gallons (US gal)	x 3.785	= Litres (l)	x 0.264	= US gallons (US gal)

Mass (weight)

Ounces (oz)	x 28.35	= Grams (g)	x 0.035	= Ounces (oz)
Pounds (lb)	x 0.454	= Kilograms (kg)	x 2.205	= Pounds (lb)

Force

Ounces-force (ozf; oz)	x 0.278	= Newtons (N)	x 3.6	= Ounces-force (ozf; oz)
Pounds-force (lbf; lb)	x 4.448	= Newtons (N)	x 0.225	= Pounds-force (lbf; lb)
Newtons (N)	x 0.1	= Kilograms-force (kgf; kg)	x 9.81	= Newtons (N)

Pressure

Pounds-force per square inch (psi; lbf/in²; lb/in²)	x 0.070	= Kilograms-force per square centimetre (kgf/cm²; kg/cm²)	x 14.223	= Pounds-force per square inch (psi; lbf/in²; lb/in²)
Pounds-force per square inch (psi; lbf/in²; lb/in²)	x 0.068	= Atmospheres (atm)	x 14.696	= Pounds-force per square inch (psi; lbf/in²; lb/in²)
Pounds-force per square inch (psi; lbf/in²; lb/in²)	x 0.069	= Bars	x 14.5	= Pounds-force per square inch (psi; lbf/in²; lb/in²)
Pounds-force per square inch (psi; lbf/in²; lb/in²)	x 6.895	= Kilopascals (kPa)	x 0.145	= Pounds-force per square inch (psi; lbf/in²; lb/in²)
Kilopascals (kPa)	x 0.01	= Kilograms-force per square centimetre (kgf/cm²; kg/cm²)	x 98.1	= Kilopascals (kPa)
Millibar (mbar)	x 100	= Pascals (Pa)	x 0.01	= Millibar (mbar)
Millibar (mbar)	x 0.0145	= Pounds-force per square inch (psi; lbf/in²; lb/in²)	x 68.947	= Millibar (mbar)
Millibar (mbar)	x 0.75	= Millimetres of mercury (mmHg)	x 1.333	= Millibar (mbar)
Millibar (mbar)	x 0.401	= Inches of water (inH₂O)	x 2.491	= Millibar (mbar)
Millimetres of mercury (mmHg)	x 0.535	= Inches of water (inH₂O)	x 1.868	= Millimetres of mercury (mmHg)
Inches of water (inH₂O)	x 0.036	= Pounds-force per square inch (psi; lbf/in²; lb/in²)	x 27.68	= Inches of water (inH₂O)

Torque (moment of force)

Pounds-force inches (lbf in; lb in)	x 1.152	= Kilograms-force centimetre (kgf cm; kg cm)	x 0.868	= Pounds-force inches (lbf in; lb in)
Pounds-force inches (lbf in; lb in)	x 0.113	= Newton metres (Nm)	x 8.85	= Pounds-force inches (lbf in; lb in)
Pounds-force inches (lbf in; lb in)	x 0.083	= Pounds-force feet (lbf ft; lb ft)	x 12	= Pounds-force inches (lbf in; lb in)
Pounds-force feet (lbf ft; lb ft)	x 0.138	= Kilograms-force metres (kgf m; kg m)	x 7.233	= Pounds-force feet (lbf ft; lb ft)
Pounds-force feet (lbf ft; lb ft)	x 1.356	= Newton metres (Nm)	x 0.738	= Pounds-force feet (lbf ft; lb ft)
Newton metres (Nm)	x 0.102	= Kilograms-force metres (kgf m; kg m)	x 9.804	= Newton metres (Nm)

Power

Horsepower (hp)	x 745.7	= Watts (W)	x 0.0013	= Horsepower (hp)

Velocity (speed)

Miles per hour (miles/hr; mph)	x 1.609	= Kilometres per hour (km/hr; kph)	x 0.621	= Miles per hour (miles/hr; mph)

Fuel consumption*

Miles per gallon (mpg)	x 0.354	= Kilometres per litre (km/l)	x 2.825	= Miles per gallon (mpg)

Temperature

Degrees Fahrenheit = (°C x 1.8) + 32   Degrees Celsius (Degrees Centigrade; °C) = (°F - 32) x 0.56

It is common practice to convert from miles per gallon (mpg) to litres/100 kilometres (l/100km), where mpg x l/100 km = 282

Spare parts are available from many sources, including maker's appointed garages, accessory shops, and motor factors. To be sure of obtaining the correct parts, it will sometimes be necessary to quote the vehicle identification number. If possible, it can also be useful to take the old parts along for positive identification. Items such as starter motors and alternators may be available under a service exchange scheme - any parts returned should be clean.

Our advice regarding spare parts is as follows.

Officially appointed garages

This is the best source of parts which are peculiar to your car, and which are not otherwise generally available (eg, badges, interior trim, certain body panels, etc). It is also the only place at which you should buy parts if the vehicle is still under warranty.

Accessory shops

These are very good places to buy materials and components needed for the maintenance of your car (oil, air and fuel filters, light bulbs, drivebelts, greases, brake pads, tough-up paint, etc). Components of this nature sold by a reputable shop are of the same standard as those used by the car manufacturer.

Besides components, these shops also sell tools and general accessories, usually have convenient opening hours, charge lower prices, and can often be found close to home. Some accessory shops have parts counters where components needed for almost any repair job can be purchased or ordered.

Motor factors

Good factors will stock all the more important components which wear out comparatively quickly, and can sometimes supply individual components needed for the overhaul of a larger assembly (eg, brake seals and hydraulic parts, bearing shells, pistons, valves). They may also handle work such as cylinder block reboring, crankshaft regrinding, etc.

Tyre and exhaust specialists

These outlets may be independent, or members of a local or national chain. They frequently offer competitive prices when compared with a main dealer or local garage, but it will pay to obtain several quotes before making a decision. When researching prices, also ask what "extras" may be added - for instance fitting a new valve and balancing the wheel are both commonly charged on top of the price of a new tyre.

Other sources

Beware of parts or materials obtained from market stalls, car boot sales or similar outlets. Such items are not invariably sub-standard, but there is little chance of compensation if they do prove unsatisfactory. In the case of safety-critical components such as brake pads, there is the risk not only of financial loss, but also of an accident causing injury or death.

Second-hand components or assemblies obtained from a car breaker or "scrapyard" can be a good buy in some circumstances, but this sort of purchase is best made by the experienced DIY mechanic.

Vehicle identification

Modifications are a continuing and unpublicised process in vehicle manufacture, quite apart from major model changes. Spare parts manuals and lists are compiled upon a numerical basis, the individual vehicle identification numbers being essential to correct identification of the component concerned.

When ordering spare parts, always give as much information as possible. Quote the vehicle model, year of manufacture, body and engine numbers as appropriate.

The *vehicle identification plate* is situated on the passenger door pillar (see illustration). It gives the VIN (vehicle identification number), vehicle weight information and paint and trim colour codes.

The *vehicle identification number* is repeated in the form of stamped numbers on the centre of the engine compartment bulkhead (see illustration), and also on a plate below the lower left-hand corner of the windscreen.

The *body number* is stamped into a plate fixed to the left-hand side of the spare wheel well, in the luggage compartment.

The *engine number* on K-series petrol engines is stamped on the front face of the cylinder block, next to the transmission casing (see illustration). On L-series diesel engines, the engine number is stamped on the upper front face of the cylinder block, at the centre.

The *Manual Transmission number* is stamped on label attached to the front face of the clutch housing.

The *Automatic Transmission number* is stamped on a plate attached to the rear top face of the transmission casing.

Vehicle identification plate on passenger door pillar

Vehicle identification number on engine compartment bulkhead

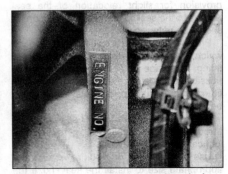

Engine number (K-series petrol engine) on front of cylinder block/crankcase

Whenever servicing, repair or overhaul work is carried out on the car or its components, observe the following procedures and instructions. This will assist in carrying out the operation efficiently and to a professional standard of workmanship.

Joint mating faces and gaskets

When separating components at their mating faces, never insert screwdrivers or similar implements into the joint between the faces in order to prise them apart. This can cause severe damage which results in oil leaks, coolant leaks, etc upon reassembly. Separation is usually achieved by tapping along the joint with a soft-faced hammer in order to break the seal. However, note that this method may not be suitable where dowels are used for component location.

Where a gasket is used between the mating faces of two components, a new one must be fitted on reassembly; fit it dry unless otherwise stated in the repair procedure. Make sure that the mating faces are clean and dry, with all traces of old gasket removed. When cleaning a joint face, use a tool which is unlikely to score or damage the face, and remove any burrs or nicks with an oilstone or fine file.

Make sure that tapped holes are cleaned with a pipe cleaner, and keep them free of jointing compound, if this is being used, unless specifically instructed otherwise.

Ensure that all orifices, channels or pipes are clear, and blow through them, preferably using compressed air.

Oil seals

Oil seals can be removed by levering them out with a wide flat-bladed screwdriver or similar implement. Alternatively, a number of self-tapping screws may be screwed into the seal, and these used as a purchase for pliers or some similar device in order to pull the seal free.

Whenever an oil seal is removed from its working location, either individually or as part of an assembly, it should be renewed.

The very fine sealing lip of the seal is easily damaged, and will not seal if the surface it contacts is not completely clean and free from scratches, nicks or grooves. If the original sealing surface of the component cannot be restored, and the manufacturer has not made provision for slight relocation of the seal relative to the sealing surface, the component should be renewed.

Protect the lips of the seal from any surface which may damage them in the course of fitting. Use tape or a conical sleeve where possible. Lubricate the seal lips with oil before fitting and, on dual-lipped seals, fill the space between the lips with grease.

Unless otherwise stated, oil seals must be fitted with their sealing lips toward the lubricant to be sealed.

Use a tubular drift or block of wood of the appropriate size to install the seal and, if the seal housing is shouldered, drive the seal down to the shoulder. If the seal housing is unshouldered, the seal should be fitted with its face flush with the housing top face (unless otherwise instructed).

Screw threads and fastenings

Seized nuts, bolts and screws are quite a common occurrence where corrosion has set in, and the use of penetrating oil or releasing fluid will often overcome this problem if the offending item is soaked for a while before attempting to release it. The use of an impact driver may also provide a means of releasing such stubborn fastening devices, when used in conjunction with the appropriate screwdriver bit or socket. If none of these methods works, it may be necessary to resort to the careful application of heat, or the use of a hacksaw or nut splitter device.

Studs are usually removed by locking two nuts together on the threaded part, and then using a spanner on the lower nut to unscrew the stud. Studs or bolts which have broken off below the surface of the component in which they are mounted can sometimes be removed using a stud extractor. Always ensure that a blind tapped hole is completely free from oil, grease, water or other fluid before installing the bolt or stud. Failure to do this could cause the housing to crack due to the hydraulic action of the bolt or stud as it is screwed in.

When tightening a castellated nut to accept a split pin, tighten the nut to the specified torque, where applicable, and then tighten further to the next split pin hole. Never slacken the nut to align the split pin hole, unless stated in the repair procedure.

When checking or retightening a nut or bolt to a specified torque setting, slacken the nut or bolt by a quarter of a turn, and then retighten to the specified setting. However, this should not be attempted where angular tightening has been used.

For some screw fastenings, notably cylinder head bolts or nuts, torque wrench settings are no longer specified for the latter stages of tightening, "angle-tightening" being called up instead. Typically, a fairly low torque wrench setting will be applied to the bolts/nuts in the correct sequence, followed by one or more stages of tightening through specified angles.

Locknuts, locktabs and washers

Any fastening which will rotate against a component or housing during tightening should always have a washer between it and the relevant component or housing.

Spring or split washers should always be renewed when they are used to lock a critical component such as a big-end bearing retaining bolt or nut. Locktabs which are folded over to retain a nut or bolt should always be renewed.

Self-locking nuts can be re-used in non-critical areas, providing resistance can be felt when the locking portion passes over the bolt or stud thread. However, it should be noted that self-locking stiffnuts tend to lose their effectiveness after long periods of use, and should then be renewed as a matter of course.

Split pins must always be replaced with new ones of the correct size for the hole.

When thread-locking compound is found on the threads of a fastener which is to be re-used, it should be cleaned off with a wire brush and solvent, and fresh compound applied on reassembly.

Special tools

Some repair procedures in this manual entail the use of special tools such as a press, two or three-legged pullers, spring compressors, etc. Wherever possible, suitable readily-available alternatives to the manufacturer's special tools are described, and are shown in use. In some instances, where no alternative is possible, it has been necessary to resort to the use of a manufacturer's tool, and this has been done for reasons of safety as well as the efficient completion of the repair operation. Unless you are highly-skilled and have a thorough understanding of the procedures described, never attempt to bypass the use of any special tool when the procedure described specifies its use. Not only is there a very great risk of personal injury, but expensive damage could be caused to the components involved.

Environmental considerations

When disposing of used engine oil, brake fluid, antifreeze, etc, give due consideration to any detrimental environmental effects. Do not, for instance, pour any of the above liquids down drains into the general sewage system, or onto the ground to soak away. Many local council refuse tips provide a facility for waste oil disposal, as do some garages. If none of these facilities are available, consult your local Environmental Health Department, or the National Rivers Authority, for further advice.

With the universal tightening-up of legislation regarding the emission of environmentally-harmful substances from motor vehicles, most vehicles have tamperproof devices fitted to the main adjustment points of the fuel system. These devices are primarily designed to prevent unqualified persons from adjusting the fuel/air mixture, with the chance of a consequent increase in toxic emissions. If such devices are found during servicing or overhaul, they should, wherever possible, be renewed or refitted in accordance with the manufacturer's requirements or current legislation.

OIL CARE
FOLLOW THE CODE
OIL BANK LINE
0800 66 33 66

Note: It is antisocial and illegal to dump oil down the drain. To find the location of your local oil recycling bank, call this number free.

The jack supplied with the vehicle tool kit should only be used for changing the roadwheels - see *"Wheel changing"* at the front of this Manual.

When using the jack supplied with the vehicle, position it on firm ground and locate its head in the relevant vehicle jacking point **(see illustration)**.

On models fitted with side skirt/sill extension trim panels, the access panel must first be removed from the trim panel to gain access to jacking points 3, 4, 5 and 7.

When carrying out any other kind of work, raise the vehicle using a hydraulic (or trolley) jack, and always supplement this jack with axle stands positioned under the indicated points. Always use the recommended jacking and support points, and refer to the following instructions:

If the front of the vehicle is to be raised, firmly apply the handbrake and place the jack head under point 1. Jack the vehicle up and position the axle stands either on the sills at points 3 and 4, or the underbody longitudinal supports at points 6.

To raise the rear of the vehicle, chock the front wheels and place the jack head under point 2, the reinforced location pad immediately in front of the rear towing eye. The axle stands should be placed either on the sills at points 5 and 7 or the underbody longitudinal supports at points 8.

To raise the side of the vehicle, place the jack head under the sill at point 3 or 4 (as applicable) at the front, then jack up the vehicle and position an axle stand under the longitudinal support at point 6. Remove the jack and position it under point 5 or 7 (as applicable) then jack up the rear of the vehicle and position an axle stand under the longitudinal support at point 8.

Never work under, around or near a raised vehicle unless it is adequately supported in at least two places.

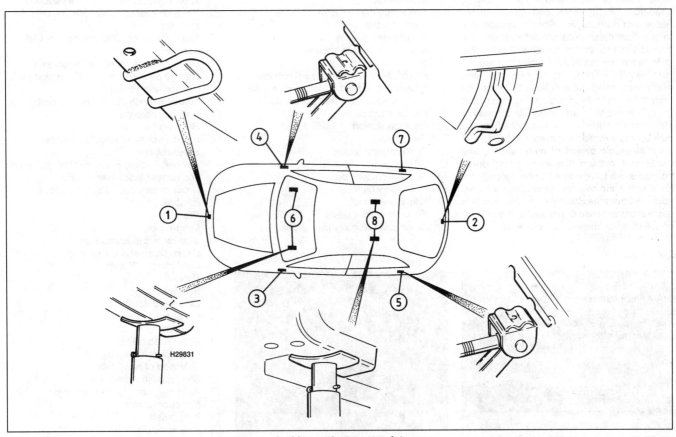

H29831

Jacking and support points

1 Front central jacking point
2 Rear central jacking point
3 Left-hand sill reinforced bracket - front
4 Right-hand sill reinforced bracket - front
5 Left-hand sill reinforced bracket - rear
6 Longitudinal members - front
7 Right-hand sill reinforced bracket - rear
8 Longitudinal members - rear

Radio/cassette Anti-theft system - precaution

The radio/cassette unit fitted as standard equipment by Rover is equipped with a built-in security code to deter thieves. If the power source to the unit is cut, the anti-theft system will activate. Even if the power source is immediately reconnected, the radio/cassette unit will not function until the correct security code has been entered. Therefore, if you do not know the correct security code for the unit, do not disconnect the battery negative lead, or remove the radio/cassette unit from the vehicle.

The procedure for reprogramming a unit that has been disconnected from its power supply varies from model to model. Consult the handbook supplied with the unit for specific details or refer to your Rover dealer.

Introduction

A selection of good tools is a fundamental requirement for anyone contemplating the maintenance and repair of a motor vehicle. For the owner who does not possess any, their purchase will prove a considerable expense, offsetting some of the savings made by doing-it-yourself. However, provided that the tools purchased meet the relevant national safety standards and are of good quality, they will last for many years and prove an extremely worthwhile investment.

To help the average owner to decide which tools are needed to carry out the various tasks detailed in this manual, we have compiled three lists of tools under the following headings: *Maintenance and minor repair, Repair and overhaul,* and *Special.* Newcomers to practical mechanics should start off with the *Maintenance and minor repair* tool kit, and confine themselves to the simpler jobs around the vehicle. Then, as confidence and experience grow, more difficult tasks can be undertaken, with extra tools being purchased as, and when, they are needed. In this way, a *Maintenance and minor repair* tool kit can be built up into a *Repair and overhaul* tool kit over a considerable period of time, without any major cash outlays. The experienced do-it-yourselfer will have a tool kit good enough for most repair and overhaul procedures, and will add tools from the *Special* category when it is felt that the expense is justified by the amount of use to which these tools will be put.

Maintenance and minor repair tool kit

The tools given in this list should be considered as a minimum requirement if routine maintenance, servicing and minor repair operations are to be undertaken. We recommend the purchase of combination spanners (ring one end, open-ended the other); although more expensive than open-ended ones, they do give the advantages of both types of spanner.

☐ *Combination spanners:*
  Metric - 8 to 19 mm inclusive
☐ *Adjustable spanner - 35 mm jaw (approx.)*
☐ *Spark plug spanner (with rubber insert) - petrol models*
☐ *Spark plug gap adjustment tool - petrol models*
☐ *Set of feeler gauges*
☐ *Brake bleed nipple spanner*
☐ *Screwdrivers:*
  Flat blade - 100 mm long x 6 mm dia
  Cross blade - 100 mm long x 6 mm dia
  Torx - various sizes (not all vehicles)
☐ *Combination pliers*
☐ *Hacksaw (junior)*
☐ *Tyre pump*
☐ *Tyre pressure gauge*
☐ *Oil can*
☐ *Oil filter removal tool*
☐ *Fine emery cloth*
☐ *Wire brush (small)*
☐ *Funnel (medium size)*
☐ *Sump drain plug key (not all vehicles)*

Repair and overhaul tool kit

These tools are virtually essential for anyone undertaking any major repairs to a motor vehicle, and are additional to those given in the *Maintenance and minor repair* list. Included in this list is a comprehensive set of sockets. Although these are expensive, they will be found invaluable as they are so versatile - particularly if various drives are included in the set. We recommend the half-inch square-drive type, as this can be used with most proprietary torque wrenches.

The tools in this list will sometimes need to be supplemented by tools from the *Special* list:

☐ *Sockets (or box spanners) to cover range in previous list (including Torx sockets)*
☐ *Reversible ratchet drive (for use with sockets)*
☐ *Extension piece, 250 mm (for use with sockets)*
☐ *Universal joint (for use with sockets)*
☐ *Flexible handle or sliding T "breaker bar" (for use with sockets)*
☐ *Torque wrench (for use with sockets)*
☐ *Self-locking grips*
☐ *Ball pein hammer*
☐ *Soft-faced mallet (plastic or rubber)*
☐ *Screwdrivers:*
  Flat blade - long & sturdy, short (chubby), and narrow (electrician's) types
  Cross blade - long & sturdy, and short (chubby) types
☐ *Pliers:*
  Long-nosed
  Side cutters (electrician's)
  Circlip (internal and external)
☐ *Cold chisel - 25 mm*
☐ *Scriber*
☐ *Scraper*
☐ *Centre-punch*
☐ *Pin punch*
☐ *Hacksaw*
☐ *Brake hose clamp*
☐ *Brake/clutch bleeding kit*
☐ *Selection of twist drills*
☐ *Steel rule/straight-edge*
☐ *Allen keys (inc. splined/Torx type)*
☐ *Selection of files*
☐ *Wire brush*
☐ *Axle stands*
☐ *Jack (strong trolley or hydraulic type)*
☐ *Light with extension lead*
☐ *Universal electrical multi-meter*

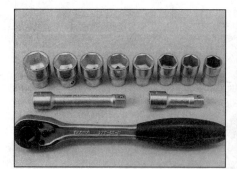

Sockets and reversible ratchet drive

Brake bleeding kit

Torx key, socket and bit

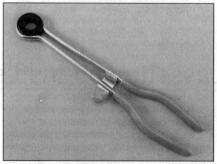

Hose clamp

Angular-tightening gauge

Special tools

The tools in this list are those which are not used regularly, are expensive to buy, or which need to be used in accordance with their manufacturers' instructions. Unless relatively difficult mechanical jobs are undertaken frequently, it will not be economic to buy many of these tools. Where this is the case, you could consider clubbing together with friends (or joining a motorists' club) to make a joint purchase, or borrowing the tools against a deposit from a local garage or tool hire specialist. It is worth noting that many of the larger DIY superstores now carry a large range of special tools for hire at modest rates.

The following list contains only those tools and instruments freely available to the public, and not those special tools produced by the vehicle manufacturer specifically for its dealer network. You will find occasional references to these manufacturers' special tools in the text of this manual. Generally, an alternative method of doing the job without the vehicle manufacturers' special tool is given. However, sometimes there is no alternative to using them. Where this is the case and the relevant tool cannot be bought or borrowed, you will have to entrust the work to a dealer.

- ☐ Angular-tightening gauge
- ☐ Valve spring compressor
- ☐ Valve grinding tool
- ☐ Piston ring compressor
- ☐ Piston ring removal/installation tool
- ☐ Cylinder bore hone
- ☐ Balljoint separator
- ☐ Coil spring compressors (where applicable)
- ☐ Two/three-legged hub and bearing puller
- ☐ Impact screwdriver
- ☐ Micrometer and/or vernier calipers
- ☐ Dial gauge
- ☐ Stroboscopic timing light
- ☐ Dwell angle meter/tachometer
- ☐ Fault code reader
- ☐ Cylinder compression gauge
- ☐ Hand-operated vacuum pump and gauge
- ☐ Clutch plate alignment set
- ☐ Brake shoe steady spring cup removal tool
- ☐ Bush and bearing removal/installation set
- ☐ Stud extractors
- ☐ Tap and die set
- ☐ Lifting tackle
- ☐ Trolley jack

Buying tools

Reputable motor accessory shops and superstores often offer excellent quality tools at discount prices, so it pays to shop around.

Remember, you don't have to buy the most expensive items on the shelf, but it is always advisable to steer clear of the very cheap tools. Beware of 'bargains' offered on market stalls or at car boot sales. There are plenty of good tools around at reasonable prices, but always aim to purchase items which meet the relevant national safety standards. If in doubt, ask the proprietor or manager of the shop for advice before making a purchase.

Care and maintenance of tools

Having purchased a reasonable tool kit, it is necessary to keep the tools in a clean and serviceable condition. After use, always wipe off any dirt, grease and metal particles using a clean, dry cloth, before putting the tools away. Never leave them lying around after they have been used. A simple tool rack on the garage or workshop wall for items such as screwdrivers and pliers is a good idea. Store all normal spanners and sockets in a metal box. Any measuring instruments, gauges, meters, etc, must be carefully stored where they cannot be damaged or become rusty.

Take a little care when tools are used. Hammer heads inevitably become marked, and screwdrivers lose the keen edge on their blades from time to time. A little timely attention with emery cloth or a file will soon restore items like this to a good finish.

Working facilities

Not to be forgotten when discussing tools is the workshop itself. If anything more than routine maintenance is to be carried out, a suitable working area becomes essential.

It is appreciated that many an owner-mechanic is forced by circumstances to remove an engine or similar item without the benefit of a garage or workshop. Having done this, any repairs should always be done under the cover of a roof.

Wherever possible, any dismantling should be done on a clean, flat workbench or table at a suitable working height.

Any workbench needs a vice; one with a jaw opening of 100 mm is suitable for most jobs. As mentioned previously, some clean dry storage space is also required for tools, as well as for any lubricants, cleaning fluids, touch-up paints etc, which become necessary.

Another item which may be required, and which has a much more general usage, is an electric drill with a chuck capacity of at least 8 mm. This, together with a good range of twist drills, is virtually essential for fitting accessories.

Last, but not least, always keep a supply of old newspapers and clean, lint-free rags available, and try to keep any working area as clean as possible.

Micrometers

Dial test indicator ("dial gauge")

Strap wrench

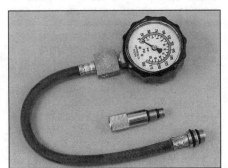

Compression tester

Fault code reader

This is a guide to getting your vehicle through the MOT test. Obviously it will not be possible to examine the vehicle to the same standard as the professional MOT tester. However, working through the following checks will enable you to identify any problem areas before submitting the vehicle for the test.

Where a testable component is in borderline condition, the tester has discretion in deciding whether to pass or fail it. The basis of such discretion is whether the tester would be happy for a close relative or friend to use the vehicle with the component in that condition. If the vehicle presented is clean and evidently well cared for, the tester may be more inclined to pass a borderline component than if the vehicle is scruffy and apparently neglected.

It has only been possible to summarise the test requirements here, based on the regulations in force at the time of printing. Test standards are becoming increasingly stringent, although there are some exemptions for older vehicles. For full details obtain a copy of the Haynes publication Pass the MOT! (available from stockists of Haynes manuals).

An assistant will be needed to help carry out some of these checks.

The checks have been sub-divided into four categories, as follows:

1 Checks carried out **FROM THE DRIVER'S SEAT**

2 Checks carried out **WITH THE VEHICLE ON THE GROUND**

3 Checks carried out **WITH THE VEHICLE RAISED AND THE WHEELS FREE TO TURN**

4 Checks carried out on **YOUR VEHICLE'S EXHAUST EMISSION SYSTEM**

1 Checks carried out **FROM THE DRIVER'S SEAT**

Handbrake

☐ Test the operation of the handbrake. Excessive travel (too many clicks) indicates incorrect brake or cable adjustment.

☐ Check that the handbrake cannot be released by tapping the lever sideways. Check the security of the lever mountings.

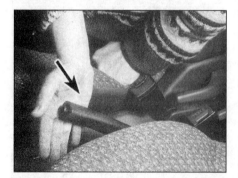

Footbrake

☐ Depress the brake pedal and check that it does not creep down to the floor, indicating a master cylinder fault. Release the pedal, wait a few seconds, then depress it again. If the pedal travels nearly to the floor before firm resistance is felt, brake adjustment or repair is necessary. If the pedal feels spongy, there is air in the hydraulic system which must be removed by bleeding.

☐ Check that the brake pedal is secure and in good condition. Check also for signs of fluid leaks on the pedal, floor or carpets, which would indicate failed seals in the brake master cylinder.

☐ Check the servo unit (when applicable) by operating the brake pedal several times, then keeping the pedal depressed and starting the engine. As the engine starts, the pedal will move down slightly. If not, the vacuum hose or the servo itself may be faulty.

Steering wheel and column

☐ Examine the steering wheel for fractures or looseness of the hub, spokes or rim.

☐ Move the steering wheel from side to side and then up and down. Check that the steering wheel is not loose on the column, indicating wear or a loose retaining nut. Continue moving the steering wheel as before, but also turn it slightly from left to right.

☐ Check that the steering wheel is not loose on the column, and that there is no abnormal

movement of the steering wheel, indicating wear in the column support bearings or couplings.

Windscreen and mirrors

☐ The windscreen must be free of cracks or other significant damage within the driver's field of view. (Small stone chips are acceptable.) Rear view mirrors must be secure, intact, and capable of being adjusted.

290mm

Seat belts and seats

Note: *The following checks are applicable to all seat belts, front and rear.*

☐ Examine the webbing of all the belts (including rear belts if fitted) for cuts, serious fraying or deterioration. Fasten and unfasten each belt to check the buckles. If applicable, check the retracting mechanism. Check the security of all seat belt mountings accessible from inside the vehicle.

☐ The front seats themselves must be securely attached and the backrests must lock in the upright position.

Doors

☐ Both front doors must be able to be opened and closed from outside and inside, and must latch securely when closed.

2 Checks carried out WITH THE VEHICLE ON THE GROUND

Vehicle identification

☐ Number plates must be in good condition, secure and legible, with letters and numbers correctly spaced – spacing at (A) should be twice that at (B).

☐ The VIN plate and/or homologation plate must be legible.

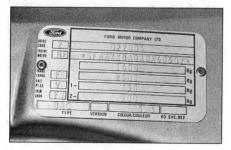

Electrical equipment

☐ Switch on the ignition and check the operation of the horn.

☐ Check the windscreen washers and wipers, examining the wiper blades; renew damaged or perished blades. Also check the operation of the stop-lights.

☐ Check the operation of the sidelights and number plate lights. The lenses and reflectors must be secure, clean and undamaged.

☐ Check the operation and alignment of the headlights. The headlight reflectors must not be tarnished and the lenses must be undamaged.

☐ Switch on the ignition and check the operation of the direction indicators (including the instrument panel tell-tale) and the hazard warning lights. Operation of the sidelights and stop-lights must not affect the indicators - if it does, the cause is usually a bad earth at the rear light cluster.

☐ Check the operation of the rear foglight(s), including the warning light on the instrument panel or in the switch.

Footbrake

☐ Examine the master cylinder, brake pipes and servo unit for leaks, loose mountings, corrosion or other damage.

☐ The fluid reservoir must be secure and the fluid level must be between the upper (A) and lower (B) markings.

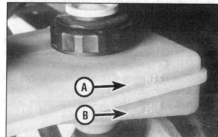

☐ Inspect both front brake flexible hoses for cracks or deterioration of the rubber. Turn the steering from lock to lock, and ensure that the hoses do not contact the wheel, tyre, or any part of the steering or suspension mechanism. With the brake pedal firmly depressed, check the hoses for bulges or leaks under pressure.

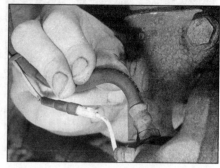

Steering and suspension

☐ Have your assistant turn the steering wheel from side to side slightly, up to the point where the steering gear just begins to transmit this movement to the roadwheels. Check for excessive free play between the steering wheel and the steering gear, indicating wear or insecurity of the steering column joints, the column-to-steering gear coupling, or the steering gear itself.

☐ Have your assistant turn the steering wheel more vigorously in each direction, so that the roadwheels just begin to turn. As this is done, examine all the steering joints, linkages, fittings and attachments. Renew any component that shows signs of wear or damage. On vehicles with power steering, check the security and condition of the steering pump, drivebelt and hoses.

☐ Check that the vehicle is standing level, and at approximately the correct ride height.

Shock absorbers

☐ Depress each corner of the vehicle in turn, then release it. The vehicle should rise and then settle in its normal position. If the vehicle continues to rise and fall, the shock absorber is defective. A shock absorber which has seized will also cause the vehicle to fail.

Exhaust system

☐ Start the engine. With your assistant holding a rag over the tailpipe, check the entire system for leaks. Repair or renew leaking sections.

3 Checks carried out **WITH THE VEHICLE RAISED AND THE WHEELS FREE TO TURN**

Jack up the front and rear of the vehicle, and securely support it on axle stands. Position the stands clear of the suspension assemblies. Ensure that the wheels are clear of the ground and that the steering can be turned from lock to lock.

Steering mechanism

☐ Have your assistant turn the steering from lock to lock. Check that the steering turns smoothly, and that no part of the steering mechanism, including a wheel or tyre, fouls any brake hose or pipe or any part of the body structure.

☐ Examine the steering rack rubber gaiters for damage or insecurity of the retaining clips. If power steering is fitted, check for signs of damage or leakage of the fluid hoses, pipes or connections. Also check for excessive stiffness or binding of the steering, a missing split pin or locking device, or severe corrosion of the body structure within 30 cm of any steering component attachment point.

Front and rear suspension and wheel bearings

☐ Starting at the front right-hand side, grasp the roadwheel at the 3 o'clock and 9 o'clock positions and shake it vigorously. Check for free play or insecurity at the wheel bearings, suspension balljoints, or suspension mountings, pivots and attachments.

☐ Now grasp the wheel at the 12 o'clock and 6 o'clock positions and repeat the previous inspection. Spin the wheel, and check for roughness or tightness of the front wheel bearing.

☐ If excess free play is suspected at a component pivot point, this can be confirmed by using a large screwdriver or similar tool and levering between the mounting and the component attachment. This will confirm whether the wear is in the pivot bush, its retaining bolt, or in the mounting itself (the bolt holes can often become elongated).

☐ Carry out all the above checks at the other front wheel, and then at both rear wheels.

Springs and shock absorbers

☐ Examine the suspension struts (when applicable) for serious fluid leakage, corrosion, or damage to the casing. Also check the security of the mounting points.

☐ If coil springs are fitted, check that the spring ends locate in their seats, and that the spring is not corroded, cracked or broken.

☐ If leaf springs are fitted, check that all leaves are intact, that the axle is securely attached to each spring, and that there is no deterioration of the spring eye mountings, bushes, and shackles.

☐ The same general checks apply to vehicles fitted with other suspension types, such as torsion bars, hydraulic displacer units, etc. Ensure that all mountings and attachments are secure, that there are no signs of excessive wear, corrosion or damage, and (on hydraulic types) that there are no fluid leaks or damaged pipes.

☐ Inspect the shock absorbers for signs of serious fluid leakage. Check for wear of the mounting bushes or attachments, or damage to the body of the unit.

Driveshafts (fwd vehicles only)

☐ Rotate each front wheel in turn and inspect the constant velocity joint gaiters for splits or damage. Also check that each driveshaft is straight and undamaged.

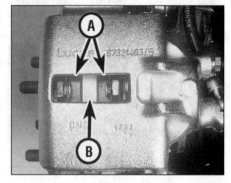

Braking system

☐ If possible without dismantling, check brake pad wear and disc condition. Ensure that the friction lining material has not worn excessively, (A) and that the discs are not fractured, pitted, scored or badly worn (B).

☐ Examine all the rigid brake pipes underneath the vehicle, and the flexible hose(s) at the rear. Look for corrosion, chafing or insecurity of the pipes, and for signs of bulging under pressure, chafing, splits or deterioration of the flexible hoses.

☐ Look for signs of fluid leaks at the brake calipers or on the brake backplates. Repair or renew leaking components.

☐ Slowly spin each wheel, while your assistant depresses and releases the footbrake. Ensure that each brake is operating and does not bind when the pedal is released.

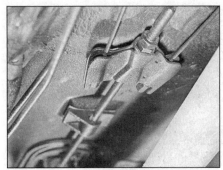

☐ Examine the handbrake mechanism, checking for frayed or broken cables, excessive corrosion, or wear or insecurity of the linkage. Check that the mechanism works on each relevant wheel, and releases fully, without binding.

☐ It is not possible to test brake efficiency without special equipment, but a road test can be carried out later to check that the vehicle pulls up in a straight line.

Fuel and exhaust systems

☐ Inspect the fuel tank (including the filler cap), fuel pipes, hoses and unions. All components must be secure and free from leaks.

☐ Examine the exhaust system over its entire length, checking for any damaged, broken or missing mountings, security of the retaining clamps and rust or corrosion.

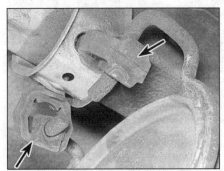

Wheels and tyres

☐ Examine the sidewalls and tread area of each tyre in turn. Check for cuts, tears, lumps, bulges, separation of the tread, and exposure of the ply or cord due to wear or damage. Check that the tyre bead is correctly seated on the wheel rim, that the valve is sound and

properly seated, and that the wheel is not distorted or damaged.

☐ Check that the tyres are of the correct size for the vehicle, that they are of the same size and type on each axle, and that the pressures are correct.

☐ Check the tyre tread depth. The legal minimum at the time of writing is 1.6 mm over at least three-quarters of the tread width. Abnormal tread wear may indicate incorrect front wheel alignment.

Body corrosion

☐ Check the condition of the entire vehicle structure for signs of corrosion in load-bearing areas. (These include chassis box sections, side sills, cross-members, pillars, and all suspension, steering, braking system and seat belt mountings and anchorages.) Any corrosion which has seriously reduced the thickness of a load-bearing area is likely to cause the vehicle to fail. In this case professional repairs are likely to be needed.

☐ Damage or corrosion which causes sharp or otherwise dangerous edges to be exposed will also cause the vehicle to fail.

4 Checks carried out on YOUR VEHICLE'S EXHAUST EMISSION SYSTEM

Petrol models

☐ Have the engine at normal operating temperature, and make sure that it is in good tune (ignition system in good order, air filter element clean, etc).

☐ Before any measurements are carried out, raise the engine speed to around 2500 rpm, and hold it at this speed for 20 seconds. Allow

the engine speed to return to idle, and watch for smoke emissions from the exhaust tailpipe. If the idle speed is obviously much too high, or if dense blue or clearly-visible black smoke comes from the tailpipe for more than 5 seconds, the vehicle will fail. As a rule of thumb, blue smoke signifies oil being burnt (engine wear) while black smoke signifies unburnt fuel (dirty air cleaner element, or other carburettor or fuel system fault).

☐ An exhaust gas analyser capable of measuring carbon monoxide (CO) and hydrocarbons (HC) is now needed. If such an instrument cannot be hired or borrowed, a local garage may agree to perform the check for a small fee.

CO emissions (mixture)

☐ At the time of writing, the maximum CO level at idle is 3.5% for vehicles first used after August 1986 and 4.5% for older vehicles. From January 1996 a much tighter limit (around 0.5%) applies to catalyst-equipped vehicles first used from August 1992. If the CO level cannot be reduced far enough to pass the test (and the fuel and ignition systems are otherwise in good condition) then the carburettor is badly worn, or there is some problem in the fuel injection system or catalytic converter (as applicable).

HC emissions

☐ With the CO emissions within limits, HC emissions must be no more than 1200 ppm (parts per million). If the vehicle fails this test at idle, it can be re-tested at around 2000 rpm; if the HC level is then 1200 ppm or less, this counts as a pass.

☐ Excessive HC emissions can be caused by oil being burnt, but they are more likely to be due to unburnt fuel.

Diesel models

☐ The only emission test applicable to Diesel engines is the measuring of exhaust smoke density. The test involves accelerating the engine several times to its maximum unloaded speed.

Note: *It is of the utmost importance that the engine timing belt is in good condition before the test is carried out.*

☐ Excessive smoke can be caused by a dirty air cleaner element. Otherwise, professional advice may be needed to find the cause.

Engine

- [ ] Engine fails to rotate when attempting to start
- [ ] Engine rotates, but will not start
- [ ] Engine difficult to start when cold
- [ ] Engine difficult to start when hot
- [ ] Starter motor noisy or excessively-rough in engagement
- [ ] Engine starts, but stops immediately
- [ ] Engine idles erratically
- [ ] Engine misfires at idle speed
- [ ] Engine misfires throughout the driving speed range
- [ ] Engine hesitates on acceleration
- [ ] Engine stalls
- [ ] Engine lacks power
- [ ] Engine backfires
- [ ] Oil pressure warning light illuminated with engine running
- [ ] Engine runs-on after switching off
- [ ] Engine noises

Cooling system

- [ ] Overheating
- [ ] Overcooling
- [ ] External coolant leakage
- [ ] Internal coolant leakage
- [ ] Corrosion

Fuel and exhaust systems

- [ ] Excessive fuel consumption
- [ ] Fuel leakage and/or fuel odour
- [ ] Excessive noise or fumes from the exhaust system

Clutch

- [ ] Pedal travels to floor - no pressure or very little resistance
- [ ] Clutch fails to disengage (unable to select gears)
- [ ] Clutch slips (engine speed increases, with no increase in vehicle speed)
- [ ] Judder as clutch is engaged
- [ ] Noise when depressing or releasing clutch pedal

Manual transmission

- [ ] Noisy in neutral with engine running
- [ ] Noisy in one particular gear
- [ ] Difficulty engaging gears
- [ ] Jumps out of gear
- [ ] Vibration
- [ ] Lubricant leaks

Automatic transmission

- [ ] Fluid leakage
- [ ] Transmission fluid brown, or has burned smell
- [ ] Engine will not start in any gear, or starts in gears other than Park or Neutral
- [ ] General gear selection problems
- [ ] Transmission slips, is noisy, or has no drive in forward or reverse gears

Driveshafts

- [ ] Vibration when accelerating or decelerating
- [ ] Clicking or knocking noise on turns (at slow speed on full-lock)

Braking system

- [ ] Vehicle pulls to one side under braking
- [ ] Noise (grinding or high-pitched squeal) when brakes applied
- [ ] Excessive brake pedal travel
- [ ] Brake pedal feels spongy when depressed
- [ ] Excessive brake pedal effort required to stop vehicle
- [ ] Judder felt through brake pedal or steering wheel when braking
- [ ] Pedal pulsates when braking hard
- [ ] Brakes binding
- [ ] Rear wheels locking under normal braking

Steering and suspension

- [ ] Vehicle pulls to one side
- [ ] Wheel wobble and vibration
- [ ] Excessive pitching and/or rolling around corners, or during braking
- [ ] Wandering or general instability
- [ ] Excessively-stiff steering
- [ ] Excessive play in steering
- [ ] Lack of power assistance
- [ ] Tyre wear excessive

Electrical system

- [ ] Battery will not hold a charge for more than a few days
- [ ] Ignition/no-charge warning light remains illuminated with engine running
- [ ] Ignition/no-charge warning light fails to come on
- [ ] Lights inoperative
- [ ] Instrument readings inaccurate or erratic
- [ ] Horn inoperative, or unsatisfactory in operation
- [ ] Windscreen/tailgate wipers inoperative, or unsatisfactory in operation
- [ ] Windscreen/tailgate washers inoperative, or unsatisfactory in operation
- [ ] Electric windows inoperative, or unsatisfactory in operation
- [ ] Central locking system inoperative, or unsatisfactory in operation

Introduction

The vehicle owner who does his or her own maintenance according to the recommended service schedules should not have to use this section of the manual very often. Modern component reliability is such that, provided those items subject to wear or deterioration are inspected or renewed at the specified intervals, sudden failure is comparatively rare. Faults do not usually just happen as a result of sudden failure, but develop over a period of time. Major mechanical failures in particular are usually preceded by characteristic symptoms over hundreds or even thousands of miles. Those components which do

occasionally fail without warning are often small and easily carried in the vehicle.

With any fault-finding, the first step is to decide where to begin investigations. This may be obvious, but some detective work may be necessary. The owner who makes half a dozen haphazard adjustments or replacements may be successful in curing a fault (or its symptoms), but will be none the wiser if the fault recurs, and ultimately may have spent more time and money than was necessary. A calm and logical approach will be found to be more satisfactory in the long run. Always take into account any warning

signs that may have been noticed in the period preceding the fault - power loss, high or low gauge readings, unusual smells, etc - and remember - failure of components such as fuses or spark plugs may only be pointers to some underlying fault.

The pages which follow provide an easy-reference guide to the more common problems which may occur during the operation of the vehicle. These problems and their possible causes are grouped under headings denoting various components or systems, such as Engine, Cooling system, etc. The Chapter and/or Section which deals with the problem is also shown in brackets. Whatever the fault, certain basic principles apply. These are as follows:

Verify the fault. This is simply a matter of being sure that you know what the symptoms are before starting work. This is particularly important if you are investigating a fault for someone else, who may not have described it very accurately.

Don't overlook the obvious. For example, if the vehicle won't start, is there fuel in the tank? (Don't take anyone else's word on this particular point, and don't trust the fuel gauge either!) If an electrical fault is indicated, look for loose or broken wires before digging out the test gear.

Cure the disease, not the symptom. Substituting a flat battery with a fully-charged one will get you off the hard shoulder, but if the underlying cause is not attended to, the new battery will go the same way. Similarly, changing oil-fouled spark plugs for a new set will get you moving again, but remember that the reason for the fouling (if it wasn't simply an incorrect grade of plug) will have to be established and corrected.

Don't take anything for granted. Particularly, don't forget that a "new" component may itself be defective (especially if it's been rattling around in the boot for months), and don't leave components out of a fault diagnosis sequence just because they are new or recently-fitted. When you do finally diagnose a difficult fault, you'll probably realise that all the evidence was there from the start.

Engine

Engine fails to rotate when attempting to start

- [ ] Battery terminal connections loose or corroded (see "*Weekly checks*").
- [ ] Battery discharged or faulty (Chapter 5A).
- [ ] Broken, loose or disconnected wiring in the starting circuit (Chapter 5A).
- [ ] Defective starter solenoid or switch (Chapter 5A).
- [ ] Defective starter motor (Chapter 5A).
- [ ] Starter pinion or flywheel ring gear teeth loose or broken (Chapters 2 and 5A).
- [ ] Engine earth strap broken or disconnected (Chapter 5A).

Engine rotates, but will not start

- [ ] Fuel tank empty.
- [ ] Battery discharged (engine rotates slowly) (Chapter 5A).
- [ ] Battery terminal connections loose or corroded (see "*Weekly checks*").
- [ ] Ignition components damp or damaged - petrol models (Chapters 1A and 5B).
- [ ] Broken, loose or disconnected wiring in the ignition circuit - petrol models (Chapters 1A and 5B).
- [ ] Worn, faulty or incorrectly-gapped spark plugs - petrol models (Chapter 1A).
- [ ] Preheating system faulty - diesel models (Chapter 5C).
- [ ] Fuel injection system faulty - petrol models (Chapter 4A).
- [ ] Stop solenoid faulty - diesel models (Chapter 4B).
- [ ] Air in fuel system - diesel models (Chapter 4B).
- [ ] Major mechanical failure (eg camshaft drive) (Chapter 2).

Engine difficult to start when cold

- [ ] Battery discharged (Chapter 5A).
- [ ] Battery terminal connections loose or corroded (see "*Weekly checks*").
- [ ] Worn, faulty or incorrectly-gapped spark plugs - petrol models (Chapter 1A).
- [ ] Preheating system faulty - diesel models (Chapter 5C).
- [ ] Fuel injection system faulty - petrol models (Chapter 4A).
- [ ] Other ignition system fault - petrol models (Chapters 1A and 5B).
- [ ] Low cylinder compressions (Chapter 2).

Engine difficult to start when hot

- [ ] Air filter element dirty or clogged (Chapter 1).
- [ ] Fuel injection system faulty - petrol models (Chapter 4A).
- [ ] Low cylinder compressions (Chapter 2).

Starter motor noisy or excessively-rough in engagement

- [ ] Starter pinion or flywheel ring gear teeth loose or broken (Chapters 2 and 5A).
- [ ] Starter motor mounting bolts loose or missing (Chapter 5A).
- [ ] Starter motor internal components worn or damaged (Chapter 5A).

Engine starts, but stops immediately

- [ ] Loose or faulty electrical connections in the ignition circuit - **petrol** models (Chapters 1A and 5B).
- [ ] Vacuum leak at the throttle body or inlet manifold - **petrol models** (Chapter 4A).
- [ ] Blocked injector/fuel injection system fault - petrol models (Chapter 4A).

Engine idles erratically

- [ ] Air filter element clogged (Chapter 1).
- [ ] Vacuum leak at the throttle body, inlet manifold or associated hoses - petrol models (Chapter 4A).
- [ ] Worn, faulty or incorrectly-gapped spark plugs - petrol models (Chapter 1A).
- [ ] Uneven or low cylinder compressions (Chapter 2).
- [ ] Camshaft lobes worn (Chapter 2).
- [ ] Timing belt/chain incorrectly fitted (Chapter 2).
- [ ] Blocked injector/fuel injection system fault - petrol models (Chapter 4A).
- [ ] Faulty injector(s) - diesel models (Chapter 4B).

Engine misfires at idle speed

- [ ] Worn, faulty or incorrectly-gapped spark plugs - petrol models (Chapter 1A).
- [ ] Faulty spark plug HT leads - petrol models (Chapter 1A).
- [ ] Vacuum leak at the throttle body, inlet manifold or associated hoses - petrol models (Chapter 4A).
- [ ] Blocked injector/fuel injection system fault - petrol models (Chapter 4A).
- [ ] Faulty injector(s) - diesel models (Chapter 4B).
- [ ] Uneven or low cylinder compressions (Chapter 2).
- [ ] Disconnected, leaking, or perished crankcase ventilation hoses (Chapter 4C).

Engine misfires throughout the driving speed range

- [ ] Fuel filter choked (Chapter 1).
- [ ] Fuel pump faulty, or delivery pressure low - petrol models (Chapter 4A).
- [ ] Fuel tank vent blocked, or fuel pipes restricted (Chapter 4).
- [ ] Vacuum leak at the throttle body, inlet manifold or associated hoses - petrol models (Chapter 4A).
- [ ] Worn, faulty or incorrectly-gapped spark plugs - petrol models (Chapter 1A).
- [ ] Faulty spark plug HT leads - petrol models (Chapter 1A).
- [ ] Faulty injector(s) - diesel models (Chapter 4B).
- [ ] Faulty ignition coil - petrol models (Chapter 5B).
- [ ] Uneven or low cylinder compressions (Chapter 2).
- [ ] Blocked injector/fuel injection system fault - petrol models (Chapter 4A).

Engine (continued)

Engine hesitates on acceleration

☐ Worn, faulty or incorrectly-gapped spark plugs - petrol models (Chapter 1A).
☐ Vacuum leak at the throttle body, inlet manifold or associated hoses - petrol models (Chapter 4A).
☐ Blocked injector/fuel injection system fault - petrol models (Chapter 4A).
☐ Faulty injector(s) - diesel models (Chapter 4B).

Engine stalls

☐ Vacuum leak at the throttle body, inlet manifold or associated hoses - petrol models (Chapter 4A).
☐ Fuel filter choked (Chapter 1).
☐ Fuel pump faulty, or delivery pressure low - petrol models (Chapter 4A).
☐ Fuel tank vent blocked, or fuel pipes restricted (Chapter 4).
☐ Blocked injector/fuel injection system fault - petrol models (Chapter 4A).
☐ Faulty injector(s) - diesel models (Chapter 4B).

Engine lacks power

☐ Timing belt/chain incorrectly fitted or tensioned (Chapter 2).
☐ Fuel filter choked (Chapter 1).
☐ Fuel pump faulty, or delivery pressure low - petrol models (Chapter 4A).
☐ Uneven or low cylinder compressions (Chapter 2).
☐ Worn, faulty or incorrectly-gapped spark plugs - petrol models (Chapter 1A).
☐ Vacuum leak at the throttle body, inlet manifold or associated hoses - petrol models (Chapter 4A).
☐ Blocked injector/fuel injection system fault - petrol models (Chapter 4A).
☐ Faulty injector(s) - diesel models (Chapter 4B).
☐ Injection pump timing incorrect - diesel models (Chapter 4B).
☐ Air trapped in fuel system - diesel models (Chapter 4B).
☐ Brakes binding (Chapters 1 and 9).
☐ Clutch slipping (Chapter 6).

Engine backfires

☐ Timing belt/chain incorrectly fitted or tensioned (Chapter 2).
☐ Vacuum leak at the throttle body, inlet manifold or associated hoses - petrol models (Chapter 4A).
☐ Blocked injector/fuel injection system fault - petrol models (Chapter 4A).

Oil pressure warning light illuminated with engine running

☐ Low oil level, or incorrect oil grade (see "Weekly checks").
☐ Faulty oil pressure sensor (Chapter 5A).
☐ Worn engine bearings and/or oil pump (Chapter 2).
☐ High engine operating temperature (Chapter 3).
☐ Oil pressure relief valve defective (Chapter 2).
☐ Oil pick-up strainer clogged (Chapter 2).

Engine runs-on after switching off

☐ Excessive carbon build-up in engine (Chapter 2).
☐ High engine operating temperature (Chapter 3).
☐ Fuel injection system faulty - petrol models (Chapter 4A).
☐ Faulty stop solenoid - diesel models (Chapter 4B).

Engine noises

Pre-ignition (pinking) or knocking during acceleration or under load

☐ Ignition timing incorrect/ignition system fault - petrol models (Chapters 1A and 5B).
☐ Incorrect grade of spark plug - petrol models (Chapter 1A).
☐ Incorrect grade of fuel (Chapter 4).
☐ Vacuum leak at the throttle body, inlet manifold or associated hoses - petrol models (Chapter 4A).
☐ Excessive carbon build-up in engine (Chapter 2).
☐ Blocked injector/injection system fault - petrol models (Chapter 4A).

Whistling or wheezing noises

☐ Leaking inlet manifold or throttle body gasket - petrol models (Chapter 4A).
☐ Leaking exhaust manifold gasket or pipe-to-manifold joint (Chapter 4).
☐ Leaking vacuum hose (Chapters 4, 5 and 9).
☐ Blowing cylinder head gasket (Chapter 2).

Tapping or rattling noises

☐ Worn valve gear or camshaft (Chapter 2).
☐ Ancillary component fault (coolant pump, alternator, etc) (Chapters 3, 5, etc).

Knocking or thumping noises

☐ Worn big-end bearings (regular heavy knocking, perhaps less under load) (Chapter 2).
☐ Worn main bearings (rumbling and knocking, perhaps worsening under load) (Chapter 2).
☐ Piston slap (most noticeable when cold) (Chapter 2).
☐ Ancillary component fault (coolant pump, alternator, etc) (Chapters 3, 5, etc).

Cooling system

Overheating

☐ Insufficient coolant in system (see "Weekly checks").
☐ Thermostat faulty (Chapter 3).
☐ Radiator core blocked, or grille restricted (Chapter 3).
☐ Electric cooling fan or thermostatic switch faulty (Chapter 3).
☐ Inaccurate temperature gauge sender unit (Chapter 3).
☐ Airlock in cooling system (Chapter 3).
☐ Expansion tank pressure cap faulty (Chapter 3).

Overcooling

☐ Thermostat faulty (Chapter 3).
☐ Inaccurate temperature gauge sender unit (Chapter 3).

External coolant leakage

☐ Deteriorated or damaged hoses or hose clips (Chapter 1).
☐ Radiator core or heater matrix leaking (Chapter 3).

☐ Pressure cap faulty (Chapter 3).
☐ Coolant pump internal seal leaking (Chapter 3).
☐ Coolant pump-to-block seal leaking (Chapter 3).
☐ Boiling due to overheating (Chapter 3).
☐ Core plug leaking (Chapter 2).

Internal coolant leakage

☐ Leaking cylinder head gasket (Chapter 2).
☐ Cracked cylinder head or cylinder block (Chapter 2).

Corrosion

☐ Infrequent draining and flushing (Chapter 1).
☐ Incorrect coolant mixture or inappropriate coolant type (see "Weekly checks").

Fuel and exhaust systems

Excessive fuel consumption

- ☐ Air filter element dirty or clogged (Chapter 1).
- ☐ Fuel injection system faulty - petrol models (Chapter 4A).
- ☐ Faulty injector(s) - diesel models (Chapter 4B).
- ☐ Ignition timing incorrect/ignition system faulty - petrol models (Chapters 1A and 5B).
- ☐ Tyres under-inflated (see "Weekly checks").

Fuel leakage and/or fuel odour

- ☐ Damaged or corroded fuel tank, pipes or connections (Chapter 4).

Excessive noise or fumes from the exhaust system

- ☐ Leaking exhaust system or manifold joints (Chapters 1 and 4).
- ☐ Leaking, corroded or damaged silencers or pipe (Chapters 1 and 4).
- ☐ Broken mountings causing body or suspension contact (Chapter 1).

Clutch

Pedal travels to floor - no pressure or very little resistance

- ☐ Broken clutch cable (Chapter 6).
- ☐ Broken clutch release bearing or arm (Chapter 6).
- ☐ Broken diaphragm spring in clutch pressure plate (Chapter 6).

Clutch fails to disengage (unable to select gears)

- ☐ Faulty clutch cable (Chapter 6).
- ☐ Clutch disc sticking on gearbox input shaft splines (Chapter 6).
- ☐ Clutch disc sticking to flywheel or pressure plate (Chapter 6).
- ☐ Faulty pressure plate assembly (Chapter 6).
- ☐ Clutch release mechanism worn or incorrectly assembled (Chapter 6).

Clutch slips (engine speed increases, with no increase in vehicle speed)

- ☐ Worn clutch cable (Chapter 6).
- ☐ Clutch disc linings excessively worn (Chapter 6).
- ☐ Clutch disc linings contaminated with oil or grease (Chapter 6).
- ☐ Faulty pressure plate or weak diaphragm spring (Chapter 6).

Judder as clutch is engaged

- ☐ Clutch disc linings contaminated with oil or grease (Chapter 6).
- ☐ Clutch disc linings excessively worn (Chapter 6).
- ☐ Faulty or distorted pressure plate or diaphragm spring (Chapter 6).
- ☐ Worn or loose engine or gearbox mountings (Chapter 2).
- ☐ Clutch disc hub or gearbox input shaft splines worn (Chapter 6).

Noise when depressing or releasing clutch pedal

- ☐ Worn clutch release bearing (Chapter 6).
- ☐ Worn clutch cable (Chapter 6)
- ☐ Worn or dry clutch pedal pivot (Chapter 6).
- ☐ Faulty pressure plate assembly (Chapter 6).
- ☐ Pressure plate diaphragm spring broken (Chapter 6).
- ☐ Broken clutch friction plate cushioning springs (Chapter 6).

Manual transmission

Noisy in neutral with engine running

- ☐ Input shaft bearings worn (noise apparent with clutch pedal released, but not when depressed) (Chapter 7A).*
- ☐ Clutch release bearing worn (noise apparent with clutch pedal depressed, possibly less when released) (Chapter 6).

Noisy in one particular gear

- ☐ Worn, damaged or chipped gear teeth (Chapter 7A).*

Difficulty engaging gears

- ☐ Clutch faulty (Chapter 6).
- ☐ Worn or damaged gear linkage (Chapter 7A).
- ☐ Worn synchroniser units (Chapter 7A).*

Jumps out of gear

- ☐ Worn or damaged gear linkage (Chapter 7A).

- ☐ Worn synchroniser units (Chapter 7A).*
- ☐ Worn selector forks (Chapter 7A).*

Vibration

- ☐ Lack of oil (Chapter 1).
- ☐ Worn bearings (Chapter 7A).*

Lubricant leaks

- ☐ Leaking oil seal (Chapter 7A).
- ☐ Leaking housing joint (Chapter 7A).*
- ☐ Leaking input shaft oil seal (Chapter 7A).*

*Although the corrective action necessary to remedy the symptoms described is beyond the scope of the home mechanic, the above information should be helpful in isolating the cause of the condition, so that the owner can communicate clearly with a professional mechanic.

Automatic transmission

Note: *Due to the complexity of the automatic transmission, it is difficult for the home mechanic to properly diagnose and service this unit. For problems other than the following, the vehicle should be taken to a dealer service department or automatic transmission specialist. Do not be too hasty in removing the transmission if a fault is suspected, as most of the testing is carried out with the unit still fitted.*

Fluid leakage

☐ Automatic transmission fluid is usually dark in colour. Fluid leaks should not be confused with engine oil, which can easily be blown onto the transmission by airflow.

☐ To determine the source of a leak, first remove all built-up dirt and grime from the transmission housing and surrounding areas using a degreasing agent, or by steam-cleaning. Drive the vehicle at low speed, so airflow will not blow the leak far from its source. Raise and support the vehicle, and determine where the leak is coming from. The following are common areas of leakage:

a) *Oil pan (Chapter 1A and 7B).*
b) *Dipstick tube (Chapter 1A and 7B).*
c) *Transmission-to-fluid cooler pipes/unions (Chapter 7B).*

Transmission fluid brown, or has burned smell

☐ Transmission fluid level low, or fluid in need of renewal (Chapter 1A and 7B).

Engine will not start in any gear, or starts in gears other than Park or Neutral

☐ Incorrect starter/inhibitor switch adjustment (Chapter 7B).
☐ Incorrect selector cable adjustment (Chapter 7B).

General gear selection problems

☐ Chapter 7B deals with checking and adjusting the selector cable on automatic transmissions. The following are common problems which may be caused by a poorly-adjusted cable:

a) *Engine starting in gears other than Park or Neutral.*
b) *Indicator panel indicating a gear other than the one actually being used.*
c) *Vehicle moves when in Park or Neutral.*
d) *Poor gear shift quality or erratic gear changes.*

☐ Refer to Chapter 7B for the selector cable adjustment procedure.

Transmission slips, is noisy, or has no drive in forward or reverse gears

☐ There are many probable causes for the above problems, but the home mechanic should be concerned with only one possibility - fluid level. Before taking the vehicle to a dealer or transmission specialist, check the fluid level and condition of the fluid as described in Chapter 1A, or 7B, as applicable. Correct the fluid level as necessary, or change the fluid and filter if needed. If the problem persists, professional help will be necessary.

Driveshafts

Vibration when accelerating or decelerating

☐ Worn inner constant velocity joint (Chapter 8).
☐ Bent or distorted driveshaft (Chapter 8).
☐ Worn intermediate bearing - where applicable (Chapter 8).

Clicking or knocking noise on turns (at slow speed on full-lock)

☐ Worn outer constant velocity joint (Chapter 8).
☐ Lack of constant velocity joint lubricant, possibly due to damaged gaiter (Chapter 8).

Braking system

Note: *Before assuming that a brake problem exists, make sure that the tyres are in good condition and correctly inflated, that the front wheel alignment is correct, and that the vehicle is not loaded with weight in an unequal manner. Apart from checking the condition of all pipe and hose connections, any faults occurring on the anti-lock braking system should be referred to a Renault dealer for diagnosis.*

Vehicle pulls to one side under braking

☐ Worn, defective, damaged or contaminated front or rear brake pads/shoes on one side (Chapters 1 and 9).
☐ Seized or partially-seized front or rear brake caliper/wheel cylinder piston (Chapter 9).
☐ A mixture of brake pad/shoe lining materials fitted between sides (Chapter 9).
☐ Brake caliper or rear brake backplate mounting bolts loose (Chapter 9).
☐ Worn or damaged steering or suspension components (Chapters 1 and 10).

Noise (grinding or high-pitched squeal) when brakes applied

☐ Brake pad/shoe friction lining material worn down to metal backing (Chapters 1 and 9).
☐ Excessive corrosion of brake disc or drum - may be apparent after the vehicle has been standing for some time (Chapters 1 and 9).
☐ Foreign object (stone chipping, etc) trapped between brake disc and shield (Chapters 1 and 9).

Excessive brake pedal travel

☐ Faulty rear drum brake self-adjust mechanism (Chapter 9).
☐ Faulty master cylinder (Chapter 9).
☐ Air in hydraulic system (Chapter 9).
☐ Faulty vacuum servo unit (Chapter 9).
☐ Faulty vacuum pump - diesel models (Chapter 9).

Brake pedal feels spongy when depressed

☐ Air in hydraulic system (Chapter 9).
☐ Deteriorated flexible rubber brake hoses (Chapters 1 and 9).
☐ Master cylinder mountings loose (Chapter 9).
☐ Faulty master cylinder (Chapter 9).

Braking system (continued)

Excessive brake pedal effort required to stop vehicle

☐ Faulty vacuum servo unit (Chapter 9).
☐ Disconnected, damaged or insecure brake servo vacuum hose (Chapters 1 and 9).
☐ Faulty vacuum pump - diesel models (Chapter 9).
☐ Primary or secondary hydraulic circuit failure (Chapter 9).
☐ Seized brake caliper or wheel cylinder piston(s) (Chapter 9).
☐ Brake pads/shoes incorrectly fitted (Chapter 9).
☐ Incorrect grade of brake pads/shoes fitted (Chapter 9).
☐ Brake pads/shoe linings contaminated (Chapter 9).

Judder felt through brake pedal or steering wheel when braking

☐ Excessive run-out or distortion of brake disc(s) or drum(s) (Chapter 9).

☐ Brake pad/shoe linings worn (Chapters 1 and 9).
☐ Brake caliper or rear brake backplate mounting bolts loose (Chapter 9).
☐ Wear in suspension or steering components or mountings (Chapters 1 and 10).

Pedal pulsates when braking hard

☐ Normal feature of ABS - no fault

Brakes binding

☐ Seized brake caliper/wheel cylinder piston(s) (Chapter 9).
☐ Incorrectly-adjusted handbrake mechanism (Chapter 9).
☐ Faulty master cylinder (Chapter 9).

Rear wheels locking under normal braking

☐ Rear brake pad/shoe linings contaminated (Chapters 1 and 9).
☐ Rear brake discs/drums warped (Chapters 1 and 9).

Steering and suspension

Note: *Before diagnosing suspension or steering faults, be sure that the trouble is not due to incorrect tyre pressures, mixtures of tyre types, or binding brakes.*

Vehicle pulls to one side

☐ Defective tyre (see *"Weekly checks"*).
☐ Excessive wear in suspension or steering components (Chapters 1 and 10).
☐ Incorrect front wheel alignment (Chapter 10).
☐ Accident damage to steering or suspension components (Chapters 1 and 10).

Wheel wobble and vibration

☐ Front roadwheels out of balance (vibration felt mainly through the steering wheel) (Chapter 10).
☐ Rear roadwheels out of balance (vibration felt throughout the vehicle) (Chapter 10).
☐ Roadwheels damaged or distorted (Chapter 10).
☐ Faulty or damaged tyre (see *"Weekly checks"*).
☐ Worn steering or suspension joints, bushes or components (Chapters 1 and 10).
☐ Wheel bolts loose (Chapter 1 and 10).

Excessive pitching and/or rolling around corners, or during braking

☐ Defective shock absorbers (Chapters 1 and 10).
☐ Broken or weak coil spring and/or suspension component (Chapters 1 and 10).
☐ Worn or damaged anti-roll bar or mountings (Chapter 10).

Wandering or general instability

☐ Incorrect front wheel alignment (Chapter 10).
☐ Worn steering or suspension joints, bushes or components (Chapters 1 and 10).
☐ Roadwheels out of balance (Chapter 10).
☐ Faulty or damaged tyre (see *"Weekly checks"*).
☐ Wheel bolts loose (Chapter 10).
☐ Defective shock absorbers (Chapters 1 and 10).

Excessively-stiff steering

☐ Seized track rod end balljoint or suspension balljoint (Chapters 1 and 10).

☐ Broken or incorrectly adjusted auxiliary drivebelt (Chapter 1).
☐ Incorrect front wheel alignment (Chapter 10).
☐ Steering gear damaged (Chapter 10).

Excessive play in steering

☐ Worn steering column universal joint(s) (Chapter 10).
☐ Worn steering track rod end balljoints (Chapters 1 and 10).
☐ Worn steering gear (Chapter 10).
☐ Worn steering or suspension joints, bushes or components (Chapters 1 and 10).

Lack of power assistance

☐ Broken or incorrectly-adjusted auxiliary drivebelt (Chapter 1).
☐ Incorrect power steering fluid level (see *"Weekly checks"*).
☐ Restriction in power steering fluid hoses (Chapter 10).
☐ Faulty power steering pump (Chapter 10).
☐ Faulty steering gear (Chapter 10).

Tyre wear excessive

Tyres worn on inside or outside edges

☐ Tyres under-inflated (wear on both edges) (see *"Weekly checks"*).
☐ Incorrect camber or castor angles (wear on one edge only) (Chapter 10).
☐ Worn steering or suspension joints, bushes or components (Chapters 1 and 10).
☐ Excessively-hard cornering.
☐ Accident damage.

Tyre treads exhibit feathered edges

☐ Incorrect toe setting (Chapter 10).

Tyres worn in centre of tread

☐ Tyres over-inflated (see *"Weekly checks"*).

Tyres worn on inside and outside edges

☐ Tyres under-inflated (see *"Weekly checks"*).
☐ Worn shock absorbers (Chapter 10).

Tyres worn unevenly

☐ Tyres/wheels out of balance (see *"Weekly checks"*).
☐ Excessive wheel or tyre run-out (Chapter 10).
☐ Worn shock absorbers (Chapters 1 and 10).
☐ Faulty tyre (see *"Weekly checks"*).

Electrical system

Note: *For problems associated with the starting system, refer to the faults listed under 'Engine' earlier in this Section.*

Battery will not hold a charge more than a few days

☐ Battery defective internally (Chapter 5A).
☐ Battery electrolyte level low - where applicable (see *"Weekly checks"*).
☐ Battery terminal connections loose or corroded (see *"Weekly checks"*).
☐ Auxiliary drivebelt worn - or incorrectly adjusted, where applicable (Chapter 1).
☐ Alternator not charging at correct output (Chapter 5A).
☐ Alternator or voltage regulator faulty (Chapter 5A).
☐ Short-circuit causing continual battery drain (Chapters 5 and 12).

Ignition/no-charge warning light remains illuminated with engine running

☐ Auxiliary drivebelt broken, worn, or incorrectly adjusted (Chapter 1).
☐ Internal fault in alternator or voltage regulator (Chapter 5A).
☐ Broken, disconnected, or loose wiring in charging circuit (Chapter 5A).

Ignition/no-charge warning light fails to come on

☐ Warning light bulb blown (Chapter 12).
☐ Broken, disconnected, or loose wiring in warning light circuit (Chapter 12).
☐ Alternator faulty (Chapter 5A).

Lights inoperative

☐ Bulb blown (Chapter 12).
☐ Corrosion of bulb or bulbholder contacts (Chapter 12).
☐ Blown fuse (Chapter 12).
☐ Faulty relay (Chapter 12).
☐ Broken, loose, or disconnected wiring (Chapter 12).
☐ Faulty switch (Chapter 12).

Instrument readings inaccurate or erratic

Instrument readings increase with engine speed

☐ Faulty voltage regulator (Chapter 12).

Fuel or temperature gauges give no reading

☐ Faulty gauge sender unit (Chapters 3 and 4).
☐ Wiring open-circuit (Chapter 12).
☐ Faulty gauge (Chapter 12).

Fuel or temperature gauges give continuous maximum reading

☐ Faulty gauge sender unit (Chapters 3 and 4).
☐ Wiring short-circuit (Chapter 12).
☐ Faulty gauge (Chapter 12).

Horn inoperative, or unsatisfactory in operation

Horn operates all the time

☐ Horn contacts permanently bridged or horn push stuck down (Chapter 12).

Horn fails to operate

☐ Blown fuse (Chapter 12).
☐ Cable or connections loose, broken or disconnected (Chapter 12).
☐ Faulty horn (Chapter 12).

Horn emits intermittent or unsatisfactory sound

☐ Cable connections loose (Chapter 12).
☐ Horn mountings loose (Chapter 12).
☐ Faulty horn (Chapter 12).

Windscreen/tailgate wipers inoperative, or unsatisfactory in operation

Wipers fail to operate, or operate very slowly

☐ Wiper blades stuck to screen, or linkage seized or binding (see *"Weekly checks"* and Chapter 12).

☐ Blown fuse (Chapter 12).
☐ Cable or connections loose, broken or disconnected (Chapter 12).
☐ Faulty relay (Chapter 12).
☐ Faulty wiper motor (Chapter 12).

Wiper blades sweep over too large or too small an area of the glass

☐ Wiper arms incorrectly positioned on spindles (Chapter 12).
☐ Excessive wear of wiper linkage (Chapter 12).
☐ Wiper motor or linkage mountings loose or insecure (Chapter 12).

Wiper blades fail to clean the glass effectively

☐ Wiper blade rubbers worn or perished (see *"Weekly checks"*).
☐ Wiper arm tension springs broken, or arm pivots seized (Chapter 12).
☐ Insufficient windscreen washer additive to adequately remove road film (see *"Weekly checks"*).

Windscreen/tailgate washers inoperative, or unsatisfactory in operation

One or more washer jets inoperative

☐ Blocked washer jet (Chapter 12).
☐ Disconnected, kinked or restricted fluid hose (Chapter 12).
☐ Insufficient fluid in washer reservoir (see *"Weekly checks"*).

Washer pump fails to operate

☐ Broken or disconnected wiring or connections (Chapter 12).
☐ Blown fuse (Chapter 12).
☐ Faulty washer switch (Chapter 12).
☐ Faulty washer pump (Chapter 12).

Washer pump runs for some time before fluid is emitted from jets

☐ Faulty one-way valve in fluid supply hose (Chapter 12).

Electric windows inoperative, or unsatisfactory in operation

Window glass will only move in one direction

☐ Faulty switch (Chapter 12).

Window glass slow to move

☐ Regulator seized or damaged, or in need of lubrication (Chapter 11).
☐ Door internal components or trim fouling regulator (Chapter 11).
☐ Faulty motor (Chapter 11).

Window glass fails to move

☐ Blown fuse (Chapter 12).
☐ Faulty relay (Chapter 12).
☐ Broken or disconnected wiring or connections (Chapter 12).
☐ Faulty motor (Chapter 12).

Central locking system inoperative, or unsatisfactory in operation

Complete system failure

☐ Blown fuse (Chapter 12).
☐ Faulty relay (Chapter 12).
☐ Broken or disconnected wiring or connections (Chapter 12).
☐ Faulty motor (Chapter 11).

Latch locks but will not unlock, or unlocks but will not lock

☐ Faulty switch (Chapter 12).
☐ Broken or disconnected latch operating rods or levers (Chapter 11).
☐ Faulty relay (Chapter 12).
☐ Faulty motor (Chapter 11).

One solenoid/motor fails to operate

☐ Broken or disconnected wiring or connections (Chapter 12).
☐ Faulty motor (Chapter 11).
☐ Broken, binding or disconnected lock operating rods or levers (Chapter 11).
☐ Fault in door lock (Chapter 11).

A

ABS (Anti-lock brake system) A system, usually electronically controlled, that senses incipient wheel lockup during braking and relieves hydraulic pressure at wheels that are about to skid.

Air bag An inflatable bag hidden in the steering wheel (driver's side) or the dash or glovebox (passenger side). In a head-on collision, the bags inflate, preventing the driver and front passenger from being thrown forward into the steering wheel or windscreen.

Air cleaner A metal or plastic housing, containing a filter element, which removes dust and dirt from the air being drawn into the engine.

Air filter element The actual filter in an air cleaner system, usually manufactured from pleated paper and requiring renewal at regular intervals.

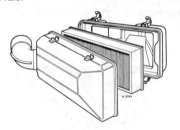

Air filter

Allen key A hexagonal wrench which fits into a recessed hexagonal hole.

Alligator clip A long-nosed spring-loaded metal clip with meshing teeth. Used to make temporary electrical connections.

Alternator A component in the electrical system which converts mechanical energy from a drivebelt into electrical energy to charge the battery and to operate the starting system, ignition system and electrical accessories.

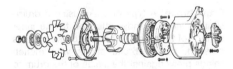

Alternator (exploded view)

Ampere (amp) A unit of measurement for the flow of electric current. One amp is the amount of current produced by one volt acting through a resistance of one ohm.

Anaerobic sealer A substance used to prevent bolts and screws from loosening. Anaerobic means that it does not require oxygen for activation. The Loctite brand is widely used.

Antifreeze A substance (usually ethylene glycol) mixed with water, and added to a vehicle's cooling system, to prevent freezing of the coolant in winter. Antifreeze also contains chemicals to inhibit corrosion and the formation of rust and other deposits that

would tend to clog the radiator and coolant passages and reduce cooling efficiency.

Anti-seize compound A coating that reduces the risk of seizing on fasteners that are subjected to high temperatures, such as exhaust manifold bolts and nuts.

Anti-seize compound

Asbestos A natural fibrous mineral with great heat resistance, commonly used in the composition of brake friction materials. Asbestos is a health hazard and the dust created by brake systems should never be inhaled or ingested.

Axle A shaft on which a wheel revolves, or which revolves with a wheel. Also, a solid beam that connects the two wheels at one end of the vehicle. An axle which also transmits power to the wheels is known as a live axle.

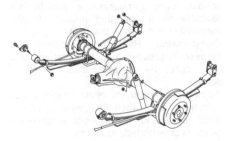

Axle assembly

Axleshaft A single rotating shaft, on either side of the differential, which delivers power from the final drive assembly to the drive wheels. Also called a driveshaft or a halfshaft.

B

Ball bearing An anti-friction bearing consisting of a hardened inner and outer race with hardened steel balls between two races.

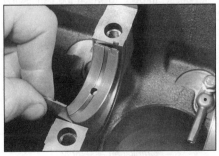

Bearing

Bearing The curved surface on a shaft or in a bore, or the part assembled into either, that permits relative motion between them with minimum wear and friction.

Big-end bearing The bearing in the end of the connecting rod that's attached to the crankshaft.

Bleed nipple A valve on a brake wheel cylinder, caliper or other hydraulic component that is opened to purge the hydraulic system of air. Also called a bleed screw.

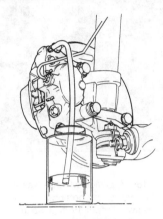

Brake bleeding

Brake bleeding Procedure for removing air from lines of a hydraulic brake system.

Brake disc The component of a disc brake that rotates with the wheels.

Brake drum The component of a drum brake that rotates with the wheels.

Brake linings The friction material which contacts the brake disc or drum to retard the vehicle's speed. The linings are bonded or riveted to the brake pads or shoes.

Brake pads The replaceable friction pads that pinch the brake disc when the brakes are applied. Brake pads consist of a friction material bonded or riveted to a rigid backing plate.

Brake shoe The crescent-shaped carrier to which the brake linings are mounted and which forces the lining against the rotating drum during braking.

Braking systems For more information on braking systems, consult the *Haynes Automotive Brake Manual*.

Breaker bar A long socket wrench handle providing greater leverage.

Bulkhead The insulated partition between the engine and the passenger compartment.

C

Caliper The non-rotating part of a disc-brake assembly that straddles the disc and carries the brake pads. The caliper also contains the hydraulic components that cause the pads to pinch the disc when the brakes are applied. A caliper is also a measuring tool that can be set to measure inside or outside dimensions of an object.

Camshaft A rotating shaft on which a series of cam lobes operate the valve mechanisms. The camshaft may be driven by gears, by sprockets and chain or by sprockets and a belt.

Canister A container in an evaporative emission control system; contains activated charcoal granules to trap vapours from the fuel system.

Canister

Carburettor A device which mixes fuel with air in the proper proportions to provide a desired power output from a spark ignition internal combustion engine.

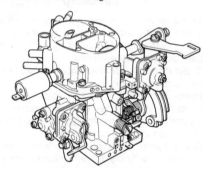

Carburettor

Castellated Resembling the parapets along the top of a castle wall. For example, a castellated balljoint stud nut.

Castellated nut

Castor In wheel alignment, the backward or forward tilt of the steering axis. Castor is positive when the steering axis is inclined rearward at the top.

Catalytic converter A silencer-like device in the exhaust system which converts certain pollutants in the exhaust gases into less harmful substances.

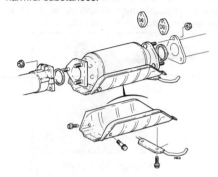

Catalytic converter

Circlip A ring-shaped clip used to prevent endwise movement of cylindrical parts and shafts. An internal circlip is installed in a groove in a housing; an external circlip fits into a groove on the outside of a cylindrical piece such as a shaft.

Clearance The amount of space between two parts. For example, between a piston and a cylinder, between a bearing and a journal, etc.

Coil spring A spiral of elastic steel found in various sizes throughout a vehicle, for example as a springing medium in the suspension and in the valve train.

Compression Reduction in volume, and increase in pressure and temperature, of a gas, caused by squeezing it into a smaller space.

Compression ratio The relationship between cylinder volume when the piston is at top dead centre and cylinder volume when the piston is at bottom dead centre.

Constant velocity (CV) joint A type of universal joint that cancels out vibrations caused by driving power being transmitted through an angle.

Core plug A disc or cup-shaped metal device inserted in a hole in a casting through which core was removed when the casting was formed. Also known as a freeze plug or expansion plug.

Crankcase The lower part of the engine block in which the crankshaft rotates.

Crankshaft The main rotating member, or shaft, running the length of the crankcase, with offset "throws" to which the connecting rods are attached.

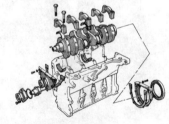

Crankshaft assembly

Crocodile clip See Alligator clip

D

Diagnostic code Code numbers obtained by accessing the diagnostic mode of an engine management computer. This code can be used to determine the area in the system where a malfunction may be located.

Disc brake A brake design incorporating a rotating disc onto which brake pads are squeezed. The resulting friction converts the energy of a moving vehicle into heat.

Double-overhead cam (DOHC) An engine that uses two overhead camshafts, usually one for the intake valves and one for the exhaust valves.

Drivebelt(s) The belt(s) used to drive accessories such as the alternator, water pump, power steering pump, air conditioning compressor, etc. off the crankshaft pulley.

Accessory drivebelts

Driveshaft Any shaft used to transmit motion. Commonly used when referring to the axleshafts on a front wheel drive vehicle.

Driveshaft

Drum brake A type of brake using a drum-shaped metal cylinder attached to the inner surface of the wheel. When the brake pedal is pressed, curved brake shoes with friction linings press against the inside of the drum to slow or stop the vehicle.

Drum brake assembly

E

EGR valve A valve used to introduce exhaust gases into the intake air stream.

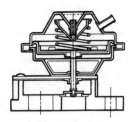

EGR valve

Electronic control unit (ECU) A computer which controls (for instance) ignition and fuel injection systems, or an anti-lock braking system. For more information refer to the *Haynes Automotive Electrical and Electronic Systems Manual*.

Electronic Fuel Injection (EFI) A computer controlled fuel system that distributes fuel through an injector located in each intake port of the engine.

Emergency brake A braking system, independent of the main hydraulic system, that can be used to slow or stop the vehicle if the primary brakes fail, or to hold the vehicle stationary even though the brake pedal isn't depressed. It usually consists of a hand lever that actuates either front or rear brakes mechanically through a series of cables and linkages. Also known as a handbrake or parking brake.

Endfloat The amount of lengthwise movement between two parts. As applied to a crankshaft, the distance that the crankshaft can move forward and back in the cylinder block.

Engine management system (EMS) A computer controlled system which manages the fuel injection and the ignition systems in an integrated fashion.

Exhaust manifold A part with several passages through which exhaust gases leave the engine combustion chambers and enter the exhaust pipe.

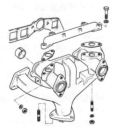

Exhaust manifold

F

Fan clutch A viscous (fluid) drive coupling device which permits variable engine fan speeds in relation to engine speeds.

Feeler blade A thin strip or blade of hardened steel, ground to an exact thickness, used to check or measure clearances between parts.

Feeler blade

Firing order The order in which the engine cylinders fire, or deliver their power strokes, beginning with the number one cylinder.

Flywheel A heavy spinning wheel in which energy is absorbed and stored by means of momentum. On cars, the flywheel is attached to the crankshaft to smooth out firing impulses.

Free play The amount of travel before any action takes place. The "looseness" in a linkage, or an assembly of parts, between the initial application of force and actual movement. For example, the distance the brake pedal moves before the pistons in the master cylinder are actuated.

Fuse An electrical device which protects a circuit against accidental overload. The typical fuse contains a soft piece of metal which is calibrated to melt at a predetermined current flow (expressed as amps) and break the circuit.

Fusible link A circuit protection device consisting of a conductor surrounded by heat-resistant insulation. The conductor is smaller than the wire it protects, so it acts as the weakest link in the circuit. Unlike a blown fuse, a failed fusible link must frequently be cut from the wire for replacement.

G

Gap The distance the spark must travel in jumping from the centre electrode to the side

Adjusting spark plug gap

electrode in a spark plug. Also refers to the spacing between the points in a contact breaker assembly in a conventional points-type ignition, or to the distance between the reluctor or rotor and the pickup coil in an electronic ignition.

Gasket Any thin, soft material - usually cork, cardboard, asbestos or soft metal - installed between two metal surfaces to ensure a good seal. For instance, the cylinder head gasket seals the joint between the block and the cylinder head.

Gasket

Gauge An instrument panel display used to monitor engine conditions. A gauge with a movable pointer on a dial or a fixed scale is an analogue gauge. A gauge with a numerical readout is called a digital gauge.

H

Halfshaft A rotating shaft that transmits power from the final drive unit to a drive wheel, usually when referring to a live rear axle.

Harmonic balancer A device designed to reduce torsion or twisting vibration in the crankshaft. May be incorporated in the crankshaft pulley. Also known as a vibration damper.

Hone An abrasive tool for correcting small irregularities or differences in diameter in an engine cylinder, brake cylinder, etc.

Hydraulic tappet A tappet that utilises hydraulic pressure from the engine's lubrication system to maintain zero clearance (constant contact with both camshaft and valve stem). Automatically adjusts to variation in valve stem length. Hydraulic tappets also reduce valve noise.

I

Ignition timing The moment at which the spark plug fires, usually expressed in the number of crankshaft degrees before the piston reaches the top of its stroke.

Inlet manifold A tube or housing with passages through which flows the air-fuel mixture (carburettor vehicles and vehicles with throttle body injection) or air only (port fuel-injected vehicles) to the port openings in the cylinder head.

J

Jump start Starting the engine of a vehicle with a discharged or weak battery by attaching jump leads from the weak battery to a charged or helper battery.

L

Load Sensing Proportioning Valve (LSPV) A brake hydraulic system control valve that works like a proportioning valve, but also takes into consideration the amount of weight carried by the rear axle.

Locknut A nut used to lock an adjustment nut, or other threaded component, in place. For example, a locknut is employed to keep the adjusting nut on the rocker arm in position.

Lockwasher A form of washer designed to prevent an attaching nut from working loose.

M

MacPherson strut A type of front suspension system devised by Earle MacPherson at Ford of England. In its original form, a simple lateral link with the anti-roll bar creates the lower control arm. A long strut - an integral coil spring and shock absorber - is mounted between the body and the steering knuckle. Many modern so-called MacPherson strut systems use a conventional lower A-arm and don't rely on the anti-roll bar for location.

Multimeter An electrical test instrument with the capability to measure voltage, current and resistance.

N

NOx Oxides of Nitrogen. A common toxic pollutant emitted by petrol and diesel engines at higher temperatures.

O

Ohm The unit of electrical resistance. One volt applied to a resistance of one ohm will produce a current of one amp.

Ohmmeter An instrument for measuring electrical resistance.

O-ring A type of sealing ring made of a special rubber-like material; in use, the O-ring is compressed into a groove to provide the sealing action.

O-ring

Overhead cam (ohc) engine An engine with the camshaft(s) located on top of the cylinder head(s).

Overhead valve (ohv) engine An engine with the valves located in the cylinder head, but with the camshaft located in the engine block.

Oxygen sensor A device installed in the engine exhaust manifold, which senses the oxygen content in the exhaust and converts this information into an electric current. Also called a Lambda sensor.

P

Phillips screw A type of screw head having a cross instead of a slot for a corresponding type of screwdriver.

Plastigage A thin strip of plastic thread, available in different sizes, used for measuring clearances. For example, a strip of Plastigage is laid across a bearing journal. The parts are assembled and dismantled; the width of the crushed strip indicates the clearance between journal and bearing.

Plastigage

Propeller shaft The long hollow tube with universal joints at both ends that carries power from the transmission to the differential on front-engined rear wheel drive vehicles.

Proportioning valve A hydraulic control valve which limits the amount of pressure to the rear brakes during panic stops to prevent wheel lock-up.

R

Rack-and-pinion steering A steering system with a pinion gear on the end of the steering shaft that mates with a rack (think of a geared wheel opened up and laid flat). When the steering wheel is turned, the pinion turns, moving the rack to the left or right. This movement is transmitted through the track rods to the steering arms at the wheels.

Radiator A liquid-to-air heat transfer device designed to reduce the temperature of the coolant in an internal combustion engine cooling system.

Refrigerant Any substance used as a heat transfer agent in an air-conditioning system. R-12 has been the principle refrigerant for many years; recently, however, manufacturers have begun using R-134a, a non-CFC substance that is considered less harmful to the ozone in the upper atmosphere.

Rocker arm A lever arm that rocks on a shaft or pivots on a stud. In an overhead valve engine, the rocker arm converts the upward movement of the pushrod into a downward movement to open a valve.

Rotor In a distributor, the rotating device inside the cap that connects the centre electrode and the outer terminals as it turns, distributing the high voltage from the coil secondary winding to the proper spark plug. Also, that part of an alternator which rotates inside the stator. Also, the rotating assembly of a turbocharger, including the compressor wheel, shaft and turbine wheel.

Runout The amount of wobble (in-and-out movement) of a gear or wheel as it's rotated. The amount a shaft rotates "out-of-true." The out-of-round condition of a rotating part.

S

Sealant A liquid or paste used to prevent leakage at a joint. Sometimes used in conjunction with a gasket.

Sealed beam lamp An older headlight design which integrates the reflector, lens and filaments into a hermetically-sealed one-piece unit. When a filament burns out or the lens cracks, the entire unit is simply replaced.

Serpentine drivebelt A single, long, wide accessory drivebelt that's used on some newer vehicles to drive all the accessories, instead of a series of smaller, shorter belts. Serpentine drivebelts are usually tensioned by an automatic tensioner.

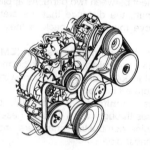

Serpentine drivebelt

Shim Thin spacer, commonly used to adjust the clearance or relative positions between two parts. For example, shims inserted into or under bucket tappets control valve clearances. Clearance is adjusted by changing the thickness of the shim.

Slide hammer A special puller that screws into or hooks onto a component such as a shaft or bearing; a heavy sliding handle on the shaft bottoms against the end of the shaft to knock the component free.

Sprocket A tooth or projection on the periphery of a wheel, shaped to engage with a chain or drivebelt. Commonly used to refer to the sprocket wheel itself.

Starter inhibitor switch On vehicles with an

automatic transmission, a switch that prevents starting if the vehicle is not in Neutral or Park.

Strut See MacPherson strut.

T

Tappet A cylindrical component which transmits motion from the cam to the valve stem, either directly or via a pushrod and rocker arm. Also called a cam follower.

Thermostat A heat-controlled valve that regulates the flow of coolant between the cylinder block and the radiator, so maintaining optimum engine operating temperature. A thermostat is also used in some air cleaners in which the temperature is regulated.

Thrust bearing The bearing in the clutch assembly that is moved in to the release levers by clutch pedal action to disengage the clutch. Also referred to as a release bearing.

Timing belt A toothed belt which drives the camshaft. Serious engine damage may result if it breaks in service.

Timing chain A chain which drives the camshaft.

Toe-in The amount the front wheels are closer together at the front than at the rear. On rear wheel drive vehicles, a slight amount of toe-in is usually specified to keep the front wheels running parallel on the road by offsetting other forces that tend to spread the wheels apart.

Toe-out The amount the front wheels are closer together at the rear than at the front. On front wheel drive vehicles, a slight amount of toe-out is usually specified.

Tools For full information on choosing and using tools, refer to the *Haynes Automotive Tools Manual*.

Tracer A stripe of a second colour applied to a wire insulator to distinguish that wire from another one with the same colour insulator.

Tune-up A process of accurate and careful adjustments and parts replacement to obtain the best possible engine performance.

Turbocharger A centrifugal device, driven by exhaust gases, that pressurises the intake air. Normally used to increase the power output from a given engine displacement, but can also be used primarily to reduce exhaust emissions (as on VW's "Umwelt" Diesel engine).

U

Universal joint or U-joint A double-pivoted connection for transmitting power from a driving to a driven shaft through an angle. A U-joint consists of two Y-shaped yokes and a cross-shaped member called the spider.

V

Valve A device through which the flow of liquid, gas, vacuum, or loose material in bulk may be started, stopped, or regulated by a movable part that opens, shuts, or partially obstructs one or more ports or passageways. A valve is also the movable part of such a device.

Valve clearance The clearance between the valve tip (the end of the valve stem) and the rocker arm or tappet. The valve clearance is measured when the valve is closed.

Vernier caliper A precision measuring instrument that measures inside and outside dimensions. Not quite as accurate as a micrometer, but more convenient.

Viscosity The thickness of a liquid or its resistance to flow.

Volt A unit for expressing electrical "pressure" in a circuit. One volt that will produce a current of one ampere through a resistance of one ohm.

W

Welding Various processes used to join metal items by heating the areas to be joined to a molten state and fusing them together. For more information refer to the *Haynes Automotive Welding Manual*.

Wiring diagram A drawing portraying the components and wires in a vehicle's electrical system, using standardised symbols. For more information refer to the *Haynes Automotive Electrical and Electronic Systems Manual*.

Note: References throughout this index are in the form - "Chapter number" • "Page number"

Haynes Manuals – The Complete List

Title	Book No.
ALFA ROMEO	
Alfa Romeo Alfasud/Sprint (74 - 88)	0292
Alfa Romeo Alfetta (73 - 87)	0531
AUDI	
Audi 80 (72 - Feb 79)	0207
Audi 80, 90 (79 - Oct 86) & Coupe (81 - Nov 88)	0605
Audi 80, 90 (Oct 86 - 90) & Coupe (Nov 88 - 90)	1491
Audi 100 (Oct 82 - 90) & 200 (Feb 84 - Oct 89)	0907
Audi 100 & A6 Petrol & Diesel (May 91 - May 97)	3504
AUSTIN	
Austin/MG/Rover Maestro 1.3 & 1.6 (83 - 95)	0922
Austin/MG Metro (80 - May 90)	0718
Austin/Rover Montego 1.3 & 1.6 (84 - 94)	1066
Austin/MG/Rover Montego 2.0 (84 - 95)	1067
Mini (59 - 69)	0527
Mini (69 - Oct 96)	0646
Austin/Rover 2.0 litre Diesel Engine (86 - 93)	1857
BEDFORD	
Bedford CF (69 - 87)	0163
Bedford/Vauxhall Rascal & Suzuki Supercarry (86 - Oct 94)	3015
BMW	
BMW 316, 320 & 320i (4-cyl) (75 - Feb 83)	0276
BMW 320, 320i, 323i & 325i (6-cyl) (Oct 77 - Sept 87)	0815
BMW 3-Series (Apr 91 - 96)	3210
BMW 3- & 5-Series (sohc) (81 - 91)	1948
BMW 520i & 525e (Oct 81 - June 88)	1560
BMW 525, 528 & 528i (73 - Sept 81)	0632
CITROEN	
Citroën 2CV, Ami & Dyane (67 - 90)	0196
Citroën AX Petrol & Diesel (87 - 97)	3014
Citroën BX (83 - 94)	0908
Citroën C15 Van Petrol & Diesel (89 - Oct 98)	3509
Citroën CX (75 - 88)	0528
Citroën Saxo Petrol & Diesel (96 - 98)	3506
Citroën Visa (79 - 88)	0620
Citroën Xantia Petrol & Diesel (93 - 98)	3082
Citroën XM Petrol & Diesel (89 - 98)	3451
Citroën ZX Diesel (91 - 93)	1922
Citroën ZX Petrol (91 - 94)	1881
Citroën 1.7 & 1.9 litre Diesel Engine (84 - 96)	1379
COLT	
Colt/Mitsubishi 1200, 1250 & 1400 (79 - May 84)	0600
FIAT	
Fiat 126 (73 - 87)	0305
Fiat 127 (71 - 83)	0193
Fiat 500 (57 - 73)	0090
Fiat Cinquecento (93 - 98)	3501
Fiat Panda (81 - 95)	0793
Fiat Punto Petrol & Diesel (94 - 99)	3251
Fiat Regata (84 - 88)	1167
Fiat Tipo (88 - 91)	1625
Fiat Uno (83 - 95)	0923
Fiat X1/9 (74 - 89)	0273

Title	Book No.
FORD	
Ford Capri II (& III) 1.6 & 2.0 (74 - 87)	0283
Ford Capri II (& III) 2.8 & 3.0 (74 - 87)	1309
Ford Cortina Mk IV (& V) 1.6 & 2.0 (76 - 83)	0343
Ford Escort (75 - Aug 80)	0280
Ford Escort (Sept 80 - Sept 90)	0686
Ford Escort & Orion (Sept 90 - 97)	1737
Ford Escort Mk II Mexico, RS 1600 & RS 2000 (75 - 80)	0735
Ford Fiesta (76 - Aug 83)	0334
Ford Fiesta (Aug 83 - Feb 89)	1030
Ford Fiesta (Feb 89 - Oct 95)	1595
Ford Fiesta Petrol & Diesel (Oct 95 - 97)	3397
Ford Granada (Sept 77 - Feb 85)	0481
Ford Granada & Scorpio (Mar 85 - 94)	1245
Ford Ka (96 - 99)	3570
Ford Mondeo Petrol (93 - 99)	1923
Ford Mondeo Diesel (93 - 96)	3465
Ford Orion (83 - Sept 90)	1009
Ford Sierra 4 cyl. (82 - 93)	0903
Ford Sierra V6 (82 - 91)	0904
Ford Transit Petrol (Mk 2) (78 - Jan 86)	0719
Ford Transit Petrol (Mk 3) (Feb 86 - 89)	1468
Ford Transit Diesel (Feb 86 - 99)	3019
Ford 1.6 & 1.8 litre Diesel Engine (84 - 96)	1172
Ford 2.1, 2.3 & 2.5 litre Diesel Engine (77 - 90)	1606
FREIGHT ROVER	
Freight Rover Sherpa (74 - 87)	0463
HILLMAN	
Hillman Avenger (70 - 82)	0037
HONDA	
Honda Accord (76 - Feb 84)	0351
Honda Accord (Feb 84 - Oct 85)	1177
Honda Civic (Feb 84 - Oct 87)	1226
Honda Civic (Nov 91 - 96)	3199
HYUNDAI	
Hyundai Pony (85 - 94)	3398
JAGUAR	
Jaguar E Type (61 - 72)	0140
Jaguar MkI & II, 240 & 340 (55 - 69)	0098
Jaguar XJ6, XJ & Sovereign; Daimler Sovereign (68 - Oct 86)	0242
Jaguar XJ6 & Sovereign (Oct 86 - Sept 94)	3261
Jaguar XJ12, XJS & Sovereign; Daimler Double Six (72 - 88)	0478
JEEP	
Jeep Cherokee Petrol (93 - 96)	1943
LADA	
Lada 1200, 1300, 1500 & 1600 (74 - 91)	0413
Lada Samara (87 - 91)	1610
LAND ROVER	
Land Rover 90, 110 & Defender Diesel (83 - 95)	3017
Land Rover Discovery Diesel (89 - 95)	3016
Land Rover Series IIA & III Diesel (58 - 85)	0529
Land Rover Series II, IIA & III Petrol (58 - 85)	0314
MAZDA	
Mazda 323 (Mar 81 - Oct 89)	1608
Mazda 323 (Oct 89 - 98)	3455

Title	Book No.
Mazda 626 (May 83 - Sept 87)	0929
Mazda B-1600, B-1800 & B-2000 Pick-up (72 - 88)	0267
MERCEDES-BENZ	
Mercedes-Benz 190, 190E & 190D Petrol & Diesel (83 - 93)	3450
Mercedes-Benz 200, 240, 300 Diesel (Oct 76 - 85)	1114
Mercedes-Benz 250 & 280 (68 - 72)	0346
Mercedes-Benz 250 & 280 (123 Series) (Oct 76 - 84)	0677
Mercedes-Benz 124 Series (85 - Aug 93)	3253
MG	
MGB (62 - 80)	0111
MG Midget & AH Sprite (58 - 80)	0265
MITSUBISHI	
Mitsubishi Shogun & L200 Pick-Ups (83 - 94)	1944
MORRIS	
Morris Ital 1.3 (80 - 84)	0705
Morris Minor 1000 (56 - 71)	0024
NISSAN	
Nissan Bluebird (May 84 - Mar 86)	1223
Nissan Bluebird (Mar 86 - 90)	1473
Nissan Cherry (Sept 82 - 86)	1031
Nissan Micra (83 - Jan 93)	0931
Nissan Micra (93 - 99)	3254
Nissan Primera (90 - Oct 96)	1851
Nissan Stanza (82 - 86)	0824
Nissan Sunny (May 82 - Oct 86)	0895
Nissan Sunny (Oct 86 - Mar 91)	1378
Nissan Sunny (Apr 91 - 95)	3219
OPEL	
Opel Ascona & Manta (B Series) (Sept 75 - 88)	0316
Opel Ascona (81 - 88) *(Not available in UK see Vauxhall Cavalier 0812)*	3215
Opel Astra (Oct 91 - Feb 98) *(Not available in UK see Vauxhall Astra 1832)*	3156
Opel Calibra (90 - 98) see Vauxhall/Opel Calibra Book No. 3502	
Opel Corsa (83 - Mar 93) *(Not available in UK see Vauxhall Nova 0909)*	3160
Opel Corsa (Mar 93 - 97) *(Not available in UK see Vauxhall Corsa 1985)*	3159
Opel Frontera Petrol & Diesel (91 - 98) see Vauxhall/Opel Frontera Book No. 3454	
Opel Kadett (Nov 79 - Oct 84)	0634
Opel Kadett (Oct 84 - Oct 91) *(Not available in UK see Vauxhall Astra & Belmont 1136)*	3196
Opel Omega & Senator (86 - 94) *(Not available in UK see Vauxhall Carlton & Senator 1469)*	3157
Opel Omega (94 - 99) *(See Vauxhall/Opel Omega Book No. 3510)*	
Opel Rekord (Feb 78 - Oct 86)	0543
Opel Vectra (Oct 88 - Oct 95) *(Not available in UK see Vauxhall Cavalier 1570)*	3158
Opel Vectra Petrol & Diesel (95 - 98) *(Not available in UK see Vauxhall Vectra 3396)*	3523

Title	Book No.
PEUGEOT	
Peugeot 106 Petrol & Diesel (91 - 98)	1882
Peugeot 205 (83 - 95)	0932
Peugeot 305 (78 - 89)	0538
Peugeot 306 Petrol & Diesel (93 - 99)	3073
Peugeot 309 (86 - 93)	1266
Peugeot 405 Petrol (88 - 96)	1559
Peugeot 405 Diesel (88 - 96)	3198
Peugeot 406 Petrol & Diesel (96 - 97)	3394
Peugeot 505 (79 - 89)	0762
Peugeot 1.7/1.8 & 1.9 litre Diesel Engine (82 - 96)	0950
Peugeot 2.0, 2.1, 2.3 & 2.5 litre Diesel Engines (74 - 90)	1607
PORSCHE	
Porsche 911 (65 - 85)	0264
Porsche 924 & 924 Turbo (76 - 85)	0397
PROTON	
Proton (89 - 97)	3255
RANGE ROVER	
Range Rover V8 (70 - Oct 92)	0606
RELIANT	
Reliant Robin & Kitten (73 - 83)	0436
RENAULT	
Renault 5 (Feb 85 - 96)	1219
Renault 9 & 11 (82 - 89)	0822
Renault 18 (79 - 86)	0598
Renault 19 Petrol (89 - 94)	1646
Renault 19 Diesel (89 - 95)	1946
Renault 21 (86 - 94)	1397
Renault 25 (84 - 92)	1228
Renault Clio Petrol (91 - May 98)	1853
Renault Clio Diesel (91 - June 96)	3031
Renault Espace Petrol & Diesel (85 - 96)	3197
Renault Laguna Petrol & Diesel (94 - 96)	3252
Renault Mégane & Scénic Petrol & Diesel (96 - 98)	3395
ROVER	
Rover 213 & 216 (84 - 89)	1116
Rover 214 & 414 (89 - 96)	1689
Rover 216 & 416 (89 - 96)	1830
Rover 211, 214, 216, 218 & 220 Petrol & Diesel (Dec 95 - 98)	3399
Rover 414, 416 & 420 Petrol & Diesel (May 95 - 98)	3453
Rover 618, 620 & 623 (93 - 97)	3257
Rover 820, 825 & 827 (86 - 95)	1380
Rover 3500 (76 - 87)	0365
Rover Metro, 111 & 114 (May 90 - 96)	1711
SAAB	
Saab 90, 99 & 900 (79 - Oct 93)	0765
Saab 900 (Oct 93 - 98)	3512
Saab 9000 (4-cyl) (85 - 95)	1686
SEAT	
Seat Ibiza & Cordoba Petrol & Diesel (Oct 93 - 99)	3571
Seat Ibiza & Malaga (85 - 92)	1609

Title	Book No.
SKODA	
Skoda Estelle (77 - 89)	0604
Skoda Favorit (89 - 96)	1801
Skoda Felicia Petrol & Diesel (95 - 99)	3505
SUBARU	
Subaru 1600 & 1800 (Nov 79 - 90)	0995
SUZUKI	
Suzuki SJ Series, Samurai & Vitara (4-cyl) (82 - 97)	1942
Suzuki Supercarry (86 - Oct 94)	3015
TALBOT	
Talbot Alpine, Solara, Minx & Rapier (75 - 86)	0337
Talbot Horizon (78 - 86)	0473
Talbot Samba (82 - 86)	0823
TOYOTA	
Toyota Carina E (May 92 - 97)	3256
Toyota Corolla (Sept 83 - Sept 87)	1024
Toyota Corolla (80 - 85)	0683
Toyota Corolla (Sept 87 - Aug 92)	1683
Toyota Corolla (Aug 92 - 97)	3259
Toyota Hi-Ace & Hi-Lux (69 - Oct 83)	0304
TRIUMPH	
Triumph Acclaim (81 - 84)	0792
Triumph GT6 & Vitesse (62 - 74)	0112
Triumph Spitfire (62 - 81)	0113
Triumph Stag (70 - 78)	0441
Triumph TR7 (75 - 82)	0322
VAUXHALL	
Vauxhall Astra (80 - Oct 84)	0635
Vauxhall Astra & Belmont (Oct 84 - Oct 91)	1136
Vauxhall Astra (Oct 91 - Feb 98)	1832
Vauxhall/Opel Calibra (90 - 98)	3502
Vauxhall Carlton (Oct 78 - Oct 86)	0480
Vauxhall Carlton & Senator (Nov 86 - 94)	1469
Vauxhall Cavalier 1600, 1900 & 2000 (75 - July 81)	0315
Vauxhall Cavalier (81 - Oct 88)	0812
Vauxhall Cavalier (Oct 88 - 95)	1570
Vauxhall Chevette (75 - 84)	0285
Vauxhall Corsa (Mar 93 - 97)	1985
Vauxhall/Opel Frontera Petrol & Diesel (91 - Sept 98)	3454
Vauxhall Nova (83 - 93)	0909
Vauxhall/Opel Omega (94 - 99)	3510
Vauxhall Vectra Petrol & Diesel (95 - 98)	3396
Vauxhall/Opel 1.5, 1.6 & 1.7 litre Diesel Engine (82 - 96)	1222
VOLKSWAGEN	
VW Beetle 1200 (54 - 77)	0036
VW Beetle 1300 & 1500 (65 - 75)	0039
VW Beetle 1302 & 1302S (70 - 72)	0110
VW Beetle 1303, 1303S & GT (72 - 75)	0159
VW Golf & Jetta Mk 1 1.1 & 1.3 (74 - 84)	0716
VW Golf, Jetta & Scirocco Mk 1 1.5, 1.6 & 1.8 (74 - 84)	0726
VW Golf & Jetta Mk 1 Diesel (78 - 84)	0451
VW Golf & Jetta Mk 2 (Mar 84 - Feb 92)	1081

Title	Book No.
VW Golf & Vento Petrol & Diesel (Feb 92 - 96)	3097
VW LT vans & light trucks (76 - 87)	0637
VW Passat & Santana (Sept 81 - May 88)	0814
VW Passat Petrol & Diesel (May 88 - 96)	3498
VW Polo & Derby (76 - Jan 82)	0335
VW Polo (82 - Oct 90)	0813
VW Polo (Nov 90 - Aug 94)	3245
VW Polo Hatchback Petrol & Diesel (94 - 98)	3500
VW Scirocco (82 - 90)	1224
VW Transporter 1600 (68 - 79)	0082
VW Transporter 1700, 1800 & 2000 (72 - 79)	0226
VW Transporter (air-cooled) (79 - 82)	0638
VW Transporter (water-cooled) (82 - 90)	3452
VOLVO	
Volvo 142, 144 & 145 (66 - 74)	0129
Volvo 240 Series (74 - 93)	0270
Volvo 262, 264 & 260/265 (75 - 85)	0400
Volvo 340, 343, 345 & 360 (76 - 91)	0715
Volvo 440, 460 & 480 (87 - 97)	1691
Volvo 740 & 760 (82 - 91)	1258
Volvo 850 (92 - 96)	3260
Volvo 940 (90 - 96)	3249
Volvo S40 & V40 (96 - 99)	3569
Volvo S70, C70 & V70 (96 - 99)	3573
YUGO/ZASTAVA	
Yugo/Zastava (81 - 90)	1453
AUTOMOTIVE TECHBOOKS	
Automotive Brake Manual	3050
Automotive Carburettor Manual	3288
Automotive Diagnostic Fault Codes Manual	3472
Automotive Diesel Engine Service Guide	3286
Automotive Disc Brake Manual	3542
Automotive Electrical and Electronic Systems Manual	3049
Automotive Engine Management and Fuel Injection Systems Manual	3344
Automotive Gearbox Overhaul Manual	3473
Automotive Service Summaries Manual	3475
Automotive Timing Belt Manual - Ford	3474
Automotive Timing Belts Manual - Austin/Rover	3549
Automotive Timing Belts Manual - Peugeot/Citroën	3568
Automotive Timing Belt Manual - Vauxhall/Opel	3577
Automotive Welding Manual	3053
In-Car Entertainment Manual (3rd Edition)	3363
OTHER TITLES	
Automotive Fuel Injection Systems	9755
Car Bodywork Repair Manual (2nd Edition)	9864
Caravan Manual (2nd Edition)	9894
Motorcaravan Manual, The	L7322
Small Engine Repair Manual	1755
SU Carburettors	0299
Weber Carburettors (to 79)	0393

CL08.09/99

All the products featured on this page are available through most motor accessory shops, cycle shops and book stores. Our policy of continuous updating and development means that titles are being constantly added to the range. For up-to-date information on our complete list of titles, please telephone: (UK) +44 1963 440635 • (USA) +1 805 498 6703 • (France) +33 1 47 78 50 50 • (Sweden) +46 18 124016 • (Australia) +61 3 9763 8100

Preserving Our Motoring Heritage

< The Model J Duesenberg
Derham Tourster.
Only eight of these
magnificent cars were
ever built – this is the
only example to be found
outside the United
States of America

Almost every car you've ever loved, loathed or desired is gathered under one roof at the Haynes Motor
Museum. Over 300 immaculately presented cars and motorbikes represent every aspect of our motoring
heritage, from elegant reminders of bygone days, such as the superb Model J Duesenberg to curiosities like
the bug-eyed BMW Isetta. There are also many old friends and flames. Perhaps you remember the 1959 Ford
Popular that you did your courting in? The magnificent 'Red Collection' is a spectacle of classic sports cars
including AC, Alfa Romeo, Austin Healey, Ferrari, Lamborghini, Maserati, MG, Riley, Porsche and Triumph.

A Perfect Day Out

Each and every vehicle at the Haynes Motor Museum has played its part in the history and culture of
Motoring. Today, they make a wonderful spectacle and a great day out for all the family. Bring the kids, bring
Mum and Dad, but above all bring your camera to capture those golden memories for ever. You will also find
an impressive array of motoring memorabilia, a comfortable 70 seat video cinema and one of the most
extensive transport book shops in Britain. The Pit Stop Cafe serves everything from a cup of tea to
wholesome, home-made meals or, if you prefer, you can enjoy the large picnic area nestled in the beautiful
rural surroundings of Somerset.

> John Haynes O.B.E.,
Founder and
Chairman of the
museum at the wheel
of a Haynes Light 12.

< Graham Hill's Lola
Cosworth Formula 1
car next to a 1934
Riley Sports.

The Museum is situated on the A359 Yeovil to Frome road at Sparkford, just off the A303 in Somerset. It is about 40 miles south of Bristol, and
25 minutes drive from the M5 intersection at Taunton.
Open 9.30am - 5.30pm (10.00am - 4.00pm Winter) 7 days a week, except Christmas Day, Boxing Day and New Years Day
Special rates available for schools, coach parties and outings Charitable Trust No. 292048